PACIFIC ON THE RISE

THE STORY OF CALIFORNIA'S FIRST UNIVERSITY

by Philip N. Gilbertson

Published by
University of the Pacific
2016

University of the Pacific
Stockton, California

Printed by CreateSpace
ISBN-13: 978-0997685404

"Most college histories are mind-numbingly tedious. They fail to recognize that all events are not equal. Gilbertson has taken the rich history of California's oldest chartered university and woven it into an interesting narrative which highlights both the challenges that the University faced and the range of innovations that were first tried on Pacific's campuses over its century and a half of history."

—Jonathan Brown, Class of 1968
President Emeritus,
Association of Independent California Colleges and Universities

CONTENTS

ACKNOWLEDGMENTS

I am especially grateful to the University for initiating and funding this project that involved many Pacificans between 2011 and 14. Presidents Don DeRosa and Pamela Eibeck, along with the Board of Regents, have supported this project since it was initially proposed more than a decade ago.

From the start, an editorial board guided me in basic decisions about this history project and offered wise counsel on each chapter. The board, headed by library dean Brigid Welch, included emeritus history professor Reuben Smith, history professor William Swagerty, alumnus and visiting professor Dave Frederickson ('66), director of alumni relations Kelli Page ('87), associate vice president for marketing and communication Richard Rojo, and head of the library's Holt-Atherton Special Collections Shan Sutton, replaced in 2013 by his successor Michael Wurtz, head of special collections and University archivist. Numerous members of the Pacific community offered memories, ideas, and delightful lore that found their way into this history.

Special thanks go to Michael Wurtz; Trish Richards, special collections assistant; librarian Nicole Grady; and (in the first year of my work) Shan Sutton, former associate dean of the library and head of special collections, for their stewardship of Pacific history through their knowledge, judgment, and organizational skills. This project could not have been accomplished without their professional skills, commitment and often daily help. They continue to build a remarkably thorough collection of Pacific archives in print, picture and digital format, building on the prodigious organizing work of Donald Walker, University archivist from 1992 to 2003.

Advisors/readers Robert Benedetti, former dean of the College, Judith Chambers ('58, '60), former vice president for student life, Jonathan Brown ('68), former president of the Association of Independent California Colleges and Universities, and Ronald Isetti ('59, '60), emeritus professor of history at St. Mary's College and author of a recent history of St. Mary's, were especially helpful critical readers. Their counsel improved the history immensely. A student of Pacific history, president emeritus Don DeRosa was always a ready responder, well beyond the specifics during his years as president.

Sheri Grimes in Marketing and Communications and editor of the *Pacific Review* has always been ready to provide important information and has been especially helpful in identifying photos and pertinent *Pacific Review* articles. University photographer Randall Gee has created massive galleries of beautiful campus images in recent years, providing me with endless attractive photo options for the 21st century portion of the history. Michael Curran, retired publications/media relations manager of McGeorge School of Law, and Dorothy Dechant, curator of the Institute of Dental History at Dugoni School of Dentistry, were invaluable in securing information from those two campuses, as were law professor Claude Rohwer and dental professor David Chambers. Special thanks to visiting professor Gene Bigler ('67), who did an immense amount of work researching milestones in ethnic diversity and in Inter-American cooperation at Pacific, as well as gathering information and remembrances from both Raymond and Covell alumni. Mike Millerick, assistant director of athletics, and his staff provided many of the images for athletics. Mike's *Pacific Football Record Book* was an invaluable and comprehensive resource on that sport. Michael Rogers, director of institutional research, and his student assistant Grace Kim (2014), compiled for the first time a nearly complete set of enrollment data for the University that informed so many aspects of the history. Katie Ismael, managing editor of publications at Pacific, partnered on planning the coordination of the history with a new photo-essay publication on Pacific.

Thanks also to those who helped me with Stockton history: Tod Ruhstaller, CEO and curator of history of the Haggin Museum in Stockton, William Maxwell, archives manager for the Bank of Stockton's Historical Photograph Collection, Steve Werner ('77), who provided several key histories of Stockton from his library, and John Bradbury ('75), for help on Stockton's Central Methodist Church history. Gary Putnam, former University chaplain and former pastor of Central Methodist Church, provided me with an armload of important books on the history of the Methodist church in California.

My office assistant, Debbie Thomas, who worked as my executive administrative assistant during my fourteen years as provost, and then as assistant on the history project from 2010-14, advanced progress greatly through interview arrangements, interview transcriptions for the archives, and various research projects. Mark Linden (2013) picked up Debbie's work and advanced it through 2013.

I formed an undergraduate student research team for spring term 2012 to research student and campus life from 1940 to the present—an invaluable help in combing through countless pages of student publications. Coordinated by member Joshua Chipponeri (2011), the research team included Christine Burke (2012), Devon Clayton (2012), Wesley Coffay (2012), Alexander Foos (2014), Caroline Gutierrez (2013), Grace Kim (2014), Mark Linden (2013), Kathryn McAllister (2012), Rudy Oliva (2012), Andrew Rathkopf (2012), and Trevor Rosenbery (2012). Thanks also to Kelli Page, director of alumni relations, and her fleet of student assistants who determined graduation years for the host of alumni named in the history.

To prepare the history for publication, I am indebted to Rich Rojo, former associate vice president for communications, and editor Anne Basye, who has a sharp eye for lack of clarity. Both generously moved this project to conclusion.

I thank Richard Baepler, my mentor and provost emeritus of Valparaiso University, whose brilliant and eloquent history of that university, *Flame of Faith, Lamp of Learning* (2001), was the initial inspiration for me to aspire to write Pacific's history. I write this history also in memory of my good friend Bob Cox, emeritus English professor and interim dean of the College of the Pacific, who was to be my compadre in writing, especially the history of the College, but passed away just as this project began.

To my wife Carole, most of all, I owe my deepest gratitude. Her love, inspiration, support, and patience empowered me to complete this project. She is an extraordinary spouse who has been a loving partner in my endeavors for fifty years.

—Philip N. Gilbertson, Provost Emeritus

INTRODUCTION

As a former provost of Pacific (1996-2010), I cannot think of a higher honor than being selected to write this new history of Pacific. I wrote this history for two primary reasons: to provide a record of the past for Pacificans to learn of Pacific's rich heritage and its lessons for the future, and to engage alumni and members of the Pacific community in this fascinating experience called Pacific. I wanted to rekindle their memories of this remarkable university and to nourish a larger interest in the story, the saga, of Pacific.

I hope that through this history readers will renew not only their appreciation for but also their friendship with this place, with this university community, and most especially with fellow alumni, now scattered across the globe, who all share the Pacific Experience: an uncommon commitment by faculty and staff to the growth and flourishing of students, a commitment that was clear to that little band who marched in the door of a simple two-story building on the edge of Santa Clara on May 3, 1852. As you read these chapters, I hope you will offer your own versions of a history that is far richer than I could possibly capture in this book.

Prior histories

The first written history of Pacific is a master's thesis, "The First Half-Century of the College of the Pacific," completed by alumnus Robert Burns ('34). When he submitted his final manuscript on May 8, 1947, he was already the twentieth president of Pacific. One of his mentors in the project was Rockwell D. Hunt, who wrote the centennial history of Pacific, *History of the College of the Pacific, 1851-1951* (1951). Hunt, an adopted alumnus of Pacific via the merger with Napa College, taught history at Pacific before spending 37 years on the faculty at the University of Southern California, 25 of them as dean of the graduate school. In 1947, he returned to Pacific at the invitation of President Burns to head the California History Foundation, and guided Burns in the final draft of his thesis while Burns was in the heady days of his new presidency. How fitting that the first history was written by a Pacific student, then serving as assistant to President Tully C. Knoles, and mentored by an alumnus who had returned to Pacific. The drawing power of this lodestar has won hearts and minds through its sixteen decades.

Kara Pratt Brewer's *"Pioneer or Perish:" A History of the University of the Pacific during the Administration of Dr. Robert E. Burns, 1946-1971* (1977) is a splendid account of the remarkable leadership of one of Pacific's most distinguished presidents and transformational leaders.[1] Kara Brewer ('69), like Burns, was simultaneously an alumna and a student, just completing her doctoral degree at Pacific. Her work was followed by Harold S. Jacoby's *Pacific: Yesterday and the Day Before That* (1989), a collection of historical essays by the first dean of the College of the Pacific. "Jake" Jacoby ('28), who had returned to join the Pacific faculty in 1933 in sociology, served until his retirement in 1976. No surprise, then, that this alumnus, son of Pacific trustee O. D. Jacoby, who had served on the Board of Regents for 53 years, turned his attention to Pacific's past with illuminating first-hand accounts.

For Pacific's Sesquicentennial in 2001, emeritus professor Charles Clerc was invited to prepare a tribute to Pacific faculty, *The Professor Who Changed My Life: A Sesquicentennial Celebration of Educational Interaction at University of the Pacific* (2001). Together with photographer James A. Sugar, Clerc, who had taught English at Pacific for 30 years, captures the essence of this place by featuring alumni tributes to their most influential professors. The "student-centered learning experience," to paraphrase Pacific's mission statement, has always been its heart.

I am not an alumnus of Pacific, nor am I a former teaching faculty member; my 14 years as Pacific's first provost were, as I often said, "the best years of my life because I have the best job in the world." Clearly outshined by my faculty colleagues in teaching and scholarship, with humble personal and academic origins, I benefitted as much as any student or graduate from the rich learning experience of Pacific, surrounded by mentors and nurturers who immersed me in the joys and the lore of Pacific. How could I not seek a second opportunity of a lifetime: to devote years to investigating and celebrating the history of this most special of schools? By 2005 President DeRosa and I knew that now was the time to recapitulate the early history from modern historical perspectives and, most especially, to render a history of the decades following president Burns that had yet to be written. It was time.

How histories are written—this one in particular

History is always interpretation, and the notion of an "objective" history is an illusion as we puzzle over the meaning of our actions and institutions, whether for our families or our nation. Yet historians have built a discipline of assumptions, theories, and practices that requires attention minimally to the following ways of writing about the history of Pacific.

Range of Sources—The array of primary sources has expanded in recent decades, and requires an increasingly broader perspective on events and institutions. Our understanding of war, for example, has shifted dramatically from World War I to Vietnam and Iraq, because so much more information—primary and secondary sources—is readily at hand. Rockwell Hunt's centennial history of 1951 cites no interviews, references few University documents, and includes few visual sources. I have worked to include a wide range of sources to attempt to give a broader and deeper view of Pacific. Using undergraduate students to research student campus life through the decades is one way I attempted to broaden the perspective, with special interest in trying to engage alumni readers. Another is oral interviews of many alumni, faculty, and staff. Recalling someone's cautionary wisdom, "Memory is an act of imagination," I recognize that reliability is the challenge in depending on these kinds of sources. I suspect some readers will find errors of fact in these pages because of it. Given the detailed accounts in Hunt's and Brewer's histories, this new history will devote less attention to day-today matters during the earlier eras and more attentiveness to the context of activities and decisions.

Institutional Perspective—Histories of the nineteenth century often favored the "great leader" approach to history, focusing on the remarkable individual, and interpreted events often from the singular perspective of the transformative leader, especially if the history was about an institution, such as a university. Kara Brewer's magnificent portrait of president Burns in "*Pioneer or Perish*" is an example of this kind of history. Some would argue that president Tully Knoles epitomized the great leader who did embody the institution and its magnetic values during that American era between the great wars. Multi-disciplinary scholar, charismatic citizen leader, voice of democratic and Christian values—Knoles was the best of Pacific in his time. Yet we know today that at this time of growth for Pacific, the University was much more and less than this man, and this reality is also an important part of the story.

In our time, we are more keenly aware of the context of any leader's work, and of the complexities that are behind the decisions of a particular leader. Most university histories understandably devote a chapter to each key president and spotlight the work of the president as the pivotal figure in defining the times and events of the school. I have attempted to avoid an excessive focus on individual leaders as embodiments of the institution partly by organizing the chapters by eras not wholly defined by presidents' comings and goings. In the end, however, I think I have not been successful in dimming the presidential spotlight, ever more persuaded by the facts that a president of a small institution inevitably leaves indelible marks on it, perhaps more than any of us would wish. Presidents end up getting more attention in this history than I had hoped because they so often shaped the discourse and direction of Pacific—toward the edge of greatness or toward the edge of collapse.

Balancing Academic, Social, and Administrative—University histories tend to dwell either on academic programs and decisions, or on administrative actions, or on campus life as captured in picture books. A contemporary history should seek a balance among these strands of university life. If there is any neglected sector in this history of Pacific, it is probably the faculty; in an effort to capture the student experience, while retaining a thematic emphasis on key institutional decisions, attention to the achievements of faculty may be slighted. For the earliest decades, the lack of primary documents cheats the coverage of both faculty and students. A special challenge for a comprehensive university like Pacific is how to cover the range of schools within it, each having its own peculiar history and typically very different starting points. One of my greatest concerns is my inadequate treatment of Pacific's individual school histories within this University history. In the long run, each of Pacific's schools will want to follow the path of the dental school in writing its own history in the context of its profession.

Context—A major shift in contemporary histories is to present research that informs events, decisions, and institutions. For example, in Hunt's 1951 history of Pacific, there is little attention to the shaping forces in higher education that had direct impact on the decisions and development of Pacific. It can be said that Hunt's history is a subtle argument on behalf of the "small Christian liberal arts college," as he put it; a noble intent that probably fit the times for what was still a small Methodist college. Likewise, the social and political context is a very thin backdrop in Hunt's history—even the world wars seem almost absent. Today, we understand that social context is a powerful lever to open understanding of our past. Dealing with the social-cultural forces on American higher education, such as professionalization, specialization, social reform, pluralism, and technology, all require some general understanding of how they come into play, while not burying the story of Pacific under analysis that is of interest only to higher education professionals.

The Story—Perhaps foremost, I am interested in telling a story, a coherent narrative, a saga if you will. What is most important for a university history, it seems to me, is to capture the heart and soul of a place and a people, to tease out the themes and traits and qualities of a community over time. I do not believe that the prior written histories of Pacific really accomplish that. This one may disappoint many on that score, but an honest attempt here is being made, and I welcome readers to respond with their own "read" of this venerable learning community. History, as some historians have noted, is about creating "meaning stories" based on available evidence. I have made an effort to focus on a history of interest to alumni, to focus on telling a story of Pacific's development without overwhelming the story with too many facts or administrative data and personages. At the same time, I am reminded of the profound truth stated by the noted historian, Barbara Tuchman: "I mistrust history in gallon jugs whose purveyors are more concerned with establishing the meaning and purpose of history than with what happened."[2] Tuchman's "history by the ounce" of concrete actions by specific people may tell more truth. Over 150 individual interviews have informed this effort to capture a larger story that interprets Pacific's character.

Pacific's DNA

Pacific is indelibly an American and a Californian institution. Every school is shaped strongly by its neighborhood, close and far, and since most schools, public or private, actually enroll students who live within a few hundred miles, each institution's identity has a regional flavor. For Pacific, the streak of American and Californian individualism, resourcefulness, independence, entrepreneurship, and innovation runs dark and deep. Were it not for that streak, Pacific would have joined the burial grounds of hundreds of private, church-related colleges of the eighteenth and nineteenth centuries. Were it not for that streak, it could well have languished in the South Bay, overwhelmed by its big-shouldered neighbors 20 miles north, Stanford and Cal, and two other competitors a mile or two east, Santa Clara University and San Jose State. Instead, she leaped over the Coastal Range in 1924 to become the university of the Central Valley, until it linked back to San Francisco in 1962 to bring aboard the dental school in another mark of derring-do, and then brought in McGeorge Law School and Sacramento in 1966 to claim its distinctive northern California identity.

But coupled with this rugged individualism was a "ragged" individualism, borne on poverty, which can only be called presumptuous. Especially among those modest Methodist men on the Board of Trustees in the first half century, there is a streak of immodest over-confidence that wanes at times but runs through the turbulent years of revolving-door presidents. The pioneering regents' unquenchable mission to achieve a respectable civility in the far west; a tough-minded commitment to a classical education; an unreachable, immodest, maybe even foolhardy goal to build a university on the outskirts of tent city San Francisco—yes, I guess you could say, dreaming the impossible dream. The pioneer spirit of the Methodist movement west is part of this complex equation. The Methodists earned respect for their determination to be part of the giant enterprise of a continental migration, a conviction that education should be for all peoples, regardless of gender or color, a resolve to make education work for human betterment, to steer a practical education toward the common good. All of this was part of Pacific's yearning for achievement that always exceeded the result.

This overreaching had of course different stanzas over the decades, but the tune is roughly the same: *we are determined to become something special while we steadily go broke.* Pacific more than most universities lived out the wry adage of Steve Muller, the former president of Johns Hopkins University, that independent colleges and universities try to operate "on the brink of solvency." Pacific's early backers believed in it enough to keep it alive, but never rallied enough support to make it well. Some say it was Pacific's Methodist identity that tended to cater to folks of lower social classes—yet many a great Methodist university in this country overcame that stereotype and learned how to gather wealth to fulfill their dreams. As a California school, Pacific grew up in the last continental frontier of boom and bust, and its hard-scrabble existence for the first 75 years feels and tastes like that early California dream: never quite within its reckless reach, a rough-hewn, audacious dream pursued doggedly decade after decade—unduly self-confident, overreaching, daring to be different to get to where it wanted to go when it grew up—if it ever could.

One hundred and sixty-some years later, it is still not altogether clear what Pacific will be when it grows up to be a mature university. Certainly its persistent lack of solid financial support from its various constituencies is a continuing theme. But its derring-do has plunged it forward again and again, beginning with the feisty half-dozen trustees who, in their very first meeting, with charter in hand from the State Supreme Court, requested the legislature to change the name from "California Wesleyan College" to "University of the Pacific." Here was this small band of visionary Methodist clergy and laity who dared to stake out their claim as the first university of the new state, and a university they were determined to be. But it took a century for Pacific finally to come to terms with its destiny as the "University of the Pacific," not the tiny Methodist liberal arts school called "College of the Pacific". That audacious dream was only realized in the 1960s with the addition of the professional schools.

One of the most dramatic changes that propelled Pacific toward a reshaped identity was the addition of academic programs that exploded enrollment from a small college to a substantial university from the 1960s to the 1980s and beyond. Equally eye opening is the enrollment growth since Pacific moved to Stockton in 1924—a nearly fivefold increase over 30 years. Humbling, perhaps, is the realization that for nearly its first 75 years, Pacific enrolled fewer than 500 students. (See the enrollment graph in Chapter 2.)

Telescoping its history, the reality we see is a school often on the edge... of rising greatness or obscure failure—distinction or extinction. Pacific actually has a kind of bipolar history: entrepreneurial, yet impoverished; innovative, yet laggard at times; both progressive and conservative from its Methodist roots; a "comprehensive" university sometimes still acting like a "small liberal arts college;" perennially well-focused on students, yet mired in identity confusion; the "Power Cat" of today, yet the quaint and slightly goofy "Tommy Tiger" of its scruffy if friendly past.

Even today, for all of its achievements, Pacific remains challenged, stressed by under-enrolled programs, dogged by inadequate facilities, underfunded by lack of major benefactors, unknown owing to timid marketing, and under-represented for its regional potential. Yet anyone who has experienced this remarkable community would not exchange it for any other school and recognizes its continuing potential.

Pacific's core identity emerges over the decades as its relentless persistence drives it forward as an anomaly in California and for much of the country. Like many other Methodist schools, Pacific saw a calling larger than its liberal arts beginning, and aspired to be a national university. Pacific certainly aspired to be more, too, than the "comprehensive" state universities populating the state and the nation. I say "more" because it is not simply a quest to be different, to be distinctive in the sense of being uncommon: Pacific is "more" in the sense of offering students, and higher education, a model of a university that provides a vibrant general education in the liberal arts coupled with strong accredited professional schools. "More" in the sense of a university committed to providing "a superior, student-centered learning experience" that joins the communal feeling of a liberal arts college with the collective richness of many professional schools equipped to prepare students for essential professions. "More" in the sense of its tilt toward pioneering the best that learning and research can apply to the practice of professions across the globe. The traditional small college identity stood for the perennial argument of liberal education for the "whole person." Could an institution that favored a holistic approach to prepare young people for life survive in an emerging materialistic, consumer society driven by utilitarian ends? Pacific aimed to try, and when it sought successfully to blend the two models—the liberal arts college and the comprehensive university—became truly a distinctive university for our times.

Pacific's DNA of self-confidence was challenged many times in its first half-century, again during the Depression and World War II years, and once again from the 1980s to the mid-1990s, but it had built such a rich heritage through all those years that it kept calling leadership among regents, faculty and staff to a higher expectation of itself, to renew its strengths and keep pushing forward, often at great sacrifice by faculty and staff. That confidence was built on its rock-solid commitment to individual students and their learning. "Educating the whole student" is a shared value for all Pacificans on the campuses today. This dedication to building people for professions of service was there in 1851, and there is no evidence, throughout its history, that this commitment to student growth and development ever waned. We have, initially, to thank the Methodist founders—trustees, faculty, and staff—for that commitment, but the vitality of the concept of "whole student learning" was of course much larger and deeper than the American Protestant higher education movement. It was part of a growing body of knowledge about how learning happens, how people become successful, and how students develop, as the mission statement says, "for responsible leadership in their careers and communities."

So these are the elements of Pacific's enduring identity—independent, innovative while overreaching, small yet comprehensive, built on a bedrock commitment to student learning and growth for professional service. *Pacific on the Rise* describes how all this came about. It is a great story I think you will enjoy. A history should enrich knowledge, add understanding, revive memories, and intensify the bond with a particular past, the life and legacy of University of the Pacific. I hope that this history will do that for you.

Note on alumni class year designations

I use the convention of *class year designation* for alumni employed by the Office of Alumni Affairs and the *Pacific Review* alumni magazine. The year listed after the name of an alumnus/a is the year (or years for multiple degrees) of graduation, or the year in which the alumnus/a would have graduated as an undergraduate within four years, or the year designated by the alumnus/a of the class with whom he/she most closely associated. If no alumni records exist for a person who is an alumnus/a, a "no date" (n.d.) designation is made. Honorary degrees are omitted. For graduates of the 20th century, the first two digits are omitted.

CHAPTER 1

"Bustletown" Mission: How the Methodists established Pacific in the wild west, and how it survived, 1849-1905

Three founders and the Charter of 1851—Co-education—
The Owen scholarship scheme—Adapting academics—Medical school
and College of Physicians and Surgeons—Move to San Jose in 1871—
Coming of Stanford and USC—Conservatory of Music of 1878—Student
"secession" of 1891—Napa College merger in 1896—
Limping into the 20th century

God vs. gold: The wild west

It all started with the Gold Rush of '49. Without that first great California burst of glory and greed, University of the Pacific would still be a dream of Methodist Christians in the East who were driven by a vision of the world that bound faith, morality and education as tightly together as the personality of Methodist founder John Wesley. Exploiting and "civilizing" the Western frontier was a massive American enterprise, but more work, money and blood went into the exploitation of the land and its civilized native peoples than into the creation of social order, civility, learning and domestic culture of the rising European-American population. Power and violence ruled over homes and schools, even in California's one city.

The six great fires of San Francisco from 1849-51 could have been minor setbacks if the citizens had bothered to set up a fire department.[1] The first public high school in California did not open until 1858 in San Francisco, well after University of the Pacific was born in 1851.[2] What was this wild world Pacific entered?

When the Jesuits returned to San Francisco in 1849 after nearly 75 years of forced absence, they witnessed a calamitous world of unregulated greed and violence that urged them to bring order and civility to it. One priest recalled:

> *What goes under the name of San Francisco, but which, whether it should be called madhouse or Babylon, I am at a loss to determine; so great in those days was the disorder, the brawling, the open immorality, the reign of crime, which, brazen-faced, triumphed on a soil not yet brought under the sway of human laws.*[3]

University of the Pacific was the first college granted a state charter on the entire West Coast, but not by much.[4] By 1855 the San Francisco Jesuits had founded St. Ignatius College (later to become University of San Francisco) with only one teacher and one student, but they at least had joined the ranks of their fellow Jesuits in Santa Clara to bring some education into play. Father John Nobili opened Santa Clara College on March 19, 1851. A scant four months later, the California Supreme Court granted a charter on July 10, 1851, to a small group of people from the Methodist Episcopal Church. These were two of only six colleges founded in the West in the 1850s. The enterprising, education-minded Methodists eventually founded over 30 schools of higher education in California, but only University of the Pacific and the University of Southern California survived.[5]

HOW THE METHODISTS STARTED PACIFIC AND WHY THEY SUCCEEDED

The three founders

Methodist ministers Edward Bannister (1814-71), Isaac Owen (1809-66), and William Taylor (1821-1902), were the three primary founders of University of the Pacific. A copy of the original charter, signed July 10, 1851, was recovered in 1984.

Jedediah Smith, the Bible-toting Methodist fur trader of great notoriety, forged the trails west to become the first European-American to find passage through the Rockies in 1827. He was quickly followed by others whose primary enterprise was saving and educating souls, not trapping beavers. The powerful Baltimore Methodist bishop, Beverly Waugh, urged the founding of an Oregon California Mission Conference, which met first in 1849.[6] As bishop of the new conference, Waugh had unusual powers to effect the growth of Methodism, a denomination that benefitted from its centralized organization.

Bishop Waugh sought out a practical, wilderness preacher in Indiana who had a passion for education, Isaac Owen, to lead the missionary effort to build churches and schools on the West Slope. As his colleague William Taylor later said, "Brother Owen is one of the greatest Beggars in the world."[7] With a good business sense and fundraising talent honed at Indiana Asbury University, Owen had the right skill set to tackle the California challenge. Owen headed west with his family by ox wagon in 1849 piled with "three hundred and fifty dozen" school books.[8] He arrived in the Sacramento Valley with six of his 15 oxen intact and was joined by Rev. William Taylor, the second Methodist missionary assigned to California. Taylor had sailed around the Horn to arrive in San Francisco, then a tent city circled by hundreds of abandoned ships. Taylor, child of a Methodist camp meeting conversion, arrived with the same venturous drive, religious zeal and high talent as Owen. Dubbed "the John the Baptist of the Gold Rush" by one California historian, he was a renowned street preacher who frequently commanded a thousand listeners on the wharves, a friend to the outcasts and democratic to the core.[9] He defended the persecuted black and Chinese ethnic minorities and championed abolition, along with Martin Briggs, another Southern Methodist preacher who was later appointed the first president of Pacific.[10]

Soon, the church missionary board appointed Dr. Edward Bannister, graduate of Wesleyan University and professor at Cazenovia Seminary in New York, to be the first educator in California. The church directed him to found an "academy" (high school) that would lead to a college, which should culminate in a seminary. Bannister landed in San Francisco the day California heard that Congress had voted it into the Union. Within months he founded the independent San Jose Academy in early 1851, housed in a large hotel purchased by families eager to start one of the first high schools in California. J.P. Durbin, head of the Methodist missionary society, and William Roberts, superintendent of the Oregon and California Mission Conference, decided that these three men—Owen, Taylor and Bannister—should head an effort to establish a Methodist academy leading to a college.

Nine of 699 launch Pacific

At the prompting of the First Methodist Church in San Francisco, the only legal Methodist church body in California, Isaac Owen, as "Presiding Elder" of California, convened an "Educational Convention" of nine Methodist clergy to recommend the founding of "an institution the grade of a university" on January 6 and 7, 1851, in San Jose.[11] This action represented a body of no less than 699 Methodist souls in the state at the time.[12] At the second session of the convention at William Taylor's home in San Francisco on May 14, four school locations were discussed: San Francisco, San Jose, Santa Clara and Vallejo, with preference directed to San Jose and Vallejo with this proviso:

> *1. RESOLVED, that we locate the University independently of present corporations on some mile square to be selected for that purpose, which shall be sold in small lots so as to secure an endowment and give such control as to prevent the sale of intoxicating liquors, the practices of gambling, of circuses, and other immoral amusement.*[13]

At the third meeting on June 26 at Isaac Owen's home in Santa Clara, the group decided on a location and formulated the application for a charter—in less than six months from their start. Owen had already been appointed "Agent" for the cause, that is, chief fundraiser. He claimed to find the most fertile territory near Santa Clara, with pledges on land purchase totaling $27,500, though there is scant evidence that he scoured the other locales for support. Santa Clara County, with about 7,000 residents, was nearly to quadruple in size within 20 years, and its number of children—and property values—exceeded any county in the state except San Francisco.[14]

Thus began Owen's fateful influence in the start-up of Pacific, and more was to originate from this strong leader. The promising location of the institution was to dog the school for years to come, prompting two relocations and, several times, schemes to move to San Francisco. The group also selected the name "California Wesleyan University," keeping in step with a common tribute to the founder of Methodism in the names of many Methodist colleges all across the country.

What's in a name?

Reverends Owen, Bannister and Hester drafted the petition to the state Supreme Court, which the state legislature had just authorized to incorporate colleges. Attorney Annis Merrill, later to become one of the longest-serving chairs of the board of trustees, brought the petition to the judges on July 10, 1851, but there was one significant glitch: the Court realized that it was authorized to incorporate "colleges," not "universities," and thus granted that day to an agreeable Merrill a charter to establish "California Wesleyan *College*," the first charter so issued in California and the first in the West.

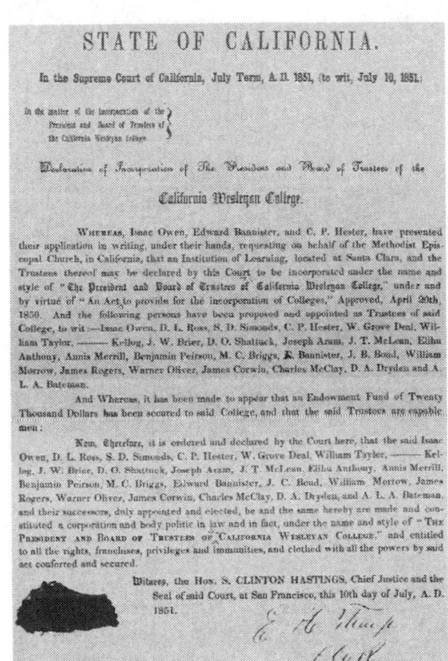

STATE OF CALIFORNIA.

In the Supreme Court of California, July Term, A. D. 1851, (to wit, July 10, 1851.)

In the matter of the incorporation of the President and Board of Trustees of the California Wesleyan College.

Declaration of Incorporation of The President and Board of Trustees of the California Wesleyan College.

WHEREAS, Isaac Owen, Edward Bannister, and C. P. Hester, have presented their application in writing, under their hands, requesting on behalf of the Methodist Episcopal Church, in California, that an Institution of Learning, located at Santa Clara, and the Trustees thereof may be declared by this Court to be incorporated under the name and style of "The President and Board of Trustees of California Wesleyan College," under and by virtue of "An Act to provide for the incorporation of Colleges," Approved, April 20th, 1850. And the following persons have been proposed and appointed as Trustees of said College, to wit:—Isaac Owen, D. L. Ross, S. D. Simonds, C. P. Hester, W. Grove Deal, William Taylor, ——— Kellog, J. W. Brier, D. O. Shattuck, Joseph Aram, J. T. McLean, Elihu Anthony, Annis Merrill, Benjamin Peirson, M. C. Briggs, E. Bannister, J. B. Bond, William Morrow, James Rogers, Warner Oliver, James Corwin, Charles McClay, D. A. Dryden and A. L. A. Bateman.

And Whereas, it has been made to appear that an Endowment Fund of Twenty Thousand Dollars has been secured to said College, and that the said Trustees are capable men:

Now, Therefore, it is ordered and declared by the Court here, that the said Isaac Owen, D. L. Ross, S. D. Simonds, C. P. Hester, W. Grove Deal, William Taylor, ——— Kellog, J. W. Brier, D. O. Shattuck, Joseph Aram, J. T. McLean, Elihu Anthony, Annis Merrill, Benjamin Peirson, M. C. Briggs, Edward Bannister, J. C. Bond, William Morrow, James Rogers, Warner Oliver, James Corwin, Charles McClay, D. A. Dryden, and A. L. A. Bateman, and their successors, duly appointed and elected, be and the same hereby are made and constituted a corporation and body politic in law and in fact, under the name and style of "THE PRESIDENT AND BOARD OF TRUSTEES OF CALIFORNIA WESLEYAN COLLEGE," and entitled to all the rights, franchises, privileges and immunities, and clothed with all the powers by said act conferred and secured.

Witness, the Hon. S. CLINTON HASTINGS, Chief Justice and the Seal of said Court, at San Francisco, this 10th day of July, A. D. 1851.

The original charter of July 10, 1851.

Within a month, at the first meeting of the board of trustees, a feisty group of 24 Methodist men immediately requested the state legislature change the name from California Wesleyan College to "University of the Pacific," reasserting its initial request to found a university, not a college, and advancing a much bolder name. About six months later, on March 29, 1852, the legislature complied by remedying its oversight to authorize the founding of "universities" as well as "colleges" and approving the name change.[15] As Pacific's centennial historian, Rockwell Hunt, observed, the name "was more than ambitious—it must have appeared decidedly fantastic to many an observer.…Who but the Methodists would have had the imagination, the audacity, the sky-limit faith to choose such a name, under such circumstances?"[16] Pacific's most venerable professor of the nineteenth century, James Martin, put it this way: "They gave her a name sufficiently expressive of their enlarged ideas of her destiny."[17]

A building rises

The trustees quickly dispatched committees to determine the faculty, degrees, curriculum, tuition and texts. A week later, the board determined construction plans for the first building, a three-story brick edifice on the northeast corner of what is now Winchester Boulevard and Bellomy Street in Santa Clara. This plan actually became the second building. The first built was two stories high and half the footprint.[18] Given the competition between Protestants and Catholics in the Bay Area, it may come as no surprise that the founders of Pacific broke ground less than a mile west of the Jesuits' Santa Clara College, as if to assert that Rome would not rule California higher education.

But the actual reason for selecting the site seems to have been a favorable land deal, local financial support and the persuasion of one man, Isaac Owen. Construction was delayed owing to title difficulties with the 11-acre land purchase, a common occurrence for former Spanish territories. Some trustees still favored building in San Francisco, but the majority agreed that a rural location was better suited to educating youth, sensibly distant from city violence, crime and temptations. Construction began in 1852. Until the building was completed, classes were held by Edward Bannister in San Jose's "What Cheer House," a refuge for people in need. Bannister was appointed the first principal, and along with three other teachers opened Pacific's first (preparatory) classes in the new building on May 3, 1852.[19]

The Methodist special power

Starting in 1784 with Cokesbury College in Baltimore, the Methodists founded 775 schools and colleges by 1899. Only 125 have survived into the 21st century.[20] This mushrooming of Methodist colleges followed the trajectory of American Methodism. In 1776, a mere three percent of U.S.

church people were Methodists; by 1850, over one-third were Methodists—by far the largest denomination in the country.[21] A vision of equality, especially for women, was there from the start. This dramatic growth in Methodism was grounded in the experiential religion of evangelical "camp meetings" and the ability to "organize to beat the devil." Methodism placed a special positive emphasis on human improvement. As one scholar summarizes, "Methodism had become the largest Protestant denomination by speaking the language of the people, winning those people to a heart-felt religion, and creating a system of circuit riders and local lay leaders and exhorters to establish societies of Methodists across the frontier."[22]

It took Methodists a while to see the value of higher education, but once they knew that schools and colleges could be an important route to human betterment, they established over the next century and a half about 1,200 schools, colleges, universities and seminaries.

PIONEER IN CO-EDUCATION

Launched by luminaries

Early trustees of the University included political leaders Governor John Bigler (left) and Congressman John Bidwell. (Bigler portrait by William F. Cogswell, public domain, from Wikipedia, The Free Encyclopedia).

On February 17, 1854, the board elected Rev. Martin Briggs as its first president and appointed the college's first faculty: Rev. Alexander Gibbons in mathematics and William Maclay in Greek and Latin languages.[23] The trustees also set the curricula for the "Collegiate Department" and the "Female Institute." Rev. Briggs was uncomfortable as president and soon became chair of the board, on which he served intermittently for three decades. Later Briggs became one of the most widely known champions of preserving the Union and keeping California a free state, along with his good friend Leland Stanford, who was governor by 1861, and the Unitarian minister Thomas Starr King.[24] Briggs headed the California delegation to the 1860 Republican National Convention to cast ten votes for Abraham Lincoln.

A breadth of California leadership promised good fortune for the state's first school of higher learning. Among the early trustees was esteemed Governor John Bigler, the only governor ever to serve on Pacific's board and a staunch leader of the state Democratic Party. He had twice been elected speaker of the first California Assembly and remained a distinguished public servant throughout his law career. Annis Merrill, board chair through the early decades, was a founder of the Republican Party of California.[25]

Another founding trustee was Joseph Aram, who helped raise the first American flag in Monterey, was a delegate at the Constitutional Convention in Monterey in 1849 and became the first sheriff of Santa Clara County. Along with Captain Aram, 14 of the first 24 trustees were Methodist clergy, three were physicians, and six were lawyers or judges. Later, the famed and wealthy pioneer of the first wagon train party to California, John Bidwell, served as trustee for a year just after he was a U.S. congressman. As a state leader, wealthy philanthropist and good friend of John Muir, Bidwell was a prominent Pacific appointment; one wonders what opportunities were lost to Pacific by his short tenure.

Co-education from the ground floor

In that first board meeting in 1851, Isaac Owen, again taking a bold lead, moved to admit female students for degree programs. His colleagues agreed. This commitment to equality of educational opportunity for men and women set Pacific ahead of almost any other school in the country. This was truly one of its pioneering milestones, especially given that educating women has become the global mandate of the twenty-first century.[26]

Within a few months the board decided to "divide the male and female departments" by separate buildings for some 50 students.[27] By the next year the "Female Institute" of the University was founded, and a handsome, wood, two-story structure was erected on one and a half acres on the Santa Clara town square next to the Methodist Church, about a half-mile from the first campus buildings. The "Female Institute" was a common way that schools taught both men and women while keeping them discreetly separate. Such was the practice at places like progressive Oberlin College as well as Pacific.

Establishing the University's collegiate Female Institute in 1851 was a pioneering act by Pacific. No known image of the male campus exists.

California's first college graduates

By 1856, Pacific already had its second president, William Maclay, the classics professor. He was replaced by the mathematics professor A. S. Gibbons, who presided over the first graduation on June 9, 1858. Gibbons, who first served two years and then returned to the presidency in 1872 for five more years, was the "first real President of the University."[28] Receiving the B.S. degree in 1858 were five women and three men, along with two men who earned the B.A. degree, the first baccalaureate degrees ever conferred in the state of California—except for one solitary graduate of Santa Clara College the prior year.[29] In a three-hour ceremony each graduate presented an oration to an audience on hard benches, a challenging end to a year when faculty took a 50 percent pay cut to make ends meet. President Gibbons was salaried at $600 annually (faculty at $400-500), "…or 1000$ if there be funds at the end of the year that can be applied to said object."[30]

Like the first graduating class, nearly half of Pacific's enrollment was female. Most of the other colleges in the country would not consider enrolling women for nearly two more decades. The decision to enroll women turned out to make great business sense; tuition income from women enrollments carried the school for many years.

Forced integration

President Briggs urged the board to unite the male and female departments as early as June 1854, but within two years the trustees rescinded the action. In 1858 and again in 1859, when Pacific enrolled 92 male and 60 female students, the trustees urged President Gibbons to "blend the classes as far as possible," no doubt owing to tight budgets that made separate classes impractical for parallel curricula, though not until 1869 were the male and female departments actually merged.[31]

The earliest known copy of the University seal, 1869.

All the evidence points to Pacific as the first co-educational institution of higher education on the West Coast, likely just prior to Methodist Corvallis College in Oregon. By the time the University of California admitted women students in October 1870, Pacific recitation classes included both male and female students.[32] Co-education was fully practiced—all classes integrated—before the move to College Park in 1871. By contrast, not until 1872 were Cornell and Wesleyan universities the first co-ed schools in the East.

What a deal

When Bannister resigned as principal of Pacific's preparatory department in 1854, he presented the board with a scholarship plan to raise endowment funds. Actually, it was a plan hatched by Isaac Owen, brought from his fundraising days at Asbury University in Indiana. While overall prep and collegiate enrollment figures looked promising—100 in the male department, 65 in the female department—the school was strapped for funds from the start. The proposal was to sell full-tuition scholarships at discounted prices that would serve as vouchers for tuition for years to come. The plan gave an investor the guarantee that his family would have the option to attend tuition-free for up to 25 years, and in some offers, in perpetuity!

This lavish scholarship program was effective in luring families to California's first college, and students from struggling farms and hardscrabble towns came in waves at the start. But of course it was too good to be good for Pacific and quickly drove the school into the ground. Owen's scholarship plan was so flawed by today's standards that it appears tragicomic in proportions: what school would ever consider selling full-tuition scholarship vouchers usable for up to six years, 25 years, not to say "perpetually," at a cost of $100, $200, and $600 respectively, guaranteed to the donor/purchaser or "his heirs or assigns," all in an effort to raise $50,000 for an endowment fund? In a pricey, inflationary Gold Rush economy, it was disastrous. The offer brought a line-up of buyers—and sunk the school into debt that dogged Pacific for decades.[33] Nearly a century later, president Burns asserted that an antique "perpetual" voucher was presented—and honored—as recently as the 1940s.[34]

Such a hare-brained plan could never have passed muster with a seasoned board, and one wonders how sensible heads on a novice board permitted it. But Owen, the only man who had any experience in collegiate fundraising, was a charismatic leader whom students affectionately called "Father Owen" for decades to come. One of Rockwell Hunt's few harsh judgments in his centennial history of Pacific is his condemnation of this example of a Methodist stumble "where pious emotionalism was permitted to prevail against sound reasoning."[35]

Imagine what this wrenching reality forced upon the board right from the start. Three years into the progam, here were the stats: seven "perpetual scholarships;" eight "25-year scholarships;" 102 "6-year scholarships;" and 18 "3-year scholarships" for a total of 135 full-tuition scholarships in a class of 165 prep and college students! This, while most of the faculty felt obliged to donate half their salaries to pay the bills to avoid collapse.

Common sense returns

Instead of folding their tents, the trustees grabbed the reins from Agent Owen. Within a year, the board voted to cease all "scholarship sales" and commanded Agent Owen to seek donations to pay off college debts. Apparently in order to underscore their resolve, the board voted again 60 days later to do the same. They declared the president as a second "financial agent" and requested of scholarship purchasers a revised agreement that would reduce "perpetual" and "25-year" scholarships to six-year scholarships.

Even this could not save the school. By fall of 1857, all board members were made "financial agents" of their respective Methodist districts to retrieve scholarship dollars in their own neighborhoods.[36] In the end, Pacific barely survived its first crisis, a threat brought on by one of its own founding heroes.

ADAPTABLE ACADEMICS AND THE START OF PROFESSIONAL SCHOOLS

Tradition rules in the classroom

The classical course of study was quite routinized across the country by the time Pacific registered its first students, so the board's first curriculum was a copy of the standard private liberal arts college fare.

Early on Pacific included "Scientific" and "Literary" "courses" or tracks for the bachelor of science (or "mistress of science") degree, introduced first by the Methodists of Wesleyan University in Connecticut in 1838. By 1876, the "bachelor of philosophy" degree was applied to the literary branch, substituting modern languages for classical ones. Written exams replaced oral exams and recitations starting in the 1860s.[37] The academic term was a couple months longer than readers of this history likely experienced; the "fall term" began in early July and the spring term ended in June.

Building Christian character was of course fundamental. Under "The Bible" course, the 1856-57 *Catalogue* stated that "Theological controversies will in no case be admitted in the course of instruction in this Institution; but weekly exercises in the History, Poetry, Religion, and Morals of the Holy Scriptures will be attended to by all the students."[38]

Pacific's medical school

In fall, 1858, San Francisco physician Beverly Cole proposed that a medical school just founded by Elias Cooper in San Francisco become affiliated with Pacific as a "Medical Department." The board endorsed the plan, which exempted the trustees of any liability, and the first "medical school" on the West Coast was born. Starting with 13 students (women were excluded, like nearly all of the 42 U.S. medical schools of the time), the four-person department headed by Dean Cole awarded two M.D. degrees within a year.[39] Thus the multiple-campus, multiple-city identity of Pacific that the world has known since the 1960s was embedded in its spirit a century earlier as part of its enterprising, adaptable character. This decision marked clearly that Pacific was not to remain simply a liberal arts college but to begin to live up to its name of "University."

18 PACIFIC PHAROS

D. QUILTY,

THE LEADING TAILOR OF SAN JOSE,

MERCANTILE GOODS AND NOVELTIES

CALL AND EXAMINE MY STOCK,

GUARANTEE TO GIVE YOU SPLENDID FITTING GARMENTS,

D. QUILTY.

COOPER MEDICAL COLLEGE.

N. E. Corner Sacramento and Webster Streets, San Francisco, California.

FACULTY.

Pacific established the West Coast's first medical school in 1858. By the 1880s, it had become Cooper Medical College on the corner of Webster and Sacramento in San Francisco.

The Civil War disrupted the school after graduating seven students in 1864, and it did not reorganize until 1870, with nine medical faculty, all with M.D.s.[40] In 1872, pressured by competing Toland Medical College (later to become the University of California medical school), the medical faculty requested they be transferred from Pacific to University (City) College, a Presbyterian school nearby with better facilities. The new school was known as Medical College of the

Pacific until 1882, when it became the independent Cooper Medical School in a new building donated by Cooper's nephew, Levi Cooper Lane. In 1908 Stanford University purchased Cooper to begin its own medical department, the founding of the current Stanford University School of Medicine.[41]

Boxton's College of Physicians and Surgeons

The story of Pacific's medical school, with its string of physician-entrepreneurs and various identities, demonstrated how San Francisco, now nearly 50 years old, was still a frontier city with a quirky individuality and independence. Charles Boxton also embodied this characteristic. Founder of the College of Physicians and Surgeons (CPS) of San Francisco in 1896, Boxton was an opportunist who saw his new school as a springboard to success in a town of entrepreneurs active with a kind of reckless energy. His initiative was part of a national movement to expand higher education in the 1890s. CPS was one of 27 dental schools in the country, up from 16 in the prior decade.[42]

Charles Boxton, Dean 1896-1923.

Charles Boxton was the quirky, entrepreneurial founder and first dean of the College of Physicians and Surgeons, which became Pacific's School of Dentistry in 1962.

The school, eventually to become the University of the Pacific School of Dentistry in 1962, was a highly successful enterprise from the start and for nearly all of its century-plus history. Boxton enrolled over 200 medical and dental students in the first year, becoming an instant success. By 1899 he had San Francisco Mayor Phelan dedicating a new building on 14th Street and saw his own political career rising as a member of the city Board of Supervisors.

The first College of Physicians & Surgeons building was rented until 1899...

...when the 344 14th Street building between Valencia and Mission was constructed and occupied, rebuilt after the 1906 fire, then occupied until 1967.

THE CIVIL WAR BRINK FORCES A MOVE

The lean Civil War years

In January 1860, Edward Bannister was elected President upon the resignation of Gibbons, whose leave-of-absence request was declined. Bannister, one of the co-founders with Owen and Taylor, remained as president for nearly eight years, far longer than his predecessors, serving throughout the difficult Civil War years. He provided the continuity absent on the board (except for Isaac Owen, Annis Merrill and Martin Briggs) and in the faculty, where turnover was routine. The exception was professor James Martin, the quintessential faculty member of the times. Always wise, levelheaded, down-to-earth, Martin was much beloved by students.[43]

Classics professor James Martin (faculty member from 1872-1890) was by far the most revered professor at Pacific in the 19th century. Pacific awarded him one of its first honorary doctorates in 1886.

At the outset of the Civil War, about half the 157 students (prep and college) were on full-tuition scholarships, yet only about one-fourth of them were Methodists.[44] Tuition was competitive—30 dollars per term for the 16 students in the "Scientific Collegiate" program and 40 dollars for the 14 in the "Classical Collegiate" program.[45] High drop-out rates were common at Pacific and across the country, especially during the war years, so while enrollment was running around 100 to 150 students, the number of actual graduates continued to be miniscule. In 1863, for example, one graduate walked for each of the four degrees, B.A., B.S., M.A., and M.S.[46]

Moving to College Park, San Jose

The Civil War had brought Pacific again to the brink. Enrollments were dropping and debts were climbing. In fact, in the 20 years from the mid-1850s to the mid-1870s, Pacific averaged fewer than 30 college students annually, and hit a low of 17 in 1864. In 1865, rather than close down Pacific, the board severed its financial obligation for the University because of "the pecuniary embarrassment of the University"—and perhaps because of such high turnover among the board itself. The trustees granted the school to the principals, Rev. Tuthill of the Female Institute, and President Bannister of the Male Institute, including the buildings and all operations—as well as all liabilities—to exempt the board from financial responsibility for one year.[47] The main male college building thrown up in 1853 was already "rickety" by 1864.[48] That the school did not close is a tribute to the determined, mission-driven handful of men who persisted when so many other schools folded under debt, duress and lack of resolve.

As the war ended, the Pacific trustees were determined to make a fresh start. Armed with a $17,000 endowment and the inspiring leadership of Rev. Greenberry Baker as their new agent-fundraiser, the board purchased 216 acres between Alameda Road and the Guadalupe River, about halfway between Santa Clara and San Jose. The land, known as "Stockton Ranch," was bought from Charles Polhemus at a very favorable price, followed

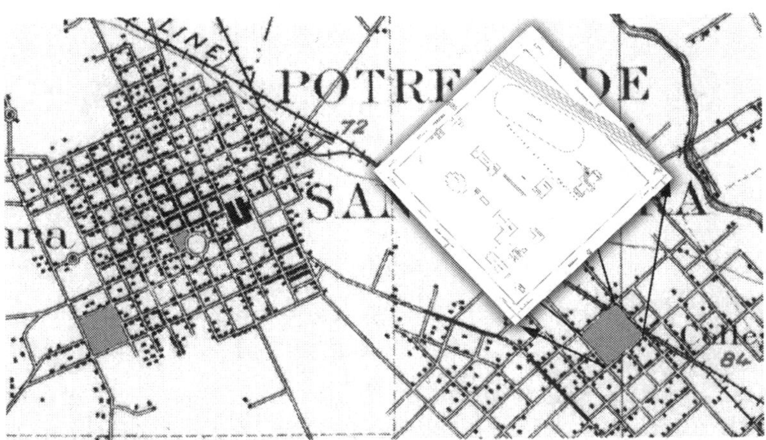

The College Park/San Jose campus was only two miles from the original Santa Clara campuses.

by another 200 acres next door sold by Mr. Newell. The total cost for 435 acres was $72,000. While close to rapidly growing San Jose, the site was, as the 1878 catalog stated, "yet removed from the excitements and scenes of temptation and dissipation found in our cities."[49] Baker's scheme was to sell one-acre lots at $550-600 each in order to build the endowment fund and a new campus that could expand to a sustainable size.[50]

Rev. Thomas Sinex, who served as President for five years, 1867-72, had the fresh opportunity to build a new campus in what was newly named College Park, a 22-acre campus on the future Union Pacific Railway line. By 1868, fifty acres had been sold for $20,000—almost enough to pay off the land debt. The old Santa Clara campus was sold for $7,375 while a new $20,000 building arose from additional pledges. Land sale income was restricted to the endowment fund.

This engraving of the College Park/San Jose campus from the 1880s was prominent in annual University bulletins.

Three-story West Hall, used for instruction, chapel and the four literary societies, opened in 1871. The board, fearing the worst, escaped liability for two years by again leasing the campus to the President and a handful of trustees to see if they could make ends meet on tuition income.[51] Board minutes for 1869 log only a single graduate, a "Mistress of Science," and in the prior year Bannister's son was one of only two graduates.[52]

West Hall, built in 1871 as the first building on the College Park campus, was the academic and social hall.

Through Pacific's many zigs and zags, the board pushed on—growing to 17 members, all nominated by the regional Methodist Conference, with staggered terms to help build continuity.

Where are the students, where are the dollars

When Sinex resigned in 1872, Rev. A. S. Gibbons, a professor at Ohio University who had been one of Pacific's first two professors and president from 1857-59 reluctantly returned to the presidency for another five years. He became the fifth "full-time" faculty member for a school that still only graduated five or six students a year. Through these years, the Methodists kept insisting that the school be a non-sectarian Christian outpost in this frontier. The board "resolved that in conducting the University of the Pacific as a school of Christian learning, we demand no other conditions of admission than those which pertain to scholarship and character."[53] They needed all the students they could get, and they did not want denominational control to doom them to oblivion like so many other schools.

NINETEENTH-CENTURY CAMPUS LIFE

The nineteenth-century student

Who were these nineteenth-century Pacific students? Prior to the appearance of the *Naranjado* yearbook and *The Pacific Pharos* biweekly student paper in 1886, there are scant records of student life. Nearly all seemed to be young white Protestant men and women from generally middle-class backgrounds, though the school was also referred to as "the poor student's friend" as it is today.[54] Mary Smith, one of those first ten graduates in 1858 and the oldest living graduate of a college in the West when she died in 1928, was probably quite typical. Arriving with her parents in Santa Clara County in 1852 after crossing the isthmus of Panama, she taught in public schools in the Foothills after graduating, married Cornelius Brooke and bore five children, and was active in a Sacramento Methodist church. Her lifelong enthusiasm for Pacific prompted her to bestow her diploma to President Knoles to commemorate that very first graduation.[55]

The 1891 Naranjado cover displays the California orange poppy, alleged source of the yearbook name and Pacific's first student color, to which black was later added. Student dress was formal through the nineteenth century, even in the science labs (1877).

Except for a few sprinklings of Chinese and especially Japanese international students, students came from Northern California towns.[56] The American-Pacific experience influenced the few Chinese and Japanese students. Two students from the 1880s credited their Pacific experience for widening their cultural views. Sanji Muto (1886), a Japanese textile magnate, became a renowned labor leader who was assassinated for his progressive reforms. Tong Sing Kow (1887, '02), active in campus affairs and Pacific's first Chinese graduate, is said to have persuaded the Chinese empress dowager to discourage the ancient practice of foot-binding.[57] Pacific's first African-American graduate, as far as we know, was William Wealthy Howard, in 1911, and the second, Mildred Jones, not until 1924, so the student body was decidedly less ethnically diverse than today.

Sanji Muto (1886) and Tong Sing Kow (1887, '02) were early Asian students who rose to prominence in their native countries of Japan and China.

After 1870, about half of the students were from the larger San Jose area. They were aspiring students, often ambitious to enroll at the University of California when it opened in 1869, then Stanford after it opened in 1891. Many graduates pursued advanced degrees at Michigan, Boston, Johns Hopkins, or became professionals in medicine, law, teaching, ministry and engineering. One became the State Librarian.

Among these nineteenth-century alumni, an 1859 graduate became the superintendent of schools for Sonoma County; an 1865 grad was a district judge in Reno, another a lawyer and legislator in Tucson; an 1876 grad was a Boston Conservatory student; an 1887 alumnus, Henry Meade Bland, was named Poet Laureate of California. The great class of 1886, the largest senior class to date, sent two to Cornell in literature, two to Philadelphia Medical College, and four to the University of Michigan. More than half of the 28 graduates planned advanced study.[58] Later, President Knoles was proud to tout that not only did Pacific produce "proportionately more leaders" than Cal or Stanford but that "the state has been run largely by Pacific legislators and Pacific judges and lawyers" and church and business leaders. Pacific presidents continue to repeat this argument to spotlight the holistic development of students that is a hallmark of the school.[59]

HENRY MEADE BLAND

Among distinguished nineteenth century alumni was Henry Meade Bland ('87), California's second Poet Laureate (1929-31).

Planting the College Park campus

Little is known about the sparse Santa Clara ("male") campus with its two buildings. Beginning in 1870, the College Park campus had its ups and downs—times of beauty, times of neglect, especially athletic fields. "Arbor Day," begun by a student groundskeeper in 1886 (not tied to the national recognition day) to spruce up a campus that had "only trees," became a university holiday when all students participated in campus grooming. True, the males cleaned up the weeds and planted the trees and the females served lemonade and noon dinner. But all joined the annual photo portrait—students hanging playfully from the balconies—followed by games, skits, musical numbers and competitions. Except for the 1906 earthquake, Arbor Day ran continuously into the 1920s.[60]

Begun in 1886, Pacific's annual Arbor Day was a campus planting and cleanup holiday that continued for decades.

Towering Monterey cypress and Monterey pines remained the signature native groves of the "beautiful shady campus," while students and staff planted non-native species such as box elder, yucca and fan palms over the years.[61]

The College Park, San Jose campus entrance in 1908—as much a campus of trees as the later Stockton Campus.

Most of the women students lodged on campus—South Hall opened in 1874—while male students boarded with families in the region. The "commuter" population was sufficient for the students to complain about a lack of parking. Yes. By 1889 the *Pacific Pharos* called for more "sheds and stalls" for horses and buggies in rainy weather.[62]

South Hall, the first residence hall on the College Park campus, opened for women in 1874. Men stayed in area homes.

Literary societies, backbone of campus life

Given its origins, character, size and the tenor of American college life at the time, not surprisingly at Pacific words carried the day. The "literary societies" were in fact literary societies for decades before they morphed into the social Greek fraternities and sororities beginning in the 1920s. The rise of "literary societies" was a tradition begun by students in the early nineteenth century and prominent at all colleges during this time.[63] Before the era of the athletic hero and rise of the "Greeks," literary societies reigned supreme as "the central institution of extracurricular life."[64] The debater, the orator and the essayist ruled the campus, not the football star, the political activist or the beauty queen.

Nearly from the start four literary societies dominated the small campus. Archania was the first collegiate society in the state and probably west of

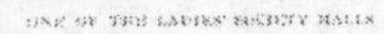
ONE OF THE LADIES' SOCIETY HALLS

ONE OF THE GENTLEMEN'S SOCIETY HALLS

Archania (1854) and Emendia (1858) were the first male and female campus societies in the west. Their "halls" were placed in West Hall, the first building on the San Jose Campus in 1871. Shown here are halls of a male and a female literary society.

the Mississippi (1854). Rhizomia (1858) was the second society for men. Emendia, the first "young ladies society" in the state and on the West Coast (1858), and Sopholechtia (1881) were the women's societies. (Phi Kappa Psi fraternity was also founded in 1881.) The founding of these literary societies with the support of the faculty and administration was Pacific's first pronounced expression of the value of what is called today "experiential learning." The Archites proclaimed in their founding charter that "no other method [is] so efficient" to achieve mature communication skills than to form a club for that purpose.

The emergence of the "Rhizites," as Rhizomia members were called, is itself a telling story of the impact of the slavery issue on antebellum Pacific. The Archites hotly debated issues of the day, including slavery. The majority of Archanians at the time favored the South and its position on slavery. Students who favored abolition and preserving the Union found debating their society brothers too combative, offensive and troublesome, so they resigned. This faction left Archania in 1858 to found the Rhizomian Society and the rivalry sparked by the divisive issue of slavery continued for decades to come.[65]

Customized student culture…

Student demonstrations were not uncommon in these early decades of American colleges, and Pacific had its share of them. More often than not, disruptive behavior was the normal erratic experiment of youth or the unstoppable urge to war with elders. Students delighted in antics like stealing the college bell clapper, and many remembered a true classic:

absconding with and burying the cornerstone for new South Hall just before it was to be laid.

More important, students created their own campus cultures. Enduring what students now would consider a harsh, boot camp atmosphere where living conditions were bare bones, structured activities limited and amenities non-existent, students fashioned a social and even academic world of their own. Organized activities for students were not provided—college staff was virtually non-existent. Students spent most of their social time informally, organizing themselves in whatever fashion suited them.

Much student impishness and tomfoolery found its way into print as student publications emerged in fits and starts. The *Pacific Pharos* and *Naranjado* were not only lavished with creative writing of every genre, they were riddled with insider cartoons and jokes like this "dictionary" item on campus dining: "Kellogg's Korn Flakes—A food made of predigested shavings and sawdust, occasionally served as breakfast food in college dining halls." And this quatrain: "A man is like a kerosene lamp, / He isn't especially bright. / He is often turned down, usually smokes, / And often goes out at night."[66] A tradition in the 1910s was an afternoon of "tie-up and tubbing" between freshman and sophomores. The class teams contested who could literally tie up opponents with four-inch cloth strips, then the winning team tagged prisoners with green paint and dunked them in a giant hogshead tub of water on the lawn.[67]

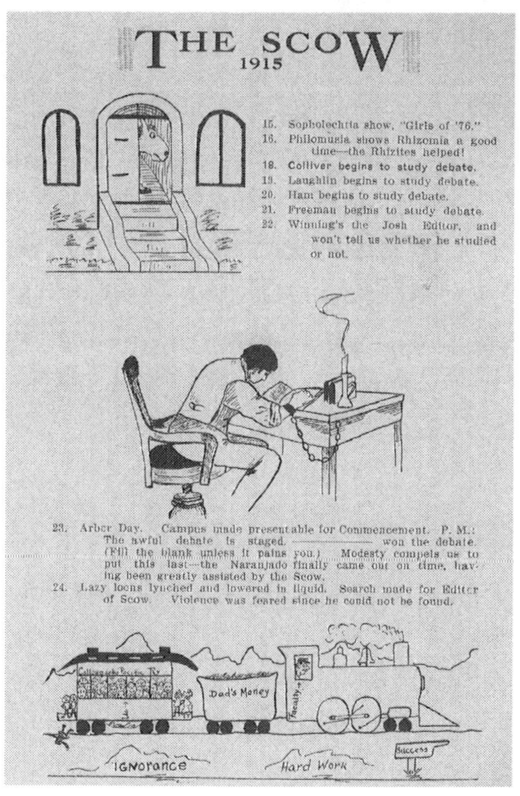
THE SCOW
1915

15. Sopholechtia show, "Girls of '76."
16. Philomusia shows Rhizomia a good time—the Rhizites helped!
18. Colliver begins to study debate.
19. Laughlin begins to study debate.
20. Ham begins to study debate.
21. Freeman begins to study debate.
22. Winning's the Josh Editor, and won't tell us whether he studied or not.

23. Arbor Day. Campus made presentable for Commencement. P. M.: The awful debate is staged. ———— won the debate. (Fill the blank unless it pains you.) Modesty compels us to put this last—the Naranjado finally came out on time, having been greatly assisted by the Scow.
24. Lazy locns lynched and lowered in liquid. Search made for Editor of Scow. Violence was feared since he could not be found.

The Naranjado yearbook (1886-) and The Epoch (1884-) and Pacific Pharos (1886-) campus newspapers were filled with creative writing, drawings, and cartoons of all sorts. Cost of college was never far from thought.

... Yet a regulated life

Pacific's "close student-faculty interaction" had a harsh edge in those early decades. Student behavior was highly regulated by the faculty through a system of demerits:

> *At the beginning of the term each student shall be credited with 100 and shall be subject to demerit for any disturbance or misconduct. Should the deportment of any student fall to 90, he shall be informed of the fact by the President; should it fall to 80, his name shall be read out in Chapel; should it fall to 70, his parents or guardians shall be informed; and, should it fall to 60, the student thereby suspends himself from the institution.*[68]

By the 1890s, late night banquets and parties, especially of the literary societies, had become lavish affairs at the best hotels in San Jose; dinner would begin at ten or later. It exercised the board enough to pass censure on them, urging the President "to dissuade all students from such injurious practices."[69] Friday morning chapel was required, as it was in nearly all public as well as private schools in the mid-nineteenth century, though *The Epoch,* the earliest student newspaper, notes longingly that Cornell, Michigan and Virginia all adopted voluntary chapel attendance by 1885.[70] Befitting this regulated decorum, students tended to dress more formally on campus—long dresses and jackets and ties were common. Yet the faculty had their playful times with students. Biology Professor Kroeck started a Halloween masquerade party that featured costumed faculty performing for the students that ran for about 30 years.[71]

Athletics begins

Pacific's character as an academic campus seems clearer by the 1880s, as student papers frequently grumbled about a lack of school spirit generally and athletics in particular. One *Pacific Pharos* editorial laments: "There is too much of a tendency among the upper class men to look upon all athletic sports as fit only for the lower class men and 'preps,' foot ball and base ball have long been neglected to the lower classes—and all other athletic games are rapidly taking the same course."[72] Actually, the annual campus "Field Day," a long Pacific tradition, saw impressive track and field performances, but when J. L. Coates (1887) set national records in the 100-yard dash (9.75 seconds) and the 220-yard dash in 1887, Field Day was discredited by the UC-Berkeley *Occident* newspaper as an unreliable amateur event.[73]

During most of the first half-century, Pacific students organized athletic contests on their own. In 1886, students organized the University of the Pacific Athletic Association "to bring the sports clubs together in one organization."[74] The YMCA organized the basketball team until 1906, when the Student Body of the University of the Pacific (the first student governing association, established in 1899) oversaw all athletic clubs. Students complained annually about the lack of campus athletic facilities until the administration began to respond after the turn of the century. The fact remained that Pacific's major intercollegiate, competitive spirit shone forth in the word, not physical prowess. When Cal refused to accept Pacific's first challenge to an oratorical contest instead of a debate in 1889, the *Pacific Pharos* called for a state oratorical association to expand competition at the podium.[75]

Demon smoking, demon rum

Tobacco and alcohol were the most worrisome of student activities on this Methodist campus. To avoid expulsion, four male students in 1897 were required to pledge in writing to president McClish that they would refrain from further smoking, card playing, drinking and playing pool in barrooms.[76] This "event" may have led the trustees to ban "the use of tobacco in any way by the students" in 1899, which was given national notoriety and disapprobation by the *New York Sun*. But the student paper supported the move against thc "cvil effects of smoking," which should result in "a great change in the character of the work done by our students," enforced, as usual, by the faculty.[77]

The least tolerated of college student excesses was intoxication, which likely brought suspension or expulsion at any school.[78] But the strict law against alcohol was absolute on any Methodist campus, since

Methodists helped to build the temperance movement, joining the Quakers in condemning excessive drinking long before other church groups. The student paper *Pacific Pharos* frequently ran articles on such topics as poverty in America, which was blamed on rum that "debauches, blotches, brutalizes, [and] makes a beastly boozy nation."[79]

Tight rules for student behavior at Pacific lasted well into the twentieth century. In the 1905-07 catalogue, the following regulation appears just before room and board policies:

> *Vicious Habits.*
>
> *In the interest of health, morals, and the profitable use of time, the Trustees and the Faculty are unalterably opposed to our students using tobacco or intoxicating beverages, visiting saloons, billiard and pool rooms, playing cards, using profane or obscene language, or spending in idleness the hours set apart for study.*[80]

JOSTLING FOR POSITION IN CALIFORNIA

Stiff local competition

The University of California opened in Oakland in 1869 with ten faculty members and nearly 40 students—an intimidating student-to-faculty ratio for Pacific! Women students were admitted the next year, and by 1873 with nearly 200 students the university moved to its new campus in Berkeley. The state university enrolled over 500 students by the 1880s, but had gone through its start-up challenges as well, with seven presidents in its first 23 years. Cal, though a public school, had its game-changing benefactor too: Phoebe Apperson Hearst, heir to the Hearst newspaper fortune. Her gifts beginning in 1891 built the core campus, funded women's scholarships and invested in quality academic programs.

How in the world could Pacific compete with these juggernauts just steps away to the north, and squeezed on both sides by Santa Clara and soon San Jose Normal? Berkeley charged no tuition as part of a statewide plan known as the "California idea" in higher education, a visionary, coordinated approach between state government and the public university to coordinate student enrollment to build the new state. "The distinguishing feature of the 'California idea' in higher education was that the utility of an educated workforce was fused with education for character and public service."[81] Even this mission seemed to compete with Pacific's ideals. In 1884, at the cornerstone laying of Pacific's East Hall, former President Sinex surveyed the impressive regional higher education landscape that looked grim for Pacific:

> *The State University was founded and started in life with a birthday present of half a million dollars from the state.... The State Normal School was removed from San Francisco to San Jose and received the generous gift from the city of thirty acres of land.... [W]ith a State University with its free tuition, with a magnificent Normal School almost within sight, with free tuition.... we were greatly at a disadvantage in seeking patronage.*[82]

Even Methodists did not always cooperate to help Pacific, and the small California band of believers—the average Methodist parish in the state had 70 to 80 eighty members between 1870 and 1900—sometimes ended up working at cross-purposes.[83] It was a Methodist minister, Rev. Oscar Fitzgerald, who helped found San Jose State Normal School (Teachers College) a couple miles from Pacific's campus, for its climate, favorable campus land, and because "the people are intelligent, hospitable and moral."[84] A fellow Methodist minister, Dr. W.T. Lucky, was the normal school's first president/principal.

The Stanford-Pacific deal

Pacific's link with Stanford was much more intimate. When Governor Leland Stanford's 15-year-old son died of typhoid fever in 1884, he and his wife Jane wanted to create a fitting monument to American youth and explored founding a university. A most fascinating story of a Leland-Pacific liaison is reported in Robert Burns' master's thesis, a story which he calls "apparently deeply rooted in the Pacific tradition" but is unable to document in writing. He cites alumnus and California Supreme Court Justice John Richards (1877) as the source of the report that Leland Stanford met with Pacific regents to explore the possibility of investing his wealth in Pacific rather than proceeding with his own university. As the story goes, he insisted that his gift would come only if Pacific severed its ties with the Methodist Church. Burns concludes, "The Trustees deliberated on the matter for some time, but could not convince themselves that money made from stock gambles, wine grapes and horse racing could be appropriated graciously for the type of Christian work in which they were committed." Stanford was turned away. [85]

In the end, Stanford decided to build on his thoroughbred horse farm (now known as "The Farm") a unique university for men and women of all economic backgrounds that extended liberal education to practical uses by focusing on the professions, not unlike what Pacific had begun years earlier.

Serious Stanford competition

The potential threat to Pacific was obvious to anyone paying attention. In Stanford president David Starr Jordan's report before opening in fall 1891 he proclaimed: "Tuition will be absolutely free. Good board will be furnished in [Encina Hall]—the best equipped dormitory in the country, electric lights, hot and cold water in every room, baths, and all modern improvements—for $4.50 a week.... No more beautiful site for a university exists in the world: the campus of 8300 acres, an arboretum of 50,000 trees, and $1,250,000 already spent on buildings."[86]

The academic program was also a lure: unlike virtually all other universities of the modern era, Stanford announced there would be no general education requirements; each student would pursue courses in a major subject area custom designed in consultation with a lead professor.[87] Despite the fact that Palo Alto as a town did not yet exist (Menlo Park held the post office, bank, and plentiful saloons), the massive Moorish-Romanesque campus located on the same rail line as Pacific captivated many California and Pacific students. Finally, Stanford set pre-college requirements at a minimum, provided generous special admission guidelines, and decided against any entrance examination, to the consternation of University of California faculty, who feared that a wealthy mediocre school would result.[88]

When the doors opened on October 1, 1891, enrollment was double what president Jordan had expected—559 students—while neighboring UC Berkeley, begun 23 years earlier, enrolled a mere 520.[89] Students came in droves to this campus paradise.

And then came Methodist USC

While not a major Pacific competitor for students in the nineteenth century, the University of Southern California's development demonstrates some of the reasons Pacific did not take off until the 1960s. By 1876, the Southern Pacific Railway ran from San Francisco to a small town called Los Angeles, established by the Spanish in 1781. Exactly a century later, the University of Southern California was born—founded by southern Methodists who bore important links to Pacific.

On September 4, 1880 when the cornerstone was laid for the first USC, Robert Widney (1863) saw his dream fulfilled. This dashing alumnus of Pacific had taught mathematics and science for his alma mater in College Park a few years before heading to Los Angeles as a lawyer, judge and real estate developer. Soon a preeminent promoter of the growing city, he knew that education would be critical to its future success. [90] Together with businessman Abel Stearns, Widney worked to secure land for a university in a little city with California-sized dreams. The local Methodist Episcopal Conference, which promoted the Los Angeles Academy founded by another former teacher at Pacific, Oliver Frambes, helped to secure property for a university campus and endowment fund. The church later merged the academy with the university, much like Pacific did 30 years earlier in Santa Clara.[91] The 144 acres of dusty desolation known as the West Los Angeles Tract, secured with the help of an Episcopalian, a Catholic and a Jew, signaled that this new university would be a more cosmopolitan enterprise than the Methodist-led Pacific.

By 1916, USC would become the second-largest denominational school in the U.S. after Northwestern near Chicago, another Methodist school founded three months prior to Pacific in 1851. In 1911, the Andrew Carnegie Foundation provided USC its first major gift, $25,000, at a time when its 2000-member student body was already larger than Stanford. By 1914, the school had set a goal of raising $10 million to build a great university for southern California, with a plan for 10,000 students by the mid-1920s.

What explains the dramatic growth and success of USC compared to Pacific? The answers are many, but the most pronounced are evident: the Methodists in Los Angeles were much more ready to work with all the brokers of the city to make it a great university, and USC had no real competition for years as Los Angeles became the next boomtown of the west, seeing its population increase sixtyfold from 1880 to 1920. UCLA was not founded until 1919. USC quickly moved out of the "small, denominational, undergraduate liberal arts college" identity to establish professional schools that denote a university, especially in the 1920s under president Rufus von KleinSmid.[92] The vision for USC was always much more ambitious than that of the founders of Pacific—to be *the* university for a rising new region.

Flourishing under Stratton

While the odds were stacked against Pacific to become a significant national university in a state where world-class universities were invented overnight, Pacific's fortunes were certainly not all grim. With solid leadership and ambition, it did right well in this era. When Rev. C.C. Stratton was elected to replace Gibbons in 1877, the University moved into better times just as the nation was

President C.C. Stratton (front center) with a thriving faculty in 1886, including classics professor James Martin (2nd from left) the most celebrated faculty member of the era, and art professor Helen Kingsbury (center, with palette), who launched the campaign to build the Conservatory building.

beginning a stumbling recovery from the "Panic of 1873," an international economic depression. Stratton instantly became a darling of the students, and no wonder. He brought everything needed to the table, including a large toolbox of skills, but most of all, he embodied the enduring mission of Pacific.

The West's first Conservatory of Music

Stratton's commitment to serving women was based on down-to-earth realities: "that school is best which most nearly conforms to actual life." He and the board thus established a Conservatory of Music in 1878, the first west of the Mississippi River and the seventh oldest in the country. It was a bold and progressive move, following the first conservatory in 1865 at Oberlin College in Ohio—both prompted by their early enrollment of women.[93] Music, after all, was woven into the fabric of the school as deeply as in the Wesleyan Methodist tradition, which thrived on hymns with folksy tunes—over 6,000 of them written by Methodist founder John Wesley's brother Charles. Conservatory dean Loui King was soon renowned in the region for his instruction, artistry and leadership.

When the Conservatory was founded, women already represented about 40 percent of the 65 undergraduates, and half of the ten graduates that year were females.[94] By 1879, six of the 14 faculty members were women. Throughout the 1880s, at a time when other colleges were just beginning to enroll women, up to 60 percent of collegiate enrollment was female as the Conservatory of Music grew in stature and popularity under Dean King's strong leadership. A key ingredient to its success undoubtedly was that the bachelor's of music degree required proficiency only in music. Not until 1911 were music students required

Art professor Etta Booth was a legendary teacher and mentor for over five decades.

to complete liberal arts courses. By 1890, 60 of 65 conservatory students seeking bachelor's degrees were female. More than a third of the college and conservatory faculty were women, led by charismatic Etta Booth, head of the art department until 1936.

While President Stratton's decade of success (1877-87) should be viewed in the context of a favorable national climate for private colleges, he was the only truly outstanding president prior to Tully Knoles. His impressive presence, magnetic personality and eloquence, like President Knoles, made him an effective recruiter of students when he was on the stump at regional churches. Enrollment soared. By 1885, the prep school enrolled over 200, and 45 percent of the 110 bachelor's degrees were awarded to women.[95]

Pacific thrives

Stratton challenged the board to erase the chronic debt, partly through his own financial pledge, and trustees responded. When the regents endorsed a plan to build a new $40,000 building that already had $23,000 in pledges raised by Stratton, he asked the Board to pledge $5,000, and they did so on the spot.[96] And the trustees launched a plan to merge the struggling

East Hall for men became the iconic campus building in 1885, surpassed only by the Conservatory building of 1890.

Methodist Napa College with Pacific, which took over a decade to accomplish. Everyone was bullish about Pacific.

Twenty-eight graduates, half of them women, crossed the platform in the Auditorium-Chapel in 1886, the largest graduating class in Pacific history to date. In 1885, editors of the first student newspaper, *The Epoch,* boasted that the school had grown from 176 students in 1881 to over 400 prep and college students, almost the size of the nearby State Normal School in San Jose. They credited Stratton—"unsurpassed in excellence"—with the many campus improvements. Three new buildings were completed in 1885: East Hall residence for men, the Dining Hall and the Observatory, which claimed the second-largest telescope in California next to Mt. Hamilton.[97]

Over his decade of leadership Stratton increased the college faculty from six to ten; improved academic programs and the culture of the campus; established the Conservatory of Music and added Art, Elocution, Education and Law; and liquidated chronic debt while producing a balanced budget.[98] The 1886 *Naranjado* closed with this proud advertisement for the University:

University of the Pacific.
Situated on Railroad, Midway Bet. San Jose and Santa Clara.
Founded 1851.
Twenty Professors and Instructors.
Four full college courses, leading to degrees of A.B., L.B., Ph.B., and B.S.
Post-graduate courses conducting to degree of Ph.D.
Complete preparatory courses connecting with classes in college.
The fullest business course in the State.
A four years' Conservatory of Music Course.
All classes open to both sexes.
Board, tuition, washing and incidentals: For young ladies, in College Hall, $250 per year; for young men and boys, in East Hall, the new building, the same.

Alluring dorm rooms attracted students in the 1880s.

Students get organized

It was America's first era of mascots, school colors and yearbooks, and Pacific was no different. In 1886 students published the first yearbook, *Naranjado,* the Spanish word for the color orange, probably adopted from the California golden poppy prolific on surrounding hillsides. It remained Pacific's school color until black was added about two years later. When the rugby team sported orange and black striped jerseys and socks, students labeled them "tigers," which instantly became the popular mascot, though not officially adopted by the students until 1925.[99]

The tiger mascot likely began with orange and black rugby jerseys as early as the 1890s. Pictured is the 1912 team.

It was a time when Pacific students got organized. Today's students should be heartened to note that in 1886, students were calling for a "student association"—like the ones at Harvard, Yale and Dartmouth—to collectively buy textbooks because the bookstore was so expensive.[100] The students first organized a student government in 1899—early compared to most colleges. In 1905, the East Hall men's dormitory established the first self-governance in residential life, finally beginning a departure from strict faculty oversight of all aspects of student life.[101]

Naranjado staff portrait, 1888. Active students had fun embracing the wild west while aiming for the sophistication of Eastern colleges, which they followed closely through publications.

Students recognized the importance of the Alumni Association, and in *Pacific Pharos* called from time to time for a stronger organization to work with students for the betterment of Pacific. While alumni meetings began as early as 1865, the Alumni Association was not founded until 1873. By the 1880s it had become better organized and effective in helping students.

Just as today, student clubs came and went with changing student interests, illustrated in this Naranjado cartoon of 1887.

It funded a new post office and bookstore building in 1888 and established clubs in Sacramento and San Jose by 1890, when it boasted 282 members.[102]

By the 1880s, student organizations sprouted across the campus: the "Oratorical Association," an "Aristotelian Society," three "football clubs," five "baseball clubs," a Glee club, a tennis club, cycle, checkers, and quoits clubs, a "military guard" club, a "Tamale club," an archery club, and even an "Eating Club" (motto: "Eat and Grow Fat"). Some of course came and went, like the "Baconian Society." The YMCA, begun in 1879 and said to be the oldest collegiate "Y" on the west coast, and the YWCA were large, robust Pacific organizations throughout the rest of the century. They flourished through the first half of the twentieth century, as they did at many other colleges.[103] The "Y" blended the Christian message with personal and social improvement especially compatible with a Methodist campus.

THE 1890s DRAMA: CONSERVATORY WOMEN, "THE SECESSION," AND THE NAPA COLLEGE MERGER

The class of 1888. Senior men wore formal top hats, called "plugs," as a signature of their class. Women had no comparable garb.

The big loss of Stratton

The vigor of Stratton's presidency, by far the most successful in Pacific's history to this point, took its toll. After completing the imposing, four-story East Hall in 1885, Stratton resigned in a long letter to the board, detailing the reasons why he was overworked and underpaid after a decade on the job. Mrs. Mills had persuaded him to become president of the West's first women's college (1852) up the road in Oakland.[104]

The signature building of the San Jose Campus in 1890, the Conservatory of Music building matched the quality of the program.

The Methodist women and the Conservatory win the day

Before the trustees appointed an impressive classics scholar and orator, Rev. A. C. Hirst, as its next president in 1887, the "Ladies Chapel Association" of Methodist women and alumni pressed the board to build a "chapel and conservatory of music." Organized by Helen Kingsbury, faculty member in languages and visual art, the women's group promised that all funds would be raised to advance the interests especially of women students, and the board signed on.

The Conservatory's elegant concert hall was unmatched in Pacific's history.

The board could see that the chapel/conservatory project required major financial commitment and they stepped up. The renamed "Ladies Conservatory of Music Society," often called the "ladies of the Pacific Coast," raised about half the $30,000 needed to complete the grand project—and grand it was. The large, graceful two-story brick building with imposing, Romanesque arch windows opened in 1890 to acclaim for its design and beauty, including 16 new pianos and an elegant auditorium seating 1,800 people.[105] The *Naranjado* reported that the dedication of the building heralded "the gift of the ladies of California to the University, in token of their appreciation of its early stand in favor of co-education."[106] The conservatory building was certainly the most impressive on the San Jose campus, a statement about the performance and prominence of Pacific's first successful professional school.

But the ladies also called for their due, and the board responded by appointing the heroic Helen Kingsbury as its first woman regent in 1896, shortly after her retirement from the faculty. In 1905, six years prior to a successful referendum granting women's right to vote in California, Pacific saw its first woman elected student body president, Elizabeth Green. She was featured with her fellow executive officers as the frontispiece of the *Pacific Pharos* of May, 1905. The second was Hazel Dixon in 1907, both thus preceding by nearly 40 years Ione Angwin Monagan, '45, who since her time was the presumed first woman student president.

The secession of 1891

President Hirst understood academics and quickly and sensibly standardized all bachelor degrees into four-year programs; however he was an inept leader. In an attempt to raise "school spirit," he instead created a campus atmosphere of tension and discord. He had promoted solidarity within each of the classes, freshmen through seniors, that culminated in fierce rivalries—a story worth telling because of its drastic outcome.

The sophomores had adopted canes as their class symbol, a common fad of the day. The seniors all had tall black top hats. One day the freshman class stole many of the canes and was accused of destroying them. The faculty, in charge of such student deportment, quickly ruled that all canes must be returned and cash paid for any destroyed. The impish freshmen, knowing they had not destroyed the canes, refused to return them. Miffed, the faculty suspended the freshmen from campus for 30 days, "except such members of the class as personally indicate to the President before 4:00 p.m. Monday next, a willingness to obey the requirements of the faculty.

To the students, this harsh sanction crossed the line. The juniors, and even the sophomores, objected. They threatened to leave the school *en masse* unless the frosh were reinstated. Forty-one of the 78 students signed a no-confidence petition against Hirst.[108] Prolonged diplomacy ensued, the canes were returned, and no suspensions occurred. But upper-class students were further reprimanded for criticizing faculty and administrative actions. The *Pacific Pharos* staff resigned in protest over this muzzling, which led to the college suspending the publication for months.[109] Throughout the incident President Hirst behaved unreliably and often harshly with all the students and utterly failed in his personal diplomacy.

All came to a head as the spring term ended in 1891. In 1886 Pacific had a record number of graduates—28, half of them women. By fall 1889, college-level enrollment exceeded 200 for the first time, nearly double the national average. But then the majority of upper-class students, whipped into a frenzied cause for justice over an inept president and a beleaguered faculty, exited *en masse* to the brand new university 20 miles up the road for the coming fall term. Stanford opened its doors, welcoming well-prepared Pacific students to its wealthy paradise, *sans* tuition, to populate its upper-classes instantly.

This mass migration, labeled "the secession" at the time, hit Pacific hard from all angles. Out of what had been a freshman class of 69 students, the class of '91 included only one original frosh among its ten graduates.[110] Pacific's fall 1891 enrollment hit a new low of 32 in the collegiate department, down from 102 two years prior. Including the Conservatory, overall university enrollment dropped by nearly 50 percent from fall 1889 to fall 1891.[111] When all but two members of the only national fraternity (Phi Kappa Psi, not a literary society) transferred, the chapter itself moved to Stanford! Of the first 120 Stanford undergraduate students with "advanced standing," over one-third (43) were transfer students from University of the Pacific.[112] Stanford's first graduating class in 1895 included Herbert Hoover, who later became a leading Stanford trustee and philanthropist after serving as U.S. President, and William Guth, who would become Pacific's president. But the real headline for Pacific was that the *majority* of the 1895 graduates were transfer students from Pacific.

The devastating impact

This crisis and the indelible mark of Stanford on the backdoor of Pacific were powerful reminders of the ongoing competitive threat to Pacific until it left town in 1924. And perhaps it is fair to say that attention to students by the faculty took on new meaning after the "secession" incident. Pacific's student-centered approach to education now went far beyond its founding fathers' commitment to educating the whole student. The student exodus gave rise to a "market sensitivity" born out of student tribulations that, if left to fester, could spell disaster. At the same time, it was a severe cautionary tale on the limits of *in loco parentis,* the role and limits of faculty and staff in regulating student conduct.

The terrible toll of Hirst's failed presidency was unrelenting. The year prior, ancient languages professor James Martin, the most venerated and senior faculty member, resigned after 18 years, reportedly over "lack of harmony with the President."[113] But the damage done by Hirst was raised to a higher power when five highly respected faculty members resigned in protest over Hirst's actions. Yes, two of them had attractive offers at that sparkling miracle called Stanford, where one, biology professor Wilbur Thoburn, became a legend as student advisor.[114] But their departure was prompted by their unwavering support for the students' just cause against Hirst.

Whereas a majority of the Alumni Association backed the faculty and called for Hirst's dismissal, the two San Jose newspapers, the *Mercury* and the *Times*, supported Hirst. The board turned a deaf ear, even imposing a requirement that the faculty or the President review any student publication that expressed views about the "administration" and demanding that every student applying for transfer be reviewed prior to honorable discharge.[115] One stinging legacy was the students' *Naranjado* yearbook, which ceased publication from 1892 until 1912.

The irony of the 1890s

In 1890, the church-related college still dominated American higher education. About 80 percent of all America's undergraduates were enrolled in church-related colleges like Pacific, and the YMCA claimed 1,300 college chapters and nearly half the student population of the time.[116] Methodist schools led the pack, with 74 colleges scattered across the continent, along with 51 Roman Catholic schools, followed in number by other denominational schools. But change was afoot. Nearly all historians agree that the 1890s was "a major turning point in the evolution of American higher education."[117]

Over the next 40 years, the seismic shift occurred as about 60 percent of all undergraduates enrolled in public and independent universities.[118] Even so, most private schools flourished as a flood of high school graduates poured onto campuses. The number of colleges and universities nearly doubled and well-established schools tended to grow in enrollment and resources as America became enamored of college life in magazines and advertising. Yet in the middle of this flowering of American higher education, Pacific was left in the dust owing to an inept president and a rigid board.

Methodist Napa College was an unwanted, distracting competitor in 1885, and eventually merged with Pacific in 1896.

THE NAPA COLLEGE MERGER

Identity crisis—again

When the Napa Collegiate Institute, bought by the Methodists in 1870, advanced to become Napa College in 1885, Pacific had a competitor within its own ranks some 80 miles north. Protracted discussions with Napa College continued into 1892 while Pacific was on edge with its enrollment crisis. Rivalry was balanced with respect for "mutual relations" and the promises of "consolidating", yet merger was inevitable. Supporting two colleges that offered parallel programs and competed for students as well as dollars as improved roads and rail lessened the distance between north and south Bay was too much for California Methodists.

The California Methodist church conference, which ratified the membership of both boards, demanded unification. The initial plan by a committee of joint regents called for two campuses with a consolidated administration located in neutral San Francisco. Napa College felt pressured to compromise and balked several times, as did the Pacific board. One favored plan was to change the name to San Francisco University, establishing its colleges of liberal arts and theology in the city, while the two existing reporting schools would continue as Napa College and San Jose College. Ambivalence about Pacific's identity rose to the forefront again. Should Pacific be a city university or a country college?

In 1894, the president of Napa College, Dr. James Beard, was elected to head the consolidated University of the Pacific as president, and Dr. F. F. Jewell was appointed chancellor to oversee business and financial affairs. At the time, the San Jose campus had 13 faculty members; the Napa site had nine. Students on both campuses were in an uproar as rumors flew back and forth about which campus would be favored or sacked, and Pacific students threatened another mass exodus when their president was deposed in favor of the Napa president.[119]

Napa College closure and innovation

To underscore the serious intent of the merger, the trustees designated the Conservatory of Music as a separate college of the University with its own dean in 1894, and classics professor Moses Cross was appointed dean of a new "San Jose College of Liberal Arts." While music would be taught only at the Conservatory, the Art School would be in Napa. Across the country dozens of small private colleges underwent moves and mergers throughout the nineteenth century, but this plan was more daring and characteristic of this jaunty state. The overriding ambition of this board recalled the first Pacific board: audacious in its vision, overreaching in its hasty planning and lack of resources, and hard-nosed in determination to advance the University through merger, reorganization and expansion.

A 36-member board was elected and all properties of the two campuses were transferred to it. But alas, after only two years, promising President Beard chose to resign abruptly, apparently because he did not share the vision of the board. Meanwhile in San Jose, after President Hirst had resigned in 1891, and his replacement Isaac Crook despaired of the job within two years, the board resorted to an acting president for months: Wesley Sawyer, German professor, Civil War amputee, and Harvard graduate, whom the students adored.

Following the numbers, the trustees had peremptorily adopted a "radical change in our educational policy in order to avert financial disaster" by closing Napa College in 1896. [120] Napa students and alumni protested, of course, but when the trustees brilliantly appointed Eli McClish to be the next Pacific president, the Napa minister beloved by the Napa College students drew many Napa students with him to San Jose, along with the esteemed young professor Rockwell Hunt, later to be dubbed "Mr. California" for authoring all his popular histories of the state, including the centennial history of Pacific. Soon McClish won over the San Jose students almost as quickly.

But Napa was not happy in losing the prestige factor of a beloved little college. Perhaps as a final nose-thumbing to the Napa closure decision, Napa College trustees voted to award B.S. degrees to all the graduates of the predecessor high school academy, Napa Collegiate Institute. This effectively granted Pacific college degrees to hundreds of high school graduates who had not spent a day in a college classroom![121]

What is most obvious to an observer over a century later is the immense struggle to make Pacific successful against all odds. Carrying off a merger during a string of weak, short-term presidents and flagging enrollment, inventing new models of organization on the fly, crafting ways to keep the constituencies together while debts continued to grow—who among us today would have had the fortitude to endure these ills, either as trustee, professor, staff or student? A pioneering spirit was certainly a prerequisite for service.

Despite this boost for Pacific through the Napa College merger, students in San Jose were dismayed and angry. McClish soon won them over, and while enrollment dropped from 1896-1901 to the lowest levels in 20 years, tight financial management and sacrificial salary reductions brought a balanced budget. Both Stanford and the University of California "accredited" the work of Pacific students who still chose to transfer out, an important validation of academic quality by respected Stanford and Cal faculty at a time when Pacific's future was in serious jeopardy. Respect from these two prestigious neighbors was always sought, and rivalry was often got. When Pacific finally played its first baseball game with Cal, without uniforms on a disgraceful home diamond, and tied the game at 12-12, Pacific students were rightly angry that Cal refused to play extra innings. In a rematch two weeks later, "old U.P." beat Cal 14-13 in Alameda, and all was well.[122]

THE SHAPING CURRICULUM

A mission—for what?

Social commentators argue that the paperback book, television, urban migration and computer technology have had greater impacts on college life than any curriculum, but the fact remains that the courses of study provided to students and the academic rigor applied to them sets the tone of any learning community even today, and that impact is never superficial for college students. The rise of science, the languishing of classical languages, the growth of professions, a rising middle class of high school graduates, the power of practical studies over piety—all these were embodied in the rise of the new curriculum, and they were played out on the College Park campus in San Jose as surely as they did at other colleges in the country.

What is remarkable is not only that Pacific survived these years, but that the essential traditional commitment to "whole student learning" embodied symbolically in the old curriculum managed to survive as well. And it was this particular flavor of Pacific that held forth amid the giant schools that surrounded it in the early 20th century. Cal, Stanford, San Jose State and USC had all shed their commitment to the individual undergraduate student, unsustainable in schools built on the scalable factory model of public universities in an industrial society. Should Pacific attempt to become a USC, or a small high-quality liberal college like Pomona? Both were false options. Pacific had no money to become either.

By the 1890s an attractive dining hall was built.

Classroom pressures

High school students were demanding options for advanced schooling, despite the fact that as late as 1905, Pacific, like most colleges, required Latin for admission into the Bachelor of Arts program.[123] By 1901, Pacific advertisements proclaimed a "Commercial College" as well as an "Art School" in addition to the "College of Liberal Arts" and the "Conservatory of Music." The Commercial College jumped from 18 to 42 students within three years, as business enrollments erupted across the nation.[124]

The curriculum was exploding on every campus: degree electives at Stanford included courses in woodworking and machine shop.[125] Pacific's Conservatory boasted a unique "Training Course for the Management of a Music Business." *Pacific Pharos,* noting that seniors at Columbia University had all elective courses, pointed to "what has long agitated the minds of students," that required courses in one program could be electives in another. "The substitution of Calculus—which is required in the Scientific and Latin Scientific courses, but not in the Classical—for Horace or Eschylus, would be very profitable, and would, in no wise, interfere with the regular workings of the College."[126] By 1903, students called for the end of the "Senior Thesis" (four of 128 units), claiming that disproportionate time was necessary to write this long paper, often requiring research in San Jose and San Francisco libraries.[127]

The *Pharos* editors also cautioned the faculty in their move to improve instruction by substituting the textbook-oriented "Recitation System" with the new "Lecture System:" "Let there be a text book for the class to follow, the subjects being studied, and then discussed by the students and the professor."[128] But not all textbooks were equal; one lighter means of thumbing their noses at academic requirements was the "Crematio Physici," the cremation of physics, a required senior course. On Friday the thirteenth of April, 1888, the seniors introduced a formal ceremony, "an Eastern innovation entirely new on the Pacific Coast—the cremation of the text book on Physics," including a dirge-droning marching band, funeral orations, last rites, incantations and finally, incineration with "a flash of smoke and crimson that filled the hall."[129]

LIMPING INTO A NEW CENTURY

Poverty breeds ambivalence

In the waning years of the century, the board and the president agonized over what to do to make Pacific more successful as it desperately sought to fill a $60,000 debt hole. The trustees approved a proposal by two college students to solicit new students at $10-15 per head—Pacific's first "admissions counselors."[130] Faculty, library, labs—all were down at the heels. Aggravated by a severe drought in the state, it seemed a losing game. The lament of the trustees in 1900 could have been the refrain nearly annually for the first 50 years: "The prevailing spirit of the School was excellent, though the limited attendance and financial embarrassments were matters for grave concern."[131] The budget that year showed a 20 percent cost overrun ($3,700). Student publications often complained that alumni lacked the generosity of support seen at other private colleges—though they complained even more often about undisciplined student disruptions during weekly chapel sessions.

President McClish cut faculty positions in biology and English, returned $500 of his own salary, and floated the idea of becoming a junior college feeder to Stanford and Cal, to face what in fact had been going on: underclass students transferring in droves to the other two schools, where tuition was nil, programs abundant and academics strong. But the trustees just could not bring themselves to downgrade Pacific from "a first-class institution of College grade."[132]

The Golden Jubilee campaign

The trustees were encouraged partly by a stable presidency: McClish, neither gifted administrator nor scholar, enjoyed a great rapport with students as a warm, down-home preacher and counselor, and stayed for a decade—as long as the hugely successful Stratton. The millennium ahead was impetus to launch a $100,000 campaign in 1899 to erase the huge debt in order to celebrate the Golden Jubilee free of this perpetual burden. The Alumni Association started a campaign of its own. Students volunteered help by selling art calendars and rallies were held across the state. San Francisco bishop J. W. Hamilton provided active leadership for "Emergency collections" in all California Methodist Conference churches before year-end. The Ladies Conservatory Association kicked in $15,000 from stock sales, and the Chinese Vice Consul and several Chinese benevolent associations of San Francisco pledged $1,000.

However, the Methodist donor list included none of the railroad, land and corporate barons who so lavishly endowed competing institutions. Crossing a shortened $60,000 goal line in 1901, the Pacific community, far and wide, now 50 years old, celebrated its "Golden Jubilee" at a gala commencement weekend. Some saw again a glimmer of hope for this fragile institution, always on the edge.

"Alleged unfavorables"

The next landmark in the fiscal journey would be to address Pacific's paltry endowment of $40,000. The board set a goal in 1905 to achieve pledges for a $100,000 endowment, about six months prior to the great earthquake. The Methodist California Conference, which had raised $20,000 to start a Pacific endowment in 1872 but held it hostage until the school paid off its debts, finally had confidence in 1902 to release the funds to the College.[133] When McClish resigned in 1905, the board reduced its membership from 36 to 21 and pondered their "alleged unfavorables:" lack of "popular interest" in the University even in its hometown, low enrollments—especially in the College—and low student morale leading to high attrition.[134]

The College had to face the fact that while most schools across the country grew dramatically in the decade prior to 1900, Pacific was stumbling to recover from the "Stanford secession" punch-in-the-stomach of 1891. Despite the spike in students from the Napa College merger in 1896, Pacific's enrollment sank to 75 college students, a 20-year low, as it limped into the twentieth century.

Adding to its woes was the "disastrous calamity of the earthquake and fire at San Francisco" on April 18-20, 1906. Pacific's San Francisco property, recently gifted to the University and valued at $35,000, nearly equivalent to the annual university budget, was destroyed. The firestorm consumed all endowment fund records held in the city, and the quake caused significant damage to several campus buildings in College Park. Miraculously, a collapsing wall of East Hall injured only two students. By tearing down the fourth floor, the hall was saved.[135]

The absent philanthropist

In turn-of-the-century California, the philanthropic temperament was resistant. For example, Pacific alumnus W. S. Clayton (n. d.), president of the largest San Jose bank, forced the University to make good on a $5,000 overdue note in 1915 despite board chair Watt's pleas. The board treasurer had to pay the debt through an annuity.[136] As historian Kevin Starr sums up the state around this time, "A restless selfishness, a preoccupation with untutored private ends which sometimes amounted to a mania, conferred a quality of instability and cranky self-absorption upon many figures of the pre-1890 period, especially upon those who, having made money, did not know what to do with it …."[137]

As the century ended, the University was still on shaky ground. President Robert Burns' blunt assessment of the first 50 years deserves repeating, especially since Burns was one of the few presidents who later advanced Pacific to achieve genuine success:

> *Even though Pacific was the first college on the scene in California and it managed to keep alive, it had not advanced with the newer institutions academically. It was considered to be academically inferior to the highest-ranking schools in Northern California and this was not remedied until a number of years later.*
>
> *The financial story was not favorable. There was a constant struggle to keep alive. It was difficult to obtain new buildings and*

equipment, the endowment was insufficient, teachers were poorly paid, and there was a debt to face practically every year. Part of this difficulty can be attributed to the fact that the college was predominantly Methodist and drew most of the support it received from the church or individuals in the church. Unfortunately, Methodism in Northern California had relatively few adherents and was considered a missionary enterprise for many years. It had a difficult time maintaining itself and the college was destined to share in this.

Possibly the most characteristic feature of this first half-century was the ability of the college to adjust itself to changing conditions ... where other protestant colleges in Northern California failed.... Certainly the college has had its fair proportion of prominent alumni.[138]

The nineteenth-century story of Pacific is perhaps more typical of small private colleges than has been stated, excepting the California flair and daring. But Pacific was never content to be a struggling little liberal arts college, while the champions of the school seemed unable to persuade their wealthy friends to invest in making it something more. In the new century, something new had to be done to pull it from the brink.

CHAPTER 2

Becoming a college, 1906-1946

Becoming COP in 1911—Outside pressures—Ups and downs in World War I—Knoles growth plan—The move to Stockton in 1924—Startling Stockton—The collegiate ideal—The professional schools begin—The Depression and the Stockton College partnership in 1935—The Stagg tradition—The Navy V-12 program—World War II takes its toll—Knoles grooms his successor—The GI Bill boom

INVENTING "THE COLLEGE"

Student protests to support their presidents

When McClish resigned as president in 1906, Moses Cross, dean and classics professor, served as acting president for two years that set up another student-school confrontation that he certainly had no fault in. Student publications, agitated that the trustees could not recognize their dean's success and achievements and appoint him president even after two years probation, lobbied hard: "… for what is a school with a dissatisfied student body?" By now this had become a student tradition—protesting the trustees' shun of three acting presidents in 15 years.

President William Guth (1909-1913) greatly strengthened Pacific as a small liberal arts college and renamed it College of the Pacific in 1911.

Under the leadership of the Archites, a crowd of students stormed the trustee meeting in Pacific Grove, prompting one trustee to report "a state of wild, rampant anarchy in the student body, [which] came near [to] convulsing the entire community."[1] In the end, Cross was named vice president as the board voted 25-3 to appoint William Guth, Stanford '95, who had followed his early San Francisco law career with Ph.D. studies in theology and philosophy at Boston University, Halle, and Berlin. Guth, who served five years as president until 1913, had a huge impact on Pacific under his dynamic, bold, optimistic leadership.

The birthing of College of the Pacific and Santa Clara University

Guth, product of an era when higher education was becoming an organized profession, reset the tone and quality of the academic program so that Pacific could regain its edge in an increasingly competitive collegiate neighborhood. He decided that the school should face up to its limitations and acknowledge that it was indeed a "college," not a "university:"

> *When the school was founded in 1851, it was hoped that it might eventually expand to the status of a university. The hope was never realized, and the institution has never undertaken university work.... Its endowment is entirely inadequate, and it would be exceedingly futile to undertake such work in the face of Stanford University and the University of California, whose magnificent incomes enable them*

to do university work. The University of the Pacific, or rather, the College of the Pacific, aims to be a college of high rank, and has a splendid equipment for first-class college work.[2]

Next door, Santa Clara College arrived at the opposite conclusion at the exact same time under the progressive leadership of president James Morrissey. Perhaps he listened carefully to Stanford president Jordan, who opined, "as time goes on the college will disappear, in fact, if not in name. The best will become universities, the others will return to their place as [high school] academies."[3] Impoverished, under-staffed (Ph.D. faculty were not appointed till the 1930s), dependent on the preparatory school, beleaguered little Santa Clara College was yanked forward to university status almost single-handedly by president Morrissey when he launched professional schools of engineering and law in 1912—nearly half a century before Pacific made its decision to grow to university status.[4]

Perhaps Pacific had a more realistic sense of its status. It certainly had more confidence in the sustainability of the liberal arts college at a time when the vast majority of the nation's college students and increasing numbers of public university students already were pursuing practical vocational studies. But the decision to adjust the school's mission came from all quarters: the California Methodist Conference, the national Methodist board for higher education and its college presidents, even the San Francisco *Chronicle.*[5] The trigger was likely another carrot from the Rockefeller Foundation: a matching gift of $50,000 if Pacific raised triple that amount—and became an independent college separate from the high school academy in order to boost college quality.[6] By action of the board, Pacific became a College on May 17, 1911.

President Guth's competitive college

The decision was well received because it followed Guth's giant steps to move the College ahead: raising the bar on new student admissions; setting higher scholarship standards for new professors hired (at the time, six of 15 liberal arts and music faculty had Ph.D.s); severing the high school Academy from the College; granting autonomy to the Conservatory of Music, which also included the School of Art and the School of Elocution (all of which included some non-degree programs); creating new departments of physics and education; expanding the campus by constructing a new women's dormitory (later named Helen Guth Hall after the accomplished first lady) and adding a longed-for gymnasium while improving campus grounds; achieving a record enrollment of over 400 students (125 in the College of Liberal Arts); balancing the budget for the first time in years; and garnering an endowment fund of $80,000. This was an astonishing record for a school that had been on the skids for over two decades. Guth declared that Pacific could be among the leading smaller colleges—*if* it were to grow to 400 or 500 college students, a long haul indeed.

Campus life in the new century

Cows still grazed the San Jose campus into the twentieth century.

By today's standards, residential life at "U.P." after the turn of the century was more rugged than Sierra camping. Students lived with crowded dorm rooms, rickety stairwells and risky heating systems, no hot water until well into the twentieth century, and student janitor services until 1918. But the school continually found ways to refurbish the halls, including electric lights in East Hall in 1917, and when the new Helen Guth women's hall opened, the president proclaimed that it exceeded a comparable hall at Stanford.

At times, the halls were invaded by strangers. George Knoles ('28), President Knoles' middle son, recounts the morning a prankster called up the president and said, "Your cow is up on the third floor of East Hall." Knoles mustered his three eldest sons to induce this unruly new student who was "not toilet trained" down three flights of stairs, leaving a trail behind her.[7] So the *Naranjado* offered this tribute to 60-year-old East Hall: "equal privileges go to all residents—including cows, cooties, and bats."

Intercollegiate athletics begins

The Bengal tiger was a popular mascot long before it was officially adopted by the student body in 1925. These examples are from 1909, 1913, and 1914 Naranjado yearbooks.

Student publications railed at and appealed to fellow students and the University to "revive" athletics, by now a national collegiate pastime. Along with cheerleaders and pep songs, a new "hymn to Pacific" appeared in every *Naranjado* annual for years. While the "Bengal" was a popular mascot, and the first football team was organized in 1894, often teams could not field a full roster of players in football or baseball because students in this small student body pursued other interests.[8]

Following Stanford, Cal, Santa Clara and Nevada, Pacific reintroduced rugby in 1907 and played mostly the California private schools. The change was prompted by a national rise in deaths and serious injuries among football players that turned even President Teddy Roosevelt against the game, and was brought home by the fatality of a Santa Clara student in a high school football game.[9] In 1916 Pacifican Dick Wright was selected as the best rugby fullback in America to play in the annual American-British game, yet the team did not get a turf field until 1919, after years of student agitation. With the new field came the resurrection of "American Football" for 76 successive seasons.[10] The 16-member traveling team had a rough start: Nevada won 134-0. From this humblest of beginnings was to come a legendary program whose heroes and alumni coaches have continued to flourish for over a century.

Basketball could only field five men—though they enjoyed a "Pajamarino Rally" to celebrate the end of the season, wearing "evening dress" in their parade across campus.[11] Men's basketball did not officially begin until 1910, when Pacific's first athletics facility, the gymnasium, was built, though YMCA teams played some years prior. The team had seven coaches in its first seven seasons. In 1913, Pacific joined the "Big Six League" of Stanford, Cal, Nevada, St. Mary's and St. Ignatius (now University of San Francisco) for some sports. Baseball came and went again in the 1920s, and the women's basketball team was restarted in 1916 when

Women's basketball began in 1905.

restrictions set in 1912 that limited women to intramural play and banned men from watching their games were lifted.[12]

OUTSIDERS MOVE IN

Rockefeller Foundation pressures relocation

The dramatic shift in higher education in this era moved amateur little colleges led by well-meaning ministers into robust schools led by professionals. Faculty with doctoral degrees became the coin of the realm, and together with the development of national professional organizations in higher education, American university education earned its global preeminence by mid-century.

The rise of private foundations that sought to improve higher education had a direct impact on the development of Pacific. The Rockefeller Foundation's General Education Board and the Carnegie Foundation for the Advancement of Teaching (CFAT) dealt directly with Pacific to face its challenges from about 1910 through the 1930s.

Rockefeller's board offered financial incentives to colleges willing to listen to them. Pacific, desperate for new funds, took the bait. The Rockefeller board urged Pacific to launch an endowment campaign and consider relocation, having concluded that the Bay Area was already overcrowded with colleges and universities.[13] Actually, the board had considered forming a task group to explore a Central Valley location as early as 1907, but did not act.[14]

President Guth prodded them with the grim facts of Pacific's sorry state: "It is the wonder of educators who come in to contact with our conditions as to how we can keep so efficient a faculty on such small pay." Given the concerns about tightening campus space, an antique library in "frightful condition," and inadequate labs to teach biology and physics, the board was ready to listen. Only add this: Guth's complaint that "the continual noise and confusion of trains make our work here far more difficult than the outsider would imagine."[15] Even the asset of rail service had become a liability.

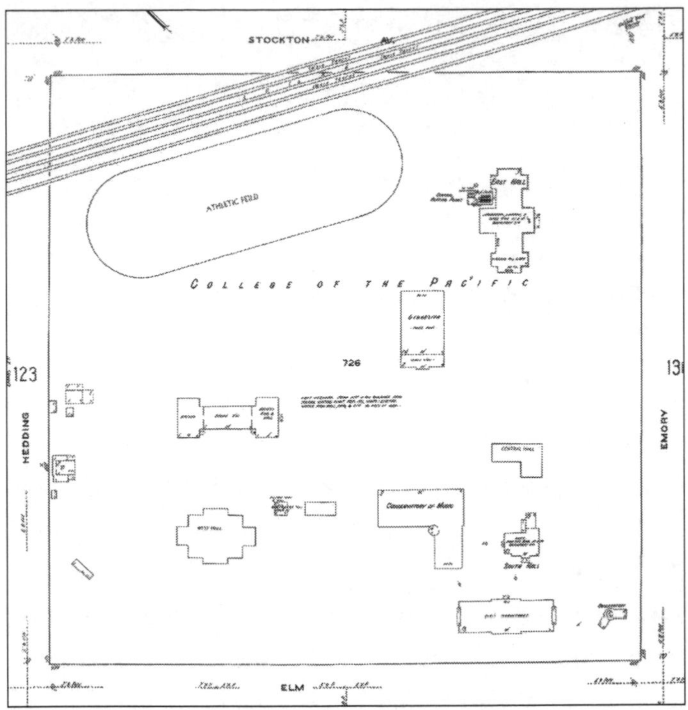

A map of the San Jose campus around 1920 shows the multiple railroad lines running through the northern edge of the campus.

Carnegie Foundation entices quality

The Carnegie Foundation for the Advancement of Teaching (CFAT) offered to fund a faculty retirement pension plan to entice talented men and women into college teaching. Its larger plan was to raise educational standards across the country through strategies to centralize, standardize, and increase educational efficiency. Pacific's trustees immediately sought eligibility for the pension fund. To qualify, the Methodist California Conference agreed to delete the article of incorporation clause that mandated a majority of the board be members of the Methodist Episcopal Church.[16]

Pacific presidents used the Carnegie enticement as leverage to increase the board's commitment to improve quality. In the end, Pacific never made it to the eligibility list and did not adopt this national faculty-staff pension program until 1946, after the foundation incentive had lapsed.

Methodist pressure

Methodist churchmen continued to dominate Pacific's Board of Trustees. Harold Jacoby, long-time Pacific faculty leader and administrator of the mid-twentieth century, observed that while the church rarely coerced a decision of the board, the trustee leadership had "so internalized the values and concerns of Methodist culture, the independently arrived at decisions and practices appear as if they had been the product of church insistence and direction."[17]

The heavy influence of the Methodist "University Senate" of education leaders also weighed in on schools like Pacific. Elected by the Church to preside over all U.S. Methodist colleges as a kind of accrediting association—the first such body in the country—the Senate joined with the national foundations to ratchet up college expectations, declaring in 1916 that "no colleges with less than $200,000 productive endowment would be allowed to grant degrees."

That same year, the Senate had the authority to close such schools. But as one of the few Methodist schools in the west, Pacific was granted a one-year reprieve to double its endowment to meet the minimum requirement. President Seaton asserted that if the school could not raise $200,000 to improve the campus, retire the debt, and increase the endowment, it would be "unwise if not impossible" to keep the doors open.[18] Seaton saw to it that these goals were accomplished, but the Methodist Senate kept raising the bar: within a few years the minimum endowment leaped to $300,000, and then to $500,000 by 1925.[19]

All these forces—the rising professionalism of higher education, the forceful imposition of national foundations, the continuing weighty hand of church educators—combined to bear down on Pacific and push it—to be better, yes, but also to the edge, fighting for its survival.

President Seaton's stride forward

By 1913 President Guth was wooed away by prestigious Goucher College, the Methodist women's school in Baltimore. Again the trustees turned to

President John Seaton (1914-19) was, along with presidents Stratton and Guth, the most important leader of Pacific before President Knoles.

the dean, now Bert Morris, for an eight-month acting presidency before appointing Dr. John Seaton in 1914. The Midwestern professor of Greek (Ph.D., Boston University) came with a reputation for raising money.

From the start, Seaton faced setbacks that challenged his determination and relentless energy. Central (Dining) Hall burned down, along with nearly all student records, days before he arrived. Dean Morris and a brigade of male students soaked surrounding buildings to save the rest of the campus. Within a year another fire burned down landmark West Hall, which housed the library. Virtually all the 14,000 books were consumed. Students raised most of the funds to replace the dining hall, thanks to a competitive campaign by the literary societies, but West Hall was never replaced, and the library became an also-ran for four decades.[20]

Pacific lost its library when West Hall (left) burned to the ground in 1915. The library was not replaced for 40 years. The prior year, Central Dining Hall (right) was also destroyed by fire.

Seaton mobilized student recruitment and added 150 new students within a year, but more important, he clarified the mission of this "liberal arts college." He affirmed the value of practical skills for specific vocations, despite the school's forfeiting several of its professional programs and university label. He celebrated ethical ideals that advanced the building of student character, a bedrock of Pacific identity, and he exploited the "development of the individual to his maximum," confirming "whole student learning" that characterizes Pacific even today.[21]

Equally important, Seaton was a shrewd budget analyst and an energetic, optimistic fund-raiser who understood that a strong faculty, robust enrollment and an "adequate" endowment were the three essentials for success. In 1916 he led a relentless endowment campaign that exceeded its goal of $300,000 in one year. Seaton's proleptic vision was evident in 1915 when he presented the board with three options for the future of Pacific: invest in the College Park campus, knowing it could accommodate at most 600 students; seek a larger campus property in Alameda; or explore "a complete change of location."[22]

UPS AND DOWNS IN WORLD WAR I

The "Safe at their College" program

Pacific's next biggest challenge was weathering World War I. When the U.S. joined the war in 1917, male collegiate enrollment dropped up to 40 percent nationally, but not at Pacific. From 1912-17, total college enrollment nearly tripled from 122 to 339. The average college had fewer than 200 students, and Cal was one of only eight schools in the country with over 5,000 students.[23] What kept Pacific and most other colleges from an enrollment

Pacific was more of a military base than a college during World War I. Women students formed a Knitters Club to make wool caps and socks for servicemen.

and financial disaster was the new Student Army Training Corps (SATC) program, aptly known as the "Safe at their College" program.

Under SATC, colleges were run as full-time army training camps. By fall 1918, 140,000 men were inducted into the United States Army at 525 colleges, including over 100 at Pacific, though about one-fourth of these were already regular students of the College.[24] Pacific was paid $900 per student soldier to cover tuition, room, and board—a windfall that meant a balanced budget for Pacific.[25]

The downside of the program was that schools were mandated to admit any applicants up to the enrollment limit. Many young men were not prepared for college work or campus life, and strain was immediate. Pacific students were offended by the behavior of the outsiders, and the commanding officer was certainly no academic dean. Schoolwork sagged. Dormitory disruptions and destructions were common. Football was suspended in favor of military drills for 60 men. As the 1919 *Naranjado* noted, "from the 5:45 a.m. bugle call till taps at 10. . . there was a formation for everything: physical exercises, mess, classes, and drill."

Even before the U.S. entered World War I, Pacific graduates worried about their futures, as this 1914 Naranjado cartoon illustrates—a worry that was relived again and again in the many decades to come.

The fallout of the War

The list of Pacific lives lost grew with each issue of the *Pacific Weekly,* and student enlistees grew more rapidly than the letters from "Pacific Tigers in the Service" printed in the paper, often asking for news from campus. Near the end of the war, nearly one-fourth of the student body had enlisted in the armed services, contributing to the "general restlessness" on campus. The count by war's end was 314 service men and women who were Pacific students or alumni.[26]

When the Armistice was announced, the national program was promptly canceled. In the end, Seaton pronounced the mix of military training and academic study "irreconcilable." Of 79 freshmen in 1916, only seven students graduated, one a fellow from Japan. In 1918, of 53 enrolled freshmen, only ten students graduated four years later.

KNOLES' GROWTH PLAN

President Knoles' promising start

After the war, Seaton was recruited to be assistant secretary of the Methodist Board of Education in New York, which positioned him to aid his successor, especially in fundraising. In early 1919, Methodist Bishop Adna Leonard reported to the board that the presidential search committee (chairman Rolla Watt, Dr. George White, former president of USC, and himself) had contacted and interviewed only one candidate, professor Tully Knoles, head of the history department at University of Southern California, who was promptly appointed president. Knoles already had a storied reputation at USC as teacher and public speaker. As assistant to the president, he was being groomed, so rumors had it, by his mentor and friend, president George Bovard, to become his successor.

Knoles had had a demanding young life that tempered him for the job at age 43. Inspired at a Methodist revival meeting at age 16, he pursued his studies at USC while holding down several pastorates. He was also a USC football quarterback while fathering two of eventually eight children with his wife Emily on a farm. He stepped into Pacific at a very favorable time: the War was over, the country was recovering, and Seaton had set an impressive record of progress over his nearly five years as president.

Students at play

And the students were happy having fun. Cosmetics were in, as the 1920 *Naranjado* noted with good humor: "Face powder used by Helen Guth [Hall] girls in one week could completely white-wash the Observatory!" Along with

Even before moving to Stockton, Pacific was drawing Filipino students; the Filipino Student Club, begun in 1921, is shown here in 1922

a surge of nearly 200 freshman students, 1921 brought a Filipino Club, three new language clubs, and new chapters of honor societies and social fraternities.

By 1923, the *Naranjado* proclaimed a "new era" in athletics: "For the first time in her history, Pacific has become a power in the athletics of the state. In football, basketball, women's basketball and tennis, Pacific has never had such a brilliant season." Which was likely accurate, though team success depended as much on a shift to the California Coast Conference of smaller schools as on athletic prowess, as Robert "Doc" Breeden ('22) became the first director.[27]

Basketball was the favorite sport as football returned. Erwin "Swede" Righter coached both sports with great success starting in 1921. As coach of the basketball team for 12 years, he won two championships in the Far West Conference.[29] In football, he had a conference championship by 1924.[30] For the women, it was quite a different story. When the national Women's Athletics Association banned intercollegiate competition for women in 1924, women's teams could play only local athletic clubs or intramurals. The ban would not be lifted for 45 years. [31]

Robert "Doc" Breeden (left, '22) became the first athletic director.[28] In the 1920s Coach "Swede" Righter led conference championships in both basketball and football.

The heyday of the Conservatory

Howard Hanson, Conservatory dean at age 23, became a renowned American composer.

The Conservatory of Music was probably at its zenith during the first two decades of the century, nearly always led by outstanding deans. Howard Hanson, elevated to dean in 1919 at the age of 23, was especially talented and ambitious. Hanson was likely the only Pacific faculty member of national distinction until DeMarcus Brown ('23) in theatre produced dozens of Broadway and Hollywood performers two decades later. A rising composer of note, Hanson founded the first national "American Music Festival" of solely American composers in 1921 at Pacific, and himself conducted the Los Angeles Philharmonic Orchestra in that magnificent conservatory auditorium, performing his own "Symphonic Rhapsody" at the climax of the four-day event.[32]

Knoles' growth model

At the same time, Knoles had key challenges that amounted to another do-or-die stake for the College. As noted earlier, Pacific had failed to ride the rising tide of U.S. college students that began in the 1870s. Major setbacks in enrollment in 1890-92, 1896-1902, and in 1910-12 placed Pacific well behind other colleges and on the edge of financial ruin.

Knoles used his gifts as a compelling public orator to immediately expand student recruitment through 45 outreach speeches within his first three months. Fervent with optimism, he envisioned one thousand students within three years.[33] His visits to countless Methodist youth gatherings were especially driven by two factors. First, Knoles identified the critical problem of college dropouts, a national issue during this era.[34] Whereas freshmen made up 40 percent of U.S. college students, they comprised two-thirds of the College enrollment. He calculated that fewer than a thousand students had actually earned a Pacific sheepskin since that first graduation in 1858.

The problem was not high cost. Knoles had made the case that Pacific had the "lowest tuition in the State" even with a $10 dollar bump to $60 per term, when Occidental, Pomona, and USC all were charging $75 per term, and Stanford, no longer tuition-free, was at $75 per quarter.[35] Students rushed in the front door—and as quickly exited out the back, many to Cal and Stanford. Pacific graduated 17 seniors in 1919, about the same number as 30 years earlier, when total enrollment was one-fourth the size.[36]

Second, California high school enrollment was mushrooming, up by one-third from 1916 to 1918. In the past, Knoles said, Pacific's appeal had been "largely to a religious constituency. Our problem is now changed." While Pacific liberal arts enrollment had increased ninefold in the last 16 years, USC had increased over thirtyfold. Knoles framed three choices for the board: continue as a "junior college" preparing students for university work at Cal and Stanford; enlarge the campus and become a small college of 500 students; or seek a new site for a "full-sized college."

From the start, a discerning listener knew that Knoles accented the third option.[37] By 1917, over a dozen school districts had established junior colleges, and Cal opened its first junior college branch campus in Los Angeles in 1919—later to become UCLA. Stanford president David Jordan had lobbied Pacific trustees to shift to junior college standing and serve as a feeder school for Stanford, given how successful Pacific transfers were in Stanford classrooms. At the same time, Knoles knew that a significant part of Pacific's stunted academic quality was owing to Stanford "flunk-outs" transferring to Pacific, welcomed to fill its empty upper-division classrooms.[38]

Quality produces quantity

Knoles' conviction was that raising academic and admission standards would lead to enrollment growth, not scare away students. This drive for academic quality to stimulate a parallel growth in quantity led Knoles as well as his successor, President Burns, to raise academic standards and open new academic programs. Part of Knoles' legacy is the truth of what became an axiom in higher education: increased academic selectivity leads to increased prestige and attractiveness of the institution, drawing in more talented students. This axiom has been lost then recovered at Pacific over the eras.

Knoles lauded the decision of the board to endorse the faculty's call for raising entrance standards to "exactly the same level as those of the University of California," and to admit transfer students only if they had not been rejected by their prior school—to end the Stanford "flunk-out" transfer problem.

Competition for students from Northern California increased when San Jose Normal School (Teachers College) opened in 1922—less than three miles from the Pacific campus. Yet Knoles reported a record enrollment of 430 (348 at the collegiate level) and expectations for continued growth.[39] Soon Knoles proudly proclaimed to the board, "the student body is changing very much." No longer accepting transfer flunk-outs meant moral as well as academic improvement, Knoles noted, observing that their behavior standards had not equaled "our own students."

FINDING A NEW HOME

Sorting options

At Knoles' first board meeting in 1919, the trustees commissioned Watt to chair a committee "to consider the future campus of the college," thus launching what would become the most significant decision for Pacific in its history, before or since.[40] Watt had earlier supported an effort by a group of fellow investors, mostly trustees, called "The New Campus Syndicate," to expand the campus beyond its 17 acres. They had purchased land surrounding the campus which linked it directly to the major thoroughfare of the neighborhood, "The Alameda" (Highway 82), two blocks to the west, where the College already owned property and planned a women's dormitory as late at 1922. The College had been drawn to its current College Park location partly because of the Southern Pacific Rail stop. Now, the rails had become a nightmare for the campus—122 passenger trains daily through the campus, along with huffing freight trains and a clacking roundhouse switching station close at hand.[41] The faculty favored the Alameda expansion plan, but Knoles' predecessor Seaton had quietly opposed it, while planning all along for a major move to a much larger campus as a preferred future.

Relocation factors

The three key factors in the plan to relocate the College to the Central Valley were financial, academic and demographic, as Knoles outlined in his letter seeking an endorsement of the move from University of California president David Barrows, an old friend from his Los Angeles YMCA days along with Stanford president Ray Lyman Wilbur.[42] Knoles gave Barrows a blunt summary of financial woes: "During the 70 years of the life of the institution in San Jose it has been enabled to gather together less than $750,000 of endowment, property, and equipment."

He cited the pressure of Stanford and San Jose Teachers' College as competitors for students and donors, and then argued that with the parity achieved in admissions standards with UC, Pacific could compete better for quality students in growing counties not served by other colleges. Finally, with no school from Chico to Fresno, the Central Valley had the dubious distinction of being the only area in the United States of equal size without a four-year college.

The Stockton bid

Within months Knoles had received letters from Stockton inviting relocation, as well as inquiries from Santa Cruz, Oakland, Lodi, Turlock, Modesto and Sacramento. But Stockton had the jump on other cities with its strong leadership of alumnus Eugene Wilhoit (n.d.), president of the Stockton Savings and Loan Bank (later to become Bank of Stockton);

Rev. Adam Bane, Pacific alumnus (1881, 1886), an old friend of Knoles, and pastor of Stockton's Central Methodist Church; and Thomas Baxter, manager of Holt Manufacturing Company and a director of the Stockton S & L Bank. The Stockton campaign was headed by the "Three B's"— Bane, Baxter, and John Burcham, the Pacific vice president who later so capably headed the relocation plan. Bane lined up generous donors of land and the solid backing of the Stockton Chamber of Commerce, which had just been formed (1921). Irving Martin's *Stockton Record* championed the cause as early as 1919.

Stockton was a promising major California city in the 1920s.

In spring 1920 Bane personally presented to the board a Stockton offer of 25 acres and $150,000. Modesto could no longer match it, and Sacramento leaders did not make a pitch.[43] From the start, Knoles had a strong bias to relocate in order to grow. At the same meeting, on March 4, 1920, the board agreed that 25 acres and a half million dollars would be the minimum to cut a deal, and Stockton was only short on dollars.[44] Perhaps Pacific historian Rockwell Hunt was correct, that weeks before this meeting the majority of trustees agreed that relocating to Stockton was the right path.[45]

San Jose deserts

A few months later Knoles wrote to Watt that the Stockton representatives were confident about raising $500,000, whereas the San Jose Chamber of Commerce voted down two-to-one a proposal to support a $300,000 campaign to retain the College in San Jose. Adding insult to injury, San Jose about the same time promised Santa Clara University support for erecting a $200,000 addition to "its already fine collection of buildings."

Student publications took up the cause. Editorials had grumbled for years about students who came only to pile up transfer credits to enroll at Cal or Stanford as juniors or seniors. The *Pacific Weekly* editorialized that it would be "shameful" if Pacific became simply a junior feeder-college for the big schools and championed relocation. Other reasons followed: as San Jose grew, the busy, loud rail yard next to campus became an increasing annoyance, and students wanted a larger campus to expand academic programs. Their only objection was the hot Stockton summers.[46]

The board chair demurs, the president balks

Ever cautious and ambivalent, the board acted in January 1921 to adopt the Alameda plan if Stockton could not meet the board's requirements, even though Stockton could now offer an additional 40 acres from the J. C. Smith family, a most generous gift solicited by Bane from his former parishioners. Knoles' ultimatum to the board was either to remedy the acute student housing conditions and shortage or to relocate to Stockton. He also got former presidents Seaton and Guth to lobby Watt to endorse the move, though Watt resisted till the end.[47]

But at this time, Knoles made clear that he would not be part of any fundraising campaign, despite the monumental importance of its success. He reiterated to chairman Watt his commitment to the College on the terms of his appointment only: "I distinctly said I was not willing to leave my position in the University of Southern California to take up financial work in connection with any College, and that your reply was that [the former president] Doctor Guth had built up the scholastic standard of the school and Doctor Seaton [the current president] had placed it on a firm financial basis, and that someone was needed to represent the school and increase its popularity before the school men of this State."[48] Knoles' flat refusal was the critical flaw in his presidency, and would place a red mark on the remainder of his tenure.

Outsiders rally

By September 1921, the Methodist California Conference had endorsed the move to Stockton with the blessing of the national Methodist Board of Education. A delegation from the Rockefeller Foundation had visited the campus, found it well run, was pleased that Knoles had leveraged its requirement for increased faculty salaries (senior professors now earned $3,000 annually), and voted to gift $250,000 toward the endowment as a matching fund if the planned fundraising campaign were successful. Rockefeller would finally reward Pacific for making the decision—if not buckling under pressure—it had favored for some years.[49] The California State Board of Education and the State Superintendent of Public Instruction added their endorsements as well.

MOVING AHEAD

An innovative move

This decision to relocate the College as a *strategic* move based on regional analysis was the single most important decision the College would make, representing an important claim about Pacific's identity. The innovative move to pull up stakes and plant itself in the middle of a region unserved by higher education, however much urged by the Rockefeller Foundation or the Methodist church, was a bold choice, a march into the unknown, a risky investment in new territory. Other schools would have either toughed it out or—more likely—folded. Pacific, resilient and ever adaptable, partly because of its poverty and remnant size, was led by a Moses of its own, into a land of new promise.

The Stockton fundraising campaign

The Board of Trustees quickly followed with its unanimous decision to relocate on September 24, 1921, including a "College of the Pacific Crusade" to raise $3 million. The fundraising started with a $1.5 million campaign among the Central Valley Methodist churches from Sacramento to Turlock, in partnership with the 1,400-member Stockton Chamber of Commerce, to raise $750,000 to construct eight campus buildings, followed by a wider state campaign for another $750,000.[50]

Sixty percent was raised by individual church member contributions, none equaling even $500. This was a sign, perhaps, of the fundraising challenge for decades to come: few major donors stepped forward.

The trustees urged student organizations to raise funds for "Club houses, Fraternity houses, and other society homes" as one way to reduce dormitory investments. So Rhizomia, Archania, and Omega Phi Alpha all planned their new Stockton houses on land designated by the Board as "fraternity row."[51] Over 99 percent of the student body and many of the faculty pledged nearly $50,000 toward the cause.[52] Students and faculty roared into Stockton on February 23, 1922, "Pacific's Day at Stockton," to showcase the College to the community—a car caravan of 180 that led a pep rally with music and speeches on the court house square.[53] While Knoles had no direct hand in it, the campaign to raise $1.5 million was successfully completed by June, 1922.

Planning the "Collegiate Gothic" campus

Stockton land donor Don Smith of the J.C. Smith Company had already donated 40 acres of land, eventually dedicated as the Harriet M. Smith Memorial Campus in honor of his loyal Methodist mother, who had homesteaded the property of 2,300 acres reclaimed from the Delta with her husband James for over 30 years. Now he added another 10 acres, between the campus and the Calaveras River, for a modest cost to the College funded with a bank loan, the first of many from the Bank of Stockton. The newly acquired Alameda property was sold for $50,000, and after a couple of false starts, chairman Watt worked through his close friend,

San Francisco Roman Catholic Archbishop Hanna, to set the stage for the Jesuits to purchase the College Park campus for $125,000. As Pacific closed its nearly 50-year-old high school academy, Bellarmine Academy was launched and still thrives today.[54]

Meanwhile, the trustees were busy planning the new Stockton campus. The architecture and engineering firm of Davis, Heller, and Pearce of Stockton won the bid and by all accounts did a splendid job. In January 1923, the board voted approval of "the Gothic Collegiate style of architecture," a powerful statement of independence in itself. The design repudiated the by-now fatigued era of Spanish-Colonial Revival structures that populated many a California courthouse and campus.[55] To this day Pacific remains the only California campus of this collegiate gothic style, adapted from Oxford, Cambridge, Harvard and Chicago, Princeton, Cornell and Northwestern. The design was streamlined—no spires to speak of, or gargoyles, and only a single tower.

Who proposed the collegiate Gothic style of architecture for the new Stockton campus, unique among California campuses, is not known. This early architectural rendering projected future buildings.

Board chair Watt asked his good friend, John McLaren, to design the landscaping. McLaren had designed San Francisco's Golden Gate Park in 1887 and achieved worldwide fame as chief landscape designer for the 1915 Pan-Pacific International Exposition in San Francisco. As a friendly gesture to Watt, he agreed.[56] Capable, energetic vice president John Burcham, assigned to oversee campus construction, pushed to add the sculptural ivory terra cotta building trim from the renowned Gladding, McBean clay works north of Sacramento.

Construction of the ten original buildings of the Stockton campus in 1923 was nearly completed in a year.

In addition to buildings for administration and the liberal arts departments (now Knoles Hall), construction crews simultaneously built an auditorium/conservatory (now the Conservatory and Faye Spanos Concert Hall), a science hall (now Weber Hall), ladies' dormitory (now South-West Hall), men's dormitory (North Hall, now renamed Hand Hall), a dining and social hall (Anderson Hall), and the president's home. Before they were finished the trustees added an "athletic bowl," a planned gymnasium, and a power plant (now Baun Hall). (Every campus wanted to have its "bowl" after Yale opened its 70,000-seat stadium in 1914.) Once again, the railroad became a college issue: the Western Pacific Railroad almost bisected the campus, but agreed to lay an additional thousand feet of track to skirt the new campus.[57] (Later, this track along the levee was removed from disuse.)

The survivor college

The first 75 years of Pacific were impoverished, turbulent and at times tumultuous—as for most colleges in the nineteenth century. What set Pacific apart was that it survived all the challenges—some self-made, others thrown at it—and crafted a few novel ways to bring itself forward. Financial collapse, negative location, close competition, internal dissension, and natural catastrophe—Pacific survived them all.

Certainly the initial decision to educate women was significant, as well as an unbending commitment to educating young people for character as well as career, grounded in a strong core faculty dedicated to this purpose. A mission-driven, visionary resolve by the Board of Trustees overcame many odds. The Methodist Episcopal Church provided a sturdy network of leadership and support, if also restraining dominance. A readiness to reach high, to innovate, to relocate, to add professional schools—all played key roles. The stimulus of stiff, close collegiate competition in a new California was another. Of the 40 church-sponsored schools and colleges founded prior to the Civil War, only four others survived: Santa Clara University, St. Ignatius (now University of San Francisco), College of California (now UC-Berkeley, originally sponsored by the Congregational church), and College of Notre Dame.[58]

In 1924, with a brand new, impressive campus and enrollment at an all-time high, the College entered its new life in Stockton with high optimism—except for the heavy millstone around its neck. As Tully Knoles said, "We have everything we need to make a great school except money.... Some means must be discovered to reach men and women of great wealth who are willing to invest in our project. I do not believe there is an institution in America that has lived so long without having received great gifts to its building fund."[59] Despite the strong vision and relentless commitment of its leaders, this great challenge would keep Pacific on the edge for years to come.

STARTLING STOCKTON, VALLEY CENTER

A Stockton community victory

The *Stockton Daily Evening Record* ran a special issue on Saturday, September 27, 1924, to celebrate the opening of the College the next Monday. Publisher Irving Martin lent a personal interest in this milestone for Stockton, as his wife Clara Goldsworthy was a Pacific alumna (1884).[60] Over 600 businesses and professional organizations advertised in the paper to trumpet the grand opening on 26 of the 28 pages, with a story on

Stockton Record

College of Pacific Opens Here Monday In New Home

Largest Pre-Enrollment in History of College Presages Immediate Growth

THE PICTURES

Greetings From President Knoles

Stockton Record *publisher Irving Martin was a strong supporter of Pacific's relocation and funded a major portion of a library addition in 1955.*

every academic department as well as photos of all 50 faculty members and all nine "Ivy League campus" buildings in various stages of construction.[61]

The headline, "Largest Pre-Enrollment in History of College Presages Immediate Growth," was on everyone's mind as the commitment of the city to meet its pledge of $600,000 had squeezed every philanthropic penny out of its citizens over a planned 10-day campaign that lasted five weeks. Stockton Chamber of Commerce president and alumnus Eugene Wilhoit of Stockton Savings and Loan Bank (renamed the Bank of Stockton in 1958) had spearheaded a highly organized campaign in 1922 that earned him a place on the Board of Trustees the following year. This relationship with the second-oldest bank in California operating under its original charter would become one of the most important partnerships in Pacific's history.

Fifteen community fundraising teams were joined by teams from the Rotary Club, Merchant's Club, the Realty Board, and 99 county schoolteachers. To push the campaign toward its goal, Wilhoit started a $100 club to name a building after Stockton's founder, Captain Weber, that produced over 600 donors and built Weber Hall. Every nickel was shaken out of the city to get to that mountainous $600,000 pledged by Stockton toward the College's larger goal of $1.5 million, half for campus buildings, half for endowment. The Central Valley region would raise another $150,000, the Methodists of Northern California $500,000, and the Rockefeller Foundation the final $250,000. The three largest donors (around

$15,000 each) were banker Wilhoit, Methodist rancher Charles H. Harrold, and the Japanese Association, a group of farmers headed by the "Potato King" George Shima, president of the Japanese Association of America for 14 years, known for championing education and funding scholarships for Japanese-American students.[62] If ever there was a community team effort for the good of Stockton, this was it—a victory for all.

A great start

In 1923 Stockton's first freshman class began at this downtown location.

The prior year, Pacific had rented a downtown building to start a freshman-only class of 39, so the Stockton pump had been primed. In 1924, a total of 201 local students registered, bumping enrollment dramatically. Of the 600 students enrolled in the College, many came from the seven county high schools, which had seen a 50 percent increase in graduates over the prior year.[63] The 200 freshmen swarming the new campus were the largest class ever, and the two residence halls were overflowing. Though ground had been broken in April 1922, construction of the imposing gothic buildings did not begin until nine months prior to opening in September 1924. The last-minute, 1,800-seat gymnasium was built in three weeks!

Cultivating the "Grand Central Garden"

What was this new world of Stockton that Pacific had entered in 1924?[64] This supply and transportation center was founded in 1847 by the methodical German immigrant Captain Charles Weber to support the southern mines of the Mother Lode. The "Grand Central Garden", as John Muir called the lush Central Valley—dotted with ancient oaks and cottonwoods, abounding in dwarf elk and pronghorn antelope, blue lupine and orange California poppies—was all but ignored by the miners, but shrewd businessmen could see what Weber was about, and set up stores to stoke the mining pipeline. The Stockton port became so choked with Weber's ships that the growing village petitioned him to move them. Weber, flush with profits, reciprocated generously by granting property for the courthouse, churches, schools and parks to a growing town.

When a fire ripped through this makeshift, gun-toting, gold-driven "linen city" of tents and sails in 1849, the town was quickly rebuilt with brick and stone, and became known as "brick city." Stockton, incorporated in 1850, was on its way to become the center of commerce for the Central Valley, and maybe even a place of civility.

Rev. Isaac Owen, the Methodist supervisor of the region who spearheaded the founding of Pacific, arrived in little Stockton one March Saturday in 1850. He heard that the Presbyterians were to organize a church the next day, so he hustled the local Methodists together to form Central Methodist Episcopal

Stockton was a leading industrial California city in the 1920s. (Courtesy of Bank of Stockton Historical Photograph Collection)

Church, the first Protestant parish in Stockton by one day—perhaps an apocryphal story. Seventy years later the Methodist church became one of the key players in bringing Pacific to Stockton.

After the frenzy of the Gold Rush, Stockton became what it has been for a century and a half: a center of agriculture and transportation for the state.[65] By 1900 three transcontinental railways linked the city to the continent East, while the San Joaquin Delta linked it to the West and continents beyond. Stockton was a bustling mill town for the grain trade, and agricultural machinery plants and boat-builders abounded. For a time, around the turn of the twentieth century, Stockton was known as the "Chicago of the West," the second most industrial California city after San Francisco.

A city of all nations

From 1910 to 1920, Stockton's population nearly doubled to 40,000—its most dramatic decade-growth spurt from 1870 to the present. Like any port city, from the start it was a cosmopolitan mix of peoples. Chinese laborers, brought in to dig the mines and build the railways, settled in town among native Yokuts and Miwoks, Mexicans and European-American immigrants. A sizable Jewish community founded Temple Israel Cemetery in 1851, the oldest continuously used Jewish cemetery west of the Rockies. Indian immigrants built the first Sikh temple on the continent in 1912. Japanese immigrant George Shima became the first Japanese-American millionaire by breaking all world records in potato yields. He made Stockton "Spud City" by the mid-1920s, featuring an annual Potato Day festival parade with a Pacific float.

By 1920, Stockton had one of the country's largest Japanese-American populations, and by the 1930s was known as "Little Manila" as the largest population of Filipinos outside of the Philippines stoked the growing agricultural workforce. Among Stockton's top employers were Holt Manufacturing, builders of the famous caterpillar tractors and other agrimachinery, a major Stockton industry since the 1850s. Sperry Flour Mills, established in 1852, became the largest miller on the West Coast, processing the famous "Drifted Snow Flour" and grain for cereals and animal feed. Alongside were the boat-builders of launches, dredges, and the Delta King and Delta Queen—the largest steamers in the West. Both Holt and Sperry had their own booths at the heralded 1915 Panama-Pacific Exposition in San Francisco. A Holt competitor for farm equipment was Harris Harvester machines, manufactured by COP trustee George Harris, an active Stockton Methodist.

This growing city was developing a civic pride and cultural engagement that has enriched the city ever since. As Stockton grew, the Methodists did also, and "Old Central," with a capacity of 1,200, was the largest city gathering place from 1891 to 1925. The Stockton Memorial Civic Auditorium replaced it and later became the Pacific basketball venue in 1963. The Stockton Symphony got off the ground in 1927 by the roll-up-your-sleeves do-it-all conductor Manlio Silva to become the third-oldest continuous symphony in the state, and the Fox California Theatre (1930), featuring the Marx Brothers, Duke Ellington, and the Dorseys, was the "largest vaudeville house in California" with three pipe organs.

One answer to Stockton's dilemma

Did Stockton civic leaders know that they must carve out more options for the city's future? Could they have foreseen in 1922, when they had finally "won" Pacific, that their top two employers would abandon the city the year Pacific opened its doors in north Stockton? First, the larger grain ships could no longer make the channel bends from San Francisco Bay to the Port of Stockton, the state's first inland seaport, so Sperry Mills closed their giant towers and moved to Vallejo, just inside the Bay.

During World War I, Holt Manufacturing had depended on government contracts from the U.S. and major Allied countries to build "armored tractors" at the Peoria plant, not in Stockton. When the war contracts ended in 1918, Holt's competitor cornered the domestic market, bought out Holt, and closed the Stockton plant in 1925, the same year the mills went silent.

As a participant in the merger, Holt's general manager Thomas Baxter, a board member of Stockton Savings and Loan, must have seen the acute need for Stockton to find new players. While no remedy for these two major losses, College of the Pacific would bring about 600 new students and faculty into this city of 40,000—roughly the same ratio of campus to city population in 2010. But there was another good reason to bring a college to town: this was an era in California when the equation of quality city growth through shared middle-class cooperation produced rising property values that led to mutual community success.[66]

Perhaps most remarkable of all the layers of decisions for the Pacific relocation was the collective decision of the faculty to uproot their families, sell their homes in College Park, and start a new life in Stockton. Apparently only two of 49 faculty members resigned to continue their lives in the South Bay.[67] All the rest stuck with Knoles and made the move, including all 16 women faculty members except three from the Conservatory. A dozen were still teaching at Pacific a quarter century later, among them Pacific icons Fred Farley, William Harris, George Colliver, Gustav Werner, DeMarcus Brown, Russell Bodley, and Warren White.[68]

With the assistance of loans from Pacific, the faculty pooled resources and purchased 30 acres off Pacific Avenue, just across the street from the new campus. Pacific Manor, as it was called, was subdivided and sold, mainly to 22 faculty and staff. The College and the faculty agreed that the $8,000 collective net profit from the sale would go not into the faculty's own poor pockets, but towards a gymnasium for the students.[69]

Building out the campus

Meanwhile, the famous landscape architect James McLaren laid out a plan to build a grand park to match the magnificence of the architecture. His plan for a horticultural mansion was stalled, however, because of its palatial expense—$11,000. Instead, it would be done the Pacific way: many small donations and a lot of sweat equity by volunteer students and staff. Total bill to Pacific: $650. A double row of eucalyptus trees—later known as the notorious "Eucalyptus curtain"—was planted on the north and west edges of campus both as a wind break and to "shut off the sight and sound of the Western Pacific Railroad."[70]

Pacific founder William Taylor is among those credited with bringing the Eucalyptus tree from Australia to California—thus Pacific's Methodist heritage may be present even in the campus "Eucalyptus Curtain," evident here by the 1930s. The railway is on the left (north), bordering the Calaveras River.

The College was bullish with full classes. Women comprised 40 percent of the 44 faculty in 1924. And the board, with Knoles objecting, decided to finance a new 6,000-seat stadium through the sale of ten-year season tickets. The fundraising plan failed by mid-year owing partly to a Valley drought and hoof-and-mouth disease that hit the local ranchers hard.[71]

1924 Baxter Stadium was the largest in the region for many years.

But this was the era when stadiums and field houses trumped many other campus projects across America. Big-time collegiate athletics was here to stay, so a stadium there would be. Board chair Baxter, no doubt envisioning what the Valley's first stadium could mean to the community, quietly wrote a check for $25,000 to fund the project.

Built on the "Stanford model" of 16-foot-high earth walls, the impressive first Valley bowl was quickly named in Baxter's honor. When the stadium was dedicated in fall 1924—the stands a sea of orange and black hats—the Bengals were led by quarterback "Rube" Maurice Wood ('27), who had 35 seconds to break a tie with the Cal Aggies. This four-letter, 5' 7" athlete drop-kicked a perfect field goal from behind the 25-yard line to win the game 17-14.[72]

Opening day

All were awed when the towering brick halls opened in the fall. These ornate monoliths of architectural splendor inspired by the best before them back to Oxford and Cambridge—a collegiate gothic style that resounded with quality, venerable beauty, and resolute stability—stood as conservators of the past.

Forty acres of land for the campus was gifted by the children of pioneer rancher Harriet Smith.

Contractors scrambled to finish up construction, but the high spirits of students and families could not be dampened. Students hauled their slender hoards into the two oak-floored dormitories, later named North Hall for men and South Hall for women. Though workers were still installing windows and doors, the women found a gleaming sink in every room! They tottered back and forth on the wooden planks that served as makeshift sidewalks, barely escaping the muddy, rubble flats that once were grain and alfalfa fields surrounding the nearly completed buildings. Things were a little chaotic, though one parent from Marysville claimed it was "ten times worse" on opening day at Stanford.[73]

House poor

As in the past and in the future, many of these students enrolled because of unfunded (tuition-discounted) scholarships and grants, which drove a red bottom line, and, yes, the campus building plan was short on money again. Between 1919 and 1926, families accommodated an increase in tuition of two and one-half times, to $220 per year. Still, the total price tag of tuition, room and board at $560 per year was 50 percent less than Mills College in Oakland.[74]

Harriet West Jackson of Stockton provided the largest gift to that time, the West Memorial Infirmary, which now houses the University's business and finance center. Nellie Smith and family donated funds to build the famous "Harriet M. Smith Memorial Campus" Gateway in commemoration of her mother's foundational gift of land. Jackson was quickly added to the board as its third woman member, with fellow Stocktonians Jessie Wilhoit and Anna Holt. Of its 33 members, 18 trustees were Pacific alumni. Fourteen were businessmen, three were bankers, two were lawyers and one a justice of the State Supreme Court; eight ministers, two physicians, and three women civic leaders rounded out the group.

THE CHARMING YEARS

A big draw

Pacific's iconic new campus, the first four-year college in the Central Valley, became a lodestar for eager students. Enrollment jumped nearly 200 students, and by 1928, had increased by 50 percent since its Stockton opening. By then there were ten campus living units—four dorms and six

Greek houses. The three fraternity and three sorority houses were all built 1925-26, following USC's lead in using Greek societies to build housing in an era when funding was tight and federal funding for college dorms had not yet been created.[75] Some students commuted from town on a new trolley car line from Tuxedo Park to the gymnasium on the west end of campus (to what is now Brubeck Way and Kensington Avenue).

Tuxedo Park, Stockton's first suburban subdivision and the city's first strip mall built in the 1920s, was an easy trolley ride from the campus. (Courtesy of Bank of Stockton Historical Photograph Collection.)

Boxing matches were popular for the men on campus, and a new fashion statement appeared on the quad: for the annual tie-up and tug-of-war, the frosh men wore "jeans for their protection."[76] Students had to be juniors before they could wear "semester cords," corduroy trousers that were washed once a term. "They could stand by themselves in the corner," reported Elliot Taylor ('28).[77] Frosh men were not allowed to strike up a conversation with fellow women students.

One important tradition that carried forward was presidential support to establish Greek societies. President Seaton had proposed a third women's literary society in 1917, Athenaea, and Knoles had proposed the Omega Phi

The annual Rhizomia campus watermelon feed went on for decades.

Alpha fraternity in 1921. The Zetagathean Club, formed in 1935 by four women, became Zeta Phi, the fourth sorority, by 1945 again thanks to support by Knoles.[78] Other long-standing traditions continued: the annual watermelon feed by Rho Lambda Phi fraternity, the annual dinner by Alpha Theta Tau for the men's basketball team. And "Piccadilly Circus," a campus English bulldog who filed into the conservatory auditorium with the students for the weekly lecture by President Knoles, lay down in the front row for a nap, then trooped out with them at the end of the hour.[79] Perhaps most significant as a bellwether of student life, however, was the formation of a women's association.

Pacific women again take the lead

In 1925, Pacific women formed the Associated Women Students, and like their female predecessors who built the conservatory into the music powerhouse of the west, went about changing the campus. Where the women at UC-Berkeley formed an AWS out of self-defense, Pacific women were determined to expand their leadership opportunities.[80] Cal women were commonly hassled and frequently ridiculed by the male-dominated Cal student press, warning UC women of fatigue and burn-out that would foil romance and sentence them to solitude. In the 1890s, the Cal yearbooks had segregated the individual photos of women students into a separate section.[81] Their first sorority was recognized in 1890, 32 years after Pacific's first sorority. Perhaps worst of all, the UC administration did not intervene when the men prohibited women students from being members of the Associated Students of UC.

The "Cub House" eventually became the "End Zone" snack shop (1948) and later the "Summit" in the McCaffrey Center (1975), that then moved to the "Lair" in the DeRosa University Center (2008).

Such banishment was inconceivable at Pacific, which included women in the student association from its start in 1899. Pacific women launched the AWS to serve fellow students: in addition to a "Big-Little Sister" orientation program, they raised funds to begin a snack bar in the bookstore building, next door to the Associated Students barber shop venture. The AWS "Tea Room" was an instant hit, and became the campus hangout, known for decades as the "Cub House."[82] The Cub House was also a popular snack spot for the "townies" who came in by streetcar seeking the best butterhorns and bear claws in town.

At Pacific's 75th anniversary celebration in 1926, President Knoles announced Pacific's membership in the Association of American Universities, the pinnacle organization of national colleges and universities that served as a quasi-accrediting body. AAU was especially impressed with this figure in the application portfolio: 41 percent of Pacific graduates since 1910 had completed at least one year of graduate or professional study.[83]

"The collegiate ideal"

Like President Burns, who rode the post-war wave of endless expansion and experimentation for two decades, Knoles served at a time when higher education was thriving in America. Knoles had all he needed to succeed: the national surge in college growth, the move to a brand new campus in a region uncharted by other schools, a climate of rising national standards for admission and graduation, and what historians call the "collegiate ideal."

This "ideal" era captured the stereotype of campus life for decades to come: students who had fun in clubs, Greek societies, athletics, parties, and shenanigans with fewer boundaries, while on a pleasant path toward a generally educated rising middle class of professionally successful graduates. Pacific had the added benefit of a faculty truly committed to student learning and welfare, who were fully accessible to students—in fact, the faculty home addresses and phone numbers were listed in the annual college catalogue. The curriculum was solid if not innovative.[84] So how could a president fail? But of course two realities were beyond his control: an unprecedented national financial collapse and then another world war. And a third reality, an unstable financial footing for the College, which always seemed unfixable.

But what did the students care. This was the age of bathtub gin, new dance crazes, the start of beauty queens and football heroes. The freshman students were required to wear their identifying "dink" caps or be in for a "ducking" in a campus water trough.

Campus heroes

"Swede" Righter, head football coach from 1921 till Stagg arrived in 1934, did right well, except for the mistake of scheduling powerhouse St. Mary's College for the 1926 Homecoming game. The famous "Slip" Madigan team creamed Pacific 67-7.[85] Pacific's big athletics stars were burly Jim Corson ('27), who as national discus champion came in third in the 1928 Olympics, and track standout Myra Parsons ('28), who nearly competed on the U.S. Olympic track team. Jim Corson had an unusual campus job that got recognition: because he daily placed a block of ice in the admissions office drinking fountain to cool drinks for prospective students, admissions staffer Pearl Piper ('57) named the drinking fountain in his honor.[86] Cecil "Moose" Disbrow ('30), track standout and football fullback was named "one of the greatest Pacific athletes" ever, leading the basketball team to its first Pacific Coast Conference championship in 1930.[87] That made for high spirits at the annual "Tiger Stag party," begun in 1922 with the founding of the Block P Society, which has run on and off since then. Disbrow must have the record for the most letters—11 in three sports.[88]

Left to right: James Corson ('27) and Myra Parsons ('28) were nationally ranked athletes, but Cecil "Moose" Disbrow ('30) was probably Pacific's most rounded champion athlete to his time.

The storied achievements of past debate teams were carried forward in these years: over a thousand people crammed into the conservatory auditorium to witness Pacific take on Cambridge University in 1927, part of a partnership with "British Empire" teams (Oxford, Sydney, Liverpool) that continued for at least four years. Hazel Kelly ('28) was the only woman debater among all teams in 30 meets that year, joining her classmates Elliot Taylor ('28) and Leonard McKaig ('28) as some of the best in the nation. Debate coach Dwayne Orton's goal for Pacific to be nationally recognized in Forensics was achieved in the 1930s, the 1960s, and the 2000s. With two women on the team, Pacific won the 1934 national Phi Kappa Delta debate tournament, and another team of women won the state trophy.[89]

New campus traditions are born

College traditions were deepened in this era and new ones arose. The College was becoming known as the "campus of camellias" (in the central quad), and the Conservatory tower chimes sang every quarter hour to enchanted students. The Homecoming bonfire was a towering giant by the mid-1920s. Many a cheer and school song was published each year, but when Bob Couchman ('22) wrote the lyrics to Russell Bodley's ('23) lively tune called "Hungry Tigers," it became an instant favorite, now known as the "Tiger Fight Song."

Students guarded the Homecoming bonfire from an early burn by UC-Davis Aggie or San Jose State Spartan students, the traditional school rivals for the Homecoming football game. Shown is the 1925 construction.

The yell handbook included many "fight songs," but "Hungry Tigers" won the day for decades. Now students hardly know it.

New college hymns were also published every year, but in 1928, Lois Warner's ('23, '58) "Pacific Hail" was officially adopted as Pacific's *alma mater*, sung after every athletic contest and rally, and "nearly all student body or school functions."[90] Some say it was the most suitable because it depicted the College so vividly in its Valley location and alludes to the torch from the College "crest" (logo) of the times. Others would nod and whisper, "and not because of its sing-ability!"

Lois Warner's ('23, '58) "Pacific Hail" (with an extra verse) was adopted as Pacific's alma mater in 1928; singing it at campus events was resurrected in the 1990s.

Curiously, *Naranjado* yearbook coverage shows that Pacific's heralded Band Frolic had to earn its way to the forefront of annual student talent events. Beloved for over 60 years, the first Band Frolic was started by band director Robert Gordon ('33) in 1928 as a band fundraiser. The concert and a skit competition among the dorm halls soon became a legendary, fierce competition among the Greek societies.

Perhaps Pacific's most popular of campus traditions was Band Frolic, begun in 1928 and beloved for over 60 years. The photo is from the 1954 competition

The other landmark annual event during this era was the Death Valley Tour, a caravan trip begun in 1932 by Arthur Bowden, chair of natural sciences, who commandeered a good 20 vehicles, often over 100 students, with loads of camping gear and crazy abandon that somehow meshed with a geology course to examine the exotic terrain of the south. Popular geology excursions to southern California continued off and on right into the 2010s.

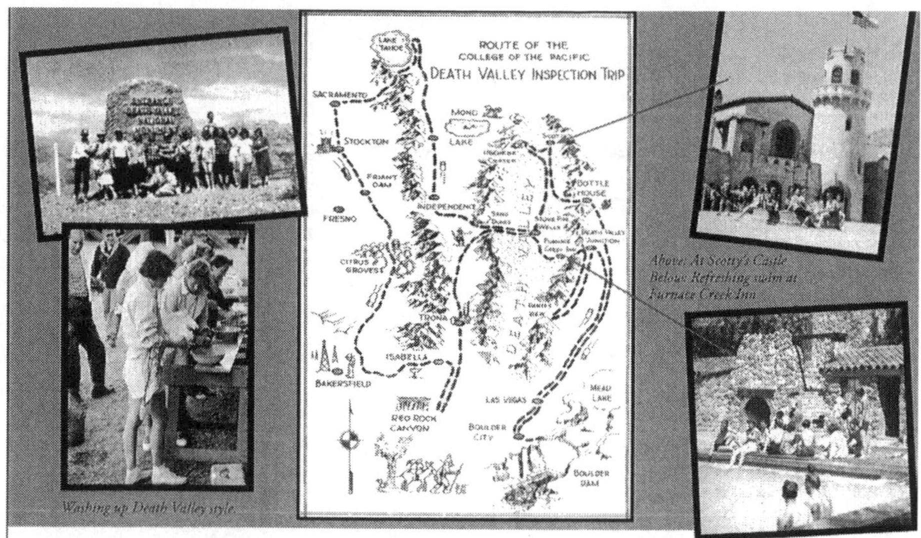

The "Death Valley Tour," began in 1932, was a popular geology excursion to southern California that continued in some fashion into the 2010s.

Equally important was the landmark decision not to banish the first married couple at Pacific. Bill and Maymie Kimes ('31), married in 1930, forced a faculty meeting on an unwritten rule against setting an "undesirable precedent." As the vote neared, a brave professor shouted, "There shouldn't be a penalty for the first offense!" The faculty roared, and Knoles never called the vote. Next year, among the five married student couples was one of Knoles' sons.[91] The shining story of the Depression years may be the "round robin" letter started by Ann Turner Stark ('31), who missed her friendship with 11 sorority sisters (now Delta Gamma) after they parted as graduates. The letter ran for 66 years.[92]

Smoking and dancing

All the fuss was about smoking and dancing in these years of abandonment to the freedom and pleasures of the era, which would not recur until the 1960s. What was a good Methodist school to do about a popular culture that imposed itself upon the campus? The smoking policy came before the trustees several times in the early 1930s, with the resolution that smoking would be allowed in the male residences (but not the women's hall), thus ending the well-worn path from the "Boys' Dorm" to the levee known as "Nicotine Lane."[93]

Dancing was another matter. As early as 1924 Knoles complained to the board, "Youth is becoming impatient in many respects. It is inclined since the war to rebel against authority of every kind." He called for "lifting of the ban on dancing."[94] The trustees were not persuaded. Starting in 1926, the Associated Students began to lobby the trustees. They determined that there was actually no *written* ban on dancing, so their vote of 275-116 on the issue was "only an expression of the student revolt against tradition."[95] The trustees deferred to the Methodist California Conference meeting for advice, and church leaders said no.[96]

The first campus dance: while President Knoles called for lifting the ban on dancing in 1924, the Board of Trustees did not approve until 1933. Forty-eight dances were held in that first year.

Even by 1931, seven years after Knoles' first appeal, the trustees tabled a motion to allow one annual off-campus dance party! Not until 1933 did the trustees finally agree to Knoles' urging to approve on-campus dancing. By the late 1930s the annual Mardi Gras dance begun in 1935 was so large it was held in the Stockton Civic Auditorium, where 600 students, faculty, staff and alumni regaled each other in an elaborate costume contest along with the queen of the ball, who topped all the other annual queens of the year.

Knoles as cowboy, statesman, and friend

In many respects, the last years in San Jose and the early time in Stockton were the glory days of the College before the Depression and another

President Knoles, a serious horse trainer since his youth, loved to parade his horses.

war. It was the time when Tully Knoles returned to his horsemanship and often roamed the campus neighborhood levees on his Tennessee walker "Little Mountain" or anyone of several horses he bought, trained and sold for another. Many remember him astride his beautiful palomino, "Ole," perhaps named after the "Ole" who was his colleague and friend, beloved dean and professor Gustav Werner. Knoles would lead parades with his full cowboy regalia, waving his gloved hand, his smart goatee under his flashing smile—a bit like Buffalo Bill Cody.

This western spectacle he rarely displayed on the stage, instead relying on his incisive mind, quick wit, direct and organized clarity without script or notes, usually addressing complex international issues. He was one of the most popular lecturers in the state, erect and vigorous in his walk as he was keen and crisp in his analysis of current world trends. Whether as Methodist church leader (national education board member for 30 years), educator (high school commencement speaker), Rotarian (district governor in 1937), Mason (thirty-third degree Scottish Rite), or Optimist club member, he was ever the statesman. Twenty-four times he addressed the

San Francisco Commonwealth Club as a respected public intellectual of his day (13 were his "Crystal Ball" annual global forecasts) and served as a board member to advance its mission to promote democratic citizenship.[97] If all this weren't impressive enough, his brand new 1930 Packard sedan, decorated by a delegation of faculty, won first prize in the annual Stockton Armistice Parade.[98]

His and his wife Emily's five sons and three daughters all became students at Pacific. Many were campus student leaders and nearly all of them became educators. Knoles was much admired, and even beloved, on campus. Genuinely friendly, he promoted "friendliness" as a mark of the Pacific campus through his annual *Naranjado* editorials. He worked collegially with faculty because he never lost touch with his own faculty roots; his son George called him a "born teacher" who loved to joke with students and colleagues.[99] He taught the required freshman orientation course "College, Man and Society" without notes. In effect, he heroically embodied the "citizen leader" ideal that became a hallmark of Pacific's commitment to general education for all students around the turn of the next century. Knoles exemplified the best of Pacific—a commitment to students and their personal development, a broad cosmopolitan view of the world grounded in a liberal education, a person of great integrity in his leadership on campus and across the state.

GROWTH THROUGH DIVERSIFICATION I: THE RISE OF PROFESSIONAL EDUCATION

The student boom

Considering all its enrollment setbacks throughout its first half-century, Pacific's enrollment trajectory in the twentieth century is especially impressive. But even from the start, Pacific roughly doubled its student body every 25 years. The two notable exceptions are 1900-1925, when despite a drop around 1910, enrollment mushroomed sixfold from 120 to 820, and then from 1925 to1950, when enrollment grew nearly sixfold again.

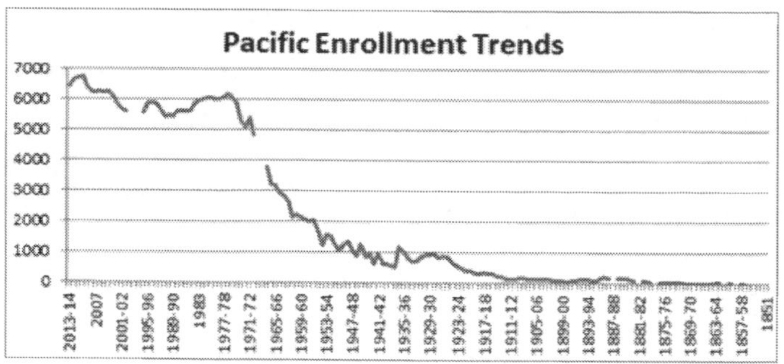

Pacific's enrollment for the first half-century was on par with most other colleges and universities. Its growth since then also matched national trends.

This surge in students duplicated a national phenomenon. Between 1890 and 1925, colleges grew nearly five times as fast as the country's population, and nearly doubled in the 1920s alone, as high school graduates exploded from nine percent of the population in 1910 to over 50 percent in 1940.[100] In the Central Valley, Pacific had gained a decided advantage. The Rockefeller Foundation pronounced, "The College of the Pacific serves exclusively a more heavily populated area, from the standpoint of high school graduates, than any other college in the United States."[101]

Baxter, Knoles' new partner

Thomas Baxter was elected board chair in 1927 after the death of Rolla Watt. Baxter was an innovator, open to new academic programs, which cleared the way for entrepreneurial leaders like Robert Burns to follow. When Baxter discovered an aeronautical engineer in the fledgling engineering department, he bought an Eagle Rock biplane, had students build a landing strip, and built a hangar on the campus to jumpstart the first accredited flight instruction on

Department of Aeronautics

Hilton F. Lask

On April 10, 1928, a group of four students received flying instruction at Pacific field, the airport of the College of the Pacific. The importance of this seemingly trivial incident is that these lessons marked the opening of the first course in flying instruction given in the regular curriculum by any American university of accredited rank.

The courses in aeronautics have been added and a full four year curriculum has been planned which offers the student an education designed to equip him for leadership in the aeronautics industry in the fields of aeronautical engineering, business administration and expert operation of aircraft.

a college campus.[102] He also took command of the institution's finances. In his first year, the College's endowment fund was moved from one of Rolla Watt's banks in San Francisco to the Stockton Savings and Loan Bank, where the fund remains today under its custodial oversight, and where Pacific could always turn to for loans.[103]

The School of Education is founded, the arts flourish

Observing the huge success of the teacher education program at USC a decade earlier, Knoles pushed to make the department of education, established in 1910, into a new School of Education for the Stockton opening, the first professional school since the Conservatory was created in 1878.[104] The new school was authorized by the state to credential high school teachers before the fall 1924 start-up in Stockton. Because the school was one of only a few in the country and even fewer in the west to offer a four-year bachelor's degree, its quality stood out among the largely two-year public and private "normal school" or "teachers college" options.[105]

Meanwhile, within the Conservatory, the art department was the first in California to be granted teacher certification by the state.[106] The Conservatory saw a 40 percent increase in students in its second year in Stockton—many a future church musician learned at Pacific. It started a band and became a charter member of the American Association of Schools of Music (now NASM) in 1928.[107] Heralded dean Howard Hanson

Dean Charles Dennis pioneered the "A Cappella choir" (no instrumental accompaniment) in the west by 1916; this portrait is of his 1933 choir.

resigned to become dean of Eastman School of Music at the University of Rochester, one of the premier music schools in the nation, only adding to the prestige of Pacific's music program. Charles Dennis, his successor, was a nationally recognized choral conductor who in 1916 pioneered the "A Cappella choir" as a collegiate ensemble west of the Mississippi and who often guest-conducted national high school choirs.[108] Some would later observe that as competition arose in the west and around the country, the conservatory would never quite match the stature it had in its first half-century as the first music school west of the Rockies.

As music luminaries moved on, DeMarcus Brown ('23) returned from the American Academy of Dramatic Arts in New York City in 1924 to develop a theater program that achieved regional acclaim for decades and produced a remarkable legacy of alumni on Broadway and in film. These achievements tended to focus attention on the liberal arts profile of the school and its many artistic performers, overshadowing what was actually afoot: a steady investment in professional programs.

Pioneer in professional programs

As elective courses of study became the national signature of colleges at the close of the nineteenth century, the early decades of the twentieth century saw the proliferation of professional degrees. Even in the liberal arts, professional programs steadily found their way into Pacific. George Colliver ('15) established the first religious education department on the west coast. Wilhelmina Harbert ('33), a pioneer in the field, began the music therapy program in the 1930s (a major by 1946), the first such program west of the Mississippi and one of the first in the nation.[109] Within the College, professional programs continued to develop, from business (a major since 1934) to home economics (nine advanced courses).[110] Radio and "speech correction" bolstered the speech department. By 1942, business had the second highest department enrollment—a sign of things to come.[111]

Engineering takes off

The first head of the new engineering department, Clarence White, sought cooperative partnerships with Stockton industries in "a scheme somewhat in the plan of Antioch College," offering industry work experience integrated into the curriculum. This partnership became a distinctive, innovative hallmark of Pacific's engineering program as it began in 1924. For the next 80 years the engineering program would be a five-year program with three terms devoted to "extension" (now called "cooperative") work for students directly with industry partners. Right into the twenty-first century, Pacific's engineering school has been the only program west of the Mississippi to require students to work in industry as an integrated part of their degree program.

As engineering enrollment jumped from 18 to 65 in its first three years, majors proliferated. By 1928 there were six in engineering: general, civil, electrical, chemical, mining, and mechanical. As noted earlier, trustee chair Baxter aided in the formation of the aeronautical engineering major by 1929 as Pacific became the first college to offer a course in flying.[112]

Boxton's dental school: Survival tales

Meanwhile, back in San Francisco, the highly successful College of Physicians and Surgeons came back quickly and strongly after its building was leveled by the 1906 earthquake, having added pharmacy to its medical and dental colleges. While "P&S" students were sent home after the quake for the remainder of the term, within four months they were back in a new building on the same site, a phoenix rebirth as remarkable as dean Boxton's. Caught on bribery as a city Board of Supervisors member in a sting operation, Boxton managed to become San Francisco mayor for one week before public disgrace forced his resignation and his ouster as dental dean. Yet in ignominy he managed to hold his place at P&S as he slowly bought out all other owners. He returned as dean and board member by 1915, becoming president of the board by 1921.[113]

When the American Dental Association forced its hand—become a public trust or shut down—Boxton sold the school in 1923 to five of his faculty members. They restructured the school as a non-profit public trust to build professional credibility at a time when accreditation requirements enforced standards of quality. The two key faculty leaders were alumni Arthur McDowell ('17) and Ernest Sloman ('21), each to become dean of the school. Decades later Dr. Sloman hired a young former student body president to the faculty, Arthur Dugoni ('48), who eventually became the most famous dean in all of dental education.

Verne and Annabel McGeorge rescued a fledgling proprietary night law school in downtown Sacramento in 1924.

McGeorge Law School gets its start

In Sacramento, another profession was developing a school foothold. After World War I, a profitable San Francisco Law School begun in 1909 explored Sacramento as a market, given its rising prominence as the state capital where crowds of young state employees were crafting and enforcing laws and regulations. In 1921, the school incorporated the Sacramento Law School in the Mull Building at 10th and L Streets with ten impressive young faculty members, including Verne McGeorge. But night-school enrollment lagged, so by summer 1924, the owners quietly packed up and removed to San Francisco.

When Sacramento law students returned in the fall to discover empty offices behind a locked door, they appealed to McGeorge, their popular contracts professor, to rescue their schooling. With his wife Annabel as registrar and comptroller, McGeorge pulled together a faculty and held classes in their living room. The couple incorporated as the Sacramento College of Law in 1924, with a board that included Judge Peter Shields, later to help found UC-Davis, and Belle Cooledge, vice president of Sacramento

McGeorge School of Law had several downtown locations until 1957, the last of which was the Ruhstaller Building at 9th and J Streets.

Junior College and later mayor of Sacramento. Repudiating any link to the fly-by-night San Francisco operation, Pacific's McGeorge School of Law has ever since referred to 1924 as its founding date.

Like the dental school, it was under pressure to end its for-profit status, and in 1927 became nonprofit McGeorge College of Law, two years after it graduated its first six bachelor of law students. Thus, while the 1920s were indeed a time of great change and advancement in higher education, the times were especially pivotal for Pacific. Between 1923 and 1927, College of the Pacific and its future schools of dentistry and law all established new and improved identities in new locations.

Liberal arts flourishes through general education

Pacific, like so many smaller liberal arts colleges, asserted its identity as a teaching institution with close interaction between students and their professors, while Stanford and Cal became big, impersonal, and research oriented. By combining a streamlined classical curriculum with a lacing of professional paths into business, law, and engineering, the College in effect paralleled its modified traditional Gothic architecture: simplified and more efficient than it Oxbridge predecessors. When, years later, COP dean Harold Jacoby called forth the College faculty to define its liberal arts goals, he admitted that there were "few traces of any clearly defined set of educational objectives" from these earlier decades. In fact, Jacoby asserted, President Knoles "openly supported the position that his educational philosophy was to have no educational philosophy."[114]

While the liberal arts undoubtedly became stronger during these years of growth, there is no evidence that the academic programs consolidated toward the liberal arts.[115] In fact, the opposite occurred: professional programs generally grew in number and size steadily under Knoles' two decades in Stockton, despite the dual setbacks of the Depression and War.

By the 1920s the Carnegie Foundation helped achieve consensus on national admission requirements for college and on graduation requirements for the bachelor's degree. Pacific joined most schools in setting general education requirements for all undergraduates. Roughly half of a student's college courses focused on the arts and humanities, natural science and mathematics, and the social sciences, while the other half consisted of courses in a subject major and electives. President Knoles taught the required freshman orientation course, "The College, Man and Society." Two courses in Bible were still required, as was English, a foreign language, history or political science, physical education (health and physical fitness were now touted to build character), and ten units of natural science laboratory courses.[116]

This "general education" curriculum molded in the 1920s became the standard liberal arts college fare for decades to come, even as Pacific began to expand its professional programs and the religion requirement faded. General education stood for the values of that old curriculum, which asserted the importance of developing personal character, of expanding a worldview, of understanding the moral and ethical responsibilities of leadership for a career and as a citizen. Lively, challenging, and engaging professors aided this goal. Malcolm Eiselen, professor of history, made general education an attraction for most students; his U.S. history course was popular not only because of his sharp knowledge but because he "radiate[d] a genial sense of humor in the classroom."[117]

THE GREAT DEPRESSION AND THE STOCKTON JUNIOR COLLEGE PARTNERSHIP

At debt's door again

Despite the steady, impressive enrollment growth, cash pledges lagged once the College opened in Stockton, and Knoles complained that the regional Methodist dollar support was weaker than any other area of the country.[118] Knoles urged exploration of an "interdenominational college" to broaden support, but no formal actions were taken.

On the brink of the Great Depression, Knoles' assessment to the trustees was unduly grim: "I do not see how we can go on unless this debt paying campaign is a success. We are hampered on every turn, and we are sailing on such thin ice."[119] The Pomona and Redlands college endowments were six to eight times greater than Pacific's, and even Occidental's was nearly three times larger. What is most troubling is that Knoles did not perceive himself as a president who either had command over the College's financial health or responsibility to rectify it. All he thought he could do was to warn of its jeopardizing the academic welfare: "It is not for me to advise in connection with the financial matters of the College."[120]

Rev. Bane, the energetic fundraiser who helped recruit Pacific to Stockton, was added as a vice president at least to push the debt out the door. This the College did accomplish, barely three months before the bank and stock market collapse brought on the Great Depression. Board chair Baxter was credited most for the campaign's success, and the school went ahead with its planned dedication of Baxter Stadium just three days after October 29. But the College did not achieve its endowment goal and was forced to forfeit nearly all the $250,000 Rockefeller Foundation grant, not for the first time. No doubt this ongoing interaction with the Carnegie and Rockefeller foundations continued to shape Pacific's shaky national reputation as a school heartfelt in its commitment, but unable to achieve the financial grounding of a national university.

The Great Depression cuts to the bone

With the collapse of October 1929, Pacific faced empty-pocket supporters and students unable to pay their Pacific bills. Inez Sheldon ('37) worked in the library, swept the gym in the heat, and babysat for faculty to help pay her tuition.[121] From 1912 to 1928, Pacific had seen its student body grow eightfold, to a record high of 978 students. By 1933, enrollment had dropped by over one-fourth. The school had to consider new options simply to survive. The country was in for 15 years of profound uncertainty and tentativeness about the future that was unprecedented since the Civil War. One campus action could symbolize this change of mood: the *Naranjado,* forever a yearbook that included 20 to 30 pages of humor, satire, and campus joshings, ended this comic tradition in 1930.

Knoles was a passive leader when it came to finances. A 1931 Methodist report had challenged the "dual administration" of the College, noting that executive vice president and comptroller O.H. Ritter had been making all the financial decisions, even those affecting the academic program.[122] The trustees then took charge. With $400,000 of unpaid campaign pledges, the board reduced all salaries by 40 percent in fall 1933 ("wholly beyond reason" said a sympathetic board), transferred $10,000 from the endowment to the annual operating budget—a sure sign of desperation—and even considered the possibility of selling the College to the state.[123] By 1934, all salaries were cut by a month, but Knoles stood firm against cutting academic programs or laying off five faculty members. A more realistic board stood their ground and cut by four.[124] The students sensed foreboding and voted to discard the Honor System, established a decade earlier requiring fellow students to report cheating.[125]

Knoles hits bottom

This was Knoles' darkest hour. Within months Knoles, self-conscious of his inability to provide financial leadership at such a perilous time, recommended that the board "secure a man of special financial abilities" as president, even naming his possible successor. As a former USC faculty member, he knew how starkly USC's amazing success under president Rufus von KleinSmid contrasted with Pacific's experience.

A USC board that like Pacific's was appointed by the Methodist church became a stumbling block to giving. Von KleinSmid had succeeded in a $10 million campaign after severing ties with the Methodist Church in 1928 to widen the appeal of USC as Los Angeles' private university. Von KleinSmid persuaded his trustees to change the bylaws to become a self-perpetuating board and to reduce its Methodist membership by one-half.[126] In the first decade of "Rufus Rex" (1921-31), von KleinSmid secured mergers with the five affiliated but privately owned professional schools of the city—law, dentistry, pharmacy, oratory, and music—then added schools of film, journalism, fine arts, education, engineering, medicine, international affairs, public administration, and philosophy, capping it off with the preeminent sign of a strong liberal arts college—a Phi Beta Kappa chapter in 1929.[127]

Knoles must have known that Pacific needed a game-changer, that time had passed him by, and that a successor might better meet the challenge. Yet during this era he reinforced the Methodist tie by insisting that the bylaws of the College require a portion of the trustees be elected by the northern and southern Methodist church conferences, and that revision of this bylaw require the consent of both Methodist conferences.[128]

Another pioneering first is launched

The board, in 1934 still confident of Knoles' talented leadership and "brilliant presidency," firmly rejected his offer to resign. Instead they embraced Knoles' novel idea that the College attempt to consolidate as a senior college by creating a public junior college eligible for state tuition funding. President Knoles, reaffirmed by his board, rewound his courage and proceeded to launch a major innovation in higher education while he held his nose.

Encouraged again by the two New York foundation juggernauts, the Rockefeller and Carnegie foundations, along with the Methodist higher education bureaucracy now headed by former Pacific president Seaton, Knoles explored the addition of a "junior college" that would open the door to students who qualified for public two-year colleges but could not achieve Pacific's admission standards.[129] Driven by economics, the innovation would be a unique private-public partnership unprecedented in American higher education. Necessity—or desperation—is the mother of invention at Pacific.

Tully Knoles (1919-46) was probably Pacific's most beloved and popular president of the twentieth century.

The College piloted a program of 73 students coming with high school diplomas or ages over 21—either credential would do. This decision matched what USC had done in 1932 by launching its University Junior College—also heavily criticized for forfeiting admission standards. But USC balanced its decision with the founding of the school of research (ironically under the key leadership of Napa/Pacific alumnus Rockwell Hunt, dean of the USC Graduate School) to foster USC's lagging reputation as a university serious about scholarship and research.

Knoles instead focused on making the junior college a success. Director Dwayne Orton ('33), the director of forensics, oversaw a skeleton of courses designed as basic, barely college-level overviews of disciplines taught by Pacific faculty faced with some empty classrooms. For a president who had repudiated Stanford's repeated overtures for Pacific to become its junior college feeder school, this venture was a huge concession that still would not fill the budget gap it was intended to address. Yet it was of monumental importance for Pacific: another ingenious, innovative move that rescued a college determined to survive regardless of the temporary setback in quality and reputation.

With 200 public junior colleges by the mid-1920s, California had become a national leader in the movement when the local superintendents huddled with Knoles and community leaders to explore how San Joaquin County might retain junior college tuition that was going to schools out of the district. Another attraction was avoiding costly construction during these hard times.[130] This would clearly be a win-win-win agreement: Pacific could survive by enrolling more underclass students who would have their tuition funded by the taxpayer. Filling classes could avoid slashing more faculty positions and also earn income through rental of under-used classrooms. Junior college students would save the hassle and expense of driving to Sacramento or Modesto for college. Local taxpayers would save around $30,000 now being spent to send their youngsters to colleges in those cities, and Stockton could have a junior collcgc without investing in facilities.[131]

The question was, would it be legal for public entities to partner with a private, church-related college? Through the summer of 1935, over 250 junior college students were admitted into the program on the hope and expectation that the state would approve, but the trustees had to fund the students' tuition in a sign of good faith that their venture would pay off.[132]

Stockton College is born

The State legislature approved this unprecedented partnership in October 1935, based on the Pacific tradition of teaching no sectarian or denominational doctrine. The state attorney general followed with a positive opinion by May 1936, opening a door for Pacific to prosper during an era that may have spelled its demise.

Opening with 301 freshman students in fall 1935, the junior college enrollment doubled to 615 students the following year, helping the joint college enrollment hit an all-time high of 1008 students. Stockton had an instant public junior college separate from Pacific without building a campus, and students could try out college locally for two years that could gain them admission into Pacific's bachelor's degree programs.[133]

Confident, Pacific quickly hired five new professors, four with Ph.D.s, and discarded the watered-down "general college" curriculum in favor of a traditional transfer curriculum.[134] Once again, Pacific was brought back from the brink by a novel and winning innovation. Knoles reminded COP that the $50,000 annual rental income from the Stockton College partnership alone was equivalent to a $1.5 million endowment. This novel public-private partnership, unique in the country, lasted until 1951, and was not duplicated by other schools for years.

TWO COLLEGES, ONE CAMPUS LIFE

"Student Affairs" begins

By the 1930s, the notion that a college was responsible for all aspects of student life—from social life to psychological counseling to job assistance—was firmly established across the country.[135] Bob Burns ('31), the young graduate who headed alumni relations, produced the first "Freshman Handbook," known as the "Frosh Bible," to orient students to college life at Pacific. In 1930, Pacific began its "deputations," 60 students in outreach teams sent to high schools to recruit students.[136] Dean of Men Olympian Jim Corson started a "Student Employment Bureau" to help graduates find jobs—a novel campus service in 1936.[137] The "Social Hall" was expanded with a new wing called Anderson Hall in honor of its donors, and it became the home of the YMCA and YWCA, which merged to form the "Student Christian Association" in 1939.[138] Anderson Hall was Pacific's "student union" until the McCaffrey Center was built, and home for a host of clubs, debates, meetings, and all the SCA's campus ministry activities.

The decision to treat Stockton College students like COP students in all aspects of campus life was critical to a positive atmosphere during the tough Depression years. Students intermingled with no distinction except the usual groupings by class level. All were members of the same Pacific Student Association. Joining students who could not afford college without state-funded tuition with students whose middle-class families could support them through the bachelor's degree stood in contrast to the social class tensions surrounding them in the Central Valley.

The campus fills out

Student pride in the campus was evident through the 1920s and 30s; the majestic campus halls were featured in formal portraits in nearly every issue of *Naranjado*. The Pacific campus still needed much mothering, so within six months of the Crash the College proceeded with a plan to pave the muddy campus streets. Thriftiness was a way at Pacific—an army of students built the grounds, the lawns and flowerbeds, under the expert direction of grounds superintendent Santino Bava.[139] The students loved Pacific, and they worked to improve the campus again and again during these years, at significant financial sacrifice. They fussed little over the peat from the asparagus fields silting under their dorm room sills but poured a good deal of sweat equity into curbs and sidewalks under engineering faculty supervision.

Several graduating classes donated to build more sidewalks across the campus.[140] But they had larger ambitions for this beautiful yard: in 1934, they persuaded the trustees to build a swimming pool underwritten by the student body, to be funded by student "bond sales." This project carried forward a student tradition. They had funded lights for Baxter Stadium and paid for a 1250-seat outdoor amphitheatre through three-year ticket subscriptions in 1933. A student used his family's horses to do the excavation![141]

Remarkably, the loss of the library in the 1915 fire had not urged Pacific to make a library a priority for the new campus. A space was found in Weber Hall along with a crowd of other uses—the snakes in the zoology lab found their way into the book stacks. When the campus heating system was decentralized in 1938, the Power House became the "temporary" library with classrooms and labs. Mrs. Herbert Hoover, who earlier had given books to the library, came to dedicate "the Power House to the House of Power."[142]

As the Depression began to ease in 1936, Childress Pool opened a new era in swimming under Chris Kjeldsen ('35) that led to national ranking in the 1940s. Many of those great swimmers like Bob Steel ('50, '61), Don

Driggs ('50) and Ken Mork ('50), along with other students, helped to start the famous "Ale and Quail" club in the Foothill town of Murphys. Hundreds of alumni have returned for an annual celebration that continues today.[143]

The gymnasium was burned down in June 1940 by a junior college student arsonist resulting in lost records, a trophy case "reduced to a lump of metal," and charred drafts of an incomplete master's thesis by a young graduate student named Gladys Benerd ('52). This is the same Gladys Benerd who much later made generous bequests to the Stockton Fire and Police Departments—as well as endowing the School of Education now bearing her name with a gift of over $9 million.[144] The gym was quickly rebuilt over the summer for $50,000 and remains a mainstay for campus recreation to this day.

Another landmark building was begun in 1939 when trustee Percy Morris offered half the funds to build a chapel. The cornerstone was laid seven days after Pearl Harbor, so the military virtually took over the rails by 1942, causing the chapel timbers to arrive late. But by 1943 the beautiful Morris Chapel was finished, graced with the stained-glass rose window of Temple Methodist Church of San Francisco as a memorial to board chair Rolla and Mrs. Watt, and a pulpit dedicated to Knoles. The first wedding in Morris Chapel was Grace Carter ('32), long-time secretary to the president and the faculty, to Leslie Richardson, local trustee; at his death, she was appointed to replace him on the board (1942-60), the only known staff person ever to serve this role.[145]

Business vice president Ovid Ritter published a small book, Morris Chapel *(1946), identifying the artifacts and symbolism of beautiful Morris Chapel, built in 1943.*

HIRING HISTORY TO MAKE HISTORY: AMOS ALONZO STAGG

Hiring "the gospel of football"

When Tully Knoles picked up the phone to invite an American icon to join Pacific in 1933, he could not have truly known the impact his decision would have, the fate he had struck. The "Old Man" of football (not yet known as the "Grand Old Man"), who in so many respects invented the big-time game of American collegiate football, in all of its glory and disgrace, also hatched a program at Pacific that would become one of its most lasting legacies and its own undoing. Amos Alonzo Stagg would invent an ambition for football at Pacific that won national admiration and spawned a roster of professional players and coaches unmatched by any school its size.[146] While at the University of Chicago he had built an industrial complex for NCAA Division I football through its power, dominance, and pervasiveness, and that complex killed the sport at Pacific.

Knoles was drawn to Stagg primarily for his fame of character, for his driving moral purpose as a mentor to young men, for his "gospel of football" that produced winning teams of successful students of moral stature. But he also was hiring the man who virtually invented the collegiate sport and all its trappings as we know it a century later—from athletic scholarships to entrepreneurial ticket sales to big-time boosterism. Stagg's and college football's success led to the 1929 Carnegie Report, the first of many national reports to come, condemning collegiate athletics as out of control. But that could not be said of Pacific, with Baxter Stadium waiting to be filled. So Tully Knoles made the call to Stagg, the second most important appointment of his presidency. (His most important hire was young alumni relations director Robert Burns ('31) as his assistant in 1942, to be groomed as his successor.)

The astonishing Stagg story

While Stagg was the star of five Yale baseball championships, he earned a place on football-inventor and Yale athletic director Walter Camp's first

All-American football team in 1889.[147] After YMCA leadership training, Stagg became the first tenured athletic director and first head of physical culture and athletics at University of Chicago in 1892, where he reigned for 41 years. President Harper offered him imperious *carte blanche* freedom to build an empire through his heroic "evangelical athleticism," his breakthrough innovations in the game itself (preeminently the nimble "open game" and forward pass), and his promotional savvy that generated soaring profits to catapult his football program and his own salary to the highest in academe. He was the very first of a long line of "celebrity-entrepreneur" coaches of wealth and power.

Some say he was the key to dissuading President Theodore Roosevelt from banning football for its brutality by inventing the less dangerous fast game of forward passes and innovative plays. He invented the huddle, numbers on uniforms, night lights, and the "T" formation while he exhorted players to "live clean" by outlawing drinking, smoking, and profanity. For Stagg, the purpose of athletics was "Christian manhood," and he preached through his coaching.[148]

The Stagg tradition at Pacific

When Chicago president Robert Maynard Hutchins forced Stagg to retire at age 70 in 1933, the most famous man in football claimed he had seven job offers. Merlin Porter ('26), secretary of the Pacific alumni club in San Francisco, had wired Stagg when he read of his Chicago ouster, and when Stagg responded, Knoles stepped in. Knoles went to Chicago to persuade him to come to Pacific, and Stagg never regretted it. The rally to welcome Knoles back from his successful recruitment trip formed a cheering parade of hundreds of students and townspeople, led by the band through the main streets of Stockton.[149] Later, during Stagg's heyday, Knoles paid tribute to Stagg in the highest terms; he wrote in the *Pacific Review* that Stagg was one of the "four greatest teachers" of his life: "He is a truly great teacher of character."[150]

Amos Alonzo Stagg more than any other person shaped intercollegiate football for the country and established the Pacific football tradition as coach from 1933-1946.

Stagg's challenge at Pacific was to start from scratch. Pacific football, which began in fits and starts in 1894, was at the top of a weak "California Coach Conference" until 1926, when it moved to stiffer competition in the region, enduring that 1927 humiliation (67-7) by famous Knute Rockne protégé "Slip" Madigan and his St. Mary's College team, on a roll with national ranking. Stagg's wife Stella was what he called his "Number One Assistant."[151] As Stagg's scout, she "sent down plays from the stands," and early on washed and mended the team's uniforms after the games.[152] He demanded Spartan discipline in his players—once he kicked a player off the team on the spot for smoking—but never cursed them. "Jack-ass"—maybe "double jack-ass"—was as hot as it got.[153] Stagg soon had the Pacific Alumni Club developing the "Pacific Athletic Revolving Loan Fund" to help recruit athletes and the Stockton Chamber of Commerce partnering to provide jobs for them.[154]

The football team on board the Lurline, Pearl Harbor, December 1939 (Coach Stagg is on far right). Pacific beat Hawaii 19-6. A decade later, Pacific would beat Hawaii 75-0.

Stagg and his "Bengals" grabbed headlines in his second year by nearly knocking off Cal and USC with Little All-American Chris Kjeldsen ('35), and in his fourth year the Tigers won the Far Western Conference championship. Threatened by this upstart, the 1936 big-time Pacific Coast Conference now added Pacific to its boycott of little powerhouses St. Mary's and Santa Clara—and Stagg left the PCC meeting after a 12-hour wait with no team schedule.[155] While the Bay area sports writers dismissed the 1938 Tigers as "a junior college squad," Pacific won its Far Western Conference championship again in 1939 and 1940, including the 32-0 victory over Stagg's old team at Stagg Field in Chicago, starring Little All-American Bobby Kientz ('40).[156] (The next year Chicago dropped football.)

Still, it must have been frustrating to Stagg that Pacific was not invited to a national bowl game, while St. Mary's and Santa Clara were both bowl champs in the 30s and 40s—SCU three times in the Sugar Bowl, SMC once in the Sugar Bowl and 1-1 in the Cotton Bowl. Yet Stagg's reputation drew top players during the war years; the Navy wanted its men to play football with the best, so according to Robert Burns they sent their stars to Stagg.[157]

The incomparable Eddie LeBaron and the vets

In 1946, when a diminutive 16-year old from Oakdale stepped onto the field as a frosh among a host of hulking vets, Stagg in his final year could see a storied contrast: Stagg the oldest, Eddie LeBaron ('50) the youngest college footballer in the nation. LeBaron admits that he turned down Stanford and came to Pacific not because of Stagg but because of his eight Oakdale buddies, including standouts like David "Bud" Klein ('47), Bruce Orvis ('50), John Rohde ('50), and Bob Moser ('52). They were having fun playing under an inventive assistant coach, Larry Siemering, who LeBaron said was one of the two best coaches he ever worked with—the other was Tom Landry of the Dallas Cowboys.[158]

For nearly 70 years, most Americans learned of the school through the fame of football quarterback Eddie LeBaron ('50).

The war years at first depleted the team of players, then became a windfall: by 1943, with the influx of beefy V-12 Navy and Marine men from around the country, Stagg produced his best season, was named national "Coach of the Year," and the Bengals ranked sixth in the nation. With nifty new plays dreamed up by Stagg, the Bengals beat UCLA, Cal, and a nationally ranked St. Mary's team, losing only to USC 6-0 on two hotly disputed touchdown callbacks.[159] Some games were radio broadcasted to the troops in the South Pacific theater.

Pacific had its first big-school All-Americans, fullback Johnny Podesto ('43) and tackle Artie McCaffray ('44), "the finest lineman I've ever coached," said Stagg.[160] But what the military machine provideth, it taketh away: two of his top players, Podesto and Earl Klapstein ('43, '53), were called up by the Marines, and football again took a backseat. The *Pacific Review* declared that the Marines' exit "closed the era of big-time FootBall" for Pacific.[161] In 1945, St. Mary's replayed the 1927 debacle,

0-61, prompting a frank review of Stagg's troubled coaching, failing eyesight and grumbling players.[162]

Knoles offered Stagg a position of "Consultant in Athletics at full faculty status," which he flatly turned down. He left to assist his son as coach at Susquehanna University.[163] In the end, Stagg lost more games than he won in his 14 years, but when he ended his coaching at Pacific in 1946, he was the "winningest" Division I football coach in history with 314 victories, until his record was broken in 1981.

The three "grand old men" of Pacific, "Mr. California" historian Rockwell D. Hunt, football coach Amos Alonzo Stagg, and Pacific President Tully C. Knoles.

With all his success, Stagg lived a modest life, mowing the lawn around his Stockton bungalow with a push mower for decades, even after his return to Stockton at age 90. He died at 102 in 1965, only one of three named to the College Hall of Fame as both player and coach. He was generous throughout his life: "No man learns the secret of life until he learns how to give gladly. . . . A man is no true giver until it has become like play to him."[164] His 1941 donation to purchase the 21 acres of land to honor Tully Knoles that eventually became Stagg Stadium, Simoni Softball Field, the Aquatics Center, and Knoles Field is only one shining example.

Stagg had made Pacific's Orange and Black famous on the national stage for the first time. His team-building task paralleled the construction years of the Golden Gate Bridge, then the largest bridge in human history. And like the enduring "International Orange" color of the bridge, which began as a temporary red lead primer, Stagg's 1933 makeshift orange and black Bengals had staying power that would last for decades. As President Burns said of him, "The rare example of his life—his philosophy, his sportsmanship, his countless achievements through physical and moral fitness will inspire Americans in the years ahead." And they have.[165]

Community supporters planted three redwoods and this sword in stone on the central quad to commemorate coach Stagg in 1944. The sword has been missing for many years.

SURVIVING THE WAR YEARS

Wishing upon a star

The eve of World War II was a time of optimism and hope, climbing out of the Depression, driven by popular culture at its best. The movies of 1940—*Citizen Kane, The Grapes of Wrath, The Philadelphia Story*—all celebrated in varying ways the heart of America. The jitterbug dance craze had high schoolers frenetic with abandon. The hit song of the year was Walt Disney's "When You Wish upon a Star," and at Pacific, you really could dream of becoming a star. Under the masterful direction of DeMarcus Brown ('23), one of Pacific's great professors, stars emerged one after the other, right on through the war. "Pacific Theatre" was open to all majors, but Brown never really had auditions. An awful classroom teacher whose artistic arrogance led to clashes with the Conservatory, Brown produced 350 plays over 44 years at a high professional level by reigning over all. His students and Stockton society adored him. He claimed President Knoles told him he could "do anything you want . . . as long as it doesn't cost anything." President Burns called him "De-Marvelous." [166]

Graduates like William Geery ('33) were headed for Hollywood even before Will Rogers came to town to film *Steamboat 'Round the Bend* in 1936, when Pacific students started the tradition of signing up as movie extras. Oscar winner Jo Van Fleet ('37) starred on Broadway before her *East of Eden* Hollywood days, along with Lois Wheeler ('41) and Margaret Ritter Sears ('37). Toni Rifberg (aka Ann Summers (n.d) and Jack Holmes ('42) were dancers on Broadway as well as in movies. Barbara Baxley ('44) starred in *Bus Stop* and *Peter Pan*, and Robert Nichols ('47) starred in 50 films before his TV roles. Darren McGavin ('48) won an Emmy among his many TV roles, and Robert Culp ('49) starred in countless TV series for decades. In the conservatory, the other one-man show was Lucas Underwood, whose heralded opera program vied for space with Brown and featured the glorious voice of June Spencer ('53). Herman Saunders ('40) started his own swing band at Pacific, played piano for Tommy Dorsey, then rose to television and film producer whose "Dragnet" featured his old Army buddy Jack Webb.[167]

Theater professor DeMarcus Brown was Pacific's most prominent faculty member in the early decades in Stockton. His outdoor "Greek amphitheatre" added a venue to increase performances.

The draft comes to campus

The military draft of college students became a contentious issue at Pacific and on campuses across the country as Army General Hershey proposed universal conscription. Many *Pacific Weekly* editorials echoed a national sentiment: why draft the cream of the crop, college students, risking the loss of a generation of future leaders? The answer was simple: U.S. military forces lacked the leadership required. Anticipating a rapid expansion of forces, many more officers were needed, and the college campus was the obvious place to get them. Though the draft was narrowed, the challenge for Pacific and many schools was the impact on male enrollment. All engineering courses were suspended for lack of students, and engineering professor Edward Gardner, one of seven faculty members to be called up, was deployed to the Panama Canal project. Ione Angwin Monagan ('45) recalled that she was elected 1943 student body president because there were few men confident enough of avoiding call-up for military service. Two more women followed her in office in 1944 and 1945.

The Navy V-12 program rescues Pacific

The Navy V-12 program rescued Pacific and many other small colleges from closing during World War II.

Enrollment was up in 1941 as students were eager to get in as much college coursework as they could before the draft pulled them out of school. Draft boards gradually called up Pacific students month by month to fill their quotas. Then the Navy and Marine Corps, followed by the Army, offered student deferments for officers in training. The huge student windfall for Pacific was the Navy V-12 Collegiate Training Program for pre-officers, one of six in the state, and the Army Signal Corps radio training program. Instantly the $108,000 COP debt was cut nearly in half with the flood of federal war training funds.[168]

The premier program was the Navy V-12 program for 227 cadets headed by Commander Burton Rokes, a Naval officer who openly despised colleges.[169] A total of 377 men began arriving by July 1943 to pursue pre-medical and deck officer training. Men's Hall became a V-12 barracks, all the pre-meds lived in "Cadaver Hall," one of the fleet of "Quonset hut" dorms, and the Marines took over Archania and Mu Zeta Rho houses. At first, half of the servicemen were Marines, but by fall 1944 all the Marines were called up.

How the Brubecks met

Dave ('42) and Iola ('45) Brubeck met at Pacific (shown here in 1942) and became a powerful team to pioneer west coast jazz and promote human rights. Dave Brubeck is Pacific's most famous alumnus; his wife Iola ('45) is credited for much of his success as an innovative composer and musician.

Iola Whitlock ('45) met Dave Brubeck ('42) in a conservatory auditorium doorway on his way to piano practice as a senior. John Crabbe's radio major, begun in 1927 as the second in the country, was a big draw for talented students like Iola who won radio awards as a student, and media luminaries like Daren McGavin ('48), Ralph Guild ('50), and David Gerber ('50).[170] Brubeck had wanted to follow in his rancher father's footsteps rather than his piano-teacher mother by pursing a pre-veterinary major. President Knoles used to join his dad on cattle drives, so the family got to know Pacific.[171]

But he floundered in the freshman biology lab. Zoology professor Dr. Arnold told him, "Brubeck, your mind's not here. It's across the lawn in the Conservatory. Please go there. Stop wasting my time and yours."[172] Later, Brubeck narrowly graduated because he could not read music, so some faculty members challenged his candidacy for a liberal arts degree. Dean Elliott knew he had a composer whiz, overruled, and prevented an historic disgrace.

Iola Brubeck invented the college tour for jazz musicians in the 1950s, with Dave Brubeck ('42) and his quartet in the lead.

Brubeck proposed marriage on his first date with Iola Whitlock, and their life-long partnership produced a global legacy in jazz and contemporary music. Dave was drafted right after graduation, so they married before he was sent overseas. The rest of the story is history, but the proper phrase is "unprecedented history:" surely worldwide, Dave Brubeck, the jazz pianist-composer who took American college campuses by storm with his quartet and appeared on a *Time* magazine cover by the time he was 34, is Pacific's most famous alumnus. Dave and Iola always credited professors for their shaping influence. For Iola it was John Crabbe, the founder of the radio program, and for Dave, it was Irving Goleman, the ever-popular humanities professor of Stockton College and COP. In fact Dave Brubeck once remarked, "Three Jewish teachers have been a great influence in my life: Irving Goleman, Darius Milhaud [the famous music composer], and Jesus."[173]

Japanese student internment

In 1924, despite Japan's diplomacy, Congress banished all Japanese from further immigrating to the U.S. In 1928, the Methodist church adopted a strong statement in support of the Japanese, objecting to the hostility as playing into the hands of Japanese military extremists, who by 1936 overthrew the Japanese government.[174] Throughout this era, Pacific remained silent on this contentious issue in all its publications while it increasingly enrolled Japanese-American students. By 1942, 26 Japanese-American students were members of the Japanese Club, and overall Japanese-American enrollment exceeded 50.[175]

Pacific's Japanese Club was large and active, seen here in the 1942 Naranjado. Japanese-American students in California were required to join their families in war internment camps from 1942-46.

All culminated in February 1942 when President Roosevelt's Executive Order 9066 authorized the removal of suspicious persons from military areas. There was special concern about people of Japanese descent in California, labeled part of "the Western military area," called by some a "combat zone," where nearly 90 percent of persons of Japanese ancestry lived. Led by attorney general Earl Warren, virtually all public leaders in California urged the roundup of all Japanese-Americans, though not Germans or Italians, and within two weeks of the Order the mass evacuation on the West Coast began. Deployed to detention camps were 100,000 Japanese residents, two-thirds U.S. citizens.

In May, 1942, the War Relocation Authority of the U.S. Department of Interior required 51 Pacific and Stockton College students, among over 4,000 Stocktonians of Japanese descent, to move to the San Joaquin County Fairgrounds, the temporary local detention camp from May to October.[176] They lived in tents, horse stalls, and makeshift buildings until assigned to one of the ten relocation centers around the country, including

Manzanar and Tule Lake in California, where they remained for the rest of the war. Students were given "proportionate credit" for work completed in unfinished classes—seven were seniors in their final month before graduation.

The war-effort campus

Every aspect of student life was affected by the war effort, including the "war curricula." The calendar switched to an accelerated trimester to fit the armed forces schedule to graduate in three years. Physical education was now four days per week, not two. Math and science courses were revamped, business courses focused on ordnance depots and supply centers instead of small business management, English classes focused on clear command memos. In the *Pacific Review*'s special "Jeep Edition," every academic department listed courses for the major that related to the war effort, and the editor exhorted alumni, "We are suffering a shortage of college graduates just as factually as we are suffering a shortage of rubber."[177] Commander Rokes was so dismissive of college officials and faculty that Knoles tried unsuccessfully to get him transferred.[178]

The "SS Pacific Victory," named for COP, was one of over 500 ships in the cargo fleet to support the war effort. (postcard photo)

The Army thanked the "French students" of the two colleges for helping to fund six Jeeps for the 471st Battalion.[179] One veteran remembered seeing a jeep with its COP bumper sticker when he was leaving the beach at Normandy.[180] As part of a national military public relations program, College of the Pacific had a merchant-marine ship named after it for donating a small library of books for the sailors, the "SS Pacific Victory." COP was assured by the military that the College was in the name, despite its ambiguous title.[181]

Student life at this time was a world away from what had been or what would be. Hazing ended, as did the Homecoming bonfire. Amid air-raid drills, students donated old keys to the "Victory Keys" jar—metal for bullets and bombers. Some students volunteered to work in the canneries but found the assembly line too demanding to return: "We were canned along with the tomatoes."[182] Gas rationing limited student outings and co-eds were rolling Red Cross bandages, though students were not about to complain, knowing how many of their fellow classmates were sacrificing their futures for the country. Basketball games and holiday dances continued with an earnest effort for a normalcy everyone knew had passed. The editors gallantly concluded, "Our college was still a college and the co-eds still wore angora sweaters and too much perfume; the men students had dirtier corduroys than ever."

The War takes its toll

The saddest day of the war for the campus was the deployment of 58 students in the Army Enlisted Reserve Corps.

On March 16, 1943, fifty-eight Pacific students in the Army Enlisted Reserve Corps boarded Greyhound buses for Monterey, to be scattered to bases all across the country for various military training. "We sang 'Pacific Hail' one last time," the *Naranjado* reported, "almost like a benediction…then stood there, our hearts in our eyes, as the buses rolled away."[183] The *Naranjado* voiced the campus lament: "Men enlisted; women wept. Studies were forgotten—What's the use?…Today, each seeks a place in national offense…not defense…with victory in his soul."[184]

Every part of the College was oriented to the war effort. Fraternity life disappeared completely, though sororities carried on as all co-curricular organizations struggled to survive. The basketball team managed with the huge help of Stan McWilliams ('50), the sixth highest scorer in the nation by 1945. The A Cappella Choir, famous for singing in the Easter Sunrise Service at Mirror Lake in Yosemite Park for 30 consecutive years, became an "all-women war-time edition." Americans listened to this renowned choir on national radio under the direction of dean Russell Bodley.[185]

On the battlefront, Pacific students lost their lives. Marine Lt. Albert Garcia ('44), outstanding football halfback on the great Stagg team of 1943, was killed in action on Iwo Jima. He wrote to his mom just days before he died: "We are now witnessing the most beautiful sight I have ever seen. That is Old Glory flying on top of the rock [Mt. Suribachi] with our boys all around it, cheering. Mom, it sends chills up and down my spine."[186] All Americans had that same thrill when the Associated Press printed that most famous visual icon of the war. In the end, over 2,000 Pacific men and women served in World War II.[187] An unknown number gave their lives.

Atherton's GI Bill of Rights

During the war, Stocktonian Warren Atherton served as the National Commander of the American Legion. He became known as the "Father of the GI Bill" for rallying support for landmark legislation to provide veterans with a college education.[188] Known as the GI Bill of Rights, the Servicemen's Readjustment Act of 1944 ended forever the notion that higher education was for the privileged few, transforming America's campuses in size and scope by bankrolling tuition plus a generous monthly stipend for any war veteran.

By 1947, veterans were 49 percent of college enrollment, roughly doubling college enrollment nationally. This surge of students seasoned by war drove the curriculum toward practical disciplines for rebuilding the country—business, engineering, and other professions. The major legacy of the GI Bill was to give any veteran, regardless of background, the opportunity to get a college education, and many enrolled at Pacific.[189]

Knoles grooms a successor

Knoles, having faced his darkest hours through the Great Depression and the War, turned increasingly to his young assistant Robert Burns ('31) for leadership across the board. By appointing Burns as "Assistant to the President" in 1942 when Knoles was 65 years old, he signaled his personal mentorship of Pacific's most promising young administrator. The age gap did not faze Knoles. He was well aware that University of Chicago had appointed 30-year-old Maynard Hutchins as president in 1929, and he openly compared Burns to his own experience as young assistant to USC president Bovard, who had groomed Knoles to succeed him.[190]

The 20 years from 1924 through the War were not only a turning point for Pacific through the Stockton College and V-12 rescues, but also signaled a clear aim to achieve institutional and financial stability through enrollment growth built on professional programs. Knoles asserted to the end that even though he avoided academic leadership, he "laid stress upon the liberal arts, and was most anxious not to expand into larger and vocational fields." But the evidence points to his blunt understanding of the need to expand professional studies, and his realization that Bob Burns could lead Pacific there.[191]

The post-war boom launches a new president

The V-12 program ended in November 1945 and within three months, the College was purchasing five "Quonset huts" for $25,000 to house 100 male veterans (and five more "huts" the next year), along with building West Hall, a new dormitory for 100 women. Stagg agreed to head a council to integrate Japanese-American students back into the campus life they had left four years earlier, and some were provided transportation back to campus.[192]

The College began to run a surplus budget, and vice president Ritter announced all debts paid by March 1946, when enrollment hit a record high. The next fall's enrollment practically doubled with nearly 450 male veterans. The trustees boosted faculty salaries substantially—and hiked tuition by nearly 25 percent. The fact was, the War had been relatively

Post-war campus construction was driven by thrifty war-surplus military barracks from bases and depots in the area. The 325-foot long Quonset hut running parallel to North/Hand Hall, called "The Tube," was not removed until 1979.

generous to Pacific, and the coming veterans would make it even stronger. It seemed a good time for Knoles, now 70, to step aside.

When Burns was recruited for a second college presidency—he had turned down the first offer a few years earlier—the board made an overnight decision at the October 1946 board meeting. A faction of the faculty were "strongly opposed" to this young non-academic as president, but trustee Bishop Baker eloquently won them over in a private faculty meeting, gaining a standing ovation.[193] The board proposed that Knoles remain as "Chancellor" as Burns moved into the presidency. Knoles would be the junior college liaison, while Burns would handle all else—yet mentor Knoles would have a desk in the same office as the young president.

Flush with GI Bill students and their federal tuition checks, Pacific was again thriving, and these were buoyant times: a five percent Christmas bonus check was handed to every employee.[194] Burns, just 37, did not deposit his Pacific master's thesis until May 1947 (though he had completed all course work by 1938!), thus was appointed president with only a bachelor's degree.[195] But he knew Pacific well, having served Pacific continuously since his graduation in 1931, devoted his master's thesis to researching the first 50 years of Pacific, and serving as an active partner of President Knoles well before he was appointed his assistant in 1942. Knoles' selecting his own successor, while certainly irregular by today's standards, was his most important personnel decision. Burns was bright, outgoing, energetic and visionary. Burns could see the limitations of Pacific's past yet see beyond them to a different future. He was about to become Pacific's greatest president.

CHAPTER 3

Building a University: On the leading edge, 1946-71

Ending the Stockton College partnership in 1951—GI Bill and Greek life—Identity crisis—Engineering reborn in 1948—Pharmacy created in 1955—Methodist separation in 1969—Football, basketball, and forensics success—Raymond College opens in 1961—the CIP Victory in 1969—Covell and Callison begin—COP asserts identity—P&S and McGeorge join—Burns' legacy

PIONEERING BURNS

The quintessential Californian

Robert Burns was born in little Flat River, Missouri, but he was a Californian through and through. His temperament and ambition matched the tumultuous, pioneer history of the State, and through him Pacific changed its character and reclaimed its infant wish to become a "university." In Pacific's 1951 centennial history, Burns' foreword noted that "the pioneering which has been the characteristic feature in the past should continue during the next 100 years." In his 1946 inaugural address, he announced one of his most quoted statements: "Pacific must pioneer or perish." He wanted Pacific to pursue "the spirit of the covered wagon, not the band wagon!"

Burns eventually would discover that two of his Flat River playmates also became California university presidents—Norman Topping at USC and Paul Leonard at San Francisco State. But he grew up in Richmond, California, and from the time he was a freshman at Pacific in 1928 until his death in 1971, he devoted his full and vigorous life to Pacific. A debate star, choir member, YMCA leader and president of the student body, he found identity and mission at Pacific while he pursued western American history as his major. Burns had joined Pacific as a jack-of-all-trades young staff person the year after he graduated, and a decade later, in 1942, President Knoles appointed him as assistant to the president and chief fund-raiser.

Knoles saw in Burns what USC President Bovard saw in young professor Knoles: a future leader of the institution. Both brought a spirited intellect to their love of history, and Burns, though Pacific's first non-clergy president, was an active leader in the Methodist church and became a 33rd Degree Mason like Knoles.

The 37-year-old Burns, "the youngest college president in the West,"[1] was open and friendly. His straightforward personality brightened the campus after the challenges of the prior decades. More accessible and engaging than Knoles, Burns never let his modest educational credentials (his doctorates were honorary) hold him back from faculty, nor did his highly energetic entrepreneurism around the region remove him from routinely befriending students on campus. As student body president John Corson ('57, later a Pacific regent) said, "The welcome sign is always out at Burns' door for students."[2] Burns' reputation for impish humor, his flair for salesmanship, and a fast and loose style of leadership continued throughout his days, and it played an important role in his winning way with people and his ability to get things done in a hurry—"charming impetuousness," as one colleague so aptly put it.[3]

"Pioneer or perish"

Burns' inaugural address also signaled a gifted visionary who matched the entrepreneurial spirit of California. He concluded with what became a signature statement: "a community of scholars is bound together by a dynamic idea. They either move forward or perish. An institution becomes great by daring to dream and then bending every effort to make these dreams come true."[4]

Burns' two signature statements defined his early overall strategy for the College that transformed it into a university, partly by design, partly by accident of a leader who could rarely say no to any new opportunity to expand and diversify the College. A decade later, he would add his third signature statement—"growing bigger by getting smaller"—that defined the pathway to transformation for Pacific. He was temperamentally perfectly suited to capitalize on the post-war boom that created the golden years of American higher education and to seize the California pioneering spirit that has shaped Pacific's identity for over a century and a half. He never lost faith in the brimming optimism that drives the California dream.

Engaging alumni

Burns had fundraising savvy (as a Pacific student he led successful bond sales to fund lights for Baxter Stadium), knew alumni relations (he had served as director), and established the first offices to deliver annual and deferred gifts. Though Pacific was hampered by the churchly focus of those activities, alumni giving jumped from five percent to a record high of 27 percent in 1960 through an incentive program for the Alumni Association: the board gifted $1000 to the fund for every percentage of annual increase in alumni giving over the prior year.[5] This achievement—a giving percentage exceeding USC's and Stanford's though not St. Mary's and Redlands' (the national average was 20.5 percent)—was the result of a reorganized Alumni Association in 1957. With 14 regional clubs, the association took on the challenge of the annual fund with gusto and a detailed plan of personal-contact teams for each region. This same year the association began its annual awards banquet, today one of the University's premier annual events. The Distinguished Alumni Award was first presented in 1956.[6] And the annual alumni summer retreats at Stockton's Silver Lake camp helped to build *esprit de corps*.

But this giving plan worked for only two years, then fell off to 15 percent, recovered again by the mid-sixties, and then apparently steadily declined until the twenty-first century.[7] Some alumni say that Burns—

focused on innovation and his own role as a leader—failed to build structures for keeping in touch with alumni. Then, as now, Pacific alumni were enthusiastic about Pacific (85 percent would choose Pacific again) and were donors in their own communities at nearly a 90 percent rate, yet giving to Pacific was never sustained.[8] There was finally no consistent program over time to engage alumni and invite philanthropy, especially alumni-to-alumni solicitation.

Regional leader

Burns had the benefit of taking the reins when the city was just beginning to become respectable after the depression and war years. Stockton was a rough-and-tumble town through the war years and after, until police chief Rex Parker ended graft and corruption on the police force, then shut down 16 gambling halls along with brothels and slot machine operations.[9] The Stockton Ports baseball team's record 26-game winning streak in 1947 lifted town spirits.

By the start of the 1950s, a new Stockton began to surround the Pacific campus. In 1949, three years before the city moved the city limits north of the Calaveras River, Greenlaw Grupe built the Lincoln Village housing development, adding a shopping center in 1951. Charles Weber III added

Lincoln Center, north of campus on Pacific Avenue, was Stockton's first suburban commercial development in 1951. (Courtesy of Lincoln Center and Daniel Kasser)

the Weberstown housing development along Pacific Avenue by 1955, later adding a shopping mall. By the 1960s, the city was booming, undergoing more growth and building between 1950 and 1965 than in its entire prior century.[10] No one was surprised when Burns was elected president of the Stockton Chamber of Commerce.

Burns was always active in the larger community. He became founding president of the Associated Independent California College and Universities, president of the Western College Association, served on the state Centennial Commission and State Parks Commission, was national chair of the Independent Colleges Fund of America and provided consistent national leadership for the Methodist Church.[11] He found a mentor/sponsor in the parks commission chair, alumnus and *Oakland Tribune* publisher Joseph "J.R." Knowland (1891). One of the state's most prominent conservative Republicans, Knowland vetted many a politician, including his son, Senator William Knowland, and Earl Warren.

The Stockton College divorce

What vexed Burns weekly was the mounting strife over policies and accounting and athletics between Knoles and his counterparts at Stockton College. Burns never really believed that the unique private-public partnership saved Pacific—after all, other schools survived the Depression without such a drastic union. In his final memoirs, Burns states frankly his "mixed emotions" about the decision to hand over half the College to an open-admission public school, now depending on this "polyglot student body" of questionable academic promise to produce students worthy of Pacific professors teaching at both levels.[12] The state pressure to move to vocational training at Stockton College was understandable, but it conflicted with Pacific's commitment to the liberal arts and higher learning.

By 1944, the school district had purchased a 43-acre campus south across the street from Pacific and added countless government surplus buildings to handle post-war enrollment growth. What aggravated the relationship was Stockton College's 1948 adoption of a 6-4-4 plan that enrolled high school juniors and seniors with the junior college students. Pacific students resented high schoolers invading their classrooms, student union and campus activities, so by 1949, a separate Pacific student association was formed. Jointly appointed Pacific faculty chafed under this system that increased teaching and advising loads and pushed against common educational goals with the high school and junior college faculty. By 1950 the public school board became what Burns called "cantankerous." A new prickly administrator caused even chancellor Knoles to throw up his hands: "cooperation is almost impossible."[13]

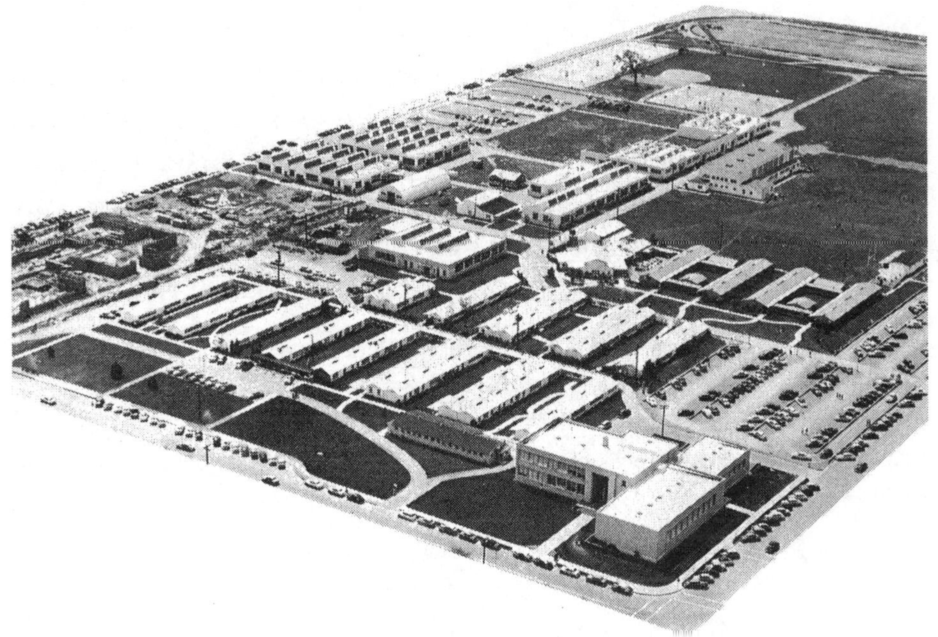

Pacific's partnership with a public two-year college was a ground-breaking innovation in American higher education in 1935, but the Stockton College campus was not built until 1947. By 1950 the junior college served 4000 students in grades 11-14 mainly in temporary war surplus buildings. This photo shows the campus in 1954.

Pacific alumni, persistently critical from the start, sharply objected to a system where their children could not enroll for a four-year experience because of state quotas for lower-division students outside the local district. Piled on this heap of distress was the Pacific Coast Conference ruling that Stockton College sophomores could not play on Pacific teams, and the ruling by the American Chemical Society that accreditation be denied

Pacific over lack of "control over the caliber and scope of the lower level courses and training."[14]

As if these tensions were not reason enough to break this marriage, Burns saw the Korean War that erupted in 1950 as the key trigger for change. The military draft pulled hundreds of students from Stockton College and other junior college feeder schools, while students at four-year institutions were generally allowed to continue their degree programs by passing a Selective Service College Qualification Test. "If the Korean War hadn't come along, I suspect we might still be an upper-division-graduate institution," said Burns, who now knew he had the right chance to act.[15]

In 1951, the board restored the freshman and sophomore years, and Pacific regained its standing as a four-year college. While enrollment had dipped to around one thousand students by 1950—a drop of nearly one-fourth within two years (and neighboring St. Mary's College was seriously considering closing its doors for lack of students and funds)—Pacific quickly rebounded. An ingenious, unique 15-year experiment had ended owing mainly to the rising pressure of a state in need of "open-admission" community colleges ill-suited to a selective liberal arts institution committed to excellence. In the end, this grand Pacific experiment was a financial convenience—perhaps a financial imperative. Stockton College continued to rent space as it evolved into San Joaquin Delta College and began to plan for a new campus, but the divorce was final.

The Burns and Baun team

While Burns engaged faculty and alumni in college planning meetings and retreats at his cabin in Columbia, he loved to operate independently, with a board that was often a rubber stamp for his dreams. His increasingly close friendship with board chair Ted Baun ('27) made this work. For the first time, Pacific was led by two alumni, and the two couples, Ted and Alice ('27) and Bob and Grace ('34), became good friends who loved to travel together.[16] Burns would often work out an idea with Baun on the run, who would then champion it with the board. Burns' "optimism without realism," as one professor observed, was not grounded by an informed,

Burns Tower, completed in 1963, symbolized the ambitious aim of its young President Robert Burns, whose office was on the top floor. The Tower became the focal point for student protests in the 1960s and remains the most widely recognized image of Pacific in the community.

actively engaged board.[17] Paul Davies, regent from 1959-90, quipped years later that he "needed a rope around his ankle" to hold Burns back because Burns never saw a new idea he didn't like: "his enthusiasm carried the day."[18] This relentless drive resulted in a near-fatal attack of hemorrhaging ulcers in 1950 that required repeated blood transfusions. Eddie LeBaron ('50), his football teammates and other students donated blood.[19]

When in 1964 financial vice president Bob Winterberg fused the need for a new campus water tower with Burns' dream of a gothic tower to match the campaniles of Cal and Stanford, Ted Baun insisted that the tower, with executive suites, be named for Burns. Scoffing students, wanting the dollars to go to the cramped biology labs, called it "Burns' Last Erection." But Burns knew better: "Symbolically it will be important."[20] No other image of Pacific is more prominent today. Burns Tower was silent until Paul Davies, Jr. paid tribute to his wife with the "Carillon of Faith."[21] The elegant Conservatory tower had finally been trumped by the Burns Tower broadcast of 122 miniature brass bells, played by Conservatory professor Charles Schilling, its *carillonneur* for 50 years.

Burns' key appointments

Burns' most important personnel decisions were his first two: to hire alumnus Elliott Taylor ('28) as Pacific's first director of admissions and local Methodist minister Jesse Rudkin as assistant to the president and director of development. He knew dependable and growing enrollment was critical to Pacific's success, and in Taylor he found the perfect match. Enrollment grew steadily, fed by Stockton College, although one-third of transfers were from other two- and four-year institutions. When total enrollment exceeded 900 in 1947 the faculty urged limiting enrollment to 1000-1200 by becoming more selective in admissions, like Methodist Willamette University was doing in Oregon. Burns knew this ceiling would be too low to accommodate his overall growth plan, so largely ignored it.[22]

Burns also knew that feet on the streets were important to fundraising, and that Pacific had a lot of catch-up work to do. Rudkin shared Burns' enthusiasm for the College as well as his endless energy and friendly assertiveness. Knoles had long lamented the lack of support from the regional Methodist churches, the California-Nevada and Southern California-Arizona Conferences. Even though many prominent Methodist leaders were Pacific alumni—including Gerald Kennedy ('29), president of the national council of Methodist bishops—Pacific ranked 44th of the 45 Methodist colleges in the level of support from its conference churches. Rudkin's approach was more personal, visiting individuals throughout the state rather than berating the church. Both men served long and well—Rudkin until 1962, Taylor until 1972. Without their strong leadership and enduring loyalty, Burns could not have achieved his dreams. Enrollment grew from under 900 to nearly 5000 under Taylor not even counting the three professional schools of pharmacy, dentistry and law. Rudkin with Burns raised over $15 million in gifts and pledges during his service. This total was given a kick-start with a "$5 Million in 5 Years" campaign in 1953 that came in the very infancy of the organized and staffed University fundraising of today.

A third key appointment came a few years later when he hired Robert Winterberg ('51) as his financial vice president in 1963. Burns increasingly relied on Winterberg to untie any budget knot, and Winterberg, who had worked his way up in the office since joining in 1950, carried that power on through three presidents to 1989. During his presidency Burns had a revolving door of academic vice presidents that he never viewed as bothersome, but in these three key positions he held trusted leaders for many years.

BUILDING IN AND BUILDING OUT

Construction site

The early Burns years were a time of rapid campus expansion, even though much of the added square footage was in "temporary" structures gifted by the War Surplus Board. By 1948, campus building space had nearly doubled in size (over 73,000 additional square feet) with seven "new" metal buildings in the center of campus, including Owen and Bannister Halls, four metal buildings called "tropical huts" for Engineering and Music and a metal Quonset hut for a small gymnasium.[23] As other temporary metal buildings were added over the next few years and their uses migrated, they all became known as "the Quonset huts," a label that became ubiquitous across the nation's campuses symbolizing rapid "growth and innovation."[24] Sears Hall (1950) was constructed as well as a student union addition to Anderson Hall (1949). Hardly a year passed when students didn't have to step around a construction site.

The most significant decision was to build a new stadium and postpone construction of a permanent library—an embarrassing absence since the fire of 1915. Students complained, accreditors scorned, and faculty lamented the postponements and delays of a library owing to lack of donors, despite a $20,000 pledged by the faculty. The long wait finally ended in 1955 when trustee and *Stockton Record* publisher Irving Martin gave $125,000 to launch the Irving Martin Library. It was the first-stage building of a master-plan library quadrangle with a tower, plans which never did get off the ground. So after 40 years with a temporary library, the last in a 1938 renovation of the power plant, Pacific finally had a home for student study—air-conditioned, no less. The Martin Library was the first Pacific structure actually designed to be a library in its 104 years!

Temporary single-story government surplus buildings populated the central campus, and were not banished until 2001.

A Northern California campus—From the Bay to Tahoe

As though planned by President Burns himself, a pebble mosaic compass pointing in all directions was built in 1950 by an art student at the very center of the rose garden between Burns Tower and the campus administration building (Knoles Hall).[25] Seeing Northern California as his campus, Burns and the College created six enduring programs that signaled Burns' wide swath of interests and his ambition to turn Pacific outward: the California History Foundation, the Pacific Marine Station at Dillon Beach, the Pacific Music Camp, the Folk Dance Camp, the Pacific Institute of Philosophy, and the Fallon House Theater.[26]

To orient new students, art instructor Susanne Scheuer and her student Elaine Stanley ('41) built the stone compass at the heart of the central quad in 1950.

Begun by Burns in 1948 the Pacific Marine Station at Dillon Beach, just north of Point Reyes National Seashore, was taking off under professor Alden Noble's able direction. Noble had declared the location to be unequalled on the West Coast in diversity of marine habitats, ideal for

Pacific's Marine Station for graduate biology students was active from 1932 until 1977. Pacific's Fallon House Theatre drew wide summer audiences to Columbia in the Foothills from 1949-1982.

study and research. Burns leased the beach property from the Lawson family to formally launch the graduate program. Two war-surplus buildings were carted to the site, and a men's dorm for 20 students was built.

Burns' ambition to expand Pacific's reputation and contacts throughout the state was realized when he was named to the five-member State Centennial Commission. Other new programs served equally well to build a regional presence. Famed California historian Rockwell Hunt brought instant prestige as the first director of the California History Foundation, which Burns created in 1947 to house library collections in western American history. The Pacific Music Camp for high school students, launched in 1946 by David Lawson from the famed Interlochen Music Institute in Michigan, brought world-renowned music conductors like Fred Waring and Percy Grainger to campus and has continued in various formats to the present day. The Folk Dance Camp headed by Lawton Harris ('22) in 1948 was the first in the West to bring dance leaders from across the globe and the second-oldest continuing dance camp in the country.[27] Philosophy professor William Nietman responded to Burns' challenge to the faculty to propose innovative programs with his novel and highly successful Institute of Philosophy, held annually at Lake Tahoe until 1970, focusing each institute on such contemporary public issues as capitalism and communism, ethics and technology, war and peace.

Burns saw the potential of regional theatre, capitalizing on the earned acclaim of DeMarcus Brown ('23) by partnering with the state to preserve the Fallon House hotel and dance hall in Columbia. Launched in 1949, the Fallon House Theatre was famous throughout the state, led by English professor Sy Kahn after Brown until 1982.[28] Noted alumni of this highpoint era of Pacific theatre were James Jewell ('51) and Alfred Muller ('53), both elected as Fellows of the American Theatre along with Brown, and Joseph Lillis ('74), who produced thirty musicals off Broadway.[29]

No limits

By 1959, enrollment was at an all-time high while 40 percent of undergraduate applicants were rejected—a selectivity ratio close to UC-Berkeley and

Stanford at the time.[30] Even as tuition took double-digit jumps, the students just kept coming. Pacific was the fourth-largest private school in California after USC, Stanford, and USF. Faculty research grants jumped, and alumni giving was up to 22 percent. Pacific was on a roll.

As Pacific was approaching a thousand students in the late forties, the faculty again asked the board to limit enrollment to 1200 and become more academically selective, but the board and Burns remained silent.[31] This ritual would be repeated over the next decade. As enrollment grew, Burns pressed the board to explore buying the 43-acre Stockton College campus and turned to the faculty to enlist their support. Appreciative of growing salaries, the faculty were ready to act, but were halted only by the Stockton school board's balk at the offer—a decision that dragged on for years as a new community college district was formed, leading to San Joaquin Delta College. This open question about the identity, size and direction of Pacific hung in the air for years to come.

"HIGH TIME"

Veterans join in

Immediately after the war, national campus life was tempered by a flood of GIs who wanted to get on with their lives and careers and had little time for undergraduate distractions. At Pacific, however, this separation between high-school grads and vets was reduced by the family spirit of the place. "We were lucky to be at a small school where most everyone was like a family," said one alumnus.[32] Youngsters like 5' 7," 16-year old Eddie LeBaron ('50) were surrounded by vets like Bruce Orvis ('50) and speedster Bob Heck who bunked with him in the barracks, and each benefitted from the camaraderie. About half of the undergraduates were veterans.

An outstanding example was David Gerber ('50), a bomber crewman who survived a German POW camp, where Pacific alumnus Stan Vaughan (n.d.), captain of Stagg's 1940 team, regaled him with stories of his wondrous years at Pacific. Gerber vowed in his prison bunk that if he got home, he would leave his cozy Brooklyn neighborhood and head for this perfect little school in California, and he did.[33] He plunged himself into campus life with a gusto that made him legendary and ended in his becoming an inspirational regent.

The huge car caravan/rally to the San Francisco newspapers organized by Dave Gerber ('50, left) in 1949 was as much about Pacific school spirit as it was a protest of sports reporters' passing over football hero Eddie LeBaron.

Gerber was a campus cheerleader in every respect. One night he and his buddies lined up cars facing South Hall. When the fire alarm blared and the women in scant nighties poured out of the dorm, Gerber signaled on all the headlights. When Eddie LeBaron's football record did not earn him All-American honors by sports journalists, Gerber was incensed that the San Francisco writers voted for Cal quarterback Bob Celeri over LeBaron. Gerber rallied 500 students in a mile-long caravan of cars headed west to besiege five sports editors' offices in the City, which got front-page headlines and praise for the "wholesome student unity".[34] The rally was all about school pride and a reminder that when Pacific left the south Bay, it forfeited opportunities for great Bay area press coverage. When LeBaron joined the Washington Redskins after graduation, Gerber got him on the popular TV show "This is Your Life."

Governor Earl Warren celebrates California's top collegiate quarterbacks in 1949: Pacific's Eddie LeBaron (right) and Cal's Bob Celeri.

Campus life

The sports section of *Pacific Weekly* dominated at this time when even swimming and track were spectator events. In 1950, the swim team led by beloved coach Chris Kjeldsen ('35) went undefeated to rousing crowds, and women like Mareen Foster (n.d.) and Helen Graham ('47) were nationally ranked swimmers. The Pacific Aquatic Club produced the first Aquacade in the newly lighted pool. In 1956 the men's water polo team won the Pacific Coast title—a high point in water polo for decades. In 1968 Mark Gardner became the fastest freshman in the country, setting a national record in the 3000 meter run.[35] But overall, football dominated the Pacific campus, with Eddie LeBaron a national phenomenon. LeBaron was active on campus in baseball, track, and Omega Phi, chaired the now-legendary Mardi Gras celebration, and hauled heavy barley sacks in the summer for big cash.

Women students had a 10 p.m. curfew on weekdays, midnight on weekends, and were "campused" to their rooms after class if they broke the curfew. Harsher was the dress code: pants for women were outlawed, as was public display of hair curlers. And frosh men, alumni say, were not allowed to wear jeans until they were sophomores. Needless to say, students had no say in these matters, nor did they expect to. They had other priorities, mostly the rising prominence of fraternities and sororities and a lively sprouting of clubs for every student interest. The *Pacific Weekly* was the communication center of the campus, with a heavy focus on social events, engagements and weddings, and club activities.

The surge of students required new housing for a school steadfastly committed to campus living. Soon the "largest building in Stockton for human use" was constructed for 400 women, Grace Covell Hall and dining facilities.[36] This was the era of "housemothers" who upheld the family atmosphere and home values of the times, including curfews and control of male-female visitations.[37]

Eleanor Roosevelt and Bob Hope were campus headlines in the late forties. *All the King's Men,* one of the great American films on politics, was filmed in Stockton in 1949. Luminaries like Stan Kenton and Les Brown bands sparkled Homecoming and Mardi Gras dances. Dave Brubeck's ('42) ensemble launched its first national tour at Pacific, thanks to Iola

Who could have guessed that the COP junior class secretary, Jeanette Morrison ('47,left, with vice president Betty Lou Cooper and president Art Carfagni), would become the international film star, Janet Leigh.

Whitlock Brubeck ('45), who sprung the idea of a first-ever national college jazz tour. His renowned 1959 *Time Out* album included "Take Five," the best-selling jazz single in history.

Pacific's most famous alumna is probably Stockton's Jeanette Morrison ('47). As a junior conservatory student she was discovered by a Hollywood star while visiting her parents who worked at the Sugar Bowl ski resort. By 1947 she was starring in films as Janet Leigh, one of the all-time favorites of Hollywood films. Her daughter, the actress Jamie Lee Curtis ('80), was nearly to duplicate her mother's path to stardom by leaping from the Pacific classroom into Hollywood films well before graduation.

Film star Bing Crosby, on the campus in 1960 for weeks shooting the movie High Time, befriended many students and faculty. (Here shown with co-stars Fabian and Tuesday Weld.)

Professor Edwin Ding, who taught economics and Asian philosophy, was a perennial favorite of students in the 1950s and 60s.

By the end of this era, circa 1960, Pacific as a small college was at its peak performance. It was in fact *High Time* for many of the students who had appearances in the famous comedy of that title, filmed on campus starring Bing Crosby, Fabian, and Tuesday Weld. Bing Crosby, who had a room in Owen Hall for weeks of filming, became an honorary Archite, joined them in a serenade and regaled Kappa Alpha Theta with piano and song.[38] Libby Matson taught him fencing.[39]

The two thousand students all seemed to own the campus—they were busy, well, as "B's." "B" words dominated the days: The incomparable Band Fest, of course. Those luscious barefoot walks on the flooded lawns in fall and spring—and belly sliding. Nancy Robinson ('59) asked, "Does putting on rain slickers over our Bermuda shorts and belly sliding on the flooded lawns count as athletics?"[40] Dick Bass ('60) and Co. beating Cal 24-20 in Berkeley in 1958. Some were calling the College "Bassific," but Dick would be the first to point out that nine of his teammates also went on to play for the NFL. Dr. Burns' friendly informality, Dr. Alonzo Baker's mesmerizing lectures on global politics, and, well, even if his name starts with "D," the profound, captivating professor Edwin Ding of economics and Asian philosophy, or sociology professor Harold Jacoby, inspiration to so many. And the Sunday morning breakfasts at the Hoosier Inn—after the Friday night beers and blanket parties on the water at "Dad's Point" in Louis Park.

Greek life goes national

The 1950s had their own frat distinctions: Archites Duane Weaver (n.d.) and Jim Lane (n.d.) "set the world teeter-totter record in front of their

Larry Wells ('55) was a pioneering black campus leader in the early 1950s (here pictured in 1954 as junior class president with officers Huberta Williams, Nancy Stowe, and Nadine Reasoner).

fraternity house at 100 hours in tribute to the golden century which crowned Pacific" in 1951.[41] The Archites still had their uniformed "Confederate Brigade," and even "captured" a Mother Lode town.[42] Everyone loved riding their antique fire engine. The Omega Phi Alpha brothers owned the annual serenade of sorority circle, adding musical instruments to a half-hour concert leading up to a spotlight on the new Omega Phi girl of the year.[43] The Brubecks, who soon became as well-known for their civil rights activism, would have been proud of Larry Wells ('55), who broke many barriers as the first black student to be class president (twice), first black member of the Blue Key honor fraternity, and first black president of a social fraternity in 1954: Archania, mind you—the celebrators of the Confederacy long after the Civil War.[44]

It wasn't that Burns lacked fraternity grief during these halcyon years. In trouble for a decade, Burns' and Baun's own Rhizomia fraternity (now Rho Lambda Phi) had been given an ultimatum to "present a good clean stunt" for Band Frolics, but somehow they could not pass muster. A few months after Stockton endured one of its worst floods in history in December 1955, when nearly all roads were closed and most streets under water, Burns was forced to suspend the Rhizite fraternity, nearing its 100th anniversary.[45] Students across campus held a memorial service while the brothers burned their flag. But it got worse: the alcohol abuse, noisy behavior, and destruction of property was so severe that the board placed all fraternities on probation for fall 1959, just as all three sororities "went national" to lead the way for the men to follow.[46] Within two years, all Greek houses had gone national and doubled in size to 40-45 to keep the houses afloat.[47]

Homecoming at Archania House, 1959 (left). Registrar Ellen Deering ('26) (1926-69) was admired and feared by students and faculty alike. Omega Phi Alpha named her one of their annual "dream girls" for over 50 years.

But students did not let social life cripple their classroom achievement for professors with high expectations. Widely known lecturer and political science professor Alonzo Baker mandated reading *U.S. News & World Report* in his required senior course, "The World Today."[48] In addition to being a CBS radio commentator and correspondent for the *Oakland Tribune,* he brought many political luminaries to campus like Barry Goldwater, Nelson Rockefeller, Pierre Salinger, and Alan Cranston to mix it up.[49] Many alumni recount the challenging religion classes of George Colliver.

Ellen Deering ('26), registrar from 1926-69, was a one-person academic police force. Deering knew everyone—faculty, staff and students—and made sure in her impatient and brusque manner that rules, regulations and standards would be met. As well, she handled student admissions and job placement after graduation. Yet she was admired and respected, fiercely loyal, an active campus historian, and generous, personally funding many students through Pacific and helped to found the annual YMCA Strawberry Breakfast fundraiser in 1932, which continues today.[50] As dean of women Kay Davis said, "she knew all the answers to everything."[51]

Few students had financial support from the College. Middle class families sacrificed to make it work, and many students had part-time jobs. Even drinking (aside from the fraternities) was muted compared to later decades. A six-pack fit neatly into a portable typewriter case. Drinking on campus could end in expulsion, so alcohol was a discreet habit, often even in the frat houses, though Burns enforced Methodist rules with "a gracious campus could end in expulsion, so alcohol was a discreet habit, often even in the frat houses, though Burns enforced Methodist rules with "a gracious hand."[52] Students would still find time to head for the "276 Club" on Pacific Avenue for a beer between classes, and a sea of frosh "dinks," those little orange beanie caps, were often seen at the local burlesque show.[53] Gay students were of course discreet—there was no "gay life style" at Pacific in the 1950s, or even the 1960s.

IDENTITY DILEMMA

The 1956 wake-up call

In 1955, the Methodist Church did a huge favor to Pacific by sending an "accreditation team" to assess the school on behalf of all Methodist institutions. The 1956 national Methodist University Senate Survey Committee report was a wake-up call and key pivot point for the College. By holding a mirror up to the institution and by careful analysis and comprehensive assessment, the visiting committee identified virtually all of the key internal issues that the College had to face in the next 15 years.[54] Among the praise and criticism, the team noted overcrowded dorms, no student union, and a campus where half of the buildings were "temporary structures."

Equally important, the prescient report also criticized the "barely average" academic profile of the undergraduate student body, the quality of the liberal arts program, the neglect of general education, and an over-extension of graduate and professional programs when senior Graduate Record Examination scores were "significantly below national averages." The report chastised the trustees for neglecting both its duties and the endowment, noting that the board had ignored a stern warning from a 1931 visit team to focus on building endowment, which had reached only one million dollars in 1951. Unrestricted gifts and bequests were routinely used to fill annual budget holes instead of invested in the future as was normal practice by building endowment and reserves. The team lamented, "This seems almost tragic."

Identity crisis

The fundamental question raised by the visit team was whether or not Pacific had a clear vision of its identity. Was it to continue its strong liberal arts tradition, or was it moving quickly to become a more comprehensive university, with engineering, pharmacy and business programs growing and demanding resources to the neglect of the liberal arts as budget deficits accumulated? During the same year, the accrediting team from the Engineers' Council for Professional Development turned down Pacific's bid to accredit its engineering program because of inadequate faculty, curriculum, and facilities. The Methodist report urged the College to limit growth in order to strengthen existing programs.

Limiting growth at a time when California higher education was booming was perhaps too much to ask, even though the faculty quickly endorsed the report's emphasis on strengthening present programs and sought a raised cap of 1750 students. Burns' response to the report was to assert that Pacific would not expand into a larger university "in the foreseeable future" and urged no additional schools "unless they are unusually well-financed." Vice president Bertholf called for bolstering the liberal arts with a separate dean and capping enrollment at 1600 for five years.[55] But this fundamental question of identity, size, quality and resources would continue to haunt Pacific as Burns and the board ignored the team's advice and tried to raise income through new schools that in the end were not self-sufficient, much less revenue generators for established programs.

Finally, the Methodist accreditation committee zeroed in on what had by now become one of the culprits in a college strapped for money: the high cost of athletics, "wholly out of proportion to that of the educational program." They fingered the football program in particular, which they called "dangerous and inappropriate." The concern was not simply an outsider judgment; surveys of students and alumni had pointed the visit team to the conclusion that football was "more divisive than unifying" and out of control. This was not welcome news to a board headed by Baun, a 1926 football captain under Coach Righter who proudly watched the march forward of football under Stagg and his successors.

The 1956 report challenged Pacific to examine its values and priorities in fundamental ways that had been ignored by a board and president justifiably proud about rising enrollment and expansion of programs. Burns and the board took seriously the harsh laundry list, but paying for upgrades was of course a dilemma. Growth would mean new dollars that just might help. Within two years, Burns set out the options to the board: cap enrollment at 1750, grow to about 2500 to become "the Stanford of the Valley," or a new idea: add separate new small colleges like the Claremont group. Option one was out; Burns could not tolerate stasis. Option two was unacceptable: his Pacific pride was too strong to copy the neighborhood. The best way to compete would be to add small liberal arts colleges—not exactly like Claremont, just outside the neighborhood, but "in the manner of Oxford University."[56]

GROWTH THROUGH DIVERSIFICATION II: ROBUST EXPANSION

The struggle to restart engineering

In his first report to the board in 1947, Burns called for the reestablishment of the engineering department. Professor Felix Wallace became revered as the true father of the engineering department starting in 1948. The small, close-knit group of faculty and students took over the old boiler building that had held the temporary library since 1938, now named Baun Hall. Graduating distinguished engineering alumni from tiny classes was a Pacific tradition running back to the 1880s: Ted Baun ('27) founded his own highly successful construction company in Fresno and chaired the board for most of the Burns years; Eugene Root ('32) became president of Lockheed Missiles and Space Center and Pacific trustee; and Carlos Wood ('33) was vice president of Sikorsky Aircraft.

In 1958 when Burns invited the College faculty to sign off on shifting engineering from department to school status with its own dean and aim for accreditation, the faculty assented—with the assurance that the new school would demand no new dollars. Burns kept his word, and the school languished under dean Adelbert Diefendorf (1957-62), who got no additional funds to build programs, not even after accreditation had been denied to civil and electrical engineering in 1955. After a consultant looked over the progress in 1961, he nixed another accreditation visit to avoid embarrassment.[57] With the explosion of "third generation" computers in the 1960s, engineering students got their first computer in 1964. Meanwhile, by 1961 neighboring Santa Clara had built a new engineering center for its school of 300 undergraduates and 700 graduate students.[58]

To gain campus visibility for engineering, Tom Duecker ('61) commandeered a band of students to haul a seven-and-a-half ton boulder from the Foothills to the front of Baun Hall, where it has been ever since. Freshman students were inducted to the "Guard of St. Patrick" (patron saint of engineers) on St. Patrick's Day by kissing the stone. Fawzi al-Saleh ('62, later a University regent), wearing his native Kuwaiti attire, was the first student to participate.[59] Faculty joined students in an annual softball game and picnic that built school solidarity. Now, as every Stockton campus student and alum knows, instead of getting kissed, "the Rock" gets a coat of spray-paint with a message nearly nightly. So does its companion rock steps away in front of Anderson Hall, a gift from Napa College to commemorate its merger with Pacific in 1896.

A distinctive co-op program

When Henderson McGee ('27) became dean in 1962, he formulated a $500,000 plan to accredit the school after years of neglect and finally threw down the gauntlet before the board in 1967: support our accreditation push or mercifully end us. Chair Baun partnered with classmate McGee to rally support for moving the school forward.

The plan included a new dean, Robert Heyborne from Utah State, who transformed the school by developing a five-year program that placed students in engineering firms in salaried positions two or three times throughout their

Painting the Engineering Rock—now dubbed "Spirit Rock"—has been a solid campus tradition since the 1960s...

... So too has been painting the rock donated by Napa College class of 1893 (five initials on the right) to commemorate its merger with Pacific in 1896. History professor Rockwell Hunt, Napa College alumnus of 1890, was instrumental in bringing the rock to Pacific. Just steps away from each other, the two rocks vie for the attention of spray painters.

campus studies. Pacific's mandatory work-study cooperative education program has been unique west of the Rockies to this day.

This distinctive signature "co-op program" launched in 1970 was a huge draw for new students: salaries for needy students paid by the sponsoring company, a maturing work-culture experience in jobs around the country, and a leg up on employment after graduation. Many grads went right into the firms or agencies where they had completed their co-ops. Under Heyborne's strong and effective leadership, school enrollment immediately jumped and by the 1980s peaked at over 700 students. Co-op placements offered students remarkable challenges that followed developing technology—

from helping to invent the HP Inkjet printer and designing the first Mars Rover, to Japanese manufacturing, to designing high-altitude aircraft for NASA at the Ames Research Center, which for John Whittenbury ('90) led to Stanford, Lockheed, and Northrop Grumman, where he worked on advanced unmanned vehicles commonly called drones.[60]

Beyond engineering, this bold decision to require practical learning on the job along with classroom studies was embraced by the dental and law schools. Thirty years later "preparing practice-ready graduates" is a hallmark of Pacific.

Building pharmacy with a bare light bulb

Burns was drawn to engineering if only to pay homage to his partner Ted Baun, who had made his fortune as a Pacific civil engineering graduate and so generously paid tribute to his college through his loads of time, take-charge leadership, and steady stream of dollars. Pharmacy was a completely new venture, and exposed to all Pacificans that the pious genuflections before the "liberal arts college" were rituals more than reality. The fact was that Burns and his board wanted the College to grow so that it could not merely survive but thrive.

Finding new stakeholders was imperative. He found them in local pharmacists and chemistry professor Emerson Cobb, who conspired together to persuade Pacific to become the third pharmacy school in the state, after UCSF and USC. Cobb elbowed local pharmacists on the need for a school that could produce professionals who would stay in the Valley. These pharmacists completed a study of need and support, made a persuasive case before the state pharmaceutical association in 1954, and kicked in $50,000 to launch it.[61]

The board was persuaded by the bottom line and approved the program: labs could take over Weber Hall classrooms vacated by Stockton College, and the program would pay for itself through tuition income. This was 1955, the first year the engineering program was denied accreditation after crawling toward it for eight years, having graduated only 31 students over seven years. Though the board anointed engineering with school status by

Dean Cy Rowland (1955-1980) matched Burns' vision and energy to build an impressive pharmacy school over 25 years.

1958, it was not Burns' priority to take care of existing programs—he always found another opportunity to start a new school, and any new dean would have to start from scratch.

Burns scoured the landscape for a strong dean. Several local pharmacists trained at Idaho State recommended their successful dean Ivan Rowland. When Rowland saw the bare-light-bulb classrooms squeezed between chemistry and biology, he balked, just as biologist-vice president Meyer would soon be "shocked" by the state of the biology labs.[62] Burns pressed him on the "challenge of a lifetime," and Rowland accepted just weeks before the pre-pharmacy students enrolled in fall 1955.[63]

He was a brilliant choice: "Cy" Rowland leaped to the challenge, brought several outstanding ISU faculty with him (Cisco Kihara, the first woman pharmacy faculty member, among them), and within four years had 250 students among hundreds of applicants. Along with Kihara, Carl Riedesel and Don Barker were the master professors of the era. When students grumbled about some campus issue, Riedesel challenged them to run a candidate for student body president. Wayne Gohl ('64) won the election.[64]

By 1959, the Doctor of Pharmacy began to replace the bachelor's degree program in a curriculum that was fittingly Pacific: "integrated, flexible, and liberal."[65] It was also practical: about 80 percent of pharmacy students planned to become retail pharmacists. Underway was a major shift in student enrollment; in 1924, four percent of all students majored in the sciences, but by 1957, 22 percent were chemistry majors alone.[66] The first commencement to be held in Memorial Stadium awarded the first Pharm. D. degrees in 1961, when Dave Brubeck was awarded his honorary doctorate.[67]

Dean Rowland on a roll

Rowland was a gifted fundraiser as well. The Long family had by now built a western regional stronghold of pharmacies, especially in the Central Valley, that made them a prime employer of Pacific graduates. Dean Rowland had the added advantage that his new wife Helen was a Pacific classmate and good friend of Tom Long's wife "Billie" (Muriel). As Helen became national president of the women's pharmacy auxiliary and Tom Long became regent in 1969, the support from the Longs grew.[68] Dean Rowland was a leader in the profession beyond the campus that brought recognition to the school. He became national president of the first pharmacy fraternity, Phi Delta Chi, and held the position for eight years, just as professor Ralph Saroyan ('64) later did in the 1980s.

New purchases of acreage bordering Pershing Avenue and the Latter Day Saints (Mormon) Church and at March Lane and Pershing helped put into place a "north campus" for a new pharmacy school in the mid-sixties.[69] Professor Jean Matuszak taught Rowland's classes so he could hit the road to fundraise for the new building, completed in 1969.

The dedication of the new pharmacy school buildings in 1971 marked a major advancement for the University.

At the urging of Burns, the pharmacy school launched a massive curriculum revision and shifted to a three-year, year-round program in 1970, following the lead of the dental school, in order to increase the efficient use of the new buildings.[70] Today the school is one of a handful that has retained a three-year program. At the same time dean Rowland introduced an "externship" program that required students to spend a year rotating among professional workplaces under faculty supervision. Like the engineering firms, Tom Long and his drugstores as well as independent pharmacies embraced the new program that gave them a leg up on recruiting new pharmacists as demand steadily grew. The curriculum by 1970 was fully "clinical," with emphases in such areas as primary care, disease prevention, and drug selection.

THE UPS AND DOWNS OF METHODIST AFFILIATION

Modernizing Meyer

The departure of dean Bertholf in 1957 for the presidency of Illinois Wesleyan University occurred just following Burns' decision to shift to a university structure, with an academic vice president to oversee five school deans. Samuel Meyer became the first academic vice president, a biologist and active Methodist like Bertholf. But Meyer was a much more dynamic and aggressive leader who challenged the faculty to increase its academic expectations and raise its scholarly activity. The *Pacific Review* began running stories about faculty research that had been meager in the past. At the same time Meyer enlisted students to meet with faculty to discuss how teaching and learning could be improved, an action that earned him the student association's "Outstanding Faculty Member of the Year."[71]

When Tully Knoles retired as chancellor in 1954 and then died in 1959, it was the passing of an era.[72] The legendary George Colliver, beloved and admired religion professor, had died two years earlier. These men had personified the spirit of the Methodist liberal arts college that now had been led in a different direction, at an opportune time to dream big in a state burgeoning with students demanding higher education. Further, the religious character of the campus shifted as well. Sam Meyer no longer sorted faculty candidates by religious commitment, even though

Popular religion professor George Colliver ('15) was not only a pioneer in religious education in the west but also a champion of the Chinese immigrant communities in San Jose and Stockton.

clergy and Methodists held leadership positions well into the 1980s. After much mulling by the trustees, Sunday morning chapel was discontinued in 1951 owing to low attendance.

A legal crisis

In 1967, the board considered the legal relationship with the United Methodist Church (UMC) in regard to the controversial constitutional issue of state and federal aid to students at church-related schools. Higher court rulings aimed to ax public aid to institutions in any way controlled by religious groups. That spelled disaster for many schools that depended on the state for everything from construction loans to student scholarships. Pacific's legal brief on the matter stated that the only change in University bylaws required to free the University of worry would be to "reduce or completely eliminate the church's control of the board," which provided that the Board of Regents be elected by the Methodist Church. To change this bylaw in itself required approval of the two regional units of the Methodist Church that presided over the College, as President Knoles had insisted: the California-Nevada and Southern California-Arizona Annual Conferences.[73]

The church relationship was certainly not fundamentally financial. Board minutes are peppered with comments and reports about the lack of financial support from the Methodist Church.[74] Yet most church-related schools found more pragmatic means of fundraising than their church bodies. Even Jesuit Santa Clara University found its most successful fundraiser in the 1960s to be its Jewish board chair, hotelier Benjamin Swig.[75]

As noted earlier, historically only one-fourth of the student body was Methodist yet the board was predominantly Methodist by its own requirement, and all presidents until Robert Burns in 1946 were Methodist clergy. Even into the 1960s, key posts were filled by academic leaders of Methodist background, such as several of the cluster college provosts. Faculty members were hired who had a sympathetic understanding of the church relationship and typically were affiliated with Protestant churches. Burns asserted in 1963, in a report titled "50 Ways in which the University of the Pacific Relates itself to the Methodist Church," that 15 ordained ministers were on the faculty and another ten on the staff.[76] (Recalling that era, professor Gwen Browne quipped, "every second person was ordained in something."[77]) Nearly all of the honorary degrees went to Methodist bishops or other clergy. No benefactors and few other prominent leaders were honored in this manner until the 1970s.[78]

By 1969, the board decided to sever its formal relationship with the UMC.[79] The board was worried that federal subvention of the dental school would be jeopardized, and funding for a planned science center had just been rebuffed by the Olin Foundation because Pacific was "too Methodist."[80] The United Methodist Church was cordial and supportive of Pacific through this difficult decision. With the urging of the national head of the Methodist Board of Education, regent bishop Tippett and other church leaders, the board ended the policy of formal election of regents by the two sponsoring regional church bodies, and they in turn endorsed the change.[81]

Only months later, the Supreme Court upheld the eligibility of church-related schools to continue to receive federal aid, but neither the University nor the Church revisited the issue. After all, the church conference election of regents had been a *pro forma* approval of the board's nominations for some time.

Pacific continued its positive relationship with the Church, even to keeping a director of church relations (begun in 1991 with the Bishops Scholarship program for Methodist students, ending in late 1990s when the incumbent retired) as well as a full-time interfaith chaplain, continuing today as a partially endowed position. Pacific remains on the roster of Methodist-associated universities, and still participates in its team-visit review process every ten years. Today, the University readily acknowledges its Methodist heritage in its publications without stating that it has any formal affiliation with the UMC.

The decline of an active relationship with the Church occurred over time, especially after the move to Stockton, where Pacific welcomed more diverse Valley students. The gradual decrease of Methodist clergy on the board was also a practical decision to diversify leadership and broaden the funding base of the University. By the 1970s, no regents were clergy members of any denomination. Church leaders understood that the

University was evolving as a comprehensive independent university and accepted that its lessening interaction with the church was a consequence of many forces.

Pacific's Methodist association

Pacific's relationship to the United Methodist Church is actually quite remarkable today. With about one percent of students declaring Methodist ties (the national average in 1998 was 18 percent at Methodist schools[82]), with no attempt to track faculty and staff religious affiliation over many decades, and with no specific educational expectations from the church body that set it apart from other smaller private institutions, Pacific has in fact remained in conformance with Methodist church expectations and therefore continues to be listed among those schools associated with the UMC. Thus, while Pacific has referenced only its "historical ties" to Methodism since the 1970s, it has embraced a heritage always openly non-sectarian, eager to broadly define its educational mission. With the passing of Burns, all subsequent presidents came with some church background, but only Atchley and Eibeck identified as Methodist.

The most important shift in religious identity began in the 1970s when Pacific moved from being a college of "Christian culture," as Knoles would often say, to a university with specific human and community values embracing all religious traditions.[83] But it would be wrong to say that Pacific is a "secular institution" in the sense that public universities must be, and that other private schools decide to be. The endowed chaplaincy position assures that attention to students' religious development is affirmed, and while Morris Chapel may be more of a charming wedding destination than a place of worship, it is still a respected campus gathering place, and remains a retreat for personal meditation and prayer for students of all backgrounds.

A continuing tradition of interfaith invocations at ceremonial events punctuates Pacific's commitment to this identity that understands students' religious values as part of their holistic education. Of the core values of Pacific planted by the Methodist founders long ago, the most important are respecting academic freedom and honoring the relationship of reason and faith, nurturing whole-student development and close community, standing for social justice, and preparing for future community leadership and service.

The University continues to affirm its Methodist heritage, and Pacific values its standing as one among many distinguished universities associated with the UMC, confirmed by the UMC's University Senate, the body of peers that represents Methodist higher education. Other such universities currently include Duke, Emory, American, Drew, Southern Methodist University, Syracuse and Denver. Some former members, such as USC, Boston, and Northwestern, choose not to be recognized by the University Senate. Pacific could choose to do so as well, but has not done so primarily because there are no pressures to do so from any constituents in the current era.

THE PROMISE AND PROBLEM OF ATHLETICS

Continuing the heroic years

Larry Siemering was an outstanding successor to Stagg and built a three-year record of unprecedented wins with Eddie LeBaron at the helm. Quick and small, LeBaron out-danced linemen, executed run and pass plays invented by Stagg, and became a national legend. Siemering had drawn talent and speed to Pacific, including eight players from little Oakdale, LeBaron's hometown. Stockton's Eddie Macon and Bob Heck were both nationally ranked sprinters

Larry Siemering, with talent like LeBaron and Eddie Macon (right), became Pacific's winningest football coach (1947-1950).

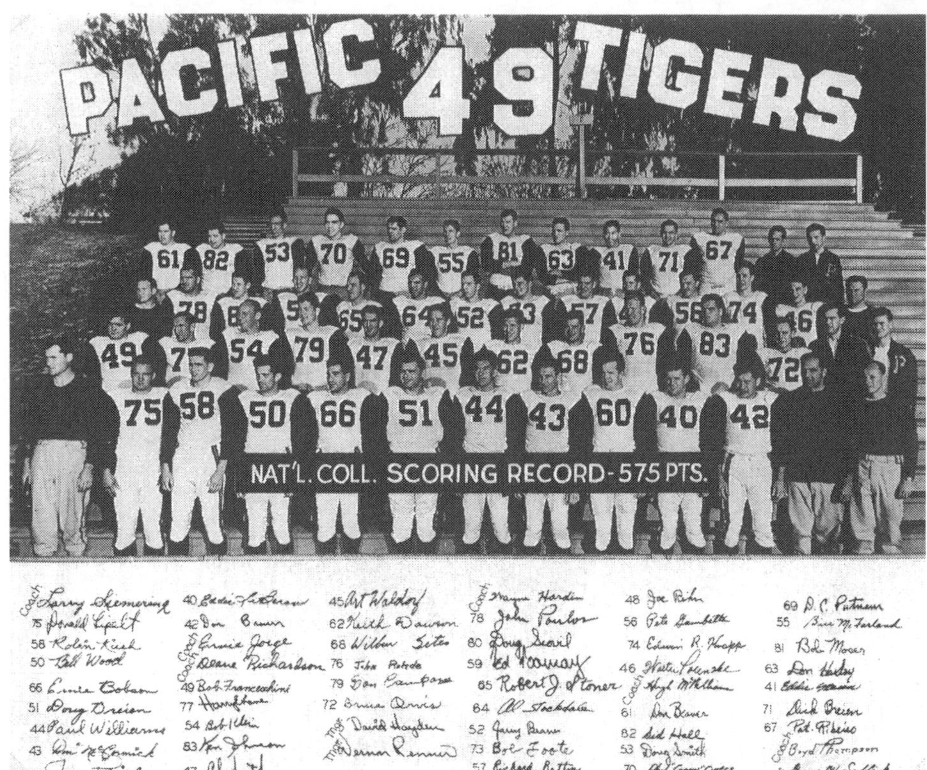

The 1949 team produced Pacific's all-time greatest football season.

(Macon, Pacific's and the Chicago Bears' first black player, held Pacific's all-time scoring record until Dick Bass came along in 1959), and Bob Moser anchored center as he did later for the Chicago Bears.

LeBaron led the Tigers to a 10-1 record in 1947, 7-1 in 1948, and racked up an astonishing record in Pacific's all-time greatest football season in 1949. The Tigers scored 576 points during a perfect 11-0 season, while their opponents collectively scored a total of only 66 points. (The only other undefeated season was in 1923.) Pacific ranked tenth in the nation—the only time the Tigers ever achieved that ranking.[84] Students were justifiably frustrated that even this record could not open the door to a major bowl game— "Undefeated, Untied, and Uninvited!" was their chant. LeBaron and Rohde were the first two in a long line of Pacific players in the annual East-West All-Star Shrine Classic. Siemering was Pacific's winningest coach and had three of Pacific's five best seasons ever.

Locally, crowds jammed Baxter Stadium, forcing some games to the Lodi Grape Bowl. Bigger name schools wouldn't play in the small stadium, and trustee Lowell Berry was convinced that a large stadium would end the spreading red ink for the sport. Berry, joined by Mike Evanhoe and the Stockton Chamber of Commerce, persuaded the trustees to launch a joint campaign for a new stadium befitting a nationally ranked team. "Two big games" in a packed new stadium of 42,000, Berry pled, would erase the deficit.[85] Burns reluctantly agreed, knowing that it would again delay a much-needed new library. The board nodded OK when fundraisers assured them the $250,000 project would not cost the College.[86]

The plan was to sell "scrip," a certificate like a bond or stock share, at $100 a share, redeemable for season tickets over a decade, much like student Bob Burns had sold to get lights into Baxter Stadium years earlier.[87] Scrip sales reached over $150,000 by spring of 1950 thanks to support from the Stockton community led by the Quarterback Club, motivated partly by the plan to name it in memory of the war dead from the region. Students raised $23,000, led by the *Pacific Weekly* student paper. Berry donated $60,000 toward the final cost of $350,000. Though the campaign goal was unmet, the stadium project was a powerful testimony to the unified effort of the

Memorial Stadium, later named Stagg Memorial Stadium, was a big boost for the campus and community in 1950.

While the live "Tommy Tiger" had a short life at Pacific, he sparked school spirit at the Memorial Stadium opening in 1950, and a costumed Tommy lived on—here pictured in 1951.

Stockton community to advance the College, which echoed the triumphant campaign to bring the school to Stockton 30 years earlier.[88]

With an April groundbreaking, the College set a goal to have the seats and turf ready by Homecoming, the first game of the 1950 season and the start of Pacific's centennial. Mountains of earth were piled to shape the bowl around 30,000 seats, including mud dredged from the Calaveras River, but much of the dirt came from scalping six feet off Knoles Field next door, ever since known as "the sunken field." In a dash to meet the deadline, they imported green-dyed sawdust from Ralph McClure's cabinet shop as imitation turf in time for opening kickoff![89]

The two-mile homecoming parade down the Miracle Mile was led by Tully Knoles on his famous white stallion named Ole and a new mascot, "Tommy Tiger," a 450-pound Bengal imported from Boston by Lowell Berry. Both animals pranced and prowled the football sidelines, though "Tommy" died mysteriously two years later.[90] Governor Earl Warren and actor Dick Powell led the dedication speeches for Pacific Memorial Stadium in remembrance of veterans.

"Moose's men"

Within two years of completion, the need for such a grand monument to the gridiron was virtually obsolete. Only four games ever exceeded 30,000, and after 1958 only one season ever averaged over 15,000 fans.[91] Pacific had never gotten beyond the College Division in national competition, and between 1951 and 1953, Pacific's four major private competitor schools dropped football—St. Mary's, Santa Clara, USF, and Loyola. Only once was the stadium ever filled to capacity, and the board considered ending radio broadcasts of the games to boost attendance.[92] The San Francisco Forty-Niners had brought professional football Sundays to Northern California in 1946, drawing fans away from local college-ball Saturdays.

Jack "Moose" Myers (1953-61), one of Pacific's most heralded football coaches, drew annual reunions of players for decades after his service.

The next year, at age 28 Jack "Moose" Myers became the youngest coach in the country (1953-61), the same age as his Athletic Director, Jerry Kirsten ('47). Ken Buck ('54) became Pacific's fourth football All-American but died of cancer the next year. Through the fifties, Pacific steadily sent players to the East-West Shriners game—including Gene Cronin ('56) and John Nisby ('57, '71). The trustees watched as both debt and football scholarships mounted. Players' room and board fees were added to tuition scholarships to meet the competition. At one meeting, the trustees simultaneously approved funds to replace "unacceptable" dorm mattresses and dining hall stoves—and added ten more football scholarships to reach 60.[93]

Burns, in response to growing national concern that big-time football had gotten out of hand, publicly defended intercollegiate football. He was convinced that athletic competition and the unifying spirit of football for an increasingly fragmented campus social life was the sole powerful common experience for all. (He momentarily forgot about Band Frolic.) In those days virtually all students did attend the games. "Football has become the spiritual core of the modern campus," Burns concluded—and indeed, into the sixties, the crowd hushed and the lights dimmed as the spotlight flashed to the robed A Cappella Choir, who sang an anthem before the kickoff.[94]

Dick Bass ('60), second only to LeBaron in Pacific football fame, led Pacific 24-20 over Rose Bowl-bound Cal in 1958.

Pacific played in post-season games in this era, making six appearances from 1946-52 in the Optimist, Grape, Raisin, and Sun Bowls.[95]

Dick Bass ('60), California's top high school player, joined Myers and the Bengals to become a superstar by clearing several rushing records. When Bass and company knocked off Rose Bowl-bound Cal in 1958 before 100,000 fans, all Pacificans celebrated one of the greatest sport highlights in its history.

Pacific finally had a profitable season, and the trustees voted ten more football scholarships to make it 70.[96] Bass led the nation in rushing that year when *Time* magazine called the All-American a "one-man show."[97] He earned the "triple title winner" award for most rushing, total offense and scoring, done for the first time since 1937. Teammate Tom Flores ('59, former regent) became the first Hispanic quarterback in pro ball, playing for the Oakland Raiders, and went on to win two Super Bowl championships as head coach of the Raiders and the first Mexican-American head coach in the NFL. Myers had a string of five winning seasons (1954-59), and 20 of his players were selected for the NFL draft.[98] To this day, "Moose's Men" gather annually to celebrate those golden seasons that nearly matched the Siemering years.

Tom Flores ('59) pioneered Latino success in college and pro football as a player, coach, and manager.

Burns draws the line

But within a few years, football again became "the Problem" for the board, which pushed for study and discussion as students and faculty began to question the return on investment. Coinciding with Burns' 1960 announcement about the change from college to university status and the start of cluster colleges was his decision to curtail football. As cost overruns had gotten out of hand when attendance and gate receipts had fallen away, Burns declared that football was his "biggest problem" as president.[99] Like so many grand Pacific enterprises, big-time football was simply out of its price range, and much-appreciated local boosters were never more than marginal funders given the size of the deficits.[100] Some students gathered in front of the president's house holding protest signs, "Let's not De-emphasize" and "We want sex, beer, and football."[101] Perhaps Burns was influenced more by one of the biggest scandals in collegiate football to date: four Pacific Coast Conference schools caught with slush funds for their football players at Cal, USC, UCLA and Washington in 1956.[102]

Burns asked three strong football supporters, Bruce Orvis ('50), Boyd Thompson ('43), and Jerry Kirsten ('47), to study the issue. Their report to the board recommended "a major readjustment…to put it [football] on a proper basis and give it back to the students."[103] He returned intercollegiate athletics to an academic department, cut back on scholarships, and ended cross-country games that piled on travel costs. Coach Myers called Burns' plan "ridiculous" and left.[104] Students, Burns said, were waning spectators more interested in academic success in the post-Sputnik era. Football for fun would include more players on fewer scholarships playing regional teams of real rivalry, hopefully in a new league "with schools of academic rather than athletic prestige."[105] In the 1960s, between Dick Bass ('60) and Bob Lee ('68), the marching band was probably the star on the field, and even got a cameo appearance on the silver screen in Bing Crosby's *High Time.*

Beckoned back

All of this was wishful thinking. Traditional students wanted football restored, and a cost analysis could not verify any dollar savings. For most students, the policy changes were lost to the weekend excitement of a home game, led to the stadium by the marching band and cheering students. In 1970 Pacific's largest band ever played for a televised Raiders game.[106] Burns' 1965 "Statement of Policy" on athletics declared that rivals USF and Santa Clara had reinstated football, that underwriting athletics was inevitable, that as an independent Pacific had no good conference options, and that he expected excellence on the gridiron.[107] Perhaps again Burns was influenced by the legacy of the Pacific Coast Conference: while the 1956 scandal ended the PCC by 1959, in no way did it trim the athletic ambitions of these schools, which soon formed the Pac-10 and entered a golden age of collegiate football in the early sixties.[108]

In the end, it was a capitulation. Pacific's longest losing streak of nine games was followed by the hiring of coach Doug Scovill in 1966. Burns gave in to pressures to find a regional conference affiliation and signed on to the Pacific Coast Athletic Conference of regional public state colleges like Fresno and Long Beach in 1969, predecessor to the Big West Conference. This football decision meant that all sports had to move from the non-football West Coast Conference of private schools, where Pacific had been a founding member since 1952, to the Big West. (Not until 2013 did Pacific finally regain membership in the WCC.) Scovill had winning seasons in 1968 and 1969, with players Bob Lee ('68) and Bob Heinz ('68) leading the way, both of whom landed in Super Bowl games (Lee for Minnesota twice, Heinz for Miami three times).

Pacific had more active professional football players than any other school except Grambling State, the most famous black college in the country for its football prowess.[109] From the 1950s to the 1990s, Pacific attracted players of remarkable talent and leadership owing to its unique profile in the West during the years the Catholic schools suspended football. Over a hundred players went on to play professional ball.[110] Pacific was the only small private university of solid academic standing that offered NCAA Division I football and an academic program of high expectations that prepared students well for coaching.[111] Of course, having around 450 "PE majors" in the seventies did not hurt recruitment either.

Still, the aspiration to be competitive in Division I football remained an elusive dream that kept pushing Pacific to the edge of academic mediocrity if not extinction right up to the suspension of football in 1995. Burns' decisions to pull back in football, then lean forward again, encapsulate the ambivalence that defined so much of Pacific's history. Football was another one of those grand dreams that kept Pacific alive in spirit while keeping it from realizing its full identity.

Pacific regents of the "greatest generation" that lived through World War II continued to believe if Pacific worked at it hard enough, they could achieve their dream of big-time football that could pay its way. They saw how USC had orchestrated its place in the sun by using national-caliber football to build a major national university. Pacific could never marshal the resources to match the institutional size and heft of its big-time competitors. The resources football demanded were captured from all the other needy programs, while the regents still ended up with red ink on the bottom line.

Basketball champion Dick Edwards

With all the triumph and turmoil of Pacific football, one of the great athletic success stories of the 1960s was in the making on the basketball court. Pacific had won a conference championship in 1947 with star Hank Pfister ('49), then Bill Wirt ('51) and George Moscone ('53, yes, *that* Moscone—later mayor of San Francisco) led the team to a record 19 wins in the 1950-51 season under Chris Kjeldsen. They played home games in the 1200-seat North Gym, dubbed the "Pacific Pavilion."[112] Leroy Wright ('60) was named conference MVP in 1959 and still holds school records

The Stockton Memorial Civic Auditorium, known as "The Pit," was notorious as one of the nation's toughest home courts for opponents from 1963-1981.

in rebounding. But basketball really became a Pacific game with coach Dick Edwards in 1963, who in nine seasons had four West Coast Athletic Conference championships and three NCAA tournament appearances.[113]

The era of coach Edwards was a raucous celebration of a 98-9 home record on the Stockton Memorial Civic Auditorium court called "The Pit." He moved from campus to The Pit in 1963 and lined the court with spectators who rallied behind his flamboyant, in-your-face behavior. In one stretch the team had over 50 consecutive home court wins. The tight downtown venue seating only 2900 excited local fans and may have discouraged student attendance, but it certainly was a home-court advantage: the Civic Auditorium floor was so lopsided that one basket was nearly eleven feet high![114] *Sports Illustrated* ranked The Pit as one of the toughest home courts in the country. [115] When Jerry Tarkanian's Long Beach State team, ranked third in the country, was routed 104-86 by the Tigers in 1972, he said the noise was so deafening "I was in a total state of shock."

Keith Swagerty ('67), pictured here with Bob Krulish ('67, left) and coach Edwards, was with John Gianelli ('72) the best of many of Pacific's basketball standouts in the twentieth century. Legendary UCLA coach John Wooden gained respect for what coach Dick Edwards' championship teams accomplished in the late sixties.

The 1960s standout was Keith Swagerty ('67), third nationally in rebounding and All-American in 1966-67 when he and Bob Krulish ('67) led the team to two consecutive conference championships and NCAA tournaments, when the "Big Dance" was only 32 teams. In 1967 Pacific upset national-champion Texas Western (now Texas-El Paso) before falling to one of John Wooden's legendary Lew Alcindor-UCLA teams. "Wooden said we gave them the toughest game they had all year," Krulish remarked.[116]

At the time, there were no NCAA scholarship limits, so Pacific had as many as 25 basketball scholarships. Pacific could gamble on players who were not heavily recruited, like Stockton's John Gianelli ('72), all-time tops in Pacific career scoring average by beating out Swagerty, second to Swagerty in rebounding, and arguably Pacific's best of basketball greats, who went on to play for the New York Knicks and other NBA teams.[117] Edwards won two more conference championships in 1970 and 1971, returning to the NCAA tournament for a third time in 1971. In addition to standout Bill Stricker ('70) one of Edwards' recruits was Bob Thomason ('71, '85), who joined Gianelli as a star in the 1971 NCAA tournament, and then returned to coach at Pacific for 25 years, exceeding Edwards' record.

Stockton's John Gianelli ('72) held the all-time career scoring average into the twenty-first century. John "the Fox" Ostrom ('66) was Pacific's only NCAA national swim champion.

So by the time Cedric Dempsey was hired to serve as athletic director in 1967, the first AD to report directly to the president, Pacific had notable success in major sports, still important to most students. After hitting rock bottom in 1963, the Tiger baseball team, which got its modern start in 1944, had its "best ever" season in 1968 (32-15)—and still the best ever—led by Terry Maple ('68), Rod Sperling ('68), and John Strohmeyer ('68), earning second place in the WCAC after nationally ranked Santa Clara. All the more remarkable was that baseball had only two scholarships among the whole team.[118] The swim team was typically very competitive, and in 1965 produced Pacific's only NCAA national swim champion, John "the Fox" Ostrom ('66), who set a national butterfly record and broke many Pacific records.

While America's high schools had organized sports for girls, collegiate women's sports did not exist at this time, so Pacific women students organized their own clubs that played other schools like Cal and Stanford informally. Professor Doris Meyer was hired in 1956 to start a formal intramural program for women, but few women were interested—the good players kept to their own clubs.[119] As women's athletics began to organize nationally, it resisted until the 1980s any association with the NCAA, viewed as corrupt and out of control. Not until the courts began applying Title IX legislation to collegiate athletics in the mid-seventies did that begin to change.

Heroic forensics

In the end, despite strong presidents' and regents' support, outstanding leadership in athletics, relatively positive support from the faculty, and talented football coaches and players, the football teams could not reach the level of achievement accomplished in forensics. Starting in 1956, debate coach Paul Winters recruited national championship debaters to set records unexcelled in any other student team activity because forensics had all the assets of football listed above—at miniscule cost.

When he took on the job, Winters persuaded Burns to double the number of scholarships from four to eight and to underwrite travel anywhere in the country in order to become the best.[120] Former debater Burns consented willingly, eager to have a champion to brag about other than football. This was a major victory for Winters and forensics because the other performance-based programs, even the Conservatory of Music, shamefully had no talent scholarships at the time, even into the 1980s.[121]

The debate team reached the pinnacle in 1964—the year of Tiger football's longest losing streak of nine games—when Raoul Kennedy('64) and Douglas Pipes ('65) won the National Debate Tournament Championship at West Point, certainly one of the high points of student achievement in Pacific history. A crowd of 50 students and faculty greeted their return at the Stockton airport and followed a police escort to Burns Tower where 150 cheering fans celebrated the victory.[122] "I was astonished. It was very humbling," said Kennedy, who went on to be ranked the top trial attorney on the West Coast.

Raoul Kennedy ('64) and Douglas Pipes ('65) won the National Debate Tournament Championship at West Point in 1964, the high point of debate coach Paul Winters' storied career. (With trophies: Pipes, Winters, Kennedy)

Earlier, Ted Olson ('62), outspoken *Pacifican* editor who later became U.S. Solicitor General, won a 1961 NBC TV contest. Once, returning from a Hawaii tournament, Olson said the team "had so many trophies we could hardly get them all on the plane." One year the Harvard team, which had falsely accused Pacific of lying in a debate, made it up to Pacific by sharing their research to enable Pacific to beat Boston College in the finals. Other top sixties debaters included Donald Duns ('58), Dennis Day ('58), John Beyer ('62), Karen Beattie (n.d.), Patty Bilbry ('66), and Angela Metropulos O'Rand ('67), now a dean at Duke University. Led by Kennedy and Pipes, the sixties team was crowned by competing in four of the PBS series of collegiate debates on national television.

By the time Winters retired as coach, his teams of men and women, black and white, had amassed 43 national first-place awards. He knew how to match strengths with students of different backgrounds and insisted on ceaseless research throughout the season, a key to team success. From just a handful of students his team had grown to 70 to 80, crisscrossing the country from Thursday through Sunday over two dozen weekends each year. Named national coach of the year at age 40 in 1964, Winters used the bully pulpit as head of the Western Forensics Association for a decade to overcome stiff opposition to integrate women and minorities into competition. Pacific led the way with standouts Brenda Robinson ('62) and Jenny Kahle ('63), Horace Wheatley ('61) and John Red Horse ('62).

REDEFINING PACIFIC—IN TWO DIRECTIONS

Time for a shake-up

While Burns had never been fastidious about the liberal arts identity of Pacific and readily supported and added professional programs of all sorts, he did conclude that the liberal arts faculty itself needed a change, with its entrenched, powerful department heads and complacent faculty. An important identity marker for Burns' new plan was a focus on the "pure liberal arts…

no specialties or vocationalism."[123] He also knew it was time to reposition Pacific, given the addition of engineering and pharmacy schools. Burns was determined to follow his mentor Knoles' lead in notching up the academic expectations of students. He declared that "the central focus should be *learning*," which itself was a new notion: the focus for decades in American higher education had been on *teaching*.[124] He did so in a bold move by creating a new college super-charged by intellectual intensity in a community setting of mutual support, not competitiveness—Raymond College.

Burns wanted to find a new way for Pacific to make its mark in California higher education, and he found it in pursuing two directions almost simultaneously—a new university identity and small-scale academic innovation. He had already made headway by staking out a regional presence, from San Francisco to Sacramento, from Dillon Beach on the coast to Fallon House Theatre in the Foothills, but these outposts could not make the difference. Changing from a small liberal arts college identity to building a university with prestigious professional schools would be notable, as would creating new versions of small liberal arts colleges within this new university.

New public competition

Two key turning points occurred in the California landscape of higher education at this time: the sprouting of University of California campuses and the state's higher education "Master Plan." The state board of education could foresee a surge in university enrollment, due to baby boomers (people born after 1945) coming of age. The University of California Board of Regents had gradually added campuses over the decades, the fourth in Santa Barbara in 1944. As early as 1948, *Life* magazine featured UC as the "Biggest University in the World" at over 43,000 students, charging no tuition for California residents.[125] Then in 1959 the state launched campuses in San Diego, Davis and Riverside, and six years later in Santa Cruz and Irvine.

The state board of education also devised the master plan in 1960 to balance quality with opportunity by providing student access to one of the three college systems and separating their functions to avoid duplication. The UCs could enroll the top one-eighth of high school graduates, the CSUs could enroll the top third, and the community colleges could enroll all applicants. This monumental investment in higher education, which produced the world's best public university system for decades to come, was a powerful driver for Pacific to assess its place in this new terrain. The California State College system added seven campuses from 1957-60, then added six more to total 23 by the mid-1960s. The California Community College System created in 1967 would become the world's largest higher education system, growing to over 100 colleges. As college-going was becoming a national consumer item on a mass scale, state-supported schools gobbled up the demand, moving from serving half the college population in 1950 to three-fourths by 1970, even as independent institutions like Pacific continued to grow.[126]

The lure of the Claremonts

Though Burns rarely publicly acknowledged it, the Claremont Colleges in southern California were the primary source of his cluster-college vision for Pacific. The Claremont Colleges, starting with Pomona (1887), grew out of a 1920s "Oxford Plan" of residential colleges, each with its own distinctive identity and educational agenda, linked by library and campus services, a kind of "corporate federation."[127]

Pomona, motivated to preserve the personal values of the small college while building a great university, added four distinctive small colleges from 1926 to 1963 called the Claremont Colleges.[128] Burns was drawn to the Claremont Colleges partly because their innovation prompted an avalanche of generous gifts in the late 1950s that built a $50 million endowment out of $5 million in a few short years. Students were pouring forth from California high schools so there would be a ready market, and, following the Claremonts, he felt strongly that new resources would come to Pacific through new and distinctive programs. There would be income to build a respectable science center, add a wing to a crowded library, and build engineering labs that met professional standards.

But rather than the Claremonts, Burns preferred publicly to hold up Oxford and Cambridge as his models for the future. Who could be criticized for plagiarizing centuries-old icons? So in 1959, Burns strong-armed Ted Baun to accompany him to visit Oxford and Cambridge first hand, and they became convinced that new colleges based on this model would be distinctive enough to bring prestige and standing to Pacific in a state overrun with large public institutions. "Something different and something unique" would retain the small-college, personalized learning that Burns had grown up with at Pacific, would add academic rigor to a college that had been justly criticized for academic neglect, and would still grow in numbers of students and tuition dollars.[129] It was no surprise, however, that Burns' key liaison with the British universities was Robert Bernard, managing director of Claremont College.

Burns envisioned as many as 15 new colleges, each with distinct identities, sharing only in one library and central administrative services. Vice president Sam Meyer summed up the century-old Pacific values they wished to perpetuate in these new colleges: "small classes, intimate personal student-faculty relationships, individual counseling and guidance, a campus residence experience, participation in a community of learning where each member is important, opportunity for exploration and experimentation, emphasis on moral and spiritual values, academic freedom."[130]

Each college should come "near to supporting itself financially" by avoiding extra-curricular programs—no fraternities or sororities or athletics. Burns' plan counted on an enrollment of 250 students; an efficient, required curriculum; a 20:1 student to faculty ratio; and an endowment for each college —all intended to produce a fairly self-sufficient unit that might not even *require* the desired endowment to back it up.

Becoming a university again

Burns' debate skills, energetic confidence, and winsome charm won over the faculty and the board. College faculty suspicious that the plan would drain their struggling programs were answered by a confident Burns, who saw donors lining up to endow both programs and fund student scholarships for something new and distinctive. He asserted that competition among schools was part of the success of both the Oxbridge and Claremont models, so friendly competition would raise all boats.

By fall 1959, the faculty unanimously endorsed the plan and in two weeks the board did the same. The College became the University of the Pacific again on January 6, 1961, at the Founders Day convocation celebrating 110 years. The "trustees" became "regents" to symbolize university status; a new liberal arts college quad would replace Baxter Stadium; and the school would aim to purchase the Stockton College campus.[131] These unanimous, landmark decisions sealed what had already been an emerging direction for Pacific.

The Raymond College experiment

The cluster college concept was the key means by which Burns could both restore the liberal arts standing of Pacific and affirm the university status that had been emerging by the restoration of engineering and addition of pharmacy. Burns had studied the early years of Pacific and concluded that survival was "a constant struggle…[because] there were no dreams big enough… . We can't let any institution move past us. It takes vision and tall thinking to keep moving and expanding in changing times."[132] Within months Mr. and Mrs. Walter Raymond, loyal Methodist benefactors, bequeathed ranchland near Sutter that was later sold for $2 million to build Raymond College—the single largest gift in Pacific history to that time.[133]

Ambitious young Warren Bryan "Dick" Martin, chair of religious studies at Cornell College in Iowa, was appointed to be the architect of Raymond's academic program, and he tore into the job of defining academic excellence through the classical liberal arts and sciences. Vice president Meyer insisted on a rigorous traditional liberal arts curriculum—a movement started at University of Chicago in the 1930s that also rejected any vocational purpose. Strong-headed Martin pressed for an intensive, three-year degree program, the first of many accelerated academic programs at Pacific.

The buildings of the new quad west of the main campus went up quickly with federal dollars. Living units included faculty apartments and a common dining hall separate from the rest of the campus. Most of the

The three cluster colleges, Raymond, Callison, and Covell (1962-1986), were separated from the rest of the campus by the infamous "Eucalyptus Curtain."

Raymond gift was plowed into the program. With 67 freshman students and a faculty of nine, the College opened in 1962 to much fanfare, with the chancellor of UC-Santa Cruz as speaker, who would soon copy the cluster college model on his campus.[134]

While admissions standards were uniform for all the colleges, Raymond attracted exceptional academic talent. Under provost Martin's inspirational leadership, Raymond students were lavished with cultural immersion, from art exhibits to poets to distinguished scholars of every stripe. The Wednesday "High Table" was a marker of the College—formal attire for dinner with faculty.

On the other side of the "Eucalyptus Curtain"—the giant gangly line of trees separating the new quad from the old campus—reports of Raymond were of experiments in fringe living, a cocktail of sex and drugs that mixed students with faculty in a social brew that grew zestier by the year throughout the decade. Actually, in the early years, as student Carter Brown ('70, later a Pacific regent) wrote, Raymond was "academically innovative and socially traditional, if not reactionary."[135] The College conformed to the double standard of restricted hours for women students and dress codes for both women and men until the second provost, Berndt Kolker, empowered the Raymond students to set their own social regulations starting in 1966.[136]

Raymond was truly a 24-hour-a-day learning town that lived up to its self-made label as the "honors college" of the campus. With bull sessions running late into the night, faculty were constantly at the behest of eager students in this immersion experiment of a long, intense, three-semester year. Economics professor Michael Wagner—older than most of the Raymond profs just out of school—was the intellectual *provocateur* for the students, riddled with the beliefs and values of a complacent American culture, that sent them spinning into debates through the lunch hour. As Dorothy Wilson Leland ('69) said, Wagner was "spectacularly offensive" to students' preconceptions.[137] Written evaluations replaced grades. The senior comprehensive written and oral exams in humanities, natural sciences, and social sciences were notoriously demanding.

Economics professor Mike Wagner was the resident iconoclast of Raymond College.

But the intense learning paid off for those headed to advanced study. Early Raymond classes ranked in the 98th percentile on the Graduate Record Examination. The first graduating class of 38 included three Fulbright and two Rockefeller fellowships and four Peace Corps placements. Of the first 416 Raymond graduates, 72 percent earned advanced degrees.[138] But they had extra help. Burns had approved Martin's lavish menu: guaranteed sabbatical leaves for faculty every five years, free faculty lunches with students, informal classrooms with carpets rather than desks, a regal Raymond

The sumptuous Raymond Common Room epitomized the feeling of a two-tiered campus: the well-funded cluster colleges vs. the other academic programs.

Common Room for after-class chats. No wonder the threadbare COP faculty and their students felt like second-class citizens and were galled by the separatist enclave on the other side of the eucalyptus curtain—all unlike the Claremont colleges, where harmonious relationships among the schools were fostered and all were well funded.[139]

Tension between the two colleges peaked at the spring 1965 COP faculty meeting that denounced the Raymond sabbatical plan as discriminatory and "violently rejected it."[140] COP dean Jacoby complained to vice president Graves about shriveled budgets for equipment, operations, and student scholarships; antique offices and labs; creeping graduate programs; increased football coaching staff and scholarships that gave "the general impression that we are 'on the way back' to big time football;" and disproportionate cluster college teaching loads and amenities—all pointed to massive neglect of the College.[141] Graves retorted to Jacoby that "the clusters' reputation and prestige [would] in the long run bring financial support to all parts of the University."[142]

But even the new "Academic Facilities Building" was named the "Wendell Phillips Center for Intercultural Studies" and reserved for Raymond and Covell College faculty and classes. (Only later would it become the COP home known as "WPC," a long-lamented name that could never be removed because of a signed agreement with the charlatan Phillips, whose global oil stocks meant to fund the new building as estate gifts cashed out to a paltry $71,000.[143]) At the same time, COP and other schools reduced a bloated roster of courses by 25 percent to try to reduce the number of costly small classes and reallocate resources to improve their departments.[144]

A new Raymond

A serious drop in enrollment in 1967—35 percent of students transferred out, and SAT scores plummeted—forced adjustments. The curriculum eased off on required courses and added more independent study. A fourth year was added to appeal to more students and spread out expenses. The new provost Berndt Kolker's accent on individualized learning and on students' self-determination of their college life and studies really turned the original prescriptive Raymond on its head.

The next major Raymond change occurred after the shift in the economy in the early 1970s, coinciding with the coming of President McCaffrey. Less involved with campus and national politics, Raymond students turned inward, focusing on personal academic pursuits, whether internships or independent studies in the now unstructured curriculum. The commonality of the three versions of Raymond was the "intensive learning in community," as former Raymond professor Eugene Rice pointed out.[145] In the end, experimental colleges like Raymond lasted about seven years, so the relative longevity of Raymond is a tribute to the immense effort to keep the vision going for 17 years, until 1979.

An emerging identity?

College of the Pacific faculty and students complained about the "superiority complex" of the Raymond community, but Burns blessed the tension and occasional clash as a tonic to raise academic expectations in all programs. And so as *Time* and *Newsweek* magazines featured the clusters and Pacific's reputation as an outstanding "liberal arts college" grew, the attention again confused pieces of Pacific for the whole. The reality was that the clusters stimulated overall improvement of admissions and academic standards for Pacific, but were dwarfed by the growth of the College and the rise of the professional schools. Still, the cluster colleges forced an identity crisis that shook Pacific out of its complacent "Methodist college family/football powerhouse/party school" image into something quite different.

Pacific's distinction lay partly in its unique little liberal arts colleges, but also in its particular combination of liberal arts and professional schools that matched large public universities in its academic diversity, yet preserved the personalized, residential campus and close interaction among faculty and students of a small college. It was this distinctive combination that was to be the enduring legacy of Pacific's place in American higher education. As vice president Sam Meyer put it, Pacific was "being transformed from a small, regional, liberal arts college into a medium-sized, multi-purposed university of national and international significance."[146]

STUDENT LIFE ERUPTS—GRACEFULLY

"Animal House" to free speech

Student life at Pacific in the 1960s was a contradiction. Yes, students still loved "lawn surfing" across the flooded main quad, a tradition that did not end until underground sprinklers replaced the flooding hydrant faucets about 2000. The usual frat shenanigans of the fifties were now raised to a higher power, counterpointed by rising student political activism. It was a time of transition, when the post-Sputnik ratcheting up of American high schools poured well-prepared students onto the campus.

"Lawn surfing" was a quick cool-down for decades during those hot fall and spring days thanks to an old-fashioned campus lawn watering system.

They were looking for ways to shirk the complacent past with erratic behavior, perhaps with the sense of foreboding captured in the comedy hit *National Lampoon's Animal House* (1978), set on a campus the year before the Kennedy assassination. For years stories have circulated that several of the movie scenes came from Pacific frat alumni who knew Hollywood writers and filmmakers. It is true that Tom Honey ('66) became friends with George Lucas (who later made his hometown Modesto famous in *American Graffiti*) at the Pacific library when both were writing high school term papers. But it was less clear if the food fight in *Animal House* re-enacted the notorious food fights in Anderson Dining Hall (affectionately known as "Burns' ptomaine domain") incited by the "Thursday Surprise" and mystery meats that made dinners miserable.[147] In a sense, these fights, at least one of which resulted in a fork-stabbed hand, were the first campus protests of the sixties. But the Rhizomia parties certainly matched those in *Animal House*, and the band that played in the movie actually played at one of their parties.

With a no-alcohol dorm policy, the famous "toga parties" memorialized in *Animal House* were held at local clubs like Jesters and the Sportsman's, where punch-drenched togas got torn off or tossed aside. Many a parent tried to use the purse to encourage better behavior. One disgusted father blared, "I am not writing the checks to that place where it's Christmas every day and New Year's every night."[149] The *Animal House* episode of the dead horse may well have come from Pacific. During Christmas break, two drunken students coaxed an old mare into an empty Tri-Delt sorority house one night—and put it out of its misery. Days later as the stench seeped out, police used a chain saw to butcher it into portable sizes.

Dean Ed Betz, the campus warden trying to stamp out the perpetual antic circus of frat life, was always in the students' cross hairs. One morning Betz had to figure out how to remove five Volkswagen beetles from the steps of the library.[150] Over the decades, part of an annual Archania pledge class ritual was stealing bells from Foothill country churches to add to their impressive collection. It was dean Betz' sisyphean task to return them—well, some of them. All the bells rang at the annual "Belle of Archania" naming ritual begun in 1941, with a crown of white carnations and a bouquet

An Archania fraternity bell became a symbol of athletic rivalry with San Jose State starting in 1949 (1989 photo).

of red roses ready for the lucky woman. An Archania bell has been part of football and basketball rivalries with San Jose State at least since 1949.[151] Alpha Kappa Lambda introduced its cannon in 1955, firing it at every home football game and at graduation.[152] The Omega Phi custom was for pledges to steal some bulldog hood ornament from a Mack truck for the house's bulldog mascot collection.[153] All the fraternities had kidnappings (called "sneaks") that were excuses for a beer blast in a remote location. Beyond the pervasive Greek culture of corporal punishment (butt paddling), every frat brother knew of bizarre hazing rituals that far exceeded the bounds of what would be tolerated in the twenty-first century.

The best: Homecoming, Mardi Gras, Band Frolic

The annual homecoming parade survived this turbulent era, but other traditions did not. Parade float and house decoration prizes continued to fuel competitions between housing units. The parade down the Miracle Mile of Pacific Avenue still drew community crowds, if only to see the quirky floats. Many alumni remember when upperclassmen charged the freshman bonfire with "Molotov cocktails" to burn it down, only to be routed by freshmen armed with air guns filled with filthy concoctions that a shower wouldn't wash off.[154] But the great homecoming bonfire tradition of decades ended in 1968 with the rise of environmental concerns. And when the feminist movement arose in the late sixties, the homecoming queen and her court vanished until the pageantry was revived in 1977.[155]

The annual Mardi Gras traditional celebration and dance continued through the decade, with its queen, "ugly man" presider, games, benefit contests with theme booths, and a costume dance that almost always lived up to its billing. Some years even included a parade. Mardi Gras was a fitting companion to the all-time favorite spring Band Frolic that crammed all living units into the Conservatory auditorium over two evenings of relished competition for the best campus musical review. To most students, Band Frolic epitomized the best of Pacific community. From Omega Phi to Raymond College, alumni of any living group that won the top prize—or barely lost it—will never forget that night.

Mardi Gras—parade and all—vied with Homecoming as the campus's favorite annual celebration in this era.

Amid the rising national turmoil of the 1960s, Band Frolic flourished.

Raymond opens the door

Raymond College was in many ways the avenue by which Pacific transitioned from the old fifties carefree college life of football, follies and fun to a campus where academics, intellectual curiosity, and serious bull sessions mattered deeply for the first time since the nineteenth century. Across the country, a carnival of clubs, ballgames and Greek life interspersed with a dabbling of classes was changing to competing campus environments and factions where no majority of students ruled the campus.[156]

While Raymond students represented a tiny minority on campus, they quickly assumed leadership of student organizations and the student newspaper. Raymondite Pete Windrem ('65) was elected student association president and other classmates won senate seats as Raymond dominated student government, even taking on the student judiciary and protesting inadequate campus health services.[157] Raymond student leadership set a new tone of serious intellectual life. Books and academic achievement mattered again, and the campus was fed by provocative guest speakers who prodded new thinking. Drugs and sex were an important part of the mix, but most Raymond students managed to survive the intense three-year accelerated curriculum of tough interdisciplinary courses while winning the intramural basketball tournament and the Mardi Gras costume contest in 1964 and Band Frolic in both 1964 and 1965.[158]

Dean of women Kay Davis' dress codes for women were highly regimented by time of day and event. From 1967-70, these rules faded fast, led by the Associated Women Students, but the contrast between antiquated campus rules versus open inquiry in the classroom was stark. Even Raymond women could not wear pants, and the tension over a women's dorm curfew was the minor difference between 11:00 p.m. for Raymond women vs. 10:30 p.m. for all others.[159] Women and minority students across the campus began to raise their voices, and the contraceptive "Pill," rainbow dress, wild hair, and folk and rock music filled the marijuana-scented air by the end of the decade. Still, these students were a minority "counter-culture" on a fast-growing campus calling for a return to big-time football.

Free speech on an open campus

The 1964 launch of the "Free Speech Movement" by Mario Savio on UC-Berkeley's Sproul Plaza, prompted by a new restriction on campus political activity, became a national movement for a student voice in campus governance. But at Pacific President Burns had always kept open lines of communication with students, both informally through his exuberant campus presence and formally by creating a forum of student, faculty and administrative leaders to air student concerns.

When Larry Meredith came as chaplain and Callison College professor in 1966 he invited Morris Chapel guests that included the most extreme voices in the country in already turbulent times. Standing-room-only crowds jammed the 400-seat chapel, hanging from the balcony beneath the blue rose window, flanked by the astonishingly detailed color and beauty of the high, wall-to-wall stained glass windows. Students stuffed themselves in among the ornately carved and painted words and images of ancient Christian heritage in the elaborate nave to hear black radicals like Angela Davis and Huey Newton, "Peanuts" cartoonist Charles Schultz, or the "God is Dead" theologian Thomas Altizer.

The Stockton community and regents were shocked when the LSD guru Timothy Leary sauntered on to the chancel preaching his disoriented drug gospel in 1967. But he won no converts among the students, who could see his dissipated mind and body. Time and again Burns, together with Methodist bishop Donald Tippett, would defend Meredith's train of witches, revolutionaries, and social outcasts against angry critics. Intellectual and cultural freedom needed to be defended on the campus. As Burns said, "This policy of freedom—to think, to hear, to discuss, to speak, is our most precious heritage."[160]

Preserving community

Burns and his leadership invented an "All University Study Day" in 1967 in the face of rising anti-war disruptions of classes and renegade "teach-ins" that left campuses deeply divided. The University-wide teach-in brought all parties together in serious debate and discussion groups that encouraged students to vent their intense feelings and frustrations. Unlike many campuses, Pacific brought speakers who represented diverse viewpoints on the war, upholding Burns' commitment to learning through honest discussion and debate.

This annual event through the war years went a long ways toward keeping the peace on the Pacific campus and building a sense of shared purpose in the face of a failing U.S. policy and campus turmoil across the land. Burns inserted himself into the student ferment by convening an informal council of two dozen campus leaders who met in his living room monthly to talk about campus issues over punch and cookies.[161]

Race and the Teacher Corps in Stockton

A deep democratic strain of equality for all became a generational mantra at Pacific and throughout the country. Amid the assassinations of black leaders Malcolm X and Martin Luther King, Jr. as well as Robert Kennedy and the Watts riots of Los Angeles, the military draft to feed the Vietnam War gobbled up college students, and anti-war activity erupted into violent confrontations beginning at Columbia University in 1968. By 1969, roughly 350 colleges went on strike, and over one-fourth of college students protested in some active demonstration during their undergraduate years.[162]

The "sit-ins," begun in the South by black students to assert their civil rights, became a hallmark of campus life for both radicals and mainline campus leaders disillusioned by the failing Vietnam War and indignant about racial inequality. Issues of women's equality were also emerging. At Pacific, only junior and senior *men* were allowed to live off campus, and some programs seemed virtually segregated by gender. The first woman to graduate in engineering was Charyl Woodward in 1968, and only three more women engineers had graduated by 1977. Only a handful of women were in each pharmacy class.[163] "

In times that called for alternatives, Pacific students already had options: the cluster colleges Raymond and Callison and Covell offered challenging small classes, coordination of meaningful co-curricular activities, interdisciplinary courses, international study, and flexible schedules. The key issue for Pacific was what is now called "student access"—the admission of students of disadvantaged backgrounds and racial minorities, especially from the local region. Pacific had hired its first black faculty members only in 1964, art professor Larry Walker, who later became chair of the National Council of Art Administrators, and education professor Juanita Curtis.[164] The traditional fraternity men had little time for the civil rights agitation coming from the clusters, even though Pacific's black students were refused lunch counter service downtown.[165] Black students on football scholarships also endured indignities from foes such as LSU, which through the 1960s required all black players to be housed outside Baton Rouge.[166] There were only a handful of Mexican-American students to organize the first Hispanic club, the Chicano "Che" club in 1969.[167] When Latino students asked the food service to honor the grape boycott of the late sixties, director Paul Fairbrook ran a referendum in each dining hall to let students determine the policy. Some said yes, some no.[168]

The School of Education, led by energetic visionary Marc Jantzen (1960 "Outstanding Educator of the Year" for the national education society Phi Delta Kappa), had already responded to regional public school needs by sending out 750 graduates who were current school administrators and teachers in San Joaquin County.[169] In the 1950s he partnered with the alumni association and the Rosenberg Foundation to fund minority scholarships for junior college students to complete their degrees at Pacific. Jantzen then created the Teacher Corps Program in 1968, federally funded to recruit junior-college minority students to graduate into elementary school teaching in low-income neighborhoods. A pioneering first such program in the country, the Teacher Corps

Exceptional art professor Larry Walker was Pacific's first black faculty member in 1964.

drew black and Latino as well as white students to Pacific. This remarkable program again set Pacific ahead of its peers through an innovative project that directly addressed the practical needs of a growing regional minority population. These students of color were the vanguard in the movement to make the University more inclusive.

The CIP victory

A coalition of black students from the Black Student Union chapters of Pacific and Stockton College—along with Raymond and Callison cluster college students, progressive COP liberal arts students and activists in Anderson Y—agreed that the most urgent need at Pacific was increasing student diversity. The key impetus was the drive for scholarships for local Stockton College students who, lacking a local CSU option, could not even afford to transfer to Sac State or Stanislaus State. These were Stockton students looking for help from their local private college, students from Hispanic, Black, and Asian American communities that collectively comprised over 40 percent of the city's population.

In the spring of 1969 a band of students stormed Burns Tower and locked it down while 25 leaders climbed into President Burns' eighth-floor office to present their non-negotiable demand to overcome a "white racist campus." Led by BSU spokesman John Stanton ('71) and MEChA leader Victor Ornelas ('71, later a regent), they called for launching an "Educational Opportunities Program" in the fall, suspending basic admissions requirements, and granting full scholarships for 250 black students and 250 "Third World" students. They gave the president 48 hours to respond. Burns was sympathetic to the cause, though not this ersatz process.[170]

The 1969 student storming of Burns Tower over minority student enrollment was a watershed event for Pacific, birthing the Community Involvement Program, continuous since 1969.

He swiftly called together the faculty Academic Council, formed just two years earlier, to present the student demand and a compromise proposal. The Council was receptive; a year earlier a group of faculty had organized campus fundraising for a scholarship fund to recruit "economically disadvantaged persons."[171] Academic vice president Jack Bevan loved this drama and played a key role in it. He met with student leaders behind the scenes to draw up a compromise that they would publicly accept. Burns, again using his persuasive powers, got the faculty to agree to Bevan's negotiated response. The program would in fact burden the faculty with additional students without new resources as well as provide a tutoring program to bolster basic skills of likely underprepared students. Within hours progressive faculty members saw this as an opportunity to change the face of the campus, and 130 volunteered to provide extra help.

Within a day, Burns met with students to announce the University's plan, the Community Involvement Program (CIP). This "bold adventure" would provide a college education for "200 culturally disadvantaged students" from Stockton on full scholarship, including a tutorial program involving faculty and students. The students were elated and the minority community of Stockton surprised by this stunning move, another first for Pacific: the first university in the country to proffer such a program for its host city. Black religion professor John Diamond and remarkable Raymond student Yvonne Allen ('69) headed the program that in its first year included nearly 50 Latinos and over 30 black students among its 115 members.[172]

As if to reinforce the difference of how Pacific handled dissent, one of the memorable movies filmed at Pacific in that era was Stanley Kramer's *R.P.M,* about a campus rebellion in the sixties starring Anthony Quinn and Ann-Margret. Over the1969 winter break, 1200 Pacific students were hired to be the roily crowd taking over Knoles Hall and facing off in the "muddy bog" of the central quad, dubbed "Kramer Lake." The football team played the police enforcers trying to drive them out, and the bloody noses and a couple broken bones were not faked. A faculty member's light-hearted quip capped off campus activism at Pacific in this era: "Our students have to be paid to riot." At $15 to $50 per day, the pay was sweeter than time with Quinn and Ann-Margret.[173]

The 1969 filming of Stanley Kramer's R.P.M. starring Anthony Quinn and Ann-Margret included 1200 Pacific students staging a campus riot.

A changed campus and a community partnership

Pacific would never be the same again. Its identity as an insular, white, upper-middle class enclave, which persisted to some degree right into the 21st century, was broken by a visionary president who turned a campus crisis into an historic commitment, a future investment of millions of dollars in the talent development of Stockton. Now over 40 years old with over 1000 graduates, the CIP program remains a monument to Burns' leadership and to Pacific's ongoing commitment to embrace students of all backgrounds.

In 1970, over 400 undergraduate students (14 percent) were "minority," triple the number of 1968.[174] Within a year, a Black Studies Department was added to COP to offer all students courses to understand racial prejudice and discrimination. Pacific boasted that it was "the first in the country to offer a course on the black man and his contribution to society."[175] The next year, Chicano Studies was offered, then canceled within a year owing to lack of appropriate faculty and student interest. In the early years, nearly all the students in professor Mark Ealey's Black Studies classes were black.

For most of the early CIP students, campus life was tough. Counseling and tutoring were critical to their success, and a skeptical faculty and

Professor Mark Ealey founded Black Studies at Pacific in 1970.

sometimes hostile students were a challenge. A group of black CIP men decided one night to break the unstated color line in Grace Covell Dining Hall, supposedly open to all students.[176] Their courage to claim their place in the hall was a path for future minority students. Many of the dorm custodians were local black women, who often served the "housemother" role for black students and offered them encouragement and support. With each succeeding wave of CIP students, together with the Latin American Covell students, a rich dialogue of cultural exchange developed at Pacific, with a struggling local black student forging a friendship with a wealthy Venezuelan. White, black and brown students discovered common bonds, certainly within the CIP program, which required regular meetings and volunteer group projects in the Stockton community, but also with diverse students across the campus.

Out of this legendary program, now if its fifth decade, have come such graduates as Jose Hernandez ('84), Pacific regent and NASA Flight

Recording and TV star Chris Isaak ('80) and NASA astronaut and regent Jose Hernandez ('84) are two of CIP's distinguished graduates.

Engineer and astronaut; Dr. Robert Acosta ('73), NASA Flight Surgeon for the space shuttle Columbia; Chris Isaak ('80), popular music and TV star for 30 years; and such Stockton leaders as celebrated high school band teacher Arthur Coleman ('81).[177] Acosta sums up the significance of Pacific for many CIP grads: "If it weren't for CIP, I wouldn't have gone on in school…it was my only chance."[178]

The L.U.V. campaign

At Pacific, the constructive atmosphere created by President Burns went beyond campus politics. Alumni from the sixties remember the great "L.U.V." campaign, launched not to create a sixties campus "love-in," but to bring voting rights to 18-year-olds during the height of the Vietnam War, when the average age of a Vietnam soldier was 19. In a campus appearance, Indiana Senator Birch Bayh challenged students to start a grass-roots movement to bring the voting age down to age 18. Dennis Warren ('70, '73), a 20-year-old political science student, stood up. He started a student movement he called "Let Us Vote," a "L.U.V." campaign popularized through the slogan, "Old enough to fight, old enough to vote."[179]

Dennis Warren ('70, '73) became a national hero of sorts for sparking the LUV ("Let Us Vote") campaign for 18-year-olds' voting rights, legislated in 1971.

Using his excellent debate skills, Warren organized student clubs that sent out packets to promote the movement, and campus chapters sprouted across the country. The widely popular TV talk-show host Joey Bishop invited him to spread the word as Bishop took up the cause. As L.U.V.'s national "Honorary Chairman" Bishop tracked progress of new campus chapters from 90 schools in the first week to 327 college chapters and 3,000 high school clubs by the end of 1970. Bishop came to Pacific for a L.U.V. rally, and Senator Bayh asked Warren, Bishop and vice president Bevan to testify in Senate hearings for election reform.

Thanks to a full-page *Time* magazine story, thousands of volunteers, Warren's determined leadership and his countless media interviews, before the year was out President Nixon signed a law lowering the voting age that was confirmed by the 26th Amendment to the U.S. Constitution in 1971.[180] Now that is Pacific student activism: citizen leadership of the highest order. It was somehow fitting that the student body president during this campaign was Chauncey Veatch ('70), who became National Teacher of the Year in 2002 for his remarkable work with Latino and limited-ability high school students in Coachella Valley.

In 1970 students conducted a memorial service in protest over the U.S. invasion of Cambodia. Many Pacific students were deeply engaged in anti-Vietnam war activities, but they upheld civility and rejected violence.

The truly open campus

The height of campus unrest culminated in spring 1970 when President Nixon authorized the military invasion of Cambodia. Students as well as citizens were outraged by the aggression. Classes were suspended or ended at over 400 colleges and universities. In May, Pacific students and faculty rallied to protest and called for suspension of classes. Jack Bevan quickly gathered student, staff, and faculty leaders to find common ground. The University would stay open, but scheduled a special "All University Study Day" to air views on the invasion. While this reduced tension, within days unarmed student protesters were killed by National Guard and police forces, four at Kent State and two at Jackson State, and every campus was paralyzed by the horror. Again, some students called for closing the school, but campus leaders decided to hold a memorial service and cancel the traditional Mardi Gras celebration.

When Governor Reagan closed all state universities and colleges to prevent further violence (two students had died in California campus demonstrations), Pacific student leaders sent him a telegram expressing "deep regret. We remain open seeking a dialogue with the community that you have so effectively attempted to stifle. We have disavowed violence and mob action. The conclusion of our rational reflection is that we must work as hard as possible to erase the polarities...."[181] Pacific's law school was apparently the only California law school to remain open till term end.[182] Even Alumni-Parent Weekend was modified to provide time for the entire community to exchange views.

Still, some students remained committed to shutting down the University, so Jack Bevan met with the "Pacific Strike Committee" to review the results of a campus poll on the issue. While a Berkeley radical called "Super-Joel...a total acid revolutionary" came to campus to foment a strike, Pacific students dismissed his extreme rhetoric.[183] To radicals, street protest and threat of violence were the only means of power; negotiation meant capitulation. Pacific students rejected this path. As student Alan O'Neal observed, "here, people think before they do something."

The group decided to keep classes running, but authorized faculty to release students committed to outreach in church and civic groups to further war opposition. The Strike Committee changed its name to the "People's Alliance for Peace" to better communicate its message. A bomb threat from disappointed campus radicals at San Jose State prompted level-headed dean of students Ed Betz to declare to the campus that he would spend all night in the targeted administration building (Knoles Hall), so that any perpetrators would have blood on their hands should they proceed.[184] Sixty percent of the graduating seniors voted to contribute extra dollars to support the election campaigns of legislators opposed to the war. Commencement that year saw many armbands with various peace emblems.

A national model

The incidents of riots, violence, and destructive behavior across the nation's campuses in the late sixties never occurred at Pacific. The campus survived intact, its community affirmed, the semester completed, academic and political freedoms preserved, campus diversity enhanced. All was owing to a diplomatic leadership team of faculty, students and administrators who were respectful of students yet courageously open to compromise, empathetic to the deep ethical issues of justice and peace that grew from a strong Methodist tradition yet tactful in dealing with youthful outbursts. Four years of Meredith's "pressure valve" weekly chapel programs had exposed students to every side of any burning issue.[185] Burns, Bevan and Betz—all poised, principled, compassionate leaders through these tumultuous episodes—stood their ground. As Kara Brewer wrote, "The result was decision-making based on ethical wisdom as well as practical exigency."[186]

When the American Council on Education sent a team of educators to Pacific in 1969 as one of seven schools in the country selected to determine how Pacific had avoided aggressive disruption, Burns laid out the policies and strategies that made it so. They included small academic units with close student-faculty interaction; his and others' open door accessibility that encouraged students to voice complaints and student representation on virtually all committees; the practice of inviting controversy on the campus to explore extreme viewpoints in structured encounters that protected all voices; the lack of military programs and research; academic programs devoted to service professions and Anderson Y programs devoted to service activities; engaged faculty and administrative leaders who knew how to work with students, drawing on a Methodist tradition of compassionate ethics and bold conscience.[187] In the end, he might have added one more strength: an exemplary student body that had risen to a genuine learning community.

"INNOVATIVE, INVOLVED, AND INTERNATIONAL": AAAS, COVELL AND CALLISON COLLEGES

AAAS: A failed first try

Flanked by flags of all nations, Burns' 1947 inaugural address saluted the value of international education with special emphasis on the Pacific region: "the College has the possibilities of pioneering as we look toward the great Pacific basin" by exchanging professors from abroad and recruiting international students. Burns' hiring of Elliott Taylor, who frequently organized study abroad trips for students, was another arrow in his quiver for internationalism.

Burns was soon to fulfill his dream by founding the first Spanish-speaking college in the United States, Elbert Covell College, with students from all the Americas, and the first college to send all its students to Asia for a full year of study, Callison College. But even before these plans were hatched, Burns had pursued another novel international venture, the erstwhile partnership with the American Academy of Asian Studies (AAAS) in San Francisco.

AAAS had a small group of international faculty offering graduate-only degrees in Asian philosophical, spiritual, cultural and artistic life—on the vanguard of Asian studies in the U.S. Two prominent faculty members were Rom Landau, a prolific scholar in Islamic studies who later helped to launch Callison College's India program, and Alan Watts, renowned writer on Zen Buddhism, who became the Academy's dean. Among its students were the founders of the Esalen Institute at Big Sur and Gary Snyder, the prominent counter-culture American poet.

This independent academy needed a larger institution to widen its appeal to students and donors and gain accreditation, so Burns brought its founder Louis Gainsborough on the Pacific board to facilitate an agreement with Pacific. Burns knew that Pacific's past ties to San Francisco extended back to the first medical college in 1858, so taking on a new San Francisco partnership was no problem. In fact, it would extend Pacific's regional

The American Academy of Asian Studies in San Francisco, affiliated with Pacific from 1954-59, was one of Burns' ventures to build international education.

footprint into the heart of northern California. The 1954 agreement set the framework for Burns' method of future Pacific affiliations: retain the identity and independence of the other partner, and protect Pacific from financial liability. Without any thorough review of its program or promise, Pacific's board adopted the Academy so that now the Academy could offer masters and doctoral degrees with the imprimatur of a well-established college, and Pacific could boast of a sophisticated Asian curriculum that catapulted Pacific's international offerings from meager to robust.

But there were details that Burns tended to downplay. The Academy was already in arrears; Watts was prancing about, unable to manage himself, much less an institution; and Burns agreed to help fundraise. The campaign was unsuccessful; adding social sciences to balance the curriculum was an expense it could ill afford, with a paltry library and low salaries; and Pacific's faculty became restless about the Academy jeopardizing Pacific's own graduate program accreditation. When the Academy's dean Alan Watts was exposed to be reckless with his personal life and a terrible administrator, the College fired him, and the Pacific's board simply ended the five-year experiment in 1959. Did the partnership advance Pacific in any important way? Despite its purported promise of internationalizing Pacific and opening doors to city donors, probably not. But it was a practice run for Burns for the ventures to come.

Pioneering with Elbert Covell College

A 1960 Burns-Meyer pilgrimage to South America surfaced an obvious need: most Latin American students studying in the U.S. struggled with both language and culture and rarely were accommodated. Only the wealthy elites with private tutors and international resort travel had access to the world's best higher education. In turn, U.S. students who became proficient in Spanish to pursue international careers rarely had a good understanding of Latin cultures. At this time, there were very few Latino students at Pacific, though the first graduated in 1938.[188] Typical of Burns, he sat down with Meyer in their Caracas hotel and outlined a 12-point program for Inter-American studies. Their plan included a new college where all instruction would be in Spanish, a proposal from Robert Woodward, U.S. Ambassador to Uruguay, that many others endorsed during their travels.

Within weeks Arthur Cullen, director of thc Latin American Center at the Inter-American University in Puerto Rico, was hired to head the Inter-American Studies program. The second new quad was opened in fall 1963, the only U.S. college before or since to offer its curriculum in a second language. Woodbridge vineyardist Elbert Covell had through a series of gifts and a bequest over the years earned the board's recognition to name the new college in his honor, though one specific Covell gift of real estate that brought in $1 million was invested to build the program. Happily for Pacific, President John Kennedy announced his new "Alliance for Progress" with Latin America during this time and sent a letter to Burns with his "warmest congratulations" on the founding of Elbert Covell College. Vision-maker Robert Woodward was Pacific's commencement speaker in 1962. Voice of America broadcasted radio programs throughout Latin America about the Covell opening to lay a pathway for student recruitment.

Ardent internationalist and admissions director Elliott Taylor made nearly annual treks South to publicize the program and recruit and interview students, most of whom wanted not a liberal education, but engineering, business and science. And only the wealthy could actually afford Pacific tuition; Burns and Meyer had not looked closely enough at the economics of middle-class Latin American families investing in a U.S. school. The only way to achieve the enrollment goal of roughly 50 percent Latin Americans of 250 students was to fund more scholarships than had been planned.

From the start, Covell was riding a thin edge of viability owing to heavy underwriting of students without an endowment fund to sustain it. In the first year, 39 students from 13 Latin American countries joined 21 U.S. students to launch this impressive experiment. By 1965, the U.S. Information Agency made a TV program about Covell to distribute throughout Latin America.[189] *Time* and *Newsweek* soon followed with Covell articles that spotlighted this unique experiment in higher education.[190]

The liberal arts core of the College was an integrated series of courses on inter-American affairs based in the social sciences and humanities that would produce "inter-American specialists."[191] The initial focus of the academic program was on science and mathematics, business and economics, and teacher education. As the Latin American students developed English language proficiency, they enrolled in COP or engineering courses beyond Covell, thus offering a degree of integration with the rest of the University that Raymond students lacked.

The signature of this college was *el Centro*, the student union of the little school, where *covelianos*, as they called themselves, talked, studied and played together, sharing their markedly different national backgrounds—a

Because of the great diversity of nationalities, covelianos not only learned about North and South American culture, they learned about the vast variety of Latin American cultures. (Left, Irene Bautista and Carlos Reyes perform.) Every Covell birthday deserved a pool toss.

united nations of the western hemisphere that bonded through shared experience. As their provost Arthur Cullen said, "your *convivencia*...has made you proud of your inter-American bond."[192] Their *comedor* and *casa residenciales* did more for inter-American understanding than any part of the course of study, though students relished their courses from international professors, some of real distinction, who constantly challenged them into discussions over meals and late night gatherings.

By 1970, Pacific partnered with University of Costa Rica to provide a Latin American semester for North American students, including a path-breaking required internship or experiential learning project, unheard of for study abroad at the time.[193] And by 1972, the Covell curriculum accommodated engineering course work, especially for Latin American students who wanted practical professional skills needed in their countries. Over time, Covell tried to balance its enrollment with half U.S. students in order to reduce the heavy dependence on scholarships for the South Americans. Covell alumni became prominent leaders in commerce, government, and education: Ecuador's minister of agriculture, Nicaragua's head of primary education, a Honduran institute director, a Costa Rican cement magnate, a Venezuelan entrepreneur, and a Uruguayan who works for the United Nations in Geneva.[194]

The real fringe: Callison College

What Burns could not accomplish through the Asian Institute in the fifties he would try to achieve in Callison College in the sixties. Burns' campaign to shake up the liberal arts had taken on Western culture (Raymond), Latin culture (Covell), and now had a chance to take on Eastern culture with a pioneering first. Callison would require a full year of study in Asia and an interdisciplinary concentration in Far Eastern studies for all students.

Burns had been counting on San Francisco surgeon Ferd Callison as a major donor for a new medical school they both ardently pursued. When UC's Clark Kerr axed a plan to fund private medical school students in the state legislature, Burns asked Callison to fund the third cluster, and Callison College was born in 1966.[195] Callison College would do for the

Pacific Basin what Covell was beginning to do for Latin America: create a bridge for building understanding between the United States and an emerging giant of over half the globe's population. Burns, as usual, had a big, audacious goal—nothing less than preparing America for a partnering role across the globe through these tiny colleges.

The Bauns and Burnses, together with new Callison provost Larry Jackson, the former chaplain, took another round-the-world tour to locate an appropriate study site in a non-western, developing nation, settling on India. The first year was devoted to an intensive, interdisciplinary study of the "Heritage of Man" along with science and economics. But Callison's unique distinction was the required year abroad—in Asia besides, and in India, no less. Each sophomore class of 60-some students booked a flight to Calcutta, and then rode to the University in Bangalore and the Shilton Hotel, where they had a rich a year of study and exploration. In their last two years on campus they integrated their experiential learning abroad with their academic, language, and professional goals.

Students in Callison College (1966-79) spent the sophomore year in Asia—India or Japan—immersed in cultural differences. Like Covell, this college was unique in American higher education.

The Callison faculty talked about "the five I's" of their curriculum: "individual, international, intercultural, interdisciplinary, and involved," just as the University launched a tag line with a new logo: "innovative, involved and international." Highly independent, open-minded students were drawn to the new college, ready for high adventure. "A high degree of self-assertion, sophistication, and great expectations" is how Pacific's counselor Beth Mason characterized the typical Callison student.[196]

The archaic instruction of Indian professors, the overwhelming poverty, the spicy food, the ubiquity of drugs—everything about the year in Bangalore was hugely challenging for students and faculty. When the students returned, chastened by the mind-blowing experience, they inevitably became campus leaders in forces for change—or dropped out and found their own private pathways of independence.

EMPOWERING FACULTY AND THE RISE OF THE COLLEGE

The faculty "Manifesto"

Ever since the Methodist accreditation report of 1956, the faculty, with 60 percent Ph.D.s well above the national average, had been restless with concern about the lack of formal faculty input into the direction of the College. [197] The addition of schools, especially the cluster colleges, was a brainchild of Burns and his tight circle—the board chair and his academic and business vice presidents. A 1961 "Manifesto" of complaints by 40 talented younger faculty members called the "young Turks" picked up the criticisms of the 1956 Methodist report and added to them.[198] Their faculty retreat report asked for more say in decisions, reasonable teaching loads, and improvements in such lackluster campus amenities as the student newspaper, bookstore and convocations. The campus of the lackadaisical fifties was being challenged on all fronts.

To champion these causes, the College of the Pacific got its own spokesman in the appointment of sociology professor Harold "Jake" Jacoby in 1962 as its first dean. He was a trusted, loyal, levelheaded advocate for the faculty and students of the College, offering some serious competition for resources among the other deans and provosts. Jacoby, who served as dean until 1968, "almost singlehandedly (and not without opposition) developed identity and academic integrity for the College" in the early years of renewal.[199] He began to dismantle the tyranny of department heads by rotating chairs and inviting the College Council to review curricula. By 1968 the one-woman department head had her home economics program ended. Many new young faculty like philosophy professor Herbert Reinelt and drama professor Sy Kahn came aboard, gathering frequently for sack-lunch intellectual debate at the Anderson Y, the active center of campus reform, "liberal activity," and community outreach for students and faculty alike.[200]

As the College's founding dean in 1962, sociology professor Harold "Jake" Jacoby had a profound influence on its development.

Academic Council is born

Prior to 1967, the faculty was represented by a Faculty Council composed of senior professors, department chairs and deans. Chaired by the academic vice president, it met monthly with the faculty of the whole.[201] There was rising criticism of its unrepresentative nature, especially as new, younger faculty members were hired for the emerging colleges and schools. Senior professors were almost all in the College of the Pacific. To many young professors, the Faculty Council was "not only *a* problem, it was *the* problem."[202] The full faculty meetings had become unwieldy as interests became less uniform. The faculty charged that they were not key players in the crafting of Pacific's comprehensive "12 Year Program" plan adopted in 1964 that envisioned over 4700 students. The faculty handbook setting forth the governance structure itself had been a creation of vice president Sam Meyer in 1964, rubber-stamped by the ossified Faculty Council.

Across the country, college professors, like government employees, were gaining rights to organize and many public university faculties unionized at this time.[203] At Pacific, the generally positive community of relationships among faculty, staff, administration and students sought a better path: shared governance that outlined the key responsibilities of the faculty in relation to the rest of the University. The Academic Council was established by vote of the faculty in 1967 with the blessing of the administration as the official voice of the faculty, with a faculty member elected annually as chair. The faculty gained increased stature as professionals who held primary responsibility over curriculum and instruction and shared roles in many other administrative matters.

COP curriculum renewal

In 1968, a College of the Pacific delegation of faculty and its new dean, William Binkley, proposed a "sweeping revision" of the general education program, including a new one-month "winter term" in January when students plunged into one course, often off-campus. They also recommended that four, four-unit classes per term, first proposed by dean Jacoby in 1966, replace a roster of innumerable one-to-three unit courses.[204] More important, the faculty voted to introduce a multi-disciplinary series of courses called "Information and Imagination" ("I and I") over the first two years to integrate student learning in four broad fields of study: historical-cultural studies, behavioral sciences, physical and natural sciences, and communicative and creative arts.

As all of these colossal changes were implemented, nearly every professor in the College had to scrap course materials in the old "survey" courses of the traditional disciplines of English or biology and team with colleagues in neighboring disciplines in theme-based courses.

Conservatory competition

The Conservatory also struggled to field a strong presence into the sixties. In 1962, the internationally famous American composer Roy Harris was hired, along with his wife Johana, a renowned pianist. Russell Bodley's choirs (1934-72) still commanded notice beyond the state. Former dean Howard Hanson urged several of his top Eastman graduates to the Pacific

Here shown in 1945, Conservatory dean Russell Bodley maintained dean Dennis' high reputation for the A Cappella choir from 1934-1972.

Conservatory over the years, including Russell Bodley, Preston Stedman, George Buckbee, Ira Lehn, and Warren Von Bronkhorst. Its storied reputation built over nearly a century hung on. Many Pacificans recall Burns telling of the time when Pacific was beating Cal in football and he overheard a Cal fan say in amazement, "And it's just a conservatory of music!"

But the lack of basic resources was taking its toll. Like football, music was being overtaken by the competition. The Conservatory was competitive nationally perhaps into the 1950s, but as more schools invested in quality music programs if not full conservatories, Pacific lagged, especially in facilities, equipment and scholarships. By the 1960s, when the California public universities took off, and certainly by 1978 when California's Proposition 13 practically ended public school music in the state, Pacific could rarely attract top students, at least in performance. One of the many ironies of Pacific history is understanding how generously-scholarshiped football, on a financial treadmill that could never catch the competition, siphoned resources from venerable programs like the Conservatory, which had no scholarships for outstanding players until the 1990s.

When Preston Stedman was hired as dean in 1966, he found a music school where faculty rarely performed in recitals and student "juries" did not exist.[205] He did expand instruction to all the orchestra instruments, an elementary advancement. But his ambitious vision to add a doctorate in piano performance and partner with the San Francisco Conservatory of Music went nowhere. Brusque Stedman won no friends for his open criticism of the cluster college budget drain. The administration was perfectly comfortable with a music service program that provided a cultural presence at campus and public events.

Another first: the John Muir Papers

While John Muir did not visit Pacific (shown here in 1913 with his friend John McLaren, designer of Golden Gate Park and Pacific's Stockton campus), his family placed his writings and library at Pacific, making it the world's foremost Muir collection.

One highlight in 1970 was the placing of the John Muir Papers at Pacific by his descendants. Six of his grandchildren and other family members are Pacific alumni. The Papers are the world's foremost collection of writings, notebooks, drawings, and correspondence of the pioneer environmental activist, writer, botanist, explorer and founder of the Sierra Club. This massive compilation of correspondence (now over 6700), travel journals, sketches, and his personal library of over 1000 books, easily makes Pacific home to the largest collection of Muir materials in the world. Muir had landed in San Francisco with malaria on his way to South America in 1868 and never really left California. Once he discovered "the Range of Light, surely the brightest and best that all the Lord had built," in Yosemite and the Sierra, he could not stop praising and preserving it.[206] Arguably California's most prominent citizen, he was a key player in establishing Yosemite and the national parks system. By 1984, Muir's complete works were available on microform, and today the richest parts of the collection are freely available online.[207] The California History Institute, begun in 1947, frequently focused its annual research conference on Muir, right up to the present.

THE RISE OF THE PROFESSIONAL SCHOOLS: ACQUIRING DENTISTRY AND LAW

The birth of P&S as Pacific

The decade from 1960 to 1970 saw a phenomenal spike in Pacific's enrollment, to nearly 5900 students. This growth was across the board, but mainly from the acquisitions of the law and dentistry schools and the creation of the cluster colleges. So even though national collegiate enrollment doubled in this decade, Pacific exceeded that increase by over half by the end of the golden age of American higher education that had begun in 1945.[208]

When the College of Physicians and Surgeons in San Francisco was acquired by Pacific in 1962, Burns was on a roll, having started schools of pharmacy, engineering and two cluster colleges, all within the last seven years. But what had turned his attention again to San Francisco after the Asian Academy debacle? Recall that in 1919 Methodist bishop Adna Leonard, a powerful Pacific trustee at the time, urged the board to consider buying the P&S dental school that was privately exploring a rescue by affiliation.

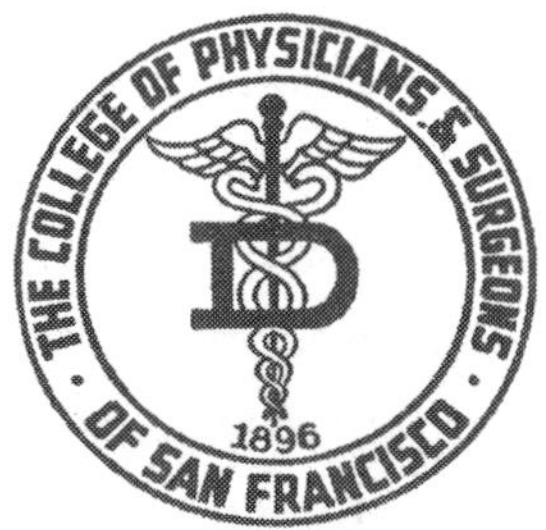

The proposal lay dormant for decades as the school found its own way as a non-profit independent, becoming a leader in dental education in the West despite another fire in

When the College of Physicians and Surgeons in San Francisco merged with Pacific in 1962, it was already 66 years old.

1926. Led by outstanding deans Arthur McDowell ('17, dean 1923-38, and national president of the American Association of Dental Schools) and Ernest Sloman ('21, dean 1938-51), "P&S" got attention with its top State Board Dental Examination scores and careful attention to alumni, whose pride, loyalty and volunteer help to P&S was higher than any other dental school. In 1942, the U.S. military requested that dental schools move to intensive, three-year, year-round programs to hasten the supply of dentists for the war effort, and P&S, along with nearly all schools, responded. By 1944, one hundred fifty eight of 160 students accepted Army and Navy commissions. After the war, the spectacular growth of the Bay area increased demand for dentists as oral health became a family priority.

By 1960, P&S, the last independent dental school in the country, was under intense pressure from the American Association of Dental Schools to affiliate with a university or forfeit accreditation. Despite the school's achievements, its disgraceful wooden building on 14th Street, thrown up after the 1906 earthquake, was condemned by the city. "It was a fire hazard. There was no running water upstairs. Students joked that the building was so feeble, the only thing holding it together must be a group of termites holding hands."[209] Still, the school was immensely popular thanks to its unrelenting focus on preparing successful practitioners and the great pride of its appreciative alumni. Among outstanding faculty was professor Charles Sweet, internationally known for pioneering pediatric dentistry.

University of San Francisco courted the school, but P&S trustees rejected an offer stiffened by restrictions.[210] Stanford's interest ran hot and cold over the years, but by 1960, Stanford was again interested in a merger. Sobered by the financial drain of its medical school, Stanford now expected P&S to raise $5 million and even to build its own new facility. Dean John Tocchini ('37) had launched a "Filling-a-Month Club" for a new building back in 1954, asking alums to donate the cost of a tooth repair toward a building fund. Steadily over the years, alumni dutifully built a war chest of over $1 million. This fundraising organization later grew into the powerful Pacific Dental Education Foundation (PDEF), the greatest fundraising machine Pacific has ever known. But five million dollars and a building in 1960? While P&S tried to cope with these impossible demands, Stanford reneged on Tocchini and moved its medical center to Palo Alto, leaving P&S in the cold.

In April, 1961, P&S board president Francis Herz met with President Burns at Masonic Order meetings to discuss a more favorable merger. While some members of Pacific's board worried about overseeing a campus two hours away, Burns could see a fresh opportunity to reclaim San Francisco after the fiasco of the Asian Institute. It could also provide him with a new footing for a possible medical school. He could see that this school offered a contrast to the state's dental schools that by now were focused on research and advanced study, not preparing professionals for practice.

The record P&S presented to the board in December was impressive: one of six applicants admitted, 96 percent retention rate of students, top scores on the national board examinations, a practice-based faculty of 117, and annual surpluses for the last six years. The problem was urgency. The American Dental Association had set a January 6, 1962 deadline for an affiliation decision to trigger an accreditation visit—handy for an eager president never too bothered by the details. At that December meeting, the Pacific board shook hands and set aside two regent positions for the P&S trustees. Frederick West ('17), one of the original five dentists to take over the school in 1923, was the first appointee. With the Burns-Baun engine behind it, Pacific found, vetted, and acquired a successful new professional school in nine months![211]

After the Pacific faculty nodded approval, the two boards quickly agreed on terms, which included $1.5 million of alumni support (and dean Tocchini had coerced each student to pledge $1,000) for a new building on the corner of Sacramento and Webster Streets in Pacific Heights. Nearly $4 million of construction funds came from the very first federal grant under President Lyndon Johnson's legislation to build medical education facilities.[212] The location was most fitting, just across the street from the original location of Pacific's medical school of 1858, which as Cooper Medical College was later acquired by Stanford to be its medical school. In July 1962, the merger was complete and construction plans began immediately. A new, nearly $9 million dental school building opened in Pacific Heights with a dedication on Pacific Founders Day, May 7, 1967.

Within five years of the merger with Pacific in 1962, the School of Dentistry had a new building in posh Pacific Heights—a huge leap forward for the school. Groundbreaking with President Burns, dean John Tocchini, and young clinic patient.

With 210,000-square feet in nine stories, the building was five times larger than the old, leaky-roofed, wooden structure downtown.

A troubled dean Tocchini, struggling with illness and leading a school of underpaid faculty with low morale who began breeding enmity among its students, finally resigned.[213] After rising leader Arthur Dugoni ('48) turned down the deanship, tough and smart Dale Retig became dean in 1969 and returned the curriculum to a three-year, year-round program by 1974. Pacific was one of 19 dental schools in the country that responded to federal grant incentives for an accelerated program in order to meet the demand of a rising middle class. Of greater significance, Retig introduced a humanistic model and science-based approach to dental education that transformed the school, and under his successor Art Dugoni, transformed all of dental education.

And why not a medical school?

If adding a dental school were not enough, Burns, now confident that his magical touch could bring success wherever he found an open handshake, saw an opportunity to start a medical school in San Francisco on the remains of the faculty and facilities vacated by Stanford. When Stanford built its new school in Palo Alto, 80 percent of the faculty remained at the Presbyterian Medical Center just across the street from Pacific's new dental school, and they urged Pacific to claim the school that Pacific had founded in 1858.

By 1962, the Institute of Medical Sciences, a freestanding research and teaching center staffed by some of these former Stanford faculty, needed university affiliation to grant graduate degrees. Pacific partnered to accommodate the need, establishing Pacific's "Graduate School of Medical Sciences" led by dean Bruce Spivey, but Burns took this as only a first step. In fact, at this very same board meeting that the medical program was approved, Burns got approval of a "School of Medical Technology" in partnership with Sutter Community Hospitals in Sacramento, which needed a bachelor's degree program for state licensure![214] This program, which enrolled students for three years at Pacific then one year at Sutter, lasted only until 1968.[215]

Despite the shortage of medical doctors in California, vice presidents Winterberg and Meyer urged Burns to forget about a medical school that would be inevitably costly for a university already over-extended.[216] Young regent Paul Davies, Jr., chair of a regent task force charged to explore it, came armed with strong objections from foundations that had seasoned experience advising cash-sucking medical schools, and joined the pair in warning against action.[217] But Burns pushed on, proposing to the state legislature that a per-student outlay of $8,000 per year to a private medical school would be half the cost of educating physicians at the public universities.

The juggernaut of Burns' ambition could hardly be stopped—and was only halted after three months in the Assembly by the powerful voice of the University of California system that decided Burns' proposal would "disrupt" the state's Master Plan for higher education. UC President Clark Kerr had it killed in committee. Most Pacific observers note with relief that UC blocked what would have been a dangerous move for Pacific, jeopardizing the health and wellbeing of a fragile, juvenile university barely able to pay its bills. Becoming beholden to the behemoth power of an endlessly expensive medical school has long been the albatross of many smaller universities. But for the unrelenting Burns, the Institute was merely a holding action for a possible future climb to a medical school.

McGeorge School of Law wins the case

Burns had been talking with the board about a law school since the mid-1950s, but failed to get strong support for a school on the Stockton Campus. By the mid-sixties, McGeorge School of Law in Sacramento was in the same situation as the P&S dental school. The American Bar Association accrediting body was pressuring all independent law schools to affiliate with comprehensive universities to broaden their base and stabilize their future. Burns asked the regents "how much of an empire" they wanted to build, laying out on the table four options of independent schools interested in affiliation, McGeorge among them.[218]

In 1965, McGeorge board chair Judge Sherrill Halbert met with Burns to explore mutual interest. The sole attorney on the Pacific board, Paul Davies, Jr., was deeply skeptical of another scheme by Burns to quickly slip another school into the fold, disregarding the burden a mediocre professional school could be for a rising Pacific.[219]

While still a small struggling school, among the 17 California law schools McGeorge ranked fifth in the percentage of graduates who passed the State Bar Exam on the first try: nearly 90 percent of the 1966 class, about 40 percent above the state average.[220] It had produced 20 percent of the attorneys practicing in the Central Valley. True, the school was still a good ways from ABA accreditation, but dean Gordon Schaber, who at age 29 succeeded John Swan (the fifth dean, 1947-57) and would serve from 1957 to 1992, had by the mid-sixties established himself as a political power broker among Democrats in Sacramento and beyond. Schaber's impressive faculty included future Supreme Court justice Anthony Kennedy and Claude Rohwer. Under Schaber's shrewd leadership McGeorge was beginning to develop a track record built on thrifty, full classes that shed unsuccessful students by the third year, so that the remaining class headed for the state bar exams would hike the pass rate. By 1963, McGeorge had earned accreditation from the State Bar Examiners. Regent Davies could not help but be impressed by both Schaber and his results.

Schaber, though hampered by polio since childhood, was immensely energetic and resourceful—a natural partner that Burns saw as a dynamic leader with a solid "commitment to diversity and innovation."[221] In his first year as dean in 1957 Schaber moved the school from its third home at the corner of 9th and J Streets in downtown Sacramento to its current location in Oak Park, starting in a former pediatric clinic building at the corner of Fifth Avenue and 33rd Street. Himself a celebrated Superior Court judge, Schaber had a vision to develop a law school built on practical skills in a clinical program of actual courtroom experience, much like the clinically based dental school. In the end, Gordon Schaber won over regent Davies despite his continuing misgivings, and Davies let the partnership proceed, much to his and other regents' high satisfaction over the years.

Dean Schaber himself was cautious about the merger, but he needed Pacific: lack of university affiliation and a day program blocked ABA accreditation. Schaber, a clever and diplomatic negotiator, worked out a deal with Burns to assure that McGeorge would pay only a flat fee of $100,000 annually and retain its own budget and any net revenue throughout the life of the lease on the one law building at the time.[222] Within months they had a deal and merged assets with Pacific in 1966, when McGeorge had the highest bar pass rate in the state.[223] Burns brought the law school to the head of the line on federal loans to build low-interest student housing on a growing campus that added acreage by the year. In its first year, the new daytime program enrolled 135 students, twice what was expected, to reach 350 students in 1967. By 1968 ABA accreditation was achieved.[224] TV actor "attorney" Raymond Burr joined 41 percent of the alumni in contributing to library and classroom construction.[225] The *Pacific Law Journal* was first published in 1970, when enrollment had jumped to 700, the 30th largest law school in the country.

THE BURNS LEGACY

Burns drives to the end

In fall 1969, Burns was diagnosed with bone cancer, but the optimistic Burns kept the news private even as he checked in as the first patient in the new Cowell Health Center on campus. After only three years at Pacific, academic vice president Bevan had a heart attack and resigned.[226] Burns reluctantly agreed to the search committee's recommendation to hire Alistair McCrone, not the obvious choice for Bevan's replacement: an inexperienced 37-year-old as well as the first non-churchman in the job. Within months he would become acting president.

Not to be held back, Burns flew to Costa Rica, then to Japan by the end of 1970. He took another world tour early in 1971, from Hong Kong to Paris, boasting that he had more stamina than the rest of his party, only to return to a hospital bed in Stockton for ten days before succumbing to heart failure.[227] He had no known succession plan. Many Pacificans were shocked to hear of his death, not surprisingly, since Burns and Baun had kept secret his advancing cancer. At the crowded memorial service, board chair Ted Baun saluted Burns for building "a university of worldwide influence," which fairly expressed the scope of his achievement. "His worry," Baun said, "was that dreams and plans of today would be so small the future would be handicapped." That worry drove Burns to the extreme in expanding Pacific's future by forging a wide pathway of innovations.

The location of Burns' ashes was a secret for years. In 2001, alumnus David Gerber pressed long-time staff reliable, Pearl Piper. She confirmed their location in the basement of Burns Tower, placed there by his devoted assistant Alice Saecker ('43), who "did not want to put his remains out where they could be desecrated" by a law at the time that forbade keeping ashes on private property.[228] They still lie there, no doubt at the request of Burns himself.

Burns' breathtaking achievement

When Burns first visited Pacific for a high school YMCA conference in the 1920s, he said "it was literally love at first sight." Burns never lost that love.[229] His favorite line of verse inscribed on a wall of the Library of Congress is a fitting epitaph for this greatest of Pacific visionaries: "Too low they build, who build beneath the stars."[230] No one ever accused Burns of aiming too low. While most informed followers of Pacific might assert that he has been Pacific's best president, he certainly has been Pacific's most transformative president.

In the end, the overall record is indisputable. Burns changed the fundamental identity of Pacific by creating a new university in the fifties and sixties while retaining the founding core values that remain today: a commitment to the development of the whole student through close interaction with faculty and staff —a "personalized education," and a residential life that grows students into responsible leaders, grounded in a Methodist tradition passionate about human possibility through education.

From 1946 to 1971, enrollment multiplied eight times, from roughly 700 students to 5500, while faculty grew sixfold to over 400 to maintain a favorable ratio for learning. Stockton campus housing quadrupled from 500 to nearly 2000 to assure a lively residential community for learning. Student aid increased tenfold to assure diverse voices and cultures in the mix. Two valuable new campuses were added in San Francisco and Sacramento, and the Stockton campus value increased from $1.6 million to nearly $40 million as 26 new buildings (12 residence halls) were constructed. The three large professional schools of dentistry, pharmacy, and law gained accreditation. Alumni donor support increased from 5 to 27 percent (for a time). And yes, endowment increased from less than $700,000 to nearly $5 million to match other growth indicators.

Here is the remarkable, indeed astonishing, record of school and college foundings at Pacific during the heart of the Burns years:

1955—Pharmacy School
1958—Engineering School
1962—Dental School
1962—Raymond College
1963—Covell College
1966—Law School
1966—Callison College
1968—Medical Sciences

Eight new schools and colleges in 13 years. And to think Burns had already fielded the American Academy of Asian Studies (1954-59), was "this close" to founding a medical school, tried the Sacramento School of Medical Technology (1963-68) and added two doctoral programs in chemistry and English. In 1970, each college and school had its own custom graduation ceremony to match the anomalous ceremonies already afoot by the Raymond, Pharmacy and Dentistry calendars. It was a breath-taking accomplishment.

Burns' four key limitations

The limits of the Burns administration were less apparent to their contemporaries, but not absent. Four areas of performance kept surfacing throughout the Burns era: a Board of Regents that failed to engage, a penchant for runaway innovation, neglect of established programs, and underfunding bold ideas. Burns loved working with people and persuaded many talented colleagues to come to an out-of-the-way college. He sought their ideas daily and welcomed honest criticism. But with the board of trustees/regents, he forged close friendships with only two leaders, Ted Baun and bishop Donald Tippett. The rest of the board supported him at nearly every turn, but lacked the serious involvement required of regents today to make wise decisions for an independent university. Impatient Burns preferred to sail his ideas through the board quickly rather than urge careful analysis and thoughtful reflection.

He built trust with a strong chair, Ted Baun, who really ran the board meetings himself as a crusty veteran who served 44 years as regent. Not infrequently he and Burns comprised the decision-making of Pacific, along with business officer Winterberg and fundraiser Rudkin and an academic vice president from time to time. This Burns-Baun partnership enabled Pacific to try experiments, move boldly ahead, change on a dime and transform Pacific without serious challenge or testing. This partnership was perhaps too close. Regents became too comfortable letting a pair of strong leaders do the creative hard work of fashioning a university, though this impairment was not uncommon for university boards across the country in this era. This culture of disengaged regents would haunt Pacific for the next 30 years.

Second, Burns' relentless pursuit of innovation, however admirable, should be tempered by recent research that identifies the limits of innovation in any organization, research that shows innovation itself not as important as other qualities to build long-term success.[231] Burns' general neglect of analysis in a hurry to act contradicts the steady reflection of mature organizations. His readiness to act without proper financial backing is easy to see in hindsight—but in the heady bubble of growth in the sixties, it seemed less to worry about. His eagerness to pursue the new meant little testing and analysis, epitomized by his serial plan to add many cluster colleges without assuring that even one could be sustainable.

Third, neglecting the needs of established academic programs was a frequent complaint, and while a familiar criticism of many college presidents, in Burns' case it was especially stark for the College and the schools of music, education and engineering. Academic quality is typically built over time by steady investment. For example, neighboring Santa Clara University had accredited law and engineering schools by 1937, and its business school founded in 1923 achieved accreditation by 1953.[232] Pacific's indecision about its identity and its future delayed for years its achievement of academic distinction. Yes, federal funds for health education coincided nicely with the acquisitions of dentistry and pharmacy, but the relentless push to fund cluster colleges in the end stunted the growth of established schools that have suffered lean years for decades since. The unachievable goal of building a big-time football program as collegiate football moved into the modern era was another audacious ambition that overran the needs of a campus hungry to achieve quality.

Finally, funding innovation was as much of a challenge as resourcing the old. As in the past, the endowment fell far short of competitor schools, but especially by the end of the sixties the endowment was woefully inadequate to sustain an array of 11 small schools and colleges.[233] Willamette University, Pacific's partner Methodist school in Oregon, by disciplining its expansion to only 1600 liberal arts students, had meanwhile grown its endowment to double that of Pacific's.[234] While some regents complained about a neglected endowment, Burns argued that new ventures would "pay for themselves," though he himself vaguely envisioned a $50 million endowment by the late 1970s.[235] Yet just as Pacific had borrowed from its endowment in the 1920s to fund residence halls, so in the sixties Pacific schools that have suffered lean years for decades since. The unachievable goal of building a big-time football program as collegiate football moved into the modern era was another audacious ambition that overran the needs of a campus hungry to achieve quality.

Finally, funding innovation was as much of a challenge as resourcing the old. As in the past, the endowment fell far short of competitor schools, but especially by the end of the sixties the endowment was woefully inadequate to sustain an array of 11 small schools and colleges.[233] Willamette University, Pacific's partner Methodist school in Oregon, by disciplining its expansion to only 1600 liberal arts students, had meanwhile grown its endowment to double that of Pacific's.[234] While some regents complained about a neglected endowment, Burns argued that new ventures would "pay for themselves," though he himself vaguely envisioned a $50 million endowment by the late 1970s.[235] Yet just as Pacific had borrowed from its endowment in the 1920s to fund residence halls, so in the sixties Pacific used bequests and major gifts to plug budget holes and feed new ventures instead of steadily building the endowment like most private universities did. This failure to adopt a disciplined plan to invest in endowment was not addressed until the 1990s.

These four limitations—a distant board, a passion for novelty, a disregard for traditional programs, a cash-and-carry funding plan—are reminders that however successful the Burns years were for Pacific, its "leading edge" identity was perilous for a school that was now, in a sense, again in its infancy as a brand new university created in 1961.

Burns' fourfold transformation

In the end, President Burns' transformative role for Pacific was massively fourfold: pushing to get Pacific out front in "active learning" that eventually flowered in a nationally regarded general education program 40 years later; focusing attention on international education that is enduring; asserting Pacific's regional footprint from the coast to the Foothills, from San Francisco to Sacramento; and especially in building an emerging university from a small, still rather quaint, Methodist liberal arts college.

call "engaged, active learning." Since the 1990s, all of higher education has joined this bandwagon, but in 1960 it was, as Burns said, a "covered wagon" frontier journey.

Burns may have himself been on the pulse of change, but most especially the academic leaders and faculty he brought to deliver this new education were pioneers in learning. As iconic civil engineering professor Dave Fletcher once remarked, "After all, as professors we don't really do a lot of teaching, but we try to get the students to do a whole lot of learning."[236] Burns himself likely did not fully understand what was developing in Raymond and the other clusters, but he relished the results of all those stellar faculty and students, and the rest followed. The three professional schools of pharmacy, dentistry and law along with engineering added to this impetus by championing practice-based programs that engaged students actively in the clinic, pharmacy store, court room, and draft table.

Burns' second transformative role was to bind international/intercultural education into Pacific's DNA. Burns saw the importance of Latin America for the U.S. just at the time the nation's new president did the same, not years later. And then he acted boldly to create a new approach to international education—a Spanish-speaking inter-American college—that remains a compelling need in the country today and could be sustainable with sufficient funding.

His own personal commitment to international and intercultural education is writ across his record, and it is part and parcel of his support for an inter-racial campus fired by his bold decision to fund the Community Involvement Program. And he anticipated by years, maybe decades, the importance of Asia for America—he talked about the "rise of the Pacific Basin century" and thus launched Callison College. Pacific's commitment to intercultural and international education has been strong and distinctive ever since.

Burns' third transformative role was to reclaim northern California as Pacific's campus, beginning with the array of programs in the late forties from Dillon Beach on the coast to Fallon House in the Foothills to his persistent aim to have an important presence in San Francisco and Sacramento through partnership acquisitions. This concept of a multicampus university began in 1858 with the San Francisco medical school and the late nineteenth-century plan to place the administration of Pacific in San Francisco with campuses in Napa and San Jose, but only Burns made that plan a reality.

Burns' final transformative role was to recreate Pacific, symbolically beginning in 1961 by reclaiming the original name of University of Pacific, but actually by rejecting the fear of parochial faculty and trustees stuck in the past, and almost single-handedly pulling in professional schools at the same time he was populating the campus with small liberal arts colleges. This combination of investing in a reform of liberal education while daring to build and acquire unaccredited professional schools made what Pacific has become today: a distinctive university that champions personalized, holistic, liberal learning across the schools to leaven professional programs with a wider world view to prepare graduates for professional practice and citizenship.

From our vantage point today, the Burns years seem almost recklessly ambitious. But for a quarter of a century Burns captured the spirit of the times and understood that Pacific would be lost in the shuffle of burgeoning California higher education unless it embraced growth and innovation, when the UCs, CSUs, and the community colleges were escalating at a record pace. He coupled this drive for change with a rock-solid commitment to intellectual freedom that helped him weather the turbulent sixties better than nearly every other college president, and a pursuit of excellence that produced some remarkable academic achievements despite a naïve understanding of the true costs of excellence. Certainly today Pacificans celebrate the brilliant decisions to launch pharmacy and acquire dentistry and law. They have been wonderfully successful and the financial anchors that have sustained virtually all other academic programs to create a unique blend of quality programs—the only private university in the country under 10,000 students with nine schools.

CHAPTER 4

Thriving through adversity, 1971-1980s

Modern Stockton—McCaffrey begins in 1971—
Delta Campus acquired—Alumni renewal—Cluster College closings—
College and schools mature—Student life organized—Diversity begins—
Dentistry and Law rise—Athletics triumphs and troubles—
Business and SIS born

A DIFFERENT WORLD

Tough times

As one historian summarized it, all universities and colleges "experienced turbulent waters between 1970 and 1980," and Pacific was part of this national instability.[1]

The bloating of American higher education through the sixties had depended on endless enrollment growth and funding. Almost from the day President Burns died, Pacific was thrown into an era of uncertainty that would not end, an uncertainty driven by a nation over-extended by runaway inflation coupled with declining productivity ("stagflation") and soaring oil prices, self-doubt from the Vietnam war, and pragmatic assessment of a possible no-growth future.

The local scene was not much better as Stockton lived through historic growth in size and decline in the streets.[2] From 1960-75, the city grew nearly as much as the prior hundred years to over 100,000, with an influx of immigrants and the emergence of a suburban commuter population that grew with highways to the Bay and the capital. The *braceros* program had assured the Mexican farm worker shuttle to and from Mexico. When the program ended in 1964, Mexican families along with many Asian immigrants settled in Stockton as year-round farm workers and manual laborers on marginal incomes. War refugees from Southeast Asia—Vietnam, Laos, and Cambodia—were welcomed by Catholic Charities and other church groups to resettle in the city. Schools, social services, and criminal justice—all had heavy loads, later intensified by the state's decision to build prisons around the county.

In many respects the city was an image of the larger region. The great Central Valley and its rich soil depended on farm laborers, often undocumented immigrants, who typically were tied to poverty and illiteracy. Leonard Gardner's novel *Fat City* (1969, movie 1972) depicted Stockton citizens who did not benefit from federal and state largess, a permanent underclass that struggled to survive amid the country's most abundant food basket. This agricultural reality destined the Central Valley to be a major national region of neglect, exceeding even the infamous eastern Appalachia region in poverty and its host of associated deprivations. The shift to suburban growth as well as the lack of civic leadership after the war left the city and county under the sway of a few powerful developers who saw rebuilding downtown as too risky. The bankers, led by Bank of Stockton's Robert Eberhardt ('57), did what they could to foster civic responsibility and downtown renewal, but there was never adequate collective action to stave off the forces of decline.

The Bay wins over the Valley

Through the Burns years, the board added as many members from the Central Valley as from the larger Bay area, so when time came to select

President Stan McCaffrey (1971-87) was popular with students because he remembered names and understood their campus needs. The tiger was starring in a movie filmed on campus, "The World's Greatest Athlete" (1973).

a new president, it came down to a Valley candidate, alumnus Robert Monagan ('42), Republican Assembly leader and former mayor of Tracy, versus the head of the influential Bay Area Council of business and civic leaders, Stanley McCaffrey, who had worked for UC president Clark Kerr as well as for his high school classmate from Whittier, vice president Richard Nixon.

Even though Eberhardt and other Valley regents promoted Monagan (Eberhardt had been Monagan's campaign treasurer for years), the vote went for McCaffrey, despite well-known realities: McCaffrey's deep loyalty to Cal, where he had been captain of the football team and a Phi Beta Kappa student body president before his many years on the staff, and his focused enthusiasm for Rotary International (vice president for ten years).[3]

But McCaffrey was a wonderful "people person" who could remember names with uncanny accuracy, and he certainly looked the part—a president "right out of central casting," as Judy Chambers put it. McCaffrey's wife Beth was an especially strong asset. She along with Grace Burns was perhaps the most admired first lady of Pacific. Lovely, bright, poised, classy, beautiful, a regent of the Pacific School of Religion in Berkeley for two decades, she had all the traits of a leader who knew how to support her president. She sat as a silent sentinel at nearly all board meetings while McCaffrey was in office.[4]

A shaky start

Just as president McCaffrey was walking in the Burns Tower door, budgets were being cut. In his first board meeting, McCaffrey called enrollment one of the most serious issues facing Pacific, knowing that the seventies would produce fewer college students than the prior decade.[5] Falling enrollments, national inflation, and squeezed budgets forced Pacific to review programs and activities across the board.

In McCaffrey's first fall on campus, a shortfall of over 200 Stockton campus students forced a salary and hiring freeze that was contentious. Not only were state schools getting 7.5 percent raises, but the board was unwilling to let the thriving Schools of Law and Dentistry off the hook to fill Stockton campus budget holes. In just three years, dean Redig argued, dentistry had doubled its budget and tripled its faculty to 92. Extra payments to Stockton would cripple a rising school. He threatened to resign.[6]

Director of dining services Paul Fairbrook, darling of the campus for his high-quality meals, service delivered with panache, and readiness to partner with any campus organization, painfully reported that skyrocketing food costs would require food portions and "second helpings" to be curtailed to make it through the year.[7] Then the first real energy crisis hit in 1973, when oil ran short and prices spiked. Heat was set at 68 degrees, carpools were started, and students were consolidated into residence halls so some dorms could be shut down.

Faculty in the crossfire

Through the seventies, Pacific tuition increases went through the roof, yet the Consumer Price Index seemed to rise even higher. One key driver was faculty and staff salaries. With hefty tuition hikes annually, the regents poured money into faculty salaries to keep Pacific competitive. By this time, the Stockton campus, with 4,000 students, 1100 employees and a $22 million payroll, was pumping $5 million a year into the Stockton economy.[8] By 1978 Stockton campus faculty salaries finally reached the long-term 60th percentile goal of comparable independent national universities. University-wide faculty salaries reached the 80th percentile. Neither achievement lasted long.[9] A salary freeze in 1983 dropped the competitive ranking, so by 1985, when Pacific had more senior professors than 40 comparable universities, salaries plummeted to about the 40th percentile.[10]

One curious note is that Pacific students at the time told the regents they wanted all faculty raises to be based on merit as an incentive to improve teaching.[11] While the faculty repelled this call, insisting that most of the increase be "cost of living" adjustment, the board adopted an all-merit salary increase policy.[12]

PACIFIC SURGES AHEAD

Against the current

To combat the national shrinkage in college-going students, Pacific expanded a strategy to recruit more transfer students. While colleges across the country faced an enrollment slump, Pacific saw the largest entering class ever in 1974, topped the next year by an even larger class of 1300 new students. Pacific's enrollment peak at nearly 6200 students in 1976 was not matched again until 2004. The influx came mainly through generous admissions for transfer students from Delta College and other community colleges as well as four-year schools: 570 students, the largest transfer class ever. This dependency on undergraduate transfer students continued and increased over the next two decades.

But the freshman class was impressive as well: 3.3 GPA (highest on record), six National Merit Scholars, and while one-fourth of the undergraduates were receiving Cal Grants from the state (comparable to USC, Stanford, and Santa Clara), still only 55 percent received some form of financial aid. Though enrollment was down by over 100 students in 1978 as interest in the cluster colleges waned, the freshman class nearly met the 1974 record as students lined up to enroll in business and engineering, while a new bachelor's in fine arts and a pre-med biochemistry major were added.

By the late seventies, 36 percent of graduates were pursuing advanced degrees, while 90 percent had jobs within six months of graduation.[13] No surprise, then, that over 80 percent of the freshman had selected Pacific as their first-choice school based on its academic reputation in the late seventies.[14] Amid the enrollment doldrums of most American universities,

Pacific was doing remarkably well through the 1970s, leading McCaffrey to declare fairly in 1978 that Pacific had "never been in a stronger position in all its history than right now."[15]

McCaffrey's fourfold agenda

When McCaffrey began his presidency, he had in mind a few key goals that translated into four objectives: improve Stockton campus facilities, build a fundraising organization, strengthen alumni and community relations, and engage the Board of Regents.

He and his vice president and executive assistant, Clifford Dochterman, saw the blatant neglect of the existing physical Stockton campus during the heyday of Burns' expansive vision to add and add again more schools to the University's portfolio and to build the academic reputation of Pacific. To two newcomers who had worked at Cal, the diminutive campus looked in desperate need of expansion. There was no student center to speak of, the library was scandalously small, the community college that flanked the campus on the south was mainly a squadron of metal army barracks, basketball games were downtown, and the 50 acres of campus were littered with Quonset huts that served as offices and classrooms for many disciplines. Where was the campus that lived up to Pacific's storied reputation across the state, built on the stature of Tully Knoles and the visionary power of Bob Burns? The dorms were shabby and faculty offices disgraceful. Foremost on McCaffrey's mind was building facilities that could match the ambitious programs Burns had created.

Second, McCaffrey saw no organized fundraising structure to execute a capital campaign to fund the bricks-and-mortar job ahead. Again, Burns' exceptional talent, energy and success masked a harsh truth: Pacific had been passed by in the development of the modern university; strong offices for fundraising, public relations, and alumni development were all essentially done by a president who thrived till 1971, well into the modern era of American universities.

When Bob Eberhardt became chair, he understood the essential philanthropic role of regents. Because an effective fundraising campaign would require improved relations with alumni and the community, outreach to both audiences became a third area of priority, one which McCaffrey and Dochterman were well prepared to tackle.

A fourth challenge was one of the most difficult to meet. The Board of Regents was an insular group committed to the school that did not offer the financial support expected by trustees of most organizations. Only one or two major donors on the board understood this philanthropic responsibility. Changing this culture of ignoring the obligation to "give or get" dollars to advance the University continued to be an issue with the board for decades.

Building begins

Before McCaffrey was appointed, the Pacific Athletic Foundation—founded in Bob Eberhardt's living room—had already begun planning a $3 million, 7500-seat basketball pavilion across the street from the new Olympic-sized swimming pool. The PAF proposed a partnership with the city for a joint sports and exposition center, but the deal fell through in 1976 because the city could not afford it.[16] By 1978, the "Events Center" had raised lead gifts from regents Alex Spanos ('48), Eberhardt and others toward a ballooning goal that grew first to $4.5 million, then to over $8 million, requiring that nearly half the cost be financed.[17]

The board's decision to name the pavilion the Alex G. Spanos Center honored multiple gifts from the Spanos family over a decade, including an endowment for the annual COP Spanos Teaching Award, which grew in prestige over the decades.[18] The Spanos Center opened in 1982. The following year, Spanos provided a generous gift to build the Pacific Center over the stadium, to fund the library, and mainly to renovate the conservatory auditorium. The hall

The Alex G. Spanos Center in 1982 was a landmark for what was to become the home of Pacific's two top sports, women's volleyball and men's basketball, along with many other sports and campus and community events.

Alex Spanos and Bob Hope were good friends—and soft-shoe dancing partners. Spanos family members have been regents from 1972 to the present.

was renamed the Faye Spanos Concert Hall in 1987 at a spectacular gala with the Spanos' Hollywood friends Bob Hope, Telly Savalas, Vic Damone, and Diahann Carroll, along with the University choir and orchestra.[19]

Delta becomes Pacific

The next stage for a campus upgrade was to add—another campus. When the San Joaquin Delta Community College Board/Stockton Unified School District finally wrung out a decision to sell the old 42-acre campus property in 1974, Pacific was of course waiting at the front of the line, as it had been for over a decade. While Pacific's campus had doubled in size to 100 acres since 1924, with 75 buildings scattered across it, Pacific needed some growing room.[20] Stockton had rescued Pacific through the Stockton College partnership, and now it would revive Pacific through the sale of the campus.

Acquiring the campus of Stockton College might have been an obvious decision to any administration and board of regents, but it was McCaffrey's role to execute it, and he did so against other Stockton community groups beseeching the city council to set aside the land for their public causes. The Chamber of Commerce, *Stockton Record*, and Pacific Avenue merchants all lined up behind the University, and Pacific was finally the only bidder.[21] Pacific patched together funds from property sales west along Pershing Avenue to fund the $4.5 million purchase and the $1 million needed to renovate the shabby facilities. Pacific removed 28 temporary buildings that had been war-surplus military barracks, lined up row upon row across the acres, leaving nine buildings standing.

A south aerial view of Stockton College shows the campus crowded with war-surplus buildings.

After the 28 temporary metal barracks buildings were torn away, the first building renovated was the old Delta College library, which now became Pacific's School of Education.[22] The Conservatory claimed education's vacated Owen Hall for student practice rooms in 1975. Owen, the old war surplus barracks, has been the heart of 24-hour musical practice ever since, despite its many drawbacks.

Gradually, as refurbishing could be afforded, departments of physics, mathematics, chemistry and biology migrated into the permanent structures that bordered Mendocino Avenue and began to gain ground. After surviving its Quonset hut life for years and enduring the resignations of two key faculty members over the football issue, physics grew when vice president Sam Meyer gave all his discretionary dollars to physics for two years to build a master's program.[23]

Drama and dance, communicative disorders, and psychology took over other existing buildings. The old Delta College auditorium became Pacific's Long Theatre when Tom Long gave nearly $700,000 to move the theatre program out of the Rotunda on the north campus to make more room for pharmacy.[24] Despite its generous renovation, the Long Theatre ever remained a second-rate facility, clearly not designed for theatre productions, unsuitable for a school that had such a storied reputation in theatre. But this was the continuing trade-off: the College of the Pacific got a new campus with improved and expanded facilities. Not what it needed, but what was the best available at the time, even if the fortunes of the campus were on the upswing with the opening of the new student University Center.

A renewed alumni board turns to Feather River Inn

McCaffrey's third priority, to improve outreach to alumni and community, began with a thorough rebuilding of alumni relations. By 1973 alumni giving had dropped from a peak of 25 percent in 1959 to 13 percent, well below the national average of 20 percent for private schools. Something new had to be done, and Dochterman went about building change. Given that half of Pacific's living alumni had graduated since 1970, this was a time for alumni renewal. The alumni board was doubled in size to 30, and phone call campaigns began. The senior class pledge was restarted, an alumni admissions representative program began, and the class agent program re-introduced, with 64 class agents identified.[25] The "Half Century Weekend" for the 50th anniversary class began at the 1977 commencement, the same year the annual "Alumni Fellows Day" dreamed up by regent George Wilson brought alumni back to thc classrooms.[26] Annual alumni awards began in 1981. Twelve regional clubs sprouted up over the next decade.

When in 1977 regent Tom Long donated the Feather River Inn Prep School, an historic railway lodge and golf course in Plumas County, he set afoot a saga that reshaped the alumni board and, many would say, diverted attention and resources away from the central role of the association for over two decades. But it certainly was an attractive resource, valued at nearly $1 million at the time, so the regents accepted the offer with enthusiasm, despite the rag-tag condition of both the students and the facilities.

The Feather River Inn in Plumas County was a popular setting for alumni and other gatherings, but it became an expensive distraction for the Alumni Association over the decades until it was sold in 2004.

The alumni board threw itself into the massive project of restoring the rustic resort to make it attractive for summer alumni family camps. When alumni director Kara Brewer called for an alumni board planning retreat at FRI in 1981, many saw this event as the "real start" of the modern alumni association. Soon-to-be board chair Nancy Spiekerman ('57) started the Orange Aide Volunteers, a group of 100 Stockton women, not all alumnae, who bolstered admissions efforts by aiding families of student prospects.[27] Alumni family camp began at FRI and thrived for nearly two decades. Soon bylaws, term limits, and younger alumni led the alumni board forward.

The Alumni Association took over the management of FRI in 1988 after the Board of Regents closed the sagging prep school and nearly sold the $1 million camp. Spearheaded by regents Walt Baun ('53) and Nancy Spiekerman, the alumni board rejuvenated its commitment to make a real go of the attractive, rustic forest retreat. Spurred on by Chris Greene ('58), Alex and Jeri Vereschagin ('57), Ken Mork ('50) and others, alumni organized dozens of Elderhostel events and booked many campus groups for retreats to build support for improvements. But the long drive to the northern Sierras made its demands, and despite organized efforts to increase its use, interest faded. Improved alumni involvement had been one of McCaffrey's four goals, and the Feather River Inn (FRI) was an avenue that presented itself. In the long run, it was never clear how the resort fit into a larger picture.

Board building

Addressing his fourth priority, McCaffrey began to recruit local wealthy businessmen like Alex Spanos ('48) and call in the chips on his Bay area and Bohemian Club friends. Among them were such prominent business and civic leaders as Robert Haas, member of the influential Levi Straus family; Stephen Bechtel, Jr. of the giant Bechtel engineering firm; Tom Witter of the Dean Witter clan; Cecil Humphreys ('27), president of Shell Oil; Jacqueline (Jack) Hume, food-processing magnate and a member of President Reagan's "kitchen cabinet;" Roy Brandenburger, Monsanto vice president; Richard Landis, Del Monte president; and Holt Atherton, now

State senate majority leader George Moscone ('53) became known for inclusive civic government as mayor of San Francisco, then was assassinated in 1978.

in Texas, who combined the powerful and successful Stockton families of the renowned tractor-inventor Benjamin Holt and the legendary leader of the American Legion Warren Atherton.[28] (Along the way, San Francisco mayor, former state senate majority leader, and Pacific alumnus George Moscone ('53) was awarded an honorary degree in 1976.)

Powerhouse corporate leadership was never so strong as during this era. This was Pacific's moment to engage the strategic vision and philanthropic interest of wealthy Bay Area families that had eluded the University from the start, now part of a region that was the fourth-largest metro area in the U.S. by the early 1970s. Not surprisingly, it came under the leadership of a president who was in no way limited by the Methodist community of friends. By 1976, only eleven of the 36 board members were alumni.

CONSOLIDATION AFTER THE 60s: CLUSTER COLLEGE ENDINGS

An era closing

By the time the Vietnam War and military draft ended in 1973, the age of campus protests was over. The market for "experimental colleges" declined dramatically in the seventies and eighties. Students had other goals in mind than the independent, personal exploration that defined the Raymond and Callison student. The steady fall-off of student interest in the cluster colleges through the 1970s was part of a national trend that tightened family decisions about the purpose of college and what it was good for. Middle-class families looked at Raymond, Callison and Covell and saw an amorphous idealism that could not assure security in middle-class professions. In fall 1971, Raymond had 61 applications.[29] America's college students settled down to a practical reality: "disciplined training leading to the professions—the curriculum—had the surest potential economic benefit."[30] For Pacific and nearly every other university, this reality became the students' polestar for the decades to come.

As the cluster college students dwindled, the other Pacific schools grew, although Covell College, with the heaviest scholarship subsidy and ties to professional programs, attracted students for a longer time and peaked at 201 students in 1975. None of the Colleges had more than about 200 freshman applicants per year, and by the mid-seventies, fewer than 100 applicants per college.[31] All three Pacific cluster colleges thrived longer than most of these experiments across the country.[32] Perhaps one reason was that Pacific clusters all valued experiential learning through internships and study abroad.[33]

Raymond College

In 1971 Raymond had to do something to broaden its appeal. The college shifted to a 4-1-4 calendar like the other undergraduate schools, discarded any major, bolstered career-oriented internships, and ended the science requirement—heresy certainly to the early Raymond ideal of a rigorous and regimented classical liberal studies program. But all these shifts helped: enrollment crept back, and the heart of Raymond endured, even if in hindsight the "open curriculum" might have fit the "self-realization" era of the sixties, not the track-oriented curriculum of the seventies.

By 1974, the Raymond faculty was forced to make more: they offered grades and pre-professional tracks for more career-minded students. After all, while 44 percent of freshman students favored abolishing college grades in 1969, ten years later only 11 percent agreed.[34] But other features of the old colleges endured: dances in the Great Hall, the joint Halloween LSD parties with Callison, "lodgeball," the "massage workshops" and co-ed showers in John Ballantyne Hall. When Callison introduced co-ed housing in 1967, it actually worked so well in promoting healthier relationships between men and women that co-ed halls expanded rapidly.[35]

But even in 1975, when all other Pacific schools saw an enrollment uptick, Raymond continued its downward slide along with the "baby bust" of the times. Vice president Hand reported to the board that Raymond would have to end and merge with COP, and asserted that the cluster college approach of starting new programs from scratch would have to end. Only new programs that built on existing faculty made sense in an era of austerity. The Academic Council supported a merger of Raymond and Callison colleges on a two-year trial basis in 1977.

"Ray-Cal," as the merger was called, preserved the interdisciplinary, non-departmental structure of the two colleges as well as Raymond's strong internship program and Callison's year of study in Japan. Of course students in these colleges protested. They marched to the Tower and took it over for a night. Their Homecoming parade float was "The Shotgun Wedding of Raymond and Callison." Christian Jutt ('79) organized a "funeral" for the two colleges, constructed two coffins labeled Raymond and Callison, and led a procession through campus, culminating in a service where chapel dean Meredith offered a eulogy.[36] By 1979, a campus committee recommended ending the Ray-Cal experiment and folding its international program into COP, ending a 17-year run. In less than a decade, this program would again move out of the College to form the core of the School of International Studies.

Raymond's legacy

As a pioneer (though not inventor) in redefining how best to learn, Raymond bestowed a profound legacy on Pacific's undergraduate program. Most important, Raymond introduced the concept and practice of learner-centered teaching which, decades later, has come to define undergraduate education. As vice president Sam Meyer said of Raymond, "The emphasis was to be on *learning* rather than on *teaching*. There is a vital difference."[37] As the Raymond approach infiltrated the College and other schools, Pacific began to adopt the focus on student learning rather than "inputs" by the professor. Raymond professors John Williams (English), Bob Orpinela (philosophy), Steve Anderson (biology) and John Smith (English) epitomized this engaged approach to learning.

Second, Raymond's emphasis on liberal education, on the importance of the core liberal arts and sciences disciplines, not primarily on skills acquisition, became a signature feature of the College, intensified by fostering independent study and student research. Third, Raymond set a higher academic standard for liberal arts learning that raised academic expectations for all of general education at Pacific, with a special accent on interdisciplinary studies that has flourished at Pacific ever since. Fourth, Raymond's three-year accelerated degree introduced the notion that the traditional four square years required for a bachelor's degree could be challenged. Intensified learning under a speedy calendar could work for certain students. Accelerated programs have become one of the signature features of Pacific, most especially in linking the College to dentistry, law, and pharmacy. Fifth, Raymond's deliberate "learning community" of students and staff, and of students living and learning together in groups and teams, has become important for the rest of Pacific's residential campus, especially the "theme" residence halls. Lastly, the deliberate effort to cultivate the undergraduate "seminar," a small class animated by intense exchange and discussion, has been kept alive in the three interdisciplinary core courses of the general education program now known as the "Pacific Seminars," required of all undergraduates.[38]

Raymond stands out as a key pioneering laboratory for the future that lay ahead for Pacific. No wonder Raymond alumni have gathered for reunions about every five years since 1985. Among outstanding alumni are Edna Turner DeVore ('67), head of the education arm of the NASA-funded Search for Extraterrestrial Intelligence Institute (SETI), Peter Morales ('67), elected as the first Latino president of the Unitarian Universalist Association in 2009, and Dorothy Wilson Leland ('66), appointed chancellor of UC-Merced in 2011.

Callison College

The vision of Callison College was to provide a liberal education accented by immersion in a non-Western culture to alter students' outlook on the world regardless of major.[39] As professor Larry Meredith said, Callison was "education for global awareness," especially through the sophomore year of living in India. In addition to Meredith, Callison was gifted with outstanding faculty like Len Humphreys and Jerry Hewitt, who led students through profound, life-changing learning, and Cort Smith and Bruce LaBrack, who both later anchored Callison's successor, the School of International Studies. The faculty fostered the independent development of each student. Callison students came eager for this kind of learning—more independent, creative, flexible, and self-assertive than most students on the campus.

Callison moved its overseas program to Kansai Gaidai University in Osaka, Japan, and later added Sophia University in Tokyo as a second center.[40] But the romping days of India were carried forward at home through the seventies, partly fostered by a cadre of young faculty who bore the temper of the times without much senior guidance.

Callison College students made their stamp on Pacific by their creative independence.

The College was a "do-your-own-thing sort of place," as Cort Smith recounts. Allan Ginsberg, leader of the Beat Generation poets, addressed a packed Raymond Great Hall followed by a party at a faculty home where students and faculty joined Ginsberg in a hot tub fest. At a freshman retreat in the Foothills students and faculty shed clothes for a game of water volleyball to "acculturate to the Japanese habit of nude bathing" that would presumably face them when they spent their sophomore year in Japan.[41]

The legacy of Callison, together with Covell, was the central importance of international education, especially oriented to the developing nations of the world, for any undergraduate student. Pacific cultivated experiential learning off the campus in all of its schools over time, but experiential learning reached its apogee in Callison's yearlong immersion in an alien culture. Callison was way ahead of its time in introducing undergraduates fully to Asian cultures. Equally important for Pacific, Bruce LaBrack's cross-cultural training for study abroad became a Pacific trademark for nearly all of its foreign study programs.

While Callison alumni reunited in 2004 and 2009, they remain more independent minded than most Pacificans. Prominent alumni in the international arena include Baxter Urist ('71), who has built businesses globally through partnerships, focusing on children. He doubled world viewership of PBS' *Sesame Street* and headed up The Smile Train among many worthy projects. Frank Young ('72) has been a leader at USAID in Bangladesh and throughout Africa for decades. Callison was a draw for creative students, so no wonder many alumni are highly successful in the arts—like filmmaker Ted Thomas ('73), award-winning children's author and musician Matthew Gollub ('82), TV executive Gavin Harvey ('80) and film location expert Dow Griffith ('72).

Callison students often led Pacific in 1960s counter-culture.

Covell College

Covell College professor Rufo Lopez-Fresquet from Cuba epitomized the infectious energy of international intellectuals who provoked debate for covelianos outside of class.

After a decade, Covell College was still the only bilingual, four-year college in the U.S., magically held together by *convivencia*, a total immersion in joyful living together. Covell students loved the intensity of their talk with faculty, especially during their long lunch hours, with students and teachers each from a different country or political persuasion. Julio Hallack ('76) recalls, "the debate was very heated. It was very common to see a table where the fumes were coming out.... We had a Dr. Rufo Lopez-Fresquet, an amazing doctor coming out of Cuba, a brilliant man on economics [who loved to host students in his home to hash out issues over a beer and a cigar]. What a joy to sit around him and have a discussion about economics and politics."[42] *El Centro* was always alive with debate, singing, dancing, dual language practice, and playful fun. Seven faculty members were from Latin American countries and all faculty had extensive experience in Latin America. In the end, the immersion in the lives of students and teachers from many countries of two continents gave meaning and purpose to *covelianos*, most of whom were transformed into missionaries for *interamericanismo*.

For all of Covell's transformative power, most agree that the quality of the faculty and the College's provost declined over the years, which contributed to its waning. The College cut its required courses in half and embraced joint programs outside the College so that over the decade students were in 21 different majors. Another problem was that Covell College was heavily subsidizing students from Latin America to maintain the balance of students from North and South America. What rescued Covell in the mid-1970s was Venezuela. An ambitious oil-fed government scholarship program sent thousands of young Venezuelans abroad, and 45 of them were enrolled in Covell by 1975 as part of an agreement with Venezuela to educate 220 students at Pacific.[43]

After its peak enrollment of 201 in 1976, Covell dwindled to 100 by 1981, and less than half of those students were fully enrolled in Covell. Most were enrolled fulltime in the Intensive English Program. Covell was able to continue into the eighties primarily because it never attempted to eliminate traditional majors like Raymond and Callison; rather, it accommodated the disciplines most needed in Latin America to appeal to international students: engineering, business and education.

The regents formed a special committee to determine the future of Covell College in 1982 to find ways to preserve the "unique and valuable" qualities of Pacific's most distinctive school. Only one Academic Council member voted against action to end the College.[44] Financially unsustainable, the College shifted into degree programs in COP (Inter-American studies) and Education (ESL and bilingual studies) to provide a certificate in "bilingual, bicultural competence" for both North American and Latin American students. By 1985, surviving Covell programs were not sustainable: 34 students vs. the planned 150, so the "Covell Program" was ended in spring 1986 after 23 glorious years, far longer than the other two cluster colleges.[45]

This audacious goal, to found a tiny college to take on the dilemmas of the Western Hemisphere, found its fruition in the hundreds of alumni, especially in Latin America, who carried the message of *interamericanismo.* At the same time, it was another overreaching vision that simply lacked the backing and resources to achieve the quality investments it deserved.

For Covell, a cornerstone of its legacy is its distinguished record of alumni leaders in Latin America in commerce, government, industry and diplomacy. Among the most prominent are economist Fernando Zumbado Jimenez ('67), ambassador of Costa Rica to the United Nations and later UN regional director for Latin America; Carlos Mazal ('74) a Uruguayan who became director for Latin America in intellectual property at the United Nations in Geneva; Martin Burt ('80), who became mayor of Asunción, the capital city of his native Paraguay, during intense national conflict, then went on to become one of the world's most prominent social entrepreneurs; and in the States, Arnoldo Torres ('75), former executive director of the League of United Latin American Citizens (LULAC).[46] Like Raymond alumni, *covelianos* have kept in touch over the years. Alumni reunions were launched in 1975 with the formation of the Covell alumni association, first held in Guatemala, then in Stockton in 1981 and 1998, and in Colombia in 1986. In 2013, nearly 200 alumni returned to the Stockton campus to celebrate Covell's 50th anniversary.

Cluster legacies

When in 1972 the *Wall Street Journal* published a front-page story, "Without Much Fanfare, University of the Pacific Tries Some New Ideas," the three cluster colleges felt they had arrived.[47] What developed in each college was a saga, a central ingredient to its identity and success as a separate academic community.[48] As with most truly distinctive colleges, the internal values, culture, and stories told about these schools, held deeply by its students and faculty and alumni, are a "mission accomplished," an achievement of a distinctive character embodied in the saga, upheld by all its loyal members. That is why, even today, alumni from these three colleges are acutely aware of their collegiate identity, their cluster saga, and why they feel still bruised and betrayed by the University that ended their colleges in the 1980s. It was not a "program closure" to them, but rather an erasing of their collegiate community identity.

Many Pacificans would assert that the cluster colleges were Burns' lasting legacy and a key contribution to innovation in American higher education. Pacific's cluster colleges were some of the most bold, path-breaking, and renowned experiments in the country. And they certainly live on among their alumni. But the harsh reality is that the cluster colleges did not survive either at Pacific or at other universities, except for the well-funded Claremont, UC-Santa Cruz, and the original models themselves, Oxford and Cambridge.[49] If Burns and the board had built sizable endowments behind these small colleges, and made them larger like Claremont did, perhaps Pacific could have funded the scholarships adequate to draw students to support them when student interest waned.

SCHOOLS MATURE: THE COLLEGE, ENGINEERING, EDUCATION, AND THE CONSERVATORY

College of the Pacific

In several respects, the seventies and eighties were good years for building the College. The College absorbed the three cluster colleges as they became unsustainable, adding talented faculty across the disciplines and fostering interdisciplinary studies and innovative teaching. Some came gladly, others were pushed. Walter Payne in Latin American history, Cortland Smith in Asian international relations, John Williams in English, Neil Lark in physics, and others—nearly all eventually became important leaders in the College. As younger faculty began to move into leadership positions, the College got stronger. Two outstanding examples were Michael Minch in chemistry and Paul Richmond in biology, who reshaped their departments for the good through their leadership. The same could be said about Arlin Hanson in English or Martin Gipson in psychology.

At the same time, the College spun off some professional programs, physical therapy the most notable, and partnered with business and engineering to offer joint programs. Purchase of the Delta College campus was a major advance for the College. The College in the mid-seventies had "horrible" facilities—rats in the Quonset huts, English department in Knoles Hall attic.[50] When the Biology department moved to the old Classroom building at the southern edge, it nearly doubled its space from Weber Hall. The department needed it, with a steady stream of pre-pharmacy and pre-dentistry students seeking a way to wealth professions, which continued for 40 years.

The decision to add a chemistry laboratory building in 1979 was another major step ahead, along with the remodeling of a south campus building for the psychology department and the freeing up of Wendell Phillips Center when Ray-Cal ended in 1979. COP could now have its own building for the first time, though it came with the tainted history of its charlatan "donor." This massive relocation of the College also finally allowed the campus to erase the long Quonset "Tube."[51]

Wendell Phillips Center is the heart of the College today, with a Humanities Center addition (on the right, 2005).

Even as departments began to populate the south campus, their enrollments generally shrank through the 1980s, from nearly half the University enrollment to under 40 percent, as the professional schools generally grew in size.[52] Through all of the University turmoil ahead, the College earned a steadily rising reputation for outstanding teaching and student mentoring. Julianne George Van Leeuwen's ('81) tribute to her English professor Bob Knighton could be passed around to dozens of COP professors: "He made us aware of the need for excellence in writing, the importance of correct thinking, the necessity for appreciating the art of reading great books. Dr. Knighton elevated our thinking to the level where we discovered the power and resources of our nature, and began to improve ourselves in order to live with self-esteem and honor." [53]

The College benefitted from strong department chairs who also served as Academic Council chairs during this era. Professor Walter Payne headed the history department for many years and was chair of the faculty in the early seventies. Physics chair Carl Wulfman, biology chair Francis Hunter, art chair Larry Walker, English chair John Smith, communication chair Donald Duns ('58)—all provided leadership in the classroom, in building their departments, and in stabilizing the College and faculty governance during turbulent and uncertain times.

School of Engineering

Through his energy, vision and bold leadership across the state, dean Heyborne brought attention to the School of Engineering, especially after finally achieving accreditation in 1971.[54] By 1975, the School had a model cooperative education program that was already a magnet for other curious deans and faculty. Heyborne received two national awards for this signature program. The new 4-1-4 campus calendar forced required courses into the summer, so 11-month teaching contracts pulled many faculty away from summer research, and pushed others out of Pacific altogether. This constraint reinforced a faculty culture where research was not the norm and muted the achievement of the School in this era.

Computer engineering was added in 1978, engineering physics in 1981, mechanical engineering the next year—and by 1986, all were accredited. Even though only four women had graduated by 1977, by 1980 twenty percent of the students were women, including its top three graduates. Pacific students were recognized across the state: nearly one-third of the top awards from the state Consulting Engineers Association of California went to Pacificans over a seven-year period.[55] Between 1977 and 1990 seven Pacific students were chosen as the annual top engineering student in state, and frequently during this era Pacific students were ranked among the annual top engineering students in the nation.[56]

Students credited their cooperative education experience in industry for their success, with over 100 employers now participating in the program, and 15 percent of graduates went on for further study at the best engineering schools in the country, such as Stanford and MIT. They thanked outstanding faculty like Bob Hamernik, Jim Morgali, Dave Fletcher, and Gary Litton, among the great ones of this era, all of whom were conferred the top faculty honor by the University, the Distinguished Faculty Award, granted to one professor annually. Fletcher was particularly uncompromising in his expectations, but no less admired. The legendary punch line carries on: when a negligent student asks, "Why did I get an 'F'?" Fletcher zings, "Because there is no lower grade."

Engineering dean Robert Heyborne (1969-90) had a powerful shaping influence that built a significant reputation for the school, especially through its distinctive, industry-based cooperative education program.

By the early 1980s, the School was overflowing with students—over 400 now, quite variable in quality—and a new building became a top University priority. Khoury Hall was completed by 1982 with a gift from Said Khoury, president of Consolidated Contractors Company, a world-wide Kuwaiti construction firm, whose son Tawfic ('80) had graduated, along with dozens of other Kuwaiti engineering and computer science students. Many of these Kuwaitis became loyal alumni over the decades. Khoury Hall was innovative in design, with solar panels and translucent roofing ahead of its time. The famous engineering rock, which had been sandblasted clean in 1974 to start anew the ritual midnight painting, was temporarily removed to construct Khoury Hall—but also to end the paint vandalism that had spread to sidewalks and benches nearby. With a new brick perimeter guard, the rock was returned in 1985.[57]

In 1981, the students founded the Association of Engineering Students (AES) and created a handful of other student organizations through the 1980s and 1990s that fed their ambition to be leaders in their fields. Also in 1981, engineering alumni formed a school association. With large classes, the early eighties produced many outstanding engineers. Paula Brown ('82) graduated in civil engineering to pursue a career in the Navy, eventually becoming a Rear Admiral in 2011. The School's most famous graduate, Jose Hernandez ('84) from Stockton, son of immigrant *campesino* parents, student body president of Franklin High School, enrolled in the CIP program and pursued electrical engineering while working part-time at a restaurant and cannery. He pursued his dream to become an astronaut who circled the globe as a flight engineer in 2009. Along the way he was appointed a Pacific regent.

But alas, enrollment peaked in 1985, and like most other engineering programs took a nosedive as student interest turned away from the technical. From 1985-1990, engineering enrollment dropped more than 50 percent.[58] Fortunately for Pacific, students flocked to the business school and to pharmacy, just as surging engineering enrollments had balanced the precipitous drop in pharmacy students a few years earlier.

After a frustrating search for a dean, Pacific appointed Ashland Brown in 1991, when he launched the Industrial Advisory Council, an important link to alumni and the professional community. Later with his resourceful, entrepreneurial assistant dean Gary Martin ('86), he introduced the Engineering Industry Fellowship (EIF) program of generous scholarships that placed students in the industry workplace as freshmen, and then continued their employment-internship throughout their undergraduate career, usually ending with a solid placement in the firm. The push for more students led to lax standards resulting in high attrition. Enrollments fell steadily into the nineties, from over 600 students to less than half that. The School needed a new strategy.

School of Education

The School of Education had long been defined by its partnerships, beginning of course with area public schools.[59] But partnerships expanded in this era as the School grew in stature under dean Jantzen's strong leadership, then dean Oscar Jarvis (1974-83). When California passed the Ryan Act of 1970, teacher credentialing was streamlined to allow liberal arts students a quicker way into teaching—and fewer students in the education classrooms. A fifth-year teacher credentialing program was added to accommodate liberal studies graduates.

Jarvis expanded community partnerships and added programs in bilingual, cross-cultural, and special education, following federal and state funding. A novel partnership with the CSUs became a model for Pacific, starting with CSU-Stanislaus, then later extended to CSU-Bakersfield and almost to CSU-San Jose. Pacific was the Valley's only provider of doctorally

Education professor Dewey Chambers was Pacific's pre-eminent storyteller.

prepared community college and public school superintendents, principals, and other executives, a massive service to prepare a diverse profession with skilled leaders. The "ed. admin. doctorate," under the storied leadership of Dennis Brennan, carried on for decades through the reputation of outstanding principals and superintendents who were its graduates.[60]

Like all other schools at Pacific, the professors always earned center stage: Alumni collectively praised nearly every school faculty member over the decades as a personal mentor or inspiring teacher. The names Marc Jantzen, Heath Lowry, Juanita Curtis, Bob Morrow, and Hugh McBride appear frequently in the School's alumni *Memory Book.* Among the luminaries Dewey Chambers was the most colorful, often on the edge of professorial decorum, a nationally known scholar, and always entertaining in "kiddie lit" as he inspired hundreds of future teachers to shun Disney stories for honest storytelling.

A lean Conservatory

When gifted but demanding dean Preston Stedman resigned, Ira Lehn became acting dean in 1976 and then dean.[61] Despite a strong faculty, the school had little visibility and no help from the University to improve itself. Even the centennial celebration of the Conservatory in 1978 lacked any University support, but conservatory students were electrified by exuberant former dean and celebrated American composer Howard Hanson conducting a west coast premiere of his "Sea Symphony" as part of the celebration. With no music scholarships and inadequate facilities, the Conservatory was in survival mode, while other west coast schools continued to build quality programs, including summer music camps, that made Pacific's Conservatory faculty work resourcefully to be competitive.

Occasionally, honors came: in the school's centennial year, Bill Dehning's A Cappella Choir won top honors in the west.[62]

Regent Eberhardt's friend Eva Buck of Vacaville funded three major capital projects for the Conservatory starting in 1983, the Rehearsal Hall, the Recital Hall, and later Buck Memorial Hall, an office-classroom building named in honor of her late husband Frank Buck. A landmark development, the new buildings meant the school could finally move out of its two Quonset huts. A high point was the generous gifts from Alex Spanos and Eva Buck to remodel the auditorium in honor of Faye Spanos, for whom the hall was named in 1987. These facilities gave the school a great lift while Carl Nosse began his long deanship from 1980 to 2001.

Through the two-decade enrollment turbulence of the seventies and eighties, the Conservatory was always "exhibit A" in student-faculty ratios, with its barely 150 students and 27 some faculty. Faculty such as Warren von Bronkhorst, Frank Wiens, and George Buckbee deserved more and better students, but even Cliff Hand had opposed music scholarships when he was acting president.[63] Its most successful growth was in its innovative joint program in music management with the business school (first on the west coast) and its master's program in music therapy. When music school accreditation required graduate work for licensure in therapy in 1980, Pacific became the first master's program on the west coast under the masterful leadership of Suzanne Hanser. Music therapy was an especially large program until the state cut funding to medical facilities and jobs dried up.

Dean Nosse called these programs and music education the "bread and butter" programs that drew students in so that the performance studio programs in voice and instruments could carry on. Music management director Dick Etlinger, a former vice president of Capital Records, linked students to the Los Angeles music scene for internships and employment.

When Dave Brubeck contacted dean Nosse in the early 1980s, Nosse quickly developed a lasting friendship built on Nosse's appreciation of Brubeck's breadth of achievement in both jazz and classical compositions as well as his famed piano playing and jazz combo. Conservatory students performed his larger works for orchestra and chorus on campus, in Sacramento and in San Francisco through the eighties and early nineties.

Nosse recognized the key role Iola Brubeck was making in Dave's work. He mounted a plaque over the side door in the concert hall (still there today) to dedicate the spot where Dave Brubeck met Iola Whitlock in 1942 and then made a lifetime of great achievement together. When the Brubecks offered their vast collection of memorabilia in 1990, the University ignored the offer for five years, except for the continuing friendship between Nosse and the Brubecks. Later, Nosse was instrumental in establishing the Brubeck Institute and became its first director.

STUDENTS IN THE DRIVER'S SEAT: HOW PACIFIC INTENSIFIED ITS MISSION

Shifting student values

In the 1970s, the school was still very attractive to students despite the steep drop in interest in the distinctive cluster colleges. With the 1980s came more students who valued job-related goals, conforming to a national trend that has continued for decades. "Being well off" financially matched the priority of becoming an "authority in a field," and pursuing "a philosophy of life" hit an all-time low at less than 50 percent.[64] And while nearly 40 percent of Pacific's entering class identified as "liberals" in 1972, only half that percentage did so in 1985, about equal to those who called themselves "conservatives."[65]

Chambers and the heyday of student life

Among McCaffrey's key actions—to make up for lost time under Burns—was to bolster campus life for students. He directed the ascendancy of an orchestrated campus life program run by professionals at a time when American higher education saw the flowering of student services. For all of Burns' successes and his passion for Pacific students, he never really understood the role of student affairs in the holistic development of students.[66]

Under McCaffrey's student-oriented presidency, Judith McMillin Chambers ('58, '60) led a national movement to place campus life—or "student affairs" as it was then called in the profession—on solid footing. Chambers had returned to Pacific in 1969 to assist president Burns, then moved into student affairs. It was a natural fit; she grasped the vitality of out-of-class learning from the start. McCaffrey understood and supported Chambers' claim that "the only real difference between us [student affairs staff] and the faculty is that we teach outside the classroom, not in it."[67]

The University Center, later named the McCaffrey Center, provided the first campus social center actually designed for student use in 1975.

McCaffrey responded to student criticism that they had no place to gather, no real student center for clubs, meetings, and "hanging out" for conversation and meeting new friends. Approval of the new $2.4 million student center came one year into McCaffrey's presidency, and when it opened in 1975, it had more meeting rooms and gathering places than the campus had ever seen, with an actual movie theater and a grocery store that was dubbed "Garden of Eatin'" in a naming contest.[68] Students felt wanted on campus. At the same time the Raney Recreation Area was added, with outdoor sand volleyball and basketball courts to expand the options to stay on campus and stay at Pacific.

McCaffrey trusted Chambers and invested in her leadership to catch up with national campus trends. She chaired the enrollment task force through the 1970s into the 1980s. He elevated Chambers from her role as assistant to the president to dean of students in 1973 and then by 1975 to vice president for student life—the first such position at Pacific—so she and student life could have standing equal to the other vice presidents.[69]

The contrast with the Pacific campus a century earlier, in the 1870s and 1880s, was stark. At that time the college controlled most all social life on the campus: no smoking, no drinking, no dancing, no co-ed activities, not much at all. But dorm life was different. Students had no residential staff, in fact, no staff specifically assigned to student life outside the classroom. Students created their own culture because they had free rein to organize themselves into private clubs and activities as they chose. Not until the mid-twentieth century were clear objectives of campus student services articulated, and national standards began in the late 1970s. Chambers was part of the national movement in her profession to set national standards through the 1980s for the some 30 professional organizations involved in this campus work.[70]

At the same time, in public social behavior the 1970s and 1980s were freewheeling compared to a century earlier. Pacific and all other colleges had given way to student desires, starting with smoking and dancing, and now a student-organized control of massive drinking under the radar, marijuana and drugs floating freely at rock concerts, co-ed living, sexual dalliances at will, and a few nude streakers crossing the central quad in broad daylight. Was all this what brought the popular "Phil Donahue Show" of daytime television to Knoles Lawn for two days in May 1977?[71]

In 1974 Chambers launched a "peer advisor" program for freshman students headed by gifted Doug Smith, a computer science professor who devised and headed the model program for over 20 years. Chambers established a new Learning Center for skills development and expanded the summer new-student orientation sessions to three days. By 1980, Pacific fielded ten orientation sessions for new students and parents from June to August, sometimes in 110-degree heat, and through the decade two-thirds of new parents participated in them.[72]

Learning halls

When respected if old-fashioned Catherine Davis retired after 31 years as dean of women and associate dean of students, Jess Marks ('65) became associate dean and earned a solid reputation for student support and shrewd administration for the next two decades. By the mid-1980s, residence hall programming included 30 different activities to engage students in learning outside the classroom—and improve retention.[73] Presumably a spate of 27 midnight false fire alarms in Grace and Southwest halls was an anomaly.[74]

Following a national trend of "theme houses" and coeducational residence halls, two co-ed theme halls were begun in the late eighties, the John Ballantyne "intercultural" hall and the Ritter/Reimer "quiet" hall. A "healthy lifestyles" hall soon followed.[75] Life in the halls was sparked by the annual "Treasure Hunt" and Halloween Ball events to build a stronger sense of community, under the leadership of over 50 resident assistants supervised by 17 head residents.[76] Cable TV did not start invading until 1991.

Character building remains

While most American universities were forgetting about their undergraduate students in favor of mega-sized factories of graduate and doctoral programs, Pacific was investing in one of its core values, educating the whole student through close interaction with faculty and staff. In the earlier Methodist era, this mission was interpreted as building Christian character, but the fundamental value had not been lost in translation over the years. Education has always involved some inculcation of values, even though many academics in the modern era tried to deny it. And Pacific never gave up on the value of what today is called "character formation."

The sixties helped to make manifest that college students will inevitably bind their personal and social lives and values together with what they learn in the classroom, on the field, in the student club, in campus debates—or on the protest march. Pacific has been successful in its personalized learning partly because it has never lost the opportunity to engage students in value questions and issues, far beyond the heyday of president Burns and the sometimes zany, always provocative chapel of dean Meredith.

Through all these initiatives, the University aimed to orchestrate student lives with professional authority and assertiveness. By 1987, Pacific was noted as one of three universities identified as successful in "turning residence halls into learning centers."[77] Most faculty understood that the majority of student life was lived beyond the borders of the classroom, lab, and studio, and the assistance of a conscientious student life staff meant that student life was more productive and character building than anyone could have dreamed of a century earlier.

The Fairbrook phenomenon

Food at Pacific in this era was celebrated because director Paul Fairbrook made it that way. "Nothing counts but quality," he would say, and no one could lay out a spread like he could. No one catered better to the special wishes of any campus group, especially the international students, whom he hired by the dozens as student help. He sponsored a "Burger Cook-off" that invited all the burger joints in town to compete. When Pacific-donor McDonald's ended up fifth (Pacific ranked fourth behind # 1 A&W), McCaffrey got a call, and Fairbrook was in the doghouse.

Raymond College students, allowed pets in their halls, drew a trail of dogs into Raymond Great Hall for lunch, and the dog pack loved cleaning up the food trays. Students would jeer as Fairbrook tried frantically to chase the hounds out the door. The assistant provost, who wore a leather jacket and rode his motorcycle around inside the dining hall, was no help. Fairbrook finally threatened a city health department closedown to get the dogs barred. He succeeded.

Fairbrook was duly famous for his lavish banquets. One of his hits was a luau with the Stockton Hawaiian Club. Fairbrook roasted a hundred-pound pig, a parent of a Hawaiian student donated 500 pineapples direct from Hawaii, and Hawaiian students put on a show for 2,000.[78] Getting off campus for eating was common on the weekends, when many campus dining halls and Greek house kitchens were closed. The Hatch Cover, The Graduate, Al the Wop's in Locke, On Loc Sam's downtown—all were popular dining spots. Happy hour at Luigi's was good and

Food Services Director Paul Fairbrook was a campus personality and mentor to many students as well as a national authority in his field.

cheap. The Black Angus had a steel dance floor that beckoned at a time when disco was the rage.

Students take charge

In the early 1970s, student leaders were activist oriented and often made their voices heard. ASUOP helped students train for citizenship, practice leadership, exercise policy-making, and gain voice in campus affairs if not in tuition setting. In spring 1972, students petitioned to cancel classes for a day to participate in a national anti-war "moratorium" protest, but campus leaders instead crafted a compromise of options for faculty that allowed a thousand students to march downtown.[79] In 1973 students held "rap sessions" that reached the ear of the board when students urged "more rigor" from the faculty.[80] Susan Harlan ('74), ASUOP president that year (the first woman in that office since 1946), launched a state lobby on behalf of private college students to match the UC student lobby begun in 1971.[81] ASUOP started one of the nation's first student-run grocery stores, "similar in format to a 7-11" drop-in snack store—in addition to a record store, travel and notary services, legal aid and a loan company.[82]

In 1974 ASUOP requested permission to secure a beer license on campus, but McCaffrey and the board, eyeing a student referendum with only one-eighth of the students voting, not to mention the liabilities of the 21-year-old age requirement, said no.[83] In the same year McCaffrey asked the board if the heads of the Alumni Association, Academic Council, and ASUOP could attend board meetings as observers, but he was refused. The board turned down another student request for a board representative in 1976.[84]

Students objected strongly in 1975 when the board spiked meal rates by $60 midyear, then another $150 for room and board for the following year as fuel and food costs soared. Student leaders claimed they heard of the plan one day prior to the board meeting—a perennial student complaint, depending on who represented them on key university committees. McCaffrey, always sympathetic with student concerns, might have delayed the decision to allow more student input, but the deadline for setting fees to determine financial aid could not be extended.[85]

In 1981, the faculty's Academic Council was finally preparing to vote on a unified academic calendar for the Stockton campus after two years of debate. In campus rallies, ASUOP, led by its president Joe Hartley—the first ASUOP president ever to be re-elected—strongly opposed the ending of the January "winter term". Many faculty and regents questioned the lax academic standards and educational value of the January forays off campus and touristy trips to other countries for the 75 percent of undergraduates who participated (COP and Education). Students loved the research of Inca ruins in South America, the ski trip to Utah, the African safari, skin diving in the Caribbean. In 1972, 108 students flew on one plane to Paris to start their studies in six courses throughout Europe.[86]

The greater problem at Pacific was the number of undergraduate professional schools that found the odd one-month term a distracting squandering of resources, and it made no sense for the pharmacy school. The Academic Council was "deeply divided" on the issue, since half of all students were in professional schools, so the Council was unable to make a recommendation to the board.[87] (The one-month January term remained popular in liberal arts colleges into the twenty-first century, so its staying power was proved elsewhere.) In the end, academic vice president Hand had to step in and choose a unified calendar over a January term, making the change to an "early semester" calendar in 1982 that has held since that time: a late-August start, ending the fall term before the winter holidays, with spring term from January to mid-May.[88]

The next year Hartley and his ASUOP company took on the regents' "special admits" program, charging that those athletes admitted under the program were unsuccessful students, that only 4 percent of undergraduates enrolled at Pacific were lured by Division I athletics, and therefore the program should end. Of course the Academic Council concurred, but chair Eberhardt stood his ground and the board affirmed the program.[89]

ASUOP feuded with the "Pacific Programs Council" on who should coordinate student activities. By 1983 they signed a truce by forming a joint council triumphantly called UPBEAT: "University Programs Board for Entertaining and Amusing Times!"[90] A "Festival of the Arts" began in 1986, with guest artists populating the campus. By the late eighties, students were listening to one of their own: Stockton native Chris Isaak ('80) had turned his English/Communication degree into songwriting and singing, and soon became a rock and roll star, including his own TV show and film appearances.

Even though in 1988 ASUOP president Norm Allen, another activist leader, introduced the "Pacific Express Card" and coped with the erstwhile *Epoch* yearbook staff (which replaced the *Naranjado* in 1982 after a three-year hiatus), the late eighties saw a decline in student involvement. ASUOP elections with poor turnouts were normal, and interest in athletic events waned.[91] Campus interest and debate were driven by specific events, such as the anti-abortion demonstration, controversy over showing the film *Hail Mary* against the objections of Christian groups, AIDS awareness actions during the raging AIDS epidemic throughout this era, or a student protest against Israeli brutality against Palestinians.[92]

Norm Allen ('88) epitomized the Pacific student leader who continued his leadership as an alumnus: keynoter for the 2009 annual Lavender Graduation and Alumni Association board president in 2012.

The Pacifican had some aggressive editors in these years, but none who matched the 1976 editor who alleged that a small group of freshman women had formed a prostitution ring in Grace Covell Hall especially designed to lure football players. The baseless allegations resulted in his dismissal by the University judicial board of students, faculty and staff.[93] The Academic Council established a publication board for *The Pacifican* to help get the straying student newspaper back on track. The paper had been unattached to an academic program for some time, and the publication board struggled for years to improve it. The paper hit another low in 1983, when the editor embezzled $22,000 of newspaper funds, while the publication board complained *The Pacifican* "lack[ed] professionalism, and is running wild."[94]

Professor Paul Winters assured that forensics would still have its presence on the Pacific stage, and McCaffrey supported "the academic football team" of Pacific. Debate was not the only star-making competition for Pacific forensics: in 1979, Dana Davenport ('79) won the American Forensics Association top national award in persuasive speaking, and two years later Scott Park ('83) won the AFA top national award in informative speaking.[95] After 20 years of giving himself to students—"you've got to care for your students, listen to them, they come first"—Winters handed the coach baton by 1980 to communication professor Jon Schamber ('74, '75), one of his former star students, but forensics would never be quite the same again after Winters' record of 43 first place national awards.[96]

Greeks flourish

"Archania is a glimpse of heaven," recalled John Franklin ('78).[97] For many a Pacifican, the fraternity/sorority experience created a lifetime bond of friendship that transcended all else from campus days. And despite the instinctive animal joy and reckless behavior that would redefine what heaven is for most people, this heartfelt reality, the lasting power of college friendships and camaraderie, lay at the heart of the all-encompassing Greek experience—perhaps even deeper than the bonds of other groups such as the baseball team, the choir, or CIP.

Greek life in the seventies was at its peak, with Pacific's four sororities and eight fraternities. From 1970-1980 Greeks doubled in numbers to 200,000 across the nation's campuses, then doubled again by 1990. When

SAE upheld the mud-wrestling tradition, and Delta Gamma's Anchor Splash was a big hit for decades—especially the Mr. Anchor Splash contest, here with Omega Phi in 1992.

Animal House hit the screen in 1978, it "confirmed the validity of collegiate life in the 1970s and helped reinvigorate it."[98] Pacific Greek houses were jammed with students, and often fraternities would have membership nearly double the house residents, up to 80 students. Sometimes they even took over a dorm hall: After the SAE turned their front lawn into a mud wrestling pit, they weren't going to trash their own bathrooms to clean up. They all ran to the showers of Grace Covell Hall, leaving a trail of mud-streaked hallways behind.[99]

The Greeks were never left behind in charity fundraising, from the Delta Gamma's annual "Anchor Splash" for Aid for the Blind launched in Kjeldsen pool in 1980, or the Phi Delta's annual "Phis and Thighs" auction for the Stockton Food Bank.[100] Archania's annual teeter-totter marathon charity still drew a big crowd through the eighties and into the nineties for causes like AIDS, and they were joined by Sigma Alpha Epsilon and Delta Gamma's "Bop till You Drop" dance marathon, both for Jerry Lewis' perennial muscular dystrophy telethon.

By the seventies Band Frolic had become dominated by the Greek houses, though other residence halls certainly shared in the tradition. The 1979 Band Frolic, a tribute to "Pops" Gordon, the band director founder of the Frolic in 1928 who had just died, was not like the early days, when the band gave a full concert followed by five or six skits judged by two professors. The modern version, as every undergraduate alumnus/a knows, could not accommodate a band concert because the conservatory stage was typically filled with a series of a dozen or so racy music and dance skits, masterfully choreographed and costumed. Based on topics or movies of the day—"Raiders of the Lost Wallet," "Grease III," and "Star Trek V: The Search for Stan" were representative—judged by a six-member panel selected in secret.[101] It was serious competition in front of a sell-out crowd (a 12-hour wait for front row tickets), with prizes for the best show from each group—frats, sororities, and dorms.

In 1985, Band Frolic moved to the new Spanos Center to handle the huge crowd, and organizers found ways to end the show before 2 a.m.[102] Alpha Kappa Lambda won first place in the men's division six years running in the mid-seventies, with its drama majors like Dean Butler ('79), who began his TV stardom the day after final exams.[103] Alpha Chi Omega had all the great singers from the Conservatory—they even recorded all their traditional sorority songs for the international sorority.[104] This competition like others spilled over into "RF'ing," rowdy fun raids to mess up another house or ring the sacred Phi Kappa Tau bell.

For Homecoming, the Greeks spearheaded float building along with the residence halls for the parade on Pacific Avenue up Miracle Mile and on to the stadium. The Greeks also "were the big event planners" of Homecoming weekend, as Steve Whyte ('79) recalls, and they would welcome all alums to Greek house circle for a dance after the ball game.[105] Throughout the year, theme parties were common among the Greek houses, like Archania's "Fireman's Fling Dance," begun with a fire truck in 1958 and going strong in the eighties. Archites would pick up girls from second story sorority house windows on the ladder rising from the flaming 1982 International fire truck.[106] Campus concerts with big-name bands played in the Conservatory auditorium or fraternity circle if not downtown at the Civic Auditorium.

The Homecoming parade up the Miracle Mile on Pacific Avenue was a long-standing tradition that lapsed in the 1990s but returned in the 2010s. By 1990, Archania fielded two fire trucks for its annual "Fireman's Fling."

Especially in the 1980s, Greek life among the pharmacy students was lively, particularly between the two founding rival professional fraternities, Phi Delta Chi, called "Boneheads" (both dean Cy Rowland and advisor-professor Ralph Saroyan had been national presidents) and Kappa Psi, called "Jellies" (professor Jim King had been national president).[107] Early one morning students found a large outhouse perched on the roof above the school door with the label, "Kappa Psi House." The Kappa Psi's quickly scrambled up and pushed it over. The Phi Delts were compelled to cart it off to the front lawn of North Hall, where they resided, and where the searching farmer owner caught the Phi Delt thieves. That probably was not the only time the Phi Delts were suspended. One time they left a fresh, dripping cow head for Kappa Psi advisor/professor Don Floriddia ('71) to discover in his lab. Alumni often instigated the pranks, as when one Homecoming the Kappa Psi's completely removed the front door of McConchie Hall, the new home of Phi Delta Chi. Later, the Kappa Psi's found a 500-pound mountain of horse manure placed squarely on the front porch of their house across the street.

The Greek houses were strong enough to show their muscle when challenged. The student life deans detested the fraternity "Little Sister" program, carried on as a remnant of earlier sexist times, and finally tried to end it in 1990. Many national fraternities had actually outlawed the practice of a Greek house selecting a freshman beauty to be their annual "mascot" of sorts. But the students won out, even though stiff regulations applied.[108] It took years for the Greek police to clamp down on the simple "hazing" practice of a pharmacy Phi Delta Chi pledge handcuffing a large bone to his wrist. Capping off this era may be the remarkable tribute to Edith Moore, the housemother of Omega Phi Alpha fraternity for 35 years. Friend and counselor to many a student who called her "Luv," the fraternity orchestrated the extraordinary approval of the Order of Pacific in 1984 for her indelible impact on the lives of so many frat men.[109]

Women rise

Recall that the seventies was still the forefront of the women's equality movement in America, so women on campus were just beginning to flex their rights. Coming as a freshman in 1972, Cindy Spiro ('76) wondered if she would be written-up for wearing her Adidas sport shoes.[110] Not until 1973 when Judy Chambers became dean was associate dean of students Kay Davis overruled to end the archaic double standard on curfew hours and restricting women's pants to Saturdays. When women's studies sprouted across the country in the seventies—150 programs by mid-decade, and as many more in the last half-decade—professor Sally Miller offered the first women's history course at Pacific in 1973.[111] Although women's studies remained a marginal program at Pacific in terms of enrollment and budget, the courses empowered hundreds of women to explore a wider sense of themselves and their possibilities.[112]

Fay Goleman, professor of sociology and state and local leader in community mental health, headed an Affirmative Action committee set up to comply with the 1972 federal regulations prohibiting sex discrimination. Chambers and a graduate student named Joan Darrah ('74), who later became Stockton's mayor and a regent, staffed the committee. McCaffrey and the board quickly adopted all committee recommendations in 1974, when women comprised 38 percent of all students and about 15 percent of the faculty.[113]

McCaffrey had encouraged Chambers to run for president of the most important national organization in her profession, National Association of Student Personnel Administrators (NASPA). She became its third woman president in 1986, when women comprised only 15 percent of student affairs professionals.[114] Chambers was one of only six student affairs leaders ever to receive NASPA's two top national awards for outstanding service. When Rotary International was placed under Supreme Court order to permit women members, McCaffrey was quick to nominate Chambers, who became one of the first women Rotarians in California in 1987.

Student life vice president Judith McMillin Chambers ('58, '60) was an inspiration and role model for countless students.

Through the seventies to the nineties, women students gradually became the majority of the Pacific student body, then not more than 56 percent in the 2000s. Dentistry, law and engineering continued to be male choices (the dental school was 39 percent women in 1990), even though pharmacy was steadily becoming a female profession. Teresa Galvez Piper

('73), the only woman among 150 electrical engineers, was part of the 1981 Columbia Space Shuttle team.[115] Through the decade of the 1980s, women increased from 15 percent of the faculty to nearly one-fourth.[116]

CIP and other growing pains

In 1978, when the CIP budget came up short, the future of the program was put under review, like all programs that could not pay their bills. Vice president Hand chaired a group to clarify goals and accountability. About 150 CIP students and Stockton community supporters rallied to save the program with a planned march. Stockton's black community was especially sensitive to access in the program for its students, now comprising only one-fifth of CIP students, less than half the number of "Chicanos."[117] Faculty were upset that CIP would be on the chopping block when the program required many "no-cost" volunteer hours of their time as tutors and mentors. And they pointed to the fact the CIP students progressed to graduation at the same rate as all other students. The Hand "Special Report" clarified issues by directing the program to enroll students "economically disadvantaged," both minority students and others. The regents agreed to sustain a revised program as long as no quota system was used to measure its success.[118]

One important inaction was the regents' response to a charter for the first Gay Student Union in 1972, during a time when gay campus organizations were proliferating across the country, forced by court rulings in support of student civil liberties. Sacramento State College was one prominent example of a resistant campus that was required to recognize a student-faculty club in 1971.[119] While the board had never rejected a request for charter approval of any student organization backed by the campus student affairs committee, on this one the regents balked, and no action was taken.[120]

The handful of gay faculty kept their sexual identities private, so the student action was brave at the time and offered a vision of campus actions adopted in the future. While a "Gay People's Union" is pictured in the 1974 *Naranjado* and a Gay Students Union is listed by the 1978 catalogue, likely allowed along the way because of favorable state court rulings opening many public campuses, it was action in the 1980s by the state bar association, requesting that all California universities add "sexual orientation" to non-discrimination policies, that prompted the Academic Council to pave the way for formal recognition of gays and lesbians in 1985.[121]

Black students gain…

Black students provided important campus leadership through the 1970s. Pictured are the Black Student Union and the UOP Songleaders in 1974.

At this time, ethnic minorities comprised only 12 percent of the Stockton campus enrollment.[122] But for black students, the 1970s was a flourishing time, with all these new programs resulting in nearly 200 black students, more than at any time until 2008. Many were students on football scholarships, others were part of the CIP surge or a result of expanded recruiting. There was a strong "can-do" attitude that picked up the positive energy in popular culture that spilled over from the Black Power movement. Black students sought out leadership positions, were cheerleaders, on the dance team, ran for ASUOP offices, or were "soul music" DJs on the KUOP radio station.

No wonder that Norma Ivey ('74) and other black alumni from this era formed Pacific's black alumni club in 2006 during a three-day reunion.[123] Morrison England ('76, '83) was a football standout who chose McGeorge over the NFL and became a federal district court judge and Pacific regent. Vincent Orange ('79, '80) also pursued law and became a longtime member of the Council of District of Columbia. Rickey Boyland ('79) helped to found the first black fraternity chapter, Alpha Phi Alpha, with four fellow campus "resident assistants" in 1978, determined to be campus leaders involved in community service that he and his fellow frat alumni continue into the present, partly by mentoring new black students at Pacific.[124]

By the mid-eighties, CIP enrolled about 100 students and was still being shuttled among vice presidents, but Pacific had undergirded the program by establishing a federally funded Supportive Services Program led by Anita Bautista that continued, thanks to her savvy and skillful leadership, for the next three decades. The SSP assisted 200 low-income students with tutoring and support services that produced persistence rates matching the rest of campus.[125] Perhaps owing to these two successful programs and the others, the faculty did not develop an actual policy on recruiting more ethnically diverse students until 1989 in response to WASC accreditation concerns.[126]

. . . *And then get stalled*

By 1978, 23 percent of the students on the Stockton campus were from some ethnic/racial background other than "white/non-Hispanic." That percentage grew slowly for the next 25 years and even more slowly University wide. More Asian American students—themselves from many ethnic groups and nationalities—were drawn to the University than other ethnic groups, tripling their percentage from 7.5 percent in 1975 to 22 percent by 1995. Latino students steadily became a larger part of Pacific during this era, if not at the pace of Asian American students. From 1975 to 1985 there were about 200 Latino students annually. The Latino student organization MEChA (Movimiento Estudiantil Chican@ de Aztlán) held a conference to address the high dropout rate of Latinos in 1985.[127] Then over the next decade, the number of Latino students doubled to 8 percent with nearly 500 students, and then rose to ten percent of all University students by 2010 with 700 students.

In contrast, right up to the present day black students have represented only 2-3 percent of the student body, dipping down to 120 students in the mid-nineties (when football was ended), and never exceeding 200 students until 2008.[128] Native American students have been a tiny minority on campus over the decades—handfuls until 1990, and since then fluctuating between 35 and 65 students across the University. From time to time a Native American club gathered, but the most notable presence was the annual Native American Pow-Wow on the south campus, first organized in 1993, with over 300 members from over 75 tribes represented.[129]

In sum, the ethnic diversity of Pacific students changed dramatically during this period and beyond, except for black students. Around 1975, only 15 percent of enrollment was non-white, rising by about 10 percent each decade since then, so that by the end of the first decade of the twenty-first century, white students were a minority of the student body.[130] Pacific reached a milestone in 1989 by electing Chinh Vu ('90) as its first Vietnamese-American ASUOP president and by appointing Tom Flores ('58) as the first Latino regent. About 300 students came from other countries, but a new goal of 10 percent of the Stockton student body—400 undergraduate and graduate students—was set with a new full-time advisor for Stockton campus international students. The goal was achieved in the early 1980s but was not sustained for long.[131]

Why the Anderson Y

The Anderson Y was still the home of student activism, outreach, and recreational activities in the seventies, a social force on campus as the oldest college Y in the West, with students running recreation excursions, international student groups, and a safe place for gay students to hang out.

The special needs of the southeast Asian communities of Stockton were brought dramatically in focus when Patrick Purdy, a disturbed, racist, criminal drifter, sprayed bullets from his assault rifle across the grounds of Cleveland Elementary School near the campus early in 1986. He apparently targeted the school because most of the children were from Stockton's Cambodian community—the third largest in the U.S.—in the nearby Park Village apartment complex where the Anderson Y had an after-school program. Five children were killed and 30 students and a teacher were wounded. (The tragedy led to the assault weapons ban in California and later to a national ban for a decade.) At the time, Pacific enrolled only three Cambodian students, but one, Christine Mouk (n.d.), redefined her life by taking charge of campus relief efforts for the victims' families that involved dozens of students from the Anderson Y volunteer force. The Anderson Y provided much of the crisis management and support for the Park Village enclave struck by the tragedy.

Anderson Y leaders sponsored a benefit rock concert to create five Pacific scholarships, named after the five victims, for future Southeast Asian students. President Atchley assured a $50,000 fund. So in addition to the volunteer tutoring and big brother/sister mentoring programs, Anderson Y volunteers took on new scout troops, translation, and even classroom coverage for the besieged school community.[132] By the 1990s, there were over 30 Cambodian-American students at Pacific, and by the turn of the century a Cambodian alumni group had been formed.[133] In 1991, President Bush named the Anderson Y volunteers the 421st "Daily Point of Light" in the country to honor their Cleveland School work and to highlight the remarkable volunteer spirit and successes in America.[134]

Drinking days

One major change in this era that also responded to student wishes was the alcohol policy. The unmanageable old policy banning campus drink except in a private room meant enforcement was lax at best. It was common now to see a kegger in frat circle, with pyramids of kegs eight or ten wide, or open frat house parties with 400 students. In 1981 the old policy was replaced by a registration requirement for all student events serving alcohol, on or off campus, and a large dose of alcohol education, particularly on the "drug of choice" for most college students, beer.[135]

The alcohol policy was revised again in 1989 to focus even more on education and training, mandatory prior to any alcohol event. Tougher was the ban on "open parties" to control the clientele and reduce the size, noise and publicity. Student monitors had to police more, and sanctions were stiffened.[136] By the mid-eighties, the campus had many alcohol awareness programs. There was a brave if futile optimism on the student life staff that students could change the culture of beer drinking just as students had, by their own leadership, practically banished tobacco from the campus.[137]

Campus safety becomes an issue

As Pacific moved through the 1970s and 80s, safety around the Stockton campus was a rising issue. As Stockton grew, gang violence, illegal drug trafficking, and other urban crime rose. To keep pace with a changing city, Stockton had a model police force by the 1970s that worked in tandem with Pacific's campus security. There was a major setback in 1972, when ASUOP sponsored another rock concert at Stagg Stadium to hear legendary rock bands The Byrds and Chicago. Over 20,000 gathered and drugs were floating everywhere. Outside the stadium a non-student was stabbed to death, and the University faced a $750,000 lawsuit. President McCaffrey and the board banned rock concerts in the stadium, and how could students disagree. The ban was lifted for country singer Garth Brooks—but not until *20 years* later.[138]

By 1988 the Stockton campus started an escort service for women's safety after dark.[139] Pacific took a path it has followed in the decades since: to beef up campus security whenever the perceived threat of increased violence risked any reputation of an unsafe campus. The number one crime issue on the Stockton campus in the eighties and nineties was bicycle theft. The rampant loss of bikes each fall steadily reduced campus bike traffic over the years; students drove cars to class, or walked.

Taking the broad view of student life in this era, the larger social issues for all campuses were alcohol abuse, AIDS, the balance of athletics and academic performance, access for disadvantaged students, and institutional accountability to external constituencies—not so different from those of the twenty-first century. If faculty insisted that Pacific still had a ways to go in regulating campus life, their supportive critique was part of the equation that kept Pacific on the front edge of national best practices for campus life. The "Judy Chambers era" was a noteworthy advancement for Pacific during this time.

PROFESSIONAL SCHOOLS ADVANCE

The triumph of dentistry

The new dental school dean, Dale Redig, had a mountain to climb. Midwest immigrant Redig fell out of faculty and alumni favor because he disrupted school culture from the start, but students adored him. When he arrived in 1969, he was appalled by the "primitive treatment of students," who were routinely demeaned by the inbred faculty—a storied tradition among American dental schools passed down through generations of merciless instructors.[140] With his handsome stature, impeccable dress, dignified demeanor, and steely resolve, he ended the abuse, and lost some good faculty members.

Redig asked faculty to treat students with respect and invited their shared authority to start the "humanistic" approach that defines the school's culture today: students treated as professional partners in learning and patient care. He added students to all the school committees and embraced their San Francisco sixties style: "I can't quite see that we can afford to get so terribly upset about a student's hair, trousers, or beard when the problems facing society are so much greater than that."[141]

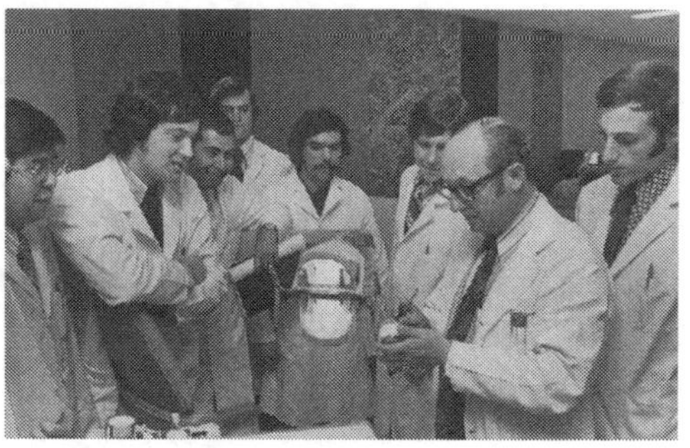

Dental dean Dale Redig was a strong advocate for students, and respected their culture (here pictured with former dean LeRoy Cagnone).

Redig re-engineered the curriculum by 1974 into an efficient, productive three-year, year-round program that students welcomed because he gave them a voice and treated them as professionals. On the other hand, the program was unpopular with loyal P&S alumni, who objected to a "cheapened" school, even though it brought in $3 million of federal subsidies as the payback for producing more graduates.

Unheard of among dental schools, Redig hired non-dentist David Chambers, a professional educator, to help him build an educational approach to teaching rather than a training camp. The plan included offering a master's in education degree program for the faculty provided by Pacific's School of Education. Professor Chambers represented the front wave in the 1970s to upgrade the quality of teaching and learning in professional schools.[142] Over four decades, Chambers, who probably published more articles on dental pedagogy than anyone, became the leading authority on competency-based dental education in the country.

Redig created three "group practice" clinics, each with teams of teachers for "comprehensive patient care." These new clinics became highly successful for students, brought new funds to the School, and gained national attention. He hired James Pride to start eight community clinics to provide low-cost dental care to needy populations in six Northern California cities and teach students community service. The Union City clinic, started in 1973, celebrated its 40th anniversary in 2013. Graduates were tops in state board examinations by the seventies, and in 1974, to pick one year, the School could accept only four percent of its 3500 applicants—14 percent of the class came from Pacific's undergraduate program. Redig's student-centered vision and stellar record earned him national stature. He was elected president of the American Association of Dental Schools in 1978.

By 1978, a small group of alumni conspired to make Redig executive director of a struggling California Dental Association to move it ahead while also creating an opening to bring in Arthur Dugoni as dean. Redig transformed the CDA from a lazy office in Los Angeles to a hugely successful enterprise in Sacramento by pioneering dental practice insurance. He later became a Pacific regent in 1986 and an important player in the ensuing saga of a board torn apart.

The appointment of Arthur Dugoni ('48) as dean had deep roots. When bright student body president Dugoni was called into the dental dean's office, he had no idea what was ahead. Dean Ernie Sloman ('21)—cigar in hand, necktie off-kilter, feet on the desk—looked young Dugoni in the eye and said, "you should think about teaching after graduation—we need you here. You have what it takes! Some day you could be sitting in this chair!"[143]

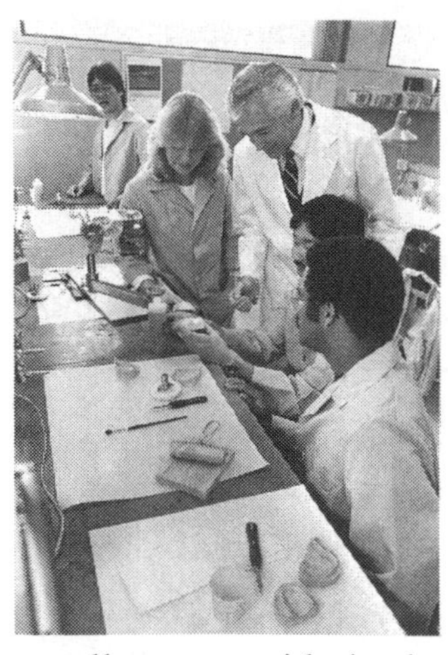

Dental Dean Arthur Dugoni ('48) became Pacific's greatest dean, serving from 1979-2006.

And of course he did: Art Dugoni, starting as dean in 1979, about the year Joe Montana started for the San Francisco 49ers, had risen from adjunct orthodontics professor to became the most renowned of the seven dental deans over 120 years of school history. Beyond that distinction, he became the most successful and celebrated of all the academic deans in Pacific's history. Dugoni brought a passion for excellence; a pride in the school, the profession, and his students; and a powerful ability to communicate and inspire that transformed the School to another level. Under his hand the School became the most highly respected practitioner-based (vs. research) program in the country.

To ease the student housing crunch, the school purchased a hospital building near the campus in 1979 to become apartments for 250 students. Some thought it another "crazy idea" of Dugoni's, but it turned out to be a big hit.

The 1980s were a time of real testing for the school, when applications fell by 70 percent.[144] The School responded with creative solutions: creating an international program that allowed practicing dentists in other countries to complete a D.D.S. degree in an accelerated program ably led by professor David Nielsen; adding a master's degree in orthodontics that became renowned; and introducing a post-DDS residency for general practice. Dugoni renewed the master's degree in education for the faculty and added an MBA program to sharpen their skills to prepare students destined become practitioners in their own small businesses.

Tall, handsome, silver-haired, with a charming smile that radiated throughout a room, Dugoni was a master of public relations who sold his "shiny car with no engine" as a way to build a powerful engine over time.[145] The three biggest draws for the School were sustained and strengthened throughout this era: the humanistic culture of caring for students, staff, and patients and honoring their dignity; a rising reputation for its clinical program; and the only three-year, year-round program in the country.[146] Of course, location also mattered, especially when your school is located in the heart of San Francisco's Pacific Heights! Through his passionate drive for excellence, clothed in a winsome personality and deep love for people, he gradually built highly effective fundraising, alumni and marketing programs that put the rest of the University to shame. As one long-time colleague observed, dean Redig was the surgeon brought into make radical change; Dugoni was the physician-healer who restored the school to wholeness. Board licensure pass rates were tops among California schools, and 95 percent of graduates passed the national examinations.[147]

Dean Arthur Dugoni moved the dental school to the top of clinically based dental schools with passion, grace, and style.

Dean Dugoni set an example for his students through his leadership in the profession. Like so many P&S alumni he became California Dental Association president, and in 1988 the third alumnus to become president of the American Dental Association. In 1998 the World Dental Federation awarded him an honor granted to only 30 living dentists in the world. Fellow dental alumni have held more professional state offices than any other California dental school. Leadership in the CDA comes as naturally as service to community, learned by every student in the dental school.

While Pacific Heights was isolated from needy populations, dental clinics were scattered in underserved communities from Oakland to Elk. The "campus" clinics in the Pacific Heights building themselves served primarily low-income people and the poor. The school has been a leader in responding to community needs, through an AIDS clinic in the city, service to migrant workers in Stockton, or distance learning across the state to treat disabled adults.

And they had fun: through most of the eighties, the students fielded the famous "Toothbrush Centipede" of 13 linked runners in the annual Bay to Breakers run.[148] Dean Dugoni summed it up in nearly every speech he made: "Education is not just about making a living. It's about making a life. At Pacific we grow people, and along the way they become doctors." Dugoni fixed the compass on core strengths: "camaraderie, flexibility, performance, and service…to students, to practitioners, to the profession, and to the community."[149] The annual glittering P&S Ball for alumni, begun in 1968 by a handful of alumni who cooked their own dinner at the St. Francis Hotel, became a lavish black tie affair at the Fairmont, Ritz Carlton, and other special venues by the nineties. To a cheering crowd of over 700, Dugoni's costumed impersonations—from Elvis Presley to King Arthur—deepened their affection for him and support for the school.

The Law School steams ahead

Dean Gordon Schaber was a great leader and strong decision-maker, with his commanding presence, his bright mind, his strong, articulate and insistently persuasive voice, and his indelible memory for names. He was also a loyal leader, helpful to president McCaffrey throughout his years. He had chaired the search committee that first identified McCaffrey, and they became good friends. As superior court judge, Schaber's reputation soared and connected him to every corner of the legal community. Schaber wielded powerful influence in Sacramento on the local, state, and even national level through his loyal work on behalf of the Democratic Party. Often sought out for his counsel by governors, legislators and state officials on both sides of the aisle, he advised Ronald Reagan as well as John Kennedy.[150] He was also in demand by celebrities of all sorts. Raymond Burr's long-time attorney and confidante, Schaber negotiated Burr's "Ironside" TV series contract, and Burr had every television script sent to Schaber for editing and approval. Conrad Hilton had his own law firm to handle transactions, but, the story goes, he would not close a deal on a hotel until Schaber looked it over.[151]

Celebrated law Dean Gordon Schaber, Pacific's longest serving dean (1957-91), was politically well connected and friends with celebrities like Raymond Burr.

More than anything, Gordon Schaber was passionate about legal education. He saw the great need for educating lawyers ready for practice, rigorously prepared to speak, write, research, analyze, and debate. He knew that experiential learning could prepare students better, and by focusing on trial advocacy experience, he made his mark on legal education. A strong believer in public service, he combined service with experiential learning in innovative community clinics led by students, always striving for ways to do it better than any other law school. The *Pacific Law Journal* started in 1969, run by 50 students, appropriately provided analysis of new California laws.

The law school achieved ABA accreditation first in 1971 with 850 students and celebrated an 85 percent pass rate on the state board exams for first-time takers. Schaber believed in the "sink or swim" approach to learning. In those days, the financial risks were less high than today, so the door was open for many students to try their hand. Schaber studied the metrics of testing to determine how best to prepare his students to pass the bar. He focused on practical skills, instilled the ethics of professional responsibility, and expected his professors to mentor students well. Many flunked out within the first year, or second or third, so that by the third year, the small senior classes were filled with smart, motivated, hard-working

Among a sea of mustached faces are two of the 20 women graduates of the 230-member class of 1974.

students who would be successful in passing the bar. Claude Rohwer and his colleagues would take all students through their paces using the Socratic method of oral inquisition that left unprepared students shredded.

Another milestone era was membership in the American Association of Law Schools in 1975, no surprise in a year when Pacific had a 92 percent bar pass rate compared to Stanford's 84 percent, followed by Boalt Hall and Hastings.[152] The bar pass rates also contributed to a strong academic profile that in 1982 earned the school the coveted Order of the Coif, an honors chapter awarded to only 58 of the 172 accredited law schools at the time.[153]

Schaber knew how to drive up quality, though it took its toll on the School. McGeorge earned a reputation as a boot-camp survival course. Unlike the dental school graduates who gloried in their student days, graduating McGeorge students did not want to relive the exhausting experience that drove out many of their friends. Alumni experiences of these two campuses were utterly different, and it showed for years in alumni participation in campus events, reunions, and alumni philanthropy.

The law school break room was all that was available for evening students until the student center opened in 1976.

Construction of the "Courtroom of the Future" was completed by 1973, a national statement about the McGeorge commitment to train trial attorneys through direct, practical experience in innovative courtroom procedures. The Center for Legal Advocacy was likely the only experiential advocacy program in the country at the time.[154] The courtroom was followed by a library addition and a classroom and office building, then a student center by 1976.

In 1973 McGeorge's "Courtroom of the Future" put the school on the map as an innovator in preparing practice-ready graduates.

During these years, the school grew dramatically, doubling the number of students in a decade to 1350 by 1978. An apartment complex was added in 1979 as well as a community legal services center with more classrooms. The faculty increased fourfold over to reduce the student to faculty ratio from 58:1 to 33:1. Jobs were plentiful in these days; the placement rate was over 96 percent. By 1985, 1500 judges volunteered for moot court, and 250 volunteered to judge in mock trials.[155] Pacific ranked third nationally in moot court competition.[156] The highly successful international law program in Salzburg was launched in 1973, typically attracting 40 McGeorge students and a dozen or so students from other universities each summer to compare U.S. and European law as well as to work in internships throughout Western Europe. A master's program in transnational business and taxation was added in 1981, with internships throughout Europe.[157]

Pacific McGeorge was a pioneer in international education among U.S. law schools, with one of the first European centers in Salzburg in 1973.

The one bump in the road was the students' request to have the controversial California chief justice and the first woman on the California Supreme Court, Rose Bird, as commencement speaker in 1980. Typically, the speaker was awarded an honorary degree, but the board set a new policy that separated the graduation speaker from honorary degree consideration as they turned down the students' request. Later, Bird became the only chief justice removed from office by voters, especially for her strong stand against the death penalty. The next year the students selected a safer bet, Anthony Kennedy, then a justice on the Ninth Circuit Court of Appeal, soon to become a justice of the U.S. Supreme Court.

Since the 1960s, the surrounding neighborhood of Oak Park in Sacramento had suffered.[158] Downtown urban renewal pushed many African Americans to this welcoming neighborhood. A solid working class district experienced demographic shifts, especially as lower income populations migrated in. When the east-west freeways were built, the area became isolated from the heart of the city. After the "Oak Park Riots" of 1969, property values dropped and sections became checkered with transient citizens well into the 1980s and beyond. Following Pacific's tradition of responding to the underserved through dental clinics and tutoring and other outreach programs, the law school set up free law clinics for underserved neighbors who could be helped by eager young law students just a walk away.

Troubling times in graduate education

Graduate programs on the Stockton campus were loose and largely unregulated because with little authority and less money, the graduate dean's ability to serve as watchdog for academic quality across departments was limited.[159] For many programs, even the essential of faculty research that undergirds graduate study was lacking. Many of the faculty leaders were not active scholars, such as Emerson Cobb in chemistry. Research grants by outside agencies though not absent were not common.[160] Yet Pacific tried to expand its graduate offerings befitting of a comprehensive university even when the prospects were slim.

In 1979, the regional accrediting agency Western Association of Schools and Colleges (WASC) visited campus to review the tiny Ph.D. program in chemistry and also the doctorate in English. WASC decided to tolerate these under-resourced programs, allowing them to drift ahead. Though they lacked a University plan to guide them, they both had some strong faculty, such as Michael Minch and researcher Paul Gross in chemistry and Arlen Hansen in English.

Other graduate programs were strengthened. The Graduate School of Medical Science in San Francisco got a fresh start in 1971 with new dean Bruce Spivey in ophthalmology. His research agenda on blindness was impressive, and soon Spivey became the head of the Pacific Medical Center. The school managed to survive into the 1980s even though it lacked the research infrastructure of a large university to support it. Back in Stockton, in 1971 the pharmacy school received a windfall of the third-largest gift in Pacific history to that time, $800,000 from Thomas and Joseph Long, whose drugstore chain had grown mightily. The gift retooled the Rotunda and research labs to strengthen the doctoral program. The gift also funded south campus remodeling to relocate the theatre program from the Rotunda to Long Theatre.

In the School of Education, the bilingual education doctoral program was one of four programs nationally recognized by the National Council for Accreditation of Teacher Education (NCATE) as outstanding in 1977.[161] The NCATE accreditation visit of 1986 was proclaimed as the best Pacific report since NCATE had started its accreditation process in the 1950s. One of the best academic additions was the physical therapy master's degree program, launched in 1985. The psychology department in the College created the Community Re-Entry Program in 1975, using undergraduates as well as graduate students to conduct research in applied behavioral analysis as well as provide voluntary assistance for over 100 mentally disabled adults in Stockton. With funding from state and federal grants, the program continues to this day under the long-term leadership of professor Cris Clay.[162]

The fundamental problem with the quality and success of graduate programs was the lack of adequate academic infrastructure, itself a product of an under-funded University. Many programs with a handful of students were just surviving. Again, Pacific found itself doing too many things with too little backing. Support for the William Knox Holt Memorial Library on the Stockton campus, much below the national norm at less than 3 percent of the campus budget, had reached a "crisis stage" by 1990, in contrast to the law school library funded at 8 percent of its budget.[163]

Like all college libraries, it always remained popular as a social hangout, but the "antiquated" library as a research tool was being abandoned owing to meager funding. "Associates of the University Library," a support group started in the early 1970s, lacked the firepower to lead a turnaround. Book circulation declined in the eighties as book buying languished, and an online catalog and computerized circulation system remained unfunded: "an institutional embarrassment." Many students as well as faculty routinely used the UC libraries in Berkeley and Davis. Library, computer and lab equipment, grant support, scholarships and assistantships—all were stunted legs to support graduate studies. Struggling graduate programs relied, as did the undergraduate program, on the quality and passion of the professors and the personal attention they devoted to their students.

ROLLER-COASTER ATHLETICS

"Cradle of coaches"

By the time of McCaffrey's presidency, the National Collegiate Athletic Association (NCAA), founded in 1910, had become the leader in intercollegiate athletics as efforts by presidents and athletic conferences failed to clean up countless abuses, especially in college football, that ran through the 1950s and 1960s. Virtually by default, the NCAA took on the task of regulating itself, which eventually led to immense power and influence in American higher education. When the NCAA shifted from a guaranteed four-year athletic scholarship to one-year renewable grants for student athletes, the new policy gave coaches much more power over athletes and did much to professionalize the college sport.[164]

At Pacific, the stakes seemed lower and the mood was positive. Those men who had the good fortune to play under Chester Caddas from 1972-78 developed a great *esprit de corps* working with perhaps Pacific's most beloved football coach. Caddas' teams were the only winners in the PCAA/Big West Conference over the quarter of a century of Pacific football in the conference. Four of his seven years were winning seasons. As Mike Millerick wrote in his comprehensive *Pacific Football Record Book,* the 1972 Tigers "had the third most wins in school history (8), and scored first against #1 Louisiana State on a blocked punt."[165] Those were the days of All-Americans Willie Viney ('74), Willard Harrell ('76), and (triple) Brad Vassar ('80). Harrell's career rushing total ranked 10th in NCAA history at the time, and Harrell was the only other player to have his jersey retired after LeBaron and Bass.[166]

Beloved coach Chester Caddas, led by All-American Willard Harrell ('76), had four winning seasons from 1972-78.

Many of Caddas' grads went on to become National Football League players as well as successful coaches, like the renowned Pete Carroll ('73, '77), who led USC to a BCS title in 2005 and then headed the Seattle Seahawks. Few universities can match Pacific's record of coaches: about 15 former Pacific coaches have coached in the NFL, including at least seven head coaches.[167] As one sports commentator remarked, "the list of coaching greats is too long to be lucky."[168] In 2014 Pete Carroll was the third Pacific coach to win the NFL championship at the Super Bowl, following Tom Flores' ('58) two crowns with the Oakland Raiders and Jon Gruden's win with the Tampa Bay Buccaneers.

Celebrated NFL coach Pete Carroll ('73, '77) was especially appreciative of his mentoring by professors Larry Meredith and Glen Albaugh, both of whom shaped Carroll's strategies for success.

This "cradle of coaches" rested on the quality of students recruited to Pacific. They were motivated by the value of education and mentored by some of the best teachers—Libby Matson, Doris Meyer, Conner Sutton, Glen Albaugh among them—and best coaches anywhere.[169] Pete Carroll got his start when coach Caddas offered him a graduate assistantship while he was just getting his feet wet in business. Carroll credits some of his unusual coaching style and success to professors Glen Albaugh and Larry Meredith.[170] Syd Church ('78) recalls tiny Libby Matson—known for her piercing blue eyes and fervent finger-wag admonitions of giant linemen and timid co-eds—writing out a check for $1000 to cover his last tuition payment for his teaching credential (paid back in full). The program was known for this kind of passionate commitment to students.[171]

But Caddas' popularity with his players did not extend much beyond them. Students and faculty had called for the end of football the year McCaffrey was appointed, the same year UC-Santa Barbara dropped it, and the campus was restless about the budget in a bad economy.[172] In 1977 Pacific made a bid to rejoin the West Coast Conference of private, selective west coast universities but was passed over. Pacific was stuck in the PCAA with all public universities. The old rivalry schools of St. Mary's, Santa Clara, and USF had all retreated from I-A football as televised games of the best collegiate teams dominated Saturdays, and the 49ers and Raiders captured the Sunday regional market.[173] At least Pacific kept rivalries with San Jose State and Fresno State that reached back to 1921. The alternative was to drop to the new Division I-AA, which cut some costs but boosted travel to obscure schools and locations.[174]

Football's fault line

According to storied athletic director Cedric Dempsey, the next stage of Pacific football all started with a big loss to UC-Davis, a non-scholarship, Division II football team in 1978.[175] Despite the stature, likeability, and respectable record of Caddas, his loss to lowly UC-Davis crossed the line for many regents, even though the following year the team placed six All-Americans, including Steve Goulart ('80), the only Pacific regent to hold such an honor.

In Burns' last years, he handed off athletics to vice president Winterberg, who continued all through the McCaffrey years. Working closely with board chair Eberhardt, Winterberg handled the cost-overruns of athletics, especially football, with quiet care, as the imposing, gregarious fan Eberhardt, "always on the field and behind the bench," standing shoulder to shoulder with the coach in his orange jacket and football shoes, plunged into the gridiron fray.[176] He and newly appointed regent Alex Spanos called in Dempsey and asked for changes about the year the NCAA split Division I into three levels. Ced Dempsey laid it on the line: if you want to notch up football at Division I-A, you will have to make investments in facilities (done with dispatch by Spanos, including building the Pacific Club above the east stadium bleachers), a next-level coach (done by hiring Bob Toledo from UC-Riverside), and—unprecedented—opening admission to junior college transfers who had not satisfactorily completed their first two years (McCaffrey agreed to a few "special admits" each year).[177]

The first *Stockton Record* interview with new coach Toledo in early 1979 immediately raised faculty concerns: would academic standards for players be lowered and the football budget raised? McCaffrey said no to the first question—academic standards were firm—and yes to the second, with more gifts as the source.[178] The executive board of the Academic Council sent a six-page letter to McCaffrey asking detailed questions on special admits, the faculty role in athletics policy, and the athletics budget. Earlier, the Academic Council had specifically called for a ban on special admissions, and that ban had been campus policy for some years. The faculty reviewed a "talent category" for special admission and rejected it in 1975 and again in 1977, even though it would have helped the conservatory stage as well as the football team.[179]

Tony Sauro's six-part series on Pacific athletics in the *Stockton Record* had reminded all that Pacific's admissions standards since 1961 far exceeded the NCAA standards that allowed "D" grades to qualify for athletic scholarships.[180] Dempsey pointed out to the faculty council that Stanford allowed 2 percent of a class to be special admits by the president, UC-Berkeley allowed 4 percent, and furthermore that scholarship athletes had graduated above the campus-wide rate for the last 15 years.[181] McCaffrey scheduled a special meeting with the faculty to present a statement explaining his decisions. He noted especially that the additional dollars for football would be funded by alumni and regents, not the University budget, and that football was part of the "overall excellence" of Pacific that was beneficial to both students and the public.[182] He said nothing of a wider door for admissions.

A few weeks into his first recruiting season, coach Toledo signed a player under the secret special admit plan, and acknowledged it to others. The faculty caught wind of it, and demanded an answer from McCaffrey before the council. The President denied knowing of any "special admit" policy, and turned to the athletic director to reinforce his cover-up. AD Dempsey had the courage to acknowledge the agreement, even though the vigilant admissions director, Les Medford, had no knowledge of it. McCaffrey was caught in the squeeze and reneged on the "special admit" policy a few days after the faculty meeting. Coach Toledo threatened to sue for breach of contract.

Board chair Eberhardt called McCaffrey and Dempsey downtown to his bank office to ask McCaffrey why he had backed down. Emotional McCaffrey said the faculty would not let him, even though the Academic Council had not set demands at the meeting. Eberhardt, already in a huff over what seemed to him to be an intransigent faculty, insisted that McCaffrey follow through to honor the Toledo commitment. Spanos called up Dempsey and told him it was time for McCaffrey to go if he couldn't back up Toledo, and would Dempsey be ready to pick up the reigns as president? Dempsey, troubled by this ersatz spectacle, quickly opted for the AD position offer at San Diego State that he had almost passed up. Toledo's contract was honored by the president, including "a limited number of exceptions" to admission standards, defined as no more than "a dozen." And the faculty chairman was left fuming.[183]

McCaffrey again met with the Academic Council in less than a week, restating his "100 percent commitment to those policies" that disallowed special admits. But he argued that Toledo had already committed to the special admit student prior to the applicant's interview with admissions director Medford, a Marine vet who ran a tight ship with high standards who declined the student's candidacy. McCaffrey said Toledo "put his career on the line," so McCaffrey decided to make one exception to the policy based on his prior pledge to Toledo, admitting that he himself "was at fault" for overstepping his bounds and claiming that he would not let it happen again.[184] The Academic Council, meeting the following week, came one vote short of censuring the president for "seriously undermining the confidence" of the faculty on academic standards and requested that McCaffrey reverse his decision.[185]

With the board and McCaffrey at tense odds, the regents required that the president quickly fashion a new policy for "special presidential admission" with "special talents, in whatever fields" and affirmed the board's role in setting policy, noting that the faculty had "too much power." This prompted another special meeting of the faculty council, drawing 100 faculty and students upset that preempting the setting of academic standards entrusted to the faculty was an action unprecedented in over 125 years of Pacific. Students pleaded, "Please don't let us down!" and the council requested that the board reconsider.

McCaffrey, himself concerned about the prerogative of the faculty and administration on setting such campus policies, quickly appointed respected communication professor Don Duns ('58) to head a task force on the "special admits" issue that concluded that switching to a NCAA Division II football program would mean little cost savings.[186] The board made clear that Pacific would be "returning to the old practice" of making special admits, limiting them to no more than a dozen per year.[187]

Toledo left after four years with twice as many losses as wins, though he did launch the Football Hall of Fame in his final year, which soon became the Athletic Hall of Fame, honored annually to the present.[188] One of the fascinating aspects of Pacific's football history ever since Stagg was that no "heroic" coach lay at the center of the vortex of support. Larry Siemering, Moose Meyers, Chester Caddas—all the revered coaches at Pacific—never stayed long enough to develop a zealous following of alumni and community fans that made the Amos Staggs and Knute Rocknes, or the John McKays (USC) and "Slip" Madigans (St. Mary's), so storied.

By the mid-1980s, coach Bob Cope was inspiring the team so deeply it even learned to sing the fight song. The 1977-79 teams garnered 12

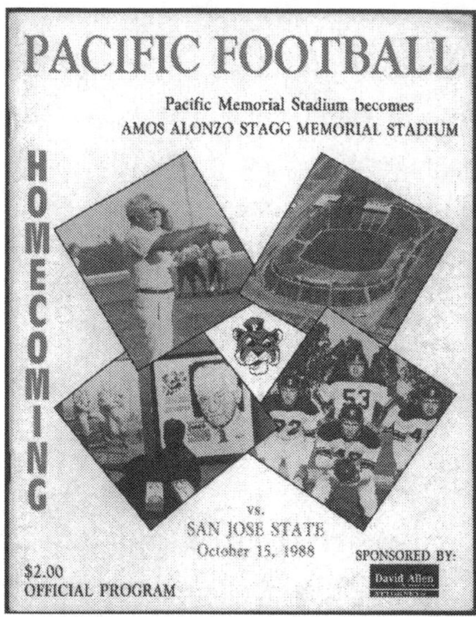

In 1959, the new public high school near Pacific was named in honor of A.A. Stagg. In 1988, his name was added to Memorial Stadium to commemorate the 100th anniversary of his coaching career.

All-American awards, led by three-time All American Brad Vassar. But 1978-93 saw the longest streak of consecutive losing seasons (the most winning streaks were 1921-26 and 1947-52).[189] The Academic Council chair in 1986 happened to be business professor Donald Bryan, also chair of the athletic advisory board, who presented a "frightening" report on athletic deficits: since 1980, athletics "consistently had an annual deficit of $1 million or more" at a time when McCaffrey had declared that deficits over $750,000 would not be tolerated amid the annual budget woes.[190]

In the last of Bob Cope's six losing seasons in 1988, at Homecoming the stadium was named in honor of Stagg on the 100th anniversary of his coaching career. It was also dedicated to all veterans: Stagg Memorial Stadium, a memorial to the man who started it all, and a salute to all the Pacificans who served in the military.[191] That was the year the federal courts ruled that football and men's basketball must be factored in to any Title IX compliance formula, so pressure intensified to invest in women's sports—and over 30 California colleges and universities dropped football.

Title IX

For all the drama and success in other sports, the crowning achievement for Pacific athletics went to the women by winning an historic two national NCAA women's volleyball titles under the odd-couple duo of coaches Terry Lyskevych and John Dunning. For 25 years, All-Americans starred on Pacific volleyball teams all but two years, and often there were two or three.[192]

When Congress passed gender equity legislation in 1972, few could have predicted how it would influence intercollegiate athletics, following a 46-year intercollegiate hiatus for women's sports. Pacific offered only women's tennis and swimming, but by 1974 basketball and volleyball were added and then softball, field hockey and cross-country running to balance the male-female participation required by Title IX. But in the early 1970s, support was slim: the three women's teams of basketball, volleyball and softball all shared the same set of game uniforms! With women's sports sprouting in high schools and California state universities leading the nation toward women's sports, athletic director Dempsey was a major player in setting up the NorCal Athletic Conference for women. His motivation was clear: to be a teacher-coach, you had to play the game, and he had a crowd of women physical education majors.[193]

Unlike many schools, Pacific's transition to comply with Title IX was not highly contentious under Dempsey's progressive approach, though actually trying to achieve equity was another matter. Pioneer physical education professor Doris Meyer, hired to coordinate women's athletics in the fifities, saluted Dempsey and dean of students Ed Betz for advancing women's athletics ahead of some other schools and for providing national leadership for women's athletics.[194] Betz chaired the NCAA Women's Intercollegiate Athletics Commission in 1976.[195] Soon Meyer, who preached "competence and confidence" to all her players and students, gradually withdrew from coaching as women athletes demanded professional coaches in each sport.

Pacific focused on tennis, golf and swimming, building on long-standing teams. For the more expensive team sports the department decided to focus on volleyball partly because Stockton had a standout city team that had won a national championship, and it was becoming popular in California high schools. In 1976 Dempsey hired 28-year-old coach Taras "Terry" Liskevych, who promised a championship in five years.

It was not easy to point to specific benefits to Pacific from president McCaffrey's personal friendship with president Nixon and his cabinet members from that era. But in 1975 the NCAA did ask McCaffrey to meet with his old friend Health Education and Welfare Secretary Caspar

Weinberger to seek a reasonable compromise on Title IX because the high bar of equal funds for men's and women's sports was insurmountable with football factored in. McCaffrey asked that football be removed from the equation.[196] The national policy issue was resolved by compromise, so by 1980, the board approved a policy statement on Title IX that assured "nondiscriminatory access" to University resources in athletics, "not equality of result or expenditure."[197]

Within the decade women's non-revenue sports received "significantly more financial support than men's non-revenue sports," as a WASC report concluded.[198] But like most universities, Pacific lagged in compliance because the bar was high. Although women edged out men in enrollment across the country, male athletes outnumbered female athletes by more than two to one and on average nationally received double the number of scholarships and three-fourths of the athletics budget.[199] All this disparity prompted Cindy Spiro ('76) and Mary Elizabeth Eberhardt ('76) to launch a booster organization, Pacific Association for Women's Sports (Tiger PAWS) in 1980.[200]

Women's volleyball heroics

Coach Taras (Terry) Lyskevych built a women's volleyball powerhouse from the ground up from 1976-85.

Liskevych saw to it that Cindy Spiro was hired as women's athletics coordinator, and they set out to launch the fast-food chain Wendy's Classic (later Bankers' Classic) women's volleyball tournament—the longest running in the country—to build fan and financial support for a championship team that now trained year round. In the early 1980s, Jan Sanders ('84), Eileen Dempster ('85), and Julie Maginot ('86) were three-time All-Americans. Liskevych grumbled about getting more funding from a single donor than he got from the University, but the team ranked second in the nation behind USC by 1981, led by three-time All-American Jayne Gibson ('82).[201]

Coach John Dunning led the women's volleyball team to two NCAA championships—the only Pacific team ever to become national champions.

Personable Liskevych had a forceful, intense style of coaching that knew no bounds. Using applied behavior modification by teaming with psychology professor Martin Gipson, he built champions and earned himself the job of U.S. Olympic coach in 1985.[202] John Dunning entered, and with an entirely different coaching style, brought the 1986 team to the NCAA national championship with Liz Hert ('88), Mary Miller ('88), Teri McGrath ('89), and Elaina Oden ('90), all two- or three-time All-Americans. This was the first-ever national championship for any Pacific sport. Liskevych later tapped Gibson and Oden, a first-team All-American as a freshman, for U.S. Olympic teams. The 1980s and early 1990s were the glory days of Pacific women's volleyball. Four of the teams in a decade are in Pacific's Hall of Fame. Julie Maginot ('85) and Oden were three-time All-Americans, and Charlotte Johansson ('95) was a four-time All-American. The teams from 1985-1991 earned 19 All-American awards.

Dunning like Liskevych had a magical manner to inspire the best team effort. Both earned NCAA national coach of the year. The team won the national championship again the very next year, when they clinched 24 straight wins by defeating Nebraska in the Spanos Center. In 1988, nine Pacific players were drafted into the professional league, one-sixth of all the league players.[203] Dunning called the powerful Oden "the most talented volleyball player ever to play," while Oden responded that Pacific was one of the few schools in the country with a top team "where everyone likes each other."[204] The team was nationally ranked in the top five for 12 years, and in the top ten for nearly two decades. Dunning had the highest percentage of wins than any Pacific coach in history.[205]

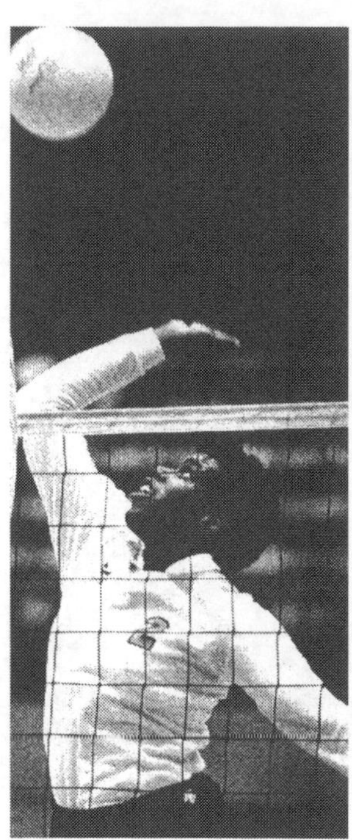

Volleyball player Elaina Oden ('90) was probably Pacific's top woman athlete of the modern era.

Men's basketball and other sports

When Pacific's great coach Dick Edwards left for the Cal coaching job in 1972, he said Pacific was in the wrong league for basketball, that the West Coast Conference Pacific had departed was a stronger league of peer private universities. Pacific basketball had always wanted to stay in the WCC, but football had won out in 1968, and all the other sports moved to the PCAA in 1971. While basketball languished for most of 25 years under Edwards' successors, the home-court advantage of "The Pit" downtown did witness the powerful Jim McCargo ('73) and earn coach Stan Morrison a 69-19 home record during his seven-year stint. His team earned one conference championship in 1979, and Morrison was named PCAA coach of the year. Led by super-star Ron Cornelius ('81), the team headed to the NCAA tournament again, now labeled "March Madness," the year ESPN was launched, and the dance was on its way to the annual billion-dollar spectacle it has become. As Pacific games moved back to the campus in

1982, Cornelius, only the third player to have his jersey retired after Swagerty and Gianelli, averaged 24 points per game. He broke Gianelli's all-time scoring record, set a PCAA conference record, earned All American honors, and was drafted by the Los Angeles Lakers.[206]

Ron Cornelius ('81) was only the third Tiger basketball player to have his jersey retired.

Tom Stubbs, baseball coach from 1966 until 1981, was the winningest baseball coach in Pacific history despite his shoestring budget, always in the shadow of football and basketball, never with a player on a "full ride."[207] By the end of his run he had five scholarships to spread among his team, competing against a fierce Big West baseball conference which routinely produced College World Series teams. Stubbs was succeeded by Quincy Noble, who coached ably for 15 years with a number of winning seasons on a bare-bones budget, until a new president took a new turn with the sport.

Coach Tom Stubbs (1966-81) had the most wins in Pacific baseball history.

Other sports had equally variable histories, but the standout for the men was the swim team of the 1970s. Led by Rick Reeder ('74), Joe Dietrich ('74), Craig Schwartz ('77, also four-time All-American in water polo), and Kevin Drake ('78), the team was ranked in the top 20 nationally three years running.[208] From 1970-76, the team earned eight All-American awards.[209] Men's varsity soccer was ended in 1986, but then in 1991 men's volleyball and women's soccer were added to its intercollegiate roster of sports.

The star-studded men's swim team of the early 1970s earned national rankings. (Pictured is 1974 team.)

RESPONDING TO THE ENVIRONMENT: BUSINESS, PHARMACY AND INTERNATIONAL STUDIES

The School of Business is born

In 1972 Pacific flirted with the idea of a "School of Administrative Science" to include business, public administration, health care and education, but instead opted for a school of business and public administration.[210] In the long run, the hero of the business school is its founding department chair, Sid Turoff, the very faculty firebrand who raised the ire of nearly all regents during the McCaffrey era for his forceful leadership on faculty governance issues. For the business program, however, he was a rough-hewn godsend.[211] Students remember his baggy forties pants and the jingle of change he fisted in both front pockets as he lectured.[212] After he arrived in 1971, he recruited a group of young professors all dedicated to building an accredited school out of an inherited faculty of six with little direction. He may have had a blunt, even gruff manner with the powers

Professor Sid Turoff was the spark to launch the School of Business and Public Administration in1978 and to light fires under the faculty on governance issues.

that be—he had been a union organizer before he headed to college and graduate school—but he was an angel to the business faculty.

Benefiting from fast-growing enrollments of talented students who loved the zesty environment of a program on the move, the business program virtually outgrew COP. One fifth of COP students were business majors.[213] This phenomenon of a new school growing out of the liberal arts college was common among many schools, and given Pacific's history, it was no surprise that this developed only in the post-sixties, post-Vietnam war era when college students poured into professional programs.

In 1978 the department was declared to be the School of Business and Public Administration with a new dean, Elliot Kline. Kline was an outstanding dean who partnered effectively with Turoff—Kline the polished diplomat, Turoff the political strategist—to build a great new school that remarkably achieved AACSB accreditation in 1983 on its first try. It was one of only 240 accredited schools among 1200 nationwide. The school then moved from North Hall into a refurbished Weber Hall with plenty of room to grow.[214]

These were the golden years of the business school, with large classes, engaged and energetic faculty, and good financial support. Mentored well by Turoff to be good university citizens, the young faculty took leadership positions across the campus. The School was highly regarded by all. From the start Turoff had led the faculty as a "committee of the whole," resisting separate departments, a practice that has continued to this day. The strong sense of common vision led the accreditation team to call the School "Camelot," and the alumni from these years, like entrepreneur Mark Bozz ('82), who founded Pete's Brewing Co. and launched Wicked Ale, are impressive exemplars of successful graduates.[215]

When Turoff retired, the School was settled in Weber Hall, and dean Kline resigned in 1986—some say out of boredom, having accomplished all his goals. The school shifted in style and tone, partly shaped by the changing agenda of the accrediting body. Faculty research was now essential, and the new dean, Mark Plovnick (1989-2006), supported a fresh engagement with the profession as well as in the local business community.[216] Looking for visibility and resources, Plovnick understood that outreach was the best means for a business school to get them. He offered great freedom and support for faculty to head off into their specialties, especially if it involved a community outreach program.

In 1989 he started the Westgate Center for Management Development in honor of regent Ed Westgate's ('33?) long-term support of the School, and the Center for Entrepreneurship funded in memory of Greenlaw Grupe, Sr. ('33). The entrepreneurship emphasis fostered the Institute for Family Business, a Real Estate Institute, and an Invention Evaluation Service, mostly run by outstanding faculty like John Knight and Cynthia Wagner Weick. Because each of these attractive new enterprises often involved one or two faculty members, over time the sense of common purpose waned, and the school stretched itself thin for a small school with less than two dozen professors.

Professors John Knight and Cynthia Wagner Weick were two of several outstanding business professors in this era who excelled at teaching and scholarship—and earned students' admiration.

Whereas other Pacific schools often struggled in the eighties and nineties to set research on its proper footing in relation to teaching, the business school was justly proud of its balance of teaching and research befitting the Pacific teacher-scholar. Plovnick set up faculty measurements for teaching, scholarship and service that increased productivity in all three areas. By the mid-nineties the provost pointed to them as a model for the other undergraduate schools. Plovnick also took a stodgy "Pacific Business Forum" of public lectures for the business community and ratcheted it up to a series of national-profile CEOs—Sony, Coors, 49ers, the Fed—that drew large crowds from a 10,000-member mailing list. This spotlight brought corporate sponsors and new school supporters as the School flowered.

At the same time, the new dean was not the open and transparent leader of the past, and the deals he cut with individual faculty members tended to undermine the collective vision and *esprit de corps* of the past. Yet students consistently rated their teachers very highly, and every accreditation team marveled at the "unprecedented" high student ratings of their faculty. The resourceful dean always found a donor for any need—especially in keeping the computer labs current despite the lack of them elsewhere on campus. Plovnick was also one of the few administrators who worked well with President Atchley during his tenure, so while other schools may not have fared so well under his leadership, the business school thrived with no interference and a good deal of support.

Pharmacy challenged

Pharmacy students were delighted to move into a new "campus" of their own north of the Calaveras in 1969. Many pharmacy students pitched in to plant the trees and shrubs that grace the campus green. In 1972, the Long brothers, Thomas and Joseph, founders of Long Drug Stores, Inc. donated nearly a million dollars, the third largest gift to Pacific to date, to complete the pharmacy complex in honor of their parents.[217] They followed this gift with another in 1976 to move drama to the south campus to open up the Rotunda for pharmacy. Through the 1970s pharmacy was thriving with nearly 500 students, many of whom moved seamlessly from liberal

The mentorship of professor Ralph Saroyan ('64) and coach Tom Stubbs enabled Scott Boras ('72, '77, '82) to achieve in baseball and complete pharmacy and law degrees at Pacific before he became the most famous professional sports agent of his time.

arts courses into pharmacy and played an active part in the campus community. In the still-heady days of the early seventies, Pacific had the only pharmacy school in the country offering an "Information Service on Street Drugs." Run by pharmacy students, they could quickly sort out the LSD from mescaline.[218]

As advisor for all the pre-pharmacy students, assistant dean Ralph Saroyan ('64) mentored a young student named Scott Boras ('72, '77, '82), who became an Academic All-American baseball star by 1972 under coach Stubbs.[219] Saroyan figured out how to get Boras through the doctoral program by 1977 while he was playing ball with the St. Louis Cardinals, and then after injury Boras returned to Pacific to earn a law degree in 1982, as he launched his career to become the most famous baseball agent ever. One of his player-clients was Stockton standout Ed Sprague, Jr., who became Pacific's baseball coach in 2004.

After 25 years of outstanding leadership, Cy Rowland retired as pharmacy dean in 1980, and the school hit troubled times. The faculty revolted with a no-confidence vote against dean Louis Martinelli, an insecure autocratic outsider who was a disorganized failure almost from the start. He was replaced in 1983 by Warren Schneider, well-liked and dedicated, who was quickly overcome by one of the longest, costliest University lawsuits on a faculty tenure denial. Coping with illness, he ended his own life within the year.[220] The School was at its lowest point, with a remnant of the early large student classes. Long's and other chain drugstores pressured to keep an anachronistic B.S. degree, but it was finally phased out, later than most schools.

When Donald Sorby became dean, the school was ready to move ahead again, and it did. Under constant pressure from the president, enrollment gradually grew back to 200 students per class. Sorby, who had already earned a national reputation as a pharmacy dean, knew immediately what to do: boost enrollment to expand the faculty and reorganize the curriculum around the professional practitioner, as the dental and law schools had already done. A good listener and facilitator, he invested in developing student leadership, now a hallmark of the school, by building the Association of Student Pharmacists, which brought top national awards in the mid-nineties.[221]

Dean Donald Sorby restored stability to the pharmacy school and advanced enrollment and student leadership through the 1980s.

The changing profession also altered the school. Small independent pharmacies began closing as chain stores took over, women were no longer content with the "hospital pharmacist" role, and drug manufacturers became mega-pharmaceuticals. While more women entered the profession, jobs in the region temporarily shrunk, and applications began to dry up. In 1986, the pharmacy program had 201 applicants for 200 positions as job saturation hit—and only 98 enrolled.[222] (At the same time, engineering was surging with record numbers. The ebb and flow of enrollments among the schools often balanced each other out—one of Pacific's perennial stabilizing strengths.)

In 1988 Jean Matuszak became the first chair of the commission on women's affairs for the American Pharmaceutical Association while Stockton's Charlie Green ('68) was national president. Pacific's pharmacy school, like the two other professional schools, began to dominate leadership positions in the profession nationally and in the state. Dean Sorby was president of the American Association of Colleges of Pharmacy in 1980. Also in the eighties alumnus John Schlegel ('67) was president and then CEO of the APhA, and professor Don Floriddia ('71) received the APhA outstanding chapter award for Pacific's Associated Students of Pharmacy (ASP). Other national presidents include professor Richard Abood in pharmacy law, Matuszak in pharmacy history, Floriddia in Kappa Psi, and Jannet Carmichael ('81) in health systems pharmacy. Professors Marvin Malone and Jeff Jellin ('74) were editors of influential journals, *American Journal of Pharmaceutical Education* (1972-80) and *Pharmacists Letter* (1985-) respectively.

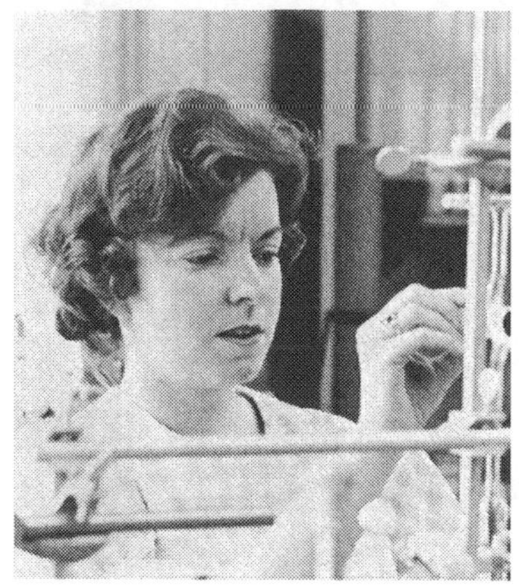

Pharmacy professor Jean Matuszak (here, 1965) was a national leader to promote women in a profession that now graduates more women than men.

In the 1970s, the school considered adding a physical therapy program, then set it aside. But in 1983, with pharmacy enrollments struggling, when Stanford decided to end all allied health programs to focus on its medical school, Pacific took a fresh look and found an opportunity.[223] The University invited the College to develop "PT" along with an emerging sports medicine program. As with other professional programs like business and communicative disorders, the College was comfortable with physical therapy being housed in COP. None of these programs were ever pushed out by the liberal arts.[224] But because the College had no space, the PT program began in the pharmacy school.

Physical therapy quickly got off the ground with many applicants and moved into the Rotunda on the north campus in 1986, the year sports medicine opened in the College with over 30 majors. The physical therapy master's program was one of only 14 in the country at the time.[225] Steady dean Sorby built the school's faculty morale by allowing them to grow and thrive as the school gradually rebuilt its enrollment and stability. The school even had its student underground newspaper, *The Suppository,* in the late eighties to air school issues.[226]

Community outreach grows

Though he knew community relations were important, McCaffrey had little time to get engaged in Stockton's growing issues. He had his sights on the path to the Rotary International presidency, a major achievement. So he urged his vice president Cliff Dochterman, a gifted leader and orator who knew how to work a room, to join the Stockton Chamber of Commerce, where he soon became president.

Stockton, lacking no more than token presence of Cal State University-Stanislaus in Turlock, has suffered from the absence of a public four-year institution for decades. But in 1973, Pacific, in an anxious and unwise attempt to keep out all competition for students, actually opposed a CSU-S branch in Stockton, a factor when the state higher education coordinating council turned down the CSU-S request.[227] By 1985, the Stanislaus campus did expand programs at Delta College, while Delta president Lawrence DeRicco ('49), eager to keep on good terms with Pacific, started a "Delta-UOP Day" to build collaboration for a transfer student pipeline.

Along with the Conservatory of Music, KUOP FM radio was the major cultural arm of Pacific. As the National Public Radio affiliate campus station on the air since 1947, the first non-commercial station in northern California, KUOP continued to provide classical music, news, and campus programming, remaining a popular if starved source of culture for an educated populace. In 1973, heavily subsidized KUOP was almost lost in a budget cut.[228]

Pacific continued as an important player in the overall welfare of the community, but it lacked the material resources—and at times even the expertise—to invest in ways that could treat social ills beyond Band-Aid projects. Sturdy ongoing programs like CIP and the steady partnerships forged by the School of Education were its most important community investments. For most citizens, football was the school's major contribution to the life of the town, and even it did not always draw many to the campus. Through the seventies and eighties crowds averaged about 10-12,000, but by 1989, the gate hit a low of under 6,000.

Innovation returns: A unique School of International Studies

When regent George Wilson announced his plan to create a $1 million endowed chair in international management in 1982, he had in mind a much more ambitious project "to foster international good will and understanding and peace." [229] The first Wilson professor was appointed in 1983.[230] For regent Wilson, who served on the board for 40 years, the commitment to international education at Pacific ran much deeper. His vision was actually to start a professional school for "foreign service" diplomats to prepare them better than the uninformed U.S. diplomats abroad he had met over the decades.

A year earlier, McCaffrey's old friend, head of the renowned international engineering firm and world traveler Stephen Bechtel, Jr., along with regent and Bechtel family member Paul Davies, pitched in to build the Bechtel International Center specifically for a growing international student population. Students from other countries had reached over 300 students in that year, then grew to over 400, 10 percent of the Stockton campus enrollment in the early 1980s.

Momentum built for establishing a school, given that 100 students were already enrolled in the three international majors of international relations, management, and interdisciplinary studies. In addition, Pacific had built faculty strength in international law and management to draw on. In the mid-eighties, ten faculty members were selected for teaching and research at institutions in other countries in the prestigious Fulbright Program.[231] Pacific was only one of ten universities nationwide that offered a cross-cultural orientation class for students about to study abroad.[232]

Shortly after he announced his intent to retire in 1987 after 16 years of service, McCaffrey presented a proposal for a School of International Studies based on a two-year study. The international faculty had initially thought McCaffrey was out of his head with this "hail-Mary" decision late in his game. He had ended all three cluster colleges just a few years earlier, forcing many of their faculty into the College. The international faculty were all "flabbergasted—and appalled.… The Callison corpse was hardly cold in the ground," as political science professor Cort Smith said. But once they knew the board would move ahead, they huddled and came up with a program that tried to avoid all the flaws of the cluster colleges. They designed an undergraduate professional program that was uniquely excellent in the country: international, interdisciplinary, intercultural, with a required study abroad semester unknown in any other program.

The ace in the hole was the opportunity to build on four current faculty members, including two talented Callison leaders, Cort Smith and Bruce LaBrack. Smith had orchestrated the international programs and study abroad office in 1981 into a nationally respected program with a proliferation of study abroad options for nearly every major. LaBrack was the pioneer developer of cross-cultural orientation for students studying abroad.

The Academic Council had its reservations: long and hot debate centered on faculty unwilling to commit wholeheartedly (once bitten, twice shy former cluster college faculty), and resources being diverted from impoverished programs. And why would you start a new school without full-time faculty even before a new president is announced, rather than begin as an "institute"? The proposal barely squeaked by the council (11-7-3 vote), and the school became a bone of faculty contention throughout its years.[233] But the more confident board, eager to honor their colleague, signed off, and the former *El Centro* of Covell College was renamed George Wilson Hall. Unlike the three cluster colleges, at least SIS had a bona fide endowment, but starting a school with $1 million in the late 1980s was itself not wholly responsible. Cort Smith became the acting dean, and the School was launched in 1987 with 104 students.

Visionary regent George Wilson and Mrs. Wilson, together with president McCaffrey and board chair Robert Eberhardt ('51), dedicate the launch of SIS in George Wilson Hall in 1987.

SIS graduates will tell you that the required study abroad for any of the three majors—typically in a less-developed country, and often extended to a second term in another country—was the most formative experience of their time at Pacific. But they would also point to rigorous interdisciplinary study, research, writing, debate and analysis with teams of teachers. They reveled in the intensity of a small, close-knit community focused on the world. In the case of SIS, the promise of the cluster colleges was carried forward, still precarious in its sustainability, but chock full of some of the best of Pacific's heritage.

CHAPTER 5

Over the edge, 1980s-1995

Board of Regents challenges—McCaffrey's Rotary presidency—McCaffrey's troubled legacy—President Atchley's promise and setbacks—General education strengthened—The College, schools and campus of the 1980s—Athletic achievements—The accreditation crisis—Faculty leadership—Football issues—Board upheaval and restoration

DETACHED LEADERSHIP

A board adrift

At the center of what became Pacific's decline in this era was an inattentive Board of Regents. Beginning with Burns and Baun, this detachment continued under Baun's aging leadership and it challenged Bob Eberhardt, who became chair in 1975. In Stockton, Eberhardt was one of the few genuine philanthropists who worked behind the scenes to make life better for downtown and for many struggling families. Devoting much of his life and energy to Pacific, Eberhardt saw his investment in Pacific football as one way to open a door to a better life for young men from south Stockton like standouts Willie Viney ('74) or Willard Harrell ('76).[1]

McCaffrey persuaded wealthy influential San Francisco businessmen he had known through the Bay Area Council and Cal alumni to join the board, but their loyalties and philanthropy were never won over. Board leaders could never quite unite this detached group of aging regents—veterans of Valley farms with country ways—with ambitious city suits who never forgot they were Cal Golden Bears or belonged to Stanford. McCaffrey too was implicated, as he himself was challenged to overcome his own Cal loyalties to build a genuine passion for Pacific. Some of the Bay Area regents drifted away, dismayed by the way the board and University were run.

Over the years, McCaffrey began a shift in board culture, but the underlying issue remained: a board disengaged in a personal way from the mission and purposes of the University, not ready to ask searching questions, unable to challenge assumptions, and unwilling to push the president to take responsibility for enlivening the University. In the end, McCaffrey lacked the vision and ambition to build a great university on the shoulders of Burns. Both McCaffrey and Eberhardt relished Pacific sports, supported conservative politics, and thrived on world travel. They also shared a discomfort for faculty and the academic enterprise. "Bay vs. Valley" carried on through the Atchley years.[2] It is not clear that the regents understood their role—many later claimed they did not.

Financial troubles percolate

As chair, Eberhardt had a trusted old friend he could count on at Pacific. Vice president for finance Bob Winterberg was a classmate of Eberhardt's, so they worked closely together. Winterberg, hired by O. H. Ritter upon graduation, chose Pacific as his "lifelong career." Winterberg had great regard for Eberhardt's leadership and admired his frankness and integrity, always keeping the interests of Pacific foremost in his mind.[3]

During the enrollment slide ahead, the regents did not realize that shrinking revenue and construction debt was becoming a severe problem. McCaffrey and Winterberg covered over the losses that built year after year, to an accumulated deficit of $13 million. It was "common practice" to juggle enrollment numbers to match annual budget needs.[4] Winterberg's unified budget reports did not fully disclose the disparities between the three campus budgets. But an attentive board would have asked questions.

Eberhardt called upon trusted successful Stockton businessmen and athletic supporters like Alex Spanos ('48), Edward Westgate ('33), and Charles Bloom ('43) to make sure "the faculty don't run the school."[5] One key mark of engaged regents is leadership in fundraising; it would not be unusual for an active university board to raise half the campaign goal around the table. Eberhardt certainly led by impressive example, as did some others. However, by the time Pacific's seven-year campaign (1977 to 1985) closed at $30 million, the regents had contributed less than 20 percent of the total.[6] The annual gift fund was chronically short of its fundraising goal through the 1970s, and by 1980 was $900,000 short of its cumulative goal.[7]

The governance issue

A special meeting of the faculty in 1976 debated a proposed new University governance policy after seven years of wrangling. Three years in the drafting, the policy reverberated through decision-making for years to come. This process was an attempt to craft Pacific's first shared governance policy, since the board had never formalized the faculty's role in University decision-making.[8] Jittery about the uncertain leadership of McCaffrey—whose famous temper could erupt in any setting—faculty leaders worried that the deans' direct accountability to the president would bypass the faculty on important budget and policy issues. Academic vice president Hand endorsed the proposal approved by a representative leadership body, but in the end the faculty voted against it for granting too much power to executives.

McCaffrey, determined to settle the matter, revised the document and sent a copy to the board and the faculty, declaring that the proposed policy, mirroring current practice, would serve as the official governance policy.[9] To help cool down the inflamed atmosphere, McCaffrey arranged for Academic Council chair Turoff to meet with the regents' academic affairs committee, a strong step toward mutual understanding.[10]

The temporary resolution to the "shared governance" issue demonstrated that when McCaffrey was so inclined, he could step up to lead Pacific forward. After all, the expectations declared by Turoff on behalf of the faculty were unrealistic and beyond the bounds of contemporary private higher education. The president *is* finally accountable to the board for the overall conduct of the institution. Any other formula is unworkable. But the means by which the faculty, staff, and students participate in the process is critically important to the welfare of a university.

The Rotary absence

A touchstone of McCaffrey's tenure was his decision to pursue the presidency of Rotary International, perhaps the most prestigious of the U.S.-founded service organizations, whose ambitious worldwide service projects promoted international understanding. In retrospect, it seems remarkable that McCaffrey would consider requesting a leave of absence in the middle of a University fundraising campaign, relaunched in 1977 at a period of great enrollment volatility. But then again he had dared earlier to ask permission of the board to run for the Rotary office in his *first* year as Pacific's president, which was promptly rejected. Now, an ambivalent Board was persuaded to assent by Baun and Eberhardt, who believed the global exposure of Pacific's president would redound to Pacific many times over.[11]

The Academic Council passed a resolution voicing formal concern about the University's capacity to raise money "in the absence of the President during the next two years."[12] If anything, it was McCaffrey's talent and preference to hold sway in the larger community—and finally the entire world—as both he (1981-82) and his vice president Cliff Dochterman (1992-93) became presidents of Rotary International.

President and Mrs. McCaffrey traveled the world as ambassadors for peace while Stan McCaffrey served as president of Rotary International in 1981-82, here shown with Pope John Paul II.

He was essentially absent from the campuses for 18 months, during which time attendance at board meetings ran about 50 percent.

Standoffs grow into the eighties

McCaffrey always looked the model president: tall, silver-haired, stunningly handsome and flawlessly dressed, he was well spoken, cordial and charming. He was gifted with a great memory for names, was at ease as much among the powerful and influential as with students, and was even connected to the White House. Yet he did not seem to understand how to lead the board, collaborate with the faculty, and feel the pulse of the students. Under his time at the helm, Pacific was often adrift.

The 1970s had been comparatively good times for McCaffrey and the University even if budget worries nagged. Enrollments held at about 6,000 until the early eighties, student campus life improved, the Stockton campus acreage increased by nearly one-half, and new buildings like the University Center, chemistry building and Spanos Center were impressive. McCaffrey launched the 1980s with his "President's Commission on the Future of the University," headed by academic vice president Hand, but it was mainly window dressing as McCaffrey prepared for his Rotary leave of absence. The 100-page report, issued just prior to the 1981 WASC accreditation visit, set no priorities, timelines or measures of success.[13] In a fluffy convocation address, McCaffrey set forth three task forces to address fundraising, academic programs, and program efficiency, all of which straggled along for years. Pacific suffered from a lack of systematic planning to set clear goals and priorities.

In 1976 Hand had presented the Academic Council with the glaring results of his study: over half the undergraduate classes enrolled fewer than 15 students, totaling only 17 percent of all students. Three-fourths of the classes enrolled 30 or fewer students.[14] Winterberg pressed for a 17:1 student/faculty ratio target when the ratio dipped to 13:1 in 1982, just as the regents were eyeing a projected enrollment decline over the next five years.[15] When Hand reported the board's decision to set a 15:1 student/faculty ratio requirement for the undergraduate schools, the faculty spurned it. The faculty's unwillingness to accept reasonable responsibility on this issue was a source of much of the board's antagonism.

In addition, the WASC report kicked into gear academic program review, but the process had no teeth to address feather-bedded programs: bland reviews recommended that University College expand its adult degree program or that the Conservatory improve its efficiency. Japanese language was retained as "effective, efficient and necessary." The most important outcome was a new policy of automatic review of any program based on low enrollment or revenue/cost ratio.[16] The faculty evaded serious program review for another 15 years.

Red ink

When McCaffrey returned to the campus in fall 1982, Stockton campus enrollment had dropped by 240 students. Despite the fact that only the Covell cluster college remained and the new business school and engineering were booming, a bad economy, uncertainty about shrinking government grants, a fall-off of transfer and graduate students, and perhaps some campus neglect contributed to the decline. Yet board decisions made Pacific now the second most expensive private university in California, even though entering students, choosing primarily between the UC campuses and Pacific, agreed Pacific lacked "high prestige."[17]

The campaign languished $10 million short of its $30 million goal, and things got worse. To handle a 5 percent budget cut, McCaffrey froze salaries in 1983. By then, 24 percent of the freshman students were "special admits," that is, students who had either lower SAT scores, lower high school GPAs, participated in the special bootstrap summer program, or athletic promise. By 1985, the faculty had successfully defended the sabbatical leave program but saw nine faculty positions cut in communication, education, pharmacy and physical therapy.[18]

McCaffrey had returned just in time for acting president Hand. Beloved for championing academic achievement with a compassionate touch since his days as honors program director, Raymond College English professor, COP dean and academic vice president, Cliff Hand had served Pacific well once again. Within weeks he was diagnosed with pancreatic cancer that took his life a few months later in 1983. To honor one of its most distinguished and gracious academic leaders, the board renamed North Hall as Clifford J. Hand Hall that year. His loss was to have a painful impact on the University for the next two years over McCaffrey's fateful appointment to replace him.

As professor, dean, and academic vice president, Clifford Hand was a wise leader for Pacific during turbulent years, including time as acting president.

The tipping point

Executive vice president Dochterman covered for McCaffrey's increasing detachment from University affairs. When Cliff Hand died, McCaffrey abruptly appointed Oscar Jarvis, the dean of the school of education, as interim academic vice president without any faculty consultation in fall 1983. He then announced to the Academic Council that he did not intend to conduct a search for a permanent replacement, and would appoint Jarvis as his academic leader as soon as the faculty signaled acceptance of the decision.

The Academic Council was confounded that a critical academic appointment could proceed without faculty consultation. Outspoken philosophy professor Gwenn Brown resigned from the Academic Council, noting to her colleagues that continuing would be "mere cooperation in a charade."[19] McCaffrey sent a written response to the council admitting his mistake in failing to consult, but stating that he would not back down. The Academic Council called for a faculty referendum to force a national search that was in effect a no-confidence vote of the president.

The council included a letter of support from six former Academic Council chairs objecting to the appointment "without significant faculty consultation." The faculty letter noted the "precarious" state of the University, highly dependent on tuition income, that now admitted nearly 90 percent of all applicants, many with low SAT scores on special admission. Good planning, the chairs asserted, would not be focused on covering costly deficits in athletics by short-term budget cuts but on investing in "innovative" programs to "maintain the University's distinctiveness."[20]

McCaffrey labeled the letter with the faculty ballot "certainly a violation of good voting or ethical procedure." The faculty vote split down the middle, though the majority rejected the call for a national search.[21] The board unanimously approved both the Jarvis appointment and a vote of confidence in McCaffrey, but McCaffrey knew his seriously damaged relationship with the faculty required mending. As one regent noted, McCaffrey was great at public relations but not at decisions. The faculty referendum to call him to account actually boosted the University to a new level of collaboration unseen for decades. In the end, though, McCaffrey was devastated by the faculty vote.[22] Undoubtedly retirement was beckoning.

Faculty leadership through collaboration

McCaffrey called for a meeting with the faculty to "bring together" the campus community, urging a joint effort to move the school ahead and welcoming joint meetings with regents and faculty. In March 1984, the Academic Council executive board sent a 40-page report on academic quality to the regents' academic affairs committee. In a searching study with seven recommendations, faculty leaders detailed the serious concerns that they saw unaddressed. The seven proposals were on governance (the need for "shared authority"), program review (the stalled appraisal of athletics), faculty quality (inadequate support for improvement), student quality (low admission standards), administrative quality (no evaluation procedures for key administrators), academic reputation (no market research and public relations campaign), and planning (a need to set priorities).[23] The central theme was the need to invest in academic quality as the highest priority in policy-making and investment.

All these issues had been mounting for some time, but the flash point of the Jarvis appointment brought all to the fore. The Jarvis jolt especially grabbed the attention of passive regents, which in turn required McCaffrey to focus on the layers of woes that had grown to become perilous for Pacific. McCaffrey and Jarvis held 23 meetings with nearly all academic departments and schools over the next few months to try to build communication and trust. As professor Turoff remarked, "A university with an uninvolved faculty is not a very good one."[24] The chief concern of faculty was the decline in academic quality. They called for an aggressive merit scholarship program and hiked admissions standards, which were adopted by the end of 1985.[25]

Faculty increased their own accountability on the most stinging criticism of the faculty in the 1981 WASC report: reduce faculty time devoted to governance and administrative issues and increase productivity in teaching and scholarly activities. At the same time, the board focused on boosting the student/faculty ratios to help balance the budget, including an early retirement program for faculty.

In fall 1984, the first joint retreat of regents, faculty and administrators was held since McCaffrey was named president 13 years earlier—another neglect acknowledged. This very constructive meeting was followed by others where regents and faculty wrestled with a major budget pinch point, the student/faculty ratio issue.

The McCaffrey legacy

Remarkably, after decades of neglect, and just as the $30 million campaign drew to a close nearly a decade after it began, in the final months of McCaffrey's presidency, the board suddenly awakened to the feeble state of the University endowment fund. The bedrock of any quality private university is a sizable endowment to provide a reliable income apart from student tuition, but Pacific's had been ignored by all its presidents since Seaton in 1919. The endowment had crept up from around $4 million to $9 million in the years since Burns departed—a disgraceful amount for a comprehensive university. McCaffrey had never been an effective fundraiser because he never devoted the time, effort, and commitment required. He certainly expressed little concern about the endowment. The board set about to double it in five years through a new endowment fundraising campaign, and by 1985 had hiked the goal to $25 million.[26] When McCaffrey retired it stood at $12 million.

McCaffrey certainly helped advance Pacific in many ways. His most important contributions were to acquire the Stockton College campus, to build out the three campuses, and to develop a first-rate student life program. He presided over the difficult and painful decline and ending of the cluster colleges while building two professional schools, business and international studies. Important enduring programs were added: physical therapy, music and entertainment management, computer and mechanical engineering, and sports medicine. The business school had grown to 600 students, the engineering school nearly to 700. The quality marker in law, Order of the Coif, was earned, and international programs in law and dentistry were added. He groomed a nationally noted residential life program, created offices for international students and programs as well as a chaplain, and elevated the student life dean to a vice presidency. He added many lasting alumni programs that stretched well beyond the Feather River Inn.

In addition, McCaffrey could well be called Pacific's "building president" as much as Knoles and Burns. He built the Student Center (named the McCaffrey University Center in 1987) and the Spanos Center, both major landmarks that lifted the University. He expanded the library and built out the "conservatory campus," both occurring at critical times in their progress. He developed the "south campus" for the School of Education and the College and supported the massive building program on the Sacramento campus (nine newly constructed buildings), including student housing there and on the San Francisco campus. The budget quadrupled to $78 million during a time in which McCaffrey handed diplomas to nearly two-thirds of all living alumni.[27] He certainly made marked progress on his fourfold agenda—Stockton campus build-out, fundraising infrastructure, alumni and community relations, and Board of Regents culture. All this accomplishment should have added up to a highly successful presidency.

Unfortunately, it did not work out that way by most everyone's account.

New construction left mounting budget deficits, the development office build-up did not survive, constituents were not inspired, and the Bay-Valley regent *rapprochement* never brought transformational philanthropy or serious engagement to the board. At the end of his term, McCaffrey presided over a university that had decidedly lost its luster and even its clear sense of direction. Without vision and academic aspiration, many of its endeavors suffered. The freshman class of 1978 had overwhelmingly selected Pacific as its "first choice" school, 87 percent of them. A decade later, barely two thirds did. And while "academic reputation" remained the top reason for selecting Pacific over other schools through these years, the percentage steadily declined.[28]

Traditions faded, quality dulled, and community values turned tepid. Shortcomings in planning, financing and governance led to troubling times. It seemed fitting that Rotary International created a monument to McCaffrey on the Stockton campus, a bronze and stone marker surrounded by a redwood grove, in tribute to his immense contributions to Rotary, just south of the Spanos Center. After his death in 2002, his ashes were placed there.

A TRANSITION ON THE BRINK

The Valley wins over the Bay

The 1987 Black Monday global stock market crash was a bad omen for Pacific. The University was about to enter its darkest days since the 1930s, beginning with the selection of a mismatched president. The events over the next eight years could have been avoided by a more engaged board, but instead the University found itself on a collision course with its accrediting agency within four years of appointing a new president.

Bob Eberhardt ('51) bled orange and black. No one was more loyal to his school and to his community. He was a highly respected community and regional leader who was pulled in to be board chair by his peers. President of the California Bankers Association by age 42, Eberhardt was a seasoned leader. He cared deeply about Pacific, was a hardworking and successful fundraiser for the school, and devoted much of his life to making it better. He, his family, and the Bank of Stockton—the only Stockton corporation to rank among the top 500 in the state—were among the very top donors to the University, supporting many programs.[29] But most of all, he was devoted to the health and welfare of the intercollegiate athletic program, and nothing more than football. Eberhardt never lost his passion for the gridiron success of his student era, and he remained determined to keep football at all costs as an important community builder for the city.

So when the Pacific community lined up in support of a winsome candidate to replace McCaffrey, Eberhardt and several fellow regents were not convinced. Polished James Appleton, eager for the job, had all the skills to be a successful president, and almost everyone saw him as a shoo-in. Appleton, USC vice president of development, had been named one of 100 "most respected emerging leaders in higher education" by the American Council on Education and *Change* magazine.

On the other hand, candidate Bill Atchley, despite his casual friendliness and folksy charm, was unimpressive in campus interviews. He had difficulty communicating clearly, despite his credentials as a successful engineering dean at West Virginia and president at Clemson University, a high-profile school that won the national football championship in 1981. But he had been a pro baseball pitcher who "looked like Mickey Mantle," was serious about all the sports that Eberhardt loved, and had proved his mettle at Clemson, a tradition-entrenched public university.

At the outset of the search, Eberhardt had formed a regents selection committee in addition to the University search committee chaired by law dean Schaber. After the campus-based search committee registered its overwhelming preference for Appleton and Schaber had nearly assured Appleton he would get the job, Eberhardt called together the regents committee in his living room to make the right decision. He knew what he wanted. Like Eberhardt, Spanos offered that Atchley was "tough—he will take on the Sid Turoffs of the faculty" and get football back on track. Were it not for the San Francisco regents around the room the decision could have gone the other way. They went with Atchley, the obvious choice, a seasoned sitting president.[30]

While the appointment of Atchley in 1987 in many ways accelerated the downward spiral of Pacific in this era, his selection made more sense than many of his later detractors admit. He brought with him a strong portfolio of good ideas for Pacific. Atchley came to the Clemson University presidency as a solid academic leader and an open, unpretentious, "genuinely likeable" personality that matched his handsome, hearty, professional-baseball athleticism. He quickly became known for his directness, passion for loyalty, and eagerness to engage faculty and students more openly in the governance of a stodgy institution that improved academically under his leadership. But he also earned a reputation for rash decisions and abrupt firings of administrators to stimulate change, as well as his "tendency toward personalizing matters" that later carried forward to Pacific.

Atchley's promise

President Bill Atchley (1987-95) shared the handsome charm of president McCaffrey as well as being a Mickey Mantle look-alike.

Initially, Bill Atchley won the affection and support of the University through his warm personality and informal, southern "good ole boy" style. Never skillful at the podium, Atchley was engaging with small groups, and could win almost anyone over one-on-one.

More important, he came with a fresh view of what Pacific needed, and set about making improvements. He was a competitive person who was not afraid to make judgments and act quickly. Atchley promised "a new beginning" by launching seven significant changes that began to address the neglect of the McCaffrey years:

1) Renewing the Board of Regents. He could see that the old guard on the board was holding back the University and needed new blood. He cut the board from 40 to 36 and urged shorter terms, in order to force turnover in a group that seemed uninformed on higher education.[31] He championed increased diversity by adding to the board two prominent alumni, Latino Thomas Flores ('58) and African-American James McCargo ('73), both firsts for the University.

2) Tackling finances. Atchley grappled openly with the accumulated deficit and flimsy budget rules. He hired new finance vice president Michael Goins in 1990 to replace Winterberg, who was beyond his control. At that point, Atchley exposed a $13 million budget deficit accumulating since 1983, a stunning bombshell. Regents said they were "surprised when they were informed of the severity of the current budget crisis."[32] How could this be? For one thing, the regents had been dealing with enrollment and budget jolts in the eighties under McCaffrey, so they thought they were grappling with it all. Annual deficits were stacking up unknown to the board because law and dental school surpluses masked the losses, as well as the elastic line of credit at the Bank of Stockton. Many of the debts were owing to facilities built without dollars in place, the Spanos Center being the most obvious example. A combination of factors added $6 million to the deficit in 1990 as enrollment plummeted. Atchley cut the budget 8 percent across the board, slashed 25 staff and 28 faculty positions, reduced salary increases for the year, and suspended faculty sabbaticals. He called to account a growing $1 million deficit owing to careless accounting of bookstore inventory over years.[33]

The 25-year contract with the law school, which had locked in any law school assets, preventing their use to fill annual Stockton campus budget holes, had just expired in 1990 with dean Schaber's retirement.[34] To replace the contract, the board adopted what seemed like a reasonable annual 10 percent overhead charge, which increased the school's contribution to University overhead to around $2 million annually. The law faculty chafed over what they viewed as an unfair deal, even though outside accrediting teams commented on a below-average rate.[35] Atchley did use current law school surpluses to help cover Stockton deficits to the tune of $1 million in 1992 alone.[36] But he let an accumulated $7 million reserve fund stand, so when Schaber passed the deanship on to Jerry Caplan, the school was strong.

Stating that the University needed to be run "more like a business," Atchley outsourced campus maintenance to Service Master to save $600,000 and food service to Aramark (ARA) to save $500,000.[37] Atchley and the board agreed to allow the Alumni Association to take over the operations of Feather River Inn in 1988 as it struggled to keep income up and maintenance costs down. The campus was perturbed by the loss of Paul Fairbrook's renowned in-house meal operation.

The shake-up in campus maintenance operations exposed grand theft among the staff resulting in four felony convictions.[38] One scam among several became known on campus as "the toilet paper caper," where a couple of staff would intercept cartloads of toilet paper headed for the residence halls and sell them to off-campus customers. Another casualty of Atchley's sweep was athletic director Carl Miller, who had taken advantage of the Pacific Athletic Foundation that his predecessor Ced Dempsey had created.[39] Atchley may have ended with wrongful termination lawsuits, but he certainly knew that many offices needed a shakedown.

3) Investing in endowment. Atchley's take-charge action to build the University's endowment, with considerable success, began in 1989. It is fair to say that Atchley was the first president in most of the century to bend his effort to build the University's endowment.[40] The board discovered that the median endowment-per-student for independent universities was four times as great as Pacific's.[41] Atchley launched a $50 million campaign in his first year (teed up by the board months earlier), soon raised to a $70 million goal. Headed by Eberhardt and Monagan, "Fulfilling the Promise" aimed to nearly double the endowment. By the time Atchley left the presidency in 1995, the endowment had grown from a mere $12 million to $56 million.

A remarkable windfall occurred early in the campaign to bolster Atchley's endowment thrust. Likely through the positive influence of Bob Eberhardt, Stockton College teacher and alumna Gladys Benerd ('52)

Gladys Benerd's gift to Pacific in 1992 was by far the largest in Pacific history to that time, endowing the School of Education, scholarships, and library acquisitions.

signed over a stock trust fund of her estate to the University in 1992 valued at $9 million. Her gift, by far the largest to the University to that time, endowed the School of Education, scholarships, and library acquisitions.[42] Benerd was able to attend the christening of the school that same year, the first school to be endowed and named after a donor.[43] By the time Benerd's former student Eberhardt sold the stocks over the phone a year later, he had shrewdly negotiated a gift now worth $14.5 million.[44]

4) Engaging the campus. Atchley moved his office out of the top of the ivory tower and placed it in Anderson Hall at the center of campus—a significant symbolic statement. He opened communication and drew in the campus to assess itself, especially through the upcoming WASC reaccreditation self-study. In the early months, he hosted informal pool parties in his backyard for the faculty Academic Council. Atchley was the first to bring systematic annual evaluation of the staff and replace a rigid salary schedule with pay based on performance.[45] While he was quick to fire staff as he made all staff more accountable, new energy came from his bold effort to clear out deadwood in the administration.

By establishing the annual "MVP" ("Most Valuable Pacifican") award, launching the Bishops Scholarship program for Methodist students in 1990 and re-establishing Founders Day to build a sense of tradition, he affirmed core values for faculty and staff. By the time of the WASC accreditation visit in 1991, the Academic Council noted improved trust between faculty and administration, and agreed that faculty morale was better than in the mid-1980s.[46]

5) Investing in infrastructure. He began to establish a reliable data base for decision-making, aiming for a real institutional research office that required a major overhaul of administrative computing from a home-grown operation to a professional, integrated system. While he botched the contract on an outsourced computing operation, he did instantly bring a common, professional system that everyone could argue over as it gradually became Pacific's electronic backbone.

6) Stimulating faculty scholarship. Faculty scholarship and research had a bumpy road at Pacific for decades. Generally, in the seventies and early eighties the published research done by many of the natural science faculty was almost resented by the humanities and social science faculty. And over the decades, presidents Burns and McCaffrey, and deans such as Schaber and Jantzen, ignored scholarship as a faculty expectation.

Atchley understood the need to help the faculty along to productive scholarship and research befitting a selective national university, including a modest teaching load and fewer hours in lengthy committee meetings. Responding to this scholarship priority, the Eberhardt family funded an endowment for faculty development in 1988, known today as the prestigious annual Eberhardt Teacher-Scholar Awards and summer research fellowships.

Atchley's commitment to faculty scholarship and creative activity was matched by the faculty's landmark policies on faculty workload, urged by Atchley in his first year. For the first time the faculty hammered out clear responsibilities in teaching, scholarship and service, noting that scholarship was "second in importance only to teaching."[47] From 1986-89, the faculty nearly doubled their research activity.[48] This led to revised guidelines for promotion and tenure, adopted in 1991 after three years of debate and drafting—the first time the faculty as a body voted on their own evaluation guidelines.[49]

7) Taking on football. While Atchley's hiring was engineered by a small cadre of regents primarily to solve the problems of athletics, Atchley was hesitant. He began by re-assigning athletics to his office to ensure closer control, but he probably did not know the community rumor that Alex Spanos met weekly with the athletics director. Immediately confronted with a mountain of debt unknown to him before he opened his office door, he was cautious about the over-investment in football. His engineer's mind eventually led him through the numbers to find the inevitable bottom line: Pacific could not afford it. When he finally took on the board chair, the football budget got jumbled with many other issues, described below.

In 1989, there was a hopeful mood at the University: *US News and World Report*, which had started its infamous school rankings just six years earlier, now ranked Pacific among the top 125 national universities, and pegged the University as 22nd among 399 "comprehensive" universities.[50] Yet for all his good intentions and impressive set of priorities, Atchley was unable to translate most of his initiatives into success for Pacific. Atchley's style of leadership undermined his declared aims in many of these projects, so much so that he worked his own way out of the presidency before most came to fruition. In the end, he was a poor match for Pacific.

Reckless decision-making

In the years of the Persian Gulf War and the collapse of the Soviet Union in 1990-1991, Pacific began its own historic years of change, among the most significant since its move to Stockton in 1924. With 16 presidents during its first 68 years, Pacific had only four for the next 76: Knoles, Burns, McCaffrey and Atchley. But the apparent stability of long-serving presidents masked serious leadership issues that wobbled Pacific toward the precipice in the eighties, finally losing direction and confidence that imperiled the identity if not the survival of the school by the early nineties. Atchley accumulated a long list of careless decisions, selected here in roughly chronological order, which dug him into a hole impossible to climb out of.

While many senior administrators likely needed to go, Atchley's secretive and reckless personnel decisions too frequently ended in lawsuits.[51] Some senior executives said he ran the University "like a plantation." As if the switch of food service were not controversial enough, there was evidence that the food contract went to ARA as a favor to an Atchley friend.[52]

One example of his abrupt, obstinate decision-making—admittedly more symbolic than substantive—was his sudden move in his second year to combine the College and all Stockton school commencement ceremonies into one after only brief conversations with ASUOP leaders and deans. The students led a campus earthquake that quickly sobered him into recalling his decree within a week.[53] After all, as McCaffrey had said years earlier, the distinctive, individual ceremonies of each of the schools and College expressed two of the University's "most important characteristics"—"the personal quality of the student's experience" and "the diversity offered by our twelve individual Schools and Colleges."[54]

Atchley never wanted a strategic plan for the University. He preferred an unwritten, fluid environment that allowed him free reign.[55] He loved to "mix it up," with units competing for attention and resources. When he arrived, he quickly disbanded the planning and budget committee the faculty had struggled long to get going, a new representative group that in 1986 had finally begun to set some guidelines for long-range planning. He tossed out five-year plans developed by each of the schools and units of the University as too detailed and costly. He asked instead for brief statements of need in 1988, never to be reviewed, as short-term financial crises enveloped the University. Finally, under pressure to have some plan, he substituted his own ten-point plan in a campus address three years into his presidency. Eventually WASC accreditation forced an end to his negligence.

With a poor University bond rating and an accreditation visit pending, perhaps Atchley had no choice but to face the music and attack budget problems aggressively. The fault was lack of serious consultation. He offered a faculty-staff early retirement program in 1989 that included lifetime health benefits for employee and spouse to encourage a swift reduction in staff to match an enrollment nose-dive. New accounting regulations required that the cost of the plan be logged at its present value in the budget, creating another massive hole of $3.5 million for 44 retirees.[56] This counter-productive action pushed the total deficit for the year to over $6 million. The program was quickly halted because of cost, and the trail of funds for retiree health coverage spun out for decades.

Most serious of all, in addition to a salary freeze in 1991 (after two salary freezes under McCaffrey), Atchley cut the University's pension contribution to every employee from 7.5% to 2.5% of annual salary. He announced the decision the morning after a meeting with two faculty representatives of the faculty compensation committee. The cut caused a firestorm of protest from the Sacramento and San Francisco campuses that felt already unduly burdened by Stockton budget problems.[57] The Academic Council rejected the plan outright, lacking any "meaningful input."[58] Within a year or two the board restored retirement funding, but the entire episode cost Atchley dearly in campus confidence, especially since such a drastic action came with feeble consultation.

One of the more serious of Atchley's hasty and unexpected decisions was the seven-year $14.6 million computer contract with SCT (Systems and Computer Technology Corporation) in 1992. No one disputed the desperate need for a centralized computer solution, especially after it was identified as a critical deficiency in the WASC accreditation process. But one weekend evening without prior consultation Atchley persuaded the board chair and vice chair to "immediately" approve the package to meet an SCT deadline on a lopsided contract his assistant John Ryan ('70) had negotiated. Atchley said, "I'll put my job on the line for it." Chair Eberhardt angrily declared that it better never happen again, but the damage was done. No users or outside experts were consulted, no due diligence, no competitive bids.[59] The SCT contract would gnaw at Pacific's craw for years to come, and because it provided only an administrative system, it did not begin to address the festering student and faculty needs.

Atchley added confusion by constantly juggling his cabinet of vice presidents, where there was no teamwork or consensus building to speak of. He had four successive executive vice presidents during his eight years in office. When Atchley appointed Joseph Subbiondo as academic vice president in 1989, Atchley undercut the position by allowing at least four of the deans to report directly to him—law, dentistry, business and education. His decision to relegate vice president Subbiondo to a secondary role reporting to the executive vice president simply increased the uncertainty about how decisions would be made right at the time when the WASC accreditation team arrived.

Many in the Pacific community remember a rash decision near the end of his term that revealed his estrangement from students and faculty: his impulsive action to move his desk out on the lawn in front of his office weekly to be more accessible to students and the campus. It was an awkward University embarrassment, noted by regents, after they laughed, as perhaps the last straw.[60]

Atchley's heart surgery in 1992 knocked him out for about nine months, aggravating the uncertainty of leadership. Throughout his service, Atchley seemed to blur the line between University and family. Among questionable acts was permitting his son to run a business out of McConchie Hall.[61] In the end, Atchley inherited most of the major problems he had to deal with, but his polarizing approach, his rash decisions, his inability or refusal to build an administrative team, and his incapacity to build consensus and direction with the board doomed his presidency to failure.

FACULTY AND STUDENTS RISE ABOVE

Pacific vs. the culture wars

The national campus "culture wars" of the 1980s and 1990s never really hit Pacific. Alan Bloom's *The Closing of the American Mind* in 1987 claimed to explain "how higher education has failed democracy and impoverished the souls of today's students." He aimed at the "openness" of relativism and all the academic movements spawned in the sixties that undermined both critical thinking and the defining values of Western culture. The book became a political football on campuses and was castigated by most academics as undemocratic and reactionary. The book touched a nerve among the educated public irritated by faculty neglect and illiteracies of all sorts among college students.

Instead, at Pacific, the rise of women's studies, though tardy, was welcomed. As noted earlier, black studies and Latino studies had already segued onto campus after the CIP launch in 1969. The fact is that while Pacific faculty generally represented politically progressive to liberal views as they had for decades, they never abdicated their responsibility to students to understand all view points, to engage on all sides, to consider alternatives to every assertion. Student learning and good teaching, in other words, trumped any ideology or political persuasion of the day. As education professor Dewey Chambers said, "A teacher touches eternity. What I do today will reach tomorrow's grandchildren and beyond."[62]

When "political correctness" entered the American lexicon in 1990, tensions between traditional scholarship ("Eurocentric" and "elitist") and politicized perspectives based on new knowledge of how marginalized peoples got left out of the classroom dialogue escalated across the land. But they never had a significant impact on the curricular debates at Pacific because faculty generally agreed on sensible change. As well, the California social and multicultural landscape and progressive views on race, gender and sexual orientation informed faculty and student understandings of themselves and their cultures.

More important, Pacific professors were reluctant to discard venerable traditions to install the new; both could be taught as important. The community of learning and generous colleagueship prevailed over the potentially divisive issues of Affirmative Action, speech codes, and the treatment of women and minorities. Not that prejudice was absent, but rather constructive action always helped to move the Pacific community ahead to more inclusion, tolerance and respect. That had been Pacific's history. And when retired UC-Santa Cruz history professor Page Smith wrote his scorching *Killing the Spirit: Higher Education in America* in 1990, indicting university professors for ignoring the classroom, avoiding undergraduates, indulging in meaningless research, and relying on the dole and dominance of corporate and government funders, he had never witnessed its lively opposite at Pacific.

General education flowers

In 1978, Pacific was one of 14 universities selected to participate in a pioneering national "General Education Models Project" headed by former Raymond College professor Jerry Gaff, now the leading guru of general education in the country. With this consortium Pacific jumped to the forefront of educational reform for undergraduates. In 1981, led by vice president Hand, the faculty adopted a revised curriculum without major contention (after an early turndown) —perhaps because there was so much other campus turbulence the time.[63] Part of Pacific's plan was so promising that Gaff used it as a model in his groundbreaking book on general education reform.[64]

General education became important again as the framer of Pacific's core values. Fresh enthusiasm for the new "Information and Imagination" framework, called the "I and I" program, drew faculty from many disciplines to team-teach paired freshman courses. Intellectual excitement was afoot on the campus. Business professor Horst (Ray) Sylvester, one of Pacific's truly outstanding faculty leaders and mentor of students over 40 years, worked for decades, often as chair of the general education committee, to build policies and procedures that increased student responsibility for their performance in and out of the classroom.

But even the promising general education reform of the early eighties foundered as so many efforts did in that unhealthy Pacific era. The misguided pledge of "I and I" faculty never to repeat a course was not sustainable, especially as budgets tightened, and the GE program went to seed again with a creeping array of course options. The WASC accreditation report of 1986 honed in on Pacific's "sprawling" program described as "loose, diffuse and unfocused."[65]

Business professor Ray Sylvester epitomized the caring professor who mentored countless students while rising as a University citizen leader in all matters of significance for students.

COP dean Robert Benedetti was more than any other person the author of the nationally recognized Mentor/Pacific Seminar general education program for all undergraduate students, 1990 - present.

Not until Subbiondo arrived as academic vice president and Robert Benedetti was appointed dean of the College (1989-2002) did solid, sustainable reform occur. Subbiondo, mindful of an upcoming WASC accreditation review that would look especially hard at general education, charged Benedetti to lead a large faculty general education committee with representatives from all the undergraduate schools. They forged a new plan for academic skills, core freshman seminars and a senior interdisciplinary seminar, and three coherent "paths" of learning in natural science, social science, and arts-humanities. Through Benedetti's skillful leadership, by fall 1990 the Academic Council *unanimously* endorsed the general education plan for all undergraduates—practically unheard of in American higher education. And the faculty had reached this agreement on universal requirements across departmental and school turfs in less than a year![66]

Benedetti had listened to the complaints of faculty about the lack of any "intellectual community" on campus, and thus proposed an extended common learning experience that had rarely been tried successfully at other universities. The genuine innovation came from Benedetti: a series of two freshman seminars followed by a senior capstone seminar required of all undergraduates regardless of school.

The "Mentor Seminars" (now called "Pacific Seminars," or "Pac Sem" to students and faculty), launched in 1992, called for intense discussion of seminal readings across the disciplines and debate of each student's short papers in a seminar format in the fall term. The senior seminar, pushed hard by Benedetti, studied the moral development of famous figures, culminating in an ethical autobiography by every student.

Thus, amid a world of fragmented knowledge that treated all ideas as equal, the seminars planted meaning, structure and coherence. In a climate where "values" were locked out of public university classrooms, ethics and character formation became central. Liberal arts faculty were elated with the focus on "great ideas," and professional school faculty celebrated the practical focus on ethics and public issues. All faculty who joined in felt renewed by embedding writing and discussion into small classes and creating new courses on public issues that grew out of their own disciplines.

Thanks to the strong leadership of successive directors of general education over the years—English professor John Smith, communication professor Jon Schamber, philosophy professor Lou Matz, history professor Gesine Gerhardt—the three-seminar core sequence endured, nourished and replenished by the faculty over more than 25 years. Pacific's general education curriculum earned national recognition several times through the Association of American Colleges and Universities. Benedetti gave the new Mentor Seminar program its signature motto of preparing "citizen leaders," which touched on the key elements that knit the program back to its Methodist roots and on into the 21st century.

All this sounded wonderful, but many an alum remembers well the bewilderment of heady readings, the pain of writing essays, the challenge of new ideas and values that defined their Mentor/Pacific Seminar experience. Like students on most campuses, Pacific students did not welcome a menu of required learning handed to them on day one. Many a frosh groused about the threat these courses posed to their GPAs. In the end, however, many students, and perhaps even more alumni upon later reflection, came to value the rigorous inquiry and debate and the autobiographical soul-searching of the Mentor seminars.

The College and schools push ahead

The central story of the College was the transformation of the general education program into a national model. Also important was the development of the freshman honors program, begun in 1981 under philosophy professor Gwenn Browne. In 1986 when professor of Spanish Bob Dash took it on, the application process was streamlined and the honors program grew. It really took off when the Regents Scholarship program attracted many more academically talented students and Price Hall became an honors residence.[67] In addition to two honors courses required in an array of liberal arts departments, students bonded through concert, lecture and special events. When the program grew to 130, a second honors hall (John Ballantyne) was added, and more courses were offered. While majors varied, the program drew most of the talented students from the health sciences, and many of them thrived in the new Mentor Seminar honor sections.

As the Stockton campus became more ethnically diverse in the early 1990s, the faculty saw a need for helping faculty integrate cultural diversity materials into their courses, especially in Mentor III (Pac Sem 3). English professor Heather Mayne was a leader in the effort, which led to her later appointment as assistant provost to head up diversity initiatives. In 1992, dean Benedetti led the faculty to formulate a strategic plan for the College built on the concept of the "citizen-leader," a framework for setting specific learning goals for all students in the College. [68]

The College continued to be an incubator for professional programs: just as it had spun off schools of education, engineering and business, so in these years computer science moved appropriately into the engineering school, and communicative disorders joined physical therapy in the school of pharmacy and health sciences. Two other large departments with master's programs chose to remain in the College: communication and sports sciences (now health, exercise, and sports sciences). Professor Tom Stubbs led the reorganization of the physical education and recreation department into five sports science tracks that enrolled more majors than any department other than biology.

Dean Carl Nosse (1980-99) oversaw many developments for the Conservatory of Music, including the west's only graduate degree in music therapy and first music management program. Like Pacific, the school fully embraced the integration of liberal arts and professional studies by emphasizing the applied areas of music. Enrollment generally grew during this era, and the quality of students improved along with increased endowed scholarships to woo them. Piano professor Frank Wiens, an anchor of the faculty into the 2010s, launched his annual regional high school piano competition in 1982 that ran over 30 years. Unevenness in the quality of the faculty meant that some programs, like the vocal program, thrived while others, like the orchestra, struggled.

Among others, Conservatory of Music professors George Buckbee and Frank Wiens marked the height of modern artistic achievement for the school.

Fay Haisley was appointed dean of the Benerd School of Education in 1984 and served for 15 years, building the school's reputation through her forceful, entrepreneurial leadership and readiness to take on all challenges. In 1989, the school of education in partnership with the college was selected as one of 30 independent universities federally funded as "Project 30" to redesign the elementary education curriculum to fit the needs of minority students and teachers. The tuition-subsidized program was aimed at reducing alarming high school dropout rates by preparing 100 local teachers in bilingual and special education.

The massive Gladys L. Benerd endowment elevated the school's resources well beyond several of the other schools for faculty development, technology equipment, and outreach. The endowment solidified the school's prominence in the state as the only school of education accredited by the National Council for Accreditation of Teacher Education (NCATE) with bachelor's through doctoral degrees. Though Haisley's friendship with the Atchleys helped her advance the school, it was not appreciated by most faculty. "My greatest legacy will be a feeling of disequilibrium that keeps the school on the cutting edge," she said at her troubled departure in 1999.[69]

Thus ended an era of stable leadership. Only four deans had served since the school was founded in 1924. While professor Marilyn Draheim's steady hand held well as interim dean, the provost finally appointed John Nagle as dean, and for the next five years the faculty lamented the bad match they had warned about.

Dean Ashland Brown (1991-1999) built sturdy foundations for advancing the School of Engineering as Heyborne's successor.[70] A former engineer at Ford and General Motors, Brown launched an enduring partnership with Lawrence Livermore National Laboratories in 1993 to promote technology transfer. He began the Minority Engineering Program (MEP) in 1991 with scholarship dollars from foundations, then brought to Pacific the regional pre-college Mathematics, Engineering, and Science Achievement (MESA) program for low-income, first-generation students in 1993 that continues strong to the present. The program served 11,000 students, "a legacy the campus has given to the community."[71] A partnership with high schools partly funded by the state, MESA provided project-based learning through competitions. Stockton high school teacher Andrew Walter ('93) guided teams to win the national MESA design competition in 2005, in 2012, and again in 2014. Maria Garcia-Sheets, director of these programs for years, oversaw steady growth in the number of MESA students who enrolled at Pacific through the MEP scholarship program.

One of dean Plovnick's landmark initiatives in the Eberhardt School of Business was the MBA program launched in 1993 that soon included a popular, accelerated five-year BS/MBA joint degree. At the time, the need for a local MBA program seemed clear, and the pent-up demand meant a gush of 100 students in an evening program. The faculty was energized, especially with the revenue flowing into the school owing to an especially attractive agreement Plovnick crafted with Atchley: the school took on all the financial risk while reaping most of the profits. The MBA was a popular first for San Joaquin county and drew better students and faculty. Soon, demand justified a full-time day program, which settled in despite uncertain enrollments and a gradual decline in the quality of applicants.

Plovnick's reluctance to place the MBA program in the much larger market of Sacramento was part of his focus on cultivating Stockton business leaders rather than regional supporters. The Eberhardt family and the Bank of Stockton became its most solid supporter, with gifts over time that culminated in the naming of the school. But Plovnick was skillful in engaging an advisory board that supported the school on all fronts and became over time increasingly broader in its membership.

In addition to the popular five-year BS/MBA program, the school crafted a partnership with the Conservatory to offer an arts and entertainment management emphasis that has been in high demand for many years. Offering only one undergraduate major in business administration, the school was free to explore concentrations that had appeal: real estate management, business law, entrepreneurship—resulting in 13 concentrations for the smallest accredited business school in the state! This broad appeal, along with great teaching and unwavering advising from Associate Dean Ray Sylvester, drove a positive momentum into the nineties.

Toward the end of this era, the Fletcher Jones Foundation funded an endowed professorship in entrepreneurship, the first fully funded endowed faculty position in University history.[72] This fact in itself is testimony to Pacific's privation: most strong private American universities began endowed faculty positions from decades to a century earlier.

In its carliest ycars, the School of International Studies benefitted from its strong faculty despite its mostly absentee dean, Martin Needler, a noted scholar of Latin America. The cornerstone of the school was its required study term abroad, typically in a non-European country, and many SIS students would add a second term in another country, often on another continent. The required orientation course prior to departure and the re-entry course upon return equipped graduates with an unusually sophisticated intercultural perspective that placed them well in their international careers. In the early nineties, SIS students represented about half of the only 80 students who participated annually in the impressive study abroad program—a national model with over 200 different programs in nearly 60 countries to select from.[73]

The two SIS "peace poles" have disappeared from the campus since they were planted in 1989.

Given Pacific's tradition of international education, the 1989 controversy over the "Peace Poles" must have come as a surprise. The SIS student group wanted to plant eight-foot poles on campus declaring "May Peace Prevail on Earth" in four languages, part of a global action that began in Japan.[74] They dedicated the poles to the memory of George Wilson who endowed their school, the future of SIS, and to students who shared his ideals. The state had declined to post a pole on the capitol grounds, and thus it was made available to SIS. Interim dean Haley and Winterberg decided that placing the other two in the front of Wilson Hall would be too political, so the poles were relegated to the side of the hall and near the library. Over time, the two campus poles disappeared, so at the 25th anniversary reunion of SIS in 2012, a new one was planted.

Students in the eighties and nineties

By the mid-1980s, the values of the sixties were just a memory, as freshmen listed "getting a better job" and "achieving financial success" as their top goals. [75] The times prompted Jim Hodge ('86) and Bret Almazan ('85) to launch the Delta Sigma Pi "Yuppie Squad," a 30-man drill team replete with dark suits and briefcases.[76]

The Delta Sigma Pi "Yuppie Squad" of 1986 poked fun at the campus culture of job obsession.

Atchley had little appreciation for the central role of the student affairs division at a university like Pacific, where the quality of living and out-of-class learning is critical to its success. Housing, meals, cultural climate, student hangouts—all the avenues of living contributed to a rich campus life.[77] When Atchley outsourced food service to ARA, the quality of meals declined notably, and the students grumbled about it more loudly every year. Dok Shoons for hotdogs, El Torito, The Shamrock, and Blackwater Cafe became local hangouts.

For students of color, the early nineties was a time of challenge and empowerment. They ended Archania's mindless flaunting of the confederate flag. Bolstered by dozens of black football players, black students ran for Homecoming king and queen. When ASUOP pulled funding from the African American Student Association for hosting a Nation of Islam speaker, black students protested and raised the ante by bringing Digital Underground and hip-hop protest singer Tupac Shakur to campus.[78]

Making the most of a dorm room, circa 1990.

Pacific recruited diverse students but still struggled to enable this diverse community to thrive together. Sometimes rituals helped. The annual Christmas event to light the redwood tree by Burns Tower now included the Vietnamese Student Association performing a traditional candle dance, and the African American Student Union presenting the Kwanzaa ceremony in chapel.[79] The "Festival of Lights" event had become thoroughly interfaith, with Muslims, Hindus, and Wiccan students joining in.

Knocking off ranked UNLV both in 1993 and 1995 was one of the all-time highs for Tiger basketball.

Campus capers of course continued. Safety officers had an extra challenge the night students stole all the license plates from the campus police cars—and never returned them. Another night, students muscled the Townhouse apartment stairways and set them out on the lawn. Was it years earlier that students stole the cement sacks near Grace Covell Hall and stacked them up to block all the doors of McConchie Hall?[80]

Pacific athletics soars

After struggling at the bottom end of the conference standings through the 1980s, basketball needed a fresh start. Bob Thomason ('71, '85) was appointed men's basketball coach in 1988 at a time when the local paper was astir about the lack of fan support for Pacific athletics. Steadily, Thomason built his way, with winning records most years. In the early nineties, the great games with Dell Demps ('92) were inspiring. Demps, presently general manager of the New Orleans Hornets, was second only to

Swimmer and water polo player Brad Schumacher (95, '97) was Pacific's only Olympic gold medal winner.

Cornelius in career scoring. But the national shocker was the Tigers beating tenth-ranked UNLV in a jam-packed, raucous Spanos Center in 1993, the first over UNLV in 21 years, then again beating them by one point in 1995, with ESPN TV SportsCenter catching the mayhem for the nation. Fans left with "UOP" ringing in their ears. They cheered Thomason on his way to becoming Pacific's all-time winningest coach.[81]

Under the incomparable coach John Tanner, swimming and water polo reached record levels from 1985-96, inheriting the record of two All-Americans in the early eighties, Mike Ennis ('84, double) and Mike Haley ('85, triple). For nearly 25 years, from 1988 through 2011, All-Americans populated the men's water polo teams every year except three.[82] Three-time All-American Todd Hosmer ('94) was the nation's leading water polo scorer in 1991.[83] Bradley Schumacher ('95, '97) was uniquely a four-time All-American in water polo and two-time All-American in individual swimming. He was the only double Olympic gold-medal winner in Pacific history and the only Pacific aquatics star to have his suit and cap retired. He earned two gold medals in the 1996 Olympics on freestyle relay teams, and then played with the U.S. water polo team in the 2000 Olympics. Notable also is that two

Tommy Tiger flying in 1985.

dental school alumni won Olympic gold medals in swimming earlier in their careers: Lance Larson ('66, gold and silver in 1960) and Ginnylee Roderick ('94, gold in 1984).

Sports psychology guru Glen Albaugh created a champion golf team from scratch, starting in 1971 with few scholarships and fewer dollars. His teams were competitive by the late seventies, and he had six consecutive years with players in the NCAA tournament by the mid-eighties, led by All-Americans Jim Rowse ('81), Ken Earle ('84), and Jeff Wilson ('84), then Aaron Bengoechea ('89). From 1982-85, Pacific ranked among the top 25 teams in the U. S.[84]

The women's softball team had a brilliant four-year run 1982-85 under Cindy "Bucky" Reynolds, with four straight trips to the NCAA national tournament. They went on to the College World Series in 1983 led by All-

The 1983 softball team made it to the NCAA World Series led by All-Americans Jennae Lambdin ('84) and Becky Suttman ('85).

Americans Jennae Lambdin ('84) and Becky Suttmann ('85). Bill Simoni Softball Field was opened in 1993, named after a local softball pitcher who was named to the all-world team in 1960 and pitched 32 years for Stockton teams. The softball team upset fifth-ranked Long Beach State in 1993. Baseball in this era struggled in one of the country's toughest leagues; even with a 22-game winning stretch in a 36-18 season in 1994, the team ranked fifth in the Big West.[85]

1992: ACCREDITATION, ACADEMICS AND FOOTBALL COLLIDE

The football subsidy

Aside from another fulfilling year for the students in the care of committed faculty, about the only good thing in 1992 was Gladys Benerd's record endowment gift. In addition to the computer contract debacle, the downgrade of the bond rating, Atchley's heart attack, and the faculty vote to end football came the WASC accreditation citations and suspension of Pacific in late February.

Ted Leland ('70, '73), renowned athletic director at major universities including Stanford, served twice as Pacific's director of athletics (1989-91, 2011-present), and was the architect for rebuilding athletics in the 2010s.

While the courts tossed about the Title IX issue for years, most athletic programs felt the pressure of gender equity and were strapped for funds through the 1970s and 1980s right along with troubled economic times. Then in walked Ted Leland ('70, '73), who along with Dempsey remained Pacific's most prominent athletic director in its history after Stagg. Coming off his years of coaching at Pacific and Stanford, then athletics director roles at Houston, Northwestern, and Dartmouth, Leland had been called back home in 1989 as an especially gifted leader in athletics. Surely he could right the ship. Leland, like

Dempsey, enjoyed enormous support from the faculty and staff because of his openness and integrity.

Atchley hired football coach Walt Harris ('68, '69) with little consultation the same year, and Pacific saw another spurt of gridiron glory. With the arm and legs of Troy Kopp ('93), running back Ryan Benjamin ('92), and receiver Aaron Turner ('91), Pacific witnessed a trio who collectively earned most Pacific records in offense. From 1989-92, Kopp and Turner set many Pacific passing and receiving records, and Kopp set Pacific records for total offense per game, season and career, while Turner captured the career scoring record. Kopp, named *Sports Illustrated* player of the week during the 1990 season, was ranked fifth nationally in all-time number of touchdowns at 79. Benjamin also set career rushing and receiving records in 1990-92. His three-year total of yards gained was still among the top in the country—no wonder he became one of only five Pacific players to garner All-American honors.[86] For the first time since 1949, Pacific had four players in three college all-star games: Kopp, Turner, Benjamin, and Greg Bishop ('95).[87] But with Harris' hostile style of leadership the program continued to suffer, and he lasted only three years. Leland moved to become AD at Stanford in 1991, much to the regret of the campus.

The trio of Aaron Turner ('91), Troy Kopp ('93), and Ryan Benjamin ('92) set most Pacific football offense records.

The regents were again zeroing in on football just as the WASC accreditation visit occurred, and the WASC team's focus on football forced action. When Atchley began as president he found that athletic expenses always exceeded McCaffrey's ceiling of 3.5% of the University's annual operating budget. The athletics budget was in the red by $200,000 to

$800,000 every year since 1980, sometimes exceeding the budget by 50 percent.[88] He cut the budget by his second year and settled on about $350,000 of annual pledges for the next four years to make football successful again.[89] The donors were mostly alumni regents stalwart in upholding this most fundamental of Pacific traditions, led by Eberhardt, Spanos, Gerber and Smith.[90] Ted Baun, never far from the action, built an Athletic Fitness Center in 1990 to provide a much-needed weight room for athletes.

The athletics advisory board was regularly reporting to the Academic Council the annual deficits in athletics, now running from half a million dollars to over a million owing to under-estimated expenses and halo estimates on revenue.[91] The advisory board also reported that the five-year graduation rate for Pacific athletes was 80 percent, far higher than the 61 percent for all students, with GPAs nearly comparable to the University average.[92] Faculty viewed it as evidence of committed students who were secure in their scholarship support, but hardly an argument for maintaining a budget-draining program.

The board's ad hoc athletics committee looked again at all the options, including dropping the program in late 1992. The investment in athletics had risen 140 percent over a decade while the library's budget rose less than 75 percent.[93] The group concluded that limiting athletics to 3.5% of the University budget would be firm this time, paid partly by student fees and other donor funds. Atchley concluded that the only certain way to reduce expenses would be to move to the NCAA Division IAA level of fewer scholarships with foes that matched Pacific's capacities.[94] The board approved an annual budget with a $700,000 football deficit to be funded by donors.[95]

Fighting against student decline

Adding to campus tension over football funding was the continuing drop in enrollment amid a national decline in the number of high school graduates, lasting until the mid-nineties. From 1988-91, undergraduate enrollment fell by 340 students, though the professional schools of dentistry, law, and pharmacy held steady at over 2,000 students collectively. Engineering had already lost nearly 200 students just from 1985 to 1987.[96] In 1989 Pacific enrolled under 3,000 undergraduates for the first time since the 1960s, and this enrollment drought lasted until 2000.

Just as serious was the decline in academic quality of undergraduates. In 1990 Pacific accepted nine out of every ten applicants.[97] By mid-year of 1992-93, 22 percent of the freshman students were on academic probation, the highest ever.[98] Retention of students was a challenge when average SAT scores and graduation rates ran significantly below Santa Clara, St. Mary's and USC.[99] Two additional pressure points mounted. The board learned that compared to other independent universities with eight or more professional schools, Pacific was undersized, running about 5,500 students during these years, while ten other comparable schools enrolled at a much more efficient level of nearly 7,000 students or more.[100] A recurrent pressure point was faculty salaries, now at or near the bottom of Pacific's national comparison group.[101]

Pacific fought back with three major student recruitment initiatives whose success continues to the present.[102] First, Pacific started a transfer program with San Joaquin Delta College, the perennial key "feeder" school of transfer students, along with an annual "UOP/Delta Day" that provided several incentives for Delta students to transfer. Then in 1992 the "Four Year Guarantee" was created, assuring any undergraduate a degree in four years during a time when the state universities were over-crowded and demand for classes often meant waiting in line for six years to earn a degree. This new program, another "first" for Pacific, was popular with California students and continued to the present.[103] Third, the Regents Scholarship program was launched to provide half-tuition scholarships to the most talented first-year students.[104]

The accreditation whistle blows

As the regional WASC accreditation visit approached, Atchley dismissed the concerns raised in the self-study report led by academic vice president Joe Subbiondo. Since Pacific had been continuously re-accredited by

WASC since 1949, the president and board chair were confident that the issues identified in the report were not grave. Atchley did not realize how assertive and progressive the accreditation process was in the Western Association, which led the nation in pressing for increased institutional accountability. Atchley asked regents Nancy Spiekerman ('57) and James McCargo ('73)—both active alums who kept in touch with the campus, Spiekerman as former alumni board chair and McCargo as a local businessman and popular former Pacific basketball star—to represent the board on the campus accreditation committee and the strategic planning task force, both headed by Subbiondo.

Soon Spiekerman and McCargo were grappling with campus issues that no regent had waded into in memory, and they were troubled. They brought their concerns to the board frequently prior to the WASC team visit of fall 1991, though one-third to one-half of the regents were absent from these meetings leading up to the visit. "You don't know the school," McCargo would complain to his colleagues, and as the pair became increasingly vocal about the mounting problems ignored by the board, a small group of newer regents began to listen. McCargo, Spiekerman and other regents got into the habit of informal conversations with faculty and a couple of administrators that may well have crossed the normal boundary of proper exchange, but the pitch of the times was bordering on brinkmanship. Many faculty felt that the accreditation process was "the last resort—the only option" to turn around Pacific.[105]

The University self-study report the WASC visiting team used as its guidebook was honest and forthright on all the key issues facing Pacific. Academic vice president Subbiondo and his associate Lee Fennell led the fight on behalf of the faculty and staff for a frank self-analysis, though scant attention was given to the quality of academics, especially mediocre graduate programs.[106] The pointed self-criticism was opposed by some top administrators and board members. While later Atchley noted to the WASC staff that the report "lacked balance" because many positives of Pacific were absent, he apparently never really worried about a possible negative outcome, so he and the board let the report proceed.[107]

The report submitted to WASC in fall 1991 focused the team's attention on three issues: planning, finance and governance.[108] The visiting team found that little had been done on the three issues since the last major visit a decade earlier, including the formal involvement of faculty in shaping the direction of Pacific. The self-study report itself had concluded that the "overwhelming theme" of the comprehensive report was the need for "coherent and sustained institutional planning," one of the signature failures of Atchley's polarizing administration.

When the WASC Commission made its accreditation decisions in February 1992 based on the visiting team report, the panel dinged Pacific on most of the nine WASC standards in a letter to the president.[109] The list was long, summed up by WASC as a "severe financial crisis" based on "structural and long-standing problems."

Pacific faced a humiliation unprecedented in its history: WASC action on re-accreditation was "deferred" until such time that the University met WASC standards. Though accreditation continued, the "sanction" was a formal "Warning... that [Pacific's] current condition is serious and reflects noncompliance with a number of Commission standards."[110] The issues were never about the academic program: the visiting team did not question the academic quality of Pacific's undergraduate, graduate or professional programs, but only the lack of planning, governance and crippling finances that undermined its promise. Pacific was again on a dangerous edge, what one regent called a "precipice," that was the outcome of a detached board, the long and increasingly distracted presidency of McCaffrey, and the briefer, turbulent years under Atchley.

The news hit the headlines, and a *Sacramento Bee* story circulated among Valley McClatchy newspapers was particularly hard-hitting.[111] Within a week vice presidents Fleming and Subbiondo fielded a campus TV/media conference, and a flurry of newspaper stories and editorials followed. Pacific was quick to respond by rightly saying that accreditation was not in jeopardy, and in fact it had acted on many issues cited by the visiting team weeks and months prior to the WASC decision. A strategic planning process was started, the current budget was balanced, a new dean of admission was hired and applications were up, and the board was conducting planning retreats. WASC pressure produced actions on the lack of diversity among its students, faculty and staff, called a "major weakness."[112] That was the year that Pacific established its first Cultural Diversity Committee. "Celebrate Diversity Week" was launched in 1992, among other actions.

Some regents called for suing WASC or other negative tactics, but cooler heads led by regent Robert Monagan turned to the future. Atchley toured the state to reassure alumni and the media that Pacific was accredited, strong and moving forward. But the Alumni Association was worried: alumni giving, a sign of alumni engagement, was still flat after the flurry of new initiatives in the eighties. While over 50 percent of alumni had graduated in the last 20 years, the percentage of donors had not increased much above ten percent. An alumni report pointed to a lack of school spirit and traditions, rapid growth, a greater diversity of students, enclaves in separate schools and alienation of the cluster college graduates as factors contributing to alumni apathy if not estrangement. Among many changes to alumni relations came a wise recognition of constituent groups as formal arms of the association, whether based on school affiliation, ethnicity or activity.[113]

Faculty win the day

An esteemed faculty member who lived through the two presidencies observed that "McCaffrey had no appreciation for academics [faculty], and Atchley had no time for them." Yet in many respects, it was the faculty who carried Pacific forward during these years. During the Atchley era, faculty not only led the way on the priority of academic quality but also in establishing a University-wide strategic planning committee and a budget committee, both of which got off the ground with helpful pressure from WASC.[114] Faculty members were critically important in insisting that the 1991 WASC accreditation self-study report be an honest document. They constantly challenged Atchley on key decisions that lacked appropriate consultation. The faculty solicited meetings with the regents to convey the severity of the University's plight to a largely uninformed board. They persistently pointed out the need for revised governance statements to clarify the rights and responsibilities of the faculty in relation to University administration.

The faculty leadership could see that investing in a distinctive, high-quality academic program based on priority setting would be more sustainable than relentless cost cutting. Faculty for undergraduate programs took on a major revision of the general education curriculum in the middle of campus turmoil and created a nationally recognized model with few extra dollars. The Sacramento and San Francisco campuses tried to steer clear of the heat, though dean Schaber continued to counsel the president, and law professor Jed Scully, a seasoned higher education administrator, chaired the Academic Council in 1993-94.

As integral players in this discordant community, faculty also contributed their share to the impasse. They were reluctant to tackle budget inefficiencies on their side of the aisle, steered clear of systematic review of programs, delayed in reordering their time and energy to engage in research, and held unrealistic hopes for their role in governance. But without their relentless vigilance and initiative, it is unclear how either the board or the administration would have turned the University around.

The faculty did all this during tumultuous times while preserving their positive, supportive relationships with students, who mercifully lived out their brief Pacific years without much direct action in the fray. With engaging professors, the heart of Pacific pulsed on: "One sentence can change the course of a student's life, implant a lifelong mission, or reveal a new interest."[115] Students consistently praised the quality of learning, the personal attention and the caring commitment the faculty gave through these stormy years.[116] Many students worried more about the morale of their teachers than they did about their own personal futures. The WASC visiting team commended a faculty that "nurtures students intellectually and personally," while noting "a genuine uneasiness among students about the Institution's commitment to faculty and to Undergraduate Education."

STUMBLING AHEAD

Football vs. the numbers

After the accreditation fiasco, the board took a more aggressive role in exploring options for athletics. Board chair Eberhardt promised a "complete review of the Athletic program and budget each year." He and other regents visited neighboring private schools like Santa Clara, which had dropped football in 1992, and St. Mary's, which had cut back to Division I-AA for football, with fewer scholarships and no big-time foes but also no cost savings.[117] Atchley had already concluded that the football program did not add up, that the hemorrhaging dollars were a serious flow, that Pacific could not be competitive, that Pacific was being kicked around, a loser on the national scene. Tensions between Atchley and Eberhardt were mounting. As expected, athletic director Bob Lee ('68), former standout quarterback for the Atlanta Falcons and for two other Super Bowl teams, argued to preserve football while Academic Council leaders urged its banishment as an "albatross."[118] But without telling Eberhardt, suddenly in December 1993 Atchley announced to a stunned regents academic affairs committee that football should end. When Eberhardt heard of Atchley's change of mind, he went "ballistic."[119]

The next day at the full board meeting Atchley presented the grim numbers: the accumulated $13 million deficit plus a $5.6 million current deficit, even after donors covered a nearly million dollar football bill from 1992, with a looming half-million dollar football shortfall this year. Add to these figures Title IX funding pressure for women's sports and a needed $500,000 stadium repair. To cap it off, the NCAA required dissolving the Pacific Athletic Foundation as a separate corporation. Atchley had reached the stern conclusion that the board eventually had to face: Pacific could not afford football.

But the resolute board voted to sustain football, led by Monagan's five-year plan to (again) cap athletics at 3.5% of the budget, with additional dollars from outside funding.[120] Three days later, the Academic Council considered 14 various motions to censure the board and the president on several counts. The council ended with a resolution asking the board to "reconsider" their decision on football amid a budget crisis where pensions had been cut and the budget slashed by 8 percent.[121]

Academic Council chair Fred Muskal noted that he and the president at least agreed on one thing: relations between board and faculty were "deplorable." After again debating "no confidence" votes against the board, the council asked for face-to-face meetings with the regents on governance and athletics.[122] Meanwhile, a sport survey of Pacific undergraduates showed that support for football came in third after volleyball and basketball.[123]

Picking up the pieces

The WASC report was a rude wakeup call to the regents to pay attention to the Stockton campus they had neglected for decades. In effect, Pacific's modern Board of Regents was born out of the WASC action of 1992, though it really took the strong leadership of Monagan to make it work. The board was never the same again. The simple equation of governance, planning and finances was the root of all the major problems that had been festering for years. Certainly the football issue, for example, was grounded in a lack of clarity in decision-making between board, administration, and faculty (governance); in undetermined priorities (planning); and dispute over how resources should be used (finances); which is why football was a perennial flash point for the campus and board for so many years.

Eberhardt charged the regent committees to scrutinize each of the WASC standards cited in the report, with special attention to these top three unresolved issues. As much as he loathed institutional planning, Atchley worked closely with regent Dale Redig, now appointed co-chair of planning with Subbiondo, to mesh the new strategic planning process with the WASC issues. By mid-1993 the board adopted a strategic plan with eight priorities, beginning with salaries and governance, based on a University "Vision Statement."[124] Crafted during the WASC self-study process in 1990, the Vision Statement actually set forth a University identity that carried forward. The six-paragraph statement identified the key ingredients of the 1996 "Mission and Vision Statement" that essentially presided over Pacific to the present.

Board upheavals

One fall-out of the WASC action was a deeper questioning of the direction of Pacific. Newer regents began to ask more questions, and when Atchley was proved wrong by the potent WASC blow to suspend re-accreditation, a small group of regents decided they must pursue changes.

At the regents' routine committee meeting to nominate officers for the coming 1994 year, Dale Redig was nominated as chair and Jim McCargo as vice chair. Redig himself was "stunned."[125] When the full board convened moments later, they were astonished that former chair Baun moved the new slate of officers effective immediately, and the board approved the change.[126] Eberhardt, who had been contemplating stepping down and had invited Monagan on the board to become his replacement, was surprised by the abrupt turnabout. If there ever was a sign of a fractured board it was this inability to gather seeming foes together, and with a sprinkle of diplomacy, work out compromises that could have provided a smoother transition.

But this was not the end of the tribulations. In early 1994, with no consultation, Atchley removed academic vice president Subbiondo from his office and installed Lee Fennell as acting AVP. The Academic Council was in an uproar again over basic governance procedures and almost cast a no-confidence vote. Instead, the council devised a faculty "evaluation survey" of the president, which welcomed comments.[127] The majority of faculty complained about his failure in communication and peremptory decision-making despite his positives of fundraising, tough decisions, and enrollment building.

Within a couple months, and prior to thc board meeting at the law school in May 1994, a few regents orchestrated a plan to elect Bob Monagan to replace Redig as chair that blindsided Redig supporters.[128] News leaked to campus prior to the board meeting, so a crowd of 100 students and faculty mostly from Stockton clamored to enter the law school meeting room to protest a call for Redig to resign as board chair.[129] In executive session the board invited into the room student and faculty leaders, who appealed for stability and continuity. Upon their departure, the regents rejected Redig and McCargo on a close vote, electing Monagan as chair and Don Smith as vice chair. The new officers had been in charge for only five months and one full board meeting.

Within a few days the ASUOP Senate unanimously cast a vote of no confidence in the board over their ouster of Redig and McCargo, fearing that the deed might prompt more severe action by WASC, who had scheduled a return visit in a few months.[130] Nearly 200 students and faculty greeted the arrival of chairman Monagan on campus with chants, "Oh, no, they've got to go!" "Pacific hails Jim [McCargo] and Dale [Redig]!" "We pay, we have a say!" "WASC is no joke!"[131]

The Academic Council held an open forum, drawing over 200 students, faculty and staff to discuss the "hostile takeover." At the commencement convocation days later, biology professor Dale McNeal stepped up to the graduation podium to thank the University for the 1994 Distinguished Faculty Award, then proceeded to lament the board action by "a nucleus of 17 regents who have been in charge for years," objected to accusations that the Academic Council had tried to damage the University and announced that he would "withdraw from the proceedings."[132] About 60 faculty members and some students followed McNeal down the center aisle on Knoles lawn that hot afternoon in a stunning display of what could have been called civil disobedience.

At the same May meeting, Atchley fought for a continuing appointment, but he was asked to resign by a narrow vote and to leave in 1995 after one more year. Certainly the votes came because he had become the flashpoint of Pacific problems, but also presumably because of his turn away from football. In any case, finally the purging had worked its way. Pacific would be resetting its direction under new leadership on the board and in the presidency, hoping this time to turn the bus away from the cliff and get it back on course, even if the football crater still loomed.

The election of Monagan was momentous, but so was the untimely death of Bob Eberhardt, who had finally persuaded his reluctant old friend Monagan to join the board in 1991. Eberhardt died of a heart attack in fall 1994 while on a hunting trip in Hungary with his brother Douglass ('59) and friends. The *Stockton Record*'s eulogy rightly concluded that Eberhardt had "not sought the public eye" had and "sought only the public good" as Stockton's most respected leader.[133] But his role as leader of the Pacific Board of Regents was difficult for most of his years.

Robert Eberhardt ('51, right) and Robert Monagan ('42, left) were giant leaders of the Board of Regents through the last decades of the 20th century.

Within months, a large tiger statue, designed as a tribute to president Knoles by art professor Richard Reynolds in 1961, was stolen from its high pedestal outside Knoles Hall. Perhaps the thief was making a statement about the misfortunes of the Bengals at this turning point in their storied history.[134] Steps away, however, stands the marker noting the naming of the Eberhardt School of Business in 1995 to honor the service of Bob Eberhardt and the Eberhardt family, a testimony to a legacy of commitment and generosity. Four family members served on the board almost continuously for 60 years, from 1953-2013, and four of six alumni family members graduated with business degrees. The family and the Bank of Stockton continued to be among the topmost supporters and benefactors of the business school and the University.

Monagan takes charge

The key to the future was Monagan's leadership for a "complete restart."[135] Monagan had served as president of the Alumni Association 30 years earlier, and was now chair of the California World Trade Commission and the Sutter Health board. He knew how to get things done collaboratively with volunteer public service groups. He immediately formalized campus representation on the board with the ASUOP president, Academic Council chair, and Alumni Association board president all as official non-voting members.[136] He encouraged the faculty to "govern themselves" as they wrapped up a three-year revision of their handbook of policies and procedures.

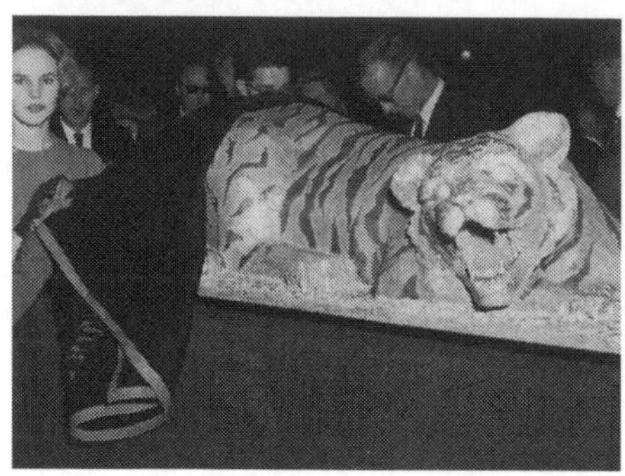

Art professor Richard Reynolds' tiger statue, unveiled by Homecoming Queen Diane Brizzolara ('62) in 1961 as a tribute to President Knoles, growled on the pedestal north of Knoles Hall for over three decades.

Monagan set regent Thomas Eres ('72) afoot to review the board's bylaws, which had not been examined in years, and to work with faculty and deans on campus governance.[137] Eres, adjutant general of the state National Guard, board member of the state bar association, and former McGeorge alumni president, waded in to tackle a "complete, utter lack of a governance system" under bylaws that were "outmoded, outdated, and irrelevant."[138] Monagan invited Stockton businessman and regent Gary Podesto to head a new review of athletics, asked the board to endorse a gender equity document for athletics and appointed a regents committee on faculty compensation. Both Eres and Podesto were fortunate to have sports science professor Margaret (Peg) Ciccolella as Academic Council chair, only the second woman to hold the office, because she had a law degree and was ready to work with them.

Monagan quoted Francis Bacon to urge change on the board: "He who will not apply new remedies must expect new evils."[139] When Monagan and Smith met with the Academic Council, the board chair was conciliatory, acknowledging the "distrust." He understood that the faculty felt demeaned by former leaders who viewed them as generic employees rather than the heartbeat of the University. Faculty responded that they did not wish "to run the University, we wish the University to be run well."[140]

The WASC Commission reaffirmed accreditation for another two years (later extended to 2000), so the accreditation crisis was ended, even if not all was back on track. The WASC letter announcing the end of the "Warning" and "deferred reaffirmation" also noted the changes in the board and progress made. The WASC letter concluded with a powerful declaration of hope: University of the Pacific had accomplished "a profound and radical shift in the way it does business," now building toward open communication and trust between board and faculty.[141]

Pacific had veered right to the thin edge of a major breakdown, but avoided a collapse through the extra efforts of a few regents, faculty and staff who with the backup of accreditation pressure turned the institution away from the brink. It was time to respond with a purposeful board and a new president chosen through care and collective action. Pacific needed to regain the stature and promise of a University that finally had most of the ingredients for greatness on the table, ready for alignment and action.

CHAPTER 6

A new era: Recovery and aspiration, 1995-2009

The Monagan-DeRosa partnership—Planning a priority—Football suspension—The "MVP" and program review—Athletics success—Rebuilding quality and stability—Stockton campus improvements—The National Commission and fundraising campaign—Naming the Dental School—The Powell legacy—The challenge of visibility—Community partnerships—The Pacific Rising plan

TEAM BUILDING

The DeRosa-Monagan partnership

When it came down to a vote for a new president in February 1995, Board of Regents chair Bob Monagan declared the winner without ever divulging the numbers. All agreed it was an exceptional search process, the first ever genuinely collective presidential search process at Pacific that relied on openness and consensus building. While Dominick DePaola, the Baylor University dental dean, was certainly a strong finalist, Donald DeRosa, like DePaola a son of New York Italian immigrants, an experienced vice chancellor for academic affairs/provost at University of North Carolina at

President DeRosa (1995-2009) worked closely with Board chair Bob Monagan to advance Pacific. Karen DeRosa was a popular and engaged first lady.

Greensboro, had a track record of solid diplomacy with faculty as well as a good understanding of finances. DeRosa's wife Karen was a distinct asset. Don DeRosa was welcomed by all as Pacific's first non-Protestant president. Whereas Eberhardt and Atchley had struggled to form a team, DeRosa shared Monagan's deep understanding of the value of teamwork, learned as a pitcher on his college baseball team. For Monagan and DeRosa, diplomacy was a foremost strength at a time when Pacific needed it most.[1]

DeRosa was the first strong academic leader since Knoles, and even Knoles frequently declined to play a leadership role in the academic realm. As a student DeRosa had experienced the value of mentors in his own development, and as chair of the psychology department at Bowling Green State University, he focused on improving teaching as a priority. No surprise, then, when he immediately announced that Pacific must be a "student-centered institution" which offered varied ways of learning, especially through internships and team projects that drew in students through experienced-based learning. He believed in the value of innovation, and saw it in accelerated programs for students looking for cost-effective education like that already provided by the dental school.[3] In his inaugural address he restated President Burns' theme by urging Pacific to "be pioneering and risk-taking."[4]

For the first few months he spent time with chair Monagan to build a trusting relationship and close personal friendship that lasted through Monagan's nine years as board chair (1994-2003). While Monagan's tenure as chair was relatively brief compared with past chairs (Watt 16 years, Baxter 14 years, Baun 23 years, Eberhardt 19 years), his impact on the turnaround of Pacific was enormous.

DeRosa, the regents, the cabinet, faculty leaders—all recognized that Monagan had exceptional leaderships skills to bring the University together behind DeRosa's vision to transform a struggling school, uncertain about its mission and how to do its job, into a vibrant, coherent university of great value. DeRosa noted that change in the past was typically in "reaction to external factors," whereas now change was driven by aspirations for quality.[5] All the more important thus was Monagan's leadership to get the regents engaged in planning the University's future rather than reacting to crises.

Setting his team in place

DeRosa, who loved reading American history, especially liked Doris Goodwin's *Team of Rivals* biography of Abraham Lincoln. He understood the value of putting together a team of leaders who complemented each other with differences and contrasting strengths as Lincoln did. DeRosa quickly completed campus-led searches for provost and business vice president at the same time that he found his executive assistant in John Stein, one of the key leaders on the WASC visitation team that had blown the whistle on Pacific and who returned again to chair the follow-up visit. When board chair Monagan heard of the hire he was outraged. How could a new president hire the enemy? But Monagan soon learned how Stein's acute mind, his wide range of executive experience in California private higher education, and his understanding of Pacific led to many shrewd decisions that benefitted Pacific.

The two other new leaders stood in obvious contrast to DeRosa's background as a New York native who devoted his career to large public universities. The new provost, Philip Gilbertson, came from the rural Midwest, most recently as a dean at Valparaiso, a mid-sized, independent comprehensive university much like Pacific. Patrick Cavanaugh, the new business and finance vice president, grew up on an Iowa farm, worked as an executive for the state of Iowa after a law degree, then served as business vice president at Drake, another mid-sized, independent comprehensive university.

These four men joined the veteran Judith Chambers, who had served Pacific since 1968 and knew the background on every issue, and whose dry wit cracked up the rest of the cabinet, if not the president, in their weekly meetings. Soon DeRosa hired a development vice president to complete his team. John Evey was a dapper, seasoned leader from Oregon State, but the position opened every few years to try to get the right match-up for the long term. It never happened under DeRosa. And because Chambers retired as vice president in a few years to become special assistant to the advancement vice president, the core team really came down to four men for a decade and more. While "team of rivals" might be a misnomer, DeRosa's team provided a solid complement of talent, all committed to making the team work for the benefit of Pacific.

DeRosa had a balanced approach to leadership, highly organized yet personable. He quickly ended the ad hoc administrative style that had earned Atchley a reputation for letting anyone in the door and making decisions based on any last-chance meeting. DeRosa insisted on a chain-of-command approach to deal with issues, which protected his time to deliberate based on the best judgments of his leaders, on up through the administrative chain. While this hierarchic approach put off some staff, he became known for thoughtful decisions based on thorough consultation. And his one-on-one meetings with people at any level, students and staff to heads of state, earned him a reputation as a warm, inquisitive, thoughtful, persuasive and charismatic leader.

Board turnaround

At the request of DeRosa, the board gathered in a retreat at Feather River Inn ten days prior to DeRosa's June 1995 start date to assess how to move forward with a new leader. They forged a list of five-year priorities, including agreement on mission, improved budgeting and governance, raising salaries, increasing endowment and overcoming fragmentation. They agreed that the most important barriers to faculty effectiveness were lack of resources and technology as well as student academic potential. At the time, the board had the uninformed view that doubling the $65 million endowment could take care of financial worries.[6]

Within months, regent judge Loren Dahl ('42) spearheaded a thorough revision of the bylaws that had been neglected for years, as regent Tom Eres ('72) ably led the regents to repair the governance system.[7] In turn, the Academic Council for the first time ever crafted bylaws for itself (completed in 1998) as a joint faculty-regent committee tackled a University governance plan, stating clearly the responsibilities for all campus constituents.[8] Term limits, while anathema to veteran politician Monagan, were adopted as best university practice, limiting regents to three three-year terms.

By 1999, DeRosa commended the regents. "You re-engineered yourself as a board," he noted. "At the core of leadership is the ability to define and articulate a mission and vision that can be shared. Then, one must empower others to carry out that mission."[9] What was happening at Pacific had been absent for some time. When the WASC accreditation team returned in 1999, it declared that all the issues of 1991 and 1994 had been resolved: "Pacific will be able to move forward, once and for all, from a difficult period in its rich history."[10] When Monagan retired as chair in 2003, DeRosa observed, "He came to a divided institution and leaves the chair with a legacy of inclusion."[11]

PLANNING FOR THE LONG TERM

A bumpy start

DeRosa said he would "take the long view" in leading Pacific, which was helpful in getting through the early years, with the mountain of challenges that had accumulated over the past 25 years. He had a shaky start financially when more undergraduates exited by his first spring term. He was informed of the $900,000 loss of tuition income abruptly in January while driving to his first board meeting in San Francisco. A culture of overestimating enrollment and gift income had to stop. Then a second unexpected drop in enrollment the next fall required a nearly 8 percent cut in the annual budget for 1997. Twenty-five positions were slashed. DeRosa insisted on creating a million-dollar operating reserve to protect the University from further unexpected jolts.[12]

Fragmentation of the campus meant voices had gone unheard. The Staff Council, just begun in 1992, asked for a voice at the table of key committees. DeRosa initially missed the significance of growing staff discontent. Many staff felt slighted by inadequate communication, a new job classification system, and low compensation. Tensions rose in 2000 when a staff movement to unionize Stockton campus clerical staff came to a head under a very unpopular director of human resources. In the end most staff voted down the union because they valued the amenities of a non-union environment, even though most staff at the dental school were unionized, as were the physical plant workers in Stockton. For many staff, it was the "family environment," as 40-year registrar veteran DeDe Sanchez noted, "helping students and each other, not competing," that made Pacific "never boring, always exciting."[13]

The "MVP"

DeRosa knew that a sturdy planning process was needed to set a long-term course for a university that had wavered in uncertainty for decades. Faculty and staff quickly agreed that two important bodies, the Strategic Planning and Steering Committee and the University Budget Committee, were not synchronized to make sure resources flowed to priorities. The makeshift strategic plan made clear another problem: the fat book of plans avoided any prioritizing.

DeRosa renamed the academic vice president position "provost" to signal the primacy of this academic position in relation to the other three vice presidencies. The appointment was just in time for Gilbertson to join in the University-wide retreat early in 1996 to clarify the University's mission with a large group of regents, alumni, students, faculty and staff. Such an exercise was unprecedented. The board adopted a new mission statement April 5, 1996 that stated succinctly the purposes of Pacific:

> *University of the Pacific's mission is to provide a superior, student-centered learning environment integrating liberal arts and professional education and preparing individuals for lasting achievement and responsible leadership in their careers and communities.*

DeRosa remarked to the board, "The statement works because in the right ways it is a big tent within which many educational initiatives can develop. It is also sufficiently restrictive. What research and creative work we do will be student-based and supportive of our teaching mission. We prize the balance of professional schools around a liberal arts core."[14] Shortly, new regent, judge Janice Rogers Brown, suggested that the phrase "student-centered learning *experience*" better reflected her own understanding of Pacific, and the mission statement was tweaked in an instant. Within eight months the board adopted a comprehensive plan, the "Mission, Vision, and Priorities" statement that captured the values and the 16 priority goals for the next five years. The plan set forth Pacific priorities clearly in print for the first time.

A critically important board retreat was held in November 1998 at Silverado Resort in Napa to focus on strategy, plan a campaign, and increase regent involvement. Regents were asked to weigh in on the Carnegie school classification issue: should Pacific be a high-ranking regional school or struggle to rise in the national university group? The president's cabinet of vice presidents saw this as a real choice: Pacific would rank highly as a regional school in such public ratings as *U.S. News & World Report*, rather than be buried in the third quartile of national universities.[15] But the regents, led by cheerleader David Gerber ('50), sounded loud and clear: Pacific must be a national university.

By 1998 the Institutional Priorities Committee (IPC), chaired by the provost, was the engine for planning and budget throughout this era.

The provost insisted the IPC track progress on all 16 priorities annually, focusing on reasonable measurements that were tied to the "MVP," the mission, vision, and priorities booklet that Gilbertson carried around in his suit pocket and practically memorized. Transparency was important. Through the era, the IPC presented its annual budget recommendations to the campus and the president, linked clearly to statements of planning priorities and budget assumptions, along with three or more years of budget comparisons. Cavanaugh was heralded by the faculty and staff as the first fiscal leader who could present an open and understandable University budget.

In fall 1998 DeRosa announced a new goal, to create "Hallmarks of Academic Excellence" and "Hallmarks of Distinctiveness." He saw special opportunities for Pacific to excel in the Brubeck Institute just created, in the general education Mentor Seminars that were gaining national attention, and in the IPC proposals for across-the-board leadership development, internships, and ethics across the curriculum.[16] Distinctiveness was defined as programs with both quality and "uncommonness."

In the end, agreement was reached on one important priority. The provost and IPC bent to faculty pressure not to *require* internships but rather to *guarantee* an internship to every student. Virtually all the professional schools required some form of work-based "experiential learning," but many college and business faculty resisted this opportunity to "brand" Pacific as a national leader in what was an increasingly popular option across the nation. The internship guarantee continues to the present, but an opportunity to become a more distinctive university through a work-based requirement was forfeited. Still, by 2001, 80 percent of undergraduates were participating in internships or other work-based learning, compared to 61 percent for national private universities.[17]

SUSPENDING FOOTBALL FOR A BALANCED ATHLETIC PROGRAM

Monagan-DeRosa leadership at work

In the late 1980s the board considered moving to division II football, but the majority of regents were resolved to play at the top.[18] They could not forfeit a great legacy that elevated 106 Tigers into professional football over a half century.[19] As regent Gary Podesto put it, the many regents who were part of that "greatest generation" of World War II veterans were convinced that if everyone pulled together and worked hard at it, the football war could be won.[20]

By the 1990s, coach Chuck Shelton had better players and better students than in recent memory. There was a spirit of optimism, at least during his one winning season in 1994 with standout Joe Abdullah ('96), the best team showing since 1977. In 1995, Craig Whelihan ('95), was the fifth Pacific quarterback drafted by the NFL.[21] Alumnus and NFL star Bob Lee ('68) had been brought in as athletic director to keep football alive through windfall income from away games against powerhouse teams awash in television revenue. As DeRosa said when he came on board, there was "unbridled optimism" that some miracle would rescue the program.[22]

But it was also "the same old, same old:" the regents had failed to raise the extra $350,000 needed to balance the 1995 football budget and admitted that Pacific could not be competitive in the Big West Conference. Lucrative income from big away games was ending. Nebraska had paid $400,000 in 1995 for the Tigers to get creamed in Lincoln, but nothing comparable was slated for 1996. And home games grew more costly: $225,000 to book Oregon for the 1996 season, for example, even as ticket sales dwindled.

Following the board commitment, Monagan had appointed Stockton regent Podesto to head a new 16-member broad-based committee on athletics in summer of 1994 to recommend action on football. Monagan, one of the die-hard supporters, thought that Podesto, a member of the Pacific Athletic Foundation, would steer the committee to a positive decision. When Marquette University dropped football in 1960, Podesto was one of the players who left. But Podesto, a smart local businessman who later was twice elected mayor of Stockton (1997-2004), scrutinized the budget as never before and as no other regent dared. His committee of regents, faculty and staff studied the numbers for six months, aided especially by Academic Council chair Peg Ciccolella. Against regent warnings, Podesto went to the Academic Council to listen, and found constructive ideas, not stonewalling. Then in January 1995, with just regent members voting, the committee recommended 6-1 to end football. Podesto was all set to present the report for board action days later when Monagan tabled it without distribution on a vote of 14-13, trying to find a way out.[23]

By June the regents committed themselves to making a decision by year-end as they continued to analyze numbers and seek outside support. Monagan, working closely with DeRosa, was beginning to understand what was at stake: if the board could not wrestle this issue to the ground, how could it ask the faculty to take a hard look at academic programs? In fact, how could Pacific move ahead on any key issue without dealing with this financial millstone? As DeRosa reflected, "Big decisions pulled us together."[24] He replaced athletic director Lee within a year. Monagan stepped up to his responsibility and began to call his regent friends one by one, asking them to look at the numbers and do what was right for the future of Pacific. More regents were recognizing that football costs were untenable, and fundraising in athletics was not what it was cracked up to be. Monagan lined up the votes. Working closely with DeRosa, Monagan made sure that the president would not vote on the issue and that he as chair would take the heat for the stunning decision ahead.

Fearing the worst, athletic director Lee had pushed for a December decision to allow players to transfer midyear. In a special "executive session" meeting on December 19, 1995, the regents endorsed a plan to achieve gender equity in athletics to comply with federal guidelines, then voted—with one negative vote—to end NCAA division I-A football for "at least one year." They retained I-A status for all other sports and asked for a viable budget model that might allow football to return, perhaps at the I-AA level of non-scholarship play like the Ivy League or University of San Diego.[25]

DeRosa's letter to the University community announcing the decision noted the obvious: that of the 105 NCAA division I-A schools, the only private ones remaining on the west coast were USC and Stanford—completely different schools in size, mission, and especially wealth. That over the 1994-95 season, football had an $800,000 cost overrun, with another $400,000 over budget in 1995-96, and a projected $600,000 deficit for the coming year. And that the University contribution of about $2 million per year did not include the cost of 82 full football scholarships. He also noted one of the chronic problems was scheduling high-profile home games: ranked teams lost computer rankings and TV income if they played weaker schools like Pacific, so they exacted a heavy tax to come to Stagg Stadium.[26] Most issues were not new. Many of the reasons that led to the decision had been identified in writing in 1979 by COP dean Jacoby.[27]

Yet the power of the tradition was hard to counter. Pacific had one impressive record on the gridiron. Over nearly a half century, Tiger teams or players racked up 14 national statistics titles and 95 top-ten stats rankings from 1948-1995, from rushing to interceptions to scoring.[28] So a letter to the president in March 1996 signed by many football alumni and coaches, including luminaries like Caddas, Carroll, and Harrell, voiced their objection that ". . . a newly elected President, not familiar with the Pacific community and it's [sic] tradition, would allow this event to occur. We are likewise troubled that a board of regents, most of whom are not alumni, would have the audacity to wield such a mighty ax."[29]

How it stuck

But the burden of changing times and dollar data could no longer be ignored. As DeRosa said, "Ultimately the decision was based on finances."[30] Through the 1990s, Santa Clara, UC-Santa Barbara and six CSU campuses also ended football. The December decision allowed for players to transfer without losing eligibility, and 40 students chose other schools. One reason the decision held is that DeRosa and the board allowed for a follow-up study in 1998 that led to a confirmation of the 1995 decision.

An ad hoc nine-member committee of regents, faculty, staff, a student and an alumnus headed by Kenneth Beauchamp, psychology professor and Pacific's NCAA athletic representative, looked again at the options. Their public report of April 1999 offered three options for NCAA Division I-AA football based on six criteria: non-scholarship, partial scholarship, and full scholarship.[31] Key issues centered on gender equity, financial impact, available competition, and intangible benefits. The committee noted the national context "is highly unsettled because of shifting student and fan interest, the rising costs of quality higher education, gender equity requirements of federal law, and the impact of television and media on the regulation and management of the sport."

After three public hearings, the athletic department rejected the non-scholarship option right about the time that Pacific won the Big West Commissioner's Cup for the most outstanding all-around athletic program. A *Pacifican* poll of 75 random students showed that about 75 percent favored bringing back football, and an editorial called for the middle-ground option of 40 football scholarships.[32] Division I fit Pacific in most sports, but the practical problem for Pacific football was a lack of peer competition in the west: what Division I competitors were at all like Pacific? Board chair Monagan and vice-chair Don Smith were both strongly opposed to non-scholarship ball. The ad hoc committee voted 7-2 to continue suspension of football, citing the daunting challenges facing Pacific: a lagging endowment, low alumni giving, an improving student academic profile with high tuition discounts, and net revenue lower than competitors.[33]

Committee member Jerald Kirsten ('47) filed a minority report, noting that 35 schools had added or re-instated football in the 1990s, whereas only ten had dropped it. He disputed the reported financial analysis and objected that the chair had denied consideration of a new plan based on private donors. The new athletic director Michael McNeely had been operating behind the scenes with Alex Spanos ('48) and others to work out a financial plan for a robust I-AA scholarship program that counted on tuition income from starting a marching band. McNeely released his report without consulting the president. DeRosa visited Santa Clara, St. Mary's, and UC-Davis to test interest, and found little. The president of Santa Clara, a school that had been in and out of football a couple of times, said "We will bring back football when the Pope ordains women." The Academic Council reported its unanimous recommendation to terminate the program, citing a faculty survey showing that 79 percent favored the shutdown.

The new athletic director made another quick move. McNeely tossed out Tommy Tiger in summer 1999 and brought in a new mascot, "PowerCat," so Pacific teams could be "identified in a strong, powerful way."[34] The dynamic and aggressive new mascot quickly caught on, even though older alumni and many current students grumbled about the loss of an old dear friend in Tommy, whose distinctive personality and look scorned the sleek contemporary logo. Within two years McNeely left to join the Spanos' professional football organization.

A new aggressive mascot, "PowerCat," replaced old-fashioned, likeable "Tommy Tiger" in 1999. The winning combination was a live "Powercat" cheerleader with the fun personality of many Tommy Tiger mascots of old.

In June 1999 the board "endorsed" a final committee report headed by Kathleen Lagorio Janssen ('68), another football holdout until now, to continue the football suspension with only one negative vote. Podesto had calculated that Pacific would need at least a $60 million football endowment to offset the television revenue and gate income of big-time programs, and even then, what conference would have them? In the end the funding was not there. The suspension cooled a relationship between the Spanos family and DeRosa, though certainly not with Pacific. Alex Spanos was always ready to make improvements to the Spanos Center when needed, and the unbroken record of a Spanos family member serving as regent since Alex Spanos was appointed in 1972 continues to the present.

Hitting gold with the 49ers

A stroke of luck for the new president was the proposal by the San Francisco 49ers professional football team to shift their summer camp to Pacific. The 49ers moved from Sierra College in Rocklin to the campus beginning the summer of 1998, just three years after winning the Super Bowl for the fifth time. DeRosa went to the Spanos compound to seek Alex Spanos' blessing. If the owner of the San Diego Chargers nixed the idea, it would go nowhere. But the 49ers' president Carmen Policy was a close Spanos friend, and they persuaded owner Eddie DeBartolo to make the move. Spanos was delighted to see this glimmer of hope for football in Stockton and immediately offered the Chargers for a scrimmage in the first season. Before the TV cameras and the SRO crowd in Faye Spanos Concert Hall, DeRosa evaded donning a 49ers helmet, while Spanos crowed, "This is the happiest day of my life."[35] With fresh memories of the 49ers' defeat of the Chargers in the 1995 Super Bowl, the 1998 scrimmage was only the second sellout crowd ever for football—a spectacular show that thrilled the campus and the city.

Hosting the San Francisco 49ers summer camp (1998-2002) was a big boost for Stockton as well as Pacific.

This windfall ten-year contract did three notable things for Pacific. Most importantly it rallied the Stockton and area community in support of Pacific and made the University a leader in rebuilding community relations that had suffered during the WASC accreditation ordeal. Second, local fans were inspired to fund the $3.5 million in infrastructure required, led by Alex Spanos' check handed over at the Pacific Club fundraiser to improve the stadium. Like so many similar projects, the dollars trailed the goal by

The 1998 San Francisco 49ers—San Diego Chargers scrimmage drew the last sellout crowd to Stagg Memorial Stadium.

nearly $1 million, which was borrowed to meet the deadline for the 49ers' arrival. Third, the contract brought much-needed new annual revenue to the University as the turnaround tackled a new Intercollegiate Athletics Center, DeRosa's first new building, and three refurbished and air-conditioned residence halls—the first dorms to be centrally air conditioned. Annual 49er payments helped fund the academic and physical plant building upgrades that came with the banishment of the Quonset huts.

Within five years the 49ers, now under new ownership and management, bickered with Pacific to get out of their contract. The 49ers Management wanted to return to new quarters in Santa Clara where they could turn summer camp expense into a revenue generator. The 49ers tried to wangle their way out of the hefty penalty fee. When DeRosa finally sat down with 49ers owner John York, York said, "so what is the number?" DeRosa quietly restated the original ten-ycar contract terms: $100,000 penalty per year for any unused years. Within days the $500,000 was in the mail.

HOUSECLEANING

Gilbertson's landmark academic program review

In his first report to the Academic Council, the provost announced that to be on the forefront of innovation, Pacific needed to tackle a serious review of academic programs that had been neglected during the *Sturm und Drang* years. The board and the president had insisted on it. He launched an academic program review with a tight, one-year timeline.[36] The Academic Council soon agreed that the tough review of academic programs should be done swiftly to avoid protracting the pain.

Using guidelines developed by the Academic Council the prior year, the provost nominated nearly half of all Stockton campus academic majors for review by carly fall 1996. At the time, these majors only enrolled about 6 percent of all students. Electrical engineering professor Louise Stark, then chair of the faculty academic affairs committee, ably coordinated eight faculty panels to review 45 programs.

Soon 16 academic programs were voluntarily withdrawn by their department faculties, mostly master's programs in education and the College. Remarkably, within an academic year, nearly all reviews were completed and decisions made following a board "hearing" on contested programs. What made the process successful was the relative agreement between the faculty panels and the novice provost, who worked hard to listen to all sides, including crowds of students besieging him into the night and piles of alumni mail defending threatened programs. In the end, the faculty and the provost agreed on enhancing, maintaining or discontinuing 29 programs. They disagreed on seven. Many of the discontinued programs were struggling with tiny enrollments. In all discontinued programs, only 49 students were directly affected, and every student was supported in each program through graduation. Seven faculty positions were also eliminated.[37]

Probably the most difficult decisions centered on two areas. Although he cherished the humanities as an English professor, the provost recommended ending most of these majors as the numbers of humanities majors were plummeting across the country. The College faculty was up in arms. To break through the impasse, a compromise was struck, one that hit Gilbertson while with DeRosa listening to a Dave Brubeck concert in San Francisco. They reached agreement during intermission to forge a "Humanities Project" that retained all majors and recruited students collectively over a three-year trial period, partly through an interdisciplinary humanities program.[38] Humanities enrollment rose 17 percent in the next three years.

The second area was the graduate program in Chemistry. At the last minute, following both internal and external review panels reaching conflicting judgments, COP dean Benedetti proposed a compromise to join the chemistry master's and Ph.D. programs with those in pharmacy. While the president and provost were skeptical, they agreed. The new joint program began in 2000 and has grown in quality ever since.

A critical decision was to enhance the struggling School of International Studies. The president and provost decided that the school lacked the leadership and support it needed to be successful in its first ten years, and that a five-year plan under a strong dean might strengthen and grow it to become sustainable. Majors in classics and German were ended, geology became environmental sciences, and music therapy was revived despite the provost's push to end it. Along the way the "January Term" for undergraduates faded away for lack of interest and calendar pressures in 1998.

The faculty were wrung out by the emotional and demanding review process and asked immediately for revisions in procedures for the future. But all in all, there was a sense of accomplishment. Academic affairs chair Louise Stark and Academic Council chair, education professor Margaret Langer, bravely championed the process week in, week out, and kept the process moving ahead. Everyone knew this "academic housecleaning," as the provost called it, had to be done. Over the first three years, 84 programs were reviewed, with a revolving schedule set for every seven years. Nineteen non-academic offices were also reviewed, from physical plant to recreation, which forced improvements and efficiencies.[39]

The review led to improved programs, including an upgrade from a master's to a doctoral program in physical therapy and beefing up computer science as it moved to the engineering school. In the School of Education the master's core curriculum was revamped and graduate scholarships increased. For the business school, an in-house career services office was created and the MBA program redesigned. A four-year honors program was phased in by 2001.

To better connect liberal arts and professional studies, new linked or joint programs grew from 13 in 1998 to 34 in 2000. This effort, prompted by the mission statement, followed a new perspective in this era of higher education: the notion that a "liberal education" was essential for all undergraduate students in every program, and that this liberating of the mind, this opening of student potential, this equipping students for responsible lives beyond their careers, should occur in all fields of study, not simply in the common learning of general education courses in the "liberal arts" disciplines dealing with culture, science, and society.

Mathematics professor Roland diFranco (1972-2001), who championed reasoned roles for faculty in University decisions, led major changes in faculty governance.

In a parallel process, the grinding work of revising the faculty governance document, the *Faculty Handbook,* finally was brought to the faculty in 2002, led by the highly respected Roland diFranco, mathematics professor who had become the campus expert on governance issues. When the Academic Council endorsed the *Handbook* before the affirmative all-faculty vote, they dedicated the monumental document to him. While amendments naturally came forth over the years, the essential work of the task group headed by law dean Jerald Caplan stood the test of time.

Salaries bring hope

Through the Atchley years students as well as the faculty had complained that the faculty was underpaid and deserved better. For years faculty compensation committee proposals, most of them unrealistic, languished unattended. At the regents urging, DeRosa made compensation for all faculty and staff a priority. The provost headed a University task group that proposed a three-year Stockton campus faculty salary plan in 1998 requiring each school to match dollar for dollar a University fund to increase salaries.[40] The goal to achieve the 60th percentile of salaries at peer institutions was met for the Stockton campus. Following this achievement, the IPC pushed for an increase in the pension benefit. Steady progress on this factor alone built University morale and competitiveness, and the goal was met.

A second four-year faculty salary plan was launched with a staff pay hike plan in 2004.[41] The faculty plan, aimed for the 50th percentile by faculty rank and discipline of comparable universities, was completed in 2007, and staff wages met regional markets.[42] This milestone in compensation bolstered morale and energized the campus community to aim higher in all their work.

A GOLDEN ERA IN ATHLETICS

A successful and balanced program

In many respects, the early to mid-2000s was a new golden era for Pacific athletics.[43] Nearly half of the 16 athletic teams were excelling at the national level. Remarkably, five teams were in post-season NCAA play in 2004: men's basketball, women's volleyball, men's tennis (third time in five years), women's swimming (third straight conference champions), and women's softball. But even more remarkable was that Pacific had five teams in NCAA post-season competition each year from 1999-2005. [44]

The most public validation of the football decision probably came in 2001 during athletic director Lynn King's first year, when Pacific won the "Sears Cup" as the top NCAA Division I non-football university for its comprehensive success across the sports in post-season play. This national award followed two Big West "Commissioner's Cup" awards in 1999 and 2000 as the top all-around athletic program based on conference standings in each sport. This same year athletic director King revived the Block P society, expanding it to all sports for both men and women.[45]

Gina Carbonatto ('07), three-time All American, led some of the great softball teams of the 2000s, including several of eight NCAA tournaments.

While sport teams did benefit from the redistribution of the football operations budget, additional support was modest. As other universities invested heavily in improving their sports—some funded by television revenues, Big West Conference public schools by hiking student fees—Pacific lost ground because fundraising could not match the competition. Stellar coach Brian Kolze, for example, brought his softball team to the NCAA national tournament eight times starting in 1998, led by two-time All-American and top player in team history, Cindy Ball ('02), who still holds most of the pitching records, and later led by All-American Gina Carbonatto ('07), Pacific's only three-time softball All-American. But Kolze did most of the fundraising himself when their operations budget received no increase over these years. In 2011, the team won its first Big West Conference championship, and Kolze was named conference coach of the year for the fourth time. Meanwhile, Simoni softball field was gradually brought to a competitive level over years of prolonged fundraising, a sluggish record compared to Kolze's 20 years of leadership, with eight trips to the NCAA tournament. Other women's sports also peaked from time to time. Keith Coleman's women's soccer team won the Big West Conference championship in 1998 with its best season in history. In 2005 women's field hockey had its best season in its history, long after triple All-American Luci Lagrimas ('86). But these teams had to make do with undersized support.

The men's and women's swim teams were conference champions in 2002 and 2003, with Shannon Catalano ('05), 14-time All-American, leading the way. Yes, Catalano, three-time All-American in individual swimming, also won 11 All-American relay awards from 2002-04, along

The 2000s women's swim teams amassed more All-American awards than any other Pacific sport, led by 14-time All-American Shannon Catalano ('05).

with her relay teammates, Sarah Marshall ('04, two individual, seven relay All-American awards), Robin Errecart ('04, nine in relays), Kris Willey ('04, six in relays), Heidi Schmidt ('04, five in relays) and Lyndsay McNamee ('05, five in relays). These women swimmers collected more All-American awards than any other Pacific sport.

Molly Smith (2000) was a triple All-American in women's water polo in the late 1990s, when triple All-American Elsa Stegemann was burning the nets in volleyball. The women's volleyball team had another peak year in 2003 with Jennifer Joines ('05), the second four-time All-American in Pacific volleyball and a member of the U.S. national team for three years, winning Olympic silver in 2008. After the team lost to Stanford in the second round of the NCAA finals, the turnover in coaches began. The quick

Four-time All American Jennifer Joines ('05) led women's volleyball back to national standing—and later earned an Olympic silver medal.

decline in women's volleyball left women's sports without a lead team, so Pacific made the strategic decision to invest in women's basketball. Not until Lynne Roberts was appointed women's basketball coach in 2006 did that sport gain ground and visibility by adding more coaching, travel, and support funds. Her team got beyond the first round in WNIT post-season play in both 2012 and 2103.

The baseball escapade

DeRosa had grown up going to Yankee Stadium to watch Joe DiMaggio and was a pretty good player himself. So he listened when his old friend and major league manager Grady Little alerted him that third baseman Ed Sprague, Jr. would soon retire and offer a great chance for Pacific to bring baseball up to a competitive level. Sprague was Stockton's most famous pro player of that era, an Olympic gold medalist and two-time World Series champion, ready to come home. As a college scholarship pitcher, DeRosa knew the value of the game for a campus, and soon found plenty of community support to build a campus diamond to clinch a deal with Sprague in 2003 just as the city was abandoning Billy Hebert Field where the Tigers played. When the Forty-niners broke their contract in 2003, the coast was clear to place the park right next to the new athletic center.

By 2004, the board approved a plan for a $3 million baseball stadium named the Klein Family Field after the lead donors. This project had not been part of campaign planning, yet all of a sudden it seemed to preempt the fundraising plan to build a multipurpose gymnasium recreation and practice facility. Behind it all was the president passionate about his sport, seizing an opportunity to make his own stamp on athletics after the burial of football. Through the persuasion of Sprague and others, and despite many cost overruns, a first-class, big-league park was built, called "the best collegiate ballpark on the west coast." Just before the new field opened, the team earned a winning overall record for the first time since 1999, so even though its operations were funded by cuts in other sports, the promise of baseball seemed bright for Pacific. DeRosa's dream was to achieve a premier program like Rice and other smaller private schools, but

Klein Family Field opened in 2005 as likely the finest collegiate baseball field on the west coast.

alas, the team struggled for years following, and the hope for a nationally competitive team in a third high profile sport remained elusive.

To the dance: Thomason basketball thrills

Coach Thomason gradually built a system of recruiting players who he knew could graduate at Pacific and produce on the floor. With its first trip to the NCAA Tournament in 18 years on the line against Nevada in the 1997 Big West Conference championship, seven-foot neophyte Michael Olowokandi ('98) and the team overcame the Reno crowd and won with command. Olowokandi was a walk-on from London, son of a Nigerian diplomat, who had never played organized basketball. A chance phone call led him to Pacific from 1995-98, an overnight sensation because of his size, strength, agility and quick development. He became a star player that landed him the number one pick in the 1998 NBA draft, and only the fourth Tiger

Sensational Michael Olowokandi ('98) broke many Pacific basketball records.

basketball player to have his jersey retired. Basketball's first All-American since 1982, Olowokandi set the single-season scoring record for Pacific, broke the single-season and career blocks records with his hands above the basket, and held the single-season and career records for field goal percentages (61 and 59 percent).[46]

Not until 2004 did the team return to the NCAA "Big Dance" by winning the conference championship with two free throws in the last five seconds. They went on to knock off a cocky, five-seeded Providence team from the Big East Conference in the first round. The win earned them a front-page story in *The Washington Post* and a doubling of traffic to the Pacific website.[47] This NCAA basketball tournament win was a first since 1971. And who will forget Myree Bowden's (2004) second place finish in the NCAA slam-dunk contest.

The next year, on a 22-game winning streak, the Tigers pushed over another Big East powerhouse, Pittsburgh, in the opening round. Then in 2006, with the great Swede Christian Maraker (2006, third in all-time Pacific scoring) leading another league championship, Pacific went to the Dance for a third time, enduring a heartbreaker to Boston College on a dreadful foul call in the final seconds of regulation play that led to a double-overtime loss. This string of three seasons under Thomason, filled with both talent and depth, was certainly the all-time high point of Pacific basketball since the Edwards era, culminating in (almost) three first-round wins at the Dance. During these years, a loyal fan base grew, but few could claim the loyalty of Koreen Freitas in food service, who on the early morning shift served athletes their breakfast for 40 years. Freitas was an institution: she never missed a single men's basketball game at home and knew most athletes. Heroes like Pete Carroll and Willard Harrell kept in touch with her long after graduation.[48]

Thomason ended his career in 2013 as the winningest coach at Pacific (437-321) and in the Big West Conference, where he won six championships, and went on to four NCAA Tournaments. His coaching was both demanding and caring, selfless and personal, building on character. His taskmaster approach softened by the 2000s. Basketball, he said, was "80 percent mental."[49] He was Big West Conference coach of the year five times and National Mid-Major Coach of the Year in 2005. Thomason was always justifiably proud of his exceptional graduation rates compared to any elite school: 85 to 95 percent of his players in recent years, and one of nine schools in the nation with 100 percent in 2013.[50] Over half a dozen of his recent graduates were playing professional ball abroad.

Coach Bob Thomason (1988-2013) was the winningest basketball coach at Pacific, with six conference championships and four NCAA tournaments.

Ron Verlin got off to a good start as the twentieth basketball coach in 2013. He had served as Thomason's top assistant for 19 years and kept on former star Adam Jacobsen ('97), top Pacific player for 3-point goals and assists, who had been an assistant coach with Verlin for 13 years.[51]

Campus recreation takes off

Despite these successes, students were increasingly less interested in attending spectator sports and more interested in their own physical conditioning through intramural competition or fitness routines. Now that the campus had a new weight room for athletes, DeRosa could move the Baun fitness center from athletics to the student life division and soon

Baun Fitness Center doubled in size in 2002, including a climbing wall.

ended the student use fee, which made it a destination for students all hours of the day and night. Then in 2002 the center was doubled in size, including a climbing wall and dance floor, now fully a fitness center for all students.

A key champion of student recreation was Karen DeRosa. While Pacific had many outstanding first ladies, few actually had a comparable impact on students. She had a major shaping influence on Don DeRosa's commitment to improving the quality of student life on campus. "Karen helped me to understand more broadly the importance of all that goes on in the lives of students," DeRosa explained.[52] Through her he saw the central importance of co-curricular involvement on student growth and development. As a former director of the student recreation center at Bowling Green State University, Karen DeRosa was a constant reminder to the president of the importance of physical fitness to improve both social and academic success.[53] Not since Helen Guth nearly a century earlier had Pacific had a first lady whose advocacy so positively influenced student life.

By the turn of the century, over 2,000 students were in intramural sports, from racquetball to bowling to Frisbee golf, along with six other "club sports," from rugby to lacrosse.[54] In 2004, over 70 percent of undergraduates participated in organized recreation (no doubt the other 30 percent had their own kinds of recreation). A record 50 teams participated in intramural volleyball. An array of wilderness sports was fed by equipment for backpacking, rock climbing, and kayaking.[55] A women's flag football team won regional play-offs, and over 100 students participated in a bowling tournament.[56] By 2008, about 4,000 students participated in organized recreation, now with a restarted rugby team and a crew team of 100 students.[57] A particular standout was José Rojas (2013), who placed third in the 2012 professional international racquetball competition, trained by Dave Ellis ('65), coach of the U.S. national team.[58]

REBUILDING QUALITY AND STABILITY

Student selectivity re-established

As enrollment sagged in the mid-nineties, Pacific devised a new financial aid commitment in 1998 that continues today. The "Cal Grant Match" offered a University scholarship equal to the state-sponsored Cal Grant, a generous, four-year undergraduate financial aid award for talented but financially disadvantaged students. This matching program immediately drew top applicants who otherwise could not afford a Pacific education, and within a year brought a one-third increase, enrolling 200 Cal Grant students.

Most regents wanted a much higher academic profile and applauded progress in selectivity to increase the value of Pacific. In 1999, Pacific set a goal to improve selectivity from 82 to 75 percent—still a modest goal, admitting every three of four applications rather than four out of five. SAT scores improved and the average high school GPA hit an all-time high of 3.43. Compared to a decade earlier, when Pacific had virtually an "open admission" policy with low admission standards, high tuition rates, unmet enrollment targets, and high dropout rates, the University had come a long way.[59]

The IPC and DeRosa—eyeing the empty seats especially in the College and in education, engineering, and international studies—set a goal of growing the Stockton campus by 400 students.[60] The first to second year persistence rate grew from a respectable 82 percent in 1994 to an impressive 88 percent four years later, and the graduation rate rose to nearly 70 percent.

A robust national economy raised all ships: the residence halls were overflowing, the tuition discount rate was moderating, transfer student enrollment increased by 13 percent, and retention improved. Even as enrollment climbed, increased selectivity stimulated an ongoing debate among regents about Pacific becoming "elitist." DeRosa noted that Pacific was simply rebuilding its academic reputation and remained a long distance from that label. Selectivity was an important element of student success. Each applicant was given a holistic review that went beyond GPAs and SAT scores, yet not all applicants were prepared to be successful at Pacific.[61] For the first time in its history, the University had a "wait list" of applicants who would have been admitted in the past but were not because the class was full to capacity with stronger students.[62] Eight out of Pacific's top ten competitors were now UCs, and the other two were Santa Clara and USC.[63]

Growth—in quality and quantity

Each year, undergraduate enrollment grew by about 100 students (~3 percent). By 2005, the SAT frosh average had increased by 80 points from the late nineties.[64] Student satisfaction surveys of freshman and senior students exceeded national private universities in nearly all categories.[65] DeRosa called for greater selectivity over growth to improve quality, in moderate disagreement with Monagan, who saw enrollment growth as the avenue to success. But both continued to happen. By 2000, the undergraduate profile steadily improved along with retention. When the application process went online in 2002, a record number of applicants, up by nearly 20 percent, produced the highest academic profile and a 70 percent admittance rate.[66]

Many regents, led by Monagan, kept questioning the creep of tuition increases when they moved above 3 percent in the early to mid-2000s. DeRosa reminded the regents of the rapid progress in enrollment: in 2002, the board set a goal of 780 freshman students with average SAT scores of 1175 in eight years, yet in only one year, 818 frosh enrolled with an SAT 1160 average, hitting a target that was downrange by five years.[67] Pacific was helped during these years by a state budget crisis that crushed the public universities with budget cuts and skyrocketing tuition, so that a typical student choosing between Pacific and UC-Berkeley saw little difference in the total cost bottom line. The freshman student discount rate settled at about 40 percent (that is, on average each freshman student received a 40 percent unfunded discount on tuition—about the national average for independent universities).[68]

By 2003, Pacific enrollment finally matched the 1976 high of nearly 6200 students, and it moved to record heights from 2005 forward. By 2005, undergraduate selectivity was improved to 56 percent, finally in the company of other "selective" universities, where Pacific should have been all along. And only half of all graduate student applicants were admitted.[69]

But then enrollment plateaued for three years, and improvement funds shrunk, raising friction again with the regents about the value proposition of Pacific with the lowest tuition among its nine California peers.[70] Competition was actually more intense than ever. Since the 1990s, with the ease of online applications, Pacific students had applied to more than three schools, often six or more.[71] Generally, competitor private universities outpaced Pacific in the eyes of admitted students, even in Pacific's areas of strength, such as personal attention, attractive campus, quality of majors and academic facilities. Especially on cost and location, Pacific often lost students to other schools.[72]

Another important dynamic was DeRosa's commitment to bringing in underserved students. As a "first-generation" college student himself, with immigrant parents who had no college education, he knew from personal experience how important support was for families new to higher education, from financial aid to mentoring. First-generation students ran 15-20 percent among freshmen in the 2000s.[73] He always kept a vigilant eye on the proportion of students from lower incomes, seeking to strike a balance between needed tuition income and scholarships for needy students. This aim to balance students from upper, middle, and lower income families—enriching the learning environment as much as ethnic and geographic diversity—became another distinguishing mark of Pacific during this era. Transfer students, mostly from community colleges, especially San Joaquin Delta College, drew 200-250 students annually (20-30 percent of first-year enrollment). Whilc transfers students were more challenged in individual courses, their overall academic performance matched freshman students, and they graduated at a higher rate.[74]

Becoming a "best value"

As the millennium turned and the nation prospered during a time of economic growth, DeRosa told the regents, "Now we have a unique opportunity to change this institution and achieve what we did not accomplish 25 years ago."[75] In 2000 the *Newsweek/Kaplan* report ranked Pacific among the top ten in the nation in responsiveness to student financial aid needs and one of six "best values" schools in the west. The report even called Pacific one of the top ten "hidden treasure" universities in the nation.[76]

National rankings never drove the president's decisions, but the metrics were tracked carefully every year, and if they pointed to appropriate investments for improvement, they were made. The ranking that DeRosa most appreciated was the annual *U.S. News & World Report* "best value" ranking for Pacific that for eight years (2002-09) ran about 30th in the nation among 249 national universities. Pacific was remarkably competitive nationally, given its size and limited resources. It typically hovered around the one-hundredth rank among these mostly public and wealthy private institutions.[77]

Fiscal stability

In the mid-nineties, the budget bleeding was felt everywhere. Nearly all the "auxiliary enterprises," as higher education jargon calls them, were red ink instead of adding dollars to a reduced budget: the bookstore, athletics, Feather River Inn, and KUOP radio station provided valued services, but were a drag on the budget. Many dorm rooms sat vacant. By fall 1997, management changes made the bookstore and FRI profitable, probably for the first time, and by 2000 the bookstore was outsourced to Barnes and Noble. Two years later the board provided a $1 million loan to lease Feather River Inn to an alumni corporation who wanted a chance to refurbish and make a go of it.

In early 1997, the board endorsed a plan devised by the president's executive assistant John Stein to eliminate the $8.3 million deficit through the sale of appreciated assets in the endowment, thanks to extraordinary dividends in a robust economy.[78] Cutting loose an albatross that hung heavy through many years of negligence not only gave a lift to the step but also bolstered the University's Moody bond rating to A3, enabling Pacific to borrow construction funds at lower rates. As another mark of progress, the board also cut the Bank of Stockton line of credit from $8 million to $4 million. By 1998, even the Stockton campus had a $900,000 surplus to crow about. Total regent giving had doubled in one year to nearly $1 million. And for the first time ever the University actually set aside 1 percent ($1.2 million) of its 1998 operating budget as an operating reserve. Confidence was building. By the new century, DeRosa annually set aside a one percent operating reserve as well as a $1.25 million "unrestricted reserve accumulation" to build financial strength and improve the bond rating for future borrowing. The endowment had now grown to $130 million by 2001, though still small by peer standards.[79]

The Cavanaugh factor

Vice president for business and finance Pat Cavanaugh arrived on campus in July 1997 to immediately take charge of facilities development as well as direct an open budget process.[80] While Ovid Ritter and Bob Winterberg served long and well, neither one could match the skill set and sharp mind of Cavanaugh, a preeminent problem solver who did not quit until the job was done. Equally important was restoring integrity to the office and building trust in his staff. Provost Gilbertson often said, "Cavanaugh was the best hire DeRosa ever made."

Cavanaugh listed "improved customer service" as a top priority for his division in his first couple years, and then proceeded to demonstrate it by streamlining the annual budget presentation and opening the books to the Academic Council and anyone else who cared to look. The faculty were stunned by this refreshing new approach to doing business at Pacific and never lost admiration for their business vice president.

High on Cavanaugh's list of "to-dos" was to reduce the high 6 percent spending rate of endowment earnings. Best practice universities had already moved to reduce spending rates below 5 percent because of long-term earnings projections, so Cavanaugh urged the board to begin an incremental rate lowering by half a percentage a year starting in 1999.[81] Pacific's endowment made impressive gains during the late 1990s but had a long ways to catch up to its neighbors. For example, in 1998, with a $95 million total endowment, the endowment dollars *per student* at Pacific were $18,000, compared to Santa Clara's $51,000 or Loyola Marymount's $43,000. USC exceeded Santa Clara's, Occidental's was over eight times greater, and Pomona's was a whopping 26 times greater.[82] Through the turn of the century, Pacific's endowment growth went through the roof under Cavanaugh's leadership, especially through the expert portfolio management of Dodge and Cox, a diligent board investment committee, and Pacific's chief investment officer Larry Brehm, long-time associate vice president in business and finance. By 2002, the endowment reached nearly $135 million on a 14.3 percent return rate, second highest among universities in the country.

Cavanaugh orchestrated each of three Moody's bond rating upgrades in his first four years to an A2 rating, based on Pacific's student market demand, diversity of programs, financial resources, fundraising success and capital improvements.[83] The bond ratings were snapshots of a university building dependable strength. By 2004 Pacific's endowment ranked fifth in the nation in market performance over the prior five years thanks to Cavanaugh's and Brehm's diligence and an engaged board investment committee now shrewd and strategic.[84]

By 2007, the endowment peaked at $225 million just prior to the Great Recession, which chopped nearly one-third of its market value over the next two years.[85] Many wealthy universities suffered greatly with this loss, but this was one time when Pacific's modest endowment, producing only 4-5 percent of its annual operating income, proved to be advantageous. Helping to steady Pacific's keel was the University's balance sheet, which over the Cavanaugh's years showed that net assets more than tripled from $185 million to over $615 million by 2013.

Cavanaugh oversaw the triennial campus master plans, critical during these years of growth and construction, to ensure that the Stockton campus made sense architecturally and improved steadily in its polished beauty.

He built out a pedestrian landscape that pushed parking lots and vehicles to the periphery of campus. Throughout the DeRosa years, Cavanaugh was the linchpin to completing all facilities projects in timely fashion and on budget. Thanks especially to Cavanaugh, alumni who returned to campus as frequently as every 24 months reacted with wonder each time at the new construction, the fresh look, the upgraded feel, and deepened beauty of Stockton's premier garden park.

Steadily through the 1990s and 2000s vehicles were pushed to the perimeter to create a more pedestrian Stockton campus. Pictured is the College's Wendell Phillips Center in 1967 and in 2006.

When Cavanaugh retired in 2014, most University leaders recognized that Cavanaugh had been a key factor in the overall transformation of Pacific in the DeRosa era, from finances to facilities to human resources. From a historical perspective, Pacific had witnessed the most effective business and finance vice president ever in Patrick Cavanaugh's 17 years of service.

REBUILDING THE STOCKTON CAMPUS

The Quonset huts finally bite the dust

Throughout the DeRosa years, construction and renovation were standard features of the campus as much as during the Burns and McCaffrey years. Cavanaugh had told DeRosa during his final campus interview, "if those Quonsets are still here in three years, you ought to fire me."[86]

In 2001 the last of the central campus Quonset huts were razed to make room for the new DeRosa Univesity Center and lawn.

Within months of DeRosa's arrival the aquatics center was built, and then the University set plans to move the departments of art and geosciences out of the last remaining four Quonset huts on the central campus into South campus renovated facilities that had housed the physical plant maintenance staff and equipment. There had been 11 tin tents in the center of campus at one time, filled with history and memories that touched nearly every one of the Stockton schools. Finally, in April 2001, the giant yellow bulldozers and claw buckets ravaged the sagging structures in front of a crowd of curious onlookers.

Here amid these crusty tin sheds had been engineering labs, conservatory offices and classrooms, the department of home economics (ended in 1968), physics and psychology faculty, student-run stores, and most recently the art and geology departments. Some cheered while others wiped a tear as they recalled their happy times, especially those whose lives had been changed by a professor in a classroom or a lifelong friend met in the dorm. "Believe it or not," said art graduate Alex Wright ('92), "I loved every minute of my Pacific life in those blistering-hot/freezing-cold tin cans." The alumni office was careful to preserve corrugated steel roof samples for loyal fans like Pam Mendoza ('97), who "spent countless hours sitting in that old and dirty Quonset with knowledge bursting out its seams." Alumni from the fifties recalled the happy times in the earlier dorm Quonsets, like football giants Eddie LeBaron ('50) and John Rohde ('50) with swim star Ken Mork ('50) and tennis star Art Larsen ('49).[87] This rising scrap heap was a powerful symbol of the end of an era, a symbol of a lost time when Pacific was a charming yet rag-tag school, caught for decades on the edge of poverty, unable to pull itself out.

Soon these scarred grounds would become a beautiful central green, spread between a new University Center to the north, a renovated McCaffrey Center for student support offices to the south, a new Baun

Fitness Center to the west and the renovated Hand Hall offices for student life to the south—truly a center of student activity. (Once vaguely known as "Bomar Commons," research into this area uncovered not a Bomar family donor, but the self-designation of the lawn by grounds crewmembers Bob and Marty!) The grounds, always attractive, had steadily been improved all around over recent years. The student survey in *Princeton Review* confirmed in that same year what all had experienced—a new level of natural and architectural beauty. Pacific was ranked sixth among the most beautiful campuses in the nation in 2001, and continued to be ranked among the top for beauty by other publications for years to come.[88] Justly earned.

Catching up with overdue projects

One of the barriers for the College of the Pacific to build coherence and *esprit d'corps* was the dispersion of departments, especially in humanities across the Stockton campus. The College's first dean, Jake Jacoby, complained about it in 1967.[89] Centralizing all in one building was a high priority for the provost and dean Benedetti, so when the local Pacific Italian Alliance proposed a shared building on campus that would promote Italian culture and provide office space for the humanities, plans proceeded in the late 1990s. But no agreement could be reached with the PI-A, so in 2005 the University built a Humanities Center attached to the Wendell Phillips Center. Gathered together were English from Knoles Hall, classics and languages from WPC, philosophy from Raymond Lodge, and religious studies from Sears Hall behind Morris Chapel. The structure was a landmark not because the building was anything but basic, but because it brought together for the first time all the humanities faculty, whose scattered status had bred second-class status.

The biggest investment was in construction of two new residential apartment buildings on the north campus, near the pharmacy school. Monagan Hall and Brookside Hall (renamed Chan Family Hall in 2014) were built within a year of each other to house a total of 400 upper-level undergrads and pharmacy students in attractive apartments.[90] Monagan Hall in 2001 was the first new residence hall in over 30 years. The board honored the leadership of Bob Monagan along with his wife Ione as he stepped down from the chair in 2003. But the renovation of venerable Grace Covell Hall in 2000 was just as historic. The interior had nearly a complete makeover to become a modern hall, with appropriate lavatories, lounges, and laundry on each floor.

Monagan Hall (2001) was the first new residence hall in over 30 years, honoring the leadership of board chair Monagan ('42) and his wife Ione ('45, student body president in 1943).

Monagan Hall on right. Brookside Hall (2002, left) was renamed Chan Family Hall in 2014.

The black hole of information technology

Starting in fall 1996, the University took a fresh look at the role of information technology. From the start, academic use had been a stepchild to administrative computing, which under the thralldom of the SCT contract had never provided adequate service to any office. As other universities invested in the central role of academic computing, Pacific languished without leadership, direction, or resources. Again through the efforts of regent and Long family member Tom Sweeney, the Thomas J. Long Foundation funded a major project to connect all faculty to the computer network, upgrade servers, and add multimedia classrooms.

The Stockton campus Library Information Commons was a major step forward in connecting students to the Internet in 2005.

Pacific had catching up to do, especially on the Stockton campus. The new Center for Teaching and Learning assisted faculty in integrating technology into their teaching, and the opening of the William Knox Holt Library "Information Commons" in 1998 was a landmark in expanding network access to all students. Under the leadership of Jean Purnell, a new wing was added to the library in 2005, the "Information Commons" of computer carrels and group study rooms were greatly expanded, and the library truly became for the first time "a teaching and learning center" for students.[91]

A decision in 1999 to end the outsourced SCT contract forced the University to face the ever-rising demand by students, faculty and staff to improve technology services. At the same time, the tenor of campus life shifted during these years, especially for the staff and student workers. As the couriering of paper documents from office to office tapered off, so too did the personal friendships among staff across each campus that were nourished by the personal greetings face to face. Now, you could work for years with a fellow staff person whom you only knew through e-mail. New also were the countless wrangles over who was "getting all the goodies" that continued for years, as each division complained that somebody else must be getting better service from all those technology dollars. Always in a catch-up mode, having started nearly a decade later than competitive schools, Pacific suffered the legacy of the McCaffrey-Atchley years, a painful reminder of lost opportunities and a daunting sense of the mountains to climb.

The dental and pharmacy schools led the campus in technology innovation. Pharmacy led the initiative for a "notebook campus" by requiring laptop computers of all its students and filling them with a library of resources that expanded learning. Dentistry soon followed, and these laptop programs continued to the present. In 1990, the law school had designated its old Oak Park Library building as the "LawLab," the largest student computer center among the state's private law schools.[92]

DeRosa had hoped to "leap frog" other universities by partnering with major technology firms to introduce innovative devices for student learning. The new millennium did bring technology partnerships that extended for at least a decade, beginning with a joint venture with Sun Microsystems and Cisco Systems. Other partnerships followed, but none got the full support of either the faculty or administration to have a major impact on the campus.

IT progress was never fast enough for faculty or students. For example, by 2006, students accessed library resources unheard of in prior generations—28 percent of library web access was between 10 p.m. and 8 a.m.[93] Yet as late as 2008, less than one-third of Stockton campus classrooms had adequate technology.[94] To make room for the Chambers Technology Center, the central University information technology offices moved in 2009 to a handsome office building about a mile from campus with a bargain lease that made room for the offices of continuing education as well.

BUILDING BLOCKS

The National Commission

In early 1999, nearing the 150th anniversary of the University, the president launched a "National Commission on the Next Level of Excellence," consisting of seven panels of alumni, community supporters, regents, faculty and staff, totaling about 250 people. The "National Commission" was headed by Ralph Guild ('50), former regent and national leader in the radio communications industry. Seven panels convened for about a year, one for each of the professional schools of dentistry, law, and pharmacy; one for the College, education and the conservatory; one for business, engineering and international studies; and one each for students and the co-curriculum and for alumni and community relations. Each panel grappled with four University objectives: to elevate Pacific to the "second tier" of national universities, to identify areas of distinction, to engage constituents, and to assess resource needs.

The panels built a new sense of trust and community among all the constituents and elevated the sense of expectation and opportunity for Pacific. The president and the board integrated the commission's 155 recommendations into planning priorities that became the menu for the upcoming fundraising campaign.[95] The National Commission was hugely successful. When the president issued a "National Commission Report Card" in 2006, all the key goals were marked as accomplished. Fourteen members of the National Commission eventually became regents of the University, and four members eventually became chairs of the board: Donald O'Connell, Dianne Philibosian ('68), Thomas Zuckerman ('64), and Kathleen Lagorio Janssen ('68).

The sesquicentennial celebration

Headed by Bob Monagan and Judy Chambers, the 150th anniversary celebration was appropriately festive. 2001 began on a high point: the National Commission wrapped up its work on January 10 and joined the sesquicentennial kickoff gala. Dave Brubeck starred in a concert with the conservatory symphony and choirs. The evening began with a black tie dinner for 750 with stunning table bouquets, chocolate pianos for dessert, all under a huge tent covering the parking area north of Greek row. The celebration, billed also as a thank you to donors and to the community for their support of Pacific in the last campaign, was such a big hit that the president, with cabinet applause, decided a gala must be continued in future years.

A splendid brief anniversary history and collection of alumni tributes arrayed a lavish photo book called *The Professor Who Changed My Life* edited by English professor Charles Clerc. Regent Gail Kautz's ('58) Ironstone Winery produced sesquicentennial wines to toast the year. The website featured a menu of memento gifts. A special recognition of charter day, July 10, 1851, was held on the Capitol steps in Sacramento on Pacific's birthday. Alumni weekend—first moved from fall to June in 2001—included a festive birthday party. An academic symposium headed by SIS dean Margee Ensign focused on "Leadership for the Common Good: The University's Role in the Global Community" in ten events over the fall term. The highlight event was Poland's liberation President Lech Walesa's powerful address. The celebration of the future came in the fall, when *U.S. News & World Report* ranked Pacific in the second tier of national universities and a "Best Value" above UC-Berkeley.

The 2001 Sesquicentennial book by English professor Charles Clerc, The Professor Who Changed My Life: University of the Pacific, *is available through the Alumni Office. The DeRosas and PowerCat cut the cake on Pacific's 150th birthday, celebrated on Alumni Weekend, 2001.*

Relentless planning

Planning was always a core element of this era, with the board and administration in sync on its importance. At another Silverado Resort retreat, the board approved the revised "MVP" for 2002-2007, asserting a vision that the University

> *will be among the best national universities, known for linking liberal arts and professional education at both undergraduate and graduate levels through distinctive, innovative curricular and co-curricular programs of exceptional quality and high value. Pacific will become a national leader in the creative use of experiential learning and leadership development.*[96]

At the retreat DeRosa presented his vision of the "next level of excellence." There was no question that his ultimate priorities focused on the individual student: "Every student's successful experience at Pacific must include a profound experience with a faculty member in an academic context."[97]

DeRosa and his provost pushed hard on increasing the distinctiveness of each school. Some schools, of course, already had long-standing distinctiveness, such as the humanistic approach to dental education, the accelerated three-year pharmacy program, or the required work-based internships (the "co-op" program) in engineering. But engineering now had a strong and unusual undergraduate bioengineering program and international internships. Law had settled on its three key strengths: international business, government affairs, and advocacy. Education had created an accelerated four-year teacher education degree unusual in the state and a new Ph.D. program in school psychology. The conservatory had its unique Brubeck Institute and music management program along with a plan to be a "Steinway campus." Business had completely retooled its MBA program almost uniquely to recruit recent graduates *prior* to employment. The College had its remarkable general education program and web of links to accelerated professional programs. SIS as a school was itself unique. Changes came in fits and starts, but the spirit of innovation began to add yeast to the schools.[98]

Another yardstick was the net financial contribution or subsidy of each school. Dentistry, law, and pharmacy were by far the greatest contributors to the University's financial welfare. Pharmacy's efficient program made it a dramatic leader, while the College was a minor contributor. All the other schools—business, education, engineering, music and SIS—could meet their own expenses, but not their share of University-wide expenses, from technology to campus grounds to registrar.

THE CAMPAIGN TO RE-ENGAGE ALUMNI AND FRIENDS

A school-driven campaign

Fundraising in the late nineties was impressive. After the "Fulfilling the Promise" campaign exceeded its goal at $77 million in 1997, a record $16 million was raised before the new campaign was even begun.[99] Advancement vice president Jonathan Meer replaced John Evey to lead this second fundraising campaign of Pacific's modern history, "Investing in Excellence: The Campaign for Pacific." The goal was set at $200 million when it went public, even though several regents doubted it was achievable. Regent Patricia Bilbrey Kennedy ('66) chaired the campaign, and committees across the schools included over half the regents.

The campaign progressed in fits and starts. While the goal was to engage an army of volunteers to solicit gifts, the volunteer campaign never really developed, and certainly did not match the outpouring of volunteer solicitation that the the Pacific Dental Education Foundation board used so successfully in the dental school campaign that had begun two years prior.[100] The law school waited two years after the University launch to begin its fundraising. The University development infrastructure and technology support was still not in place, and many staff members were new. Still, the first three years produced over $30 million each year.[101] Each spring a black tie "gala" in the Spanos Center thanked donors and celebrated major benefactors, with music and theatre students performing.

Adding to the challenge, the president had three major illnesses in three successive autumns midway in the campaign, but he bounced back within weeks of each with a disciplined diet and daily, brisk, four-mile walks along the Calaveras River levee with his golden retriever Jessie. Never once considering early retirement, he was eager to get back to the job of a lifetime. In the end, these health setbacks probably reduced his time with prospective benefactors who, if they had gotten to know DeRosa, would have entrusted their generosity to Pacific. But it must be said that the cancer illness he shared with Robert Powell was an important bond of their friendship, which led to Pacific's most astonishing gift (see page 416).

The law school struggled through the campaign, starting late, hustling to get a staff in place and finding resistance among older alumni who still had a sour taste in their mouths from dean Schaber's "boot camp" approach to produce top bar pass rates. While law school fundraising achieved new highs, beating the mediocre record of the past was a modest achievement. The law library expansion project limped along with funding from annual surpluses as much as from donations for several years.[102]

Still, the overall campaign rolled forward. The regents noted that since 1851, only 34 over $1 million had been received, yet in 2003, over 40 percent of campaign dollars came in this category, and 250 volunteers were involved in some fashion.[103] In 2005, the campaign hit an all-time record high of over 3,000 alumni donors to the annual fund, but since the number of alumni had grown dramatically in recent years, the percentage was still a meager 13.2 percent.[104] "Most alumni aren't disaffected, they're just disconnected," declared the campaign consultant.

Despite all these drawbacks, the campaign was astonishingly successful under DeRosa's leadership. The $200 million goal was exceeded one year early, with 23,000 donors giving a total of $330 million. The campaign that started with much doubt and a sense of overreach ended with breathtaking success, exceeding its goal by nearly two-thirds.[105] Even without the Powell gift, the campaign exceeded the goal by $30 million. Yes, there were issues—weak data systems, missed goals, a high percentage of deferred gifts, uneven board and staff support, lack of coordination and effective communication—but no one would challenge the remarkable achievement.[106] And the biggest triumph coincided with the Powell gift, which raised the University's endowment by $188 million—a landmark achievement, especially given Pacific's woeful endowment history. According to external evaluators, despite "the failure over many years to build *robust and consistent* [italics original] alumni relations and development programs…the key to the spectacular success," from the National Commission to the Powell gift, was President DeRosa's leadership.[107]

"Advancing to greatness": The Arthur A. Dugoni School of Dentistry

In 2000, the Pacific Dental Education Foundation (PDEF) was fully realizing its potential under the strong leadership of Donald O'Connell, a Johnson & Johnson corporate vice president who adopted the dental school through a friendship with dean Dugoni.[108] O'Connell set the bar higher and higher, challenging a motivated PDEF board to do more, culminating in their decision to dare to raise $50 million to name the dental school after Dugoni. PDEF board members joked that O'Connell elevated expectations for the board from a spaghetti supper gang to a Morton's Steakhouse dining group. O'Connell approached DeRosa and the board with their plan, and despite consultant advice against the venture, Pacific said yes, knowing the powerful loyalty Dugoni had earned from thousands of grateful graduates. It was no surprise to anyone that the PDEF board sought to name the school after Dugoni.

That campaign was one of the most remarkable fundraising landmarks in Pacific's history. Ronald Redmond ('66), who headed the PDEF board and the campaign until he became a regent in 2003, virtually left his orthodontics practice to join with Dugoni to meet with all the major donors—and many of the minor ones—to make the four-part ask: an annual gift, a campaign gift, a bequest gift, and the gift of names of friends who should be contacted. The Earl and Tannia Hodges estate and James and Carolyn Pride were important donors. Both Redmond and Dugoni themselves became among the school's most generous benefactors. Their tireless travels throughout the west led a PDEF board-wide effort, now headed by effective Colin Wong ('65), to solicit alumni and friends. The dental school "naming campaign" was perhaps the only truly volunteer-driven campaign in Pacific's history, matched only by the city of Stockton's 1922 campaign to bring Pacific to the city.

Halfway through the dental school campaign when giving plateaued, some wanted to lower the goal, but Redmond knew that could not be compromised. After all, the Dugoni naming was the heart of the campaign and had to remain untarnished. Redmond rallied the PDEF and the giving took off again. Unlike the University board, the PDEF members were nearly all active fundraisers. Meanwhile, the University campaign was flagging, so DeRosa asked the school to extend its campaign for another year, and then a second year to help meet the overall University goal by 2007. The contrast was painful: PDEF board members were scheduling donor meetings, while many University regents barely got involved. But the extra time meant that the PDEF exceeded the $50 million goal by $15 million or 30 percent. This astounding accomplishment was a resounding affirmation of Dugoni's leadership—and Redmond's bold persuasion. As Redmond, himself a first-generation college student, reflected, "It's not often in life that you have the chance to be an important part of something you really believe in.... We have changed the way in which we define philanthropy at Pacific, and because of that, future generations will benefit from what we have done. It's incredible to be part of that change."[109]

In 2004, two years before he retired after a 28-year deanship, Dugoni was honored with a gala naming event unprecedented in dental education—and perhaps in any field of study: naming a school after a sitting dean. Following a celebrity-studded symposium on leadership, the Conservatory of Music and comedian Bill Cosby entertained all at San Francisco's Davies Symphony Hall. Along list of other dental deans attended, and Dugoni tributes came from across the country.

The dental school was at the top of its game. The naming event of the Arthur A. Dugoni School of Dentistry topped off the stellar career of Pacific's most famous and honored dean, and its financial undergirding was stronger than any Pacific school by far. By 2005, with annual tuition

The unprecedented naming of a school for a current dean was a tribute both to the remarkable trajectory of the Dugoni School of Dentistry under Arthur Dugoni (1978-2006) and to loyal and generous school alumni led by regent Ron Redmond, here pictured with President DeRosa and Arthur and Kaye Dugoni at the naming event.

nearing $62,000, the school grew by nearly 100 students to nearly 550. A dental hygiene program had been added, masterfully organized by founding director, dental practice professor Cindy Lyon ('86).[110] More importantly, the school was clearly a top leader in dental education. In 2005, professor Thomas Indresano was named outstanding national educator of the year by the American Association of Oral and Maxillofacial Surgeons, and student body president Blake Robinson ('06) was elected vice president of the American Student Dental Association.[111]

When Patrick Ferrillo, Jr., was named dean in 2006, the school began a new era of leadership that honored all that Dugoni had accomplished but advanced new initiatives as well.[112] Ferrillo, a seasoned dental dean from two other universities and former president of the American Dental Educators Association, brought women into leadership positions (half the students were now women) to build a strong leadership team. He launched a new strategic plan, "Advancing Greatness," that integrated the curriculum by shrinking departments from 17 to seven and invested in smaller classes for active learning under the leadership of associate dean Nader Nadershahi ('94).

Ferrillo launched a new customized master's and doctoral program in education with the Benerd School of Education to better equip faculty and staff; revamped the clinics into "group practices" that simulated current professional private practice; invested in technology to create a "paperless clinic;" and set forth to find a solution to the problems of an aging building. As an endodontist, he enabled a post-doctoral certificate program in his field by 2012, just as orthodontist dean Dugoni had done for his field years earlier. As president of the International Federation of Dental Educators and Associations, he saw the profession developing worldwide and would expand the school's global role in that progression.

Getting it done: The DeRosa University Center and the Biological Sciences Center

When DeRosa challenged the regents to follow his lead in pursuit of a new student center and a biology building, there was plenty of reluctance. DeRosa called the two buildings "key elements" in his vision and must-dos for the campaign. "There is a special character to Pacific; we value every person that is a member of our community," DeRosa said, and thus championed a new university center to foster an "important sense of community and family" among the now 4400 students on the Stockton campus.[113]

The going was tough, but DeRosa had a few aces in the hole. In 1998 alumnus Arnold Scott ('39) offered his 56 acres of family farmland that now happened to be surrounded by a growing upscale Petaluma community. Scott, who lived alone in a mobile home on the property, was delighted when DeRosa delivered a letter jacket to this loyal alum who played for Stagg. He wanted to give back to the school that had prepared him under sociology professor Jake Jacoby's mentorship to be a social worker. When the property was sold in 2002, it brought in over $12 million.[114] At the same time, DeRosa was visiting another friend of Pacific whom legendary development officer Kara Brewer had also befriended for years along with Scott. Even though Kent Lathy had only attended Stockton College, many of his family members graduated from Pacific, so when DeRosa sat down with him in his little farmhouse kitchen heated by a wood stove,

Lathy, a retired Fresno Public Works employee, talked with enthusiasm about Pacific. He, like Scott, found his 40-acre farm now surrounded by Clovis subdivisions, so when he moved out of his home to gift his acreage to Pacific, it sold for $6.6 million.[115] These gifts emboldened DeRosa to commit to the board in 2004—midway in the campaign—that he would raise half the cost of the two major buildings, $24 million.[116]

Behind the scenes, vice president Cavanaugh scoured the assets to see what could be put together. The KUOP public radio station, on air since 1947, was popular in the community but woefully unsupported, running annual deficits that sometimes exceeded $200,000. Despite many efforts by local citizens to keep the station going with its abundant local programming, the University leased the station to Sacramento State's Capital Public Radio in 2000. When it was finally sold to CPR in 2007, it brought $4 million. For the University center, in the end the only lead gift was from regent Joan and Dino Cortopassi. Cavanaugh cobbled all together to produce a finance plan that worked.[117] These new projects pushed the DeRosa facilities upgrade total to over $150 million.

When the University center was named for Don and Karen DeRosa at its dedication one year after its opening in fall 2008, everyone knew immediately why this nomination from board chair Dianne Philibosian was appropriate. Both DeRosas had been champions of a closer campus community and the co-curricular experience. Karen had been the special champion of campus life, and Don had been the campaigner for a town square. Now what the president called "the campus living room" was ready, with massive, laced wood beams that echoed the Ahwahnee Hotel dining room in Yosemite Park, the spectacle of elevated light hinting of John Muir's outpouring of praise: there "rose the mighty Sierra . . . so gloriously colored and so radiant, it seemed not clothed with light but wholly composed of it, like the wall of some celestial city. . . the Range of Light." Indeed, John Muir was infused in the structure, from the restaurant River Room to the giant fire pit, a popular student gathering place. Muir would have been proud of the minute attention to environmentally sustainable products and practices, from large scale to small. The building of 52,000 square feet cost $40 million, about double the original estimate.

The DeRosa University Center (2007) captured something of the spirit of John Muir and the Sierra in its elevated, massive exposed wood beams and showers of natural light. The Center drew students from the start, and typically was booked up every week.

The DUC—students immediately pronounced it the "duck"—was indeed the crowning glory of the campus, matching the majestic Knoles Hall and joining with the northern campus by nearly spanning the Calaveras river. The Lair, an informal cafe and cabaret, served beer and wine after 5 p.m. for those over 21. (Rumor had it that Don and Karen DeRosa's handprints can be found in the concrete floor near a Lair exit door.) The Marketplace food service daily featured Latin American and Asian dishes, though Tater Tots were always the number one favorite, according to 45-year veteran food server Koreen Freitas.[118] The outdoor "rooms" of furniture were perpetually popular through the endless sunny days. The dark old University Center appropriately became the McCaffrey Center, where all decentralized student services were brought together in a gracefully efficient, remodeled building.

The Biological Sciences Center was an equal challenge to engage major donors. DeRosa kept reminding the regents why the new building was so important. By 2004, over one-fifth of the entering dental school class were Pacific undergraduates (many top students in accelerated two- or three-year pre-dent programs), and over half the annual pharmacy class of 200 were marching over from the central campus.[119] Critical to fundraising success was DeRosa's inviting old friends to join the challenge. For example, regent Tony and Virginia Chan, generous benefactors of the pharmacy school, stepped forward with a major gift for biology, and with the help of regent Peter Zischke, the president restored the interest and generosity of former regent Paul Davies, Jr., who had left the board in disgust over Atchley's decisions. But gifts still lagged far behind the $27 million that the building would cost. Though a plain vanilla building in its exterior, the lab and classroom designs were faithful to the legendary biology chair Paul Richmond's plans.

Everyone in the College was grateful that the board named a laboratory after the beloved Richmond, who had built biology into the largest and arguably the strongest department of the College, and who personally designed the layout of labs, classrooms and offices that maximized the interaction of students in research with the faculty. He died suddenly in 2005 before the building was begun, but he would have been proud of his colleagues, who filled their labs with undergraduate teams active in faculty research.

THE POWELL LEGACY

The DeRosa friendship

One day in 1988, alumnus Douglass Eberhardt ('59) was having lunch in the Bohemian Club in San Francisco with his friend Robert C. Brown, who owned a highly successful investment firm in the city. Brown suggested that Eberhardt consider his client Robert Powell for the Pacific Board of Regents.[120] Powell was a very successful Sacramento real estate developer who had used Brown's help managing his sizeable investments. Soon Doug's brother Bob, the board chair, was asking regent Edward Westgate ('33) to approach his friend, Rutherford neighbor, and fellow real estate developer, and within months Bob Powell was on the Pacific board. He hated it, and was eager to get off at the end of one term. He was a shy, meticulous person who valued his privacy and found decisions by committee messy and burdensome. But Powell was inspired by the young people who stuck it out to get a college degree—something he had never done. After graduating from Sequoia High School in Redwood City he left school behind for good. To help middle-class Pacific families who were pinched by the rapid tuition hikes, as a regent he created a Pacific loan program targeted to middle-income families that was very popular. One of the last casualties of the Atchley years was the faculty's tabling of an honorary degree for Powell proposed by an unwelcome Atchley for a regent they did not know. They certainly did not know of his capacity to serve Pacific.

When DeRosa came on board, he quickly went to the Academic Council to invite their reconsideration, and Powell was honored to receive the recognition for his philanthropy and regional leadership in 1996. That began a decade-long friendship between Bob and Jeanette Powell and Don and Karen DeRosa that grew stronger as both men dealt with serious illnesses. Then, as Bob Powell saw his life waning from cancer, he met more frequently with DeRosa to design the single most important gift in Pacific's history, and the 32nd largest gift in higher education across the globe at the time. He passed over many options DeRosa presented, favoring endowed scholarships and an incentive challenge fund to match gifts in the next campaign. DeRosa announced the gift on May 7, 2007, just months before Bob Powell died. The humble Powells were notably absent by their wishes, and just hours before the announcement Bob Powell considered making the gift anonymous.[121] The President's Room was packed with cameras, reporters, and campus leaders when DeRosa announced the $100 million gift, "a magnificent gift that will transform our University."[122] When board chair Dianne Philibosian called to thank the Powells that day, Jeannette Powell said, "Bob and I are so gratified to be able to make a difference in young people's lives." [123] As DeRosa later said, for Bob Powell, it was "always about others, not himself."[124]

Bob and Jeanette Powell's transformative gift eventually totaled $125 million, devoted mostly to endow student scholarships.

Powell Scholars

Jeannette Powell, who served as a regent from 1999 until her death in 2012, poured herself into Pacific with a gusto not seen prior, especially concerning the visual art department and campus landscaping. She brought a willful determination and elegant sense of design to every project, which often came in unannounced campus visits. The Powells funded a major renovation on the south campus to create the Jeannette Powell Art Center in 1999. But she delighted most especially in the Powell Scholars, a program their endowment established in 2008 to attract the most talented students to Pacific. This premier program, initiated by DeRosa in 2003 as the Founders Scholars, offered a full scholarship, study abroad funding, generous undergraduate research support, and a collective opportunity for campus leadership with other Powell Scholars. The Powells were drawn to the possibility of underwriting a top scholarship program that would produce outstanding graduates in perpetuity and build the academic ambition of undergraduates.

Cynthia Wagner Weick, holder of the Neven C. Hulsey ('57) Endowed Chair in Business Excellence and one of Pacific's most outstanding professors, led the program masterfully and engaged Jeannette Powell personally with the students. The first Powell Scholars themselves crafted their mission statement, "to develop responsible leaders who excel academically and take the initiative to understand and serve the University, local and global communities. Our individual achievements are complemented by uniting others to make a difference in the world." As Wagner Weick put it, "We address leadership in all its complexity. It is not always about position, but about being out ahead, pushing boundaries of

Jeanette Powell (center) felt deep affection for the students in the Powell Scholar program (2008), a distinctive top scholarship program accenting leadership, ably led by business professor Cynthia Wagner Weick.

a field. We tailor the program to the students' own interests and abilities." Each scholar took on nine requirements—what the Powell students called "a roadmap of opportunities."

Jeannette Powell told Weick, "We must help these students find and follow their passions."[125] No better purpose statement was ever made for this powerful program. It also described one of Pacific's two preeminent benefactors. Jeannette Powell was "continuously curious and learning," as President Eibeck observed, and became a devotee of John Muir through her Pacific experience, among her many interests. As she fought bouts of serious illness, her friendship with Karen DeRosa increased. Pacific truly became a home for her, where she built "ties of love and caring" as important as her philanthropy. President Eibeck noted that the Powell Scholars "loved her, not for her generous gift, but because of her generous spirit."[126] Without family, Jeannette Powell had only Karen DeRosa holding her hand when she died.

When the estate was finally settled in 2013, the gift had grown to $125 million, which increased Pacific's endowment by over 50 percent to $337 million—well over the 2010 goal. The Powells designated over $90 million for student scholarships, a $25 million matching fund to inspire others to create endowments for academic programs, and a $3 million endowment for the University's art collection, including works of art from their personal collection valued at nearly $500,000. The Powell Scholars program itself funded ten $35,000 scholarships annually. Of the $90 million scholarship fund, over $60 million was earmarked for a separate matching campaign as an incentive for future donors of scholarship endowments, a particular personal interest of Bob Powell. The gift remained among the largest gifts in higher education. Only 15 other private schools in the country had received gifts of this size since 2005.[127]

PERENNIAL CHALLENGES: FUNDRAISING AND VISIBILITY

The challenge of the campaign

Despite the massive success of the "Investing in Excellence" campaign, concerns remained. The campaign never really became "volunteer driven." Few board members were actually engaged in solicitation. Many individual goals were not met. No group of regents or other philanthropists stepped forward to lead the campaign with vision and commitment, even with ambitious Don O'Connell starting as board chair in 2002. These factors did not bode well for future campaigns.

The modest size of gifts conformed to past Pacific experience. In addition to the Powell gift, the only gift above $10 million was from the Thomas J. Long Foundation to build the new Health Sciences Learning Center. The only gifts above $5 million were the remarkable gifts of property by Arnold Scott and Kent Lathy. Beyond the generous work of the National Commission volunteers, the lack of fundraising volunteers was also a legacy issue: the lack of significant alumni involvement (dental school excepted) was a consequence of the University's failure over time to invest in alumni staff, training, and infrastructure. The lack of philanthropic leadership was perhaps the most vexing. These challenges were met by many other institutions. A comparison with Chapman University in southern California during this same time period is instructive.[128]

Until the 1990s, Chapman University was known for its storefront approach to higher education throughout the state, a low-quality, high volume money-maker that helped advance the small Disciples of Christ college in Orange. But it had a talented, entrepreneurial president in James Doti, a libertarian economist widely known in the southern California business community for his economic forecasts, and a board chair, George Argyros, an alumnus in real estate who was chair for 25 years. Through Argyros' own philanthropy, he brought together trustees who decided to transform the college into a quality comprehensive university much like Pacific. Over the decade and beyond, Chapman doubled its enrollment to 7,000 as it built seven schools, nearly all endowed by major donors, as well as spun off Brandman University as the for-profit arm with many branch campuses. The culture of the Chapman board was very different from Pacific's: every member understood the importance of personal philanthropy and most were major contributors. Local support was critical. Orange County, with pockets of great wealth amid many average-income towns, adopted Chapman as its private school and supported it as a major investment.

The campaign at Pacific—setting aside the spectacular performance of the dental school—was different. When Pacific alumnus Russell Leatherby ('75) joined Pacific's board in 2001 at the start of the campaign, he was stunned by the low level of philanthropy on the board, especially compared to his personal experience with southern California boards and with Chapman. In the prior Pacific campaign, for example, one third of the board members had made no financial pledge.[129] As chair of Pacific's regent recruitment committee, he sought candidates who could lead in philanthropy, but found even resistance from fellow members to the notion that wealth capacity should be such a high priority. Where was the entrepreneurial passion to achieve greatness? The focus was on a wide representation of backgrounds and informed citizens—not wealth capacity.

Wealth was not lacking in San Joaquin County and the surrounding region, but the commitment and passion and collective effort experienced at Chapman or USC were still generally absent. Pacific had never had its George Argyros to command high-level philanthropic leadership. The culture of support without major philanthropy remained one of the defining characteristics of Pacific and a major reason that an aspiration to greatness had always eluded the University. Always on the edge of distinction, but never quite there. Pacific had yet to cultivate the collective aspiration of a donor community to make Pacific a leading edge university of its kind. Pacific's board may have had stronger governance policies and greater diversity than most, but it lacked a critical mass of regents with the capacity, passion, and entrepreneurial spirit to lift Pacific truly to the next level.

A new identity focus

In 1996, Pacific filed a patent infringement against for-profit behemoth, University of Phoenix. A judge ruled that the service mark "UOP" was protected for Pacific, at least for the west coast if not the country. But this worry was minor compared to the results of market research showing that Pacific did indeed suffer from a serious malady of "identity confusion."[130] Another mark of years of neglect, Pacific was a disarray of identities in its publications and public media. DeRosa and Gilbertson both were bothered by the moniker "UOP," which lacked national recognition needed to put the school on the map. It seemed more logical and emotionally stronger to capture the name "Pacific," the name by which the school was known nationally in athletics.

In 1998—the same year the regents declared that Pacific would be a national university—DeRosa called for a massive marketing effort to create a "standard identity package" for "Pacific" (not "UOP") that would rein in the bewildering range of word and image identifiers used for each school and program. This rampant fragmentation of message was another mark of the degree of disintegration that had been tolerated during the McCaffrey years and openly fostered by the Atchley regime. By 2001 a "branding" program to market the University was underway, and a new "name mark," logo and seal for the University were unveiled in fall 2002.[131] The regents spent hours debating the redesign of the University seal, finally opting for one of simplified elegance.

The basic design of the modern seal was created in 1910 and adapted periodically as the name and locations changed. In 1970, the torch was replaced by a mace among several modifications (upper right). With a new name mark came a new University seal in 2002.

DeRosa was determined that the University itself be clearly identified, not simply known by the arbitrary labels and logos of its schools. Law dean Parker endorsed the new identity markers and championed a new moniker for the school, "Pacific McGeorge," that pulled the most reluctant of the schools into the tent. The new name mark and identifiers stuck, but the investment in actually marketing the University with this unified message was still years away.

DEFINING ITS REGIONAL LEADERSHIP

Pacific on the edge in Stockton

Being on the edge of the Bay Area had its challenges for Pacific. Its preeminence in clinical dental education made it sensible for the Dugoni School of Dentistry to continue in San Francisco as one of only 64 American dental schools. Pacific McGeorge School of Law was ideally situated on a splendid campus in the state capital of one of the world's ten largest economies. It truly was Sacramento's law school, irreplaceable in providing legal education for state government. Both the School of Engineering and Computer Science and the Long School of Pharmacy and Health Sciences benefitted from the Stockton location. As the only pharmacy school in the Valley for over 40 years, the pharmacy school had an opportunity to serve a new region, secure the support of the Long Drug store family based in the Valley, dominate regional employment opportunities and provide health care service to an underserved region. Engineering also served the mid and southern Valley as the only school in the profession, carving out an identity in the basic engineering disciplines that fed the growth and development of the region. Both schools pushed many of their students beyond the region for their required work-based learning experience, so the Valley was no barrier to learning. The Benerd School of Education devoted its energies to providing educational leadership, from classroom teachers to superintendents, throughout the Valley, and creating many avenues for advancing a beleaguered region steeped in poverty and illiteracy. Truly, the school of education had a special mission to the region.

But for the Conservatory of Music, Stockton had severe drawbacks. All the great conservatories except for Oberlin were in large major cities rich with employment opportunities for their musicians. [132] (And in this era the endowment of Oberlin College was twice the size of Pacific's with less than half the enrollment.) For the Eberhardt School of Business, the challenge was finding a critical mass of MBA students to sustain a robust program and providing a rich range of internships and sponsorships. For the range of liberal arts programs encompassing the College of the Pacific, extensive learning opportunities and internship options in the natural sciences, social sciences and the humanities were circumscribed, especially for a university that urged every student to have an internship or other community-based learning. The School of International Studies always struggled to recruit students interested in the globe to this semi-rural setting, hours from a major world city.

Since the 1960s, student recruitment had dealt with negative perceptions of Stockton. When *Forbes* magazine listed Stockton as one of America's most miserable cities in the late 2000s, the campus like the city generally viewed it as quirky sensationalism that ignored all the positives. As recently as 2007, an in-depth survey found that for prospective and enrolled students, the city was not a major factor in their decision, but for those who chose to ignore Pacific, it was a significant factor based on traditional stereotypes as well as civic realities. In 1849, Stockton was on the front edge of California and the Gold Rush. A hundred years later, the city, the Delta, and the Valley were generally treated as second-class citizens by a state that used its water to flood the growth of Southern California while degrading its water, air and soil, sequestered its farm workers in poverty and illiteracy, and jeopardized its land to build sprawling suburbs close enough to the Bay. For decades federal and state subsidies and investments to this region were disproportionately low for its population and national agricultural importance—little more than half what comparable regions received in federal dollars.[133]

Perhaps the city itself resisted federal programs and political organization, as its citizens grew uneasy about the powerful grip of real estate developers and public employee unions. Three Valley cities ranked among the nation's top five metro areas with the highest percentage of residents in poverty, while the region enjoyed the highest farm revenues in the country.[134] Stockton had about half as many citizens with two- or four-year college degrees as the south Bay did (27 vs. 53 percent.)[135] Cal State-Stanislaus launched a satellite program at Delta College in the 1980s, then a satellite campus in downtown Stockton in 1998, but only a few hundred students were served. So the city reaped the results of this neglect in a higher crime rate even in pockets surrounding the University.

Still, Stockton was the perfect environment for developing responsible global citizens. There was a down-to-earth reality about the smaller city in a rural Valley that was lacking in larger metro areas, where the glitz of city life sometimes masked the day-to-day existence that is important for students to touch and feel. Certainly the wide range of ethnic groups and social and economic strata for Stockton—nearly 62 percent of the city was either Latino or Asian in 2013—was a rich resource for students from more homogeneous areas. Its 15 distinct cultural communities and 44 languages spoken were extraordinary, and thousands of Pacific students have benefitted richly from their interaction with these communities, often through volunteer service.[136]

Partially in recognition of the strong Hispanic presence in the Valley and city, Pacific worked for years to attract the president of Mexico, Vicente

Pacific awarded Stockton College alumna Dolores Huerta ('50) an honorary degree in 2010 to recognize her influential role in improving the lives of migrant farm workers as co-founder of the United Farm Workers (pictured at commencement with president Eibeck).

Fox, who finally appeared as the 2011 commencement speaker and received an honorary degree, to the delight of the community.[137] Perhaps even more significant was honoring Stockton College alumna Dolores Huerta, renowned and revered organizing leader of the Valley farm worker movement, with an honorary degree in 2010. Every college and university is shaped by its city and locale and typically bears the traits, positive and negative, of its region. The Stockton campus of Pacific is no exception. Stockton over the decades has held Pacific back and pushed it forward, just as Pacific has done for the city.

Water down the river: the Natural Resource Institute and the Calaveras River Project

When Tom Zuckerman became a regent in 2002, he wanted to contribute something unique to advance the school. His years as a Stockton water law attorney made him a strong conduit to the crowd of water stakeholders across the Valley and the state. He urged the president to marshal the strength of Pacific to help address Delta water issues.[138] Forty percent of the state's waterways drain through San Joaquin County. The Delta bordering the west of the city, the only inland delta in the United States, is the largest estuary on the west coast of the Americas, and the second largest in the United States after the Chesapeake Bay. Pacific's role in water research was substantial. In engineering alone, $6 million of external grants funded research in water quality and conservation 2003-07.[139] The law school had four faculty experts in water law, and other disciplines like biology had specialists. Alumnus Mark Jordan ('78) chaired the board of Waterkeepers for Northern California, an umbrella organization for several water resource watchdog groups that employed Pacific student interns.[140]

By 2003, the Natural Resources Institute was formed of faculty from engineering, the College, law, and business. Pacific became the "honest broker" where all factions on Delta water issues could sit together to seek common solutions to the state's most vexing challenge. The NRI joined with the Business Forecasting Center (see page 420) to conduct an economic sustainability plan for the Delta Protection Commission.[141] Zuckerman also brokered a lengthy effort in 2007-09 to seek state funds to restore the Calaveras River for the half-mile running through the campus as a demonstration project for restoring natural habitat to many Valley rivers. After much planning and effort, funding fell through, though the dream of a restored Calaveras winding through the campus lived on. As Zuckerman moved off the board and school leadership changed, the NRI lost momentum.

Community partnerships and student service

While it is accurate to describe the DeRosa years as mildly engaged with the surrounding community, the concrete steps DeRosa took were positive and enduring. "University College," a degree program for older working students, was formally ended as a separate college in 1999 to become the Center for Professional and Continuing Education, now focused more on training programs, on reviving and expanding summer school, and on conference coordination. With new goals, outreach and net revenue increased dramatically in the early 2000s. The Bernard Osher Foundation funded a million dollar endowment for "re-entry" scholarships for working adults. One of DeRosa's early actions was to initiate "Pacific Experience," an ongoing series of lectures and mini-courses for seniors organized by the continuing education office. The program grew to over 500 members and qualified for a second Osher endowment grant in 2010 to sustain the program, one of 117 such centers at universities across the country.

But DeRosa knew that Pacific should become a more active player in the local economy, and as the applied research of faculty developed, new opportunities for start-up companies seemed on the horizon. DeRosa created a position for regional economic development in the early 2000s that linked University research to community interest and capital, but neither faculty research nor the investment interests of the county were sufficient to get much off the ground. From the start he felt that Pacific's primary contribution was to re-establish the strength of Pacific, and then to help improve K-12 education in the county, and therefore supported all the initiatives to further those two goals. For example, the communicative disorders program, under the entrepreneurial leadership of professor Robert Hanyak, signed a 15-year contract with Stockton's Scottish Rite Center for Children's Language Disorders in 1997 to direct the center and provide vital services to local children while offering internships and scholarships for Pacific students in the program.[142]

Pacific's community partnerships grew dramatically, nearly doubling in two years from 22 to 43 by 2000. The Jacoby Center for Community and Regional Studies launched in 2001 engaged students in interdisciplinary, applied research and experiential learning that also included an option in Sacramento with state agencies or in Washington DC. One of the high-profile projects was the Jacoby Center's Magnolia District Community Development Project that brought faculty and students from the College's social science, arts, and humanities departments into collaboration through a federal HUD grant to build community after-school programs, conduct research, and aid small business development near the center of downtown Stockton. The Jacoby Center was modified in 2005 as the Jacoby Center for Public Service and Civic Leadership to better align with University priorities.[143] With funding from the California Council for the Humanities, the Jacoby Center conducted "STOCKTONSpeaks" in 2006, publishing stories of three-generational families of nine ethnic groups. Another of some 20 projects involved funded research on county voting patterns.

The expansion and better organizing of student volunteers through the Center for Community Involvement and other student life offices in this era meant that more people of Stockton were touched by Pacific students, but equally, Pacificans were moved and matured by transforming experiences in the city. Law and dental school outreach to their surrounding communities are described in the next chapter.

September 11, 2001 and other turmoil

For all the sesquicentennial anniversary celebrations, 2001 turned out to be a difficult year. In February, 200 students poured out of Grace Covell Hall at midnight to escape a fire started by an unattended candle in a dorm room. Miraculously no student was injured, thanks to a student who carried out a disabled classmate. Later in the year, one student was lost to suicide, another in an auto accident. Then when the terrorist attacks on the World Trade Center and the Pentagon took their toll on September 11, the campuses were traumatized with the rest of the nation. The event called forth Pacific to provide a community space to cope with the ordeal.

The Spirit Rock was not painted over for a month following the September 11, 2001 attacks.

The Faye Spanos Concert Hall was open all afternoon—at times nearly filled—with open mikes for the campus and local community to gather to mourn, to grieve, to reflect together on what this could mean for the nation and the world. President DeRosa said, "The University is a place to come together and express our collective grief and feelings."[144] In the evening as DeRosa visited all the residence halls, students gathered to talk through the trauma. Five days later a forum on the historical, political, and religious context drew a packed hall led by nine faculty from seven disciplines and two students from the Mideast. Five students from Mideast countries temporarily returned to their home countries. Deora Bodley, daughter of conservatory professor Darrill Bodley, was on airline Flight 93 downed in Pennsylvania, and alumni families were lost in the Pentagon crash. With the spontaneity one expects of a committed and caring community, prayer vigils, memorial services, counseling sessions, musical benefits, blood donations, student debates—all arose in a dirge of lamentation that went beyond words.

Throughout the fall, Pacific sponsored seven community forums, "Responding to Global Tragedy." The forums welcomed the city to join the campus community to consider the meaning of the world-changing events with campus and national experts on sources of terrorism. Conservatory students performed Mozart's *Requiem* as a benefit, and dental students partnered with "Smiles Against Hate" volunteers to promote intercultural understanding. Perhaps the most singular event occurred just hours after the tragedy, when leaders of the Muslim student association asked President DeRosa if they could meet safely on campus. DeRosa assured them that they would always be safe at Pacific and accepted their invitation to join them. When he arrived at their meeting, he was overwhelmed to see a small band of Jewish students from the Hillel club who had also come to join in sympathy and support. This was the Pacific community that the University could be proud of, recalling the civility and mutual support during the sixties' teach-ins on the Stockton campus.[145]

The Iraq War began about a year later, and again the campuses were in turmoil. Thc provost and the student life vice president organized responses: the Crisis Response Team handled noon-time discussions, faculty conducted two public forums, the wellness center offered counseling assistance, and an online dialogue was organized. The provost encouraged faculty to enable students to express their views and emotions in class: "If students bury doubts and fears, we may lose important teachable moments."[146]

Government relations and the Business Forecasting Center

By early 2000s Pacific launched activities to support regional economic development. The key community liaison for years was business dean Mark Plovnick, who served on a host of boards. He became Pacific's director of economic development and founding president of the San Joaquin Angel Capital Fund, created to invest in promising new business proposals through annual competitions in an eight-county region, from 2008 until his retirement in 2014.

Pacific had never connected to state and federal legislators except for Burns' and McCaffrey's personal links to some state leaders. Yet Pacific stood in four congressional districts among its three campuses, and law dean Parker came with Washington credentials. DeRosa launched a government relations initiative in 2003 by swooping down on the California congressional delegation in Washington with president, provost, advancement vice president and four deans, armed with two Washington lobbyists. He set a committee to track opportunities for state and federal grants and contracts and hired the lobby firm to help in Washington for at least five years. The focus was on Pacific's strengths in K-12 education, health care, entrepreneurship, public finance, and water.[147] About the time these liaisons were well established, federal funds for such programs began to shrink. Pacific's overall success in government relations was very limited—with one outstanding exception—and the lobby efforts ended.

The one remarkably successful regional business and government partnership started at a campus lunch with the city's economic development staff around 2002 to plan a business forecasting center. The provost was stunned to learn that the only forecasting center in the state was at USC. Here was truly an opportunity to combine what universities do best with a deep need for northern California. When the Business Forecasting Center was launched in 2004 with over $1 million in federal grants over its first few years, it quickly became Pacific's lead story. Aside from athletics, the BFC was in the press and media more than any other Pacific program, with its projections for business and government based on economic and demographic data analysis. The two directors in this era, professors Sean Snaith and Jeffrey Michael, were first-rate communicators who had their pulse on the region and its needs.[148] Former business dean Plovnick called the BFC the single most successful project of the business school.[149]

A BOLDER FUTURE

Pacific Rising, 2008-2015

Planning continued to drive the direction of Pacific. On DeRosa's tenth anniversary as president, the fourth Board of Regents retreat of his administration in January 2005 in San Francisco was a kind of turning point of this era. Bullish from increasing enrollment, $100 million of facilities projects, improved faculty and staff compensation and technology, the regents debated five different models for the future out to 2015 and selected a conservative blend of two: retaining a balanced university of nine schools along with an increased focus on distinctiveness through innovation. The push for greater coherence translated to more interdisciplinary programs, and expanded diversity, leadership development, and international education across the schools.[150] Campus retreats followed to process these aims, backed by a $1 million innovation fund to pilot new interdisciplinary proposals. Board planning, DeRosa noted, was done "with a pioneering spirit that defines what makes us distinctive."[151]

Pacific Rising, 2008-2015, adopted by the board in early 2007, also asserted six commitments to focus priorities: innovation, distinctive programs, collaboration among liberal arts and professional education, preparation of the whole student, partnerships, and resource growth and management.[152] In 2009, the plan won the first national award for "institutional innovation and integration" granted by the Society for College and University Planning (SCUP), the premier planning association in higher education.[153]

Out of the board's interest in innovation came 14 "collaboration vision teams" of six to a dozen faculty members from four to eight different disciplines that proposed new interdisciplinary "Innovation Initiatives." One of the most successful innovations was the "Legal Studies Program" begun in 2007 that guaranteed admission to McGeorge law school for entering undergraduates in a three-year accelerated program, built on the successful models in dentistry and pharmacy.

Board pride

Earlier in 2004, the board relieved the ailing O'Connell of his two-year stint as chair, and witnessed the beginning of something quite new: a woman academic leader as chair. Dianne Philibosian ('68), a dean at California State at Northridge and the only academic on the board, was a seasoned Pacific leader, having served on the alumni board, as a regent since 1998, and as chair of the National Commission panel on alumni and community relations. With a deep love of Pacific, she had witnessed how DeRosa had rescued her University. It was time to step up and champion his initiatives. She and DeRosa saw eye to eye on nearly every issue, so she led as a close member of the team to move Pacific ahead. The board itself had changed in important ways, if not in its gender, alumni and age profiles. Compared to 1998, the number of regents outside northern California jumped from two to ten, and the number with business/administrative expertise grew from four to 20.[154]

The 2005-06 academic year was an important high point in the tenth year of the DeRosa era. *Pacific Rising, 2008-2015* outlined more boldly than ever the values, commitments, and measurable goals. While the Powell gift had not yet arrived, the campaign was headed for success. The endowment had increased three-fold during this thriving decade, reaching over $200 million in 2007, and net assets more than doubled. Undergraduate enrollment had grown by nearly 25 percent over the decade, now with its highest academic profile, and the student to faculty ratio moved from under 13:1 to 16:1, a better fit for Pacific's still modest resources. Stanford athletic director Ted Leland was surely welcomed back to Pacific as vice president for institutional advancement. For the first time in decades a University-wide commencement ceremony was held in the Spanos Center. "We are at an apex," chair Philibosian toasted, as "we celebrate a decade of transformational leadership."[155]

Nearly all regents were part of the regal commencement procession in 2006, when famed film maker Clint Eastwood and astronaut Jose Hernandez ('84) received honorary degrees, and Dave Brubeck ('42) was awarded the University's first President's Medal of Achievement. Just days earlier the Klein Family Field opened to the first campus baseball game in 60 years, and heralded Cisco Systems CEO John Chambers provided a major gift for the John T. Chambers Technology Center. This indeed was a wonderful era to be a proud Pacific regent. So it was not easy when five senior regents retired from the board in 2007, including Monagan and Don Smith, leaving no continuing regents since DeRosa's arrival in 1995. DeRosa captured the board's intent when he observed that "Board leadership has helped secure our future as the West's leading student-centered national University."[156]

The 2006 commencement was arrayed with luminaries. Here Dave Brubeck assists in bestowing an honorary degree to filmmaker Clint Eastwood, chair of the Brubeck Institute honorary board (with Board of Regents chair Diane Philibosian and president DeRosa).

Alumni association comes into its own

Alumni giving was 8.4 percent in 1997, a remarkably low response from vast groups of alumni who had great experiences and solid preparation for their lives and careers. James Jewell ('51) took command without much staff support to restart the class agent network to achieve a goal of 15 percent. This program was part of a four-year plan to get to 30 percent—an audacious and unachievable goal to change a long history of sluggish financial support from alumni.[157] While alumni giving did increase over the years, it was by inches. For the Stockton campus bachelor's graduates, giving never got above 14 percent from 1996-2008. Giving rates for the other two campuses was about comparable: in 2007, about 10 percent of law alumni and about 15 percent of dental alumni were donors.[158]

When Bill Coen and Kelli Page ('87) took the helm of the alumni office in 2000, the alumni association became more focused on serving the University, more diverse in its leadership, and more attuned to expanded services. The practice of alumni board members also serving as University regents ended, as did the "clubby" social group who for years hung on to board membership as well as the Feather River Inn. All the activities a contemporary alumni association should provide came under the support and direction of Coen and Page, with the wise counsel of earlier presidents Bob Berryman ('83) and James Jewell ('51). It started their first year with alumni board president Alex Vereschagin ('57), who, as Bill Coen said, helped them turn "a huge aircraft . . . 180 degrees to head in a new direction."[159] Dale Young ('73) and Randy Hayashi ('85, '88) followed as presidents to quicken the pace and improve accountability. Under Hayashi's visionary leadership the board revamped the bylaws and set term limits. Younger presidents that followed also showed strong leadership, such as Sydney Young ('85), who commandeered the first successful alumni weekend event, and Elizabeth Johnson ('87), who upgraded the annual alumni awards event. Mary Margaret Simpson ('73) and Allie Baker ('99) helped create the faculty mentor and honorary alumnus awards. Michael Kattelman ('94), Denny Stilwell ('88), and Norm Allen ('88) were among others who led the association ahead with energy and vision.

The board created a student alumni association, grew 16 regional or affinity clubs, improved communications with alumni especially through the alumni website, expanded career programs for alumni, focused attention on fundraising for the University, and promoted an alumni center on campus.[160] Ted Leland revamped the annual fund into the "Pacific Fund" in 2006 to bolster annual loyalty giving, and the senior class gift program hit a record 41 percent participation, which rose to 57 percent in 2007.[161] But like an aggravating sore foot, even the well-designed and promoted Pacific Fund could not jump annual alumni giving much above 10 percent, and it drew staff away from major donors.[162]

A comprehensive alumni survey in 2007 was a "mythbuster" to University leaders because it dispelled numerous misconceptions about Pacific alumni attitudes.[163] The most important confirmation was that 83 percent of graduates were "very satisfied" with their student experience, a higher percentage than surveyed alumni of three dozen other prestigious national universities. But chronic fears that Pacific alumni were disengaged turned out not to be true: nearly 80 percent felt that the University valued its alumni, and two-thirds of alumni surveyed felt an emotional tie to Pacific. Well over half identified primarily with the University over their home department or school (except for the professional schools of dentistry, law and pharmacy), dispelling the notion that alumni did not feel connected to Pacific as a university. Nearly all alumni stated their interest in what was happening at Pacific and 70 percent were interested in participating in certain alumni activities. Most felt informed and wanted to keep in touch and be more involved. The disconnect was with current University outreach beyond basic information. They wanted better online connections and more socializing with other alumni. But among non-donors, nearly 70 percent felt their donations had a greater impact on other needier organizations. Only 14 percent withheld gifts because of the ending of football.

Alumni weekend, moved to June in 2001, featured the San Francisco pop rock band Huey Lewis and the News in 2002 that was a big hit for the alumni from the eighties, even though the weekend turnout was a disappointment. But as "affinity group" reunions were added, each year attendance improved, aided by a new alumni website. Greek alumni, CIP alumni, World War II vets, football or choir—each group drew more alumni to campus for the special weekend. In 2005, fifteen alumni vintners from the region started an annual tradition of wine-tasting at the reunion.

The National Commission panel on alumni and community relations offered another opportunity to notch up support. Regent and chair Dianne Philibosian coined a resounding phrase that captured alumni interests: alumni wished to be "inside the house" in both literal and figurative terms. Panel recommendations led to the Alex and Jeri Vereschagin ('57) Alumni House in 2010, but equally important alumni were asked to be inside stakeholders with students, faculty and staff on behalf of Pacific. As Philibosian said, "alumni are the lifeblood of the University, linking the past to the present and the present to the future."[164]

The Alumni Association had come a long ways from the 1980s when the alumni board, populated by regents, had an almost obsessive focus on the Feather River Inn. By 2002 the University took over the lease from the alumni group as debts mounted. The FRI was finally sold for $2.8 million in 2004.[165] At the start of the campaign, the alumni board wanted to raise funds for an alumni center, but DeRosa asked them for their help to raise funds for the new University center, a more immediate priority. They agreed to lend a hand as long as there was a good chance that an alumni center could be folded into the old McCaffrey Center building once it was vacated.[166] After many twists and turns in the planning, the Vereschagins made a major commitment that brought forth a magnificent alumni house in the center of campus, right at the pivot point between the main and south campus areas. Of all the new construction in this era, the DeRosa University Center and the Vereschagin Alumni House were the most impressive in architectural design and notable amenities, thanks especially to regent Jeannette Powell.

The opening of the Alex (center) and Jeri Vereschagin Alumni House in 2010 culminated years of building the Alumni Association into a vital and effective organization.

The Alex and Jeri Vereschagin Alumni House, with a commanding presence at the head of the south campus in Stockton, hosts a broad array of events.

The alumni board in turn began a new annual award in 2008 to honor faculty mentors, an important part of teaching at Pacific. Each year three faculty were honored among nominees by alumni. And to honor the achievements of the DeRosa era, the alumni board bestowed honorary alumni status to Don and Karen DeRosa in 2009, the first to be so honored.[167]

CHAPTER 7

Rising achievement, 1995-2009

Student life in the new millennium—Student diversity grows and matures—Faculty scholarship—The Schools and the College grow in quality—The Brubeck Institute—National recognition for Mentor/Pacific Seminars—The College achieves Phi Beta Kappa—DeRosa's legacy—Welcoming President Eibeck

FOCUSING ON STUDENTS

Needy Students

As the millennium approached, students complained about food, shelter and books; dining services rated low, the dorm rooms were antiquated, and the library was again crowded and inadequate.[1] With high expectations for their personal comforts, they were ready to seek remedies, mostly through parents. The term "helicopter parents" entered the vocabulary to describe the national phenomenon of hovering parents actively advocating on behalf of their children on campus issues from class schedules to roommates. Equally, most students had daily phone chats with

The wireless generation represented a major shift underway in higher education.

a parent tracking their campus life, since a mobile phone in the pocket was as common as a wallet.

Student surveys hammered at the old dorm rooms that lacked network connectivity, air conditioning and adequate restrooms. Everyone knew that undergraduate enrollment took a hit because of the residence halls. Upgraded halls became a top priority. "Theme communities," residence halls devoted to distinct groups like honors (1994), pharmacy (1992), and graduate students (1996), were expanded to special interests such as "intercultural" (1997) and "LINC" (Leadership in Community, 1997) to widen the appeal and raise the occupancy rate. Meanwhile, gradually all halls were wired to the network—"a port per pillow" was the refrain—and cable television was finally a plug-in away in all the halls by fall 1999.

Complaints about the food were equally harsh, so the University brought in a new vender, Marriott. Student satisfaction surveys in 1997 jumped from 30 to 50 percent and more students moved back on campus, but within two years the rating dropped again.[2] By 2002 the University decided to bring the high-end Bon Appetit to campus, named the top college food service in the country by *Princeton Review*. Prices rose, but so did quality, variety and service. When Pacific became the first western campus to add a food truck to serve the South

The E.A.T. (easy, artisan, takeout) food truck on South campus was another pioneering project at Pacific, with Bon Appetit campus food service.

campus, student complaints about food service at Pacific virtually ended—though not complaints about cost.

A changing campus profile

In this era, Pacific students were increasingly more academic-minded, less inclined to treat college as a play period in life. The concerns were practical: more studious degree-seekers who could literally not afford to fiddle away their college days, more students working their way through school, more rigorous degree programs, and faculty who required more homework. The number of top Regents Scholars had doubled to nearly 100 since the program began three years earlier. Compared to other private universities, Pacific enrolled half as many students from wealthy families and over twice as many students from poor families.[3] Most students were focused on professions that paid well. Nearly 40 percent were pursuing rigorous majors for health professions. In the late seventies, less than half the frosh listed "being well off" as a top priority; in the late nineties, 75 percent did, though priorities varied widely among the schools.[4] Ten years later, about 85 percent of them ranked financial success, preparing for graduate/professional school, and raising a family as their top priorities.[5]

This student profile would have sounded alien to the students of the seventies and eighties, though Greek enrollment actually rose to 24 percent of undergraduate students in this era.[6] The bipolarity of undergraduate student behavior was evident in a 2000 survey that revealed about 30 percent indulging in binge drinking—below the national average, but rising in the 2010s as academic pressures pushed drinking to the weekends, while 42 percent said they had no alcohol in the prior month.[7]

These patterns generally held through the decade, changing only in the sharp rise in marijuana use. As medical marijuana became more common and the legalization of marijuana began to be discussed, students joined in the loosening of use. Some came with medical marijuana cards.[8] Increasingly, like all other American campuses, students came to Pacific with medical issues, a menu of psychoactive drugs, mental health disorders and documented learning disabilities, which forced increases in the counseling and support staff from 2000 forward. *The Pacifican* introduced a weekly sex column in 2013. Graphic accounts of condom options ("don't be a fool, wrap your tool"), sexually transmitted disease (STD) symptoms, and online videos of "twerking," a sexually provocative pop culture dance, were tossed about to prove that Pacific was not out of the mainstream. As this generation focused on self-identity, "body art," both tattoos and piercings, moved from the social fringe to the mainstream.

Regulating Greek life

DeRosa was particularly keen on strengthening the alcohol policy along with recreation opportunities described earlier. Noting the high risk of liability that hit every campus, he acted early to ban hard liquor and kegs in the frat houses. When Judy Chambers retired from heading student life in 2000, energetic vice president Julie Sina led a more aggressive effort to enforce the 21-year legal age requirement on campus and hold Greeks accountable to their increasingly restrictive national society policies. When stringent regulations for parties were enforced, Greeks especially complained about hoop jumping and shifted more of their social life off campus.[9] Closely tied to substance abuse was training for students on sexual assault and sexual diseases that often were outcomes of excessive alcohol use. For the first time sexual assault was handled with openness and directness. Sina took on tough issues but still had the support of the students, who liked her open-door friendliness.

In 2002 Sina, a fountain of fresh ideas, created a master's program in college student affairs through the School of Education. This elevated the quality of student life staff, especially residence hall directors—a milestone in the quality of leadership in residential living.[10] She placed resident directors in each Greek house to add support and supervision for maturing behavior. Greeks, chafing under these crackdowns, were placated some by the University's installing air conditioning in the houses. The graduate program was a landmark in the continuing, nationally recognized high quality of Pacific's student life division.

The Pike's annual "Hit of Reality," three nights "homeless" on campus to raise funds for the local food bank, was one of many Greek charity fundraisers of this era.

The Greek houses had their usual ups and downs. By this time, Sina had phased out all local fraternities, and nationally, Greek organizations moved to reduce their liability risk by cracking down on risky behavior, especially involving alcohol.[11] Archania went national as Sigma Chi in 2002, the year Sigma Alpha Epsilon had their charter pulled by the national office for alcohol infractions.[12] In 2005, the same ending happened to Phi Delta Theta. Delta Upsilon was also closed by the national organization in 2011, replaced by Beta Theta Pi, which banned alcohol in the chapter house.[13]

Consistent enforcement and strong supervision since then have built a more stable Greek culture, and the tradition of community service never waned. Pi Kappa Alpha won a national leadership award in 2001 in part because of their annual "Hit of Reality," when members went "homeless" on campus for three days and nights in makeshift cardboard boxes to raise money for the San Joaquin Food Bank.[14] By the 2010s, Pacific had eight traditional fraternities and sororities with houses, four of each, and six multicultural societies.

Generally, these societies were more responsible and accountable than on most campuses. Another notable difference from other campuses was the mix of various ethnic, socio-economic and sexual identities of members in Pacific's Greek clubs. The prominence of the professional societies in pre-dentistry, pre-pharmacy and in the pharmacy school (four co-ed "fraternities" in the school alone) was also unusual. The reality was that among all these societies, the tendency especially by alumni to protect and perpetuate questionable secret legacy practices persisted.

By the nineties, interest in Band Frolic waned, and participation declined from 15 or 20 acts to seven. The Greek Council took charge, elevating the Greek Week "Lip Sync" contest to replace it. Lip Sync was immediately popular because it required only dance rehearsal to recorded music, not a

"Lip Sync" replaced "Band Frolic" as the annual stage competition among living units—perhaps not quite as original as Band Frolic, but just as lively and fun.

musical number built from the ground up. It was moved to Homecoming, and then vice president Sina opened it to residence halls and other organizations, much like the Band Frolic. As someone wisely observed, "The subtle rhythm that binds the two traditions—Pacific Pride, Pacific Passion, and Pacific's Penchant for the Playful"—conveyed a sense of continuity with Band Frolic, but to older alumni, nothing could replace it.[15]

A changing campus life

A resurgence in student activities leadership brought two high-profile bands to the campus in 2000. "Reel Big Fish" was the first major concert in six years, and the "Third Eye Blind" concert, a huge sell-out success at the recently renovated Bob Hope Fox Theatre downtown, was the first-ever partnership with the city of Stockton.[16] The hit band of 2005 was "Flogging Molly" playing to another sell-out house at the Bob Hope Fox Theatre. Alice Walker, Michael Moore and other marquee figures populated the special events rosters throughout this era. Movie director Spike Lee and Nobel Peace Prize winner Archbishop Desmond Tutu drew overflow crowds. One year DeRosa interviewed television journalist icon Walter Cronkite, ensconced in easy chairs on the concert hall stage. Another year President Bill Clinton spoke (the first U.S. president to visit Pacific), and then Nobel Peace Prize awardee Rigoberta Menchú for Latino Heritage Month.

A "sea change" occurred in the late 1990s: a new underground irrigation system invaded the central quad and other parts of the central campus to replace the regular flooding of the lawns. All the carefree slip-sliding on those warm sunny afternoons ceased. When he arrived in 1995, DeRosa had not been informed of the old practice common in the Valley. One morning on his way to the office he saw water gushing from the bowels of Knoles Hall and immediately called physical plant to alert them to a "broken water main." Well, orientation of a new president cannot cover everything.

Conservation of water was exceeded by a conservation of energy, especially the cursed summer of 2001 as the rolling blackouts hit California when the state experimented with deregulating energy prices. Instead of buying expensive backup generators, conservation was the Pacific way: thermostats were elevated, lights lowered, occupants consolidated, and hours shortened. Still, for 2001 the gas bill was five times higher than the prior year, and the electricity bill quadrupled the following year. Adding to the anxiety was the burst of the "dot-com bubble" in 2001 centered in the Bay that brought on a bumpy economy. By 2004 students paid an "energy surcharge" tacked on to the standard fees.[17]

On the Stockton campus, ASUOP president Matt Olson, one of the few re-elected to a second term, initiated an annual "Safety Walk" with public safety and campus facilities leaders to tag areas needing additional lighting or other hazards.[18] A tiger "Stripe" student night patrol with escort service began in 2002.[19] Public safety director Mike Belcher (2003-present), a seasoned police officer with the heart of a counselor, steadily improved campus safety and services to students despite an occasional setback. The bicycle theft epidemic of the eighties waned for two reasons: better protection and a steady rise of another campus vehicle, the skateboard, brought initially by the southern California students, but gradually becoming a common transportation choice for men and women of all backgrounds. The 2007 Virginia Tech University massacre by a demented student leaving 32 dead frightened every American campus, and even though Pacific had systems in place to prevent such a tragedy, a new "crisis response team" held practice runs more frequently. Safety cameras and card-swipe locks appeared on campus, and a University-wide emergency alert system via phones was installed.[20]

Skateboards became ubiquitous on the Stockton Campus as a common mode of transportation.

Sustainability arises

The 2000s was the era of "sustainability," whether in building construction or the curriculum. The value of preserving the natural environment amid global degradation of climate, soil, air and water rose to high campus importance. Pacific lagged a few years in the uptake, but when sustainability took hold, campus practices earned Pacific national recognition. Not until 2001 did ASUOP lead a Stockton campus-wide effort to begin a recycling program with the residence halls and physical plant staff, but little else was done during the decade.[21] A University sustainability committee was finally formed in 2009 along with a sustainability coordinator.

The Robb organic garden on the south end of campus, coupled with a similar garden at the law school, was part of the ethos of the era: natural, local foods were served in the cafeteria.

Recycling, energy and water conservation, the "MOVE" freshman orientation program, an environmental sciences major and an engineering minor in sustainability, the law school's Institute for Sustainable Development and environmental law program, the Natural Resources Institute and water quality research—all were part of a University-wide effort. Perhaps most important of all, "sustainability" was named one of seven University-wide learning objectives for all students. An annual "Sustainability Month" began in 2010 with lectures and symposia on all three campuses. University purchasing of goods, ride shares, measuring the campus carbon footprint, a residence theme hall, bike sharing for the San Francisco and Stockton campuses, a food service that was a national leader in the industry for using local produce, including a farmers market in the DeRosa University Center—all contributed to a change in campus culture. With funding from regent and CEO of Whole Foods, Walter Robb, a student organic garden opened in 2012 right in the heart of the South campus, and then the law school started one as well.

Recycling half the trash began in earnest in 2002 prompted by student activism, and by 2008 nearly 70 percent of solid waste was recycled. The dental school transitioned to a paperless clinic in 2009. Under sustainability leader Scott Heaton, director of physical plant staff, physical plant operations invested in energy savings upgrades starting in the 1990s—from boilers to windows to lights—that would pay back over time.[22] Even noise pollution entered the mix: the Academic Council complained that just about every Stockton student and faculty member had a daily class joined by a strident leaf blower out the window keeping the campus beautiful, and figuring out quiet hours was always an issue.[23] The 2008 University Center was the first LEED-certified (by U.S. Green Building Council) sustainable building constructed at Pacific and in the county. Board policy in 2009 required LEED certification in all new construction and major renovations, thus every building that followed also attained one of the LEED levels of sustainability certification in design, including a LEED Gold for the Chambers Technology Center.

The John Muir Center, established in 1989, had been redefined by the College back in 2001 to focus on environmental studies rather than California history. Then in 2007, under the leadership of history professor and noted western Americana scholar William Swagerty, a thorough program review set an ambitious agenda to "co-brand" John Muir with Pacific, integrating Muir's vision into the general education curriculum (every new undergraduate was given an anthology of Muir's writings), and engaging undergraduates in Muir research. Student life staff incorporated Muir into the new University center under construction, identifying the campus landscape through Muir's eyes, and physical plant staff built a garden of Muir botanicals within the quad just north of Callison Hall.[24]

The thousands of items in the Muir collections, 75 percent of

As the world's foremost holder of John Muir collections, Pacific began to embed the Muir legacy into its campus identity; pictured is an example in the DeRosa University Center.

his known papers, continued to win acclaim for Pacific and draw many scholars to its use. For years, Pacific history professors Sally Miller and Ronald Limbaugh and other international scholars published influential books on Muir based on the Muir Papers.

THE 21ST CENTURY PACIFICAN

Zesty cultural mix

The academic and student life offices forged a close partnership throughout the DeRosa years to bolster support for ethnic groups and multicultural awareness. Pacific's strategic plan, *Pacific Rising, 2008-2015,* had set a priority to cultivate diversity, intercultural competence and global responsibility, including "making diversity an integral part of curricula and student life" and "increasing training" in diversity and intercultural competence. Vice president for student life Elizabeth Griego had replaced Sina in 2006 when Sina became for a brief time the President's assistant and secretary to the board. Griego was especially effective in assessing whole student learning through all campus life activities overseen by her highly professional team, fed by the student life master's program. She had a sophisticated understanding of diversity issues and how they linked directly to student learning.

The Asian American/Pacific Islander population increased from 38 to nearly 52 percent of all University students. Underrepresented minorities (African American, Latino, Native American and multi-ethnic) increased from about 12 to 18.5 percent. Among undergraduates only, underrepresented minorities increased by nearly 10 percent of the student body, up to 23 percent. Among Asian American first-year undergraduates, one-third was of Chinese background, followed by Vietnamese, Korean, Indian and Japanese descent as predominant, among a dozen nationalities. Throughout this era, over 20 percent of undergraduate students came from families whose native language was not English, double the national average.[25]

In 2007, provost Gilbertson launched a Hispanic Initiative to build Latino enrollment through community partnerships, tied also to an innovative Inter-American program that prepared students to be bi-cultural in their selected profession.[26] A Spanish-speaking house was resurrected, named Casa Covell in honor of the 800 alumni of the earlier Spanish-speaking cluster college, three of whom served on the robust School of International Studies advisory board. A Latino alumni club was started in 2007, and the next year a Latino student council formed for the seven Latino student organizations, all under the driving force of Hispanic outreach coordinator Ines Ruiz-Huston.[27] When Pacific's undergraduate enrollment of Latino students reached ten percent in 2006, Pacific became eligible to join the national organization, Hispanic American Colleges and Universities (HACU), the pre-eminent higher education organization serving L

In 1998 a broad-based United Cultural Caucus was created out of the Multicultural Council to add joint programming and build support for ethnic clubs. In 2005 the ALANA Center (African, Latino, Asian and Native American) was created as an umbrella space for leaders of all the various ethnic organizations.[28] Ethnic and cultural clubs flourished as enrollments mounted. The UCC-sponsored International Spring Festival in 2000 brought 14 cultural groups together to celebrate, from the Hmong and Cambodian clubs to the Middle Eastern student association and Latin American Dance club.[29] The annual Pilipino culture night, begun in 1999 with a cast of 65 students in song, dance and story, drew nearly 500 students.

Many of the cultural clubs held annual festive celebrations to share ethnic performances, such as Kilusan, the Pilipino Club shown here in 2010.

A rich range of campus programming and student organizations made the campuses look and feel fundamentally different from 20, even 10 years earlier. While black Greek societies began at Pacific in the 1970s and flourished in the 1980s, the first Latino fraternity and sorority were not founded until 2003. They always struggled to maintain membership, and many chapters came and went over the years, often lacking a critical mass of students to support them. In 2013, for example, five multicultural Greek societies existed, a frat and sorority each for Latino/as and Asian-Americans and a black sorority, most with no more than a dozen members.[30] Student ethnic associations became strong at the law school. Certainly student government reflected this increasing ethnic diversity. In 2014 only two of 12 new ASUOP elected officers and senators for the coming year were of Anglo background, and the president and vice president, Marselus Cayton (2014) and Marquis White (2014), were both African Americans.

Religious diversity also increased. It would not have been a surprise to any student to know that in 2000, Pacific now had more freshman Buddhist students (7 percent) than Methodists; roughly one-fourth were Roman Catholic and one-fourth with no religious identity, while Baptists matched the Methodists at 5 percent.[31]

The federal TRIO program of the U.S. Department of Education to serve 200 low-income, first-generation college students, known at Pacific as "SUCCESS," became a major force in this era under the expert leadership of Anita Bautista, who managed always to re-earn the competitive four-year $1 million program for over 30 years. Only two other California schools were funded in 2005, for example.[32]

Thanks in great measure to the work of assistant provost Heather Mayne Knight, by 2008, the number of women faculty members had increased from 26 to 41 percent over a decade, and faculty of color increased from 10 to 23 percent over the same time period. Among all University employees, over 35 percent were from ethnically diverse backgrounds.[33] A "diversity" course requirement for all undergraduates now included some 55 approved courses across every school.

Flashpoints. . .

Students were alert to California policy issues that occasionally erupted into action. It was a tradition at Pacific to invite the governor to be commencement speaker, so when Pete Wilson was invited in 1998,

Latino and other students met with the President to demand that Wilson be dis-invited. Wilson supported California Proposition 187, adopted to prohibit undocumented workers—mostly Latinos—from using health care, public education and other social services. Eventually it was declared unconstitutional. DeRosa stood ground, noting that people of all views were welcome on a university campus, echoing the openness that President Burns had insisted upon decades earlier. During the event, students marched forward with placards to directly challenge Wilson standing on the platform, but they were quickly hustled away and the ceremony proceeded.[34]

Gay and lesbian awareness and participation grew rapidly. In 1999, when a national "family values" movement called "Promise Keepers" sought to rent Stagg Stadium, many faculty and students erupted in protest that Pacific would host a group that opposed gay legislation and was perceived to be demeaning of women's equality. The rental (not hosting) was approved, an academic symposium on the development of such national groups was held and the event for 30,000 transpired without incident. This was typical of Pacific's way of dealing with conflict through civil debate, through teaching and learning. In 2000 and again a decade later the "Gay Straight Alliance" was awarded "Student Organization of the Year."

One turning point on the Stockton campus came in 2002—a year when the chairs of the Academic Council and the Staff Council happened to be sports science professor Becky Beal and student life staffer Jennifer Sexton, personal partners—when the rainbow flag, universal symbol of gay rights, was stolen. The flag was bestowed to the alliance by benefactor alumnus Bill Jones ('51), the first single man in the United States to adopt a child as a single parent. A large rally of students from organizations across the campus, including the Greek Council, gathered in the McCaffrey Center patio to denounce the theft and express solidarity with lesbian, gay, bisexual and transgender students.[35] The Academic Council condemned the "desecration" and declared "tolerance, inclusiveness, and a unified community are core values of the University of the Pacific."[36] The flag was later found, urine-stained, in a campus trash bin.

That event more than any other catapulted forward the acceptance and celebration of gay students on the campus. The alliance grew into the

THE PACIFICAN

acific battles hate crimes during Pride Week

Letter from DeRosa

A pivotal event for Pacific and the LGBT community was the campus-wide rally to denounce the theft of the PRIDE flag in 2002.

PRIDE resource center in 2003, a space for "Promoting Respect In Diverse Environments," to provide support and education for LGBTQIA students. Initially located in a residence hall basement, the center moved into the McCaffrey Center by 2008. A faculty and staff organization, Out at Pacific, was also formed in 2003 with over 40 members. The first annual Lavender graduation ceremony was held in 2005 and an annual "Coming Out Week" soon followed. Especially with the leadership of student life associate vice president Steven Jacobson, Pacific's Pride Alliance became a regional leader on LGBT collegiate issues, hosting Northern California collegiate conferences starting in 2008.[37] The theatre department produced *Romeo and Juliet* with an all-female cast in 2009, the year a gay alumni club was formed and the president of the Pride Alliance, Ashley Stubblefield, was elected ASUOP president. Gender-neutral housing and restrooms came the following year.

It was no surprise that by 2012 the national Campus Pride Index awarded University of the Pacific 4.5 out of 5 stars overall on its LGBT-Friendly Campus Report Card in recognition of its policies, programs and practices for LGBT students. Although the city had only one gay bar, citizens of Stockton started a Pride center in 2012. Among leading LGBT alumni, Paul Kawata ('79) was one stand out; as executive director of the National Minority AIDS Council Kawata has had national and global impact on AIDS policies.

Another turning point was reaction to a *Pacifican* column in 2007 dismissive of the "Black National Anthem." The Black Student Union response sparked ensuing anonymous insults online. Student life staff organized three town hall meetings on racial stereotyping, out of which came a splendid, student-created documentary video on Pacific's diverse students, a larger student voice in Pacific Seminar course content and increased collaboration among diversity groups.[38]

. . . And more to be done

By 2010, the University adopted a "Diversity Statement" as policy, asserting, "diversity and inclusion are essential to the fulfillment of our institutional mission."[39] Pacific's understanding of diversity had grown with the national conversation, informed by an outpouring of research on diversity in higher education. This big step was followed by the most comprehensive review of diversity at Pacific through a taskforce headed by vice president Griego in 2012.[40]

Student surveys documented that especially in the twenty-first century, despite some bias incidents to the contrary, Pacific students typically reported positive experiences of "campus climate," and they valued the benefits of living in a diverse environment. Students of various identities felt a welcoming and supportive atmosphere in their residences that exceeded peer institutions, and they realized how they grew in their respect and appreciation of people from different backgrounds. So while students of color continued to report racial incidents on campus, they usually stayed at Pacific if they could continue to meet costs. Mario Fuentes (2003), whose home was five minutes from campus, experienced "culture shock" as a freshman, but gained footing to become a coordinator of a mentoring program. Danielle Procope (2014) found a residence hall unwelcoming, but flourished as an undergraduate researcher in African American literature, presenting at six national meetings, then chaired the first student-run undergraduate research conference on campus in the humanities and social sciences.[41]

By 2010, the University recognized designated heritage/history months for the following communities: Latino, Lesbian-Gay-Bisexual-Transgender

(LGBTQIA), Native American, Black, Women, and Asian Pacific Islander. *U.S. News & World Report* consistently ranked Pacific among the top 50 national universities on diversity factors (ranked eighth in 2012), and in 2013 Bloomberg's *Businessweek* ranked the business school ninth among accredited business schools in the diversity of its student body.[42]

An interfaith campus

The Muslim Student Association was named top student organization of 2014.

DeRosa created a task force on religious life in 1999 to examine the health and welfare of students' spiritual development at a time when the interfaith campus ministry program had run out of steam. Actions from the task force brought all student campus ministry organizations under the chaplain to help them flourish. In 2001 chaplain Joy Preisser formed the "Interfaith Council" that included 13 faith-based organizations across the Stockton campus, from the established Anderson Y, Newman House, Muslim Student Association and Fellowship of Christian Athletes to the newer Hillel, Wicca, Hindu and Buddhist groups.[43] The Interfaith Council took annual trips abroad to share in their various religious heritages. Soon the Muslim Student Association was selected as the annual outstanding campus student organization, and later the Hindu association was so named.

The practice of including Methodist clergy on the board was revived as an institutional decision in the 1980s and 1990s, though it had never been required by bylaws or pressured by the Church. Funding to Pacific directly from the Methodist church itself had ended many decades earlier. Pacific did not solicit church funds for the Bishops Scholarship for 25 to 30 outstanding undergraduate Methodist students. In 2004, the Anderson Y was incorporated directly into the student life division and renamed the Center for Community Involvement. With over a hundred student volunteers under the impressive leadership of Erin Rausch, the center was still devoted to tutoring children in the Stockton community and coordinating student volunteers for the city, never forgetting its incubator role for social justice causes, especially under Fran Abbott in the 1980s and 1990s.[44] The center's annual "Strawberry Breakfast" had been a trusty fundraiser since registrar Ellen Deering ('26) and co-workers started it in 1932. In 2008 and again in 2009 and 2012 the CCI earned recognition as a member of President Bush's "Higher Education Community Service Honor Roll," the top government award for universities in community service, based on the 750 students, faculty and staff volunteering thousands of hours in an array of projects.[45]

The DeRosa University Center continued to be a vital central gathering place for the Stockton Campus.

Students unwired

The impact of social media made campus life easier and harder. Global self-exposure on Facebook was the rage by 2004; as Andrew Westbrook (2008) said, "it's the best willing invasion of privacy ever."[46] As communication moved beyond email and instant messaging, collaboration and inclusion through instant networking and knowledge sharing exploded. Campus events were advertised through video promotions on the campus's Prowl TV, Facebook, YouTube, and Twitter. ASUOP adopted the internet application

"Orgsync" as a clearinghouse and scheduler for all campus organizations, and 233 groups registered.

Affinity groups could form in an instant, and they did, from Dumbledore's Army of Harry Potter novel fans with over 200 members, to a group called Knitting for Peace. Progressive Christian Alliance, a campus child-care advocacy group, Electronic Dance Community, Social Media Club, Students for Farm Workers and Environmental Sustainability, Veterans Writing Circle—you name it, there probably was a Pacific campus club in this era of rapid change, social awareness, and social networking through electronic media. ASUOP senators did weekly polling on issues. Campus reaction on issues was immediate, so personal abuses and social conflicts went "viral" instantly across the campus and beyond with these devices, inflating petty issues and distracting students. Marketing and student life staff conducted "threat assessments" and measured damage control of viral incidents.

Electronic learning

Earlier, technology staff kept responding to student demand for "hot spots" on campus for wireless access to the internet. By now wireless access was a given anywhere on the campuses and beyond. The dynamic uncertainty of technological innovation—new must-have "smart phones" seemed to emerge almost annually—made global information retrieval ubiquitous, simple, and abundant. "Millennials" were young people impatient with delays in service, expecting 24/7 access to everything by always staying connected. How could professors keep up with their students?

An emerging competition from a vast array of online education options available—most likely accessible even on a shirt-pocket "smart phone"—was forcing another potential major shift in the University's culture. The shift came with the research validation that "blended learning"—the combination of personal, face-to-face interaction of professor and student coupled with a rich array of global resources orchestrated by several mentor/teachers available on "hand-held devices"—was offering an optimal education that neither the traditional professor in the classroom nor the complete online degree could provide. In an era when undergraduates had never lived without the internet, reconciling online learning with personal interaction was a major challenge for all teaching-centered institutions.

Students now expected ease for doing most anything on campus, especially in transactions, from admissions to graduation. The notion of a "one-stop shop" for doing business with the University had long been part of administrative planning for a revamped Knoles Hall, but when places like University of San Diego and Pepperdine made the one-stop shop a reality, pressure increased to complete the work at Pacific.[47]

But online learning was also part of their world. Fully one-fourth of all U.S. students in higher education by 2012 were learning online.[48] The world experienced the ubiquity of information and the spreading of knowledge in all fields of study through elaborate electronic networks accessible anytime, anywhere, in almost any fashion, given the mobility of wireless internet tools. Library services took on a whole new level of sophistication. Universities began to sponsor refined college-level coursework conveyed electronically, much of it free of charge, available to any Pacific student who wanted a special course or the convenience of taking it anytime from a top professor at an international university. Electronic classes became handy fill-ins for Pacific students in this era, whether as a summer class or late night addition to their Pacific classes.

The library transformed

The University Library became a key player in the explosion of information access. Under the direction of library dean Brigid Welch beginning in 2008, the library was a hub of intense use.[49] By this time, the ubiquity of electronic access to library resources was a given, but many students marched to the library because it was a welcoming place conducive to interactive learning—and socializing—with fellow students. Group study rooms grew to over two dozen as compact shelving shrunk the need for book space. The Davey Cafe in the foyer kept students fueled late into the night. A second floor "study commons" was littered with white boards—group notes or strategies for accounting class or pharmacology. A student

The Library's "Information Commons" and a cafe in the mid-2000s signaled a merging of library and student center activities in the digital age.

Writing Center was relocated to the library for easy access. A digital multi-media lab offered specialized software and printers for engineers or musicians. Budget constraints ended an experiment with 24-hour service, even though dozens of students were in the library at 3 a.m.—not even during final exams!

Yet the deeper transformation was outside the building. The 24-hour availability of the library's electronic sources on all three campuses—now nearly three-fourths of all library resources—made access to information transparent. Electronic books had become standard in fields such as business and the sciences as nearly half of all book publishing had gone electronic by the mid-2010s. When the library consolidated access to all of the library's content through a unified, web-based search tool called "Pounce," no student could complain about information barriers. The library poured its funds into expensive electronic database subscriptions to keep sciences faculty and students happy.

Yet the building housed two important treasures that also brought students inside: special collections of archive materials and talented staff to build students' library literacy. The precious, unmatched collections of

John Muir and Dave Brubeck were backed by a host of unique California collections, from Western Americana to the World War II Japanese internment. Increasingly, professors incorporated these primary materials into their courses so students could get a first-hand feel for the stuff of Pacific history. At the same time, "library literacy" was included among University's priorities to integrate research and information competency skills into the curriculum. Research skills training became embedded into the undergraduate Pacific Seminars, cycling through library classrooms headed by library faculty and staff where orientation could easily occur.

The Stockton campus library often ran at 100% capacity from 9:30 in the evening till 1 a.m.

FACULTY EXPECTATIONS

The "teacher-scholar"

A generation of professors retired around the millennium—19 alone in 1999, opening many positions for young faculty eager to secure their place at Pacific. Many faculty were troubled by the provost and President denying tenure to candidates recommended by their departments. The tension between administration and faculty on the appropriate roles of research and service at a teaching university was typically at the heart of the conflict. Many faculty members felt that research was overemphasized and service undervalued.

By early 2004, the Academic Council had developed a plan to strengthen the "teacher-scholar" model. Key points were mentoring, a uniform student course evaluation system, and clarifying faculty "service" requirements. The Council also appealed for a center for teaching where faculty could learn ways to improve student learning. The deans rallied behind this plan. DeRosa said fine, but asked faculty find a way to fund the priority through reallocation.[51] The deans gulped and the provost acted. The Center for Teaching and Learning was open within a year and its fulltime director, Jace Hargis, quickly made the center a hub of teaching innovation and faculty scholarship on teaching and learning, with an accent on emerging technologies.

University accreditation review again was looming, this time with a focus on student learning outcomes, part of a national movement toward greater accountability in higher education. The University, confident that there was alignment across Pacific on institutional values hammered out in strategic planning, dared to take on University-wide learning outcomes. The list of seven learning outcomes for every student in every program was notable: competence in a major field, critical and creative thinking, communication, collaboration and leadership, intercultural and global perspectives, ethical reasoning, and sustainability. The faculty set two to four specific learning objectives for each of these outcomes, an ambitious exercise. The "intercultural perspectives" outcome, for example, included "engagement in the civic life of the local, national, and global community."[52]

Faculty research surges

Faculty scholarship had come a long ways over the decades. When Pacific moved to Stockton, it came with no tradition of active faculty scholarship. There was scant evidence of published faculty scholarship before the 1930s. Gradually, faculty so inclined began to become active as time permitted, especially in the sciences, but not until President Atchley was faculty scholarship set as an expectation, and not until the late 1990s was reasonable support for faculty research provided.

By the turn of the century, most of the resistant senior faculty who questioned the research requirement had retired, and junior faculty could not imagine their work without active agenda of scholarship. The persuasive power of highly effective teachers who were also productive scholars pushed the issue out the door. Many if not most professors found ways to engage their students in their research, a known avenue for deeper, more exciting learning.

For example, engineering professors Gary Litton and William Stringfellow represent a strong trend of Pacific faculty to involve undergraduate and graduate students in their research. These professors had a long list of grants and contracts that deployed teams of undergraduate and graduate students on water quality research in Valley rivers and the Delta. Stringfellow's team even found a new bacterium that ate much of the oil from the historic BP oil disaster on the Gulf Coast in 2010. Biology professor Craig Vierra deployed $2 million in funded research to analyze the molecular structure of black widow spider silk, five times stronger than steel. Over a decade he mentored dozens of undergraduate and graduate students in his labs. One of those undergraduates, Kristin Kohler (2004), published three papers and in 2013 was back in Vierra's lab as a visiting professor completing her Ph.D. at Yale.[53]

Through the 1990s, economics professor Dennis Flynn and Spanish/history professor Arturo Giraldez teamed to sponsor major international conferences on campus exploring Pacific Rim history, keying off their landmark research on early trade between China and Europe. This kind of research collaboration across departments flourished throughout the University, especially after the turn of the century. Among the College, dentistry and pharmacy schools, science faculties produced dozens of joint research results, some from the 60 joint school projects of various sorts involving 140 faculty and staff by 2012.[54]

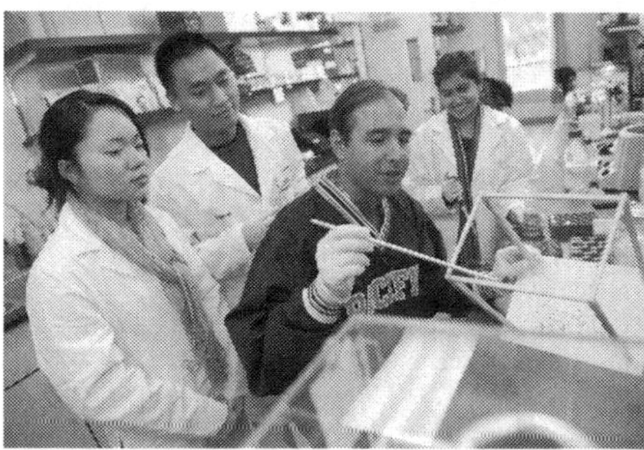

Biology professor Craig Vierra epitomized many faculty members who were outstanding in teaching, scholarship, and service. He engaged dozens of undergraduate students in his ground-breaking spider silk research.

Popular English professor Courtney Lehmann, a world expert on Shakespeare in film, was known on campus for her props—and commencement costumes.

The range and depth of scholarship across the schools is rather impressive, given the primacy of teaching and mentoring of students. Typically at Pacific, outstanding scholars were also superb teachers. Professor Caroline Cox was a noted historian on the American Revolution and war; Courtney Lehmann, English professor and director of the humanities scholars program, was one of a handful of world experts on Shakespeare and film and had completed her fifth book in the field. Sports science professors Staci Stevens ('91, '97) and Chris Snell rose to national prominence for their "Pacific Fatigue Lab" that did groundbreaking research on chronic fatigue syndrome, placing them on the national CFS Advisory Committee of the U.S. Department of Health and Human Services. Popular history professor Ken Albala was one of the foremost global authorities on food history whose 20 books included a world encyclopedia on food cultures. His book on Italian, Mexican and Chinese cuisines was named the 2012 best foreign cuisine book in the world by Gourmand International. Business professor Cynthia Wagner Weick was a noted expert in strategic management and innovation. Music education professor Ruth Brittin was the chief editor for the *International Journal of Music Education: Research.* Law professor John Myers, one of America's foremost authorities on child abuse, produced eight books and was cited by more than 150 courts, including the U.S. Supreme Court.

Equally notable was the rise of what is called the scholarship of teaching and learning, where published research was based on studies of how students learn better—research often conducted through Pacific classrooms. Dental practice chair and professor Cindy Lyon ('86), who founded the dental hygiene program, was an example of faculty who built their research on their teaching. This research was so extensive, across the College and every school, that it may be fair to say that this scholarship of teaching and learning was becoming a hallmark of Pacific.

LEADERSHIP AND THE SCHOOLS' THRUST IN QUALITY

Dean leadership and the dental school model: "Knock your socks off"

If ever one needed proof of the significant role of a dean, the School of Dentistry was the shining example. Dean Dugoni's exemplary leadership set the bar so high that many Pacific deans thought it unreachable, though his example and his generosity and supportive spirit inspired them to advance their schools. The dental school had built its reputation on core humanistic values, a program focused on clinical skills for professional practice, and a three-year, year-round program unique in the country.

The dental catalog statement defined the humanistic values as "Dignity, Integrity, and Responsibility."[55] Faculty pledged "honest communication of clear expectations along with positive support for diligent effort." They committed to "actualize individual potential" for each student by placing "great responsibility on each member of the dental school community." Faculty "must teach in a way that encourages and energizes students. Students, in turn, are expected to set very high standards, to work hard, and to take personal responsibility for their own learning process."

These values lived out every day set Pacific apart, and prospective dentists knew it. Typically, one in 20 applicants could be accepted. No matter that graduates averaged around $250,000 in federal loans by the 2010s. Rising income for dentists could comfortably manage repayment. Dean Dugoni unleashed alumni leadership, added students to the alumni board and expanded alumni chapters throughout the west under the steady leadership of

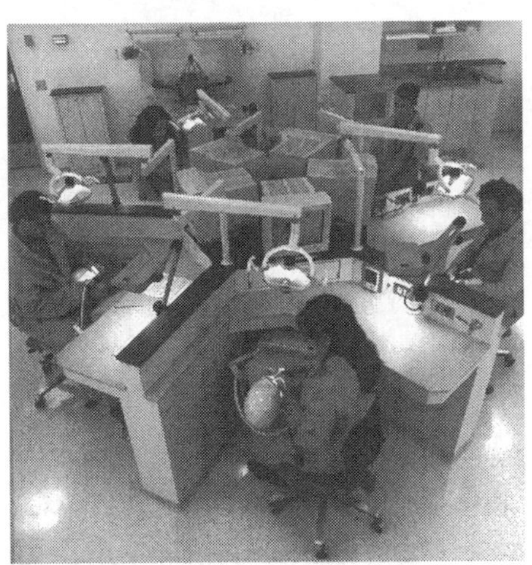

The dental school's pioneering simulation laboratory built in 1995 set a new national standard for clinical education.

alumni director David Nielsen. Of all Pacific's schools, dental school alumni stood out with exceptional pride. They graduated with zeal about their school and gave back through generous philanthropy. Under the superlative leadership of Art Dugoni, the school was so exceptional in every respect that it became the provost's model for Pacific's other schools in its quality, values, distinctiveness and success.

In 1996 the School of Dentistry celebrated its centennial in a sparkling history by Eric Curtis ('85), *A Century of Smiles*. This era of the dental school was one of high achievement and prosperity. Pacific was producing 25 percent of the state's dentists though there were five other California schools. In the early nineties, when *U.S. News & World Report* began to rank universities and professional programs, Dean Dugoni led the charge to have all 54 U.S. dental schools boycott the magazine by refusing to participate in a process so flawed in its design. After all, Dugoni had clout: he had been elected president of the American Dental Association in 1988 and headed the American Dental Education Association among many positions and awards. He was awarded the List of Honour, the highest recognition the World Dental Federation bestowed on a member, limited to 30 living members. Dugoni was arguably the most prominent dental educator in the country in this era—some would say in the world. Not surprisingly, he was

By 2014, Dugoni School of Dentistry was the only school at Pacific with an authorized history, ***A Century of Smiles*** *(1995) by alumnus Eric K. Curtis ('85).*

persuasive, and since then there have been no *U.S. News* dental school rankings.[56]

A dental hygiene bachelor's degree program, one of only two or three in the state, was launched in 1998 in preparation for the new Health Sciences Learning Center on the Stockton campus. The University embraced this new health program because it linked to liberal education through the bachelor's degree requirement, it linked two campuses directly for the first time to deliver a degree program (the real start of the "three-city campus"), it diversified the health sciences to provide students more options to stay at Pacific, and it accented partnering with the regional dental community.[57] The program opened in 2003 along with an advanced post-graduate program in the new Stockton clinic, which could deliver dental care to the disadvantaged of Stockton.

The California Endowment funded a $2 million project headed by professors Paul Glassman and Christine Miller to expand a community-based treatment and prevention program for people with disabilities in 11 centers across the state. This and other programs like it helped to keep the

Physiology professor Joseph Levy (1973-2009), a passionate and brilliant teacher, was beloved by dental students for many reasons, including his 1978 Ford Pinto.

dental school in the forefront of clinical education in the country. James Pride was a leader in developing programs in dental practice management, first at Pacific, then across the nation, to prepare students to manage successful dental practices.

In 1998 dentist Bernard Molinari ('23) gave $5 million, the largest single gift to the dental school to that time, to spark planning for a new addition for post-degree education to be called the Molinari Pavilion. Even at age 73, Dugoni was eager to tackle a new capital project to advance the school, just as he oversaw the $3 million renovation of the 30-year-old Union City clinic in 2003. The Pacific Heights campus clinic was expertly run by strong faculty like Bob Christoffersen, Jim Pride, Ron Borer and Richard Fredekind. Dugoni continually pushed for updated equipment—except for physiology professor Joe Levy's 1978 Ford Pinto, which he drove to school well into the new century.

In 2000, Dugoni forged a partnership with Highland Hospital in Oakland to launch a certificate program in oral and maxillofacial surgery, with the hope of eventually offering a joint program with UC Davis for an M.D. degree.[58] That did not happen, but the surgery program, headed by professor Thomas Indresano, quickly became a leading program in the country. It joined other special advanced programs: the international DDS degree for practicing dentists from other countries begun by Robert Gartrell and honed by David Nielsen, the master's program in orthodontics headed by renowned professor Robert Boyd, who helped to invent invisible teeth braces, and two other certificate programs in advanced education in general dentistry and in advanced clinical experience.

The provost would often say that dean Dugoni was the most remarkable educator he had ever known. Anyone associated with the dental school would likely agree. On every front, from admissions to advising to outreach to fundraising, the dental school was the gold standard for Pacific. In 2000 the school's accreditation report included a record-setting 18 commendations and no recommendations for improvement. Gilbertson engaged Dugoni to serve as mentor to the deans, most of them new. The deans of pharmacy and law, Oppenheimer and Parker, both sought out Dugoni to model school improvements.

Thomas J. Long School of Pharmacy and Health Sciences earns the spotlight

An important decision to relocate the physical therapy and communicative disorders (aka speech pathology) from the College of the Pacific to form the School of Pharmacy and Health Sciences marked a step forward in 1998 to broaden and strengthen the school as it sought a new dean. While there was controversy among the faculty over the final candidates, everyone soon rallied behind dean Phillip Oppenheimer, who provided the leadership that has advanced the school ever since.

Oppenheimer, previously associate dean at USC, brought seasoned experience and a broader, more entrepreneurial approach to the job than his predecessors. When he arrived, the school was on "Cautionary Notice," one step away from de-accreditation, for failing to meet promises to hire more faculty members. State board licensure pass rates were low. The school desperately needed a boost in achievements and morale. The new University administration made commitments to transform the school, and the new dean brought the leadership to accomplish it.[59]

Within months, dean Oppenheimer had to cobble together an accreditation report and endure an external review that came with plenty of criticism. After he worked with faculty to set the school's first strategic plan in place, including a major overhaul of the curriculum, Oppenheimer hired new faculty and staff steadily to meet accreditation promises and shape a new curriculum based on the needs of the practicing pharmacist in the new century. He added a review course for graduating seniors to catapult the licensure pass rate from the sixties to the mid-ninetieth percentile within a year. The next year the pass rate was tops in the state. The school upgraded the third-year clerkship model to be more accountable. While accreditors had challenged the 13 regional centers in 1998, six years later they named the dispersed centers a "national model" for other schools to follow.

Oppenheimer linked with both pharmaceutical companies and chain drug store giants to create funding partners and active employers, moving beyond the obvious and strong partnership with the Long family, their foundations, and their drug stores. A development office was begun and grew under the skillful enthusiasm of Nancy DeGuire ('89), herself a

Thomas J. Long (left) and his brother Joseph M. Long were key benefactors in the development and success of the Thomas J. Long School of Pharmacy and Health Sciences.

pharmacist, who in a dozen years built a model external relations office. Under the dean's leadership, the Thomas J. Long family and foundation became Pacific's largest single donor in history with its $13 million gift to build the Health Sciences Learning Center and Clinics in 2000. This transformative gift, aided by the help of regent and Long family member Tom Sweeney ('62), added to numerous major prior Long Foundation gifts. Joseph and Robert Long were also major donors. The board recognized this family of loyal, long-standing benefactors by naming the school the Thomas J. Long School of Pharmacy and Health Sciences in 2000.

Alumni Tony ('77, former regent) and Virginia ('77, regent) Chan funded a generous gift to name the first floor of the new learning center. About a decade later the Chans made another major gift to the school to place them among the most generous to Pacific.[60]

Shortly after, dean Oppenheimer secured an endowed faculty chair in health care management for a new Pharm D/MBA program with the business school funded by the Joseph M. Long Foundation. This unique program added to the school's distinctive three-year curriculum—one of only nine among 130 pharmacy schools in the country—with mandatory clerkships across the west. And by 2002 the physical therapy faculty elevated their master's program to a professional doctorate, the DPT, as student demand for the program increased following state legislation that authorized licensure of the "autonomous practitioner" with advanced training. Following pharmacy and dentistry, the DPT was distinctive as a compressed, accelerated program over 25 months.[61]

The three most important keys to the pharmacy school's dramatic rise to prominence were the massive revision of the Pharm. D. program to an

The Long School of Pharmacy and Health Sciences opened its Chan Family Health Sciences and Learning Center in 2000 for instruction and as a community clinic for pharmacy, dentistry, physical therapy and speech pathology. Pictured also is the Chan Family Hall for pharmacy student residents, and the dedication celebration with the Chans and President Eibeck.

innovative, integrated, practice-based curriculum; the new learning center and building upgrades like the new library funded by Rite Aid; and most especially investment in hiring talented faculty. Supporting faculty research was critical to sustaining the singular University Ph.D. program. Externally funded research tripled by 2003.[62] In 2007, professor William Chan, outstanding teacher in medicinal chemistry, was the first Pacific professor to be awarded a prestigious million-dollar National Institutes of Health (NIH) grant to conduct research in cancer drugs and the immune system. This grant spurred on a range of funded research by teams of chemistry and pharmacy professors, finally living out the dream of a decade earlier to combine the two disciplines into one distinctive, high-quality doctoral program in pharmaceutical and chemical sciences.[63]

Pharmacy professor William Chan (1996-present) was exceptional in both his teaching and research.

Leadership development was part of the bedrock of the school's program. Around the turn of the millennium, the school was setting new records for leadership, with Pacific's chapter of Associated Students of Pharmacy winning the top national student leadership award in nine of the previous 12 years. The students would say their success was owing in great measure to "Dr. Flo," professor Donald Floriddia ('71), champion of all pharmacy student organizations for over 40 years.[64] The school's state leadership role, begun back in the 1960s, continued well into the present. Students and alumni often swept annual CPhA awards, and by 2001 a Pacifican was selected state "Student of the Year" for the fifth year running.[65] Just as with the dental school, the accent on leadership was led by the dean. Oppenheimer, nominated by his students, became the first dean ever to be named California Pharmacist of the Year by the California Pharmacists Association in 2004, and no one on campus was

Dean Phillip Oppenheimer (1998-present) transformed the Thomas J. Long School of Pharmacy and Health Sciences through his comprehensive leadership. He was awarded national dean of the year by the Academy of Student Pharmacists in 2014.

surprised when a decade later his students' nomination brought him national Outstanding Dean of 2014 by Academy of Student Pharmacists of the American Pharmacists Association.[6]

Alumni leadership in the profession throughout the state perhaps was no wonder: 40 percent of the practicing pharmacists in the state were Pacific graduates.[67] Among many professional offices, three alumni, Charles Green ('68), John Schlegel ('67), and Lawrence Brown ('99) have served as national presidents of the premier American Pharmaceutical Association. Two alumni served on the national pharmacy board of trustees in 2013, and nine alumni have served as state presidents. The dean's leadership council included such leaders as Royce Friesen ('65), who was instrumental in forming the state pharmacy association among many state leadership posts; former faculty member Jeff Jellin ('74), who headed the Therapeutic Research Center, the leading medical and pharmaceutical publishing organization in the country; and Pacific regent Clark Gustafson ('66), who served on the board of the American Pharmaceutical Association. The school developed a branded "culture of success" in all aspects of a student's life and work, capped off by a commitment to be engaged in the profession, in community service, and in driving the profession ahead through leadership and innovation. This "success-centered" culture would assure continuing leadership in the profession at all levels.

Community outreach was also an increasingly important leg of the school, whether offering immunization clinics, conducting no-charge medication reviews, or training public school science teachers through a $1.5 million National Science Foundation grant, using students in the joint graduate program.[68] In 2007 pharmacy seniors began an annual service to provide free coaching for senior citizens on the complicated federal Medicare prescription drug plans.

When the $18 million Health Sciences and Learning Center opened in 2003, the school had more applicants and a higher graduation rate (97.5 percent) than any other pharmacy school in the country. Pacific students also had the highest pass rate on the state board examinations and more graduates than any other pharmacy school in the state.[69] At this point, the President was pointing to the school and its "distinctive programs of exceptional quality" as a model of what could be achieved. Indeed, the school had come from its glumly neglected, borderline accreditation status in 1996 to the star of the Stockton campus. In the national *U.S. News & World Report* rankings of the 2010s, Pacific ranked in the low forties among 130 pharmacy schools, but most were large public research universities. Among the 65 private schools, Pacific ranked eighth.

The law school rises

Gerald Caplan, appointed dean in 1992, brought seasoned experience in public administration with the Federal Trade Commission and U.S. Department of Justice. A conservative force for nine years during the post-Schaber era, Caplan managed, consolidated and modernized all the operations of the school that had been controlled by dean Schaber for decades. Caplan began to engage faculty in collaborative decision-making and sponsored a star-studded speaker series to enrich the curriculum. The bar pass rate in 1994 was 89 percent, one of the highest in history. By 1995, with a student body exceeding 1,200, McGeorge was one of the 15 largest law schools in the country.[70]

Caplan began hiring faculty who could elevate the school's reputation through their scholarship, an increasingly important ingredient for ongoing accreditation that had been neglected in the past. Stephen McCaffrey, Brian Landsberg, John Sprankling, Franklin Gevurtz, John Myers, Michael Malloy joined the school, and over time their presence and

In this era, law professor Stephen McCaffrey (1977-present), one of the world's foremost authorities on international water law, was likely Pacific's most prominent and renowned professor. Among many key positions, he was a member of the United Nations International Law Commission and represented countries before the International Court of Justice.

active scholarship altered the culture of the school even as quality teaching remained pre-eminent.

When dean Caplan decided to hold tuition low to become the "least expensive" accredited California law school in the mid-nineties, he thought McGeorge's impressive bar pass rate, then the third-highest in the state, would make the school a "best value" investment for students reluctant to take on more school debt[71] Besides, by 1996 the school's rank in "student satisfaction" had risen from 74th to 50th among 170 accredited law schools.[72] The multiyear strategy was questioned by University leadership but allowed to play out—to quite detrimental consequences. The school was soon viewed as "cheap," discouraging talented applicants who perceived it as a sign of lower quality. From 1997 to 1999, enrollment dropped from 1,200 to 1,100. With pressure from the president and provost, the school quickly spiked its tuition to return to the middle of the pack among California law schools, but by then the bar pass rate was plummeting.[73]

When it came time to join the University in the comprehensive campaign of 2000-2007, the school was also ill prepared. Caplan, expected to be an outgoing fundraiser, shied away from campaign receptions and alumni gatherings. Caplan had disbanded the development office some years earlier as a cost-cutting measure, and now it had to be rebuilt. The school had no endowed faculty positions until the Gordon Schaber Chair in Health Care Law and Policy, begun in 2000, which took three years to fully fund.[74] Meanwhile, to honor one of its outstanding citizen leaders, Sacramento County renamed the courthouse as the Gordon D. Schaber Courthouse in 2002, five years after his death.[75] He had been advisor not only to Pacific presidents, but also to governors Reagan, Deukmejian and Wilson, and tutored future governor Jerry Brown for the bar exam. In an eloquent eulogy, friend and Supreme Court Justice Anthony Kennedy noted "the simple humanity of the man counts the most."[76]

What did give the law school a lift were its government contracts, which far exceeded any others in University history. Beginning with steady Social Security Administration contracts in the 1990s, associate dean Glen Fait's Institute for Administrative Justice (IAJ) captured a three-year $24 million contract with the state's Department of Education, begun in 2000 and renewed in 2003, to conduct hearings on special education student cases for five years.[77] The school had acquired the Muddox Building to the northeast of the campus in 1992 to accommodate the growing IAJ staff. Then in 2005, the IAJ was awarded a $37 million two-year contract to conduct parole revocation hearings across the state, extended for several more years at roughly $20 million per year to fund 200 attorneys. This windfall offered internships for students, research projects for faculty, employment for alumni and income for the school that infused many programs and projects with investment funds.[78]

Given the sluggish start of the fundraising campaign, the contract income was an important factor in advancing the school during these years, including the much-needed renovation of the law library. Students called the crowded, shabby library space "pathetic" and "embarrassing."[79] The library project became the top priority for the campaign, needed to capture the interest of increasingly talented and competitive students who were picking and choosing among school options. The $10 million Legal Studies Center expansion and renovation was the largest facilities project the school had ever undertaken.[80]

Another major public service initiative began in 1995 when the school

The splendid new Legal Studies Center and expanded library opened in 2012.

launched a state governmental affairs program. The program, which had several aliases, most recently the Capital Center for Public Law & Policy, offered new courses, a research institute and an array of internships in over a dozen state agencies, capitalizing on the prominence of alumni in state government. The center, headed by versatile professor Clark Kelso, exploited the school's unique connection with state government, including a new master's program in 2001 in government law and public policy, overdue for a law school that fed off the state capital. A parallel move was the annual California Initiative Review begun in 1998, using two dozen students to provide nonpartisan legal analysis of all state ballot propositions, a vital service to the state and remarkable practical policy experience for students.

Ronald George, chief justice of the state supreme court, called the Capital Center "an excellent example of Pacific's ability to create learning experiences that greatly benefit our citizens."[81] And the story was known around the capital: state senator Bill Lockyer ('86) was writing law as chair of the Senate Judiciary Committee while he was a student at McGeorge. He went on to become one of the state's most prominent and outspoken politicians as state senate president, California attorney general, then state treasurer. When Kelso got deeply involved in state government himself as "Mr. Fix-it" during the 2000s—he served as emergency state insurance commissioner, the state's chief information officer, then overseer of the California prison health care system—the center perhaps lagged for a few years, but it remained an important priority for incoming dean Parker, who planted an outpost in federal government in Washington, D.C. as well.

The McGeorge focus on linking law students with practical experience in the larger community continued in other ways. The Business and Community Development Clinic was begun in 1998 for students to help its struggling Oak Park neighborhood and other Sacramento-area small businesses. Soon the community legal services and immigration clinics, run by students, assisted hundreds of low-income families in the neighborhood. Then there was the can drive. Students, armed with canned food items to donate to the school's Thanksgiving holiday food drive, could dodge a classroom question on a designated "Can Immunity Day"—unless the

Three of many prominent law school alumni include Bill Lockyer ('86), California attorney general and treasurer; Consuelo Callahan ('75, former regent), justice of the Ninth Circuit U.S. Court of Appeals (here addressing the Latino Alumni Club); and Morrison England ('77, '83, former regent) chief judge of the U.S. District Court for the Eastern District of California.

professor decided to trump them with a couple of cans. While one professor quipped, "it was one day when faculty members could not complain about getting canned answers in the classroom," the big winner was the local food pantry.[82]

In the early nineties, McGeorge student teams won their way to five consecutive national advocacy competitions, finishing third in 1995 and second and third in 1996 under the strong leadership and teaching of professors Joseph Taylor and Jay Leach. Mock trial teams were built from a trial advocacy course that included citizen jurors and real judges, a mark of distinction for the school. By the early 2000s, the school's mock trial teams emerged as national competitors, vying in the national finals three times in four years in the late 2000s.[83] In 2003, the trial advocacy program ranked 11th in the nation by *U.S. News & World Report.*

McGeorge got another shot of national publicity with the unprecedented Supreme Court case deciding the presidential election of 2000, when COP graduate Ted Olson ('62) as U.S. Solicitor General argued for George W. Bush vs. Al Gore in the Florida election process, with McGeorge professor Anthony Kennedy casting the swing vote.[84] So too did McGeorge get the spotlight when Johnnie Rawlinson ('79) was appointed to the U.S. Ninth Circuit Court of Appeals in 1997 to became the first McGeorge graduate ever to serve on a federal appeals court. Connie Callahan ('75), then president of the school's Alumni Association, was appointed to the same court in 2003. That year the school unveiled the elegant "Anthony M. Kennedy

U.S. Supreme Court Justice Anthony Kennedy continued his close association with the law school throughout his distinguished career (here teaching a class at Pacific McGeorge).

Alumni Judicial Wall of Honor" in the student center both to recognize the 350 alumni who served as judges in 18 states and territories and to honor Justice Kennedy's 40 years of teaching at McGeorge.[85]

As Caplan retired to a teaching position, and following a two-year search, Elizabeth Rindskopf Parker was appointed dean in 2002, the top choice of every constituency, a rare feat in any dean search. Parker, an expert on national security law and terrorism, had served as legal counsel to the National Security Agency and the Central Intelligence Agency. Immediately the appeal of the energetic, high-profile woman dean drew over 40 percent more student applications, building on a woman-majority student body for the first time in 2000.

She inherited other good news as well: the school's state bar exam pass rate had bottomed out in 2000, task force recommendations had been enacted and the bar pass rate jumped from an alarming 54 percent low in 1999 to 73 percent in 2001. In addition the percentage of recent graduates employed increased from 70 to 97 percent through support and improved recordkeeping.[86] Enrollment for fall 2002 jumped nearly 10 percent to

A campus swearing-in ceremony for new graduates who successfully completed the bar examination became a popular annual tradition around 2000.

1,036 students, with higher academic credentials from an applicant pool twice the size of four years earlier.[87] Caplan and the faculty had prepared a strategic plan for the new dean that focused on strengths in advocacy and international law. And the school launched an annual feel-good tradition on campus by sponsoring a festive swearing-in ceremony for graduates who had passed the state bar exam, inducting them into the legal profession among their families and faculty.[88]

The law school was on a roll, energized in part by talented young faculty hired as seniors retired, fed by budget surpluses and state contract income. Then in 2004, dean Parker made a strategic decision to add five new faculty and two staff positions to beef up the school, and great faculty were hired to advance the three program priorities in government, advocacy and international law. She also hired Mary Lou Lackey, an unusually talented and seasoned executive, to professionalize the staff, oversee all campus operations and build community relations (she later was appointed a University vice president and secretary to the board). Applications were rising and the average LSAT score was up to 158. McGeorge finally became tough to get into; only three in 10 applicants were admitted. Among 40 student organizations, from societies on environmental, sports and entertainment law, to military, water and wine law, there was a group

The renowned McGeorge courtroom continued to be updated to live up to its name as the "Courtroom of the Future."

for every interest, including a cigar society and a rugby club.

As Parker spruced up the campus with renovated classrooms (even McGeorge House and the Courtroom), high-end technology, paint and banners, students thrived on a refreshed and active campus with a new master plan. Her goal, like it or not, was to achieve a "top 100" ranking by *U.S. News & World Report* among the 187 ABA-accredited law schools, given how important national rankings had become to prospective students. By 2005, the school was ranked 90th overall in the country based on student achievement, lower student to faculty ratios and impressive placement rates.[89] As dean Parker later said about McGeorge's potential, "I simply took the cap off the bottle. . . . Well, I shook it first."[90] The school remained in the top 100 rankings for the next six years.

Parker's commitment to Pacific's student-centered education of the whole person was a personal passion. The first dean to live on campus, Parker gained popularity with students by regularly popping in on student events and welcoming conversations. Further, she certainly never lost sight of the importance of preparing "practice-ready graduates," even as the younger faculty viewed it askance. She used an influential Carnegie Foundation report critiquing legal education to reinforce the central importance of equipping students with practical skills and ethical and social responsibility.[91]

The immense challenge was maintaining the school's lofty position. The state bar examination pass rate again dropped below the state average in 2005 to a mediocre 64 percent. The school launched a bar review course now permitted by the ABA and committed to achieving an 80 percent pass rate, which was actually exceeded in 2009 for the first time in 15 years.[92] As enrollment began to sag—averaging about 1,000 students through the 2000s—the school invested heavily in smart marketing, exceeding the University's sluggish marketing efforts.[93]

The shady quad has become a central feature of one of the country's largest law school campuses, here shown in the 1970s (above) and today.

Parker's vision was wide and deep. She wanted to alter legal education by engaging what she called "the continuum," from pre-college to alumni. An early project started in 2003 was the St. Hope charter high school partnership in Oak Park with former NBA star Kevin Johnson, who later was elected Sacramento mayor.[94] She championed a national "Education Pipeline" movement among law deans and gained a small following to create ethnic diversity in a profession woefully lacking it. In 2006 she formed a unique pipeline partnership with Sacramento's law-themed charter school, Natomas Pacific Pathways Prep, to promote interest in legal education among disadvantaged students. Partnering with both McGeorge and the Benerd School of Education—dean Lynn Beck was chair of the school board in the 2010s—helped transform "NP3", which was named a California Distinguished School in 2011.[95] No wonder *U.S. News & World Report* ranked it as one of the top 100 public-charter high schools in the country.[96] But most law faculty saw the pipeline effort more a distracting pipedream and did not engage.

Fundraising was a perpetual challenge for an alumni base that was equivocal about their experience during the dean Schaber era. Some alumni wore pins declaring "not one red cent" in response to gift appeals as a repudiation of the Draconian treatment of the earlier years. Dean Parker was effective in securing project grants but less so in fundraising. As a national figure of considerable persuasion, she brought McGeorge to the national stage, but perhaps neglected the attention of practicing lawyers in the region who could have responded with dollars. It took the length of her tenure just to secure funds for the library expansion project.

Nonetheless, Parker built an alumni outreach program, including regional clubs, to try to remedy two decades of "serious neglect" of alumni.[97] The *de facto* alumni reunion had been the school's annual sponsorship of a "mandatory continuing legal education" (MCLE) program for alumni that provided required state bar continuing education credits at no charge to alumni. Begun in 1996, the event drew over 500 alumni; venues were added in southern California and the Bay area. But providing this free professional service did little to encourage giving back to the school. Nonetheless, Parker's personal vitality and the renewed sense of optimism about the school did result in a significant increase in alumni giving, which doubled from seven percent in 2005 to over 14 percent in 2008.[98]

Whereas dean Schaber envisioned McGeorge as a strong but regional law school and dean Caplan began to aim for a more national profile, visionary Parker had strong national and international ambitions for the school, and international programs became the centerpiece of her efforts. She built on the long tradition of its European programs, including its LL.M. in transnational business practice that enrolled 50 students in the early nineties.[99] Of course, the Salzburg summer institute, ever highlighted by a course taught by Supreme Court Justice and McGeorge professor Anthony Kennedy, was still going strong after 35 years. Given the faculty strength in international law and water law, the school added both a master's and a doctorate in international water resources law, only the second such program in the world. The new programs built on the stature of professor Stephen McCaffrey, arguably Pacific's most outstanding and influential scholar in this era, who had counseled durable water treaties on four continents through the United Nations, including the Danube and Nile rivers.[100]

The summer program at the University of Salzburg in Austria remained attractive in part because Supreme Court Justice Anthony Kennedy continued on the faculty for decades.

Parker pioneered partnerships in China starting in 2002 that were unprecedented among U.S. law schools, funded by a first-ever USAID grant to a law school in 2006-2012. She met with University of Beijing Law School dean Zhu Suli ('87), no doubt the most prominent law school alumnus in China, ever grateful for the shaping influence McGeorge had on his view of the law.[101] A new degree program, an LL.M. in teaching of advocacy under the direction of professor Brian Landsberg, was created explicitly to train 150 law faculty in China to reform their legal education curriculum. The school's strengths in advocacy training and international legal education earned the faculty a U.S. State Department contract to coach lawyers and judges in Chile. In 2005, Parker launched the *Journal of National Security Law and Policy* to demarcate McGeorge as a broad center of international affairs.

Dean Elizabeth Rindskopf Parker discovered that the dean of the prestigious University of Beijing Law School, Zhu Suli ('87), was a proud alumnus of Pacific McGeorge's international program.

The most important initiative, headed by professor Frank Gevurtz, was a series of 23 *Global Issues* casebooks on international law to supplement all the standard core courses in law schools, written mainly by McGeorge professors. Here Parker accomplished three goals in one: remodel the fundamental law school curriculum, internationalize it and advance faculty scholarship, which had lagged for years. Strength in international law was finally recognized in the *U.S. News & World Report* ranking of 19th in the country in 2006 and 17th in 2012.[102]

Early in Parker's tenure, associate dean John Sprankling proposed cutting enrollment by one-third and thereby automatically raising the credentials and academic profile of the school. Tuition-driven as much as any Pacific school, McGeorge would have to forfeit millions in revenue and cut faculty and staff severely to achieve this goal. Dean Parker and the provost were attracted to the proposal to upgrade the school by a pen stroke, but it seemed ill-timed as the school was experiencing rising success by investing heavily to improve facilities, programs, scholarships, marketing and curb appeal. There were few programs she and the provost did not support, contributing to a sense that the school might be becoming a spendthrift operation spread too thin, but investment in building the school's national profile seemed to be working, as enrollment, student quality and faculty talent kept growing. The drastic downsizing proposal to elevate its national standing was never more than an option presented to the Board of Regents and was not pursued.[103] As if anything were possible, in 2010 graduates at the commencement ceremony in Sacramento's Memorial Auditorium witnessed the oldest and youngest graduates ever: Alice Thomas, age 79, and Zachary Powell, age 19, both equally deserving of extended applause.[104]

Benerd School of Education partners for success

When dean Haisley retired in 1999 after 14 years as Pacific's first woman academic dean and returned to her native Australia, the Benerd School of Education entered a period of turbulence. The provost made an unfortunate mismatch in his appointment of a new dean and insisted that faculty promotions require substantial scholarship for a school so reliant on its doctoral programs. But the resilient faculty during these years experimented with many new programs in response to a dynamic state and local environment that required nimbleness.

In 2000 the school offered a doctoral program jointly with CSU-Bakersfield that continued until the CSU system won its own right to offer doctoral programs in education. For superintendents and principals hungry for advanced study to improve their schools and their own employment, Pacific was a life-changer, and the public school students of the Bakersfield area have been the real beneficiaries.

In 2001 the Board of Regents approved a Ph.D. in school psychology, a result of re-engineering the educational psychology programs to focus on a distinctive, high-quality program, one of only 13 in the west. The difficult decision to add a second Pacific Ph.D. program (the other was in pharmaceutical chemistry) was based on accreditation requirements. Along with this decision came the scuttling of the traditional counseling psychology program. But the challenge to attract strong faculty and students in school psychology proved difficult, and the program was abandoned after a decade. Dean John Nagle was unable to work well with most faculty and public school partners from the start, which blunted the school's progress.

By 2004, the state allowed local school districts to offer their own certification programs, a milestone in broadening the base for advanced education and intensifying competition for schools of education. The Benerd School, now with highly regarded interim dean Dale Anderson, responded creatively by forming a successful joint certification/master's program with the San Joaquin County Office of Education designed for school principals.[105] Later, however, the state authorized the county office to form its own "college" with its own master's degrees as well as certification. The competition for Pacific continued to heat up.

In another kind of partnership, the Spanos-Berberian family initiated annual performances by the Kennedy Center professional children's musical theatre from Washington, which packed 4500 school kids into the concert hall annually beginning in 2003, bringing scholarship income to the school and the conservatory.[106] Also in 2003, Chauncey Veatch ('70)

President George W. Bush named Army veteran Chauncey Veatch ('70) National Teacher of the Year in 2003, earning him an honorary degree from Pacific.

was a star COP alumnus feted at School of Education events to salute his being named National Teacher of the Year. A 22-year veteran and decorated Army colonel, Veatch had started teaching mostly immigrant families in the Coachella schools only seven years earlier. "Having served my country, I know that there is no work in my entire life that I have done that is more patriotic than being a teacher," he said as he received an honorary degree and presented the University commencement address that year.[107]

When Lynn Beck arrived as the new dean in 2005, the fortunes of the school improved immensely under her superb leadership.[108] Not since Marc Jantzen had the school had such a can-do attitude about its mission. With Beck's energetic, outgoing, positive spirit the school thrived beyond any past success. Despite severe enrollment challenges in the undergraduate programs—closing the bachelor's programs was discussed in the late 2000s—Beck crafted entrepreneurial partnerships to reach new populations. Eight new competitors arose for certification and master's programs in Stockton. USC began to offer an online teacher credential program, and the CSUs were authorized to offer doctorates in education in 2006. While most schools of education saw declining enrollments in this era, Beck increased enrollment in most programs, nearly doubling the school's population by 2013. At the same time she dramatically increased the ethnic diversity of the students, faculty and staff.

She recruited strong faculty who elevated the quality of both teaching and scholarship and created a strong culture of collaboration that motivated the school to be flexible, responsive, and entrepreneurial. Senior faculty like professor Linda Webster provided pragmatic leadership. Professor Marilyn Draheim's passionate attention to student advising and retention was an anchor for the school for decades. Beck consolidated the curriculum so faculty could be deployed to emerging new programs.

The school developed a successful accelerated evening degree program for paraprofessionals in the schools called EdPro2 that enabled diverse cohorts of paraprofessionals to become certified teachers. Beck launched new master's programs in the Bay area and in partnership with the dental school to provide training for dental educators worldwide. She started a successful M.Ed. and Ed.D. program in Shanghai, China with the help of graduate dean Jin Gong.[109] The school began a unique partnership with Aspire charter-public schools to improve retention of urban school teachers by offering a customized master's program that included a yearlong residency.[110]

Community partnerships, always part of the school's mission, grew in number and importance, especially as President Eibeck chose early childhood literacy and college readiness as her focus for the Beyond Our Gates community outreach program. In addition to coordinating Eibeck's Tomorrow Project, the school developed a teacher apprentice program in mathematics for underserved students with the county and Delta College, and they partnered with the County Office of Migrant Education to provide enrichment programs for 200 families to nurture college dreams.[111] Just as important, the school's graduates often led in progressive reform, such as Khushwinder Gill (2005), named California "Principal of the Year" in 2011 for lifting test scores and physical fitness through after-school programs.

All these efforts were in the context of a bleak landscape for public school teachers. The federal "No Child Left Behind" project of the era turned out to be damaging to teachers and students, the economic recession pink-slipped many young teachers, and the public only intensified its complaints about schools. Yet the Benerd School of Education placed all graduates who sought jobs in 2013. Dean Beck instilled a positive spirit and even joyful celebration in the school's community, including "Harry Potter" parties with faculty and staff costumed as characters in the novels, delighting city youngsters. The synergy of the school with its flexible,

Dean Lynn Beck (2005-present) enlivened the Benerd School of Education with her zesty spirit of optimism, entrepreneurial leadership, and partnerships with area schools.

diversified portfolio of programs had been the key to dean Beck's success in making the school responsive to change. A key to maintaining and increasing quality in all these programs was relentless focus on learning assessment embedded in every course. In many ways, the school was a model for how to thrive in the turbulent world that the next Pacific president would inherit.

The School of Engineering and Computer Science flourishes

The arrival of Ravi Jain as dean in 2000 began a school trajectory over 12 years that rivaled dean Heyborne's heralded era.[112] Jain was an accomplished international scholar in environmental impact and managing technology innovation, author of 13 books, and the only Pacific faculty member ever elected to the American Association for the Advancement of Science (AAAS). Yet he had a practical focus on what needed to be done to make the school, struggling since the late 1980s, robust and engaged. With patience, persistence, and adaptability, Jain took on the culture of the school to lift research expectations, build stronger links with industry, improve facilities, increase diversity and raise funds. He knew he had to grow the faculty to strengthen the school, and that meant increasing enrollment. To be more competitive, he streamlined the undergraduate curriculum and the co-op program to reduce the bachelor's program from five and one-half years to four years.

Yet the commitment to challenging and supporting individual students was a deep tradition continued by dean Jain as well as the "old guard" like professors Richard Turpin and David Fletcher. Professor Joe King was as popular for his teaching as for his famous massive toothpick creations, from spaceships to the Eiffel Tower, that got him on TV's *Tonight Show* and in *People* magazine.[113] The engineering industry fellowship program,

Each school has its traditions. The "Cardboard Regatta" was one of the most popular in the School of Engineering and Computer Science in this era.

begun under dean Ashland Brown in 1997, was ramped up to become a premier program, a $50,000 value that matched top students with industry partners for five years of internship and scholarship support, beginning the summer prior to the freshman year. For example, current engineering professor Elizabeth Basha (2003) spent five years at Hewlett Packard during her bachelor's work, prior to her MIT graduate degrees. One of the most fun traditions of the school was the annual fall "Cardboard Regatta", with pairs of first-year students competing in boats of cardboard and duct tape. A big crowd of faculty and students cheered them across Kjeldsen pool. Of course several never quite made it. At the end of the year, the fun was "Senior Project Day," when graduating students presented their capstone engineering projects on the engineering lawn, where they were judged by industry volunteers.

But the required co-op program was still the jewel in the crown. As part of their degree programs, over the years students worked at NASA, Bechtel, Lawrence Livermore and Sandia Labs, helped to develop the Hewlett Packard Inkjet printer, improved work processes at Gallo Wine, worked on the Mars Rover, and tweaked the Disneyland "Pirates of the Caribbean" ride.[114] Because of their work experience, Pacific graduates always had an edge over graduates of other universities in career choices.

Dean Jain was eager to diversify his student body and faculty, enrolling and hiring more women and minorities than most Pacific schools. He provided strong support for the Mathematics Engineering Science Achievement (MESA) program and created the Heyborne Leadership

The Pacific Society of Women Engineers chapter won several national awards in the 2000s. Electrical and computer engineering professor Louise Stark, advisor since 1992, was named top SWE advisor in the nation in 2010.

Academy to develop student leadership in 2004. Among the many engineering student organizations, the Pacific chapter of Society of Women Engineers (SWE) was particularly outstanding. In 2005 and again in 2009 Pacific's SWE won first prize in the national Boeing Team Technology competition with a ten-student team, inventing new technologies under the guidance of do-it-all professor Louise Stark.[115] Stark and colleagues also prepared "Team Venus," six undergraduates selected to compete in a global supercomputing competition, one of eight teams from around the world, and the only all-women team.[116]

No wonder that Stark was selected as the nation's outstanding advisor in 2010 by the Society of Women Engineers. The chapter won SWE's national outstanding collegiate activities award for sponsoring "Expanding Your Horizons" for over 20 years, a program for sixth to twelfth-grade girls to explore math and science.[117] Elizabeth Basha (2003) and James Martin (2004) both won Tau Beta Pi fellowships for graduate study in successive years, of only 30 annual awards granted nationwide by the engineering honor society.[118] By the time Jain ended his deanship, he had doubled the number of students from underrepresented groups.

Dean Jain was a leader not only in championing campus domestic diversity but also in internationalizing engineering education. He established strong if small co-op programs in Germany and Japan. He refreshed relations with over 200 alumni in Arab states of the Persian Gulf by establishing a Gulf alumni club in 2006, which culminated in the appointment of Fawzi Al-Saleh ('62) as a Pacific regent.[119]

Dean Ravi Jain (right) built closer ties with Mideast alumni, led by Fawzi Al-Saleh (left, '62), who became a Pacific regent in 2011, here shown with Tawfic Khoury ('80), whose family led in the building of Engineering's Khoury Hall.

In 2002, computer science was moved from the College into the engineering school to strengthen both programs. In the same year the bioengineering program got underway, developed by professor Richard Turpin when he was interim dean just prior to Jain's coming. Linking two strong programs in biology and engineering, this was one of only a handful of undergraduate programs in the country. Professor Abel Fernandez brought the engineering management to accredited status in 2004, one of only 11 such programs in the nation.[120]

A priority of dean Jain's was laboratory expansion and improvement. By 2005, the 26 labs required additional support, so a lab fee was added to tuition, like the conservatory, pharmacy and dentistry schools.[121] A landmark was the completion of the John T. Chambers Technology Center in 2010, with LEED gold certification for sustainability. Jain was the first to thank President DeRosa for bringing Cisco CEO John Chambers close to the University. His naming gift was a generous thank you from a proud parent of a Pacific graduate. The school's Engineering Advisory Council, headed for years by Pete Wallace ('59), was a steady source of support and funding. Jain was more successful in fundraising than any of the other undergraduate schools in this era.

Another landmark was the master's degree in civil engineering approved by the board in 2009 after years of preparation. Electrical/

The John T. Chambers Technology Center not only advanced the School of Engineering and Computer Science but paid tribute to the quality of a Pacific education that drew Cisco CEO John Chambers to Pacific as a parent of a Pacific alumnus. The Center was Pacific's first LEED gold-certified building.

computer and mechanical were soon added. This distinctive accelerated program allowed undergraduates to blend their bachelor's and graduate work to complete the master's degree in only one additional year.[122] The popular master's program, with over 120 students, led to record school enrollment approaching 800 by 2013 with SAT scores averaging over 1200.

Years of building the research capacity of the school made the program possible. Over the years, Jain and the faculty led all the schools in securing $17 million in research and program grants from 2000 to 2012. In recent years, *U.S. News & World Report* ranked the school among the top 20 percent in the country of universities without doctoral programs. When Steven Howell returned to Pacific as dean (he had been a founding faculty member of the mechanical engineering department in 1983, serving until 1991) after dean Jain retired in 2013, he found a school well positioned to be a competitive player among many fine engineering schools in the state.

The School of International Studies makes a run

DeRosa's decision to invest in SIS following the first program review meant finding a strong dean with a clear vision of how to improve and grow the school. In 1998 Margee Ensign came with strong credentials and an energetic, purposeful drive that the school needed. Immediately she insisted on beefing up the quantitative skill requirements and sparked an inspirational vision to innovate. By 2001 the school partnered with the Portland-based Intercultural Communication Institute to offer a distance-based master's program in intercultural relations with 100 students across the world.[123] The partnership with the Institute brought both visibility and revenue to a school that lacked the clout of the handful of other IS schools, which had large graduate programs.

Another option to quickly expand international studies arose again in 2003 when the board of the Monterey Institute for International Studies discreetly invited Pacific's interest. This encounter with MIIS stood in marked contrast to President Burns' almost careless pick up of the American Academy of Asian Studies (AAAS) in San Francisco in 1954 that survived for only a few years. MIIS was a small independent graduate school of a few hundred students that had grown up around the high-end Naval Postgraduate School and the military's Defense Language Institute Foreign Language Center in Monterey. In 1972, MIIS had asked Pacific to consider a merger. The board sent a delegation to campus and concluded that its goals were unclear, its quality "rather shallow," some credentials "lightweight." And given Pacific's financial woes at the time, it was easy for the board to pass it up.[124]

Now, in 2003, MIIS again approached Pacific through regent contacts to consider acquisition. DeRosa sent a stream of senior staff to examine every aspect of the school, from faculty to facilities to technology, and found much wanting. But before a decision could be made, MIIS backed away, thinking that the University of California would step in with its powerful resources. When UC withdrew, MIIS came back to Pacific. Monterey was certainly an appealing location with distinctive programs, attractive to a university that was learning how to manage efficiently campuses in three cities. The investment required to make it successful, however, would be enormous, and the provost had serious reservations about the future demand for its programs. Pacific declined in the end, burdened by its own financial challenges to complete a campaign whose outcome was uncertain.[125]

Dean Ensign also brought the state-sponsored California Institute for International Studies Program (CISP) from Stanford to Pacific to lead the state in international education training for hundreds of K-12 teachers.[126] She re-engaged Callison and Covell College alumni, promoted the Inter-American Program, developed an undergraduate emphasis in international law linked to the law school, and launched the Global Center for Social Entrepreneurship despite her faculty's misgivings. As SIS expanded programs through Ensign's entrepreneurial efforts, George Wilson Hall was squeezed for space. With donor approval, SIS switched buildings with the Bechtel Center for International Programs and Services in 2002.

By the turn of the century, anthropology professor Bruce LaBrack was widely known for his study abroad orientation and re-entry courses.[127] Remarkably, Pacific's SIS remained the only international studies school to require study abroad. "What's Up with Culture?", LaBrack's online self-assessment for study abroad, became a world standard, adopted by the Peace Corps as well as universities in many countries. In the mid-2000s, cross-cultural training conducted by SIS faculty expanded to student life staff and to most of the schools.

Dean Ensign cultivated retired regent David Gerber's passionate interest in SIS, leading to his endowment for the annual Gerber Lecture Series, which brought heads of state and other global luminaries to the

Awarding an honorary degree to Rwandan president Paul Kagame in 2005 was a high point for the School of International Studies, which had several ties to the country, including Dean Margee Ensign's book on Rwanda's post-genocide recovery.

campus. Mary Robinson of Ireland was the first, then Paul Kagame of Rwanda, where dean Ensign had forged a partnership with higher education in the post-genocide reconstruction. Kagame was the first head of state to be awarded an honorary degree by Pacific, in 2005.[128]

The provost supported most of Ensign's initiatives, including a proposed experimental doctoral program that went nowhere, but the overall outcome was a school overstretched, especially given its small size, peaking at 150 students. Ensign, challenged by administrative tasks and over-extended, was often on her own. In the end, dean Ensign did all she could to grow the distinctive school and lift its stature, but the demand for such a professional school, at least in its location, was not in the cards. It was no surprise to anyone who knew dean Ensign that she accepted the challenge to become president of American University of Nigeria in 2010. A dean search was extended while the new president and provost determined how to proceed.

The Conservatory of Music sparkles

One signature of the conservatory in this era was the annual piano recital of professor Frank Wiens, one of the few conservatory faculty members who actually conducted national and international tours. His impeccable playing would always draw a full house. The music school hit a high point

Opera professor James Haffnor's production of Rossini's La Cenerentola, starring Laura Lendman (2002) as Cinderella, was the first opera ever to win the American College Theatre Festival competition at the Kennedy Center in Washington, D.C.

in 2001 when its production of Rossini's opera *La Cenerentola* was the first opera ever to be selected as a national winner by the prestigious American College Theatre Festival, performed in the Kennedy Center in Washington. Professor James Haffner teamed with colleagues in the theatre arts department for this production, and this multi-year partnership won other regional awards. But the lack of commitment by the theatre department to become professionally accredited forced the two programs to part ways, given the conservatory's professional expectations. Despite deans' and the provost's active advocacy for a joint musical theatre program, the two faculties could not come to agreement, and the provost could not assure sufficient funding to grease the skids.

But this never held Haffner back. He and his opera students continued to earn regional and national awards for professional-level productions. In 2013, the 135th anniversary year of the conservatory, his 70-student production of *The Merry Wives of Windsor* with the conservatory symphony was named the nation's top university opera by the National Opera Association, albeit in the lowest-budget category of schools. Thanks to outstanding professors of vocal music Lynelle Wiens, Daniel Ebbers and Burr Phillips, three graduates in recent years debuted at the San Francisco Opera. They followed in the footsteps of former Pacific students like Susanne Mentzer ('76), who sang leading roles at the New York Metropolitan Opera for twenty years; Elizabeth Vrenios ('62), who toured the world as a soloist and was president of the National Opera Association; and Linda Watson ('78), one of the most sought-after sopranos for Wagner operas.[129]

When Stephen Anderson replaced Carl Nosse as dean in 2000, he quickly upgraded the equipment and management of the concert hall to generate income for the school and embraced the Brubeck Institute as an important asset. Soon dean Anderson brought a proposal to upgrade the worn pianos throughout the conservatory. The goal was to make the conservatory a "Steinway campus" funded as part of a bond issue, paid off by a student equipment and service fee. While the school-wide replacement plan did not materialize because of cost, many new practice room and concert grand pianos did upgrade the school. The instrumental program also improved in this era. Steadily, the orchestra matured from a small collection of novices to a robust, cohesive ensemble. Eric Hammer, director of bands, was a key reason students kept coming. His boundless enthusiasm for Pacific students kept high the spirit and performance of groups, from wind ensemble to pep band.

Music management professor Keith Hatschek lifted his program to a high professional level, aided by a first-rate advisory board of mostly alumni working in the industry in Los Angeles, including Denny Stilwell ('88), past president of the Alumni Association, whose recording company Mack Avenue Records had four Grammy nominations, and Nick Phillips ('87), a vice president at Concord Music Group. The Leasure Recording Studio (2008) funded by regent Larry Leasure opened opportunities for the music management students to do actual CD production that could lead to careers like the one of Marco Barbieri ('91), president of Century Media Records, a leading heavy metal recording label.[130] In 2013, students were recording the wind ensemble's CD at George Lucas' Skywalker Studio in Marin.[131] A small music composition program run by professors Robert Coburn and Francois Rose gained a reputation for outstanding student works, like those of Petra Anderson (2012), who miraculously survived the Aurora, Colorado movie theater mass shooting shortly after she graduated.

When Steve Anderson opted to step down as dean in 2007 to become director of the Brubeck Institute, the school was well-served by two-year interim dean Bill Hipp, who set the school to planning its future. When Giulio Ongaro stepped in as dean in 2009, he had a faculty ready to move ahead. Ongaro, the most effective leader the school had seen in decades, worked well with all constituents to build a sense of aspiration the conservatory needed. Enrollment grew by 50 students to 220, and support for faculty performances lifted spirits. The New Pacific Trio of women faculty (now called Trio 180), for example, was thriving after a decade, following the Pacific Arts Woodwind Quintet, still going strong for 45 years.

The school began planning for a major renovation of the Spanos concert hall and new facilities to replace the outmoded Owen Hall practice rooms—candidates for the next fundraising campaign. Ongaro's initial fundraising success was more promising than any prior dean, building special support for students to increase their opportunities in the profession.

The unprecedented success of nearly all the conservatory programs boded well for the future. For example, the thriving music therapy program, on the chopping block less than a decade earlier, held its first alumni reunion on its 75th anniversary. The program was featured on national public television (PBS) in 2012, and alumna Jennifer Geiger ('98) was elected as national president of the American Music Therapy Association in 2014. Beloved Audree O'Connell ('84), legendary music therapy professor of the 1980s and 1990s, would have been so proud.

Music therapy professor and faculty leader Audree O'Connell (1984-2002) was beloved by faculty across the University as well as by her students.

The Brubeck Institute stands out

Among 20 or so centers, institutes and clinics across the schools, the Brubeck Institute in the conservatory stood out because it was so distinctive and prestigious. DeRosa's strong hand shepherded the generosity of Dave and Iola Brubeck to place their entire collection of scores, recordings, awards, manuscripts, files and letters at Pacific. As noted earlier, the relationship with Pacific had begun under conservatory dean Carl Nosse, who had befriended the Brubecks for years and performed many of his larger works for orchestra and chorus. Nosse held the first directorship of the Brubeck Institute and named the collection a "living archive" to denote its use by performers, scholars, and jazz *aficionados.*

But it was the second director, J. B. Dyas, who defined the institute by creating a full-tuition fellowship for five top-notch jazz players out of high school, a summer jazz colony for promising high schoolers, and an educational outreach program, in addition to the Brubeck Collection and an annual festival. The Brubecks had been pioneers to integrate their combos early in the civil rights movement and to reach across the Iron Curtain in mid-twentieth century. Thus they wanted the Institute to embody their commitment to human rights and global peace through interdisciplinary symposia and collaborations, which typically occurred at the annual multi-day festival.

This ambitious program demanded more resources, even after Dyas and others were able to create a national honorary board headed by film star Clint Eastwood, a Brubeck devotee, along with jazz greats Herb Alpert, Quincy Jones, Ramsey Lewis, Wynton Marsalis, Marian McPartland, not to mention TV producer Norman Lear, filmmakers George Lucas and Ken Burns and cellist Yo-Yo Ma. Never had Pacific had such a cast of luminaries for a program. And the annual Brubeck Institute Jazz Quintet (BIJQ) routinely began to produce recordings and play at the best jazz clubs and festivals, including annual performances at the Monterey Jazz Festival. The BIJQ consistently won the most prestigious national performance awards by *Downbeat* magazine—18 from 2007-13, including best collegiate jazz group for five of those years.[132] By 2003 the Brubeck Fellows recorded an album at Steve Miller's studio, did a benefit concert at Clint Eastwood's ranch, and performed at the Library of Congress when Brubeck received the Library's Living Legend Award. Among the annual

Consistent Downbeat award winners, the Brubeck Institute Jazz Quintet's annual Commencement performances thrilled audiences in recent years.

Brubeck Festival highlights were those in 2003 and 2008 when a weeklong campus celebration was followed by a week in Washington, DC, with performances at the Smithsonian Museum, the Library of Congress, and the Kennedy Center.

By 2012 the institute was uncoupled from the conservatory but remained dependent on the strong partnership for it to thrive. Over $6 million had been raised from generous donors such as James Bancroft and Gordon Zuckerman toward a $10-15 million goal to endow the institute and its programs.[133] As if to salute this remarkable commitment to—and by—his alma mater, Brubeck featured the "Pacific Hail" tune on his 2007 album, *Indian Summer.* When he died in 2012 the day before he turned 92, the BIJQ was already booked for the United Nations the next spring, and for Wynton Marsalis' Jazz at Lincoln Center tribute to Brubeck in 2014.

Eberhardt School of Business: Downs and ups

This was the era in the business school when a few senior professors did everything well: Stephen Wheeler, John Knight, and Cynthia Wagner Weick led the way for many talented junior faculty. A high point was the 1996 naming dedication event of the Eberhardt School of Business, touting the legacy of a family of graduates that included four members each of the

The Eberhardt family has been a multi-generational supporter and benefactor of Pacific and the business school for many decades, including Robert Eberhardt's leadership as board chair, 1975-1993. In 1996, the school was named to recognize this legacy.

Robert and Douglass Eberhardt families along with their sister Mary Alice. The naming was wholly appropriate to honor the support provided to the University and the school by the families and the Bank of Stockton for decades. But the start of this era was also muted by a number of challenges. As enrollment wanted and the school began withdraw from its leadership position on the campus, three decisions soured much of the school faculty over time and made many resentful of the University administration if not the campus as a whole.

One of DeRosa's early decisions was to end the favorable agreement on MBA program revenues that funneled cash into the school. Then, in the early 2000s, after extensive planning for a new addition to Weber Hall to handle the school's specialized programs, the administration pulled the plug on the building plan for good reasons, reduced it to the renovation of a floor of Knoles Hall, and then reneged on that plan. When the President then opposed a proposal to fund MBA scholarships to recruit stronger students, many business faculty gave up hope for University support. The dean did not discourage the view that the school had been undercut by the University and bereft of financial incentives prized by business faculty at many other schools. These attitudes led to increased isolation. As well, a growing separation within the school developed as talented and assertive new faculty, enthusiastic about both teaching and research, were favored over some of the loyal but less-active long-term members. The one major collaboration with another school was led by pharmacy dean Oppenheimer, the Pharm. D.–MBA joint program.

When Plovnick retired as dean in 2006, dean Chuck Williams quickly found a faculty suspicious of any new collective effort. Williams came with an ambitious agenda that required common purpose. Unfortunately, he found that purpose only in his own ideas, not those crafted together with the faculty, and by the second year he was impatient to implement his own way without collaboration. The faculty dug in its heels, no strategic plan was approved, and the faculty shut down. Outstanding faculty like Wheeler and Knight provided steady hands to keep work focused on students.

The only real headway was the remarkable Student Investment Fund established in 2007 by a gift from regent Douglass Eberhardt ('59), later raised by the board to $2.5 million. The fund offered a team of undergraduate and graduate students a chance to handle investments on their own. Their reports to the Board of Regents showed it outperformed the S&P and many other fund managers.[134] Regent Eberhardt was especially proud that students also learned philanthropy by turning their handsome profits back to Pacific programs.[135] By the end of his second year, Williams resigned, and the school spent two years recovering under the supportive leadership of a seasoned interim dean, Richard Flaherty. He stabilized the school, dissipated the dissention, and completed a school plan. In 2008, *Princeton Review*'s student survey rankings listed the school among the top 290 in the country, and *Business Week* ranked the undergraduate program among the top 120.

The Student Investment Fund, launched by regent Douglass Eberhardt for business students, was another example of the practice-oriented student experience at Pacific. SIF students consistently outperformed the indexes.

A new chapter of the school began in 2010 with Lewis Gale's appointment as dean. His openness, transparency and collective vision restored in great measure the buy-in and group spirit of the Turoff-Klein era. Gale appealed to nobler motives, engaged in collective planning and sought campus collaborations that had been neglected for years. The school came forward in 2013 with its first significant new program in years, a bachelor's and master's degree in accounting to meet new CPA standards, including a blended program like the engineering master's that accelerated degree completion by one year. With careful listening, renewed attention to students, and a plan to establish programs in Sacramento, the school was finally off to a promising start for the twenty-first century. And again, the possibility of a new building to accommodate growth and current technology appeared on the horizon for the next fundraising campaign. Capturing the entrepreneurial spirit of students in this era was Vanessa Gabriel (2014), who during her years at Pacific founded a new fashion start-up company pitched to millennials' online shopping.[137]

ACADEMIC MILESTONES OF THE COLLEGE

General education reigns

The required multi-course Mentor Seminars always fought for student enthusiasm. "I Hate Mentor" T-shirts were peddled by sophomores in prior years, but by 1998 student satisfaction with the seminars nearly doubled to 67 percent.[138] The faculty across the schools held remarkably steady commitment to these mandatory interdisciplinary courses, and over time pride in the program grew under the skillful leadership of communication professor Jon Schamber.

When Gary Miller was appointed College dean in 2002, he soon organized an effort to reclaim general education as a program sponsored by the College rather than by the provost. The President and provost opposed moving GE back to the College, fearing that it would lose its hold with faculty in the other schools. Miller presented a detailed plan to assure that the distinctive program would regain its central role with full-time college faculty and ensure that faculty in all the schools would stay on the team. The College won the day and received strong support: from 2006-08, over $400,000 was invested to add seven faculty for the Pacific Seminars to keep classes small and staffed by fulltime professors. When Thomas Krise was appointed COP dean in 2008, he inherited a COP faculty stronger and more vibrant than it had ever been in its history.

The faculty revised the seminars to focus on "What is a Good Society?" in the mid-2000s, and the new general education director, philosophy professor Lou Matz, gained the program national recognition as one of 18 schools in an elite consortium that collectively set a new national benchmark in general education. The freshman seminar focused on what it means to be "engaged citizens" by examining the "good society" question, using a text

Part of the national distinction of the Pacific Seminars was a series of custom-created texts by the Pacific faculty teaching in the program.

the seminar faculty created, just as the senior seminar faculty created their own text, *What is an Ethical Life?* The GE program was cited as a national model for achieving "essential learning outcomes" in knowledge, skills, social responsibility and integrated, applied learning.[139] By the 2010s, "Pacs," as the students called the seminars, were as well established a core feature of Pacific as the stone columns fronting the library.

The College achieves Phi Beta Kappa

Back in the 1960s when Cliff Hand was dean of the College, he picked up President Knoles' challenge to seek a chapter of Phi Beta Kappa, the nation's first collegiate honor society, and by far the most prestigious and selective in membership. A half-century after Knoles failed, dean Roy Whiteker took on the challenge in 1976. Unlike nearly all the other schools at Pacific, the College lacked an accrediting process distinct from the regional all-university accreditation review to measure its excellence. Phi Beta Kappa was the default national benchmark for the liberal arts and sciences since the society was formed in 1776. In retrospect dean Whiteker admitted that even though the College had plenty of Phi Beta Kappa faculty to meet that crucial requirement for sponsorship, "We were nowhere near ready for a chapter. We had . . . too much money going to football, too little money going into the library resources, and too few students that were top notch."[140] He made another attempt in the 1980s, but finances were even worse. Both DeRosa and Gilbertson had it on their list of to-dos as part of upgrading every school, but postponed action until both felt confident Pacific could be successful.

Not until 2003 did they try again, this time with dean Miller and the inspired leadership of Gregg Camfield, English professor and director of the undergraduate honors program. Twenty-six PBK faculty members—many talented recent recruits passionate about the liberal arts—also contributed. From the student academic profile, to faculty scholarship, to library resources, the College had never been stronger. In fall 2006, the national council voted a chapter to Pacific, "Chi Chapter of California," a landmark achievement as one of only 276 chapters across the country. Phi Beta Kappa was the highest recognition a liberal arts college could attain and spelled the coming of age of the College. As 21 students were inducted into the first class, provost Gilbertson, who always strived for a relative parity of quality among the schools, congratulated the College on achieving a clear identity and a level of quality that matched or exceeded the other schools.

The Phi Beta Kappa process drove forward another milestone: the appointment of Pacific's first fulltime national scholarship advisor in 2005 to mentor and coach the most talented and ambitious undergraduates to pursue national and international scholarships. While Pacific had yet to

The awarding of a Phi Beta Kappa chapter to the College of the Pacific faculty in 2006 was national recognition of the College's academic quality.

produce a Rhodes Scholar, seven Fulbright, three Goldwater, and six Boren scholars were Pacific graduates from 2009-14.[141]

The College builds interdisciplinary studies

One outcome of the 1997 academic program review was the formation of the humanities center, a collective effort by the humanities disciplines—art history, English, film, theatre, modern languages, philosophy, classical and religious studies—to plan joint courses and programs as well as joint student recruitment under English professor Courtney Lehmann. The new humanities building brought all disciplines together physically in 2005. The center produced the annual award-winning literary and arts magazine, *Calliope.*[142] The Pacific Humanities Scholars program, begun in 2011 for high-achieving students who wished to complete a degree in a compressed three-year curriculum, was only the second such program in the U.S. and the most recent of many accelerated programs at Pacific.

What followed were centers in the other major liberal arts divisions: the John Muir Center sharpening its focus on the Muir legacy and the Jacoby Center for Public Service and Civic Leadership on the social sciences, described in chapter six. Even as these three centers moved in different directions, they endured as forums for faculty and students to explore how the liberal arts disciplines actually interacted in society.

Steadily gaining strength were two other interdisciplinary clusters, ethnic studies and gender studies, both begun years earlier. As more diverse faculty were hired in the 1990s and 2000s, these clusters gained strength to offer a wider range of courses and special programs, like the student research conference on gender and war that became a regional draw for college students, or a forum on women's leadership, and various symposia. Ethnic studies offered an interdisciplinary minor to equip students with skills to advance "social equity, inclusive democracy, and global citizenship." The program was robust and well led over time by English professor Xiaojing Zhou. Ethnic studies provided over 50 courses offered by 33 professors spread across 14 disciplines in four schools by the 2010s.

English professor Xiaojing Zhou's ethnic studies courses had a powerful impact on many students (2002-present).

Gender studies provided an interdisciplinary minor to explore sex and gender identity in society through a dozen courses taught by 15 faculty. The program thrived for years under the able leadership of history professor Gesine Gerhardt, who then became associate dean for general education. In 2009, the gender, humanities, and ethnic studies programs joined together to form the GHES Center in the WPC for students and faculty to interact and build joint events. The high level of scholarship among faculty in these interdisciplinary programs made the centers vibrant with currency and innovation.

Forensics back in the spotlight

Through the 2000s and beyond, the new forensics coach, communication professor Marlin Bates ('96, '99), who had debated under coach Jon Schamber ('74,'75), again built a nationally competitive program starting in 2004 that nearly matched the Paul Winters era when Schamber was a star. Debate teams were consistently among the top ten in the country in the National Parliamentary Debate Association (NPDA), and other forensics teams also achieved national rankings. Standouts during these years were Jeff Toney (2006, 2009) and Kathleen Bruce (2007, 2009), each ranked 12th in the country in debate in successive years 2006-07, Steve Farias (2009, 2011), ranked

The storied national ranking of the forensics program returned to Pacific in this era with coach Marlin Bates ('96, '99 right), who debated under Jon Schamber ('74, '75, left), himself a debater for the legendary Paul Winters

12th nationally and named parliamentary debater of the Year in 2009, and William Chamberlain (2010), ranked 2nd in debate and among the top eight in extemporaneous speaking in the nation in 2010.[143]

By 2009 Pacific ranked third in overall season sweepstakes in the NPDA, the nation's largest intercollegiate debate organization. In 2013, Bates, now executive secretary of the NPDA, had Pacific hosting the largest national debate tournament in the country, the NPDA national championship tournament, with over 500 debaters from across the country. In that tournament Pacific again finished in the top ten.

DEROSA'S ACHIEVEMENT

The "Burns Effect:" Tenuous innovation

The President and provost became increasingly convinced of Burns' fundamental vision that Pacific's success would depend upon its differentiation from other regional schools. Differentiation meant inventing distinctive identities for all the schools and the College: how could Pacific capitalize on its historic pioneering character to forge new ways of accomplishing its mission through all its programs? This orientation to "distinctive programs," DeRosa's refrain for the last third of his presidency, spawned a process of innovation that led, finally, to an array of new programs that would not survive either the resources they demanded or the vision of his successor president.

One important innovation begun by DeRosa in 2007 was the social-emotional leadership development program that grew out of the 2005 board retreat and Stockton native Daniel Goleman. The board had asked the president what Pacific was doing to make "whole person learning" a distinctive strength of Pacific. DeRosa was impressed by the work of Dan Goleman, son of two Pacific professors, who had developed a wide national following for his books on social emotional intelligence. As a psychologist, DeRosa was drawn to the essential insights of research that Goleman martialed to argue for the importance of "EQ" as well as "IQ," and that emotional intelligence could be learned. He had lectured on campus in 2001, then returned as commencement speaker the next spring.

To enact his vision for Pacific to become a "national leader in whole student learning through social and emotional competency development," DeRosa funded a Center for Social and Emotional Competence to provide training and coaching for faculty and staff, stimulate joint research and offer workshops and curricula for students.[144] With the support of the provost and student life vice president, a task force of 50 faculty and staff implemented a program for students, while some developed a first-ever reliable *collegiate* measure of social-emotional competence.[145] DeRosa, sensing that he had little time to embed the program in a lasting way, formed a high-profile national board including Goleman, and pushed ahead, hiring a director for the center to coordinate teaching, research and co-curricular activities.

While the professional schools generally bought into the program, most liberal arts faculty remained skeptical. The business school was conflicted by the strong support of the social-emotional competence initiative by their very unpopular dean. The program never gained the solid footing in key academic departments to deepen faculty research and gain broad campus approval. As DeRosa began his exit, the program paused, and all it took was a reluctant new president and provost to end the social-emotional competence initiative.

Another innovation was the Global Center for Social Entrepreneurship, devised by the provost and SIS dean Ensign in 2006 to capture growing interest among young adults in non-profit entrepreneurship in an international context. A recently retired head of a highly successful local social entrepreneurship organization, Jerry Hildebrand, joined the staff and quickly became a pied piper for students from all the schools, especially undergraduates, who fed on innovation and youthful idealism to tackle societal problems.

Social entrepreneurship applied business and management skills to develop sustainable solutions through creative entrepreneurship, especially in developing countries. Soon students were engaged in internships on four continents, from microfinance and sustainable agriculture to human trafficking, eco-tourism and community-based engineering projects. A

Covell College alumnus Martin Burt ('80), student body president in 1979, became mayor of his native Paraguay's capital city and a world-renowned social entrepreneur.

three-course online Pacific certificate program was built by alumnus Martin Burt ('80), renowned Paraguayan social entrepreneur—a first in the field. The center got national attention through the robust, student-centered constellation of 20 center programs generated by Hildebrand.[146]

By 2007 DeRosa embraced what soon became a prominent University student organization of 80 students and a high-profile advisory board of successful social entrepreneurs, mostly from the Bay Area, led by regent Ron Cortes. As one of a tiny handful of emerging social entrepreneurship programs across the country, the "Global Center" quickly became known as a resource for other universities, while on the campus the SIS faculty could not embrace its activist bent.

Amid the war in Afghanistan (2001-2014), Pacific partnered with one of Pacific's most illustrious alumnae and an advisory board member, global award-winning social entrepreneur Sakena Yacoobi ('77). The University supported her groundbreaking Afghan Institute of Learning for women and girls by funding scholarships for Afghani students. Over 40 speakers from 25 countries visited campus to meet with students.

Like the social-emotional development program, social entrepreneurship was viewed by social science faculty as suspect,

Alumna Sakena Yacoobi ('77), renowned for her groundbreaking schools for girls and women in Afghanistan and Pakistan, was a well-received visitor on campus during the time of the war in Afghanistan (2001-2014).

and especially under the leadership of Hildebrand, who lacked a feel for how to integrate passionate student interest with academic programs. Provost Gilbertson recognized the divide that emerged as Hildebrand and his inspired students met a skeptical, forceful faculty. But he fed the program as a promising enterprise that combined four important University priorities: innovation, experiential learning, cross-disciplinary inquiry, and international education. Student life vice president Griego, a highly effective collaborator and community builder, also championed the initiative and integrated the program into the campus co-curricular learning agenda. Meanwhile, Cortes and other foundations funded ten student interns each summer to participate in social enterprises in developing nations and sent large delegations to President Bill Clinton's Global Initiative.[147]

Finally rejected by SIS, and lacking commitment of leaders in other academic programs who could integrate the students' experiential learning with theory and research, the project was headed for an uncertain future with the imminent departures of DeRosa, Gilbertson and Griego. Later in 2013 center director Hildebrand resigned to continue the program at the Monterey Institute of International Studies. Again, as with the social-emotional competence initiative, the failure to tie the program to committed tenured faculty with an academic champion left the program with an uncertain future. Just as President Burns had piled the University high with promising new programs of the day, but failed to secure them with financial anchors, so too these innovations had administrative champions but neither the faculty commitment and expertise nor the financial anchors to make them enduring.

The restoration of traditions

One of the surprises for DeRosa when he arrived at Pacific was the scarcity of campus traditions that typically abound at smaller private schools. Sure, there were Greek traditions and the carillon, Tommy Tiger and the Fight Song, but actual campus rituals were few. Band Frolic had just faded away, and the pageantry of football was soon absent. He sensed that one reason alumni support for Pacific was historically weak, despite alumni enthusiasm

The Pacific Pep Band was revived by music professor Eric Hammer in the 1990s to play at athletic events, including "Pacific Hail!"

for their days at Pacific, was the lack of campus-wide experiences that bonded the community in common identity as Pacificans. So he set about to build traditions, beginning with the singing of the alma mater, "Pacific Hail!", nearly forgotten because the tune was difficult if not unsingable. DeRosa insisted it be sung not only at every commencement ceremony but also at the end of each basketball game, accompanied by the Pep Band. Gradually over time the practice became part of the campus fabric.

Another new tradition was a unified commencement, which took years of effort to build both the support and the infrastructure to manage. The Friday evening commencement on Knoles Lawn was an annual embarrassment—a tiny crowd sweltering in the heat for a renowned honoree like the celebrated writer Maya Angelou (whose mother, Vivian Baxter, was a notable Stockton community activist) or movie star Janet Leigh (perhaps Pacific's most famous alumna), while graduates who could see no point in coming prior to their individual Saturday school graduation ceremonies headed out to last-night partying.

But by 2006 the President and provost had cajoled every school, including dentistry and law, to participate in a spectacular morning event in the cool Spanos Center where degrees were conferred to the graduates of each school and the College. This was followed by "Diploma and Hooding

Moving the all-University Commencement to the Alex G. Spanos Center in 2006 was a welcome "new event" for the conferring of degrees in undergraduate and graduate programs.

Ceremonies" held for all the Stockton schools and the College throughout the day. The law and dentistry school ceremonies continued to be held on other weekends. The all-school commencement event displayed another mark of the DeRosa years: a classy high-quality production, like the galas, receptions, dinners and other ceremonial events throughout the era. Every detail was attended to, and quality performances, menus and wines were part and parcel of Pacific "pride of ownership." As Dianne Philibosian remarked, DeRosa "notched up everything."

In 2003, vice president Sina persuaded a reluctant DeRosa to re-establish the tradition of an opening convocation, which had lapsed years earlier. Billed as a "Welcome Back Weekend and Frosh Convocation," all first-year students were required to attend this event in Faye Spanos Concert Hall that carried something of the pageantry of commencement events. Large, colorful school banners hung across the stage, a small voluntary faculty processed in academic regalia and the President addressed the students with a brief, inspiring history of Pacific. An alumnus, alumna or regent spoke, the provost formally inducted the students into the academic community and everyone sang "Pacific Hail!" The event was capped off with the now famous "Tiger Roar" that welcomed the freshman students as they poured out into the late August heat, the sidewalk lined by veteran

The annual freshman convocation, ending in the "Tiger Roar," has become a celebrated tradition since it was instigated in 2003.

students, alumni, staff and faculty, applauding and cheering the newest class to Pacific, stunned by the roar and celebration, on their way to an all-campus barbeque on the lawn.

The DeRosa legacy

President DeRosa did not create a new school, did not add a new campus. He never set more than seven annual goals for his office. But his success in transforming the University was arguably the most significant in its history second only to Burns. The comprehensive array of successes was overwhelming in the context of a University that had struggled to find its way for the prior quarter century. As retiring regent John Corson ('57) noted, "The transformation of Pacific from a conflicted institution without a clear sense of mission into a rigorous, mission-driven university has been an exciting journey!"[148] DeRosa's temperament, skills, interests and resolve matched what Pacific needed at the time.

First and most importantly, DeRosa deepened the mission and values of Pacific throughout his 14 years and built a vision on that mission and values. DeRosa was sensitive to and appreciative of Pacific's rich history and its value for the present. He and Monagan overcame a quarter century of uncertain direction, lack of committed leadership and a neglectful board, then moved Pacific ahead with confidence.

Second, DeRosa profoundly understood what it meant to educate "the whole person," to embrace the development of character, of responsible leadership, of physical and social growth as part of what prepares students for professional and personal fulfillment and "responsible leadership in their careers and communities," as declared in Pacific's mission

Like Judith Chambers, vice president Elizabeth Griego (2006-13) was elected president of the national student affairs association (NASPA). President DeRosa was selected for NASPA's national president's award in 2009.

statement. In 2009, he received the annual President's Award presented by the National Association of Student Personnel Administrators as the outstanding collegiate president most instrumental in advancing student affairs. Coinciding with the year that vice president Griego was elected NASPA president, Pacific was recognized as a leader in student-centered education. Anyone could see in DeRosa's record the determination to make student campus life a part of his lasting legacy and a deepened cultivation of Pacific's core identity.

Third, he professionalized the University from top to bottom. Atchley had begun that effort by clearing out dead wood and attempting to diversify the board, but undercut it with his own lack of good administrative judgment. With Monagan's leadership, DeRosa engaged the board and helped them learn their responsibilities according to best practice in higher education, with the possible important exception of its key fundraising role. His administration reviewed and reinvigorated office after office to move it from mom-and-pop operations toward best current practice in the professions. His trust, mentorship, integrity and teamwork established effective offices functioning on behalf of students. Progress was slow in some offices, and he certainly retired with more work to be done by his successor. As the first President since Knoles to bring *academic* leadership, this professionalizing effort meant improving the quality of both faculty performance and dean leadership by raising higher expectations for teaching and research.

Fourth, he broadened Pacific's base by stabilizing its finances in every dimension and vastly improved its facilities. He urged the board to address the football hemorrhage and held steady on the suspension decision based on financial evidence. He insisted on a balanced budget and counted on building annual reserves. He addressed the neglect of the endowment head-on and built it dramatically, especially through the Powell gift. He did not hesitate to take on needed facilities when there was little appetite among constituents to do so.

Fifth, he heightened Pacific's aspiration through careful planning and resolve to achieve excellence and distinctiveness through "innovation, collaboration, and interdisciplinary integration." Among the "hallmarks of distinction," he was especially proud of the excellence and distinctiveness of the dental school, the undergraduate Pacific Seminars and the Brubeck Institute. The combination of experiential learning, accelerated programs and international outreach through an unusual mix of schools collectively brought a distinctive identity that few universities could match.[149] The experiential learning guarantee in all academic programs asserted the value of practical learning. Championing accelerated programs was a key means to address the "access" issue—to insist that a Pacific education be affordable to a full spectrum of students regardless of means. By the time DeRosa left office, Pacific had 14 accelerated degree programs spread across six of its nine schools. He understood the legacy of international education that was a part of Pacific at least since the days of President Burns, and he sought to carry it forward in fresh new ways. He worked to strengthen every one of the nine schools.

Notable, finally, was the achievement of miraculously meeting a bundle of competing enrollment goals: steadily growing the undergraduate and graduate programs each by 21 percent (over 800 students), raising the academic profile of students by increasing selectivity to 40 percent of 15,000 applicants, maintaining a strong commitment to access for disadvantaged students by maximizing financial aid while moderating tuition increases and increasing net revenue.[150] This was a landmark achievement in itself, especially after the decline in both size and academic quality over the prior 25 years. In all these efforts, DeRosa exemplified many features of exceptionally successful corporate leaders analyzed in Jim Collins' and Morten Hansen's *Great By Choice*.[151]

The limitations of his administration are less obvious, but marketing, development, and community relations top the list. Marketing was never a strength among his cabinet or most of the turnstile marketing and advancement leaders who came and went. Yet for the first time in Pacific's history DeRosa corralled all the disparate visual and print identities of the schools and offices to create a consistent University "identity" and led a "branding" initiative to promote the University. But penetrating public awareness of Pacific remained a challenge to the end, and DeRosa was reluctant to invest in it. Neither he nor his provost advanced Pacific's national standing through personal leadership in higher education, either regionally or nationally, choosing to stick close to campus and build from within. Even among surveyed alumni, fewer than half could name DeRosa as president after he had served a dozen years, or mention anything he focused on as president.[152] He inherited a neglected advancement/development office that was decades behind and understaffed, but DeRosa was unable to build an effective development office, never finding quite the right leader to turn the corner, never investing sufficiently to build its infrastructure.

While bringing the San Francisco 49ers summer camp was certainly a coup that electrified the community, and he and his new leadership team advanced many community partnerships through Pacific's schools and programs, they never seriously engaged with the community in important civic leadership roles, as, for example, Judy Chambers and McCaffrey's vice president Cliff Dochterman had done. For all the talk about preparing students as "citizen leaders," the personal demonstration of that civic engagement in the city of Stockton did not develop.

While the University endowment leaped forward, endowments for specific programs languished for lack of donors or collective effort. The 2000-2007 "Investing in Excellence" campaign, despite its sensational triumph, was dampened by DeRosa's health issues. Many would cite the overall decline in athletics success after the early 2000s as a squandering of a distinct asset for Pacific. Others complained about the lack of bold, strategic advancement in information technology during this era, despite often channeling a million dollars annually to meet rising technology demands across the campuses. DeRosa kept up with students' basic needs and demands, but lacked the confidence in the technology staff to do much more. The business school and others would certainly point to presidential decisions that discouraged entrepreneurial academic programs, and his backing away from a proposed budget model to create financial incentives seemed to support that judgment.

At times his penchant for careful deliberation stood in the way of leading the University forward, such as the tardy move to join the "sustainability" movement that swept across campuses. Yet he made tough decisions in a timely way when he had to, as when he joined with the board in suspending football within months of his appointment. His holding back both his provost and his business vice president, when they were eager to make a quick decision and move ahead, was on balance, they both agreed, a positive for Pacific. The initiative to pursue innovation in the last several years suffered, as it did under Burns, by having too many irons in the fire and insufficient resources to fully launch them at a level of quality the best ones deserved.

In sum, during his first five years DeRosa rebuilt—often from the ground up—the basic structures for a solid, professional university, financially stable, based always on a clarified mission and vision determined through collective planning. In his second five years he worked to identify and sharpen the quality and distinctiveness of Pacific to differentiate it from its peers. In his final phase, DeRosa focused on ways to deepen that distinctiveness through innovation, based on Pacific's pioneering tradition. It is easy to understand why he was revered by the board and honored by all constituencies as one of Pacific's great presidents.

Eibeck's promising start

When DeRosa announced in April 2008 that he intended to step down the following year, the Regents launched a national search for a successor. The University was on solid financial footing, enjoyed stable enrollments and had built strengths in a number of academic areas. Pacific was ready for an experienced and accomplished leader to build upon the foundation of the DeRosa era. In February 2009, the board announced that it had found that leader in Pamela Eibeck.

DeRosa stayed on for one last year, and upon his retirement became President Emeritus – the first time the Board of Regents had bestowed such an honor. He continued to serve Pacific as a member of the Powell Advisory Committee and the Brubeck Institute Advisory Board, representing two of his most cherished legacies.

Eibeck was appointed Pacific's 24th president in early 2009 with a good deal of excitement and anticipation: the first woman president, a multiple graduate of Stanford, an engineering dean with an outgoing, personable, energetic personality, ready for a first presidency. When the Board of Regents appointed her among highly contested finalists, they chose a leader well experienced in California higher education—the first such president since McCaffrey, but unlike McCaffrey, one well-versed in academic culture.

While not a native Californian, Eibeck had Stanford mechanical engineering degrees and a decade as professor at UC-Berkeley doing research in heat transfer before she became department chair. She then became vice provost at Northern Arizona University while advocating for reforms in engineering education. Since 2004, she had served as dean of a massive engineering school at Texas Tech University. She had been awarded the Society of Women Engineer's Distinguished Engineering Educator Award in 1996 and Boeing's Outstanding Educator Award in 1999.

Beyond these notable credentials she brought boundless energy and a warm openness that quickly won the affection of the University community. A fit and vigorous outdoorswoman who hiked and skied, she was out daily for her morning run at 5:30 a.m. with her new golden retriever Gracie, named after Pacific's legendary Grace Covell. She was as crisp and spontaneous in the office as she was at the round of receptions she began with alumni and the community.

Like her predecessors since President Burns, she developed her leadership at large public universities, yet she came with a passion for students and their learning that matched Pacific's core commitments: teaching focused on the individual student, learning based on a zesty student-faculty interaction, and many doors to grow as a whole person. She was immediately drawn to Pacific when her youngest son Will found Pacific on the web while searching for an engineering school that "fit."

She had served on an ABET accreditation team for Pacific's School of Engineering and Computer Science a few years earlier, so she already had a taste of the campus. She knew that Pacific's student-centered education was right for her, so when she and her son Will both "applied," then both were "accepted," Will, ready to enroll at Pacific, wanted to let his mom fulfill her dream. He understandably chose a different option—Santa Clara, where DeRosa's son Michael graduated.

Pacific started the Eibeck years with more and stronger students: a record 20,000 undergraduate applications, a record freshman class that peaked at 1,010 in 2010, and a record University enrollment that peaked at 6,733 in 2011.[153] For entering first-year students in 2012, the average SAT score was a record 1200, and the high school GPA was 3.54 for the first time. Pacific had indeed become more selective.

And the campus was more diverse than ever. Over the previous two decades, the University's student body shifted from two-thirds white students to nearly 60 percent non-white students. Asian American students doubled their percentage to nearly one-third of total enrollment during those 20 years.[154] Undergraduate Latino enrollment grew modestly but steadily, while Pacific continued to be ranked by *U.S. News & World Report* among the top 25 universities for diversity.[155] Based on national research, this surge in diversity, especially at Pacific, where students reported more interaction with students of other backgrounds than their peer institutions, enhanced students' critical thinking and problem-solving skills and increased their community engagement.[156] Graduates of 2013 witnessed an historic event at commencement when seven Japanese American students who were forced to leave Pacific in 1942 (described in Chapter 2) were awarded honorary degrees, six of them posthumously. Ida Takagishi Inouye, age 91, was the one living alumna to receive her degree.[157]

Starting her presidency in the depths of the Great Recession, Eibeck announced that part of her first-year "listening campaign" would focus on the city of Stockton. At this time, one-fourth of all Pacific undergraduates came from San Joaquin County. In her inaugural address in March 2010, Eibeck announced "community" as her theme, from campus to globe. Calling her civic partnership "Beyond Our Gates," she marshaled staff

President Pamela Eibeck immediately launched her "Beyond Our Gates" civic partnership with Stockton mayor Ann Johnston and other civic leaders in 2010 to signal a renewed partnership to advance Stockton.

to coordinate six public forums on top city issues: education, the economy, healthcare, energy and the environment, diversity, and arts and culture. With enthusiasm she launched her "listening campaign" with great success.

Pacific's impact in the community was profound: the Stockton Campus was the second largest private employer in San Joaquin County and the fifth largest overall. A "Community Impact" report based on 2008 data showed direct University expenditures amounted to $326 million annually, which supported nearly 5,000 jobs and produced $736 million in sales.[158] The report also logged over a hundred community partnerships and programs across the three campuses. From continuing education for 23,000 people, to clinical services for 14,000 citizens, to research in law, health, and international affairs, Pacific demonstrated impact. Accenting this economic impact, Eibeck set a policy to give preference to local vendors for needed services.

In a sign of increasingly visible support for the community, Pacific held a party for the city on the University Center lawn around a giant screen to witness the launch of regent Jose Hernandez in the NASA Space Shuttle Discovery in August 2009. Though the launch itself was delayed a few days because of rain, it never dampened the party in Stockton.

A number of challenges awaited Eibeck's administration. The U.S. housing price bubble of 2006 had become the credit crisis and housing foreclosure collapse of 2007, cascading into the massive economic breakdown of the 2007-09 Great Recession. Because Stockton-Modesto was the nation's center of the housing mortgage collapse, the recession inflicted more loss in economic value in the Central Valley than the Great Depression of the 1930s.[159] Almost solely dependent on student tuition dollars amid a broken global economy—and facing stiff competition for students from California private university competitors and online delivery systems that were rapidly changing the face of American higher education—the University was vulnerable. National economic distress was beginning to impact enrollment.

As well, in an era when undergraduates had never lived without the internet, reconciling online learning with personal interaction was a major challenge for all teaching-centered institutions, including Pacific. Concerns about environmental sustainability also arose, prompting not just campus recycling but also investments in energy savings and transitions to a "paperless" dental clinic.

Although the University plan, *Pacific Rising, 2008-2015,* had just been adopted by the board in 2007, many issues indicated that a new planning process was needed: the rapidly changing higher education environment, the woeful state of the economy, the decline in federal and state student aid dollars, the rising sense of public accountability for student success, the shrinking pool of high school graduates as the adult learner population grew, the softening support of families for private higher education whose cost was outstripping its value, and students' ravenous expectations for accessible technology-rich learning.

In response, Eibeck launched a planning process that culminated in a new strategic plan, *Pacific 2020: Excelling in a Changing Higher Education Environment. Pacific 2020* set the course to expand academic programs built on historic strength in the health sciences and to deliver them to "new students in new ways, leveraging our three-city presence." Throughout the process, Eibeck was transparent about decisions. She posted frequent speeches and letters on her website for all to read and view. The degree of openness was unprecedented.

MATURITY ACHIEVED

The board and president partnership

The development of the modern Pacific, beginning with its move to Stockton, demonstrated the powerful impact that a strong president coupled with a strong board chair could have to advance the University. As noted in earlier chapters, while the Board of Regents was disengaged and at times simply neglectful in the early decades of the Stockton era, the saving grace was a solid chair in partnership with a vibrant president. Across the country, this pattern of strong leadership between board chair and president bypassing a detached group of regents was more common than not through the eras up to the 1960s. President Knoles had the steady wisdom and diplomacy of Rolla Watt (1919-26) and forceful Thomas Baxter (1926-1941), who may have made all the difference in the early success of Pacific in Stockton. President Burns' close partnership with Ted Baun (1953-71) intensified the leverage those leaders could have in transforming Pacific from a small liberal arts college to a university at a time of great growth in American higher education, despite a lagging board.

The severe challenges of the McCaffrey and Atchley years perhaps proved the point: that without a close trusting partnership and shared vision between president and chair, it was difficult to move a complex institution ahead. Chair Eberhardt had difficult relationships with both presidents. The commanding DeRosa and Monagan partnership (1994-2003) restored that relationship and got Pacific back on track, again turning around Pacific just in time to avoid an intractable decline. Philibosian and DeRosa brought greater transparency and increased board engagement on key issues based on their "trust, understanding, and collaboration."[160]

As of the writing of this history, President Eibeck enjoyed a close partnership with board chair Kathleen Janssen, and both were proving to be strong.[161] Significantly different from the past, however, was that Eibeck's partnership was really with the board, not simply with the chair. Throughout the DeRosa era, the capacity of the board increased substantially with the introduction of "best practices" and of term limits leading to a broader range of regents. The board itself selected regents more systematically to reflect a diversity of backgrounds, skills, and experiences, including many more members who had leadership track records in business or professional organizations sharing the complexity of a university. Ethnic and gender diversity remained a challenge, as it did for nearly every private university board, but progress was made.[162] Progress on philanthropy was less clear. Over time, these changes led to an increasingly capable and engaged board that developed a solid working relationship with DeRosa. But there is evidence that the DeRosa-Monagan partnership and a few other regent insiders kept many regents at arm's length when needed, even avoiding documentation behind key decisions. When Eibeck joined them, the full board was ready for active engagement, and she welcomed it.

The gradual and delayed process of board maturity is a key theme of this history. In the Eibeck era, there was greater alertness to transparency, to shared leadership, to collective decision-making unprecedented in Pacific's modern history. As regent Connie Callahan observed, Eibeck respected each regent's expertise and engaged it—and expected hard work from all of them. She called on the board to focus on its culture rather than

The Board of Regents focused more on academic programs than in some prior eras.

its structure, on long-term strategic thinking over strategic planning.[163] The board streamlined committees and shortened its meetings to focus on policy and strategy, not reports. New regent orientation was rigorous, and Eibeck nearly always included background readings on national best practices for regents with board meeting agendas. Eibeck welcomed regent input frequently; all board decisions at least went through the board's executive committee, which now met monthly. Through all these notch-ups, the board became increasingly task-oriented, nimble, and accomplished. All Pacificans can be gratified to know that the present era featured the most engaged, effective, and focused Board of Regents in its history.

CHAPTER 8

The Pacific community: Stronger than ever

Ask Pacific alumni what was special about their time at Pacific and they will tell you quite a consistent story: It's all about personal attention; great and lasting friendships, often including professors; the academic challenge

Individual attention to students is one of the hallmarks of Pacific. Shown here are law professor John Myers, political science professor Cynthia Ostberg, and dentistry professor Cindy Lyon (center right) with their students.

of great professors who insisted on quality in teaching and learning; a friendly and beautiful campus, whether in Stockton, Sacramento, or San Francisco; the focus on their development as individual persons in a holistic education; the mentoring by faculty and staff; and solid preparation for careers and professions.

Most of these special traits of Pacific might be shared with some smaller colleges, but they were remarkably uncommon for schools the size of Pacific and larger. Most notable was that this faculty commitment to students prevailed even through the turbulent years, 1971-1995.

But the history of Pacific turns out to be more than these common threads of attention to individual student learning and development that run back over 150 years. The following, too, are central themes that emerge from this saga of a most unusual university in the west, themes that serve as a kind of evolving DNA for the University:

- A plucky *spirit of innovation* that created opportunities all along the way, from the first decision to enroll women students to the more recent accelerated programs to make Pacific more affordable. Some might say that Pacific was less the pioneering university on the leading edge of changes in higher education than an inventive California school "going it alone," that Pacific was creating novel practical solutions for its own survival or success that other schools would not emulate, such as the Stockton College partnership or acquiring professional schools in neighboring cities. Whether as pioneer or lone venturer, Pacific used innovation well to realize its potential, often at critical junctures when even survival was the tension of tomorrow. When Pacific chose to be bold, its nimbleness enabled it to move swiftly to regain its footing and thrust ahead.

- The gradual *rise from utter poverty* through its first century, to reasonable survival from the mid-1940s to the turn of the 21st century, then a significant gain in endowment growth and prosperity that at least placed the school more competitively with its private peers. It appears that the fundamental reason Pacific had not been able to vault forward in quality and prominence was not owing to a lack of boldness, but rather the lack of resources to make leading-edge actions enduring and of sufficient quality.

- A strong dose of *over-reaching ambition*—perhaps a corollary of the first two traits—that set unrealistic aims given its sparse resources, from its early forays into professional schools to intercollegiate football dreams. This impulse, especially under certain leaders, put Pacific in tension with a practical realism that continually called the University back to its modest bankroll.

- The gradual shaping of an *identity as a comprehensive university* that only became clear in the 1980s, after the cluster college experiments ended. Becoming a university was its original intent for its first 50 years, demonstrated initially by starting a medical school in 1858, but that intent was lost when poverty slowed momentum. Pacific then conceded itself to be a small liberal arts college for a half century, lasting until the Burns' transformation of Pacific into what today is commonly called a "comprehensive university" beginning in the 1950s.

- The *centrality of the liberal arts college*, even when it was challenged most in the 1950s and 1960s as the transformation to a university was taking place. The impact of its leavening—from the values of civil discourse in a respectful community that presided over bumpy times, to the "citizen leader" themes that defined University-wide learning outcomes in recent years—has never stopped strengthening the quality, stature and success of all the professional schools, despite its modest enrollment and occasional self-doubt.

- The *development of the Board of Regents to maturity*, from a parochial, detached, rubber-stamp board into a diverse, active, engaged and accountable group of leaders, especially since 1995. The rapid turnover of members in the nineteenth century suggests that the Board was a significant challenge in the early years, and it is clear that through the first 70 years in Stockton, the board was unable either to set appropriate aspirations or fulfill its obligations.

- The gradual but certain *loosening of ties with the Methodist church,* especially since the formal ending of church sponsorship in 1969. Like so many institutions, Pacific's heritage has been a mixed blessing: the Methodists provided the core values of whole student learning, increasing inclusiveness built on social justice, and a commitment to service in its communities (begun through the Anderson Y in the early 20th century) that still abide at Pacific. But the church, at times at cross-purposes, held back Pacific from a balanced student social life and from building a broader partnership with the region for success, especially in fundraising.

- *A readiness to claim northern California as its campus,* beginning with Pacific's San Francisco medical school in 1858, right on up to the present aspiration to expand its academic footprint in Sacramento and San Francisco. This inclination was motivated partly by entrepreneurial expansion and partly by a commitment to community building beyond the campus—to be an important player in the development of a state whose chronology paralleled the University's.

- The *migration of Pacific from the South Bay to the Central Valley,* a tremendous shaping influence on the development of the institution. As

Pacific's Burns Tower is one of Stockton's iconic images—everyone knows where it is and what it stands for.

with the Methodist tie, the location of the main campus in Stockton has been an anchor of Pacific's success—especially in the early decades of the last century—and a weight slowing its progress, again like the church, especially in financial support. The city has never been quite large or robust enough to help lift Pacific to the competitive level of most other peer private universities in the state, all located in much larger cities.

- *A genuine sense of community among faculty, staff, students and alumni* on each of its three campuses, built on mutual respect and genuine friendliness. The Pacific community has been largely free of the divisive factions or chronic divisions common on many campuses, and it often expressed itself in volunteer outreach to its surrounding communities. This strong bond of community fostered faculty collaboration across departments and schools to an unusual degree, which is one reason why the general education program has achieved national distinction and the University's common learning outcomes were so readily affirmed.

Eddie LeBaron, here at his induction into the Half Century Club at the 2011 commencement, remained a Pacific icon throughout his life of high achievement.

- A steady *growth as an inclusive learning community* based on social justice, beginning with women students, then the early championing of slavery abolition and protection of Asian immigrants, to the creation of the Community Involvement Program in 1969 and steadily opening up to all expressions of inclusion from the 1990s to the present. Pacific has consistently raised aspirations and opened pathways for students of disadvantaged backgrounds.

- A *sports history noted for its storied, unique achievements* in football, its unmatched triumphs in women's volleyball, and its successes in men's basketball. Many other sports have been notable, marked by over 180 All-American honors and Olympic players.

Alumni never forget the sweet memories. . .

- *Affectionate alumni who treasure their Pacific experience,* over time and through thick and thin. While Pacific alumni's gratitude has often exceeded their philanthropy, that was certainly partly a consequence of the University's uneven connection with alumni over many decades, and also perhaps an expression of a state not known for its citizens' patronage of private higher education.

- Remarkable *alumni leadership in professional service to the citizens of California and beyond* for many decades, especially in dentistry, law, pharmacy, and education. The rising achievement of Pacific's professional schools, grounded in preparing the professional practitioner and in fostering leadership at all levels, is in large measure the reason Pacific has grown in success as a university over the last half century.

While these themes may overlap, they especially speak to each other, helping to understand Pacific's powerful progress over time, its peculiar strengths and liabilities, its triumphs and setbacks. Readers may well discern others to add to the list.

The promise

The One Word project, invented by Pacific and then adopted by other universities, asked students to select one word to capture their personal essence to accompany their photo portrait. Students invited president Eibeck to join in when she arrived. She quickly chose her word: community, the key theme of her inaugural address. "Community," she reflected, "brings

President Eibeck joined the One Word project for undergraduates and chose community to capture her personal essence. Student Gerald Jones (2012) chose focus.

power to a common purpose." And the One Word project itself seemed to capture the common purpose of Pacific, its devotion to the growth of the individual student, a commitment to treat each one with dignity and care. As Eibeck added, "Our Pacific community is transforming the world, one student at a time."[1] A community focused on the human development of the individual person.

A San Francisco graduate will never forget the magnificent ivory vistas of everyone's favorite city glimmering out the windows of the Webster Street building, nor will a Sacramento student lose the vivid memory of those pristine emerald afternoons on the quad, amid the towering redwoods and volleyball play. A Stockton campus student will keep forever the glow

Pacific's three campuses are all memorable places that transformed thousands of student lives.

Pacific continues to aspire to be a great university, building on a rich heritage, ever pioneering its future.

of the old central quad, surrounded by stately gothic buildings, shaded by sycamores and redwoods protecting the rose garden, sliding through the wet lawns or meditating on the benches to the Tower carillon tunes. Student time at Pacific was different because the people and the places were a world away from the public university factories. Lives changed here, amid beauty and a caring community that challenged you to strive.

However many decades pass, the Pacific Experience will be carried forward in every living graduate, with gratitude for the rich history of sacrifice that sustained this experience decade upon decade, with admiration for the spunk and invention of this school, regularly adapting itself to assure that every student from any background is served "a superior, student-centered learning experience integrating liberal arts and professional education and preparing individuals for lasting achievement and responsible leadership in their careers and communities."

That little band we now call a "community of learners" that began in Santa Clara in 1851 has continued right into the twenty-first century, with abundant tools for learning undreamed of a century and a half ago. Pacific has remained faithful to a learning community sized for personal interaction, protective of faculty who enable passionate learning with individual students, one that builds a lasting bond of friendships and loyalties. But Pacific has also been faithful to a rich tradition of innovation, a pioneer in the west for more inclusive, more varied, more responsive educational options for students. It is a grand heritage. Every Pacific graduate should be proud of this heritage and proud that Pacific is now a stronger university than it has ever been.

The trajectory of Pacific since 1995 has been steadily upward, despite occasional setbacks. University of the Pacific may be ready to move to that edge of greatness it has always aspired to, but it most assuredly has come a great distance from the other edge, the edge of mediocrity and dysfunction that in the past pointed to decline. The vigilance to rigorous student learning, to community building, to mutual trust among leaders with integrity—the constant attentiveness to excellence and striving to perform better cannot falter for a school built on core values that draws diverse students to invest family income for their education. The real test ahead for Pacific is to blend the best of Pacific's student-centered heritage with forward-looking programs that make it stand out from the crowd. Pacific is well on its way. May that pioneering spirit that thrust Pacific to the leading edge continue to lift her forward.

APPENDIX 1

Interview List

Note: The author personally interviewed the following individuals 2009-14. Many more alumni were interviewed by members of the student research team.

ALUMNI

BIDDIG, Bill
BLAIR, Bob & Dolly
BOYLAND, Rickey
BROWN, Jonathan
DeRICCO, Lawrence
HINRICHS, Marguerite
HOLT, Inez Sheldon
HONEY, Tom
ISETTI, Ron
IVY, Norma
JEWELL, James
JONES, William
KNOLES, George
LE BARON, Eddie
MARZETTE, Russell
MORK, Kenneth
MUHAMMAD, Tommie Ware
MULLER, Alfred
PARSONS, Kendall
PROCOPE, Danielle

FACULTY/STAFF/ ADMINISTRATORS

BAUTISTA, Anita
BENEDETTI, Robert
BEAUCHAMP, Ken
BECK, Lynn
BETZ, Helen
BIGLER, Gene
BREHM, Larry
BRENNAN, Dennis
BROWNE, Gwenn
CAPLAN, Gerald
CAVANAUGH, Pat
CHAMBERS, Dave
CHAMBERS, Judith
CHILDS, Roy
CICCOLELLA, Peg
CLAWSON, Elmer
DASH, Bob
DAY, Patrick
DEMPSEY, Cedric
De ROSA, Don
Di FRANCO, Roland
DOCHTERMAN, Cliff
DUGONI, Art
EIBECK, Pamela
ELLIS, Ben
FAIRBROOK, Paul
FENNELL, Lee
FERRILLO, JR., Patrick
FILIPPONE, Dee
FLETCHER, David
FLORIDDIA, Don
FOX, Lynn
FRADEN, Rena
FREITAS, Koreen
GARCIA-SHEETS, Maria
GOINS, Mike
GRIEGO, Elizabeth
HALL, Darlene
HAMERNIK, Robert
HANNON, Roseann
HEATON, Scott
ISETTI, Duane
JACOBSON, Steve
JAIN, Ravi
KING, Lynn
LaBRACK, Bruce
LARK, Neil
LEHN, Ira
LELAND, Ted

MARKS, Jesse
MASON-GREGORY, Beth
MATUSZAK, Alice Jean
McCAFFREY, Beth
McNEAL, Dale
MEDFORD, Les
MEREDITH, Larry
MEYER, Doris
MILLER, Sally
MILLERICK, Mike
MORGALI, Jim
MUSKAL, Fred
NACCARATO, Tim
NIELSEN, David
NOSSE, Carl
OPPENHEIMER, Phillip
PARKER, Elizabeth Rindskopf
PEARSON, Gene
PHILLIPS, John
PIPER, Pearl
PLOVNICK, Mark
PUTNAM, Gary
REINELT, Herbert
ROHWER, Claude
ROSSON, Peggy
SANCHEZ, Dede
SAROYAN, Ralph
SCULLY, Jed
SCULLY, Glee
SMITH, Cortlandt
SMITH, Reuben
SORBY, Don
SPIRO, Cindy
SPREER, Larry
STUBBS, Tom
SUBBIONDO, Joe
SYLVESTER, Ray
THOMAS, Darrell
TOCCHINI, John
VAN HOUTEN, Marty
WELCH, Brigid
WHITEKER, Roy
WILLIAMS, John
WINTERBERG, Bob
WINTERS, Paul
WULFMAN, Carl

REGENTS

BARTON, Hugh
BLOOM, Charles
CALLAHAN, Connie
DAVIES, JR., Paul
EBERHARDT, Douglass
EBERHARDT, Mary
ERES, Tom
JANSSEN, Kathleen
LEATHERBY, Russell
McCARGO, Jim
MONAGAN, Ione (spouse)
NELSON, Fredric
PHILIBOSIAN, Dianne
PODESTO, Gary
REDIG, Dale
REDMOND, Ron
SMITH, Don
SPIEKERMAN, Nancy

COMMUNITY

ANDERSON, Alice
DARRAH, Jim
FITZGERALD, Mike
FONG, Robert
MAXWELL, Bill
REA, Dave & Liz
RUHSTALLER, Tod

APPENDIX 2

Presidents, 1852-2015

Edward Bannister (Principal)	1852-1854
Martin C. Briggs	1854-1856
William J. Maclay	1856-1857
Alexander S. Gibbons	1857-1859
Edward Bannister	1859-1867
Thomas H. Sinex	1867-1872
Alexander S. Gibbons	1872-1877
C.C. Stratton	1877-1887
A.C. Hirst	1887-1891
Isaac Crook	1891-1893
Wesley C. Sawyer (Acting)	1893-1894
James N. Beard	1894-1896
Eli McClish	1896-1906
Moses S. Cross (Acting)	1906-1908
William W. Guth	1908-1913
Bert J. Morris (Acting)	1913-1914
John L. Seaton	1914-1919
Tully C. Knoles	1919-1946
Robert E. Burns	1946-1971
Alistair McCrone (Acting)	1971-1971
Stanley E. McCaffrey	1971-1987
Clifford Hand (Acting)	1981-1982
Bill L. Atchley*	1987-1995
Donald V. DeRosa	1995-2009
Pamela A. Eibeck	2009-

*Executive vice president Horace Fleming briefly served as acting president during Atchley's illness.

APPENDIX 3

Key: (date)=unverified, h= honorary, e= emeritus, of=officer only
There is no data for 1872, 1871, 1862, 1859, and pre-1857.

Board of Regents Chronological, 1851-2014			
Name of Board Member	**Dates of Board**	**Earliest**	**Latest**
Corwin, James	1851-1856	1851	1856
Aram, Joseph Captain	(1851) 1857-1870	1857	1870
Bigler, John	(1856) 1857-1858 (1859)	1857	1858
Blain, J.D.	(1856) 1857-1866	1857	1866
Bland, Adam	(1856) 1857-1870	1857	1870
Briggs, Martin C.	(1851) of1857-of1861, 1863-1870, 1876-1891	1857	1891
Buffington, John M.	(1856) 1857-1858 (1859)	1857	1858
Gibbons, Henry	(1856) 1857-1858 (1859)	1857	1858
Headen, B.F.	(1856) 1857-1860, of1861-of1863, 1864-1874	1857	1874
Lent, William M.	(1852-1856) 1857-1860	1857	1860
Maclay, Charles	(1851) 1857-1861, of1863, 1864-1873	1857	1873
McLean, John T. Dr.,	(1851) 1857-1875	1857	1875
Merrill, Annis, Esq.	(1851) 1857, 1863-1894	1857	1894
Owen, Isaac	(1851) 1857-1864	1857	1864
Phillips, G.S.	(1856) 1857-1858, of1860	1857	1860
Simonds, S.D.	(1851-1856) 1857-1864	1857	1864
Taylor, William	(1851) 1857-1860	1857	1860
Thomas, Eleazer	(1856) 1857-1870 (1871) & 1873	1857	1873
Gibbons, A.S.	1858, 1873-1877	1858	1877
Benson, Henry C.	1860-1863, 1870-1894	1860	1894
Maclay, William J.	(1859) 1860-1874	1860	1874
Morison, J.	1860-1861 (1862)	1860	1861
Peck, Jesse T.	1860-1861, of1863, 1864	1860	1864
Saxe, A.W.	of1860, 1861-1870 & 1873	1860	1873
Webb, Captain G.S.	(1859) 1860-1861 (1862)	1860	1861
Bannister, E.	(1851) of1861-1870	1861	1870
Jacks, David	1861-1889	1861	1889
Thomas, J.B.	1861-1870	1861	1870
Cooper, E.S.	1863	1863	1863
Cole, R. Beverly	1864-1869	1864	1869

Name of Board Member	Dates of Board	Earliest	Latest
Widney, Robert M.	of1864	1864	1864
Pomeroy, A.E.	of1866, 1870-1880, 1882-1883	1866	1883
Ross, J.W.	1866-1873	1866	1873
Baker, G.R.	of1868, of1869	1868	1869
Bidwell, John	1868-1869	1868	1869
Hines, J.W.	of1868, 1902-1912	1868	1912
Pierce, J.P.	1868-1869	1868	1869
Sinex, T.H.	1868-1876, of1877, of1878, 1880-1887, 1889-1894	1868	1894
Barris, A.	1870-1875	1870	1875
Bailey, A.M.	of1873	1873	1873
Davis, Schuyler	1873-1875	1873	1875
Dennett, Wesley	1873-1875	1873	1875
Spence, Edwin T.	1873	1873	1873
Afflerbach, C.H.	1874-1885	1874	1885
Hinds, J.W.	(1870-1873) 1874-1885	1874	1885
Jewell, F.F.	(1870-1873) 1874-1899	1874	1899
Moore, E.	(1870 & 1873) 1874-1875	1874	1875
Harrison, G.S.	1875	1875	1875
Hough, A.M.	1875 -1877	1875	1877
Widney, John	1875-1894	1875	1894
Baker, G.F.	1876-1877	1876	1877
Bohl, Peter	1876-1894, 1900	1876	1900
Clayton, James A.	1876-1894	1876	1894
Wythe, J.H.	1876-1878	1876	1878
Zuck, James C.	1876-1878, 1895-1907	1876	1907
Stratton, C.C.	1877-1888	1877	1888
Bowman, G.B.	1878-1889	1878	1889
Todd, E.S.	1878-1880	1878	1880
Whiting, J.W.	1878-1894	1878	1894
Davisson, R.G.	1879	1879	1879
Forderer, J.F.	1897-1915	1879	1915
Rogers, W.H.	1879-1882	1879	1882
George, T.C.	of1880-of1889	1880	1889
Gober, W.R.	1881-1883	1881	1883
Richards, John E.	1883-1887, 1927-1932	1883	1932
Goodall, Charles	1884-1894	1884	1894

Name of Board Member	Dates of Board	Earliest	Latest
Sims, J.R.	1884-1886	1884	1886
Greeley, Justus	1886-1894	1886	1894
Playter, E.W.	1886-1892	1886	1892
Gibson, W.F.	1887-1895	1887	1895
Fowler, Henry	(1870-1873) 1888-1892	1888	1892
Hirst, A.C.	1888-1894	1888	1894
Afflerbach, C.N.	1890-1895	1890	1895
Kirk, Theophilus	1890-1892, 1898-1901	1890	1901
Krafft, L.P.	1891-1894	1891	1894
Evans, S.C., Jr.	1893-1898	1893	1898
McClish, Eli	1893-1907	1893	1907
Truman, I. J.	1893-1918	1893	1918
Beard, J.N.	1895, 1897	1895	1897
Bland, H.M.	1895-1897	1895	1897
Bovard, F.D.	1895	1895	1895
Buck, M.D.	1895-1904	1895	1904
Cantine, R.S.	1895-1897	1895	1897
Coyle, John	1895-1897	1895	1897
Dennett, E.P.	1895-1897	1895	1897
Dille, E.R.	1895-1933	1895	1933
Filben, Thomas	1895-1911	1895	1911
French, Henry	1895-1900	1895	1900
Grigsby, J.W.	1895-1899	1895	1899
Hart, R.G.	1895-1897	1895	1897
Hayes, D.A.	1895-1896	1895	1896
Heacock, H.B.	1895-1915	1895	1915
Holden, S.E.	1895-1900	1895	1900
Husband, Robert	1895-1896	1895	1896
Kellogg, George D.	1895-1920	1895	1920
Kummer, Alfred	1895	1895	1895
Leiter, Jere	1895-1923	1895	1923
MacChesney, T.C.	1895-1911	1895	1911
McCreary, E.D.	1895-1897	1895	1897
Needham, A.H.	1895-1910	1895	1910
Norton, L.J.	1895-1902	1895	1902
Percy, John A.	1895-1928	1895	1928
Perkins, C.B.	1895-1896, 1905-1910, 1916-1918	1895	1918

Name of Board Member	Dates of Board	Earliest	Latest
Tool, S.M.	1895-1896	1895	1896
Watt, Rolla V.	1895-1926	1895	1926
Willis, E.R.	1895-1911	1895	1911
Woodward, T.H.	1895-1900	1895	1900
Hutchinson, T.B.	1896-1904	1896	1904
Kingsbury, Helen Mrs.	1896-1900	1896	1900
Patton, J.R.	1896-1897	1896	1897
Stephens, H.W.	1896-1898	1896	1898
Welch, J.R.	1896	1896	1896
Blauer, H.	1897-1898	1897	1898
Holcomb, Myron T.	1897-1898	1897	1898
Kuns, H.L.	1897-1905	1897	1905
Newman, John P.	1897-1899	1897	1899
Bailey, C.P.	1898-1909	1898	1909
Brush, J.H.	1898-1918	1898	1918
Case, W.W.	1898-1903	1898	1903
Richardson, Alpheus	1898-1900	1898	1900
Tantau, Fred	1898-1900	1898	1900
Turner, Theodore	1898-1905	1898	1905
Turpin, F. L.	1898-1914	1898	1914
Evans, W.C.	1899-1905, 1908-1915	1899	1915
Hanson, A.J.	1899-1911	1899	1911
Sheppard, Joseph	1900-1904	1900	1904
Williamson, H.E.	1900-1918	1900	1918
Wilson, John A.B.	1900-1903	1900	1903
Crummey, D.C.	1901-1928	1901	1928
Lewis, J.R.	1901-1907	1901	1907
Taylor, Volney	1901-1909	1901	1909
Hestwood, J.O.	1902-1911	1902	1911
Tyrrell, R.S.	1902	1902	1902
Wenk, R.E.	1902-1911	1902	1911
Bell, H.H.	1903-1910	1903	1910
Brace, Henry	1903-1908	1903	1908
Hayes, E.A.	1904-1909	1904	1909
Wilson, Carl G.	1904-1909	1904	1909
Milnes, H.E.	1905-1944	1905	1944
Osborne, J.H.	1905	1905	1905

Name of Board Member	Dates of Board	Earliest	Latest
Collins, E.S.	1907-1909	1907	1909
Dennett, L.L.	1907-1909	1907	1909
Goseby, P.F.	1907-1915	1907	1915
Hutsinpiller, S.D.	1907-1911	1907	1911
French, W.G.	1908-1910	1908	1910
White, G.W.	1908-1924	1908	1924
Hughes, E.H.	1909-1910, 1916-1918	1909	1918
Gilman, G.D.	1910-1943	1910	1943
Hamilton, J.W.	1901-1908	1910	1908
Briggs, A.H. Dr.	1912-1934	1912	1934
Hale, R.B.	1912-1915	1912	1915
Stratton, R.T. Dr.	1912-1924	1912	1924
Williams, E.S.	1913-1914	1913	1914
Dunn, C. H.	1915-1925	1915	1925
Jacoby, O.D.	1915-1967, h1968-h1972	1915	1972
Holden, R.S.	1916-1918	1916	1918
Hopkins, M.F. Dr.	1916-1927	1916	1927
Hotle, W.M.	1916-1960, h1962-h1966	1916	1966
Kirkbride, C.N.	1916-1950	1916	1950
Pearson, G.L.	1916-1923	1916	1923
Stephens, John	1916-1929	1916	1929
Warner, Carl M.	1916-1944	1916	1944
Burcham, J.L.	1917-1939; h1940-h41, e1942-e1947	1917	1947
Childs, C.E.	1917-1924	1917	1924
Kern, F.W.	1917-1918	1917	1918
Leonard, A.W.	1917-1924	1917	1924
Parmalee, C.A.	1917-1926	1917	1926
Van Allen, L.K.	1917-1928	1917	1928
Waste, William H.	1917-1930 & 1933-1939	1917	1939
Batchelor, J.A.	1918-1924	1918	1924
Morrish, W.F.	1919-1929 & 1937-1944	1919	1937
Williams, B.J.	1919-1933	1919	1933
Williamson, H.E. Mrs.	1919-1943	1919	1943
Brown, Homer C.	1920-1948	1920	1948
Bane, Adam Clark	1922-1940	1922	1940
Crummey, John D.	1922-1959, h1960- h1972	1922	1972
Holt, Benjamin Mrs. Anna	1922-1949, h1950-h1952	1922	1952

Name of Board Member	Dates of Board	Earliest	Latest
Kelly, Roy Dr.	1922-1928	1922	1928
Anderson, W.C.	1923-1940	1923	1940
Harris, George H.	1923-1934	1923	1934
McCallum, J.H.	1923-1942	1923	1942
Turner, Henry G.	1923-1934	1923	1934
Wallace, Ben C.	1923-1962 & h1964-h1966	1923	1966
Wilhoit, E.L.	1923-1951, h1952-h1960	1923	1960
Wilhoit, George Mrs. Jessie	1924-1938	1924	1938
Burns, Charles Wesley	1925-1932	1925	1932
Baxter, Thomas F.	1926-1941	1926	1941
Richardson, Grace C. (*aka* Grace M. Carter, Mrs. Leslie V. Richardson)	of1926-of1942, 1942-1960, h1962-h1966	1926	1966
Watt, Rolla V. Mrs.	1926-1939	1926	1939
Jackson, Harriet Mrs. Charles	1927-1948	1927	1948
Pierce, Lyman L.	1928-1940	1928	1940
Shurtleff, Charles A.	1928-1941	1928	1941
Smith, Charles A.	1928-1932	1928	1932
Truman, Charles H. J.	1928-1940	1928	1940
Hawke, E.R.	1929-1941	1929	1941
Hale, Marshall	1931	1931	1931
Segerstrom, Charles	1931-1947	1931	1947
Baker, James C.	1932-1959, h1960-h1968	1932	1969
Matthews, Alfred	1932-1944	1932	1944
Mills, Edward Laird Dr.	1933-1940	1933	1940
Morris, Percy F.	1933-1943	1933	1943
Hamilton, Hugh K. Dr.	1934-1954, h1956-h1964	1934	1964
Sylvester, C.B.	1934-1955, h1956-h1964	1934	1964
Lowther, E.A.	1935-1955, h1956	1935	1956
Fricot, D.	1937-1940	1937	1940
Kenney, John Dr.	1939-1955	1939	1955
Gearhart, A.W.	1940-1952	1940	1952
Morris, William E.	1940-1956	1940	1956
Pruner, Alstyne E..	1940-1976	1940	1976
Warmer, George A.	1940-1949	1940	1949
Berger, Jess A.	1941-1968	1941	1968
Davies, Paul Mrs. Faith	1941-1980	1941	1980

Name of Board Member	Dates of Board	Earliest	Latest
Marks, Fillmore	1941-1950	1941	1950
Parr, Fred D.	1941-1946, 1948-1952	1941	1952
Wilson, George H.	1941-1988	1941	1988
Chatters, Ford	1942-1963	1942	1963
Christensen, N.A.	1942-1950	1942	1950
Hole, J. Wesley	1943-1948	1943	1948
James, Stanley	1943-1962	1943	1962
Lange, Harry W.	1944-1972	1944	1972
Morris, Lillie Mrs. Percy	1944-1954, h1956-h1972	1944	1972
Wood, Clyde	1944-1953	1944	1953
Yates, John W.	1944-1957	1944	1957
Harvey, Gerald B. Dr.	1945-1956	1945	1956
Berry, Lowell W.	1946-1954	1946	1954
Le Roque, Noel C.	1946-1949 & 1968-1986	1946	1986
Griffin, Robert M.	1948 -1949	1948	1959
Jespersen, Harry V.	1948-1967	1948	1967
Armacost, Marion	1949-1953	1949	1953
Clay, Russell E.	1949-1954	1949	1954
Orvis, William	1949-1964	1949	1964
Tippett, Donald H.	1949-1973	1949	1973
Toothaker, Frank	1949-1951	1949	1951
Weaver, Roy Mrs.	1949-1956	1949	1956
Baun, Ted F.	1951-1994	1951	1994
Grove, Elois Mrs.	of1951	1951	1951
Hamman, K.L.	1951-1952	1951	1952
Kesterson, Irving	1951-1956 & h1957-h1958	1951	1958
Saeker, Alice	of1952-of1972	1952	1972
Tiss, Wayne	1952-1954	1952	1954
Wagner, Clarence R. Dr.	1952-1960	1952	1960
Eberhardt, R.L.	1953-1963	1953	1963
Hornage, Simpson	1953- 1969	1953	1969
Kennedy, Gerald	1953-1972	1953	1972
Laird, Francis N.	1953-1956	1953	1956
Prewitt, C. Russell Dr.	1953-1965	1953	1965
Brewer, Gene C.	1954-1958	1954	1958
Rutherford, Newton	1954-1957	1954	1957
Thurman, Arthur V.	1954-1981	1954	1981

Name of Board Member	Dates of Board	Earliest	Latest
Covell, Grace A.	1955-1958, h1964-h1972	1955	1972
Gainsborough, Louis P.	1955-1958	1955	1958
Orton, Hubert E.	1955-1972	1955	1972
Price, Chalmers, G.	1955-1970	1955	1970
Hollenbeck, Dale G.	1956-1964	1956	1964
Countryman, J.E.	1957-1972	1957	1972
Fisher, Elliott L. Dr.	1957-1965	1957	1965
Hansen, C. Vernon	1957-1977	1957	1977
Harrington, Arthur	1957-1958	1957	1958
Wilson, Melvin D.	1958	1958	1958
Ballard, Lynn E.	1959-1960	1959	1960
Nelson, Marshall O.	1959-1963	1959	1963
Raney, Winifred G. Olson	1959-1991	1959	1991
Bagby, Grover C. ,Jr.	1960-1963	1960	1963
Carter, Thomas J.	1960-1962	1960	1962
Clarke, C. Robert	1960-1988	1960	1988
Covell, Elbert	1960-1967, h1968-h1970	1960	1970
Danielson, Philip A.	1960-1965	1960	1965
England, A.E.	1960-1971	1960	1971
Carlson, George O.	1961-1968, h1970-h1972	1961	1972
Root, L. Eugene Dr.	1961-1971	1961	1971
Wheatley, Melvin E., Jr..	1961-1971	1961	1971
Eberhardt, Robert M.	1963-1994	1963	1994
Herz, Francis J. Dr.,	1963-1971	1963	1971
Malouf, Bert B.	1963-1964	1963	1964
Merwin, William H.	1963-1966	1963	1966
Buerge, Maurice	1964-1984	1964	1984
Moon, Wally	1964-1966	1964	1966
Palmquist, Theodore H. Dr.	1964-1973	1964	1973
Teichert, Adolph Jr., Mrs.	1964-1967	1964	1967
West, Frederick T.	1964-1982	1964	1982
Herold, Henry R.	1965-1972	1965	1972
Rupley, J.W.	1965-1968	1965	1968
Callison, Ferd W. Dr.	1966-1969	1966	1969
Cole, Fred H. Dr.	1966-1968, h1970-h1972	1966	1972
Painter, Alfred W. Dr.	1966-1968	1966	1968
Westgate, Edward W.	1966-1994	1966	1994

Name of Board Member	Dates of Board	Earliest	Latest
Adams, Kenneth W.	1967-1975	1967	1965
Halbert, Sherrill	1967-1973	1967	1973
Smith, Myron E.	1967-1969	1967	1967
Early, Marguerite Mrs.	1968-1995	1968	1995
Humphreys, Cecil W. Dr.	1968-1982	1968	1982
Roberts, Mason M. Dr.	1968-1983	1968	1983
Davies, Paul L. Jr.	1959-1960, 1990	1969	1990
Golden, Charles F.	1969-1976	1969	1976
Beatie, Kenneth D.	1970-1991	1970	1991
Long, Thomas J.	1970-1979	1970	1979
McGavren, Daren	1970-1977	1970	1977
Wood, Don B.	1970-1972	1970	1972
McGeorge, Eugene	1971-1992	1971	1992
Wood, Carlos C.	1971-1991	1971	1991
Gamble, John R.	1972-1982	1972	1982
Haas, Robert D.	1972-1981	1972	1981
Spanos, Alex G.	1972-1982	1972	1982
Stuart, R. Marvin	1972-1988	1972	1988
Yee, Herbert K.	1972-2005	1972	2005
Brandenburger, R.L.	1973-1988	1973	1988
Hume, Jacqueline	1973-1982	1973	1982
Neitzel, Wilmere	1973-1977	1973	1977
Wallace, Bing Mrs. Ben C.	1973-1990	1973	1990
Landis, Richard G.	1974-1984	1974	1984
Witter, Thomas W.	1974-1992	1974	1992
Richardson, Frank	1976-1989	1976	1989
Ritter, Lucy	1976-1991	1976	1991
Darrah, Joan Mrs.	1977-1989	1977	1989
Jongeneel, Albert M. (Fum)	1977-1983	1977	1983
Pardee, George M., Jr.	1977-1982	1977	1982
Hansen, Wilmere Mrs.	1978-1982	1978	1982
Atherton, Holt	1980-1986	1980	1986
Dahl, Loren S.	1980-2003	1980	2003
Saunders, Herman	1980-1993	1980	1993
Choy, Wilbur W.Y.	1981-1984	1981	1984
Long, Robert	1981-1995	1981	1995

Name of Board Member	Dates of Board	Earliest	Latest
MacLean, Angus L., Jr.	1982-2005	1982	2005
Allen, William E.	1983-1985	1983	1985
Berwick, Andrew S., Jr.	1983-1985	1983	1985
Gianelli, Louis F.	1983-1988	1983	1988
Grupe, Fritz, Jr.	1983-1997	1983	1997
Shaw, Maryanna G.	1983-1987	1983	1987
Spanos, Dean A.	1983-1992	1983	1992
Smith, Donald J.	1984-2006	1984	2006
Altman, James	1985-1994	1985	1994
Barton, Hugh P.	1985-1998	1985	1998
Baun, Walter	1985- 2006	1985	2006
Kelly, Leontine T.C.	1985-1988	1985	1988
Redig, Dale F.	1986-1997	1986	1997
Spiekerman, Nancy	1986-2001; 2003	1986	2003
Gerber, David	1987-2001	1987	2001
Guild, Ralph	1987-1996	1987	1996
Flores, Tom	1989-1994	1989	1994
McCargo, James S.	1989-1999	1989	1999
Moss, Weldon T.	1989 -1999	1989	1999
Powell, Robert	1989-1992	1989	1992
Spanos, Michael	1990-1994	1990	1994
Yamada, Bob	1990-1999	1990	1999
Banks, Jeff	1991- 1992	1991	1992
Corson, John	1991-2006	1991	2006
Eres, Thomas W.	1991-2006	1991	2006
Ferguson, Frances	1991-1999	1991	1999
Hulsey, Neven C.	1991-1997	1991	1997
Monagan, Robert T.	1991-2006	1991	2006
Williams, Marjorie	1991, h1992-h1993	1991	1993
Yao, Hilda	1991-1998	1991	1998
Bloom, Charles	1992-1999	1992	1999
Brown, Carter	1992-1997	1992	1997
Conti, Gene	1992-1993	1992	1993
Nikkel, Robert	1992-2006	1992	2006
Hunton, Steven L.	1993-2003	1993	2003
Podesto, Gary	1993-2001	1993	2001
Zischke, Peter H.	1993-2006	1993	2006

Name of Board Member	Dates of Board	Earliest	Latest
Cortopassi, Joan	1994-2005	1994	2005
Janssen, Kathleen Lagorio	1994-2006; 2011-	1994	
Kautz, Gail	1994-2006	1994	2006
Berberian, Dea Spanos	1995-2006	1995	2006
Eberhardt, Mimi	1995-1997	1995	1997
Sweeney, Tom	1996-2003	1996	2003
DeRosa, Donald V.	1998-2011	1998	2011
Koff, Howard M.	1998-2003; 2007-2012	1998	2012
O'Connell, Donald E.	1998-2005	1998	2005
Philibosian, Dianne L. Dr.	1998-2008; 2011-	1998	
Brown, Janice R.	1999- 2008	1999	2008
Powell, Jeanette	1999-2014	1999	2014
Eberhardt, Douglas M.	2000-2013	2000	2013
Goulart, Steven J.	2001-2011	2001	2011
Leatherby, Russell E.	2001-2011	2001	2011
Kennedy, Patricia	2002-2005	2002	2005
Moyer, Hayne R.	2002-2011; 2012-2013	2002	2013
Ornelas, Victor F.	2002-2008	2002	2008
Zuckerman, Tom	2002-2011	2002	2011
Leer, Steven	2004-2013	2004	2013
Callahan, Connie M.	2006-2014	2006	2014
Chan, Tony	2006-2014	2006	2014
Leasure, Larry	2006-2014	2006	2014
Sawdon, Lori Best	2006-2011	2006	2011
Abelson, Sigmund H.	2007-2013	2007	2013
Corkern, Robert J.	2007-2015	2007	2015
England, Morrison C. Jr.	2007-2015	2007	2015
Hernandez, Jose M.	2007-	2007	
Miller, Diane D.	2007-	2007	
Nelson, Fredric C.	2007-	2007	
Ruhl, Barry L.	2007-	2007	
Sanders, Elizabeth A. "Betsy"	2007-2011	2007	2011
Mair, Jim	2008-	2008	
Cordes, Ron	2009- 2013	2009	2013
Ushijima, Nick	2009-2013	2009	2013
Al-Saleh, Fawzi	2011 -	2011	

Name of Board Member	Dates of Board	Earliest	Latest
Eibeck, Pamela	2011 -	2011	
Ferris, Noel	2011 -	2011	
Flores, Armando	2011 -	2011	
Hayashi, Randy	2011 -	2011	
Huber, Kevin	2011 -	2011	
Philibosian, Dianne L. Dr.	1998-2008; 2011-	1998	
Robb, Walter	2008	2008	2015
Berberian, Ron	2012	2012	
Fleming, Richard H.	2012 -	2012	
Mitchell, Gary	2012 -	2012	
Gustafson, Clark	2013	2013	
Stirling, Susanne	2012-	2012	
Bowman, D. Kirkwood	2002-2010; 2013-	2002	2015
Gustafson, Clark	2013	2013	
McShane, Kathleen	2013	2012	
Redmond, Ronald, DDS	2004-2012; 2013-	2013	
Allen, Norm	2014	2014	
Berolzheimer, Charles	2014	2014	
Chan, Virginia	2014	2014	
Spears, Janet	2014		

Following are the Unverified Members

Anthony, Elihu	(1851-1856)
Bateman, A.L.S.	(1851-1856)
Hester, Craven R. Hon.	(1851-1856)
Hutton, J.A.	(1870-1873)
Kellogg, F.E., Esq.	(1851-1856)
Linn, George	(1870-1873)
Lippitt, E.S.	(1870-1873)

APPENDIX 4

Academic Council Chairs 1967-2015

1967-68	Richard Reynolds
1968-69	Larry Pippin
1969-70	Donald Duns
1970-71	Dr. MacIntyre
1971-72	Walter Payne
1972-73	Carl Wulfman
1973-74	Margaret Cormack
1974-75	Jack Mason
1975-76	Walter Zimmermann
1976-77	Roger Reimer
1977-78	Francis Hunter
1978-79	Tapan Munroe
1979-80	Sid Turoff
1980-81	Larry Walker
1981-82	David Fletcher
1982-83	Greg Buntz
1983-84	John Smith
1984-85	Sid Turoff
1985-86	Ron Limbaugh
1986-87	Don Bryan
1987-88	Dale McNeal
1988-89	Roland di Franco
1989-90	Robert Cox
1990-91	Don Bryan
1991-92	Curt Kramer
1992-93	Fred Muskal
1993-94	Jed Scully
1994-95	Peg Ciccolella
1995-96	Herb Reinelt
1996-97	Peg Langer
1997-98	Audree O'Connell
1998-99	Gene Pearson
1999-2000	Christopher R. Snell
2000-01	Marisa Kelly
2001-02	Ron L. Ray
2002-03	Becky Beal
2003-04	Larry Spreer
2004-05	Glendalee Scully
2005-06	David Fries
2006-07	Brian Klunk
2007-08	Lydia Fox
2008-09	Kojo Yelpaala
2009-10	Cathy Peterson

ENDNOTES

Abbreviations used in the endnotes

UA = University of the Pacific Archives

BOR=University of the Pacific Board of Trustees (1854-1961) and Board of Regents (1961-present) Minutes and Board meeting reports, in UA boxes 11.4.5.1-2 (1854-1925), 1.1.1.3 (1917-61), 1.1.2.2-3 (1961-present).

PAR=Pacific alumni publications, *The Pacific Alumni* (1923-1929) and *Pacific Review* (1929-present) in UA boxes 10.3.1.1 series.

AC=Academic Council Minutes and earlier periodic Faculty Council Minutes, 1922-present, in UA boxes 3.1.2.1-11.

Record = *Stockton Daily Evening Record* newspaper and its descendant names, most recently *The Record.*

Student Reports 1940s-2000s = Final reports of the undergraduate student research group of spring term 2012, UA 11.1.1.2.2. I formed teams of two to research campus student life and interview alumni from a designated decade from 1940 to 2010. Group members were Christine Burke (2012), Devon Clayton (2012), Wesley Coffay (2012), Alex Foos (2014), Caroline Gutierrez (2013), Grace Kim (2014), Mark Linden (2013), Kat McAllister (2012), Rudy Oliva (2012), Andrew Rathkopf (2012), and Trevor Rosenbery (2012). Josh Chipponeri (2011) oversaw their work and gathered much information.

All interview transcripts and notes are located in Pacific Archives. The Emeriti Society oral interviews of selected former faculty and administrators are available on the library special collections website.

INTRODUCTION

1 In 1962 President Burns asked Reginald Stuart, author with his wife Grace Stuart of the tribute biography *Tully Knoles of Pacific* (Stockton: The College of the Pacific, 1956), to begin writing a book on the Burns years, but the manuscript never got much beyond an outline and brief sketches. (UA 11.1.1.1.)

2 Barbara W. Tuchman, *Practicing History* (New York: Alfred A. Knopf), 1981, p. 35.

CHAPTER 1

1 Frank Soule, John Gihon, and James Nisbet, *The Annals of San Francisco* (San Francisco: D. Appleton & Co., 1855), 598-925.

2 The term "Bustletown" in the chapter title is a variation on "Bustledom," the name of any California city in *The California Pilgrim* (1853), a religious allegory by Joseph Benton, a leading California clergyman at this time.

3 Lewis F. Byington and Oscar Lewis, eds. *The History of San Francisco* (San Francisco: S.J. Clarke Publishing Co., 1931), Vol. III, pp. 277-78.

4 Roger Geiger, "The Era of the Multipurpose Colleges in American Higher Education," in Roger Geiger, ed. *The American College in the Nineteenth Century* (Nashville: Vanderbilt University Press, 2000), p. 133 ff. Santa Clara College was finally chartered on April 28, 1855 (Robert E. Burns ('31), "The First Half-Century of the College of the Pacific," College of the Pacific master's thesis, 1946, p. 22.). Willamette University in Oregon claims to be "the oldest university in the West," citing the founding of a pre-collegiate institute in 1842, but the evidence provided in Willamette's own recorded history disproves this assertion. Willamette was chartered in 1853, its first collegiate classes were begun in 1856, and its first graduate was in 1859. See Robert Moulton Gatke, *Chronicles of Willamette: The Pioneer University of the West* (Portland: Binfords & Mort, 1943), vol. I, p. 172-76, 195.

5 Pearl Shaffer Sweet ('28), "Methodist Higher Education In Northern California: A Source Book," Masters Thesis for Master of Arts Degree, California State University, Long Beach, 1993, p. 1-3.

6 Sweet, pp. 4-8.

7 William Taylor, *California Life Illustrated* (1890), pp. 108-14, quoted in Burns, p. 2. I rely heavily on the Burns' master's thesis and on Rockwell D. Hunt's *History of the College of the Pacific, 1851-1951* (Stockton, CA: College of the Pacific, 1951, hereinafter noted as Hunt, *History*) for much of the early history of Pacific.

8 Burns, p. 4.

9 Kevin Starr, *Americans and the California Dream, 1850-1915* (New York: Oxford University Press, 1973), pp. 78-82. Two of the five featured clergy in Starr's account of early California are Isaac Owen and William Taylor (p. 105-09.)

10 Leon L. Loofbourow ('13), *Cross in the Sunset: The Development of Methodism in the California-Nevada Annual Conference of The Methodist Church* (San Francisco & Berkeley: Historical Society of the California-Nevada Annual Conference of The Methodist Church, 1966), Vol. 1, p. 26-27.

11 Burns, p. 15.

12 Loofbourow, *In Search of God's Gold: A Story of Continued Christian Pioneering in California* (San Francisco: The Historical Society of the California-Nevada Annual Conference of the Methodist Church in cooperation with the College of the Pacific, 1950), p. 115.

13 Burns, p. 18.

14 Frederic Hall, *The History of San Jose and Surroundings* (San Francisco: A.L. Bancroft & Co., 1871), p. 442-43.

15 UA 1.1.1 and Burns, p. 24. Unfortunately, the minutes of the Board of Trustee meetings 1851-54 have been lost, and student publications, *The Review* and *The Epoch*, did not begin until 1884, hence specific information on Pacific's earliest history is sketchy at best.

16 Hunt, *History*, p. 8.

17 J.N. Martin, "Address of Welcome," in "Addresses, Delivered on Installation of Rev. C.C. Stratton as President of the University of the Pacific, June 5, 1878" (San Francisco: Joseph Winterburn & Co., 1878), p. 4.

18 Burns, p. 27. A concrete and bronze historical marker constructed October 30, 1960, by the "State Society Daughters of Founders and Patriots of America" stands at the corner. Head of Special Collections and University archivist Michael Wurtz deserves credit for determining in 2011 the actual location of the Santa Clara (male) campus and the structures on both the Santa Clara and College Park campuses.

19 Hunt, *History*, p. 9-10.

20 Roger Finke and Rodney Stark, *The Churching of America, 1776-1990: Winners and Losers in our Religious Economy* (New Brunswick, NJ: Rutgers University Press, 1992), p. 45.

21 Finke and Stark, p. 45. For African-Americans, it began in 1864 with the formation of the Methodist Freedman's Committee, which led to the founding of 225 Black Methodist colleges—eleven have survived to the present. As the "General Conference" confederation of Methodist Episcopal churches grew stronger in New England, Wesleyan University (1831) became the dominant Methodist college of the North, while the Southern branch, formally separated over the slavery issue in 1845, rallied around Vanderbilt University as the feeder school for faculty of southern schools, eventually leading to other regional higher education centers—Emory University in Atlanta and Southern Methodist University in Fort Worth. (Conn, pp.28-32.) It is helpful to note that, just as the Methodists got college-founding fever, so too the Roman Catholic Church college building took off during this era. As Roger Geiger notes, "From 1850 to 1890 an average of 33 [Catholic] colleges were started each decade, 70 percent of which ultimately closed." (Geiger, "The Era. . .," in *The American College in the Nineteenth Century*, p. 139.)

22 Conrad Cherry, *Hurrying Toward Zion: Universities, Divinity Schools, and American Protestantism.* Bloomington: Indiana University Press, 1995, pp. 19-20.

23 Hunt, *History,* p. 23.

24 Hunt, *Personal Sketches of California Pioneers I Have Known* (Stockton, CA: University of the Pacific, 1962), pp. 30-234.

25 Oscar T. Shuck, ed., *Representative and Leading Men of the Pacific* (San Francisco: Bacon & Co., 1870), p. 829-32

26 It is difficult to pin down when and where women first earned college degrees in the U.S., though all evidence points to Pacific as the first college west of the Mississippi to enroll women. Oberlin College, the first co-educational college, was founded in 1837, and graduated its first three women in 1841. Mills College, the first women's college west of the Rockies, started in 1852 as the Young Ladies Seminary (high school) but was not chartered as Mills College until 1885, and College of Notre Dame in San Jose (now in Belmont), founded in 1851, was the first chartered women's college in California in 1868. Hillsdale (1844) and Lawrence (1847) were among the very few co-educational schools to precede Pacific. The state universities were reluctant followers. As Solomon notes, "The first eight state universities to accept women were Iowa (1855), Wisconsin (1867), Kansas, Indiana, Minnesota (1869), Missouri, Michigan, and California (1870)" (p. 53). It is highly unlikely, given Pacific board's periodic directive to integrate classes through the 1850s and 1860s, that women could have achieved degrees without participating in integrated classes. The precursor of Oregon State University, Corvallis College, also founded by the Methodists, enrolled women students by fall 1867 and graduated its first woman in 1870. University of California began admitting women students in October, 1870 and apparently began their academic work in January, 1871, according to Pacific archivist Michael Wurtz. The state normal schools all grew with the rise of women pursuing school teaching as careers.

27 No enrollment records exist for the early years; the brief history of Pacific in the 1928 *Naranjado* states that 54 students enrolled in 1851, but how many of those were at the collegiate level is unknown.

28 Hunt, *History,* p. 27.

29 Hunt, *History,* p. 27.

30 BOR, September 18, 1857.

31 BOR, August 25, 1856, June 10, 1857, and December 13, 1859. A brief history of Pacific in the 1928 *Naranjado* (p. 12) states that co-educational classes began in 1869, probably based on Rockwell Hunt's statement in his "Golden Jubilee of the University of the Pacific, San Jose, California, 1851-1901" (San Jose, n.d.), reprinted from *Overland Monthly* (May, 1901), p. 6. (UA 11.1.1.1.)

32 An 1873 alumnus, J.H. White, writes that when he entered Pacific in September, 1870, class sessions were integrated. (PAR (vol. 1, no. 4), February, 1924, p. 2).

33 Burns, pp. 29-30. The other pioneer Methodist college in the west, Willamette in Oregon, launched a similar misguided scheme, offering ten-year scholarships for $200 and "perpetual" scholarships for $500. See Gatke, p. 193-95.

34 Burns, p. 36.

35 Hunt, *History,* p. 24. In his history or St. Mary's College, Ronald Isetti recounts how Catholic Archbishop of San Francisco Jose Alemany scorned both Santa Clara and its sister Jesuit college St. Ignatius (now University of San Francisco) by founding his own college south of San Francisco in 1863, St. Mary's College. He irritated his competitors by setting total costs at $150 per year to serve the lower classes of all church denominations, while nearly driving his school into bankruptcy within three years. Ronald Isetti, *On These Promising Shores of the Pacific: A History of Saint Mary's College* (Charleston, SC: The History Press, 2013), p. 11-22. St. Mary's College moved to Moraga in the north Bay in 1928.

36 James Findlay, "Agency, Denominations, and Western Colleges, 1830-1860: Some Connections between Evangelicalism and American Higher Education," in Geiger, "The Era...," in *The American College in the Nineteenth Century*, p. 115-126. Findlay describes the "college agent" model in the 1840s at Methodist Indiana Asbury University, now DePauw University.

37 Frederick Rudolph, *Curriculum: A History of the American Undergraduate Course of Study Since 1636* (San Francisco: Jossey-Bass Publishers, 1977), p. 146.

38 *University of the Pacific Catalogue*, 1856-57, p.15.

39 BOR, September 13, 1859.

40 BOR, May 4, 1870.

41 See a detailed history of the medical school and its stormy history in John Long Wilson's "Stanford University School of Medicine and the Predecessor Schools: An Historical Perspective," Lane Medical Library, Stanford School of Medicine, 1998, at http://elane.stanford.edu/wilson/index.html

42 Geiger, "The Era...," in *The American College in the Nineteenth Century,* pp. 130.

43 *Naranjado,* 1890, p. 14-15.

44 BOR, September, 12, 1860.

45 BOR, March 14, 1861.

46 BOR, June 10, 1863.

47 BOR, June 6, 1865.

48 See Hunt, *History,* p. 35.

49 *University of the Pacific Catalogue,* 1877-78, p. 34.

50 BOR, June 6, 1865 and March 27, 1866.

51 BOR, June 6, 1871.

52 BOR, December 12, 1868.

53 BOR, September 15, 1876.

54 Editorial, *Pacific Pharos* 1, no.5 (April 14, 1886): 69.

55 PAR vol. III, #2, p. 1. (UA 4.4.2.1.1)

56On early international student enrollment, see Harold S. Jacoby ('28), *Pacific: Yesterday and the Day Before That* (Grass Valley, CA: Comstock Bonanza Press, 1989), Chapter 5, "The Muto Fund Mystery: Pacific's Early Japanese Invasion", p. 82-91. Jacoby notes that 42 Japanese students enrolled between 1885-1900, but only seven were in college-level programs. For some unknown reason, Jacoby shuns the notion that the highly successful Methodist missionary work in Japan resulted in these enrollments. From 1886-1950, Methodist missionaries in Japan were highly regarded leaders; Dr. Herbert Johnson ('06) was superintendent for 21 years in the 1920s and 1930s and awarded the highest decoration to a foreigner by Emperor Hirohito. (Loofbourow, *Cross,* Vol. II, p. 30-31.)

57 PAR (vol. VII, no. 2), February, 1933, p. 2. (UA 8.2.K2)

58 Editorial, *Pacific Pharos* 1, no.10 (August 25, 1886): 132.

59 *Pacific Weekly* 12, no.18 (March 4, 1920)

60 *Pacific Weekly* 14, no. 23 (April 27, 1922).

61 *Naranjado,* 1889, p. 11, and "The Trees on Our Campus," *Pacific Pharos* 13, no.6 (February, 1909): 24-25.

62 Editorial, *Pacific Pharos* 4, no. 3 (September 25, 1889): 51.

63 Thelin, pp. 65 ff.

64 Rudolph, *Curriculum,* p. 95.

65 Hunt, *History,* p. 31.

66 *Naranjado,* 1914.

67 *Pacific Weekly* 12, no. 1 (October 9, 1919).

68 Quoted from Minutes of the Faculty, 1876, in Burns, p. 56.

69 BOR, May 27, 1890. (UA 11.4.5.1)

70 Editorial, *The Epoch* 2, no.3 (November 9, 1885): 45.

71 *Pacific Weekly* 12, no. 2 (October 16, 1919).

72 Editorial, *Pacific Pharos* 1, no.1 (February 10, 1886): 4.

73 *Naranjado,* 1887, p. 51, and Editorial, *Pacific Pharos* 3, no. 1 (August 15, 1888): 2.

74 Jacoby, *Pacific,* p. 150. See Jacoby's Chapter 10, "Pacific Athletics in the Pre-Stagg Era," p. 148-165.

75 Editorial, *Pacific Pharos* 3, no.16 (March 27, 1889): 184-85.

76 Four signed student letters to President McClish located in the University's "Faculty Minutes, 1886-98." (UA 1.4.3.1)

77 BOR, January 4, 1889. Editorial, *Pacific Pharos* 4, no.1 (August 28, 1889): 3, and Editorial, *Pacific Pharos* 4, no.14 (March 12, 1890): 158. (UA 11.4.5.1) Yet the Trustees Minutes of May 20, 1903 and June 28, 1904 suggest that a subsequent ban was required.

78 Roger L. Geiger with Julie Ann Bubolz, "College As It Was in the Mid-Nineteenth Century," in Geiger, *The American College in the Nineteenth Century,* p. 82.

79 C. H. von Glahn, "Poverty in America," *Pacific Pharos* 4, no. 13 (February 26, 1890): 151.

80 *University of the Pacific Catalogue, 1905-06, 1906-07*, San Jose, CA, p. 17.

81 Thelin, pp. 139-140.

82 *San Jose Daily Mercury*, October 4, 1884, quote in Burns, p. 62-63.

83 Loofbourow, *Cross,* Vol. I, p. 46.

84 See San Jose State University Website: http://www.cob.sjsu.edu/nellen_a/Lucky.pdf

85 Burns, p. 80-81.

86 Elliott, p. 57.

87 Elliott, p. 71

88 Elliott, 94.

89 Elliott, p. 93-94.

90 Manuel P. Servin and Iris H. Wilson, *Southern California and Its University* (Los Angeles: The Ward Ritchie Press, 1969), p. 7.

91 Servin and Wilson, p. 9 and 19.

92 Servin and Wilson, p. 63. Only two small colleges, Pomona College (1857) and St. Vincent's College (1865, predecessor to Loyola Marymount University), were founded earlier. UCLA began in 1927.

93 Randolph, p. 138-42. As far as I am able to determine, here are the founding dates of the earlier conservatories: Oberlin (1865), Peabody (1857), Cincinnati (1867 and 1878), Boston (1867), New England (1867), and Lawrence (1874). The first school of fine arts began at Yale in 1869 as a means to offer women an avenue for college study at the all-male school.

94 *University of the Pacific Catalogue,* 1877-78.

95 *University of the Pacific Catalogue,* 1884-85.

96 BOR, June 4, 1884.

97 Editorial, *The Epoch* 2, no.1 (September, 1885): 2.

98 Burns, p. 69.

99 *Pacific Pharos* published a list of "college colors" from across the country (e.g., "Brown—Brown"), including Pacific as "Orange," a single color like two-thirds of the schools on the list (*Pacific Pharos* 2, no.8 [November 2, 1887]: 88). According to Cindy Spiro's ('76) unpublished manuscript, "Tigers, Traditions and Teams: Football and its Influence on School Customs at the University of the

Pacific"(1992, UA Box 9.2.1.1), Orange is first noted in 1866, black not till 1888; however, while both colors are mentioned together as early as the 1890s, in 1899, the board adopted "Royal Purple Chevron on Orange Ground" as the official colors, with the approval of the Alumni Association and the students pending (board of Trustees Minutes, June 7, 1899). The student body designated orange as the school color as late as 1905. The song "The Orange and Black" appears in the Pacific Pharos of April, 1907 without comment. The first stanza reads:

Although Stanford favors only
The Cardinal's brilliant hue
And the lusty sons of Berkeley
To the Blue and Gold are true,
We will stand by old Pacific,
No honor shall she lack
While the tiger stands defender
Of the Orange and the Black.

The 1915 *Catalogue* announced the first annual "Orange and Black Day" (September 8).

100 Editorial, *Pacific Pharos* 1, no.4 (March 24, 1886): 59.

101 Editorial, *Pacific Pharos* 9, no. 5 (January, 1905): 9, and 11, no.5 (January, 1907): 16-17. See Rudolph, *History*, p. 369, on the rise of student governments after 1900.

102 *Naranjado,* 1890, p. 12. For a detailed history of the Alumni Association, see Jacoby, *Pacific,* Chapter 3, "Alumni Associations: The Species and the Specimens," p. 34-64.

103 "Anderson Y" history, *Naranjado,* 1967, p. 297. The article claims that the YMCA was founded at Pacific in 1879 (other sources say 1880), and "within a decade" the YWCA was established.

104 After Pacific, Stratton had troubled presidencies at both Mills College and Willamette College.

105 One of the stained glass windows was recently discovered in Baun Hall on the Stockton campus. See the story, PAR (vol. 99, no. 1), Spring 2013, back cover.

106 *Naranjado,* 1887, p. 51.

107 Minutes of the Faculty, September 27, 1890, p.134, quoted in Burns, p. 77.

108 Editorial, *Pacific Pharos* 2, no.4 (September 1, 1887): 37.

109 Editorial, *Pacific Pharos* 5, no.20 (June 3, 1891): 230.

110 Editorial, *Pacific Pharos* 5, no.18 (May 6, 1891): 205. Pacific of course was not alone in stumbling through the adolescence of higher education in the nineteenth century; Bledstein recounts the expulsion of nearly half the Yale class of 1830 over a petty math pedagogy dispute between students and faculty (p. 231).

111 Hunt, *History,* p. 72.

112 Elliott, p. 97. See Gerald McKevitt, *The University of Santa Clara: A History, 1851-1977* (Stanford, CA: Stanford University Press, 1979), p. 128-29. McKevitt describes Santa Clara College suffering similar enrollment losses to tuition-free Berkeley and Stanford in the 1890s, as well as the impact of the 1888 collapse of the California real-estate bubble.

113 Editorial, *Pacific Pharos* 5, no.20 (June 3, 1891): 231.

114 Elliott, p. 117.

115 BOR, August 5, 1891. The Faculty fingered seven students whom they felt met the trustees' threshold to question their right to honorable certification of dismissal, including the editor and assistant editor of *Pacific Pharos* for anti-Hirst articles, and a student activist who "incited rebellion against the constituted authorities of the University" by making anti-Hirst comments at a fraternity dinner. ("Faculty Minutes," January 28, 1892. (UA 1.4.3.1)

116 Douglas Sloan, *Faith and Knowledge: Mainline Protestantism and American Higher Education* (Louisville: Westminster John Knox Press, 1994), p. 20.117 Geiger, "The Era . . .," in *The American College in the Nineteenth Century,* pp. 127-39.

118 Sloan, p. 24.

119 Hunt, *History,* p.80.

120 Burns, p. 89.

121 Hunt, *History,* p. 99.

122 Editorial, *Pacific Pharos* 1, no. 16 (November 24, 1886): 235-36; no. 17 (December 8, 1886): 251; 2, no.6 (October 5, 1887): 61-62; and 2, no. 8 (November 11, 1887): 90.

123 Arthur M. Cohen, *The Shaping of American Higher Education: Emergence and Growth of the Contemporary System* (San Francisco: Jossey-Bass, Inc. 1998), p. 117.

124 BOR, May 20, 1903.

125 Rudolph, *Curriculum,* p.167.

126 Editorials, *Pacific Pharos* 1, no.4 (March 24, 1886): 59 and no. 3 (March 10, 1886): 36.

127 Editorial, *Pacific Pharos* 7, no. 6 (March, 1903): 225.

128 Editorial, *Pacific Pharos* 1, no.11 (September 8, 1886): 153.

129 Editorial, *Pacific Pharos* 2, no.17 (April 30, 1888): 195. For an account of similar campus rituals, see Simon J. Bronner, *Piled Higher and Deeper: The Folklore of Campus Life* (Little Rock, AR: August House Publishers, Inc., 1990), p. 209-210. Bronner's book includes an excellent bibliography, but is primarily an anecdotal catalog of student pranks and rituals over the past fifty years with little analysis.

130 BOR, May 21, 1903.

131 BOR, January 31, 1900.

132 Burns, p. 9.

133 Loofbourow, *Cross,* Vol. II, p. 29.

134 BOR, July 6, 1905.

135 BOR, May 25, 1906.

136 Letter from Rolla V. Watt to W. S. Clayton, May 24, 1915, and to Jere Leiter, June 29, 1915. (UA 1.1.1.1)

137 Starr, *Americans and the California dream, 1850-1915* (New York: Oxford University Press, 1973, 1986), p. 443.

138 Burns, pp. 98-99.

CHAPTER 2

1 Hunt, *History,* p.110.

2 Hunt, *History,* p.114.

3 Lucas, p. 227.

4 McKevitt, p. 170-74.

5 Rudolph, *Curriculum,* p. 210. Rudolph points out that even at Yale, Harvard, and Princeton, struggling to maintain enrollments, nearly 60 percent of the freshman students in 1909 were admitted "on condition" because of inadequate high school preparation (p. 213). Jacoby notes the name change from "university" to "college" among five Methodist schools between 1906 and 1915. (p. 5)

6 BOR, March 7, 1911.

7 Personal Interview with George Knoles, March 27, 2011. *Naranjado,* 1921, p. 124.

8 PAR (vol. 82, no. 1), Fall, 1994, p. 3.

9 Jacoby, p. 155.

10 Hunt, *History,* p. 177.

11 *Naranjado,* 1911, p. 84.

12 Joe Wills, "Pacific Early Women's Sports: A Tale of Perseverance," PAR (vol. 83, no. 2), Winter, 1995, p. 18. Cole Field is mentioned in Jacoby, *Pacific,* p. 125.

13 Stewart and Stewart, p. 71.

14 BOR, January 29, 1907.

15 BOR, May 10, 1913.

16 BOR, May 25, 1906 and January 29, 1907.

17 Jacoby, p. 106.

18 BOR, January 26, 1916.

19 BOR, June 8, 1920.

20 Jacoby, p. 87.

21 Hunt, *History,* p.125.

22 BOR, January 26, 1915.

23 Figures appear to be unreliable. Roger L. Geiger states 374 students as the average college size in 1910, in "The Ten Generations of American Higher Education," Philip G. Altbach, Robert O. Berdahl, and Patricia J Gumport, eds., *American Higher Education in the Twenty-First Century: Social, Political, and Economic Challenges*, 2nd ed., (Baltimore: The Johns Hopkins University Press, 2005), p. 54.

24 *Pacific Weekly* 10, no.17 (February 27, 1918): 1, and John Seaton, "Report of the President," January 16, 1919, in BOR, January 17, 1919.

25 Levine, p. 28.

26 *Naranjado*, 1919, p. 52-53.

27 Breeden was hired when he graduated to be the first "Graduate Director" of athletics; by 1935, he had been promoted to "Director of Athletics" according to the 1935 *Naranjado.*

28 Breeden was hired when he graduated to be the first "Graduate Director" of athletics; by 1935, he had been promoted to "Director of Athletics" according to the 1935 *Naranjado.*

29 "2011-12 University of the Pacific Tigers Men's Basketball Media Guide," p. 74.

30 *Naranjado,* 1934, p. 166; "History of Pacific Athletics," p. 158-60.

31 Wills, 1995, p. 19.

32 *Pacific Weekly,* 13, no. 29 (June 2, 1921).

33 Letters from Dr. Tully C. Knoles to Rolla V. Watt, July 15, 1919; October 4,1919; September 29, 1920. (UA 1.2.1.3-7)

34 Thelin, p. 176-77.

35 *Pacific Weekly,* 13, no.24 (April 21, 1921).

36 BOR, September 20, 1919 and June 8, 1920.

37 BOR, September 20, 1919 and March 4, 1920.

38 Hunt, *History,* p. 135-36 and Kara Pratt Brewer, *"Pioneer or Perish:" A History of the University of the Pacific During the Administration of Dr. Robert E. Burns, 1946-1971* (Fresno, CA: Pioneer Publishing Co.), p. 16.

39 Report of the President, January 31,1922. (UA 1.2.1.3.2)

40 BOR, June 11, 1919.

41 Stewart and Stewart, p.75.

42 Letter from President Knoles to President David P. Barrows, February 2, 1922. (UA 1.2.1.3.2)

43 Stewart and Stewart, p. 72-74.

44 BOR, March 4, 1920.

45 Hunt, *History*, p. 138.

46 *Pacific Weekly* 6, no. 11(January 8, 1920) and no. 18 (March 4, 1920).

47 Letters from Dr. John L. Seaton to Dr. Tully C. Knoles, September 23. 1921, and from Dr. Tully C. Knoles to Dr.

John L. Seaton, September 8, 1921. (UA 1.2.1.3.1)

48Letter from President Knoles to Mr. Rolla V. Watt, June 1, 1921. (UA 1.2.1.3.2)

49 BOR, October 24, 1921 and January 21, 1922.

50 President Reports to the Board, June 21 and September 24, 1921. (UA 1.2.1.3.13)

51 BOR, May 13, 1922.

52 Letter from President Tully C. Knoles to Dr. John W. Hancher, May 17, 1922. (UA 1.2.1.3.2)

53 Hunt, *History,* p. 140.

54 BOR, June 19, 1923, and Correspondence of Rolla Watt, August 1, 1924. (UA 1.1.1.1)

55 Pacific leaders must have known of architect Myron Hunt's grand gesture in designing the entire campus of Occidental College in 1913 when it moved from Highland Park to Eagle Rock in Los Angeles. But Hunt, who also designed the Rose Bowl, Hollywood Bowl, and Huntington Library, stuck with the "Mediterranean" style of architecture that blended the classical Beaux Arts style with Mission Revival.

56 Manuscript by Ellen Deering, University Registrar, n.d. (UA 1.2.1.3.1)

57 Hunt, *History,* p. 139.

58 See Clifford M. Drury, "Church Sponsored Schools in Early California," *The Pacific Historian*, vol. 20 (Summer, 1976), 158-66, and McKevitt, p. 130.

59 BOR, June 17, 1924.

60 PAR, vol. XVI, no. 4 (December 1942), p. 22.

61 *Record*, September 27, 1924.

62 The largest gift was $17,000 from Charles Harrold, an early member of Central Methodist Church of Stockton (confirmed by records in The Haggin Museum of Stockton). On George Shima and his support for college scholarships, see Maury Kane, "Stockton's Potato King," *Record*, February 22, 1992, p. B3-4; H.T. Hammond, editor, "World Famous Japanese Potato King," *Byron Times,* 2nd special edition, 1910 [n. p.]; and Donald Hata and Nadine Hata, "George Shima: The Potato King of California," *Journal of the West* (vol. 25), January, 1986, p. 55-63, on his championing Japanese Americans during hostile times.

63 *Record,* September 27, 1924, p. 12.

64 This portrait of Stockton is based on numerous sources. For a quick overview of the ethnic communities of the city, see *The Guide to Stockton* by Cheryl Lewis, Toni di Franco, and G. H. Lewis (Mercer Island, WA: The Writing Works, 1979), a unique, comprehensive orientation to the city, from history to shopping and services.

65 The Stockton portrait here is based on a personal interview with Tod Ruhstaller, CEO and Curator of History, The Haggin Museum, Stockton, February 12, 2012; Gilbert, p. 12-71; and Raymond W. Hillman and Leonard Covello, *Cities & towns of San Joaquin County since 1847* (Fresno, CA: Panorama West Books, 1985), p. 3-30.

66 See Lee M. A. Simpson, *Selling the City: Gender, Class, and the California Growth Machine, 1880-1940* (Stanford: Stanford University Press, 2004), p. 4, *passim.* Mills College is used as an example of how a college had economic impact on property values in 1920s Oakland (p. 85-7). See also Andrew E. G. Jonas and David Wilson, *The Urban Growth Machine: Critical Perspectives Two Decades Later* (Albany: State University of New York Press, 1999), confirming the essential insights of Harvey Molotch's assertions in 1976 about the "urban growth machine" dynamics linked to rising property values.

67 An analysis of the Pacific "Bulletin" faculty rosters for 1923-24 and 1924-25 indicates that ten members did not continue on the faculty after the Stockton move; eight may not have been re-appointed. Eleven new faculty members were hired for 1924-25.

68 Hunt, *History,* p. 141.

69 BOR, June 17, 1924, and Jacoby, *Pacific,* p. 141

70 BOR, January 15, 1923, report by vice president Burcham.

71 BOR, June 17, 1924.

72 PAR, vol. 11, no. 1 (October 1976), p. 7, and *Naranjado,* 1925, p.116-17.

73 *Record,* September 27, 1924, p. 14.

74 Knoles Report to the Board of Trustees, January 25, 1927. (UA 1.2.1.3.7)

75 Starr, *Material Dreams,* p. 155.

76 *Naranjado*, 1926, passim.

77 "Campus Landmarks and Traditions," PAR, vol. 13, no. 8 (May 1979), p. 8.

78 Devon Clayton, "Pacific's Sisterhood: The History and Development of Women's Greek Life at University of the Pacific," unpublished undergraduate research paper, Fall, 2011, p. 18-23. (UA 11.1.1.1)

79 Personal interview with Inez Sheldon Holt ('37), March 29, 2011.

80 Thelin, p. 182-86.

81 Lynn D. Gordon, "Co-Education on Two Campuses: Berkeley and Chicago, 1890-1912," in *Woman's Being, Woman's Place: Female Identity and Vocation in American History,* ed. by Mary Kelley (Boston: G. K. Hall & Co., 1979), p.173. Gordon documents the discriminatory practices against women at Cal vs. Chicago.

82 *Naranjado*, 1925, *passim*, and PAR (vol. 90, no. 2), Summer, 2003, p. 32, which reports that Hazel Glaister ('24) and Grace Connor ('25) were the founders

83 Hunt, *History,* p. 143. The AAU began the first national collegiate accrediting process in 1913, well after the Methodist Senate had begun its accreditation role for Methodist schools in 1892.

84 Russell Thomas, *The Search for a Common Learning: General Education, 1800-1960* (New York: McGraw–Hill Book Co., 1962), p. 61-91. The first national reform of general education occurred in the 1920s, but Pacific apparently did not participate in this effort to trim electives to assure a broad liberal education, perhaps because, by national standards, Pacific had conservatively retained appropriate requirements while other schools had let them lapse.

85 *Naranjado,* 1927, p. 76.

86 Personal interview with Pearl Piper, November 15, 2010.

87 *Naranjado,* 1929, p. 161-75, and 1930, p. 148.

88 PAR (vol. 69, no. 1), September, 1981, p. 12. Bob Breeden recalls helping to found the Block P Society in this article.

89 *Naranjado,* 1934, p. 134-40.

90 PAR, vol. 3, no. 1 (September, 1928), p.1, and personal interview with Eddie LeBaron, November 28, 2011.

91 PAR (vol. 74, no. 1), September-October, 1986, p. 6.

92 PAR (vol. 85, no. 2), Winter, 1997-98, p. 18-19.

93 *Naranjado,* 1929, p. 240.

94 BOR, June 17, 1924.

95 *Naranjado,* 1926, p. 96. See Jacoby, *Pacific,* Chapter 7, "Dancing, Smoking and Alcohol: *Coming to Terms with Sin on the Campus,*" p. 105-24, who describes the issues in detail as a former student participant.

96 BOR, June 15, 1926.

97 "Commonwealth" [Journal of the Commonwealth Club], XXX, #2 (January 11, 1954) and "Board of Trustees Resolution," January 13, 1960. (UA 1.2.1.3.15)

98 PAR, vol. 5, no. 1 (November, 1930), p. 1.

99 Personal interview with George Knoles, March, 27, 2011.

100 Rudolph, *History,* p. 442, and Geiger, "The Ten Generations of American Higher Education," in *American Higher Education in the Twenty-First Century: Social, Political, and Economic Challenges,* ed. by Philip G. Altbach, Robert O. Berdahl, and Patricia J. Gumport, 2nd ed., (Baltimore: The Johns Hopkins University Press, 2005), p. 57 and 60.

101 Quoted in a booklet, *College of the Pacific,* n.d., [1932], p. 7.

102 Ellen L. Deering, "Thomas Francis Baxter," unpublished manuscript, May 1, 1976, p.2 (UA 7.1.1) and PAR (vol. 70, no. 2), October, 1982, p. 5.

103 BOR, March 27, 1928.

104 BOR, April 5, 1910

105 Cohen, p. 141. Lucas notes that only nine schools of education existed in 1906, and even the University of Michigan did not establish its school until 1921. (p. 234)

106 *Record,* September 27, 1924, p. 4.

107 *Bulletin of the College of the Pacific,* "News Bulletin," December 1928, p. *6. Naranjado,*1929, p. 24.

108 "One Hundred Years of Music, 1878-1978," (Stockton, CA: Conservatory of Music Publication, 1978), p. 3, and PAR, vol. VI, no. 1 (October, 1931), p. 4.

109 PAR, vol. XVIII, no. 3 (June, 1945), p. 2, and no. 4 (August, 1945), p. 7.

110 *Naranjado,* 1934, p. 238, PAR, vol. VIII, no. 3 (May, 1934), p. 4.

111 PAR, vol. XVI, no. 1 (February, 1942), p. 6.

112 *Bulletin of the College of the Pacific, Catalogue 1927-28,* p. 64, and *Catalogue 1928-29.*

113 Curtis, p. 27-30.

114 Harold Jacoby, "Toward An Understanding of the College of the Pacific," unpublished manuscript, May 5, 1967, p. 1. (UA 7.2.J17)

115 *Naranjado,* 1929, p. 25 and 31.

116 *Bulletin of the College of the Pacific, Catalogue 1928-29,* p. 30-35.

117 PAR, vol. VI, no. 3 (January, 1932), p. 1.

118 Hunt, *History,* p. 146.

119 Knoles, "Trustees Report of the President," March 26, 1929, p. 2.

120 Knoles, "Report of the President to the Board of Trustees," June 7, 1928.

121. Interview with Inez Sheldon Holt.

122 Quoted in Brewer, p. 59, cited as F.W. Reeves et al., *The Liberal Arts College: Based Upon Surveys of Thity-Five Colleges Related to the Methodist Episcopal Church* (Chicago: University of Chicago Press, 1932), p. 97.

123 BOR, June 11, 1932, September 28, 1932, and October 25, 1932.

124 BOR, July 27, 1934.

125 PAR, vol. V, no. 4 (April, 1931), p. 2.

126 Servin and Wilson, p. 113-16.

127 Servin and Wilson, p. 103-30.

128 Stewart and Stewart, p. 99-100.

129 BOR, June 10, 1935 and March 24, 1936.

130 Lucas, p. 229.

131 Bloch, p. 4.

132 Bloch, p. 8.

133 The 1948-49 *Stockton College Catalogue* is the first to include a map of the "South Campus," and other archive documents confirm that construction began in 1947, continuing through the early 1950s.

134 Bloch, p. 9, and BOR, October 27, 1936. The senior college admission requirement was an Associate in Arts degree with a minimum of 'C' grade work in courses approved for admission into University of California schools.

135 Cohen, p. 121.

136 *Naranjado,* 1933, p. 40.

137 *Naranjado* 1937, p. 13.

138 See Rick Garlinghouse, "An Overview of Anderson 'Y' Center," unpublished manuscript, May, 1985, p. 1-3. (UA 5.1.2.1) Another source says the merger occurred in 1934 ("Anderson Y," *Naranjado* 1967, p. 297). In 1952, the SCA changed its name to the "Anderson Y" in honor of the donors, Mr. and Mrs. W. C. Anderson; Mr. Anderson was a Pacific trustee.

139 PAR, vol. VXI, no. 2 (May, 1942), p. 4. Bava, who served as grounds head till 1954, had farmed the land that became the campus. (See Stewart and Stewart, p. 76.)

140 "Campus Landmarks & Traditions," p. 9.

141 For a full story of the outdoor "Greek theatre," see PAR (vol. 84, no. 3), Spring, 1997, p. 32. It was demolished in 1984 to make room for the Recital Hall.

142 PAR, vol. XII, no. 4 (Fall, 1938), p. 3.

143 Kenneth Mork ('50), oral remembrance at the memorial service for Bob Steel in Morris Chapel, December 21, 2011. The historic Murphy's Hotel was purchased by 32 members in the 1970s and sold in the 1990s.

144 PAR, vol. XIV, no. 2 (May, 1940), p. 3.

145 *Naranjado* 1942, p. 91.

146 While this assertion is difficult to document, Mike Millerick's ('91) *Pacific Football Record Book* (Lodi, CA: Duncan Press, 2002) is loaded with persuasive lists, and he and others like former Pacific athletic director and NCAA executive director Cedric Dempsey think that this assertion could be documented.

147 Clifford Putney, *Muscular Christianity: Manhood and Sports in Protestant America, 1880-1920* (Cambridge, MA: Harvard University Press, 2001), p. 60.

148 Robin Lester, *Stagg's University: The Rise, Decline, and Fall of Big-Time Football at Chicago* (Urbana: University of Illinois Press, 1995), p. 17-19, 41, 87-88, 102-03.

149 PAR, vol. VII, no. 2 (February, 1933), p. 5.

150 PAR, vol. XVIII, no. 1 (June, 1944), p. 5.

151 PAR (vol. 71, no. 5), March-April, 1984, p. 9.

152 Lester, p. 21. Personal interview with Eddie LeBaron, November 28, 2011 and June 22, 2012.

153 Considine, p. 139, and personal interview with Eddie LeBaron, June 22, 2012.

154 Lester, p. 147-48.

155 Randy Andrada, *They Did it Everytime: The Saga of the Saint Mary's Gaels: The Story of a Vanished College Football Empire* (Piedmont, CA: Randy Andrada, 1987), p. 126.

156 *Naranjado,* 1938, p. 88 and 1939, p. 86.

157 Robert E. Burns, "Notes Written by Robert E. Burns shortly before his death," [n.d.], p. 10. (UA 1.2.1.4.4.1)

158 Interview with LeBaron in 2011, confirmed in 2012.

159 PAR, vol. XVII, no. 3 (December, 1943), p. 14 and 26.

160 *Naranjado,* 1944, p. 38.

161 PAR, vol. XVIII, no. 2 (December, 1944), p. 9.

162 Memorandum from Dr. A. T. Bawden to Dr. Tully C. Knoles, December 17, 1945. (UA 1.2.1.3.14)

163 Report of the Chancellor to the Board of Trustees of the College of the Pacific," March 25, 1947, p. 3. (UA 1.2.1.3.15)

164 Considine, p. 151.

165 "Amos Alonzo Stagg," University of the Pacific Athletic Department unpublished manuscript, n.d., p. 2-3.

166

This portrait of Brown is informed by a personal interview with one of his mentees, Alfred Muller ('53), January 30, 2013.

167 PAR (vol.67, no. 6), March, 1980, p. 1-3.

168 BOR, October 26, 1943.

169 Joe Wills, "It was the best of times, worst of times for Pacific V-12's during World War II," PAR (vol. 82, no. 1), Fall, 1994, p. 10, and PAR (vol. 88, no. 3), Fall, 2001, p. 8-9.

170 *Naranjado,* 1928, p. 99, 110 and 1940, p. 142; PAR, vol. XVIII, no. 2 (December 1944), p. 18; and PAR (vol. 75, no. 2), November-December, 1987, p. 3.

171 PAR (vol. 72, no. 5), May-June, 1985, p. 16.

172 Fred M. Hall, *It's About Time: The Dave Brubeck Story* (Fayetteville: University of Arkansas Press, 1996), p. 16-17.

173 Dave Brubeck, "Notes by Dave Brubeck (1968), p. 4," *The Light in the Wilderness.*

174 Loofbourow, *Cross,* Vol. II, p. 150.

175 *Naranjado* 1942, p. 165.

176 According to University Archives, three Japanese-American students actually graduated in Spring, 1942. Eight other Japanese-American students were enrolled in the College; the rest were Stockton College students.

177 Arthur Farey, "Shall I Go to College Now?" PAR, vol. XVII, no. 1 (February, 1943), p. 3.

178 Joe Wills, "It was the best of times . . . ."

179 Letter from Lt. Col. Archibald Barrett to College of the Pacific, October 6, 1943. (UA 1.2.1.3.12)

180 Devon Clayton and Mark Linden, "The 40s," p. 10, Student Reports 1940s-2000s. (UA 11.1.1.2.2)

181 Various letters and documents in the Knoles file, 1943-45. (UA 1.2.1.3.13) The ship, one of 531 "Victory ships" in the cargo fleet, is known to have continued in service into the 1950s.

182 Sally Rinehart Nero, *We* (n. p., 1988), p. 102-03. This memoir, in University Archives, recounts the lives of ten women who bonded as Pacific students, 1941-45, and remained in touch at least through the 1980s.

183 *Naranjado* 1943, p. 131.

184 *Naranjado* 1942, p. 23.

185 "One Hundred Years of Music," p. 3, and PAR, vol. XVIII, no. 3 (June, 1945), p. 12.

186 PAR, vol. XVIII, no. 3 (June, 1945), p. 16-17.

187 PAR, vol. XVIII, no. 4 (August, 1945), p. 6

188 See Keith W. Olson, *The G.I. Bill, the Veterans, and the Colleges* (Lexington: University of Kentucky Press, 1974), p. 15-24. Olson documents Atherton's and the American Legion's "decisive role" in the legislation.

189 On the 60th anniversary of the GI Bill (2004), Pacific's Benerd School of Education sponsored a major symposium honoring Atherton's role and all WWII GI Bill veterans in the Central Valley.

190 PAR, vol. XVI, no. 3 (October 1942), p. 15.

191 Stewart and Stewart, p. 91.

192 Clayton and Linden, "The 40s," p. 12-13.

193 As recalled by Olin Jacoby at age 100, who was Board chair at the time of the appointment. PAR (vol. 68, no. 2), October, 1980, p. 3.

194 BOR, November 11, 1946, March 25, 1947, and April 19, 1947.

195 1945 government documents relating to Burns' draft deferment. (UA 1.2.1.3.14)

CHAPTER 3

1 Brewer, "*Pioneer or Perish,*" p. 1-3.

2 PAR (vol. 44, no. 2), February, 1957, p. 4.

3 Personal interview with professor emeritus Larry Meredith, January 19, 2012.

4 Burns, "The Inaugural Address," p. 19.

5 BOR, October 28, 1958. PAR (vol. 45, no. 10), December, 1958, p. 10-13; (vol. 46, no. 2), February, 1959, p. 9; (vol. 47, no. 6), June, 1960, p. 4-5; (vol. 49, no. 11), October, 1961, p. 12.

6 Other alumni awards were added in each decade since then. As of 2014, there were eleven different alumni awards.

7 BOR, March 7, 1966.

8 Based on a 2007 alumni survey report; see Chapter 6, note 162.

9 Davis, p. 85-86.

10 Davis, p. 87-89.

11 Brewer, p. 76, BOR, March 25-26, 1957, and various archival documents. (UA 1.2.1.4.4.1)

12 Burns, "Notes Written by Dr. Robert E. Burns shortly before his death" [n.d.], p. 5. (UA 1.2.1.4.4.1)

13 BOR, March 21, 1950.

14 BOR October 20, 1950, and Brewer, p. 96-99.

15 Robert Burns' recorded statement for Robert A. Altman's "A Study of the Establishment of Upper Divisional Colleges in the United States," Teachers College, Columbia University, as transmitted in a letter from Altman to Burns, October 18, 1968. (UA 11.1.1.1)

16 Much later, Ted Baun married Grace Burns in 1988--their first date was President Atchley's inaugural ball. (PAR [vol. 76, no. 1], September-October, 1988, p. 2.)

17 Reuben Smith interview.

18 Davies interview, May 2, 2012.

19 Personal interview with Eddie LeBaron, November 28, 2011.

20 Brewer, p. 167 and BOR, November 7, 1961.

21 PAR (vol. 52, no. 3), April, 1964, p. 4, and PAR (vol. 86, no. 1), Fall, 1998, p. 8-9.

22 BOR, February 2-3, 1948.

23 BOR, February 2 and April 6, 1948.

24 Thelin, p. 261.

25 PAR (vol. 13, no. 8), May, 1979, p. 9.

26 See Brewer, p. 71-75, and J. Marc Jantzen, *A Dean's Memoirs* (Stockton CA: University of the Pacific, 1997), p. 41-53. (UA 7.1.6)

27 PAR (vol. 84, no. 3), Spring, 1997, p. 19.

28 Since 1997, Fallon House has been the independent Sierra Repertory Theatre headed by Dennis Jones ('71, '74).

29 PAR (vol. 85, no. 3), Spring, 1998, p. 4 and 27.

30 BOR, June 20, 1959 and October 27, 1959. There is no documentation to verify the admissions selectivity ratio.

31 BOR, February 3, 1948.

32 C. Hamrol, in "Class of 1959 50th Reunion and Memory Book," p. 20. Some of these highlights are from Clayton and Linden, "The 40's.".,

33 PAR (vol. 19, no. 1), April, 1946, p. 12.

34 PAR (vol. 36, no. 7 & 8), December, 1949, p. 12 and PAR (vol. 88, no. 3), Fall, 2001, p. 11-13.

35 *Naranjado,* 1968, p. 242.

36 PAR (vol. 45, no. 5), May, 1958, p. 2.

37 Interview with Bruce Shore ('56) by Chipponeri ('11), April 16, 2012, recorded in his "Pacific in the 1950's," p. 9.

38 PAR (vol. 71, no. 6), May-June, 1984, p. 13.

39 PAR (vol. 68, no. 1), September, 1980, p. 4.

40 This quotation (1959, p. 14) and the "B" list come from the "50th Reunion Memory Book," compiled of alumni self-portraits for the 50th Anniversary reunions for the classes of 1959-61, held each Stockton commencement weekend, 2009-2011.

41 Josh Chipponeri summarizing from the story "Archania Belle to be chosen," *Pacific Weekly,* October 26, 1951, p. 6, in his "Pacific in the 1950's: A Home, and a Family," p. 11, Student Reports 1940s-2000s. See also PAR (vol. 41, no. 10), December 1954, p. 7

42 PAR (vol. 41, no. 10), p. 7.

43 Interview with R. Marchetti ('59) by Chipponeri, February 10, 2012, in "Pacific in the 1950's," p. 12. This section draws on Bruce Shore's ('56) 14-page manuscript, "Omega Phi Alpha Fraternity," a profile of the fraternity in the 1950s. (UA 5.2.1.2.1)

44 Gene Bigler, "Pioneering in Diversity—Strengthening Community: Some of the Milestones at the University of the Pacific," unpublished manuscript prepared for a diversity symposium in 2010, p. 2. (UA 11.1.1.1)

45 Wood and Covello, *Stockton Memories,* p. 160, and BOR, March 25-26, 1957. Rhizomia was reactivated 21 months later (BOR, October 28, 1958).

46 BOR, June 20 and October 27, 1959.

47 BOR, June 17, 1961.

48 Personal interview with Bob ('51) and Dolly Eaton ('50) Blair, January 11, 2011.

49 PAR (vol. 52, no. 4), June, 1964, p. 5.

50 Harold S. Jacoby, memorial tribute, March 24, 1977 (UA 7.3.1), and "Anderson Y," *Naranjado,* 1967, p. 297.

51 Interview of Catherine Davis by Doris Meyer, September 27, 2003, for the Emeriti Society Oral History Project.

52 Anecdotes and campus life come from personal interviews with alumni, such as James Jewell, May 31, 2012. See Jacoby, *Pacific,* p. 118-23 on the evolution of Pacific's alcohol policy from the 1960s to the 1980s.

53 Personal interview with Charles Bloom ('46), retired regent, May 21, 2012.

54 "Survey Report to the President and the Board of Trustees of the College of the Pacific," University Senate and Board of Education of the Methodist Church, January 1956. (UA 11.5.4.1) The five-member team included a UC dean, a college president, a Syracuse University faculty member, and two members of the church's Board of Education.

55 BOR, October 23-24, 1956.

56 BOR, Executive Committee, December 1 and 12, 1958.

57 Personal interview with engineering emeriti professors Robert Hamernik and James Morgali, October 29, 2012.

58 McKevitt, p. 290.

59 Robert E. Hamernik, *Engineering at Pacific during the 20th Century: Memories of a Faculty Member* (Stockton,CA: Robert E. Hamernik, 2011), p. 12, and PAR (vol. 93, no. 2), Spring 2006, p. 40.

60 The co-op examples are taken from a personal email from Gary Martin ('86), assistant dean and former co-op placement director in engineering, January 25, 2013.

61 BOR, March 22, 1955.

62 BOR, Executive Committee, August 1, 1958.

63 Brewer, p. 112. See her detailed account of the founding, p.109-13.

64 Personal interview with Ralph Saroyan, November 9, 2011.

65 PAR (vol. 48, no. 2), January, 1961, p. 17.

66 BOR, Executive Committee, August 1, 1958.

67 PAR (vol. 49, no. 9), June, 1961, p. 2.

68 Saroyan interview, and personal interview with emerita professor Jean Matuszak, February 17, 2012.

69 BOR, April 27, 1961, March 26, 1963, March 8, 1965, and March 7, 1966.

70Saroyan interview; the portrait of the pharmacy school's early years is informed by this interview and the interview with Jean Matuszak,

71 PAR (vol. 46, no. 9), October, 1959, p. 7.

72 To honor Knoles, President McCaffrey asked the Board to name the Administration building Knoles Hall in 1972. (BOR, May 16, 1972).

73 BOR, December 6, 1967. Harold Jacoby states that in the 1940s Pacific solicited the sponsorship of the Methodist Southern California Conference as USC was pulling away from church affiliation (not fully completed until 1957), and that Pacific granted the conference the opportunity to elect two members to Pacific's Board of Trustees beginning in 1944. ("The University of the Pacific and the United Methodist Church," unpublished manuscript, July 26,1990, p. 22-24.) (UA 11.1.1.1.)

74 BOR, March 11-12, 1951.

75 McKevitt, p. 288.

76 Burns, "50 Ways in which the University of the Pacific Relates itself to the Methodist Church," speech manuscript, 1963. (UA 1.2.1.4.3.)

77 Interview between emeriti professors Gwenn Browne and Sally Miller, December 8, 2008, Emeriti Society Oral History Collection.

78 Jacoby, "The University. . .," p. 26. Jacoby provides much detail about Methodist financial help (the maximum budgeted was $50,000 in 1960 [p. 17-18, 24]) and participation with the University in this manuscript.

79 BOR, January 28, 1969.

80 BOR, March 6, 1967.

81 BOR, March 19, 1968 and January 22, 1969.

82 Burtchaell, p. 264.

83 See, for example, "UOP Task Force on Religious Life: Report to University President Donald DeRosa," unpublished report, February 1, 1999. The task force recommends a University statement on faith and religion that is comprehensive, p. 3. (UA 4.3.5.3)

84 For a detailed account of this greatest season in Pacific football, see *The 500 Club: College of the Pacific Football, 1949,* ed. by Carroll Doty [Stockton: n.p., 1950]. (UA 9.2.1.1)

85 BOR, March 21, 1950.

86 Jacoby, *Pacific,* p. 128.

87 "Amos Alonzo Stagg Memorial Stadium," Athletic Department Manuscript, 2011, p. 1. Much of the information on the stadium is taken from this manuscript.

88 For a fuller account of this project, see Carroll R. Doty's "The Valley Bowl," in "A Golden Century Crowns Pacific," the dedication booklet for Pacific Memorial Stadium, October 21, 1950. (UA 9.2.2.2) and Jacoby, *Pacific,* Chapter 8, "The Biography of a Sunken Field: How Pacific Got a Second Stadium," p. 125-33.

89 Bloom interview. According to alumnus Bob Collett ('50), six engineering students worked on the stadium design and construction, under the mentorship of professor Felix Wallace. (Robert Collet remarks at the dedication of the Robert and Bette Collet Challenge Event for the Dr. Felix Wallace Structures/Systems Laboratory, October 14, 2004.) For a detailed history of the Stagg Memorial Stadium, see the Pacific website, 2013: http://www.pacific.edu/About-Pacific/Newsroom/2012/February-2012/Stagg-Stadium-Feature.html

90 On the tiger's arrival, see *Pacific Weekly*, October 27, 1950, p. 1. During the filming of *World's Greatest Athlete* on campus, Disney Studios brought a live tiger used in the movie and also for Pacific publicity. The most well-known photo is of President McCaffrey petting the tiger on the central quad lawn.

91 Mike Millerick, *Pacific Football Record Book* (Lodi, CA: Duncan Press, 2002), p. 25.

92 BOR, Executive Committee, October 27, 1952. The largest crowd was 41,607 in 1951 against USF, when the capacity was 36,000. See Millerick, p. 25.

93 BOR, March 24, 1953.

94 Burns, "The Place of Football in the Modern College," *Pacific Review* (41, #2), February, 1954, p. 35. See also the Emeriti Society Oral History Project Interview with emeritus professor Charles Schilling, 2001.

95 Millerick, p. 31-32.

96 BOR, Executive Committee, December 12, 1958.

97 *Time*, November 10, 1958, p. 66.

98 Millerick, p. 33.

99 BOR, December 2, 1960.

100 Personal interview with former Athletic Director Cedric Dempsey, November 28, 20012, who stated that the average crowd for popular games was about 12,500 paid admissions in the late 1960s and 1970s.

101 *Naranjado,* 1961, p. 9.

102 Thelin, *Games Colleges Play,* p.128-54.

103 BOR, September 2, 1960.

104 *San Francisco Examiner,* January 22, 1961, p. III 5. (UA 1.2.1.4.15)

105 BOR, September 2, 1960. Burns' major eight-page report on athletics is recorded in the Board minutes of December 2, 1960.

106 See PAR (vol. 4, no. 1), January, 1970, p. 20, and Christine Burke and Kat McAllister, "A High Time at Pacific: University of the Pacific in 1960-69," Student Reports 1940s-2000s, for 1960s anecdotes based on review of the *Naranjado* and *Pacific Weekly* and interviews with alumni, including Frank Beardon ('63), Duane Isetti ('63, '65), Dave Frederickson ('67), and Terry Maple ('68).

107 Burns, "Statement of Policy of Robert E. Burns Relative to University of the Pacific Intercollegiate Athletics," [1965]. (UA 1.2.1.4.3.1.)

108 Thelin, *Games Colleges Play,* p.156-57.

109 Dempsey interview, October 12. 2012.

110 Millerick, p. 45-46.

111 Both Cedric Dempsey and Ted Leland, outstanding athletic directors at Pacific during these eras, agree on these points, based on personal interviews of October 12, 2012 (Dempsey) and May 29, 2012 (Leland).

112 Jagdip Dhillon, "The Pacific Men's Basketball program reaches a milestone this season," *Record,* November 111, 2010. C1. See *Record*'s six-part series on the history of Pacific basketball in from November 2010-March, 2011.

113 Jason Anderson, "The '60s: A decade of change,"*Record*, November 25, 2010, C1.

114 Dempsey interview, November 28, 2012.

115 PAR (vol. 68, no. 6), March, 1981, p. 8.

116 Jason Anderson, "The '60s: A decade of change," *Record,* November 25, 2010.

117 Dempsey interview, November 28, 2012. See Jason Anderson, "Picking top 20 Tigers not easy," *Record*, March 3, 2011, p. C3.

118 Personal interview with Tom Stubbs, January 22, 2013. On the 1944 start date, see Popham, p. 29-34.

119 Personal interview with emerita professor Doris Meyer, March 18, 2011.

120 Personal interview with emeritus professor Paul Winters, September 2-3, 2012. This account of forensics triumphs relies partly on the sharp recollections of Winters.

121 Personal interview with emeritus professor and former dean, Ira Lehn, November 20, 2012.

122 *Pacific Weekly,* May, 1, 1964, p. 1, 7. This paragraph is heavily informed by Sheri Grimes, "No Arguing with Success," PAR (vol. 99, no. 2), Winter, 2014, p. 16-19.

123 Burns, Speech Manuscript, 1961. (UA 1.2.1.4.3.)

124 PAR (vol. 52, no. 5), October, 1964, p. 3.

125 Thelin, *History,* p. 286.

126 Thelin, *History,* p. 322.

127 Thelin, *History,* p. 236.

128 The added Claremont colleges are Scripps, a women's college (1926), Claremont McKenna, accenting international political economy (1946), Harvey Mudd, engineering and computer science focus (1955), then later added Pitzer, interdisciplinary social justice emphasis (1963) during the launch time of Pacific's clusters. The Claremont cluster also has two graduate units: Claremont Graduate University (1925) and the Keck Graduate Institute (1997). Professor Gene Bigler perceptively makes the following correlations: "Claremont McKenna opened in 1946, just as Burns became president of COP, and Harvey Mudd started in 1955, just as Burns' frustrations over his fundraising difficulties and efforts to promote reform and change were beginning to grow. . . . Indeed, the record supports the conclusion that the Oxford model did not fully enter the picture until the actual size of the new college student body and faculty, the architecture, and design of such facilities of the dining hall were actually under consideration." Bigler compiled a chronicle of Raymond College for the 50th anniversary alumni reunion, "Some Reflections on the Raymond College Experience: From Launching to Legacy," unpublished manuscript, August 1, 2012, p. 6. (UA 2.2.2.1) I am deeply indebted to Gene Bigler for his extensive research on both Raymond and Covell Colleges as well as on campus diversity milestones.

129 BOR, October 27, 1959.

130 Samuel L. Meyer, "The University of the Pacific and Its 'Cluster Colleges," in *Experimental Colleges: Their Role in American Higher Education* (Tallahassee: Florida State University, 1964), edited by W. Hugh Stickler, p. 75.

131 BOR, October 27, 1959.

132 BOR, April 27, 1961.

133 On the property sale, see BOR, May 15, 1973. This section is informed by a personal interview with emeritus professor Neil Lark, October 3, 2013.

134 See [UC Santa Cruz Chancellor] Dean E. McHenry, "The University of California Santa Cruz," in Stickler, p. 133-44. McHenry attributes to UC President Clark Kerr the UCSC planning goal to "*try to organize the campus that it will seem small as it grows large*" (original italics, p. 136).

135 Brown, p. 3.

136 Brown, *passim.*

137 Oral comment as a member of the panel on "The Changing Nature of the College Experience," at the 50th Anniversary Celebration of the Founding of Raymond College, August 4, 2012. (UA 2.2.3.1)

138 Personal interview with Raymond alumnus and visiting professor Gene Bigler ('67), May 8, 2012.

139 Personal interview with COP dean emeritus Roy Whiteker, who had been a founding member of the faculty at Harvey Mudd College, one of the Claremont colleges, June 21, 2012.

140 Jerry Gaff, "A Study of Raymond College, University of the Pacific," a Report for the U.S. Department of Health, Education, and Welfare, Office of Education, August 31, 1967, p. 186.

141 Jacoby memorandum to Wallace B. Graves, "Analysis of the faculty load situation, Fall 1966," December 9, 1966. See also Graves' memorandum to President Burns of April 25, 1967. (UA 7.2.J17.4)

142 Letter from Walter Graves to Robert Burns, April 25, 1967. (UA 7.3. J17.4)

143 BOR, January 15, 1980 and October 7, 1980.

144 BOR, January 21, 1965.

145 "The Impact of the Experimental Colleges and the Raymond Experience," address at the 50th Anniversary Celebration of the Founding of Raymond College, August 4, 2012.

146 Samuel Meyer, "Academic Progress: 1958-1964," PAR (vol. 52, no. 5) October 1964, p. 6.

147 Personal interview with Tom Honey ('66), November 19, 2012, who claims the *Animal House* food fight was "mild by comparison." Anecdotes are from Honey and a personal interview with Kendall Parsons ('63), April 25, 2012.

148 Interview with Duane Isetti ('63, '65) by Chipponeri, n.d. [2012], in "Pacific in the 1950's," p. 11.

149 Personal interview with Kendall Parsons.

150 Personal interview with Helen Betz, former staff member and widow of dean Ed Betz, February 22, 2012.

151 Betz interview. The story of the origin of the "Belle of Archania" is described in PAR (vol. 43, no. 5), May,1956, p. 25. A history of the San Jose bell rivalry is described in PAR (vol. 97, no. 2), Summer, 2011, back cover, but there is evidence that the bell rivalry extends back to 1910.

152 *Epoch,* 1991, p. 125.

153 Shore, "Omega Phi Alpha Fraternity."

154 Burke and McAllister, recounting an interview with Douglas Pipes ('64).

155 "Campus Landmarks & Traditions," p. 8.

156 Helen Lefkowitz Horowitz, *Campus life : undergraduate cultures from the end of the eighteenth century to the present* (New York, Alfred A. Knopf, 1987), p. 19.

157 Bigler, "Some Reflections," p. 18.

158 Bigler, "Some Reflections," p. 19.

159 Bigler interview.

160 Elliott Taylor quotes these lines in his eulogy to Burns, PAR (vol. 5, no. 3), Spring, 1971, p. 14.

161 David Frederickson ('66), who was a member of this informal student council, noted this to me on December 11, 2012.

162 Horowitz, p. 223.

163 Hamernik, p. 19.

164 BOR, June 13, 1964 and PAR (vol. 13, no. 5), February, 1979, p. 6.

165 Personal interview with Jess Marks ('65), retired associate vice president for student life who served Pacific from 1967-2001, January 31, 2011.

166 Dempsey interview, November 28, 2012.

167 Bigler, "Pioneering in Diversity—Strengthening Community: Some of the Milestones at the University of the Pacific," p. 3-4.

168 Personal interview with Paul Fairbrook, December 10, 2010.

169 PAR (vol. 53, no. 7), August, 1965, p. 4-5.

170 PAR (vol. 42, no. 2), February, 1955, p. 5 and PAR (vol. 95, no. 1), Winter, 2009, p. 3.

171 "Historical Overview of the Community Involvement Program," [1975] (UA 6.1.2.1)

172 Bigler, "Pioneering," p. 2.

173 PAR (vol. 4, no. 2), Spring, 1970, p. 11-13, and (vol. 94, no. 4), Summer, 2008, p. 40.

174 Bigler, "Pioneering," p. 4.

175 AC, March 26, 1969.

176 Personal interview with Tommie Muhammad ('72), November 29, 2012, who was in the first CIP class.

177 Inez Ruiz-Huston, " What Can the Community Involvement Program Tell us About Alumni Giving at the University of the Pacific," University of the Pacific doctoral dissertation, 2010, p. 15.

178 Tim Turpin, "UOP's Commitment to the Community," PAR, (vol. 76, no. 2), November-December. 1988, p. 7

179 "L.U.V. Story," *Pacific Review,* Winter 2009, p. 40.

180 Interview by Patrick Giblin of Dennis Warren, September 30, 2008, posted at http://web.pacific.edu/media/marketing/Dennis_Warren_Interview.mp3, and "L.U.V. Story," PAR, Winter 2009, p. 40. The *Time* magazine story was in January, 1969.

181 Doyle Minden, "Two Weeks in May—1970," PAR (vol.4, no. 3) Summer, 1970, p. 15.

182 BOR, May 19, 1970.

183 W. J. Rorabaugh, *Berkeley at War, the 1960s* (New York: Oxford University Press), 1989, p. 170. See a Pacific student's journal of May 2-29, 1970, Alan Lindsay O'Neal, "The People's Alliance for Peace, A Personal Chronicle" (UA MS306).

184 Based partly on Betz interview.

185 Meredith interview.

186 Brewer, p. 197. See also history student Daniel Guerra's ('06?) detailed account, "A Moderate Upheaval: Student Protest at University of the Pacific," unpublished manuscript, [2006], (UA 11.1.1.1)

187 Burns lists 12 reasons in his report to the Board (BOR, October 22, 1968 and October 27, 1970).

188 Bigler, "Pioneering," p. 2.

189 BOR, March 8, 1965. A 1963 Spanish-language recruitment film is viewable at www.youtube.com/watch?v=eyvaL3kvqFO

190 "Total Immersion," *Newsweek,* September 30, 1963, p. 59-60; and "Reform on the Coast," *Time,* October 11,1963, p. 71.

191 Meyer in Stickler, p. 73-89.

192 *Naranjado,* 1968, p. 162.

193 PAR (vol. 5, no. 4), Summer, 1971, p. 9.

194 See the website, www.covelianos.com for Covell College alumni information.

195 Personal interview with emeritus professor, Callison College provost, and graduate dean emeritus Reuben Smith, June 15, 2012; BOR, March 27, 1962 and BOR, December 17, 1974.

196 PAR (vol. 4, no. 1), January, 1970, p. 15.

197 The percentage of faculty with doctorates is from BOR, March 9, 1963. By 1965, 62 percent of 168 full-time Stockton Campus faculty held doctorates. (BOR, March 8, 1965)

198 See Jacoby, "The Faculty Manifesto: Turmoil in the Academic World," in his *Pacific,* p. 92-104.

199 Professor Malcolm Moule retirement tribute, quoted in Kara Brewer, "Foreward," in Jacoby's *Pacific*, p. xi.

200 Interview with Reinelt.

201 The history of the Academic Council is based on the history approved by the Academic Council in 2000 included in the University Faculty Handbook, Section 5.1. In 1948, new bylaws of the Board increased the membership from 21 to 36 and added a member of the faculty as an advisory member to the executive committee of the Board (BOR, April 6, 1948). The Board turned down a request by the student body president to attend board meetings, but left the door open if the topic merited (BOR, March 22, 1949).

202 Jacoby, *Pacific,* p. 94.

203 Cohen, p. 220-22. The National Labor Relations Board ruled in the 1980 that only public college and university faculty could engage in collective bargaining because private college faculty were too involved in shared governance to be judged strictly as non-management.

204 "Report of the Danforth Committee to the Faculty of the College of the Pacific," unpublished report, n.d. [1968]. See Harold S. Jacoby's memorandum to the College faculty, April 26, 1966, and his memorandum to the College faculty, "Toward an Understanding of the College of the Pacific," of May 5, 1967.

205 Personal interview with emeritus music professor Wolfgang Fetsch, December 10, 2012.

206 Quoted in PAR (vol. 4, no. 3), Summer, 1970, p. 9. Information on the Muir Collection is primarily from this *Pacific Review* article, p. 2-9.

207 PAR (vol. 70, no. 1), September, 1982, p. 6.

208 Thelin, *History,* p. 261.

209 Curtis, *A Century of Smiles,* p. 73. Again for this era of the dental school, I am indebted to Curtis's splendid history of the school.

210 Personal interview with dean emeritus John Tocchini, June 13, 2004.

211 BOR, December 15, 1961.

212 Winterberg worked out a complex land swap with the Presbyterian Medical Center and Stanford to avoid building on PMC land that would have reverted to PMC or Stanford in 40 years. Personal interview with Robert Winterberg, November 9, 2011.

213 Personal interview with dean emeritus Arthur Dugoni, January 27, 2011. This portrait of the dental school relies heavily on Eric Curtis' *A Century of Smiles* and the Dugoni interview.

214 BOR, October 23, 1962.

215 Various documents in UA 6.1.1.2.

216 Brewer, p. 175-77.

217 Davies interview, June 20, 2012.

218 BOR June 13, 1964. The other institutions were California College of Arts and Crafts, San Francisco College of Music, and the California College of Podiatry in San Francisco.

219 Davies interview, June 20, 2012.

220 Brewer, p. 177-78.

221 Brewer, p. 179.

222 Rohwer interview; the "lease agreement" lasted until 1990. The dollar amount of the annual law school fee is not stated in the agreement. Some other sources claim the amount was $250,000.

223 Rohwer, resident law school historian, notes that the McGeorge corporation sold its assets to the University with a clause that provided for the assets to be returned if the University did not live by the financial agreement. At some point, the corporation lapsed. (E-mail of December 20, 2012)

224 BOR, October 24, 1967.

225 PAR (vol.3, no. 2), April, 1969, p. 11.

226 Personal interview with emeritus professor Carl Wulfman, September 9, 2012.

227 Burns wrote of his world tour in letters to his office assistant Alice Saecker. (UA 1.2.1.4.3.) He concluded his final letter (January 25, 1971) with his usual impish wit, "You do all the work while I run around. Alice Burns while Burns roams!" See also Ted Baun's brief tribute on his final days in BOR, October 7, 1971.

228 Personal letter from Pearl Piper to David Gerber, January 5, 2001. (UA 11.1.1.1)

229 Burns, "Notes Written," p. 5.

230 Edward Young, "The Complaint, or Night Thoughts on Life, Death, and Immortality" (1742), noted as his favorite quotation in the archives. (UA 1.2.1.4.4.1.)

231 See Jim Collins and Morten T. Hansen, *Great By Choice: Uncertainty, Chaos, and Luck—Why Some Thrive Despite Them All* (New York: HarperCollins, 2011), esp. Chapter 4. Brewer identifies the limitations of Burns' presidency briefly but with great accuracy, p. 208-09.

232 McKevitt, p. 210, 278.

233 Brewer, p. 207, BOR March 26, 1963 and *passim,* and the1956 Methodist Survey Report. Meanwhile, Willamette University, the other pioneering west coast Methodist school in Oregon, had achieved a $10 million endowment by 1968.

234 Gregg, Vol. II, p. 31.

235 Davies interview June 20, 2012, and BOR, October 23, 1962.

236 PAR (vol. 68, no. 6), March, 1981, p. 12.

CHAPTER 4

1 Thelin, *History,* p. 317.

2 This portrait of Stockton comes from Davis, p. 105-27, and interviews with various civic leaders, the most important of which were Duane Isetti ('63, '65) (March 3, 2013), Michael Fitzgerald (May 15, 2013), and Robert Benedetti (May 16, 2013).

3 Personal interview with Paul Davies, Jr., May 2, 2012. Other regent interviews confirm the portrait of McCaffrey.

4 Personal interview with Hugh Barton, March 6, 2013.

5 The U.S. high school graduation rate peaked in 1974 at 78 percent and did not reach that level again until 2013. See Cameron Brenchley, "High School Graduation Rate at Highest Level in Three Decades," January 23, 2013, on "Homeroom" blog of the U.S. Department of Education at http://www.ed.gov/blog/2013/01/high-school-graduation-rate-at-highest-level-in-three-decades/. See also James J. Heckman and Paul A. LaFontaine, "The American High School Graduation Rate: Trends and Levels," *Review of Economics and Statistics,* May 2010, 92(2), p. 244–262, for problems with high school graduation statistics.

6 BOR, October 24, 1972.

7 PAR (vol. 8, no. 1), October, 1973, p. 4.

8 PAR (vol.. 68, no. 6,), March, 1981, p. 3.

9 BOR, January 10, 1978.

10 AC, November 14, 1985 and November 13, 1986.

11 BOR, January 10, 1978.

12 BOR, January 13, 1984 and October 11, 1985.

13 BOR, May 8, 1979.

14 BOR, March 8, 1977; in 1979, 87 percent of freshman students listed Pacific as a first choice (BOR, March 13, 1979).

15 BOR, October 14, 1975 and October 10, 1978

16 BOR, March 9, 1976. Board chair Bob Eberhardt was very disappointed that the city and county could not find their way to partner with Pacific on the Spanos Center. This information and the note on founding the PAF is from Rick Weber, "Eberhardt bleeds orange and black," *Record,* May 22, 1982, p. 22.

17 BOR, May 9, 1978.

18 BOR, October 9, 1979

19 BOR, May 13, 1983 and January 10, 1986.

20 PAR (vol. 8, no. 6), April, 1974, p. 2.

21 BOR, January 22, 1974, and PAR (vol. 8, no. 8), June, 1974, p. 1.

22 Personal interview with Bob Winterberg, November 9, 2011.

23 Wulfman interview.

24 BOR, May 11, 1976.

25 BOR, May 11, 1982.

26 PAR (vol. 74, no. 5), May-June, 1987, p. 17.

27 Personal interview with Nancy Spiekerman, March 16, 2011

28 Through the help of regents, Pacific presidents from Burns to DeRosa were members of the all-male San Francisco Bohemian Club, which put them in touch with many wealthy and influential (mostly) Californians among its some 2000 members.

29 BOR, August 18, 1971.

30 Horowitz, p.18.

31 Cluster college document, UA 2.2.0.

32 The renowned Meiklejohn experimental college at University of Wisconsin ran only five years, 1927-32. See Rudolph, *Curriculum,* p. 277.

33 See "Experience: An Extension of Curriculum," the lead article in PAR (vol. 9, no. 4), February, 1975, p. 1.

34 BOR, March 13, 1979.

35 PAR (vol. 6, #2), November 1971, p. 2.

36 "Beyond the Eucalyptus Curtain," p. 20 and 61.

37 Meyer, in Strickler, p. 78.

38 Given this rich heritage, it is no wonder that the Raymond alumni have formed their own organization called the Raymond Phoenix Institute (RPI--the emblem of Raymond is a Phoenix rising from the ramparts of Oxbridge), "incorporated in January 2006 to help Raymond College alumni, faculty, and associates connect with old friends, meet other alumni, coordinate events, find resources, develop educational programs, and engage in ongoing dialogues. It's our personal, private alumni association." See the RPI website at www.raymondcollege.org.

39 Personal interview with Reuben Smith, June 15, 2012.

40 A personal e-mail message from Cortland Smith, May 25, 2013. This written commentary from Cort Smith informs much of the characterization of Callison College. Actually, classes and internships occurred in Tokyo, while language training was held in Kyoto. (PAR [vol. 9, no. 8], June, 1975, p. 8.)

41 Personal interview with Gil Schedler, January 19, 2012.

42 Interview by Trevor Rosenbery ('12), recorded in an unpublished manuscript, p. 2, Student Reports 1940s-2000s.

43 BOR, March 11, 1975.

44 AC, March 15, 1982.

45 BOR, March 8, 1985

46 See the website, www.covelianos.com for Covell College alumni information. The papers of Covell alumnus Arnoldo Torres ('75) reside in the University Library's Special Collections.

47 *Wall Street Journal,* December 26, 1972 lauded the clusters as "distinctive pockets of excellence."

48 See Burton R. Clark, *The Distinctive College: Antioch, Reed & Swarthmore* (Chicago, Aldine Publishing Co, 1970), "Chapter 10. The Making of an Organizational Saga."

49 As Jerry Gaff, the former Raymond faculty member (1964-67) and eminent scholar on liberal education programs sums up the 1960s innovative liberal arts college movement, ". . .the bad news is that most of the innovative institutions of the time disappeared. There are many reasons: the times changed, a recession of the 1970s hit, students and their parents focused on jobs and career preparation. Liberal education was seen as irrelevant, a luxury, or impractical, and enrollments dropped. Leaders left and their replacements were less committed to innovation. They became too expensive." ("The Impact of Raymond College, University of the Pacific," 50th Reunion of the Founding of Raymond College, August 4, 2012, p. 3.)

50 This portrait of the College relies in part on the Whiteker interview.

51 PAR (vol. 87, no. 2), Winter, 2000, p. 24.

52 BOR, January 26, 1988.

53 Clerc, p. 44.

54 Again in this chapter, this section on engineering relies heavily on Robert Hamernik's *Engineering at Pacific during the 20th Century,* pp. 28-59. A personal interview with David Fletcher, January 18, 2013, also informs this section.

55 BOR, March 18, 1983.

56 "CEAC Scholarship Competition [1977-87]," School of Engineering document. (UA RG 2.5.5.2.2)

57 "Campus Landmarks and Traditions," p. 8, and PAR (vol. 72, no. 6), August-September, 1985, p. 2.

58 "WASC Self-Study Report, 1991," p. 220-21. All the WASC reports and documents for this era are located in UA 11.5.1.4-6.

59 This section is informed by personal interviews with emeriti education professors Dennis Brennan, June 13, 2013, and Elmer Clawson, October 7, 2013.

60 BOR, May 9, 1989. The School of Education awarded 130 doctoral degrees between 1953-1977. (PAR [vol. 11, no. 6], April 1977, p. 11.)

61 This portrait of the Conservatory is based in part on personal interviews with Ira Lehn, November 20, 2012, and Carl Nosse, May 16, 2012.

62 PAR (vol. 12, no. 4), February, 1978, p. 12.

63 Personal interview with emeritus music professor Wolfgang Fetsch, December 10, 2012.

64 BOR, May 11, 1984.

65 BOR, March 8, 1985.

66 Personal interview with Judith Chambers, January 18, 2011. As Chambers put it, Burns "never really 'got' student affairs."

67 Chambers interview and BOR, October 12, 1982.

68 *The Pacifican,* March, 22, 1999, p. 3.

69 While Chambers claims that Pacific was lagging in its development of the student services staff, she pulled the University forward dramatically during her years of leadership. No published history of student affairs in American higher education has yet been written. Sources are R. H. Fenske, "Historical Foundations," in U. Delworth and G. R. Hanson & Assoc., *Student Services: A Handbook for the Professions* (San Francisco: Jossey Bass, 1980), p. 3-24; and Helen T. Meyer, "A National Effort to Build Standards for the Student Services/Development Functions: An Historical Analysis," doctoral dissertation, The State University of New Jersey, New Brunswick, N. J., 1986. Sources on leadership in the field are Arthur Sandeen's works, *The Chief Student Affairs Officer: Leader, Manager, Mediator, Educator* (San Francisco: Jossey Bass Pub., 1991; and *Making a Difference: Profiles of Successful Student Affairs Leaders* (*n.p.,* National Association of Student Personnel Administrators, Inc., 2001). Sandeen (2001) notes that nearly all of the fifteen student affairs leaders presented in his book point to the president as the most critical factor in their success (p. 9).

70 Meyer, p. 15-31. "CAS Standards" were formalized by the Council for the Advancement of Standards for Student Services/Development Programs in 1984.

71 PAR (vol. 11, no. 8), June 1977, p. 2.

72 BOR, October 9, 1987.

73 BOR, March 11, 1986.

74 *The Pacifican,* November 10, 1988.

75 BOR, May 8, 1990. Personal interview with Jess Marks ('65), January 31, 2011.

76 BOR, October 10, 1988.

77 BOR, May 1, 1987, noted in Ernest Boyer's *College: The Undergraduate Experience in America* (1987).

78 Personal interview with Paul Fairbrook, December 10, 2010. The quotation is from PAR (vol. 68, no. 1), September, 1980, p. 6.

79 BOR, May 16, 1972.

80 BOR, May 15, 1973.

81 PAR (vol. 8, no. 1), October, 1973, p. 3.

82 PAR (vol. 9, no. 4), February, 1975, p. 3, and (vol. 11, #4), February, 1977, p. 1.

83 BOR, May 14, 1974.

84 BOR, March 9, 1976.

85 BOR, March 11, 1975.

86 PAR (vol.6, #5), February, 1972, p.1.

87 AC, April 30, September 17, and October 8, 1981.

88 BOR, October 13, 1981.

89 BOR, May 11, 1982.

90 BOR, October 14, 1983.

91 The *Naranjado* yearbook ceased publication in 1974, replaced by slender versions 1975-78 (called *Recuerdos* for two years), then lapsed until the *Epoch* was published from 1982-93. After a lapse from 1994-2001, the *Naranjado* was reborn for two years, 2002 and 2003; a yearbook has not been published since. For this history, see PAR (vol. 88, no. 3), Fall, 2001, p. 18. Occasionally, the last issue of *The Pacifican* has served as a "year in review" issue; see, for example, the May 2, 2013 and May 6, 2014 issues.

92 Wesley Coffay, "Student Life at the University of the Pacific. 1985 to 1989, p. 3, Student Reports 1940s-2000s, based on *The Pacifican* articles, 1985-1989.

93 BOR, May 11, 1976.

94 AC, May 12, 1976 and March 15, 1984.

95 Award winners noted by professor Marlin Bates, forensics coach, in a personal e-mail of November 3, 2014.

96 PAR (vol.13, no. 8), May, 1979, p. 10, and the Winters interview.

97 Personal comment to me at the Morris Chapel memorial service for classmate James Darnall ('78) in 2012.

98 Murray Sperber, *Beer and Circus: how big-time college sports is crippling undergraduate education* (New York, H. Holt, 2001), p. 16.

99 Personal interview with Scott Heaton, May 15, 2014.

100 *The Pacifican,* October 17 and November 14, 1991.

101 "Band Frolic 1979." (UA 2.3.1.3.1)

102 *The Pacifican,* December 11, 1986. Band Frolic ended in 1995, replaced by "Lip Sync," an ongoing annual event.

103 PAR (vol. 10, no. 6), April, 1976, p. 13, and (vol. 70, no. 2), October, 1982, p. 1-3.

104 Interview by Trevor Rosenbery of Deborah Veatch Latasa ('78), recorded in an unpublished manuscript, p. 6, Student Reports 1940s-2000s.

105 Interview by Trevor Rosenbery, recorded in an unpublished manuscript, p. 4, Student Reports 1940s-2000s.

106 PAR (vol. 71, no. 5), March-April, 1984, p. 5.

107 Personal interview with Donald Floriddia, May 15 2014. This section is informed by this interview.

108 BOR, October 9, 1990.

109 BOR, October 12, 1984.

110 Personal interview with Cindy Spiro ('76), April 5, 2013.

111 Lucas, p. 266.

112 Personal interview with Sally Miller, December 6, 2011.

113 BOR, January 22, 1974

114 Chambers interview.

115 PAR (vol. 69, no. 7), April, 1982, p. 1-3.

116 "University of the Pacific Self-Study Report, 1991," October 1, 1991, p. 15. Hereinafter referred to as "WASC Self-Study, 1991," in the endnotes.

117 PAR (vol. 68, no. 5), February, 1981, p. 7.

118 BOR, January 10, 1978 and AC, May 2, 1982.

119 For a detailed history of the Sacramento State case in the context of the national campus movement, see David A Reichard, "'We Can't Hide and They are Wrong:' The Society for Homosexual Freedom and the Struggle for Recognition at Sacramento State College, 1969-71," *Law and History Review* (vol. 28, no. 3) August, 2010, 629-74

120 BOR, October 24, 1972.

121 AC, September 12, 1985.

122 BOR, March 16, 1971.

123 This paragraph is based on a personal interview with Norma Ivey ('74), March 28, 2014.

124 Personal interview with Rickey Boyland ('79), April 30, 2014.

125 AC, May 11, 1989.

126 AC, May 11, 1989.

127 *The Pacifican,* March 21, 1985.

128 Data on ethnicity prior to 1975 is sketchy at best, but it is possible that some classes in the early 1970s exceeded 200 black students.

129 *The Pacifican,* April 8, 1993, p. 1. The club was also known as the American Indian Student Association (see PAR, [vol. 80, no. 4], Summer, 1993, p. 8-9.)

130 Nearly all these data are from "Pacific Enrollment Trends, 1970-2010," Office of Institutional Research.

131 BOR, May 9, 1978. Peak international student enrollment was 406 in 1984.

132 BOR, March 14, 1989.

133 This section is informed by personal interviews with Rosson and John Phillips, February 27, 2013; BOR January 10, 1989.

134 BOR, May 7, 1991.

135 BOR, March 9, 1982. Based in part on interviews by Andrew Rathkopf ('12) of Randy Hayashi (May 14, 2012) and Kurt Blakely (April 22, 2012) in an unpublished manuscript, spring, 2012, p. 1, Student Reports 1940s-2000s.

136 BOR, January 10, 1989.

137 BOR, January 11, 1985.

138 BOR, December 9, 1992.

139 *The Pacifican,* March 3, 1988.

140 Personal interview with Dale Redig, February 6, 2013. Much of the information in this account of the dental school is from the Redig interview.

141 Curtis, p. 87.

142 Personal interview with David Chambers, February 27, 2014. This section is informed by the Chambers interview.

143 Personal interview with Arthur Dugoni, January 27, 2011. For Sloman's strong influence on Dugoni, see Martin Brown's biography, *A Quest for Excellence: The Arthur A. Dugoni Story* (San Francisco: Pacific Dugoni Dental Education Foundation, 2014), p. 31 and 52.

144 BOR, January 10, 1989.

145 Personal interview with Arthur Dugoni, January 27, 2011.

146 BOR, January 10, 1989.

147 AC, October 12, 1989.

148 PAR (vol. 73, no. 6), July-August, 1986, p. 2.

149 Curtis, p. 109.

150 The portrait of Schaber is mainly based on interviews with Claude Rohwer (February 28, 2011) and Tom Eres (March 20, 2013).

151 Personal e-mail from Claude Rohwer, January 17, 2013.

152 BOR, January 14, 1975.

153 BOR, January 12, 1982.

154 PAR (vol. 8, no. 1), October, 1973, p. 4.

155 PAR (vol. 72, no. 6), August-September, 1985, p. 9.

156 BOR, May 9, 1978.

157 PAR (vol. 68, no. 5), February, 1981, p. 11.

158 This portrait of Oak Park is from William Burg, "A Brief History of Oak Park," *Midtown Monthly,* February 1, 2010, found at http://www.midtownmonthly.net/life/a-brief-history-of-oak-park/

159 This brief portrait of graduate studies relies on my interview with Reuben Smith.

160 For 1970-71, the University apparently had 36 external grants for a total of $2.5 million. (BOR, March 16, 1971.)

161 BOR, March 8, 1977.

162 PAR (vol. 12, no. 4), February, 1978, p. 12.

163 "WASC Self-Study Report, 1991," p. 163 and 177. Quotations are from this report.

164 Michael Oriard, *Bowled Over: Big-Time College Football from the Sixties to the BCS Era* (Chapel Hill: University of North Carolina Press, 2009), analyzes this change in detail in "1973: The NCAA Goes Pro," p. 127-41.

165 Millerick, p. 34 and 10. Actually, the one other winning season during 26 years in the conference was under coach Shelton in 1994.

166 PAR (vol. 9, no. 4), February, 1975, p. 13 and Millerick, p. 44.

167 See Millerick, p. 39.

168 Eric Adelson of Yahoo Sports, "Pete Carroll can extend University of the Pacific's Super Bowl legacy among coaches." See http://ca.sports.yahoo.com/news/pete-carroll-can-extend-university-of-the-pacific-s-super-bowl-legacy-among-coaches-045534604.html

169 Stubbs and Leland interviews.

170 See Jagdip Dhillon, "Super Connection," *Record,* February 2, 2014, A1, A5, and PAR (vol. 91, no. 1), Spring, 2004, p. 16.

171 Charles Clerc and James Sugar, *The Professor Who Changed My Life, a sesquicentennial celebration of educational interaction at University of the Pacific* (Louisville, KY: Harmony House Publishers, 2001), p. 31.

172 BOR, January 18, 1972.

173 See Jacoby, *Pacific*, Chapter 11, "In Search of a Viable Athletic Policy: The Impossible Dream, p. 166-77. Jacoby summarizes football policy from 1961 to 1979, when Pacific had to make a decision on its divisional affiliation, as "a period of drift" (p. 170).

174 PAR (vol. 12, no. 8), September, 1978, p. 19.

175 This account is based primarily on personal interviews with Cedric Dempsey, October 12 and November 28, 2012.

176 Personal interview with former regent Mary (Mimi) Eberhardt, May 29, 2012, and PAR, vol. 70, no. 6 (May/June, 1983), p. 1-3.

177

178 BOR, January 9, 1979. The Toledo interview was by Tony Sauro, "UOP Names Toledo Coach, Boosts Program," *Record,* December 13, 1978, p. 51.

179 Letter from E. Leslie Medford, Jr. to President McCaffrey, January 16, 1979. (UA 1.21.5.3.37)

180 Tony Sauro, *Record* six-part series, August 16-21, 1978, cited here as "Sauro Series."

181 AC, December 21, 1978 and "Sauro Series."

182 AC, January 29, 1979, and McCaffrey's "Statement Regarding Intercollegiate Athletics at University of the Pacific," December 13, 1978.

183 BOR, May 8, 1979.

184 AC, January 29, 1979.

185 AC, February 8, 1979.

186 AC, March 15, 1982.

187 BOR, May 8, 1979.

188 PAR (vol. 69, no. 1), September, 1982, p. 12.

189 Millerick, p. 10.

190 AC, February 11, 1986.

191 Millerick, p. 34 and BOR, May 10, 1988.

192 See the Pacific athletics website, 2013: http://www.pacifictigers.com/information/traditions/all_americans. The only absent years were 1995 and 1997.

193 Spiro interview. Most of the information on women's athletics is from interviews with Doris Meyer, Spiro, and Dempsey.

194 Personal interview with Doris Meyer, March 18, 2011. This section on women's athletics is based on the Meyer interview.

195 PAR (vol. 10, no. 8), June 1976, p. 4.

196 BOR, January 14, 1975.

197 "University of the Pacific Title IX Policy Statement on Collegiate Athletics," May 13, 1980.

198 "WASC Visiting Team Report," November 1992, p. 59.

199 Douglas Lederman, "Men Get 70% of Money Available for Athletic Scholarships at Colleges That Play Big-Time Sports, New Study Finds," *The Chronicle of Higher Education,* March 18, 1992, p. A1, A45-46. The best analysis of the spending gap between women's and men's athletics is Deborah L. Brake, *Getting in the Game: Title IX and the Women's Sports Revolution* (New York: New York University Press, 2010). See esp. p. 158-68.

200 PAR (vol. 67, no. 6), March, 1980, p. 7.

201 PAR (vol. 68, no. 5), February, 1981, p. 12.

202 Some of this information is from a personal interview with Bob Dash, March 12, 2013.

203 PAR (vol. 76, no. 2), November-December, 1988, p. 5.

204 PAR (vol. 77, no. 5), May-June, 1990, p. 5.

205 PAR (vol. 94, no. 1), Spring, 2007, p. 11. 4

206 "2011-12 Media Guide," p. 88.

207 Stubbs interview.

208 PAR (vol. 7, no. 6), April, 1973, p. 5.

209 PAR (vol. 10, no. 7), May, 1976, p. 5.

210 BOR, May 16, 1972.

211 This section is informed by personal interviews with Ray Sylvester, February 21, 2013, and Mark Plovnick, March 25, 2013. Turoff died in 1989. The Turoff portrait is informed by a joint personal interview with emeriti professors Roseann Hannon (psychology) and Roland diFranco (mathematics), February 19, 2013.

212 Interview by Trevor Rosenbery of Steve Whyte ('79), recorded in an unpublished manuscript, spring, 2012, p. 2, Student Reports 1940s-2000s.

213 BOR, March 8, 1977.

214 BOR, May 13, 1983.

215 PAR (vol. 82, no. 2), Winter, 1994-95, p. 5.

216 Much of the school portrait is from a personal interview with Mark Plovnick (March 25, 2013) and Ray Sylvester (February 21, 2013).

217 PAR (vol. 7, no. 7), p. 3.

218 PAR (vol. 6, no. 6), March, 1972, p. 4.

219 This section is informed by a personal interview with Ralph Saroyan, November 9, 2011. See the Boras article in PAR (vol. 87, no. 3), Fall, 2000, p. 11-13.

220 Ralph Saroyan and Don Sorby (January 28, 2013) interviews, and BOR, March 9, 1984.

221 PAR (vol. 82, no. 3), Spring, 1995, p. 13.

222 Rosson interview.

223 BOR, March 9, 1984.

224 Personal interview with Roy Whiteker (dean of the College 1976-1989), June 21, 2012.

225 PAR (vol. 72, no. 3), January-February, 1985, p. 7.

226 *The Pacifican,* March 16, 1989.

227 BOR, May 15, 1973.

228 BOR, March 20, 1973.

229 BOR, January 14, 1983.

230 PAR (vol. 70, no. 4), January-February, 1983, p. 8.

231PAR (vol. 74, no. 2), November-December, 1986, p. 7. About twenty-five Fulbright Scholar appointments were awarded to Pacific professors from the 1960s to through the 1980s, an impressive number given the size of the University. Drama professor Sy Kahn had four, each to a different country.

232 BOR, January 10, 1986.

233 AC, September 11, 1986.

CHAPTER 5

1 Spiro interview.

2 Personal interview with former regent Don Smith, January 24, 2011. Smith was particularly helpful in providing a balanced view of the board and University leadership during these years.

3 Winterberg interview.

4 President Atchley report letter to WASC, April 13, 1993, analyzing how the $13 million deficit accumulated through the 1980s.

5 Bloom interview.

6 BOR, January 11, 1985.

7 AC, May 8, 1980.

8 "WASC Visiting Team Report," January 6, 1992, p. 26-27 (UA 11.5.1.4-6).

9 AC, December 9, 1976 and January 13, 1977.

10 AC, May 10, 1979.

11 BOR, October 12, 1976 and January 15, 1980.

12 AC, May 8, 1980.

13 The 1980s planning process is described in "WASC Self-Study, 1991," p. 28-42.

14 AC, May 27, 1977.

15 BOR, October 12, 1982.

16 BOR, October 12, 1984.

17 BOR, January 14, 1983

18 BOR, October 11, 1985.

19 Gwenn Brown memorandum to the College of the Pacific faculty, November 11, 1983.

20 Memorandum from council chairs to President McCaffrey, November 9, 1983, in AC, November 10, 1983.

21 BOR, January 13, 1984 and AC, December 15, 1983. As a result of the tiff over three-campus voting privileges, the Academic Council initiated annual meetings at the dental school and law school in 1985 (see AC, March 14 and April 11, 1985), which has generally continued to be practiced.

22 Dochterman interview.

23 Memorandum from the Academic Council Executive Board to the Regents Academic Affairs Committee, March 8, 1984, in AC, March 10, 1984.

24 PAR (vol. 73, no. 3), January-February, 1986, p. 3.

25 BOR, May 11, 1984, and AC, November 14, 1985.

26 BOR, May 11, 1984 and May 10, 1985. In 1982, 88.7% of the annual budget was tuition income, only 1.8% was endowment earnings. (Advancement Report, BOR, May 6, 1982)

27 PAR (vol. 74, no. 5), May-June, 1987, p. 2. This issue of the *Pacific Review* is devoted to summing up the McCaffrey presidency.

28 Student Life Report, BOR, March 10, 1992.

29 PAR (vol. 70, no. 6), May-June, 1983, p. 1-3.

30 From interviews with Davies, Smith, Spiekerman, and Mary (Mimi) Eberhardt.

31 BOR, January 26, 1988.

32 "WASC Visiting Team Report," January 6, 1992, p. 9.

33 "WASC Visiting Team Report," January 6, 1992, p. 15.

34 BOR, October 9, 1990 and January 9, 1991.

35 BOR, November 9, 1992.

36 BOR, March 10, 1992.

37 BOR, January 10, 1989 and BOR, May 18, 1995.

38 BOR, January 9, 1990.

39 Stubbs interview.

40 Quoted in Hunt, *History*, p. 127.

41 For the "Fulfilling the Promise" campaign Pacific hired the campaign consulting firm Marts and Lundy in 1986, which has continued to serve Pacific in this capacity off and on to the present. In 1990, the endowment-per-student at Pacific was $4750, while the national median for independents was $20,000. (Advancement Report, BOR, March 13, 1990)

42 Finance Committee Report, BOR, September 4, 1992. Judy Chambers notes the Eberhardt connection in her private correspondence of July 16, 2013.

43 PAR (vol. 80, no. 1), Fall, 1992, p. 1.

44 BOR, February 9, 1993.

45 "WASC Self-Study Report, 1991," p. 155.

46 "WASC Self-Study Report, 1991," p. 59.

47 "Recommendations on Workload," Ad Hoc Faculty Workload Committee," chaired by David Fletcher, December 2, 1988, filed in BOR, January 10, 1989.

48 PAR (vol. 76, no. 5), May-June, 1989, p. 10.

49 AC, April 12, 1990.

50 "President's Open Letter" to University Faculty and Staff, January 30, 1989, filed with BOR, January 10, 1989.

51 Dochterman interview.

52 *The Pacifican,* February 16, 1989, and Fairbrook interview.

53 As Wesley Coffay summarizes, "The outcry was almost deafening, even coming off the page of a newspaper twenty-five years later, in the basement of the library." (Coffay, p. 5, citing *The Pacifican*, October 8 and 15, 1987)

54 McCaffrey annual letter to "Friends," June, 1976. (UA 1.1.2.3.1)

55 Subbiondo interview.

56 BOR, October 9, 1990. In the 1970s and 80s many California public employers granted lifetime employee health benefits, ignoring how much that would cost or how to pay for it. Unlike independent institutions, the public schools were not required to book the future expense at that time. San Joaquin Delta College, for example, installed the plan in this era and did not end it until 2007, the year in which public institutions were required to fund their programs. (*The Record,* February 21, 2013, p. A1.)

57 BOR, October 3, 1991, and personal interview with Ken Beauchamp.

58 AC, November 14, 1991.

59 Memo from the Computer Outsourcing Committee to President Atchley, April 28, 1992, and memo from Ad Hoc Faculty Committee for SCT Review to Academic Council Chair Fred Muskal, October 29, 1992. Both documents are filed with AC, November 12, 1992.

60 As interim president of Southeast Missouri State University in 1995-96, Atchley initiated his "traveling office" at different locations around the campus periodically through the year.

61 These observations come from consistent comments in a variety of interviews.

62 PAR (vol. 73, no. 4), March-April, 1986, p. 11.

63 AC, April 9, 1981.

64 Jerry G. Gaff, *General Education Today: A Critical Analysis of Controversies, Practices, and Reforms* (San Francisco: Jossey-Bass, 1983), p. 73-75.

65 Quoted in "WASC Self-Study Report, 1991," p. 114.

66 AC, May 10, 1990 and October 11, 1990. The description of the program is informed by my interviews with Benedetti.

67 This account of the Honors Program relies heavily on a personal interview with Bob Dash, March 12, 2013.

68 Sections on the College and general education as well as on Stockton in chapters 5-7 are informed by personal interviews with Robert Benedetti, May 16 and June 5, 2013.

69 PAR (vol. 86, no. 2), Winter, 1998, p. 17. The first quotation is by education professor Marilyn Draheim.

70 This summary of dean Brown's years is from Hamernik, p. 55-65.

71 Personal interview with MESA director Maria Garcia-Sheets, September 25, 2013.

72 PAR (vol. 81, no. 1) Fall, 1993, p. 2.

73 Memorandum and annual report from Patricia J. Liddle, Director, Office of International Programs, to the Deans Council, December 1991. (UA 11.5.1.5)

74 PAR (vol. 98, no. 3), Fall 2012, back cover, and (vol. 99, no. 1), Spring 2013, p. 3. Letter from Robert Winterberg to President Atchley, March 30, 1989. (UA 1.3.2.2.1.3).

75 BOR, March 11, 1986.

76 PAR (vol. 73, no. 5), May-June, 1986, p. 30.

77 Chambers interview.

78 Personal interview with Marguerite Hinrichs, February 29, 2014.

79 Dortha L. Ingham, "UOP students, faculty attend Christmas carol singing, tree lighting ceremony," *The Pacifican,* December 8, 1994.

80 Personal interview with grounds supervisor and project manager Martin Van Houten, June 5, 2012.

81 Matt Neuenburg, "Men's basketball shocks UNLV," *The Pacifican,* February 11, 1993.

82 Pacific Athletics website, 2013.

83 PAR (vol. 81, no. 2), Winter, 1993, p. 6.

84 PAR (vol. 92, no. 3), Fall, 2005, p. 16.

85 PAR (vol. 81, no. 4), Summer, 1994, p. 7.

86 Millerick, p. 43.

87 PAR (vol. 80, no. 3), Spring, 1993, p. 10.

88 "WASC Self-Study Report, 1991," p. 222.

89 AC, November 21, 1988. The amount donated varies by source, from $250-500,000 because not all donors kept their pledges.

90 "President's Special Football Fund Four-Year Commitment, $2 Million, August 27, 1991," document in Michael Goins papers. (UA 1.3.2.3.1)

91 AC, October 8, 1987.

92 BOR, March 10 and May 1, 1987. The rate is reported as 75% for athletics, 62% for campus in 1989. (PAR [v. 77, no. 1], September-October, 1989, p. 7)

93 "WASC Self-Study Report, 1991," p. 183.

94 BOR, December 7, 1992.

95 BOR, December 7, 1992 and February 9, 1993.

96 PAR (vol. 75, no. 5), May-June, 1988, p. 9.

97 "WASC Self-Study, 1991," p. 72.

98 BOR, February 9, 1993.

99 BOR, October 12, 1993. Pacific's average SAT was 943, the other schools was 1020-1100; Pacific's five-year graduation rate was 63%, vs. 75% for SCU and SMC.

100 BOR, October 12, 1993.

101 BOR, April 13, 1993.

102 *The Pacifican,* October 11, 1990.

103 The program was adopted by fourteen other institutions by 2008 . (See AC, November 13, 2008.)

104 BOR, October 8, 1991 and March 10, 1992.

105 Personal observations by emeriti faculty at an Emeriti Society meeting of September 27, 2013.

106 Many faculty members credit Lee Fennell with the bulk of the WASC report, though Fennell is quick to grant major authorship to Subbiondo and others. (Fennell interview)

107 Atchley's hand-written notes for the WASC meeting of February 19, 1992, filed in WASC (UA 11.5.1.4-6).

108 "WASC Visiting Team Report," January 6, 1992, p. 3; "WASC Self-Study, 1991," p. 239. Commentary on the WASC visit in the following paragraphs is from this report prepared primarily by Joe Subbiondo, Reuben Smith, and written by Lee Fennell.

109 Letter from Stephen S. Weiner, WASC executive director, to Bill L. Atchley, president, March 16, 1992.

110 Weiner letter of March 16, 1992. Weiner said only 15% of WASC-accredited schools have ever been issued such a Warning , as reported in Lisa Lapin, "Reviewers question stability of UOP," *Sacramento Bee,* March 24, 1992, p. 1.

111 Lisa Lapin, "Reviewers question stability of UOP, *The Sacramento Bee,* March 24, 1992, p. A1 and A9.

112 "WASC Visiting Team Report," November, 1992, p. 12.

113 Alumni report to the Institutional Advancement Committee, BOR, January 11, 1995.

114 See, for example, AC, September 10 and October 22, 1992.

115 Trevor Rosenbery (2012), summing up his research and interviews with 1970s alumni, unpublished manuscript, spring, 2012, p. 1.

116 "WASC Visiting Team Report," January 6, 1992, p. 33-34, 43, and *passim.*

117 BOR, December 9, 1993.

118 AC, December 3, 1992 and BOR, December 9, 1993.

119 Smith interview.

120 BOR, December 9, 1993 and February 2, 1994.

121 AC, December 10, 1992.

122 AC, December 17, 1992.

123 AC, February 25, 1993.

124 "WASC Self-Study, 1991," p. 25-26.

125 Redig interview.

126 BOR, December 9, 1993, and interviews with Smith, Hugh Barton (March 6, 2013), Jim McCargo (March 21, 2013), Dale Redig (February 4, 2013) , Gary Podesto (December 20, 2012).

127 AC, February 24, 1994. The quotations are from the transcription of the survey comments, March 18, 1994.

128 Smith interview.

129 Interview with Hugh Barton.

130 AC, May 16, 1994.

131 Rudy Oliva, unpublished manuscript of Pacific campus life, 1990-95, spring, 2012, citing Allison Kajiya, "Students protest removal of Regents Redig, McCargo," *The Pacifican,* May 13, 1994.

132 Personal interview with Dale McNeal and manuscript of his commencement remarks, November 28, 2012. See story in PAR (vol. 81, no. 4), Summer, 1994, p. 8-9.

133 Editorial, *Record,* November 22, 1994, p. A6.

134 PAR (vol. 82, no. 30), Spring, 1995, p. 32 and (vol. 94, no. 2), Fall, 2007, p. 40. The tiger has not been recovered; the pedestal with the Knoles tribute remains at the north entrance to the hall.

135 Eres interview.

136 BOR, August 9, 1994.

137 Eres interview.

138 Eres interview.

139 BOR, October 20, 1994 and March 10, 1995.

140 AC, June 9, 1994.

141 WASC letter from Stephen S. Weiner, Executive Director, to Bill L. Atchley, March 13, 1995, filed in WASC. (UA 11.5.1.4-6)

CHAPTER 6

1 A number of observations in this chapter and the next chapter are based on five personal interviews with Donald DeRosa, May 5 and October 31, 2012, and April 15, June 24, and November 19, 2013.

3 PAR (vol. 82, no. 3), Spring, 1995, p. 4-7.

4 PAR (vol. 83, no. 4), Summer, 1996, p. 16.

5 President DeRosa Report to the Board, May 15, 2000, in BOR, June 9, 2000.

6 Personal e-mail from Donald DeRosa, May 4, 2012.

7 Quotations are from a personal interview with retired regent Tom Eres, March20, 2013.

8 Personal interview with Roland diFranco, December 7, 2011.

9 President DeRosa Letter to the Board, March 25, 1999, in BOR, April 16, 1999.

10 BOR, June 9, 2000.

11 BOR, April 5, 2002.

12 Finance committee report, BOR, October 16, 1996.

13 Personal interview with Dolores (DeDe) Sanchez, June 18, 2012.

14 President DeRosa Report to the Board, May 15, 2000, in BOR, June 9, 2000.

15 BOR, October 13, 2000.

16 BOR, October 16, 1998.

17 BOR, October 12, 2001. National data are from *The LEAP Vision for Learning: Outcomes, Practices, Impact, and Employers' Views* (Washington, D.C.: AAC&U, 2011).

18 Spiro and other interviews.

19 Millerick, p. 47.

20 Personal interview with Gary Podesto, December 20, 2012. Some observations in this section are based on this interview.

21 Millerick, p. 47.

22 Personal interview with Donald DeRosa, March 10, 2011.

23 BOR, January 13, 1995.

24 Personal interview with Donald DeRosa, March 10, 2011.

25 BOR, December 19, 1995.

26 Underscoring the financial challenge, Oriard's analysis concludes: "In short, no non-BCS school breaks even on athletics; most lose money on football as well. Most BCS schools make money on football, but less than a third of them make enough to cover the overall athletics budget." (*Bowled Over,* p.174). See also Jeff Benedict and Armen Keteyian, *The System: The Glory and the Scandal of Big-Time College Football* (NewYork: Doubleday, 2013).

27 Jacoby, *Pacific,* Chapter 11, "In Search of a Viable Athletic Policy: The Impossible Dream, pp. 166-77.

28 Millerick, p. 26.

29 Letter to President Donald DeRosa from "Pacific Football Reunion Alumni and Coaches," March 3, 1996. (UA 1.2.1.7.3)

30 PAR (vol. 83, no. 3), Spring, 1996, p. 3.

31 At the time, 115 schools were NCAA Division IA with the full 85-player scholarships and a 30,000 seat stadium, 123 schools were at the Division IAA level with 0-63 scholarships, and 83 at the IAAA level with no football.

32 *The Pacifican,* May 6, 1999, p. 1 and 5.

33 "Report of the Ad Hoc Committee on the Feasibility of Football at Pacific," Ken Beauchamp, chair, May 25, 1999, p. 1. (UA 1.2.1.7.3)

34 PAR (vol. 86, no. 1), Fall, 1998, p.15. See this article for a full story on the Tiger mascot tradition. The Benerd School of Education created a children' book, *Powercat, The Pacific Tiger,* by Lynn G. Beck and SESA (Herndon, VA: Mascot Books, 2011).

35 PAR (vol. 85, no. 2), Winter, 1997-98, p. 3.

36 BOR, May 17, 1996.

37 BOR, June 6, 1997.

38 Special meeting of the board executive and academic affairs committees, BOR, April 28, 1997. The number of students in the seven humanities majors languished in this era, as it did nationally; from 1998-2003 the number of degrees actually dropped from 63 to 47, while the number of majors increased from 178 to 227 (BOR, October 8, 2004). For a national perspective on the decline of humanities majors to 7.6 percent of the nation's bachelor's degrees in 2010, see "The Heart of the Matter," a report by the American Academy of Arts and Sciences, 2013, at http://www.amacad.org

39 BOR, October 16, 1998.

40 BOR, October 16, 1998. The benchmark was the American Association of University Professors AAUP) rankings of "II-A" institutions, schools with diverse graduate and first professional programs but not significant doctoral-level education.

41 BOR, January 10, 2003.

42 BOR, October 6, 2006.

43 These sections on athletics are informed by personal interviews with Lynn King, June 3 and 14, 2013.

44 PAR (vol. 91, no. 2), Fall, 2004, p. 20-21.

45 PAR (vol. 88, no. 3), Fall, 2001, p. 13.

46 "Men's Basketball 2011-12 Media Guide," p. 89

47 BOR, January 22, 2005.

48 Personal interview with Koreen Freitas, September 30, 2013.

49 PAR (vol. 92, no. 2), Summer, 2005, p. 24-25.

50http://www.pacifictigers.com/genrel/Pacific_Excels_In_NCAA_Graduation_Success_Rate . Pacific's overall 2013 NCAA Graduation Success Rate (GSR) is 87 percent.

51 See the College Hoops Journal website, ttp://www.collegehoopsjournal.com/2013/08/28/wcc-basketball-q-and-a-with-university-of-pacific-head-coach-ron-verlin/

52 "A Tribute to the Presidency of Donald V. DeRosa, Celebrating 14 years of transformational leadership, 1995-2009," (Stockton, CA: University of the Pacific, 2009), p. 10.

53 For a feature story on Karen DeRosa, see PAR (vol. 84, no. 2), Winter, 1996, p. 14-15.

54 BOR, October 15, 1999.

55 BOR, January 23, 2004 and October 8, 2004.

56 BOR, January 22, 2005.

57 BOR, October 3, 2008.

58 PAR (vol. 99, no. 1), Spring 2013, p. 9.

59 Memorandum to the Board of Regents from President DeRosa, December 14, 1999, included with BOR, January 14, 2000.

60 President's Report, September 3, 1997, in BOR, October 17, 1997, and BOR, January 10, 1998.

61 BOR, January 14, 2000.

62 BOR, April 7, 2000.

63 BOR, April 23, 1998.

64 BOR, January 22, 2005.

65 BOR, October 11, 2002.

66 BOR, June 7, 2002

67 President DeRosa Report to the Board, April 19, 2004, in BOR, May 7, 2004.

68 BOR, January 10, 2003. The University-wide tuition discount rate was 22 percent.

69 BOR, October 7, 2005.

70 BOR, January 18, 2008.

71 "Pacific CIRP Freshman survey trends since 1970," *IDEA Report Series* (vol. 10, no. 1). October 2009, http://iris.pacific.edu/idea/

72 "Recruitment Strategies: What Brings New Students to Pacific?" based on the "Admitted Student Questionnaire, *IDEA Report Series* (vol. 13, no. 1), September, 2012, http://iris.pacific.edu/idea/

73 See the Office of Institutional Research report: http://iris.pacific.edu/data_public/KPI_demographics_10_years.pdf

74 "New Student Cohort Comparison: new freshmen and transfer student findings," *IDEA Report Series* (vol. 12, no. 2), September 2011, http://iris.pacific.edu/idea/

75 President DeRosa's report to the Board, March 15, 2000, in BOR, April 7, 2000.

76 BOR, October 13, 2000.

77 BOR, January 10, 2003. For updated rankings and additional national rankings, see http://www.pacific.edu/About-Pacific/General-Questions/Pacific-Rankings.html

78 BOR, January 9, 1997.

79 BOR, April 6, 2001.

80 This section is informed by a personal interview with Larry Brehm, May 23, 2012.

81 BOR, October 17, 1997.

82 BOR, October 15, 1000.

83 BOR, June 7, 2002.

84 BOR, January 22, 2005.

85 BOR, January 23, 2009 and April 24, 2009.

86 Personal interview with Patrick Cavanaugh, October 23, 2013.

87 PAR (vol. 88, no. 1), Spring, 2001, p. 11-13.

88 BOR, October 13, 2001. For example, in 2013, "bestcolleges.com" listed Pacific among the top 18 most beautiful in the country, and "thebestcolleges.org" listed Pacific among the top 50.

89 Harold S. Jacoby, "Toward An Understanding of the College of the Pacific," May 5, 1967, p. 6. (UA 7.2.J17.4)

90 BOR, January 14, 2000.

91 BOR, April 29, 2005.

92 Curran, p. 1.

93 BOR, April 28, 2006.

94 BOR, January 18, 2008.

95 BOR, April 6, 2001.

96 BOR, April 6, 2001.

97 BOR, April 6, 2001.

98 BOR, October 11, 2002.

99 BOR, June 6, 1998.

100 Personal interview with Ronald Redmond, November 9, 2013.

101 BOR, May 7, 2004.

102 BOR, April 24, 2009.

103 BOR, October 10, 2003.

104 BOR, October 7, 2005.

105 BOR, October 5, 2007.

106 BOR, January 23, 2009. The report by L. Timothy Portwood and Charles P. Howland, "Investing in Excellence: The Campaign for Pacific Post-Campaign Assessment," January 29, 2009, is found in BOR, January 20, 2012.

107 Portwood and Howland.

108 This section is informed by a personal interview with Ronald Redmond ('66), November 9, 2013.

109 "Dean's Report," Arthur A. Dugoni School of Dentistry, Spring 2006, p. 34.

110 BOR, April 29, 2005.

111 BOR, January 20, 2006.

112 This section is informed by a personal interview with Patrick Ferrillo, Jr., February 28, 2014.

113 President DeRosa's Report to the Board, [n.d.] in BOR, October 11, 2002.

114 BOR, January 11, 2002.

115 BOR, May 7, 2004.

116 President DeRosa Report to the Board, September 17, 2004, in BOR, October 8, 2004.

117 BOR, October 7, 2005.

118 Freitas interview.

119 President DeRosa Report to the Board, September 17, 2004, in BOR, October 8, 2004.

120 Personal interview with Douglass Eberhardt, February 11, 2013.

121 Hayne Moyer oral remarks at the Board "Tribute to the Powells," January 17, 2013, The Ritz-Carlton Hotel, San Francisco, California.

122 PAR (vol. 94, no. 1), Spring, 2007, p. 13-14.

123 Dianne Philibosian oral remarks at the Board "Tribute to the Powells."

124 Donald DeRosa, oral remarks at the Board "Tribute to the Powells."

125 Remarks by Cynthia Weick at "A Salute to Jeannette and Bob Powell," The Jeannette Powell Art Center, University of the Pacific, February 14, 2013. Eibeck's remarks were also made at this event.

126 Pamela Eibeck oral remarks at the Board "Tribute to the Powells."

127 According to the *Chronicle of Philanthropy*'s "America's Top Donors" database; 2005 is the earliest year for which the database provides gift information. See University Press Release, October 17, 2013.

128 The portrait of Chapman University is based on Chapman's websites and a personal interview with Russell Leatherby (November 1, 2013). In 2011, the school also added affiliation with the United Church of Christ.

129 Report of the vice president for institutional advancement, BOR, March 8, 1996.

130 BOR, October 17, 1997.

131 BOR, October 11, 2002.

132 Personal interview with Carl Nosse, May 16, 2012.

133 Michael Fitzgerald, "Where are the federal tax dollars?" *The Record,* March 23, 2014, A3-4, based on research by Congressman Jerry McNerney's office.

134 Gosia Wozniacka, "Valley areas among poorest," *The Record,* September 21, 2012, p. A1, A7.

135 The Lumina Foundation, "A Stronger Nation Through Higher Education," 2013. See http://www.luminafoundation.org/stronger_nation/report/

136 See Kevin Parrish, "Rich Tapestry," *The Record,* February 24, 2013, p. A1, and Kevin Parrish, "Asians, Latinos fuel S.J. growth," *The Record,* June 16, 2013, p. A3-4.

137 See *University of the Pacific, The Visit of Vicente Fox, May 6-7, 2011* (Stockton: University of the Pacific, 2011).

138 On Delta water issues, see Philip Garone, *Fall and Rise of the Wetlands of California's Great Central Valley* (Berkeley: University of California Press, 2011). Chapter 5 deals with the San Joaquin Delta. See also Norris Hundley, Jr., *The Great Thirst: California and Water, A History* (Berkeley: University of California Press, 2001).

139 BOR, January 22, 2005 and April 27, 2007.

140 PAR (vol. 88, no. 2), Spring, 2001, p. 28.

141 PAR (vol. 97, no. 2), Summer, 2011, p. 5.

142 BOR, June 4, 1999.

143 BOR, April 29, 2005.

144 *The Pacifican*, September 13, 2001, p.1.

145 PAR (vol. 88, no. 3), Fall, 2001, p. 2, and PAR (vol. 90, no. 1), Winter, 2003, p. 4.

146 Memorandum from Philip N. Gilbertson, Provost, and Julie A. Sina, Vice President for Student Life, to Stockton Campus Faculty and Staff, March 24, 2003. (UA 1.3.1.1.10.1)

147 BOR, January 22, 2010.

148 See Mary Williams Walsh, "How Plan to Help City Pay Pensions Backfired," *The New York Times,* September 4, 2012, p. B1 and B5, which describes BFC director Jeffrey Michael's exposing Wall Street's role in pushing Stockton into bankruptcy.

149 Personal interview with Mark Plovnick, March 25, 2013.

150 President DeRosa Report to the Board, April 15, 2005, in BOR, April 29, 2005.

151 President DeRosa Report to the Board, January, 2006, in BOR, January 20, 2006.

152 *Pacific Rising, 2008-2015.*

153 See http://www.scup.org/page/awards/iiia/2009/recipient

154 BOR, October 8, 2004. Of a Board of about 28 members, the number of women remained seven to eight, alumni 18-20, and members over sixty years of age, 17-19.

155 BOR, October 7, 2005.

156 President DeRosa Report to the Board, April, 2007, in BOR, April 27, 2007.

157 BOR, January 16, 1998.

158 BOR, October 5, 2007.

159 Personal e-mail from Bill Coen, February 13, 2014.

160 BOR, October 13, 2000. The initial proposal was to find an off-campus home for the president and turn the president's residence into the alumni house, but no favorable options were identified, and the DeRosa family decided it preferred the campus setting.

161 BOR, October 6, 2006 and April 25, 2008.

162 BOR, April 24, 2009.

163 "University of the Pacific Alumni Survey, May 2007," a confidential report by Jerold Pearson of eAdvancement, a development consulting firm, henceforth referred to as "2007 Alumni Survey." (UA 4.4.2.1.3) The telephone interview survey of May 2007 was a random sample of 700 alumni from 1955-2005. The data cited are from p. 1-25.

164 Personal interview with Dianne Philibosian, November 7-8, 2013 and *Vision 2010* [2002], p. 21.

165 BOR, April 29, 2005.

166 BOR, January 23, 2004.

167 PAR (vol. 95, no. 2), Spring, 2009, p. 12-13.

CHAPTER 7

1 BOR, October 13, 1995.

2 BOR, January 15, 1999.

3 BOR, October 13, 1995. Compared to 35 comparable private universities, Pacific enrolled half as many students from families earning over $150,000 per year (18 percent), and over twice as many students from families earning less than $20,000 (16 percent).

4 BOR, April 23, 1998. It is important to note that "reasons for going to college" in the annual freshman survey vary widely among the individual schools. For example, "make more money" was a top reason for 82 percent of the business majors, but only 41 percent of the conservatory majors; pursuing a "general education" was important to 73 percent of the SIS majors vs. 55 percent of the pre-pharmacy students. (BOR, April 7, 2000) In 2000, pursuing "a philosophy of life" was the lowest to date at 40 percent among all first year students, and becoming "well off financially" has been 75 percent or higher since 1982.

5 "Pacific CIRP Freshman survey trends since 1970," *IDEA Report Series* (vol. 10, no. 1), October 2009, http://iris.pacific.edu/idea/

6 BOR, March 6, 1997.

7 BOR, January 14, 2000.

8 BOR, January 23, 2009.

9 This section is informed by personal interviews with Steven Jacobson, June 6, 2013, and Benjamin Ellis of the student life staff, April 12, 2014.

10 BOR, October 11, 2002.

11 See Caitlin Flanagan, "The Dark Power of Fraternities," *The Atlantic,* February 19, 2014, and Richard D. Bickel and Peter F. Lake, *The Rights and Responsibilities of the Modern University: Who Assumes the Risks of College Life?* (Durham: Carolina Academic Press, 1999), esp. Chapter VI, "The Facilitator University," p. 159-213.

12 BOR, June 7, 2002.

13 BOR, October 7, 2005.

14 *The Pacifican*, August 30, 2001, p. 3.

15 PAR (vol. 90, no. 3), Fall, 2003, p. 19.

16 BOR, April 7, 2000.

17 BOR, January 23, 2004.

18 BOR, October 12, 2001.

19 BOR, October 11, 2002.

20 AC, April 26, 2007.

21 BOR, April 6, 2001.

22 Heaton interview.

23 AC, November 10 and December 8, 2011.

24 BOR, January 19, 2007.

25 BOR, January 20, 2006.

26See Gilbertson's position paper, "Hispanic/Latino Initiative for Pacific," March 28, 2007. (UA 1.3.1.1.10.1) This program became a conventional Latin American/Latino studies minor in 2012.

27 BOR, October 3, 2008.

28 BOR, April 29, 2005.

29 BOR, April 7, 2000.

30 Personal interview with Danielle Procope ('14), December 11, 2013.

31 BOR, April 7, 2000.

32 BOR, October 7, 2005.

33 BOR, October 10, 2003 and October 3, 2008. See also a consultant's report, Sheila O'Rourke, "University of the Pacific Report on the Representation of Women on the Faculty, Fall 2011," December 5, 2011. O'Rourke states that close to 50 percent of new faculty hired in the past decade were women and that Pacific is "equivalent or better" than peer institutions in the hiring and retention of women faculty (p. 2).

34 PAR (vol. 86, no. 1), Fall, 1998, p. 3.

35 BOR, June 7, 2002.

36 AC, April 11, 2002.

37 BOR, April 25, 2008.

38 BOR, April 27, 2007.

39 BOR, October 3, 2008.

40 "Report of the Strategic Task Force on Diversity and Inclusive Excellence," June 1, 2012, available on the University website at http://www.pacific.edu/Campus-Life/Diversity-and-Inclusion.html . All observations and data in this section are from this 76-page report, which includes a rich presentation of current research on the measurable benefits of diversity in higher education.

41 PAR (vol. 90, no. 3), Fall, 2003, p. 8; *Pacifican*, October 24, 2013, p. 2; and Procope interview.

42 PAR (vol. 90, no. 3), Fall, 2003, p. 4, and http://www.businessweek.com/bschools/rankings#5

43 BOR, January 12, 2001. See also history student Taylor Hitt's ('13) "Pacific's Student Christian Groups from the 1950s to Today: A Continuing Tradition in the Post-Methodist Era," unpublished manuscript, December 14, 2012. Hitt's study is a valuable account of the various conservative Christian campus groups. (UA 11.1.1.2.2)

44 PAR (vol. 93, no. 2), Spring, 2006, p. 12.

45 BOR, October 8, 2004, and April 25, 2008.

46 *The Pacifican*, December 2, 2004, p. 9.

47 See "One Stop Shops," in "EV Perspectives," an online newsletter by EduVentures at www.eduventures.com, January 13, 2014.

48 Brian Fleming and Kelley Ross, "What Happened to the Online Market?" in "EV Perspectives," January 10, 2014, an online newsletter of EduVentures, Inc., at www.eduventures.com.

49 This section is especially informed by a personal interview with Brigid Welch, June 25, 2014.

50 BOR, January 23, 2004. A faculty survey in 2009 showed that over 90 percent of faculty respondents believed that service to the University did not count in performance reviews (BOR, April 24, 2009).

51 BOR, January 23, 2004.

52 The WASC report is on a secure Pacific website, http://iris.pacific.edu/wasc/cpr.report.html#Essay_Three

53 PAR (vol. 99, no. 1), Spring, 2013, p. 14-15.

54 "Educational and Effectiveness Review--University of the Pacific," December 23, 2011, p. 14, in BOR, January 20, 2012.

55 These quotations are taken from the school's website, fall, 2013.

56 Informal polls and listings exist online without stated criteria, thus there are wildly disparate ratings for most of the California dental schools.

57 BOR, October 13, 2000.

58 BOR, June 9, 2000.

59 This section is informed by personal interviews with dean Phillip Oppenheimer on January 27 and February 3, 2014.

60 BOR, April 29, 2005 and PAR (vol. 4), Summer, 2008, p. 26.

61 BOR, October 11, 2002.

62 BOR, January 10, 2003.

63 PAR (vol. 94, no. 1), Spring, 2007, p. 11.

64 BOR, January 10, 2003.

65 BOR, April 6, 2001.

66 BOR, May 7, 2004, a March 18, 2014 news bulletin: http://www.pacific.edu/About-Pacific/Newsroom/2014/March-2014/Oppenheimer-Named-Pharmacy-Dean-of-the-Year.html.

67 BOR, April 4, 2003.

68 BOR, April 4, 2003.

69 BOR, January 10, 2003.

70 Curran, p. 5.

71 PAR (vol. 83, no. 2), Winter, 1995, p. 3.

72 BOR, September 13, 1996.

73 BOR, April 23, 1998.

74 BOR, April 4, 2003.

75 BOR, January 11, 2002.

76 PAR (vol. 85, no. 2), Winter, 1997-98, p. 7.

77 BOR, October 13, 2000 and April 4, 2003.

78 BOR, January 22, 2005.

79 BOR, January 22, 2005.

80 Curran, p. 15.

81 Address at the "Charter Day" ceremony, a celebration of the 150th anniversary of the founding of the University, Court of Appeals Building, Sacramento, July 10, 2001, quoted in Curran, p. 30.

82 Curran, p. 8.

83 PAR (vol. 95, no. 1), Winter, 2009, p. 8.

84 PAR, (vol. 88, no. 2), Spring, 2001, p. 24-27.

85 Curran, p. 6,10, and 12, and PAR (vol. 90, no. 3), Fall, 2003, p. 7.

86 BOR, April 5, 2002.

87 BOR, October 11, 2002 and April 4, 2003.

88 Curran, p. 30.

89 "Library of Charts," University of the Pacific McGeorge School of Law, August 2013, p. 15.

90 Remarks by dean Parker, "Tribute Celebration honoring Dean Elizabeth Rindskopf Parker benefiting the Pacific McGeorge Public Legal Services Society," Sacramento, California, March 3, 2012.

91 The Carnegie report is by William M. Sullivan, Anne Colby, Judith Welch Wegner and Lloyd Bond, *Educating Lawyers: Preparation for the Profession of Law* (San Francisco: Jossey-Bass, 2007). The lead author, William Sullivan, was an ongoing consultant for the school over several years.

92 BOR, April 28, 2006 and April 24, 2009.

93 BOR, April 27, 2007

94 BOR, January 23, 2004.

95 BOR, October 6, 2006 and PAR (vol. 98, no. 1), Winter, 2012, p. 6.

96 PAR (vol. 99, no. 2), Fall, 2013, p. 6.

97 BOR, October 8, 2004.

98 BOR, October 9, 2009.

99 Curran, p. 2.

100 BOR, April 6, 2001.

101 PAR (vol. 90, no. 1), Winter, 2003, p. 7.

102 PAR (vol. 93, #2), Spring, 2006, p. 5.

103 Based on personal interviews with John Sprankling and Gerald Caplan on September 19, 2013, and personal recollections.

104 PAR (vol. 96, no. 3), Summer, 2010, p. 9.

105 BOR, May 7, 2004.

106 BOR, January 22, 2005, and PAR (vol. 98, no. 2), Summer, 2012, p. 8.

107 PAR (vol. 90, no. 1), Winter, 2003, p. 10-13.

108 This section is informed by personal interviews with Lynn Beck, December 19, 2013, and Dennis Brennan, June 13, 2013.

109 BOR, April 24, 2009.

110 PAR (vol. 98, no.1), Winter 2012, p. 14-15.

111 BOR, April 25, 2008.

112 Some of the observations of this section are based on the Hamernik book and a personal interview with Ravi Jain, November 19, 2013.

113 PAR (vol. 83, no. 3), Spring, 1996, p. 2.

114 Personal e-mail from assistant dean Gary Martin, including information from Calvin Chen, co-op director, January 25, 2013.

115 PAR (vol. 92, no.1), Winter, 2005, p. 5 and PAR (vol. 95, no. 1), Winter, 2009, p. 7.

116 http://www.pacific.edu/About-Pacific/Newsroom/2012/December-2012/Team-Venus-Super-Computing-Team.html. The SWE teams were finalists in 2005-07 competitions.

117 Hamernik, p. 69

118 Hamernik, p. 69.

119 PAR (vol. 97, no. 2), Summer, 2011, p. 27.

120 Hamernik, p. 68.

121 BOR, October 7, 2005.

122 BOR, January 23, 2009.

123 BOR, January 12, 2001.

124 BOR, March 21 and October 24, 1972.

125 BOR, May 7, 2004.

126 PAR (vol. 96, no. 3), Summer 2010, p. 5. Stanford was ready to rid of a program that did not generate high revenue.

127 See Laura Bathurst and Bruce La Brack, (2012) "Shifting the Locus of Intercultural Learning: Intervening Prior to and After Student Experiences Abroad," in M. VandeBerg, M. Paige, and K. Lou (editors), *Student Learning Abroad: What Your Students Are Learning, What They're Not, and What You Can Do About It* (Sterling, VA: Stylus Publishing, 2012) p. 261-283.

128 BOR, April 29, 2005.

129 2013: http://www.pacific.edu/The-Sounds-of-Success.html

130 PAR (vol. 91, no. 1), Spring, 2004, p. 13. This section is informed by a personal interview with Anita Bautista, October 4, 2013.

131 PAR (vol. 99, no. 2), Fall, 2013, p. 12.

132 Personal e-mail from Joseph Gilman, Brubeck Institute Artistic Director, to Melissa Riley, February 5, 2014, forwarded to me.

133 BOR, October 5 2007.

134 PAR (vol. 94, no. 4), Summer, 2008, p. 6.

135 PAR (vol. 99, no. 2), Fall, 2013, p. 24-27.

136 PAR (vol. 94, no. 3), Spring, 2008, p. 5.

137 Alice Scarlett Baker, "How to: Master the ways of entrepreneurship," *The Pacifican,* April 24, 2014, p.15.

138 BOR, April 23, 1998.

139 BOR, April 29, 2005. For example, Pacific's general education program was one of eighteen in the nation to participate in the Association of American Colleges and Universities' "Core Commitments Leadership Consortium" in 2007, one of eleven universities featured by AAC&U for best educational practices, one of six schools profiled in *Integrated General Education: New Directions for*

Teaching and Learning, ed. by Catherine Wehlberg (San Francisco: Jossey-Bass, 2010), and one of seven institutions profiled in EduVentures report, "Innovations in General Education Redesign Collaborative Report Case Study Analysis," March 2010. A listing of national recognitions can be found at http://www.pacific.edu/Academics/Majors-and-Programs/General-Education-Program/General-Education-Program-Recognition.html.

140 I rely on Doris Meyer's interview with Whiteker (July 18, 2011) for this early account of PBK.

141 Personal e-mail from Susan Weiner, Fellowship Advisor, December 4, 2013.

142 *Calliope* XLIII, 2013, notes that while the journal was founded in 1970, its predecessors were *the Pharos* (1893-1912) and *The Hieroglyph* (1931-33). The 2009-2012 editions each won "Apex Awards for Publication Excellence." (preface, p.3).

143 Personal e-mail from professor Marlin Bates, director of forensics, April 17, 2014.

144 BOR, January 23, 2009.

145 BOR, October 8, 2010.

146 See Jerry Hildebrand's report, "ROI for the Global Center," April 9, 2013. (UA 1.3.1.1.10.1)

147 PAR (vol. 96, no. 1), Fall, 2009, p. 10.

148 Personal letter from Rev. John E. Corson to Phil Gilbertson, May 1, 2006.

149 President DeRosa Report to the Board, April, 2009, in BOR, April 24, 2009.

150 President DeRosa Report to the Board, April, 2009, in BOR, April 24, 2009.

151 Jim Collins and Morten T. Hansen, *Great By Choice: Uncertainty, Chaos, and Luck—Why Some Thrive Despite Them All* (New York: HarperCollins, 2011). They identify three "core behaviors" of these mission-driven leaders: "fanatic discipline," "empirical creativity," and "productive paranoia." (p. 36-37).

152 "2007 Alumni Survey," p. 11.

153 BOR, October 7, 2011.

154 "Data for Regents' Diversity and Inclusion, Internationalization, and Community Partnerships Strategy Committee," in BOR, October 8, 2010.

155 BOR, October 8, 2010.

156 Daryl G. Smith and Natalie B. Schonfeld, "The Benefits of Diversity: What the Research Tells Us," *About Campus,* November-December, 2000, pp. 16-23, in BOR, October 8, 2010.

157 See http://www.pacific.edu/About-Pacific/Newsroom/2013/April-2013/Pacific-to-Award-Honorary-Degrees-to-Japanese-American. California passed a law in 2009 requiring all public colleges to grant honorary degrees to Japanese-American students forced to leave campuses throughout the state in 1942.

158 Thomas E. Pogue, et al, *University of the Pacific: Community Impact* (Stockton, CA: University of the Pacific, 2010), p. 5. This report may be found on the Pacific website: http://www.pacific.edu/Documents/marketing/community-impact-report.pdf

159 Based on data shared by Douglass Eberhardt in a personal interview, October 16, 2013.

160 Personal interview with Dianne Philibosian, November 7-8, 2013.

161 The characterization of the board's working relationship with the president in this section is based primarily on the personal interviews with regents Kathleen Janssen, January 8 and 14, 2014, Connie Callahan, May 23, 2014, and Fredric Nelson, June 17, 2014.

162 The Association of Governing Boards surveys showed that 70-85 percent of private university boards were white males over 50 years of age. See Paul Fain, "Diversity Remains Fleeting on Colleges' Governing Boards, Surveys Find," *Chronicle of Higher Education,* November 29, 2010, reprinted in BOR, January 21, 2011.

163 The reading was Richard Chait's "The Gremlins of Governance," *Trusteeship* (vol. 17, no. 4), July-August, 2009, p. 1-4.

CHAPTER 8

1 "With Only One Word," PAR (vol. 97, no. 1), Winter, 2011, p. 20-23. See http://www.pacificoneword.org

BIBLIOGRAPHY

"Addresses, Delivered on Installation of Rev. C.C. Stratton as President of the University of the Pacific, June 5, 1878," 1878. San Francisco: Joseph Winterburn & Co.

Altbach, Philip G., Robert Oliver Berdahl, and Patricia J. Gumport. 2005. *American Higher Education in the Twenty-First Century: Social, Political, and Economic Challenges*. 2nd ed. Baltimore: Johns Hopkins University Press.

American Committee of Justice. 1920.

California and the Japanese: a Compilation of Arguments Advertised in Newspapers by the American Committee of Justice, in Opposition to the Alien Land Law, Together with the Memorial Addressed to Congress by the Said Committee, the American Committee of Justice. Oakland: Japanese Association of America.

Association of American Colleges and Universities. 2002. *Greater Expectations: A New Vision for Learning as a Nation Goes to College*. Washington, D.C.: Association of American Colleges and Universities.

________. 2011. *The LEAP Vision for Learning: Outcomes, Practices, Impact, and Employers' Views*. Washington, D.C.: Association of American Colleges and Universities.

Bean, Walton and James J. Rawls. 1983. *California: An Interpretive History*, New York: McGraw Hill Book Co.

Beck, Lynn and SESA. 2011. *Powercat, the Pacific Tiger*. Herndon, Virginia: Mascot Books.

Bellah, Robert N. 1985. *Habits of the Heart: Individualism and Commitment in American Life*. Berkeley: University of California Press.

Benedict, Jeff, and Keteyian, Armen. 2013. *The System: The Glory and Scandal of Big-Time College Football*. New York: Doubleday.

Bickel, Richard D. and Peter F. Lake. 1999.

The Rights and Responsibilities of the Modern University: Who Assumes the Risks of College Life? Durham, North Carolina: Carolina Academic Press.

Bledstein, Burton J. 1976. *The Culture of Professionalism: The Middle Class and the Development of Higher Education in America.* New York: Norton.

Bloch, Charles. 1990. *A History of San Joaquin Delta College from College of the Pacific Beginnings to 1990.* Stockton, CA: San Joaquin Delta College.

Brake, Deborah L. 2010. *Getting in the Game: Title IX and the Women's Sports Revolution*. New York: New York University Press.

Brewer, Kara Pratt. 1977. *"Pioneer Or Perish": A History of the University of the Pacific during the Administration of Dr. Robert E. Burns, 1946-1971.* Fresno, CA: Pioneer.

Brokaw, Tom. 1998. *The Greatest Generation.* New York: Random House.

Bronner, Simon J. 1990. *Piled Higher and Deeper: the Folklore of Campus Life*. Little Rock, AR: August House Publishers, Inc.

Brown, Martin. 2014. *A Quest for Excellence: the Arthur A. Dugoni Story.* San Francisco: Pacific Dugoni Dental Education Foundation.

Burns, Robert E. 1946. "The First Half-Century of the College of the Pacific." Master of Arts thesis. Stockton, CA: College of the Pacific.

Burtchaell, James Tunstead. 1998. *The Dying of the Light: The Disengagement of Colleges and Universities from their Christian Churches*. Grand Rapids, Mich.: W.B. Eerdmans Pub. Co.

Byington, Lewis F. and Oscar Lewis eds. 1931. *The History of San Francisco*. Vol. 3. San Francisco: S. J. Clarke Publishing Co.

Cherry, Conrad. 1995. *Hurrying Toward Zion: Universities, Divinity Schools, and American Protestantism*. Bloomington and Indianapolis: Indiana University Press.

Christensen, Clayton M. and Henry J. Eyring. 2011. *The Innovative University: Changing the DNA of Higher Education from the Inside Out*. San Francisco: Jossey-Bass.

Clark, Burton R. 1970. *The Distinctive College: Antioch, Reed & Swarthmore*. Chicago: Aldine Publishing Co.

Clerc, Charles and James Sugar. 2001. *The Professor Who Changed My Life, a Sesquicentennial Celebration of Educational Interaction at University of the Pacific* . Louisville, KY: Harmony House Publishers.

Cogan, Frances B. 1989. *All-American Girl: The Ideal of Real Woman-Hood in Mid-Nineteenth-Century America*. Athens: University of Georgia Press.

Cohen, Arthur M. 1998. *The Shaping of American Higher Education: Emergence and Growth of the Contemporary System*. San Francisco: Jossey-Bass, Inc.

College of the Pacific, n.d. [1932]. Stockton, CA: College of the Pacific.

Collins, Jim and Morten T. Hansen. 2011. *Great by Choice: Uncertainty, Chaos, and Luck—Why Some Thrive Despite Them All*. New York: HarperCollins Publishers.

Conn, Robert and Michael Nickerson. 1989. *United Methodists and their Colleges: Themes in the History of a College-Related Church*. Nashville, TN: United Methodist Board of Higher Education and Ministry.

Conservatory of Music. 1978. *"One Hundred Years of Music, 1878-1978,"* Stockton CA: University of the Pacific.

Considine, Bob. 1962. *The Unreconstructed Amateur; a Pictorial Biography of Amos Alonzo Stagg*. Illustrated by Ray Sullivan. Edited by Ralph Cahn. San Francisco: Amos Alonzo Stagg Foundation.

Cookingham, Mary E. 1984. "Bluestockings, Spinsters and Pedagogues: Women College Graduates, 1865-1910." *Population Studies,* 38 (3): 349-364.

Curran, Michael. "Pacific McGeorge History." Unpublished history of University of the Pacific McGeorge School of Law. Stockton, CA: University of the Pacific.

Curtis, Erik K. A Century of Smiles, 1896-1996, One Hundred Years of Excellence at the College of Physicians and Surgeons. 1995. San Francisco: University of the Pacific School of Dentistry.

Danforth Committee. 1968. "Report of the Danforth Committee to the Faculty of the College of the Pacific." Stockton, CA: University of the Pacific.

Davis, Olive. 1984. *Stockton: Sunrise Port on the San Joaquin.* Woodland Hills, CA: Windsor Publications.

Deering, Ellen L. "Thomas Francis Baxter." Unpublished manuscript. Stockton, CA: University of the Pacific.

Demographia: "US Cities Population 1850-1900", 2010: www.demographia.com.

EduVentures. 2010. "Innovations in General Education Redesign Collaborative Report Case Study Analysis." Boston, MA: EduVentures.

Fass, Paula S. 1989. *Outside in: Minorities and the Transformation of American Education.* New York: Oxford University Press.

Finke, Roger and Rodney Stark. 1992. *The Churching of America, 1776-1990: Winners and Losers in our Religious Economy.* New Brunswick, NJ: Rutgers University Press.

Flanagan, Caitlin. 2014. " "The Dark Power of Fraternities," *The Atlantic*, March, 313 (2): 72f.

Gaff, Jerry G. 1967. "A Study of Raymond College, University of the Pacific," A Report for the U. S. Department of Health, Education, and Welfare, Office of Education. Stockton, CA: University of the Pacific.

________. 2012. "The Impact of Raymond College, University of the Pacific." Unpublished manuscript, 50th Reunion of the Founding of Raymond College, University of the Pacific, August 4, 2012. Stockton, CA: University of the Pacific.

________. 1983. *General Education Today: A Critical Analysis of Controversies, Practices, and Reforms.* San Francisco: Jossey-Bass Publishers.

________. 1991. *New Life for the College Curriculum: Assessing Achievements and Furthering Progress in the Reform of General Education.* San Francisco: Jossey-Bass Publishers.

________. 1970. *The Cluster College.* San Francisco: Jossey-Bass Publishers.

Garone, Philip. 2011. *Fall and Rise of the Wetlands of California's Great Central Valley.* Berkeley: University of California Press.

Gaston, Paul, et al. 2010. *General Education and Liberal Learning: Principles of Effective Practice.* Washington, D.C.: American Association of Colleges and Universities.

Gatke, Robert Moulton. 1943. *Chronicles of Willamette: the Pioneer University of the West.* Vol. I. Portland: Binfords & Mort.

Geiger, Roger, ed. 2000. *The American College in the Nineteenth Century.* Nashville: Vanderbilt University Press.

Gilbert, Frank T. 1879. *History of San Joaquin County, California: With Illustrations Descriptive of its Scenery, Residences, Public Buildings, Fine Blocks and Manufactories from Original Sketches by Artists of the Highest Ability.* Oakland, CA: Thompson & West.

Ginzberg, Lori D. 1990. *Women and the Work of Benevolence: Morality, Politics, and Class in the Nineteenth-Century United States.* New Haven: Yale University Press.

Glazer, Penina Migdal and Miriam Slater. 1987. *Unequal Colleagues: The Entrance of Women into the Professions, 1890-1940.* New Brunswick, NJ: Rutgers University Press.

Gonzales, Annie. 2008. *Stockton: Renewed, Revitalized, Redefined. Encino, CA: Cherbo Publishing Group.*

Greenberg, Milton. 2004. "How the GI Bill Changed Higher Education," *The Chronicle of Higher Education,* June 18, 50 (41): B9-11.

Gregg, Robert D. 1970.

Chronicles of Willamette, Vol. II: Those Eventful Years of the President Smith Era. Vol. II. Portland, OR: Durham & Downey.

Gregory, Beth Mason. 1972. "Development of a Typological Description of the Charter Class of Callison College, Fall 1967." Doctor of Education dissertation. University of the Pacific.

Guinn, J. M. and George H. Tinkham. 1909. *History of the State of California and Biographical Record of San Joaquin County*. Vol. I. Los Angeles: Historical Record Co.

Hall, Fred. 1996. *It's about Time: The Dave Brubeck Story.* Fayetteville: University of Arkansas Press.

Hall, Frederic. 1871. *The History of San Jose and Surroundings: With Biographical Sketches of Early Settlers.* San Francisco: A.L. Bancroft and Co.

Hamernik, Robert E. 2011. *Engineering at Pacific during the 20th Century: Memories of a Faculty Member*. Stockton, CA: Robert E. Hamernik.

Hammond, George P. 1982. *The Weber Era in Stockton History*. Berkeley, CA: The Friends of the Bancroft Library, University of California.

Hewitt, Nancy A., ed. 2005. *A Companion to American Women's History.* Maiden, MA: Blackwell.

Hillman, Raymond W. and Leonard A. Covello. 1985. *Cities & Towns of San Joaquin County since 1847.* Fresno, CA: Panorama West Books.

Hollis, Ernest V. 1838. *Philanthropic Foundations and Higher Education*. New York: Columbia University Press.

Horowitz, Helen Lefkowitz. 1987. *Campus Life: Undergraduate Cultures from the End of the Eighteenth Century to the Present.* New York: A.A. Knopf.

Hundley, Jr., Norris. 2001. *The Great Thirst: California and Water, A History*. Berkeley: University of California Press.

Hunt, Rockwell D. 1951. *The College of the Pacific, 1851-1951.* Stockton, CA: College of the Pacific.

________. 1962. *Personal Sketches of California Pioneers I Have Known.* Stockton, CA: University of the Pacific.

Isetti, Ronald. 2013. *On These Promising Shores of the Pacific: A History of Saint Mary's College*. Charleston, SC: The History Press.

Jacoby, Harold S. 1990. "The University of the Pacific and the United Methodist Church." Unpublished manuscript. Stockton, CA: University of the Pacific.

Jacoby, Harold S. 1989. *Pacific: Yesterday and the Day Before That.* Grass Valley, CA: Comstock Bonanza Press.

Jantzen, J. Marc. 1997. *A Dean's Memoirs*. Unpublished manuscript. Stockton, CA: University of the Pacific.

Johnson, Susan Lee. 2000. *Roaring Camp: The Social World of the California Gold Rush.* New York: W.W. Norton.

Jolly, Michelle E. 1999. *Inventing the City: Gender and the Politics of Everyday Life in Gold-Rush San Francisco, 1848-1869.* Doctoral dissertation, University of California, San Diego. Ann Arbor, MI: UMI Co.

Jonas, Andrew E. G. and David Wilson, eds. 1999. *The Urban Growth Machine: Critical Perspectives Two Decades Later.* Albany: State University of New York Press.

Kelley, Mary, ed. 1979. *Woman's Being, Woman's Place: Female Identity and Vocation in American History.* Boston: G. K. Hall & Co.

Kuh, George D. 2008. *High-Impact Educational Practices: What They Are, Who Has Access to Them, and Why They Matter.* Washington, D.C.: Association of American Colleges and Universities.

Lagemann, Ellen Condliffe. 1983. *Private Power for the Public Good: A History of the Carnegie Foundation for the Advancement of Teaching.* Middletown, CT: Wesleyan University Press.

Lester, Robin. 1995. *Stagg's University: The Rise, Decline, and Fall of Big-Time Football at Chicago.* Urbana: University of Illinois Press.

Levine, Arthur and John Weingart. 1973. *Reform of Undergraduate Education.* San Francisco: Jossey-Bass Publishers.

Levine, David O. 1986. *The American College and the Culture of Aspiration, 1915-1940.* Ithaca, NY: Cornell University Press.

Levine, Lawrence W. 1988. *Highbrow / Lowbrow: The Emergence of Cultural Hierarchy in America.* Cambridge, MA: Harvard University Press.

Lewis, Cheryl, Toni Di Franco, and George H. Lewis. 1979. *The Guide to Stockton.* Mercer Island, WA: Writing Works.

Loofbourow, Leonidas Latimer. 1961. *Cross in the Sunset: The Development of Methodism in the California-Nevada Annual Conference of the Methodist Church and of its Predecessors, with Roster of all Members of the Conference.* Vols. I and II. San Francisco and Berkeley: Historical Society of the California-Nevada Annual Conference of the Methodist Church.

________. 1950. *In Search of God's Gold; a Story of Continued Christian Pioneering in California.* Stockton, CA: The Historical Society of the California-Nevada Annual Conference of the Methodist Church and the College of the Pacific.

Lowen, Rebecca S. 1977. *Creating the Cold War University: the Transformation of Stanford.* Berkeley: University of California Press.

Lucas, Christopher J. 2006. *American Higher Education, A History.* 2nd ed. New York: Palgrave Macmillan.

Marsden, George M. 1994. *The Soul of the American University: from Protestant Establishment to Established Nonbelief.* New York: Oxford University Press.

________ and Bradley J. Longfield, eds. 1992. *The Secularization of the Academy.* New York: Oxford University Press.

McCaffrey, Stanley E. 1985. *World Understanding and Peace through Rotary: People to People Efforts for Peace*. Fresno, CA: Pioneer Publishing Co.

McKale, Donald M., ed. 1988. *Tradition: A History of the Presidency of Clemson University.* Macon, GA: Mercer University Press.

McKevitt, Gerald. 1979. *The University of Santa Clara: A History, 1851-1977.* Stanford, CA: Stanford University Press.

Meyer, Helen T. 1986. ""A National Effort to Build Standards for the Student Services/ Development Functions: an Historical Analysis." Doctoral dissertation. New Brunswick, N. J.: The State University of New Jersey.

Millerick, Mike. 2002. *Pacific Football Record Book.* Lodi, CA: Duncan Press.

Moody's Investors Service. "Private College and University Medians Highlight Challenges in Post-Recession Era." Accessed August 14, 2013. https://www.moodys.com.

________. "Moody's Affirms University of the Pacific CA's A2, Outlook Stable." Accessed February 6, 2014. https://www.moodys.com.

"Music at the University of the Pacific." August 14, 1909. *Pacific Coast Musical Review* 16 (20): 4-7.

Nero, Sally Rinehart. 1988. *We*. n.p.: n.p.

Niebuhr, H. Richard. 1987, reprinted from 1929. *The Social Sources of Denominationalism.* Gloucester, MA: Peter Smith.

Olson, Keith W. 1974. *The G.I. Bill, the Veterans, and the Colleges.* Lexington: University Press of Kentucky.

Oriard, Michael. 2009. *Bowled Over: Big-Time College Football from the Sixties to the BCS Era*. Chapel Hill: University of North Carolina Press.

________. 1993. *Reading Football: How the Popular Press Created an American Spectacle.* Chapel Hill: University of North Carolina Press.

Pfaelzer, Jean. 2007. *Driven Out: The Forgotten War Against Chinese Americans.* New York: Random House.

Pogue, Thomas E., et al. 2010. *University of the Pacific: Community Impact*. Stockton, CA: University of the Pacific.

Putney, Clifford. 2001. *Muscular Christianity: Manhood and Sports in Protestant America, 1880-1920.* Cambridge, MA: Harvard University Press.

Rensch, Hero Eugene. 1929. *Educational Activities of Protestant Churches in California, 1849-1860.* Stanford, CA: Stanford University.

Rorabaugh, W. J. 1979. *The Alcoholic Republic, an American Tradition.* New York: Oxford University Press.

________. 1989. *Berkeley at War, the 1960s.* New York: Oxford University Press.

________. 1986. *The Craft Apprentice: From Franklin to the Machine Age in America.* New York: Oxford University Press.

Rothman, Sheila M. 1978. *Woman's Proper Place: A History of Changing Ideals and Practices, 1870 to the Present.* New York: Basic Books.

Rudolph, Frederick. 1977. *Curriculum: A History of the American Undergraduate Course of Study since 1636. Carnegie Council on Policy Studies in Higher Education.* San Francisco: Jossey-Bass Publishers.

________ and John R. Thelin. 1990. *The American College and University: A History* Athens: University of Georgia Press.

Ruiz-Huston, Inez. 2010. "What Can the Community Involvement Program Tell Us about Alumni Giving at the University of the Pacific." Doctoral dissertation. Stockton, CA: University of the Pacific.

Sandeen, Arthur. 1991. *The Chief Student Affairs Officer: Leader, Manager, Mediator, Educator.* San Francisco: Jossey-Bass Publishers.

________. 2001. *Making a Difference: Profiles of Successful Student Affairs Leaders.* n.p.: National Association of Student Personnel Administrators, Inc.

Schaef, Anne Wilson and Diane Fassel. 1988. *The Addictive Organization.* San Francisco: Harper & Row.

Selingo, Jeffrey J. 2013. *College (Un)Bound: The Future of Higher Education and What it Means for Students*. New York: Houghton Mifflin Harcourt Publishing Co.

Servin, Manuel P. and Iris Wilson Engstrand. 1969. *Southern California and its University; a History of USC, 1880-1964.* Los Angeles: Ward Ritchie Press.

Shebl, James M. 1993. *Weber: The American Adventure of Captain Charles M. Weber.* n.p.: San Joaquin Historical Society.

Silver, Mae. 1995. "Women Claim the Vote in California."

Http://foundsf.Org: 201.

Simpson, Lee M. A. 2004. *Selling the City: Gender, Class, and the California Growth Machine, 1880-1940.* Stanford, CA: Stanford University Press.

Sloan, Douglas. 1994. *Faith and Knowledge: Mainline Protestantism and American Higher Education*. Louisville, KY: Westminster John Knox Press.

Solomon, Barbara Miller. 1985. *In the Company of Educated Women: A History of Women and Higher Education in America.* New Haven, CT: Yale University Press.

Soule, Frank, John H. Gihon, and James Nisbet. 1855. *The Annals of San Francisco: Containing a Summary of the History of the First Discovery, Settlement, Progress and Present Condition of California, and a Complete History of ... its Great City; to which are Added, Biographical Memoirs of some Prominent Citizens.* New York: D. Appleton & Co.

Sparks, Edith. 2006. *Capital Intentions: Female Proprietors in San Francisco, 1850-1920.* Chapel Hill: University of North Carolina Press.

Sperber, Murray. 2001. *Beer and Circus: How Big-Time College Sports is Crippling Undergraduate Education.* New York: H. Holt.

Spiro, Cynthia Bava. "Tigers, Traditions, and Teams: Football and its Influence on School Customs at the University of the Pacific." Unpublished manuscript. Stockton, CA: University of the Pacific.

Stadtman, Verne A. 1970. *The University of California, 1868-1968.* New York: McGraw-Hill.

Starr, Kevin. 2005. *California, A History*. New York: Random House.

________. 1973, 1986. *Americans and the California Dream, 1850-1915.* New York: Oxford University Press.

________. 2002. *Embattled Dreams: California in War and Peace, 1940-1950.* New York: Oxford University Press.

________. 1996. *Endangered Dreams: The Great Depression in California*. New York: Oxford University Press.

________. 1985. *Inventing the Dream: California through the Progressive Era.* Oxford University Press.

Stauss, William, and Howe, Neil. 2000. *Millennials Rising: the Next Great Generation.* New York: Random House.

Stickler, W. Hugh, ed. 1964. *Experimental Colleges: Their Role in American Higher Education.* Tallahassee: Florida State University.

Stuart, Reginald R. and Grace Dell Stuart. 1956. *Tully Knoles of Pacific: Horseman, Teacher, Minister, College President, Traveler, and Public Speaker. Stockton, CA:* College of the Pacific.

Sullivan, William M., Anne Colby, Judith Welch Wegner, and Lloyd Bond. 2007. *Educating Lawyers: Preparation for the Profession of Law.* The Carnegie Foundation for the Advancement of Teaching Series on Preparation for the Professions. San Francisco: Jossey-Bass Publishers.

Sweet, Pearl Shaffer. 1993. *Methodist Higher Education in Northern California: A Source Book*. n.p.: n.p.

Sykes, Charles J. 1988. *Profscam: Professors and the Demise of Higher Education.* Washington, D.C.: Regnery Gateway.

Thelin, John R. 1994. *Games Colleges Play: Scandal and Reform in Intercollegiate Athletics.* Baltimore: The Johns Hopkins University Press.

________. 2004. *A History of American Higher Education.* Baltimore: The Johns Hopkins University Press.

Thomas, Russell Brown. 1962. *The Search for a Common Learning: General Education, 1800-1960.* New York: McGraw-Hill.

Tuchman, Barbara W. 1981. *Practicing History: Selected Essays by Barbara W. Tuchman.* New York: Alfred A. Knopf.

University of the Pacific, the Visit of Vicente Fox, May 6-7, 2011,

2011. Stockton, CA: University of the Pacific.

Watts, Alan. 1972. *In My Own Way; an Autobiography, 1915-1965.* New York: Pantheon Books.

Wehlberg, Catherine, ed. 2010. *Integrated General Education: New Directions for Teaching and Learning*. Vol. 121. San Francisco: Jossey-Bass Publishers.

Wilson, John L. "Stanford University School of Medicine and the Predecessor Schools: an Historical Perspective." Lane Medical Library, Stanford School of Medicine, accessed October 14, 2013. http://elane.stanford.edu/wilson/index.html.

Wood, R. Coke and Leonard Covello. 1977. *Stockton Memories: A Pictorial History of Stockton, California.* Fresno, CA: Valley Publishers.

Worster, Donald. 1985. *Rivers of Empire: Water, Aridity, and the Growth of the American West.* New York: Pantheon Books.

Yogi, Stan, ed. 1996. *Highway 99: A Literary Journey through California's Great Central Valley*. Berkeley, CA: Heyday Books.

Made in the USA
San Bernardino, CA
03 August 2016